Collins
gem

English
School
Thesaurus

A

Published by Collins
An imprint of HarperCollins Publishers
Westerhill Road
Bishopbriggs
Glasgow G64 2QT

HarperCollins Publishers
Macken House
39/40 Mayor Street Upper
Dublin 1, D01 C9W8, Ireland

Sixth Edition 2019

10 9 8 7 6

ISBN 978-0-00-832118-5

Collins® and Collins Gem®
are registered trademarks of
HarperCollins Publishers Limited

www.collins.co.uk/dictionaries

Typeset by Davidson Publishing
Solutions

Printed in India by
Replika Press Pvt. Ltd.

Entered words that we have reason to
believe constitute trademarks have
been designated as such. However,
neither the presence nor absence of
such designation should be regarded
as affecting the legal status of any
trademark.

The contents of this publication
are believed correct at the time of
printing. Nevertheless, the Publisher
can accept no responsibility for errors
or omissions, changes in the detail
given or for any expense or loss
thereby caused.

HarperCollins does not warrant that
any website mentioned in this title
will be provided uninterrupted, that
any website will be error free, that
defects will be corrected, or that the
website or the server that makes it
available are free of viruses or bugs.
For full terms and conditions please
refer to the site terms provided on
the website.

A catalogue record for this book is
available from the British Library.

If you would like to comment on any
aspect of this book, please contact us
at the given address or online. E-mail:
dictionaries@harpercollins.co.uk

Acknowledgements

We would like to thank those authors
and publishers who kindly gave
permission for copyright material
to be used in the Collins Corpus.
We would also like to thank Times
Newspapers Ltd for providing
valuable data.

Contents

Editorial Staff

How to Use the Thesaurus

Collins Gem School Thesaurus is easy to use and understand. On the outer edge of each page there is a marker highlighting the letter of the alphabet featured on that page. At the top of each page, the first and last words entered on the page spread are clearly shown.

Below are some entries showing the thesaurus's main features, along with an explanation of what they are.

The entry word

The word class

horse NOUN
an animal kept for riding • *a fall from a horse*
brumby (AUSTRALIAN AND NEW ZEALAND) • *There's a mob of about 30 brumbies up there.*

Coverage of English from different parts of the world

equine (FORMAL) • *the history and uses of equines*
moke (AUSTRALIAN AND NEW ZEALAND; SLANG) • *a tired old moke*
nag (INFORMAL) • *He unhitched his sorry-looking nag from a nearby post.*

Advice on when to use the synonym

pony • *Peter trotted about on the fat pony he had been given.*
RELATED WORDS:
• ADJECTIVES equestrian,
• NOUN equitation
• MALE stallion
• FEMALE mare
• YOUNG colt, filly, foal

Words related to the entry word

continued on next page

Each sense of a word is shown as a separate entry

vain ② ADJECTIVE
not successful in achieving what was intended • *He made a vain effort to cheer her up.*

An example of the entry word being used

abortive • *the abortive coup attempt*
fruitless • *It was a fruitless search.*

Synonyms

futile • *their futile attempts to avoid publicity*
unproductive • *an unproductive strategy*
useless • *a useless punishment which fails to stop crime*

Antonym

ANTONYM:
• successful

Themed list of words connected with the entry word

valley NOUN

TYPES OF VALLEY
canyon
chasm
coomb
cwm (WELSH)
dale
defile
dell
depression
dingle
glen
gorge
gulch
gully
hollow
ravine
strath (SCOTTISH)
vale

What the word means

nice ADJECTIVE
attractive or enjoyable • *Did you have a nice time, dear?*

Cross-reference to expanded Word Study section at the end of the book

▶ see *Word Study* **nice**, *page 720*

vi

Aa

abandon ① VERB
to leave someone or
something • *a charity for pets
that have been abandoned*
desert • *a soldier who had
deserted his post*
jilt • *She was jilted by her first
fiancé.*
leave • *I am leaving my job to
concentrate on music.*
leave behind • *He would never
walk out and leave his children
behind.*

abandon ② NOUN
lack of restraint • *He began to
laugh with abandon.*
recklessness • *the headstrong
recklessness of youth*
wildness • *Her wildness just
needed to be channelled properly.*
ANTONYM:
• control

abate VERB
to become less • *The four-day
flood at last abated.*
decrease • *The pain had
decreased considerably.*
diminish • *The attacks on the
village did not diminish.*
ebb • *Her strength was ebbing
fast.*
lessen • *After a while, the
cramps lessened.*

subside • *Their enthusiasm was
beginning to subside.*
wane • *His popularity shows no
sign of waning.*

ability NOUN
the skill needed to do
something • *the ability to get on
with others*
capability • *We have the
capability of going out and
winning.*
competence • *They have a high
level of competence.*
expertise • *legal expertise*
skill • *the skill to play at a higher
level*
talent • *a talent for music*
ANTONYM:
• inability

able ADJECTIVE
good at doing something • *He
proved himself to be an able
politician.*
accomplished • *an
accomplished pianist*
capable • *a very capable
manager*
efficient • *a team of efficient
workers*
expert • *My mother was an
expert baker.*
first-rate • *This run is only
suitable for first-rate skiers.*
skilled • *a skilled craftsman*
talented • *a talented actor*

abolish VERB
to do away with something
• *Their objective was to abolish
capital gains tax.*
annul • *The marriage was
annulled last month.*

A

do away with • *the proposal to do away with nuclear weapons*
overturn • *criminals seeking to overturn their convictions*
put an end to • *efforts to put an end to poverty*

about ① PREPOSITION
of or concerning • *anxiety about his sick son*
concerning • *documents concerning the estate*
on • *his book on Picasso*
regarding • *strict rules regarding the disposal of food*
relating to • *the rules relating to transfer fees*

about ② ADVERB
not exactly • *The procedure takes about thirty minutes.*
almost • *Their wages have almost doubled.*
approximately • *It was approximately three times the size of a domestic cat.*
around • *The crowd here is around 12,000.*
nearly • *a tradition going back nearly 20 centuries*
roughly • *A byte is roughly equivalent to one character of text.*

above ① PREPOSITION
over or higher than something • *above the clouds*
higher than • *There are no hotels higher than four storeys.*
over • *the picture over the fireplace*
ANTONYM:
• below

RELATED WORDS:
• PREFIXES super-, supra-, sur-

above ② PREPOSITION
greater than a certain level or amount • *The death toll will rise above 50.*
beyond • *I expect to live way beyond 100.*
exceeding • *a floor area exceeding 50,000 square feet*

abrupt ① ADJECTIVE
sudden or unexpected • *the abrupt resignation of the prime minister*
sudden • *this week's sudden thaw*
unexpected • *His career came to an unexpected end.*
unforeseen • *unforeseen difficulties*

abrupt ② ADJECTIVE
unfriendly and impolite • *He was taken aback by her abrupt manner.*
curt • *"The matter is closed" was the curt reply.*
rude • *He was frequently rude to waiters.*
short • *She seemed tense and was definitely short with me.*
terse • *He received a terse one-line rejection.*
ANTONYM:
• polite

absent ADJECTIVE
not present • *absent from work*
away • *She is away on a business trip.*
elsewhere • *Four witnesses can prove he was elsewhere at the time.*

gone • *I'll only be gone for ten minutes.*

missing • *Another 44 passengers are still missing.*

ANTONYM:
• present

absent-minded ADJECTIVE
forgetful or not paying attention • *Her absent-minded stepfather left the camera on the bus.*

distracted • *He seems distracted, giving the impression of being elsewhere.*

forgetful • *She's getting rather forgetful, and living mostly in the past.*

random (NEW ZEALAND) • *I'm sorry, I'm a bit random these days.*

absolute ① ADJECTIVE
total and complete • *He is talking absolute nonsense.*

complete • *The operation was a complete success.*

downright • *That's a downright lie!*

pure • *a work of pure genius*

sheer • *It would be sheer madness to carry on after this.*

thorough • *He has a thorough knowledge of the subject.*

total • *the total destruction of the city*

utter • *He stared at me in utter disbelief.*

absolute ② ADJECTIVE
having total power • *an absolute ruler*

dictatorial • *a dictatorial system of government*

supreme • *supreme commander of the enemy forces*

tyrannical • *popular uprisings against tyrannical rulers*

absorb VERB
to soak up or take in something • *Plants absorb carbon dioxide.*

digest • *Fats are hard to digest.*

soak up • *Stir until the wheat has soaked up all the water.*

take in • *A growing tree takes in light and processes it for food.*

abstain VERB
to choose not to do something • *The patients had to abstain from alcohol.*

avoid • *Heartburn sufferers should try to avoid fatty foods.*

deny yourself • *I won't deny myself some celebration tonight.*

forgo • *My wife and I have to forgo holidays now.*

give up • *She gave up smoking last year.*

refrain • *He appealed to all factions to refrain from violence.*

absurd ADJECTIVE
ridiculous or nonsensical • *an absurd waste of money*

crazy (INFORMAL) • *It would be crazy to tinker with a winning team.*

illogical • *his completely illogical arguments*

ludicrous • *It was ludicrous to suggest that the visit could be kept secret.*

nonsensical • *He says many diets are harmful and nonsensical.*

ridiculous • *The programme is too ridiculous to take seriously.*

A

abundance NOUN
a great amount of something
• *an abundance of wildlife*
bounty • *autumn's bounty of fruit, seeds and berries*
plenty • *Allow plenty of time to get home.*
wealth • *a wealth of opportunities*
ANTONYM:
• shortage

abundant ADJECTIVE
present in large quantities • *an abundant supply of cheap labour*
ample • *ample space for a good-sized kitchen*
copious • *copious amounts of fruit juice*
plentiful • *a plentiful supply of vegetables*
ANTONYM:
• scarce

abuse ① NOUN
cruel treatment of someone
• *physical abuse*
exploitation • *Most human life involves the exploitation of animals.*
harm • *the harm caused by lies and deceit*
hurt • *The emotional pain was worse than the physical hurt.*
ill-treatment • *the ill-treatment of political prisoners*
oppression • *the oppression of black people throughout history*

abuse ② NOUN
unkind remarks directed towards someone • *I was left shouting abuse as the car sped off.*

curses • *The crowd screamed curses at her.*
derision • *He was greeted with shouts of derision.*
insults • *They shouted insults at each other.*
invective • *A woman had hurled invective at the family.*

abuse ③ VERB
to speak insultingly to someone • *He was verbally abused by other soldiers.*
curse • *We started cursing them under our breath.*
insult • *I did not mean to insult you.*
scold • *Later she scolded her daughter for having talked to her father like that.*

abusive ADJECTIVE
rude and unkind • *abusive language*
disparaging • *He made some disparaging remarks about the team.*
insulting • *She was charged with insulting behaviour to a police officer.*
offensive • *The book was seen by many as being deeply offensive.*
rude • *He is rude to her friends.*
scathing • *He made some particularly scathing comments about the design.*

abyss NOUN
a very deep hole • *He crawled to peer over the edge of the abyss.*
chasm • *The climbers strung a rope across the chasm and crawled along it.*

fissure • *The earthquake opened large fissures in the ground.*
gorge • *The valley narrowed to a gorge with cascading crags.*
pit • *Eric lost his footing and began to slide into the pit.*
void • *His feet dangled in the void.*

accelerate VERB
to go faster • *She accelerated away from the kerb.*
hurry • *He shouted at me to hurry.*
quicken • *Her pulse quickened in alarm.*
speed up • *It is designed to speed up transactions.*
ANTONYM:
• decelerate

accept VERB
to receive or agree to something • *All those invited to next week's conference have accepted.*
acknowledge • *He was willing to acknowledge her as his child.*
agree to • *They'll never agree to my going alone.*
concur with (FORMAL) • *I concur with her opinion.*
consent to • *The family consented to the picture being used.*
take • *He took the job.*
ANTONYM:
• refuse

acceptable ADJECTIVE
good enough to be accepted • *an acceptable standard of living*
adequate • *a lack of adequate facilities*

all right • *The meal was all right for the price.*
fair • *He is a fair player, but not outstanding.*
good enough • *I'm afraid that excuse just isn't good enough.*
passable • *She can speak fluent Spanish and passable French.*
satisfactory • *The workmen have done a satisfactory job.*
tolerable • *a tolerable level of noise*

accidental ADJECTIVE
happening by chance • *The fire was accidental.*
casual • *a casual remark*
chance • *a chance meeting*
inadvertent • *She giggled at the inadvertent pun.*
random • *the random nature of death in war*
ANTONYM:
• deliberate

accommodate VERB
to provide someone with a place to stay • *a hotel used to accommodate guests for the wedding*
house • *The building will house 12 boys.*
put up • *I wanted to know if she could put me up for a few days.*
shelter • *There were no facilities for sheltering the refugees.*

accommodating ADJECTIVE
willing to help • *his polite, accommodating manner*
considerate • *I try to be considerate to those around me.*
helpful • *The staff in the Newcastle office are very helpful.*

A

hospitable • *He was very hospitable to me when I came to New York.*

kind • *It was very kind of you to come.*

obliging • *an extremely pleasant and obliging man*

accommodation NOUN

a house or room for living in • *Travel and overnight accommodation are included.*

house • *He sold his house in London and moved to the country.*

housing • *a serious housing shortage*

lodgings • *At the moment the house provides lodgings for Oxford students.*

quarters • *the officers' quarters*

accompany ① VERB

to go somewhere with someone • *Children must be accompanied by an adult.*

conduct (FORMAL) • *He asked if he might conduct us to the ball.*

escort • *They were escorted by police to their plane.*

go with • *I haven't asked my friend to go with me yet.*

usher • *I ushered him into the office.*

accompany ② VERB

to occur with something • *severe pain accompanied by fever*

come with • *Stress comes with this job.*

go together with • *Excellence in athletics can go together with academic success.*

accomplish VERB

to manage to do something • *If we'd all work together, I think we'd accomplish our goal.*

achieve • *Achieving our aims makes us feel good.*

bring about • *the only way to bring about political change*

complete • *She has just completed her first novel.*

do • *Have you done it yet?*

fulfil • *All the necessary conditions were fulfilled.*

manage • *40% of children managed the required standard in reading.*

accurate ADJECTIVE

correct to a detailed level • *Quartz watches are very accurate.*

correct • *The correct answers can be found at the bottom of the page.*

exact • *an exact copy*

faithful • *a faithful translation*

precise • *precise sales figures*

right • *That clock never tells the right time.*

strict • *The book is not a biography in the strict sense of the word.*

true • *a true account of what happened*

ANTONYM:
• inaccurate

accuse VERB

to charge someone with doing something wrong • *He accused her of stealing.*

blame • *The police blamed the explosion on terrorists.*

censure (FORMAL) • *The Stock Exchange took the unusual step of censuring him in public.*

charge • *Police have charged Mr Smith with murder.*

cite • *He was banned for 30 days after being cited for foul play.*

denounce • *He publicly denounced government nuclear policy.*

accustomed ADJECTIVE
used to something • *The manager has become accustomed to abuse of late.*

adapted • *The camel's feet, well adapted for dry sand, are useless on mud.*

familiar • *He was very familiar with contemporary music.*

used • *I'm used to having my sleep interrupted.*

ANTONYM:
• unaccustomed

achieve VERB
to gain by hard work or ability • *She has achieved her best tournament result for years.*

accomplish • *halfway towards accomplishing an important career goal*

carry out • *debate about how such reforms should be carried out*

complete • *The commission completed this task in March.*

do • *I have done what I came here to do.*

fulfil • *The army has fulfilled its objective.*

perform • *He has not performed his administrative duties properly.*

achievement NOUN
something which someone has succeeded in doing • *His presence here is an achievement in itself.*

accomplishment • *The list of her accomplishments is staggering.*

deed • *His heroic deeds were celebrated in every corner of India.*

exploit • *His wartime exploits were later made into a TV series.*

feat • *A racing car is an extraordinary feat of engineering.*

acquire VERB
to get something • *I have recently acquired a digital camera.*

attain • *students who attain the required grades*

gain • *He gained valuable experience from the job.*

get • *My toaster's broken – I'll have to get a new one.*

obtain • *I couldn't obtain a ticket at any price.*

pick up • *You can pick up some real bargains at the January sales.*

procure • *It was still difficult to procure food and fuel.*

secure • *The team have secured a place in the semi-finals.*

act ① VERB
to do something • *The bank acted properly in the best interests of the depositors.*

function • *All the computer systems functioned properly.*

operate • *In the first half he operated effectively in defence.*

A

perform • *He performed well in a World Cup match last summer.*
work • *All sides will work towards a political solution.*

act ② VERB
to perform in a play or film • *He acted in 91 films altogether.*
act out • *It was made using real people to act out the scene.*
perform • *She performed the role on television twice more.*
play • *He plays a Danish detective in the film.*
play the part of • *She agreed to play the part of Evita.*
portray • *His mean, moody looks are perfect for the cynical anti-hero he portrays.*

act ③ NOUN
a single thing someone does • *an act of disloyalty to the King*
accomplishment • *Winning the tournament would be an incredible accomplishment.*
achievement • *She was honoured for her achievements as a film-maker.*
deed • *forgotten deeds of heroism*
feat • *an outstanding feat of athleticism*
undertaking • *Organising the show has been a massive undertaking.*

action ① NOUN
the process of doing something • *He had to take evasive action to avoid being hit.*
activity • *the electrical activity of the brain*
operation • *It is quite a tricky operation.*

process • *the peace process*

action ② NOUN
something that is done • *He did not like his actions questioned.*
accomplishment • *sporting accomplishments*
achievement • *If we can win the league it will be a great achievement for me.*
deed • *daring and heroic deeds*
exploit • *the stories of his wartime exploits*
feat • *prodigious feats of engineering*

active ① ADJECTIVE
full of energy • *Having an active child around the house can be exhausting.*
energetic • *an energetic, happy young girl*
lively • *a lively and attractive teenager*
restless • *On Christmas Eve the kids are too restless to sleep.*
sprightly • *The striker looked sprightly despite his injury.*
vivacious • *He was very vivacious and great fun to work with.*

active ② ADJECTIVE
busy and hardworking • *people who are active in local politics*
busy • *My husband lived a full and busy life.*
engaged • *The contenders are now fully engaged in their campaigns.*
enthusiastic • *As a student he was an enthusiastic member of the Communist party.*

hardworking • *a team of hardworking and dedicated volunteers*

industrious • *It is a happy and industrious community.*

involved • *She is heavily involved in local fundraising projects.*

occupied • *A busy social life will keep you fully occupied.*

activity ① NOUN

a situation in which lots of things are happening • *There is an extraordinary level of activity in the office.*

action • *a film full of action and excitement*

bustle • *the hustle and bustle of a busy hospital*

energy • *I love the energy you find in big cities.*

liveliness • *a restaurant with a wonderful atmosphere of liveliness*

activity ② NOUN

something you do for pleasure • *sports and other leisure activities*

hobby • *My hobby is birdwatching.*

interest • *Amongst his many interests are angling and painting.*

pastime • *You need a more active pastime than playing computer games.*

pursuit • *I like art, cooking and outdoor pursuits.*

actual ADJECTIVE

real, rather than imaginary or guessed at • *That is the official figure: the actual figure is much higher.*

authentic • *music played on authentic medieval instruments*

genuine • *a store selling genuine army clothing*

realistic • *a realistic picture of Dublin life*

true • *The film is based on a true story.*

verified • *verified reports of serious human rights violations*

acute ① ADJECTIVE

severe or intense • *an acute shortage of supplies*

critical • *suffering from a critical illness*

extreme • *a crippling disease which causes extreme pain*

grave (FORMAL) • *His country faces grave problems.*

great • *He died in great agony.*

intense • *I felt an intense loneliness.*

serious • *It increases the risk of serious injuries.*

severe • *Nuts can trigger a severe allergic reaction.*

acute ② ADJECTIVE

very intelligent • *an acute mind*

alert • *He has a very quick and alert mind.*

astute • *She has a remarkably astute brain.*

bright • *You don't need a bright mind to figure that one out.*

keen • *a competent economist with a keen intellect*

perceptive • *a perceptive analysis of the situation*

quick • *a child with an enquiring mind and a quick intelligence*

A

sharp • *His gentle manner disguised a sharp mind.*
shrewd • *He demonstrated a shrewd understanding of human nature.*

adapt VERB
to alter for a new use • *Shelves were built to adapt the library for use as an office.*
adjust • *He had to adjust the driver's seat.*
alter • *The government has altered the rules.*
change • *The law needs to be changed.*
convert • *a table that converts into an ironing board*
modify • *Our workshop is busy modifying the tanks for desert conditions.*

add ① VERB
to put something with something else • *Add the grated cheese to the sauce.*
attach • *Don't forget to attach the completed entry form.*
include • *Please include details of your previous experience.*
supplement • *I suggest supplementing your diet with vitamin A.*

add ② VERB
to combine numbers or quantities • *Banks add all the interest and other charges together.*
add up • *adding up calories on a calculator*
count up • *They counted up all the hours the villagers worked.*
total • *They will compete for prizes totalling nearly £300.*

ANTONYM:
• subtract

addition NOUN
something that has been added to something else
• *recent additions to their range of cars*
increase • *a substantial increase in workload*
supplement • *a supplement to their basic pension*

adequate ADJECTIVE
enough in amount or quality for a purpose • *an adequate diet*
acceptable • *These are all acceptable answers.*
ample • *You've had ample time to discuss this matter.*
enough • *enough money to live on*
satisfactory • *a satisfactory bid for the company*
sufficient • *One teaspoon of salt should be sufficient.*

ANTONYM:
• insufficient

administer ① VERB
to be responsible for managing something • *people who administer large companies*
be in charge of • *Who is in charge of this division?*
command • *Who would command the troops in the event of war?*
control • *He controls the largest publishing house in the country.*
direct • *Christopher will direct day-to-day operations.*
manage • *Within two years he was managing the shop.*

run • *This is no way to run a business.*
supervise • *the teacher who supervised the project*

administer ② VERB
to inflict or impose something on someone • *He administered most of the blows.*
carry out • *You are not authorised to carry out disciplinary action.*
deal • *His attacker dealt him a severe blow to the face.*
dispense • *They have set up military courts to dispense swift justice.*
execute • *the brutal fashion in which these orders were executed*
impose • *The judge had no choice but to impose a stiff sentence.*
inflict • *Inflicting punishment to stop crime is not the answer.*
perform • *He had to perform emergency surgery.*

admiration NOUN
a feeling of great liking and respect • *I have always had the greatest admiration for him.*
appreciation • *gifts presented to them in appreciation of their work*
approval • *His son had an obsessive drive to gain his father's approval.*
esteem • *Their public esteem has never been lower.*
regard • *He has always been held in high regard.*
respect • *We all have so much respect for her.*

admire VERB
to like and respect someone or something • *All those who knew him will admire him for his work.*
appreciate • *the need for children to appreciate their mother tongue*
look up to • *A lot of the younger girls look up to you.*
respect • *We have to respect people as individuals.*
value • *She genuinely values his opinion.*
ANTONYM:
• scorn

admit ① VERB
to agree that something is true • *The driver admitted to falling asleep at the wheel.*
accept • *I accepted the truth of all that Nicola had told me.*
acknowledge • *Belatedly the government has acknowledged the problem.*
grant • *The magistrates granted that the RSPCA was justified in bringing the action.*
ANTONYM:
• deny

admit ② VERB
to allow to enter • *He was admitted to university after the war.*
accept • *Stephen was accepted into the family.*
let in • *Turnstile operators were accused of letting in fans without tickets.*
receive • *He was received into the priesthood.*

adult

take in • *The monastery has taken in 26 refugees.*

ANTONYM:
• exclude

adult NOUN

a grown-up person • *Becoming a father signified he was now an adult.*

grown-up • *Las Vegas is the ultimate playground for grown-ups.*

man • *He is now a man of 42.*

woman • *a woman of child-bearing age*

ANTONYM:
• child

advance ① VERB

to move forward or develop • *Rebel forces are advancing on the capital.*

make inroads • *They have made impressive inroads in the movie business.*

press on • *Poland pressed on with economic reform.*

proceed (FORMAL) • *He proceeded down the spiral stairway.*

progress • *the ability to progress from one step to the next*

advance ② NOUN

progress in something • *scientific advance*

breakthrough • *a breakthrough in cancer treatment*

development • *the development of the car*

gain • *a gain of nearly 10%*

progress • *signs of progress in his reading*

step • *the first step towards peace*

advantage NOUN

a more favourable position or state • *We have a competitive advantage.*

ascendancy (FORMAL) • *The extremists are gaining ascendancy.*

benefit • *For maximum benefit use your treatment every day.*

dominance • *the battle for high-street dominance*

superiority • *military superiority*

ANTONYM:
• disadvantage

advertise VERB

to present something to the public in order to sell it • *Doctors cannot advertise on television.*

plug (INFORMAL) • *If I hear another actor plugging his latest book I will scream.*

promote • *What are you doing to promote your new film?*

publicise • *He never publicised his plans.*

push • *a publisher who knows how to push a product*

advertisement NOUN

a public announcement to sell or publicise something • *She recently placed an advertisement in the local newspaper.*

ad (INFORMAL) • *an ad for a minicab company*

advert (INFORMAL) • *She appeared in a coffee advert.*

banner ad • *Only one per cent*

of internet surfers click on banner ads.

commercial • *She has turned down a small fortune to do TV commercials.*

notice • *The request is published in notices in today's national newspapers.*

plug (INFORMAL) • *a shameless plug for his new film*

advice NOUN

a suggestion as to what to do • *Take my advice and stay away from him!*

counsel (FORMAL) • *He had always been able to count on her wise counsel.*

drum (AUSTRALIAN; INFORMAL) • *What's the drum on this?*

guidance • *The nation looks to them for guidance.*

opinion • *You should seek a medical opinion.*

suggestion • *She made suggestions as to how I could improve my diet.*

advise ① VERB

to offer advice to someone • *The minister advised him to leave as soon as possible.*

caution • *The researchers caution against drawing general conclusions from this study.*

counsel • *My advisers counselled me to do nothing.*

recommend • *We strongly recommend reporting the incident to the police.*

suggest • *He suggested a visit to the Cézanne exhibition.*

urge • *We urge that vigorous action be taken immediately.*

advise ② VERB

to notify someone • *I think it best that I advise you of my decision to retire.*

inform • *My sister informed us that she was pregnant.*

make known • *The details will be made known by the end of August.*

notify • *The skipper notified the coastguard of the tragedy.*

adviser NOUN

a person whose job is to give advice • *The President and his advisers spent the day in meetings.*

aide • *a presidential aide*

consultant • *a management consultant*

guru • *She was given fashion advice by a style guru.*

mentor • *He is my friend and musical mentor.*

tutor • *my college tutor*

advocate VERB

to publicly support a plan or course of action • *Mr Smith advocates animal rights.*

back • *The newspaper is backing the residents' campaign.*

champion • *He passionately champions our cause.*

endorse • *We are reluctant to endorse such drastic measures.*

favour • *those who favour lowering the voting age*

promote • *He promoted the idea of Scottish independence.*

recommend • *I can't recommend such a course of action.*

A

support • *people who supported his policies*
uphold • *a commitment to uphold certain standards*

affair NOUN
an event or series of events • *The funeral was a sad affair.*
business • *This business has really upset me.*
event • *A wedding should be a joyous event.*
issue • *a major political issue*
matter • *I never interfere in these business matters.*
question • *the difficult question of unemployment*
situation • *The whole situation is now under control.*
subject • *a subject which had worried him for some time*

affect VERB
to influence something or someone • *More than 7 million people have been affected by the drought.*
act on • *This drug acts very fast on the central nervous system.*
alter • *The earth's climate appears to have been altered by pollution.*
change • *It was to change the course of my life.*
impinge on • *My private life does not impinge on my professional life.*

affection NOUN
a feeling of fondness for someone or something • *She thought of him with affection.*
attachment • *Mother and child form a close attachment.*

fondness • *his fondness for cats*
liking • *a liking for flashy cars*
love • *My love for all my children is unconditional.*
warmth • *He greeted us both with warmth and affection.*
ANTONYM:
• dislike

affectionate ADJECTIVE
full of fondness for someone • *She gave me a long and affectionate hug.*
caring • *a loving, caring husband*
fond • *She gave him a fond smile.*
loving • *The children were very loving to me.*
tender • *a tender kiss*
ANTONYM:
• cold

afraid ADJECTIVE
scared of something unpleasant happening • *I was afraid of the other boys.*
apprehensive • *People are still terribly apprehensive about the future.*
fearful • *Bankers were fearful of a world banking crisis.*
frightened • *She was frightened of flying.*
nervous • *Emotionally, he left me a wreck, nervous of everyone.*
scared • *I was too scared to move.*
ANTONYM:
• unafraid

after ADVERB
at a later time • *Shortly after, police arrested five suspects.*

afterwards • *He was taken to hospital but died soon afterwards.*

following • *We shared so much, not only during the war, but in the many years following.*

later • *He resigned ten years later.*

subsequently • *She subsequently became honorary secretary.*

ANTONYM:
• before

RELATED WORD:
• PREFIX post-

again ADVERB
happening one more time • *He kissed her again.*

afresh • *The couple moved abroad to start life afresh.*

anew • *She's ready to start anew.*

once more • *Rage overcame him once more.*

against ① PREPOSITION
in opposition to • *I am against animal cruelty.*

averse to • *He's not averse to the idea.*

hostile to • *countries that were once hostile to South Africa*

in opposition to • *radio stations set up in opposition to the BBC*

versus • *Portugal versus England*

RELATED WORDS:
• PREFIXES anti-, contra-, counter-

against ② PREPOSITION
in preparation for or in case of something • *precautions against fire*

in anticipation of • *His school was one of several which closed in anticipation of Arctic conditions.*

in expectation of • *The hotel was being renovated in expectation of a tourist boom.*

in preparation for • *The army massed troops and guns in preparation for a counter-attack.*

aggressive ADJECTIVE
full of hostility and violence • *These fish are very aggressive.*

assertive • *an assertive style of management*

hostile • *The prisoner eyed him in hostile silence.*

ANTONYM:
• peaceful

agile ADJECTIVE
able to move quickly and easily • *He is as agile as a cat.*

lithe • *a lithe young gymnast*

nimble • *He built his career around quick reflexes and nimble footwork.*

sprightly • *The striker looked sprightly despite his injury.*

supple • *She is as supple as a dancer.*

ANTONYM:
• clumsy

agitate ① VERB
to campaign energetically for something • *The women had begun to agitate for better conditions.*

campaign • *an organisation which campaigns for better consumer rights*

A

demonstrate • *marchers demonstrating for political reform*
protest • *If you don't like the rules, protest for change.*
push • *Some board members are pushing for the merger.*

agitate ② VERB
to worry or distress someone • *Everything she said was beginning to agitate me.*
bother • *It really bothers me when you talk like that.*
distress • *sudden noises which distressed the animals*
disturb • *These dreams disturb me for days afterwards.*
trouble • *Are you troubled by thoughts of the future?*
upset • *The whole incident upset me dreadfully.*
worry • *I didn't want to worry you with my own problems.*

agree ① VERB
to have the same opinion as someone • *So we both agree there's a problem?*
assent (FORMAL) • *I assented to the request of the publishers to write this book.*
be of the same opinion • *All the other players are of the same opinion.*
concur (FORMAL) • *Four other judges concurred.*
see eye to eye • *He has not always seen eye to eye with his brother.*
ANTONYM:
• disagree

agree ② VERB
to match or be the same as something • *His second statement agrees with facts as stated by the other witnesses.*
accord (FORMAL) • *I cannot support policies that no longer accord with my principles.*
conform • *It doesn't conform with current building regulations.*
match • *Attendances do not match the ticket sales.*
square • *Does that explanation square with the facts?*
tally • *The figures don't seem to tally.*

agreeable ① ADJECTIVE
pleasant or enjoyable • *I found it a most agreeable experience.*
delightful • *I've had a delightful time.*
enjoyable • *an enjoyable meal*
lovely • *I hope you have a lovely holiday.*
nice • *It would be very nice to get away from it all for a few days.*
pleasant • *This restaurant offers good food in pleasant surroundings.*
pleasurable • *the pleasurable task of deciding where to go on holiday*
ANTONYM:
• disagreeable

agreeable ② ADJECTIVE
willing to allow or do something • *She said she was agreeable to this plan.*
game • *Are you game to try something a little bit different?*
happy • *I'm happy to go along with what everyone else thinks.*

prepared • *Would you be prepared to queue for hours for a ticket?*

ready • *I'm ready to take over if he resigns.*

willing • *Are you willing to take part in a survey?*

agreement NOUN

a decision reached by two or more people • *The two countries have signed agreements on fishing and oil.*

arrangement • *Eventually we came to an arrangement that suited us both.*

contract • *She has signed an exclusive solo-album contract.*

deal (INFORMAL) • *The company recently won a five-year deal to build runways.*

pact • *He ruled out any formal pact with the government.*

settlement • *She accepted an out-of-court settlement of £4000.*

treaty • *negotiations over a treaty on global warming*

aim ① VERB

to plan to do something • *The company aims to sign 1 million customers within five years.*

aspire • *people who aspire to public office*

attempt • *He will attempt to win the title for the second year running.*

intend • *I intend to go to university.*

plan • *Mr Beach was planning to sue over injuries he received.*

propose • *And where do you propose building such a huge thing?*

strive • *He strives hard to keep himself very fit.*

aim ② NOUN

what someone intends to achieve • *Our main aim is to offer a superior product.*

ambition • *His ambition is to sail round the world.*

goal • *I have to keep setting goals for myself.*

intention • *It was always my intention to stay in Italy.*

objective • *His objective was to play golf and win.*

plan • *His plan was to acquire paintings by the best artists in Italy.*

target • *his target of 20 goals this season*

alarm ① NOUN

a feeling of fear • *The cat sprang back in alarm.*

anxiety • *anxiety about crime*

apprehension • *I tensed every muscle in my body in apprehension.*

fright • *The birds smashed into the top of their cages in fright.*

nervousness • *I smiled warmly so he wouldn't see my nervousness.*

panic • *There was panic in the streets of the capital.*

scare • *Despite the scare there are no plans to withdraw the drug.*

ANTONYM:

• calm

alarm ② NOUN
a device used to warn people
of something • *a burglar alarm*
distress signal • *The pilot was
trying to send a distress signal
when the aircraft crashed.*
siren • *a police siren*
warning • *A second air raid
warning sounded over the
capital.*

alarm ③ VERB
to fill with fear • *We could not
see what had alarmed him.*
distress • *He is very distressed
by what happened.*
frighten • *The future frightens
me.*
panic • *He was panicked by his
wife's behaviour.*
scare • *Horses scare me.*
startle • *startled by a gunshot*
unnerve • *Investors had been
unnerved by the country's ailing
stock market.*

ANTONYM:
• calm

alert ① ADJECTIVE
paying full attention
• *apprehended by alert security
staff*
attentive • *an attentive
audience*
observant • *an observant
police officer*
on guard • *on guard against the
threat of invasion*
vigilant • *letter bombs
intercepted by vigilant post office
staff*
wary • *He kept a wary eye on the
dog as he passed the gate.*

ANTONYM:
• unaware

alert ② VERB
to warn of danger • *I was
hoping he'd alert the police.*
forewarn • *The guide had
forewarned me what to expect.*
inform • *The patient was not
properly informed of the risks.*
notify • *The passengers were
notified of the bomb threat.*
warn • *They warned him of the
dangers of sailing alone.*

alike ① ADJECTIVE
similar in some way • *You and
your father are so alike.*
analogous • *a ritual analogous
to those of primitive cultures*
close • *a creature close in
appearance to a panther*
identical • *Nearly all the houses
were identical.*
similar • *These two cheeses are
very similar in taste.*
the same • *products which are
almost the same in every respect*

ANTONYM:
• different

alike ② ADVERB
in a similar way • *I punish all my
pupils alike if they misbehave.*
equally • *Democracy calls for all
people to be treated equally.*
in the same way • *He speaks
in the same way to his boss as to
his own employees.*
similarly • *All the children were
dressed similarly.*
uniformly • *The rules apply
uniformly to everyone.*

alive ① ADJECTIVE
having life • *Do you think he's still alive?*
animate • *animate beings*
breathing • *Not only is he still breathing, but he lives right here in New York.*
living • *The blue whale is the largest living thing on the planet.*
ANTONYM:
• dead

alive ② ADJECTIVE
lively and active • *I never expected to feel so alive in my life again.*
active • *Half an hour's physical activity, five times a week, will keep you active.*
alert • *A brisk walk will make you feel more alert.*
animated • *He becomes animated when talking about his work.*
energetic • *a vital and energetic man*
full of life • *She was so chatty and full of life.*
lively • *Cheryl was a very lively and attractive girl.*
vivacious • *a vivacious personality*
ANTONYM:
• dull

all PRONOUN
the whole of something • *Why did you have to go and say all that?*
each • *Each of us received a free gift.*
every one • *Every one of you must take a share of the blame.*

everything • *Sit down and tell me everything.*
the whole amount • *Have you paid the whole amount of the fine?*
the (whole) lot • *The whole lot of you are under arrest.*
RELATED WORDS:
• PREFIXES pan-, panto-

allow ① VERB
to permit someone to do something • *Smoking will not be allowed.*
approve • *The Housing Minister approved the building of the flats.*
authorise • *authorised to carry weapons*
let • *They won't let her leave the country.*
permit • *Unauthorised personnel are not permitted to enter.*
stand for • *We won't stand for it any more.*
tolerate • *I won't tolerate sloppiness.*
ANTONYM:
• forbid

allow ② VERB
to set aside for a particular purpose • *Allow four hours for the paint to dry.*
allocate • *an efficient method of allocating resources*
allot • *We were allotted just 15 minutes.*
assign • *the full amount of economic aid assigned for the year*
grant • *Funding had been granted for the project.*

set aside • *money set aside for education*

all right ADJECTIVE
acceptable • *It was all right but nothing special.*
acceptable • *We've made an acceptable start, but it could have been better.*
adequate • *Our accommodation was adequate.*
average • *I was only average academically.*
fair • *The overall standard of the entries was fair.*
okay or **OK** (INFORMAL) • *The prices here are okay.*

almost ADVERB
very nearly • *Over the past decade their wages have almost doubled.*
about • *I was about nine at the time.*
approximately • *The family owns approximately 8% of the company.*
close to • *He spent close to 30 years in prison.*
nearly • *The beach was very nearly empty.*
not quite • *It's more than a hill but not quite a mountain.*
practically • *I've known him practically all my life.*

alone ADJECTIVE
not with other people or things • *He was all alone in the middle of the hall.*
detached • *I felt oddly detached from what was going on.*
isolated • *Talking things over in a group meant none of us felt isolated.*

separate • *They were kept separate from the other prisoners.*
single • *Not all single people are looking for partners.*

aloud ADVERB
out loud • *Our father read aloud to us.*
audibly • *Hugh sighed audibly.*
out loud • *I tried not to laugh out loud.*

also ADVERB
in addition • *He is also an army doctor.*
as well • *She published historical novels as well.*
besides • *You get to sample lots of baked things and take home masses of cookies besides.*
furthermore • *Furthermore, they claim that any such interference is completely ineffective.*
into the bargain • *It's a great story and it is funny into the bargain.*
moreover • *They have accused the government of corruption. Moreover, they have named names.*
too • *I was there too.*

always ADVERB
all the time or forever • *She's always moaning.*
continually • *Malcolm was continually changing his mind.*
every time • *You can't get it right every time.*
forever • *He was forever attempting to arrange deals.*
invariably • *Their teamwork was invariably good.*

perpetually • *The two groups are perpetually at loggerheads.*

amaze VERB
to surprise greatly • *He amazed us by his knowledge of Welsh history.*
astonish • *I was astonished by his stupidity.*
astound • *I am astounded at the comments made by the Chief Superintendent.*
shock • *She was shocked by the appalling news.*
stagger • *He was staggered by the sheer size of the crowd.*
stun • *Many cinema-goers were stunned by the film's tragic end.*
surprise • *We'll solve the case ourselves and surprise everyone.*

amazement NOUN
complete surprise • *Much to my amazement, he arrived on time.*
astonishment • *They looked at each other in astonishment.*
shock • *I am still getting over the shock of winning.*
surprise • *To my surprise, I found I liked it.*
wonder • *Cross shook his head in wonder.*

amazing ADJECTIVE
very surprising or remarkable • *some of the most amazing stunts you're ever likely to see*
astonishing • *an astonishing display of physical strength*
astounding • *The results are quite astounding.*
staggering • *a staggering 17% leap in sales*

startling • *startling new evidence*
stunning • *a stunning piece of news*
surprising • *A surprising number of customers order the same sandwich every day.*

among ① PREPOSITION
surrounded by • *The bike lay among piles of chains and pedals.*
amid • *a tiny bungalow amid clusters of trees*
amidst • *She could see the bell tower jutting out amidst the trees.*
in the middle of • *a tiny island in the middle of the Pacific*
in the thick of • *a restaurant built on stilts in the thick of a vast mangrove swamp*
surrounded by • *surrounded by bodyguards*

among ② PREPOSITION
between more than two • *The money will be divided among seven charities.*
between • *Proceeds from the auction will be shared between the artists.*
to each of • *£2,000 to each of the five winners*

amount NOUN
how much there is of something • *I still do a certain amount of work for them.*
expanse • *a vast expanse of grassland*
quantity • *vast quantities of food*
volume • *the sheer volume of traffic and accidents*

ample ADJECTIVE

of an amount: more than enough • *There is ample space for a good-sized kitchen.*

abundant • *providing abundant food for local wildlife*

enough • *Do you have enough money for a taxi home?*

plenty of • *You've had plenty of time to make up your mind.*

sufficient • *The police have sufficient evidence to charge him.*

ancestor NOUN

a person from whom someone is descended • *He could trace his ancestors back 700 years.*

forebear • *our Victorian forebears*

forefather • *the land of their forefathers*

anger ① NOUN

extreme annoyance • *She vented her anger at the umpire.*

fury • *She screamed, her face distorted in fury.*

outrage • *The decisions provoked outrage from human rights groups.*

rage • *An intense rage was burning inside her.*

wrath • *He incurred the wrath of the referee.*

anger ② VERB

to make someone angry • *remarks which will anger his critics*

enrage • *He enraged the government by renouncing the agreement.*

infuriate • *Peter's presence had infuriated Gordon.*

outrage • *Customers are outraged by the bank's soaring profits.*

ANTONYM:
• calm

angry ADJECTIVE

very annoyed • *He gets angry with me if I'm late.*

cross • *She was rather cross about having to trail across London.*

enraged • *The enraged crowd stoned the car, then set it on fire.*

furious • *He is furious at the way his wife has been treated.*

mad (INFORMAL) • *I'm pretty mad about it, I can tell you.*

animal NOUN

a living creature • *He was attacked by wild animals.*

beast • *the threat our ancestors faced from wild beasts*

creature • *sea creatures*

RELATED WORD:
• PREFIX ZOO-

animosity NOUN

a feeling of strong dislike towards someone • *There is no animosity between these two players.*

antagonism • *a history of antagonism between the two sides*

antipathy (FORMAL) • *our growing antipathy towards our manager*

dislike • *She looked at him with dislike.*

hatred • *He didn't bother to conceal his hatred towards my mother.*

hostility • *unacceptable hostility towards minority groups*

ill will • *He didn't bear anyone any ill will.*

malice • *There was no malice in her voice.*

resentment • *There is growing resentment towards newcomers.*

announce VERB

to make known something publicly • *He will announce tonight that he is resigning from office.*

advertise • *He did not want to advertise his presence in the town.*

make known • *Details will be made known tomorrow.*

proclaim • *He loudly proclaimed his innocence.*

reveal • *They were now free to reveal the truth.*

tell • *She was relieved that she'd finally told the full story.*

announcement NOUN

a statement giving information about something • *There has been no formal announcement by either government.*

advertisement • *an advertisement placed in the local newspaper*

broadcast • *In a broadcast on state radio the government announced its plans.*

bulletin • *At 3.30pm a bulletin was released announcing the decision.*

declaration • *a public declaration of support*

report • *Local press reports estimate that at least sixteen people have died.*

statement • *a short statement by her solicitors*

annoy VERB

to irritate or displease someone • *Try making a note of the things which annoy you.*

bother • *I didn't think it would bother me so much to see Brian again.*

displease • *Not wishing to displease her, he avoided answering the question.*

get on someone's nerves (INFORMAL) • *That song gets on my nerves.*

hack off (BRITISH AND NEW ZEALAND; SLANG) • *This will just hack people off more.*

irritate • *The flippancy in her voice seemed to irritate him.*

plague • *We were plagued by mosquitoes.*

vex • *Cassandra was vexed at not having noticed it herself.*

annoyance ① NOUN

a feeling of irritation • *He made no secret of his annoyance.*

displeasure • *She voiced her displeasure at her treatment.*

irritation • *He tried not to let his irritation show.*

annoyance ② NOUN

something that causes irritation • *Snoring can be more than an annoyance.*

bore • *It's a bore to be off sick.*

drag (INFORMAL) • *A dry sandwich is a drag to eat.*

A

nuisance • *He could be a bit of a nuisance when he was drunk.*

pain (INFORMAL) • *The peacocks are a pain – beautiful but noisy.*

pain in the neck (INFORMAL) • *Traffic jams are a pain in the neck.*

pest • *He climbed on the table, pulled my hair, and was generally a pest.*

answer ① VERB

to reply to someone • *I knew Ben was lying when he answered me.*

reply • *He replied that this was absolutely impossible.*

respond • *"Mind your manners!" I responded.*

retort • *Was he afraid, he was asked. "Afraid of what?" he retorted.*

ANTONYM:
• ask

answer ② NOUN

a reply given to someone • *Without waiting for an answer, he turned and went in through the door.*

reply • *I called out a challenge but there was no reply.*

response • *There has been no response to his remarks from the government.*

retort • *His sharp retort clearly made an impact.*

ANTONYM:
• question

anxiety NOUN

nervousness or worry • *our growing anxiety about their safety*

apprehension • *a feeling of apprehension about the future*

concern • *growing concern about the environment*

fear • *His fears might be groundless.*

misgiving • *She had some misgivings about what she had been asked to do.*

nervousness • *I smiled, trying to hide my nervousness.*

unease • *a deep sense of unease about the coming interview*

worry • *a major source of worry to us all*

anxious ADJECTIVE

nervous or worried • *He admitted he was still anxious about the situation.*

apprehensive • *Their families are apprehensive about the trip.*

bothered • *I'm still bothered about what she's going to say.*

concerned • *a phone call from a concerned neighbour*

fearful • *We are all fearful for the security of our jobs.*

nervous • *I still get nervous before a visit to the dentist's.*

troubled • *He was troubled about his son's lifestyle.*

uneasy • *an uneasy feeling that something was wrong*

worried • *His parents are worried about his lack of progress.*

apathetic ADJECTIVE

not interested in anything • *apathetic about politics*

cool • *The idea met with a cool response.*

indifferent • People have become indifferent to the sufferings of others.
passive • His passive attitude made things easier for me.
uninterested • unhelpful and uninterested shop staff

ANTONYM:
• enthusiastic

apologise VERB
to say sorry for something • I apologise for being late.
ask forgiveness • He fell to his knees asking for forgiveness.
beg someone's pardon • I was impolite and I do beg your pardon.
express regret • Mr Galloway expressed regret that he had caused any offence.
say sorry • I wanted to say sorry to her.

appeal ① VERB
to make an urgent request for something • The police appealed for witnesses to come forward.
beg • I begged him to leave me alone.
call upon • Frequently he was called upon to resolve conflicts.
plead • I pleaded to be allowed to go.
request • She had requested that the door to her room be left open.

appeal ② VERB
to attract or interest • The idea appealed to him.
attract • What attracted you to research work?

fascinate • Classical music had fascinated him since the age of three.
interest • It was the garden that really interested me.
please • It pleased him to talk to her.

appeal ③ NOUN
a formal request for something • an appeal for peace
petition • The court rejected their petition.
plea • his emotional plea for help in solving the killing
request • France had agreed to his request for political asylum.

appear ① VERB
to become visible or present • A woman appeared at the far end of the street.
come into view • Nearly fifty gliders came into view to the south of the plateau.
crop up (INFORMAL) • Problems will crop up and hit you before you are ready.
emerge • The postman emerged from his van.
show up (INFORMAL) • He failed to show up at the ceremony.
surface • The same old problems would surface again.
turn up • This is like waiting for a bus that never turns up.

ANTONYM:
• disappear

appear ② VERB
to begin to exist • small white flowers which appear in early summer

become available • *In 1950, legal aid became available in Britain.*

be invented • *The lawnmower was invented in 1830.*

come into being • *Fireworks first came into being with the invention of gunpowder.*

come into existence • *before our solar system came into existence*

come out • *The book first came out in 2010.*

appearance ① NOUN
the time when something begins to exist • *the appearance of computer technology*

advent • *the advent of satellite and cable channels*

arrival • *the arrival of modern technologies*

coming • *the coming of the railways*

debut • *the debut of the new channel*

emergence • *the emergence of pay-per-view TV*

introduction • *the introduction of the minimum wage*

appearance ② NOUN
the way that a person looks • *He used to be so fussy about his appearance.*

bearing • *a tall man with a military bearing*

image • *He urged the rest of the band to update their image.*

look • *She is so much happier with her new look.*

looks • *youthful good looks*

application NOUN
a computer program designed for a particular purpose • *applications for mobile devices*

app • *The app allows the phone to store songs even without access to the internet.*

software • *Download the software onto your phone.*

appointment ① NOUN
an arrangement to meet someone • *She has an appointment with her accountant.*

date • *I have a date with Wendy.*

interview • *a job interview*

meeting • *Can we have a meeting to discuss that?*

rendezvous • *I had almost decided to keep my rendezvous with Tony.*

appointment ② NOUN
the choosing of a person to do a job • *his appointment as manager*

election • *the election of the government in 2015*

naming • *the naming of the new captain*

nomination • *They opposed the nomination of a junior officer to the position.*

selection • *his selection as a parliamentary candidate*

appointment ③ NOUN
a job • *He applied for an appointment in Russia.*

assignment • *my first assignment for The New York Times*

job • *He's trying for a job in the Civil Service.*

place • *All the candidates won places on the ruling council.*
position • *She took up a position at the Arts Council.*
post • *He has held several senior military posts.*

appreciate ① VERB
to value something highly • *He appreciates fine art.*
admire • *All those who knew him will admire him for his work.*
prize • *Military figures made out of lead are prized by collectors.*
rate highly • *The four-year-old mare is rated highly by her trainer.*
respect • *I respect his talent as a pianist.*
treasure • *She treasures her memories of those joyous days.*
value • *I value the work he gives me.*

ANTONYM:
• scorn

appreciate ② VERB
to understand a situation or problem • *I didn't appreciate the seriousness of it at the time.*
be aware of • *I am well aware of the arguments on the other side.*
perceive • *to get pupils to perceive for themselves the relationship between success and effort*
realise • *People don't realise how serious this is.*
recognise • *They have been slow to recognise it as a problem.*
understand • *They are too young to understand what is going on.*

appropriate ADJECTIVE
suitable or acceptable for a given situation • *Jeans are not appropriate wear for work.*
apt • *an apt title for his memoirs*
correct • *the importance of correct behaviour and social niceties*
fitting • *a fitting tribute to a great man*
proper • *the proper course for the court to take*
suitable • *a suitable location*

ANTONYM:
• inappropriate

approval ① NOUN
agreement given to something • *The plan will require approval from the local authority.*
agreement • *The clubs are seeking agreement for a provisional deal.*
authorisation • *We didn't have authorisation to go.*
blessing • *The head teacher appeared to give her blessing to the plan.*
endorsement • *His endorsement has been fervently sought by all the main presidential candidates.*
permission • *They cannot leave the country without permission.*
sanction • *The King cannot enact laws without the sanction of Parliament.*

approval ② NOUN
liking and admiration of a person or thing • *He wanted to gain his father's approval.*

admiration • *a strategy that is winning admiration from around the world*

esteem • *Their public esteem has never been lower.*

favour • *He has won favour with a wide range of groups.*

praise • *She is full of praise for the range of excellent services available.*

respect • *We all have so much respect for her.*

ANTONYM:
• disapproval

approve ① VERB
to think something or someone is good • *Not everyone approves of the festival.*

admire • *I admire him for his work.*

favour • *The opposition parties favour constitutional reform.*

praise • *He praised the fans for their continued support.*

respect • *I want him to respect me as an individual.*

think highly of • *He thought highly of his brother.*

ANTONYM:
• disapprove

approve ② VERB
to agree formally to something • *The court approved the compensation plan.*

authorise • *to authorise the use of military force*

consent to • *He finally consented to the visit.*

endorse • *I can endorse their opinion wholeheartedly.*

permit • *The doorman is not*

allowed to permit them entry to the film.

sanction • *He may now be ready to sanction the use of force.*

ANTONYM:
• veto

approximate ADJECTIVE
close but not exact • *We believe that an approximate figure of 20% is nearer the mark.*

estimated • *Our estimated time of arrival is 3.30.*

inexact • *Forecasting is an inexact science.*

loose • *a loose translation*

rough • *a rough estimate*

ANTONYM:
• exact

ardent ADJECTIVE
full of enthusiasm and passion • *an ardent supporter of capital punishment*

avid • *an avid follower of the team*

devoted • *surrounded by devoted fans*

enthusiastic • *He was a knowledgeable and enthusiastic collector of fine china.*

fervent • *a fervent admirer of his*

intense • *his intense love of football*

keen • *a keen supporter of the cause*

passionate • *He developed a passionate interest in motor racing.*

ANTONYM:
• apathetic

area ① NOUN
a particular part of a place
• *a built-up area of the city*
district • *I drove around the business district.*
locality • *All other factories in the locality went on strike in sympathy.*
neighbourhood • *She no longer takes evening strolls around her neighbourhood.*

region • *a remote mountainous region of Afghanistan*
zone • *a war zone*

area ② NOUN
the size of a two-dimensional surface • *The islands cover a total area of 625 square kilometres.*
expanse • *a huge expanse of blue-green sea*
extent • *the extent of the rain forest*
range • *a driver's range of vision*
size • *a country nearly three times the size of ours*

argue ① VERB
to disagree with someone in an angry way • *They argued over the cost of the taxi fare.*
bicker • *They bickered endlessly about procedure.*
disagree • *They can communicate even when they strongly disagree.*
fall out (INFORMAL) • *Mum and I used to fall out a lot.*
feud • *feuding neighbours*
fight • *We're always fighting about money.*
quarrel • *My brother quarrelled with my father.*

row • *We started rowing about whose turn it was next.*
squabble • *The children were squabbling over the remote control.*
wrangle • *Delegates wrangled over the future of the organisation.*

argue ② VERB
to try to prove • *She argued that her client had been wrongly accused.*
assert • *The defendants continue to assert their innocence.*
claim • *Statisticians claim that the book contains inaccuracies.*
debate • *Parliament will debate the issue today.*
maintain • *He had always maintained his innocence.*
reason • *I reasoned that if he could do it, so could I.*

argument ① NOUN
an angry disagreement • *She got into an argument with one of the marchers.*
barney (BRITISH, AUSTRALIAN AND NEW ZEALAND; INFORMAL) • *We had such a barney that we nearly split up.*
blue (AUSTRALIAN; SLANG) • *He gets into more blues with authority than I do.*
clash • *clashes between police and demonstrators*
dispute • *a dispute over ticket allocation*
feud • *a two-year feud between neighbours*
fight • *We had another fight about money.*

row • *Maxine and I had a terrible row.*

squabble • *a family squabble over Sunday lunch*

argument ② NOUN
a set of reasons presented for something • *There's a strong argument for lowering the price.*

case • *the case for his defence*

grounds • *facts providing grounds for an unfair dismissal complaint*

logic • *The logic is that, without more growth, the deficit will rise.*

reasoning • *the reasoning behind the decision*

arrange ① VERB
to make plans to do something • *Why don't you arrange to meet him later?*

fix up • *I fixed up an appointment to see her.*

organise • *She organised the trip to the museum.*

plan • *She planned to leave in August.*

schedule • *Our appointment is scheduled for Tuesday.*

arrange ② VERB
to set things out in a particular order • *He started to arrange the books in piles.*

classify • *Weather forecasters classify clouds into several different groups.*

group • *The fact sheet is grouped into seven sections.*

order • *Order the names alphabetically.*

organise • *He began to organise his materials.*

sort • *The students are sorted into three ability groups.*

arrest ① VERB
to take someone into custody • *Police arrested five men in connection with the attack.*

apprehend • *Police have not apprehended her killer.*

capture • *Her accomplice was captured by Dutch police.*

nick (BRITISH; SLANG) • *Keep quiet or we'll all get nicked.*

seize • *Two military observers were seized by rebels yesterday.*

take prisoner • *He was taken prisoner in 1940 at the fall of Dunkirk.*

arrest ② NOUN
the act of arresting someone • *The police made two arrests.*

apprehension • *information leading to the apprehension of the killer*

capture • *He was trying to evade capture by security forces.*

seizure • *the mass seizure of diplomats as hostages*

article ① NOUN
a piece of writing in a newspaper or magazine • *There's an article about it in today's paper.*

feature • *a feature about climate change*

item • *I read an item about this only last week.*

piece • *I disagree with your recent piece about Australia.*

story • *Most newspapers had a story about the film's premiere.*

article ② NOUN
a particular item • *household articles*
item • *Various items have gone missing from my desk.*
object • *everyday objects such as wooden spoons*
thing • *I have a few things to buy for the trip.*

ashamed ADJECTIVE
feeling embarrassed or guilty • *He was not even ashamed of what he had done.*
embarrassed • *I'm not embarrassed to admit I cried.*
guilty • *When she realised I was watching, she looked guilty.*
humiliated • *I felt humiliated at the scene he was causing.*
sheepish • *"I'm afraid it was my idea," he admitted, looking sheepish.*
sorry • *She's really sorry for all the trouble she's caused.*

ANTONYM:
• proud

ask ① VERB
to put a question to someone • *She asked me if I'd enjoyed my dinner.*
inquire • *I rang up to inquire about train times.*
interrogate • *I interrogated everyone even slightly involved.*
query • *He queried whether it could have been sabotage.*
question • *He was questioned by police.*
quiz • *He was quizzed about his eligibility for benefits.*

ANTONYM:
• answer

ask ② VERB
to make a request to someone • *We had to ask him to leave.*
appeal • *The police appealed for witnesses to come forward.*
beg • *I begged him to leave me alone.*
demand • *I demanded an explanation from him.*
implore • *I implored him not to give it up.*
plead • *She pleaded to be allowed to go.*
seek • *Always seek legal advice before entering into any agreement.*

ask ③ VERB
to invite someone • *Not everybody had been asked to the wedding.*
bid (LITERARY) • *They all smiled at him and bade him eat.*
invite • *She invited him to her 26th birthday party.*

aspect NOUN
a feature of something • *Exam results are only one aspect of a school's success.*
consideration • *The cost involved will be a chief consideration in our choice.*
element • *Fitness is now an important element in our lives.*
factor • *an important factor in a child's development*
feature • *the most significant feature of his childhood*
part • *Respect is an important part of any relationship.*

point • *There is another point to remember when making your decision.*

side • *He had a darker side to his character.*

assemble ① VERB

to gather together in a group • *a convenient place for students to assemble between classes*

collect • *We all collected round him to listen.*

come together • *a common room where we can come together and relax*

congregate • *Young people love to congregate here in the evenings.*

convene • *A grand jury has convened to gather evidence.*

gather • *We all gathered in the board room.*

mass • *Troops were massing on both sides of the border.*

assemble ② VERB

to fit the parts of something together • *Workers were assembling planes.*

build • *A carpenter built the shelves for us.*

construct • *He had constructed a crude explosive device.*

erect • *Stagehands are employed to erect the scenery.*

make • *I like making model aeroplanes.*

put together • *You can buy the parts and put it together yourself.*

assistant NOUN

a person who helps someone • *His assistant took over while he went out.*

aide • *a presidential aide*

ally • *her political allies*

colleague • *a business colleague*

helper • *volunteer helpers*

right-hand man • *the resignation of the manager's right-hand man*

associate ① VERB

to connect one thing with another • *We associate summer with holidays.*

connect • *a common problem directly connected with stress*

couple • *He had great business talents coupled with deep political convictions.*

identify • *Candidates want to identify themselves with reform.*

link • *Our sense of well-being is linked to how confident we feel.*

associate ② VERB

to spend time with a person • *I began associating with different crowds of people.*

hang out (INFORMAL) • *People want to hang out with you for the wrong reasons.*

mingle • *reporters who mingled freely with the crowd*

mix • *local youths who want to mix with the foreign tourists*

run around (INFORMAL) • *What's he doing running around with her?*

socialise • *She made little effort to socialise with other staff.*

associate ③ NOUN

a person known through work • *the restaurant owner's business associates*

colleague • *learning from more experienced colleagues*
co-worker • *Their co-workers often worked seven days a week.*
workmate • *employees who expose dishonest workmates*

association ① NOUN
an organisation • *a research association*
body • *the chairman of the police officers' representative body*
club • *the local Young Conservatives' club*
company • *a major motor company*
confederation • *the Confederation of British Industry*
group • *an environmental group*
institution • *a member of various financial institutions*
league • *the World Muslim League*
society • *the Royal Society for the Protection of Birds*
syndicate • *a syndicate of international banks*

association ② NOUN
a connection or involvement with a person or group • *his association with a political group*
affiliation • *He has no affiliation with any political party.*
attachment • *Mother and child form a close attachment.*
bond • *There is a special bond between us.*
connection • *He has denied any connection with the organisation.*

relationship • *Ours was an excellent professional relationship.*
tie • *I had very close ties with the family.*

assume ① VERB
to accept that something is true • *I assumed that he would turn up.*
believe • *I believe she'll be back next week.*
guess (INFORMAL) • *I guess she thought that was pretty smart.*
imagine • *You tend to imagine that you cannot put a foot wrong.*
suppose • *I see no reason to suppose that it isn't working.*
think • *They thought that they had the match won.*

assume ② VERB
to take responsibility for something • *Mr Cross will assume the role of Chief Executive.*
accept • *He accepted the role of player-captain.*
shoulder • *We must shoulder much of the responsibility for the damage.*
take on • *Don't take on more responsibilities than you can handle.*
undertake • *He undertook to edit the text himself.*

astute ADJECTIVE
very intelligent or perceptive • *an astute judge of character*
alert • *She has a very quick and alert mind.*
clever • *a clever business move*

keen • *a keen understanding of politics*

perceptive • *his perceptive analysis of the situation*

quick • *He has an enquiring mind and a quick intelligence.*

sharp • *His gentle manner disguised a sharp mind.*

shrewd • *He demonstrated a shrewd understanding of human nature.*

smart • *a very smart move*

attach VERB

to join or fasten things together • *The gadget can be attached to any surface.*

affix • *His name was affixed to the wall of his cubicle.*

connect • *Connect the pipe to the tap.*

couple • *The engine is coupled to a gearbox.*

fasten • *The shelves are fastened to the wall with screws.*

join • *two sticks joined together by a chain*

link • *tree houses linked by ropes*

tie • *He tied the dog to a post with its leash.*

ANTONYM:
• separate

attachment ① NOUN

a feeling of love and affection • *Mother and child form a close attachment.*

affection • *the affection between a pet and its owner*

bond • *There has always been a strong bond between us.*

fondness • *I have a great fondness for all animals.*

liking • *He has never shown any liking for his colleagues.*

love • *A deep love gradually developed between them.*

attachment ② NOUN

a part attached to something else • *The drill comes with a wide range of attachments.*

accessory • *a range of accessories for your mobile phone*

component • *Additional components are available as listed.*

fitting • *bathroom fittings*

fixture • *The box can be adapted to take a light fixture.*

part • *Extra parts can be added later.*

unit • *The unit plugs into any TV set.*

attack ① VERB

to use violence against someone or something • *I thought he was going to attack me.*

assault • *The gang assaulted him with iron bars.*

charge • *He ordered us to charge.*

invade • *The allies invaded the Italian mainland at Anzio.*

raid • *He was found guilty of raiding a bank.*

set upon • *As the lorry drove east it was set upon by bandits.*

storm • *The refugees decided to storm the embassy.*

attack ② VERB

to criticise someone strongly • *She attacked the government's economic policies.*

blast • He blasted the referee for his inconsistency.

censure (FORMAL) • The bank has been censured and fined by the authority.

criticise • The regime has been harshly criticised.

have a go at (BRITISH; INFORMAL) • If they made a mistake the crowd would have a go at them.

put down (INFORMAL) • He was always putting me down.

vilify (FORMAL) • He was vilified, hounded and forced into exile.

attack ③ NOUN

violent physical action against someone or something • a vicious attack on an unarmed man

assault • The rebels are poised for a new assault.

charge • a bayonet charge

invasion • the Roman invasion of Britain

offensive • the government's military offensive against the rebels

onslaught • civilians trying to flee from the military onslaught

raid • a raid on a house by armed police

attempt ① VERB

to try to do something • They attempted to escape.

endeavour • I will endeavour to arrange it.

seek • We have never sought to impose our views.

strive • The school strives to treat pupils as individuals.

try • I tried hard to persuade him to stay.

try your hand at • He'd always wanted to try his hand at writing.

attempt ② NOUN

an act of trying to do something • one of his rare attempts at humour

bid • a bid to save the newspaper

crack (INFORMAL) • his third crack at the world heavyweight title

go (INFORMAL) • My mum suggested I should have a go at becoming a jockey.

shot (INFORMAL) • We'd like a shot at winning the league.

stab (INFORMAL) • Several tennis stars have had a stab at acting.

try • That makes the scheme worth a try.

attitude NOUN

someone's way of thinking and behaving • negative attitudes to work

outlook • behaviour that seems contrary to his whole outlook

perspective • It gave me a new perspective on life.

point of view • Try to look at this from my point of view.

position • What's your position on this issue?

stance • the Church's stance on social issues

attract VERB

to appeal to or interest • The trials have attracted many leading riders.

A

attractive

appeal to • *The idea appealed to him.*

draw • *The match drew a large crowd.*

entice • *She resisted attempts to entice her into politics.*

lure • *They were being lured into a trap.*

pull (INFORMAL) • *They have to employ performers to pull a crowd.*

tempt • *Can I tempt you with some chocolate cake?*

ANTONYM:
• repel

attractive ADJECTIVE

pleasant, especially to look at • *an attractive woman*

appealing • *a sense of humour that I found very appealing*

charming • *a charming little village*

fetching • *a fetching outfit*

handsome • *a handsome man*

lovely • *a lovely island*

pretty • *a shy, pretty girl*

ANTONYM:
• unattractive

attribute NOUN

a quality or feature • *a normal attribute of human behaviour*

characteristic • *their physical characteristics*

feature • *the most striking feature of his music*

property • *the magnetic properties of iron*

quality • *His humility is one of his most endearing qualities.*

trait • *personality traits*

augment VERB

to add something to something else • *a good way to augment your basic wage*

add to • *A fitted kitchen adds to the value of your house.*

boost • *people who boost their earnings by working part-time from home*

complement • *an in-work benefit that complements earnings*

increase • *He is eager to increase his income by any means.*

reinforce • *measures which will reinforce their current strengths*

supplement • *I suggest supplementing your diet with vitamin A.*

top up • *compulsory contributions to top up pension schemes*

authentic ADJECTIVE

real and genuine • *an authentic French recipe*

bona fide • *We are happy to donate to bona fide charities.*

dinkum (AUSTRALIAN AND NEW ZEALAND; INFORMAL) • *a place which serves dinkum Aussie tucker*

genuine • *Experts are convinced the manuscript is genuine.*

real • *It's a real Rembrandt.*

true • *Of course she's not a true blonde.*

ANTONYM:
• fake

automatic ① ADJECTIVE

operating mechanically by

itself • *Modern trains have automatic doors.*

automated • *highly automated production lines*

mechanical • *the oldest working mechanical clock in the world*

robot • *a robot telescope*

self-propelled • *self-propelled artillery*

automatic ② ADJECTIVE

without conscious thought • *automatic body functions*

instinctive • *an instinctive reaction*

involuntary • *involuntary muscle movements*

natural • *the insect's natural instinct to feed*

reflex • *Blushing is a reflex action linked to the nervous system.*

automobile NOUN

(AMERICAN)

a vehicle for carrying a few people • *the Japanese automobile manufacturer*

car • *My dad's promised me a car if I pass my finals.*

motor (OLD-FASHIONED) • *He's bought himself a flash new motor.*

vehicle • *A child ran straight out in front of the vehicle.*

available ADJECTIVE

ready for use • *There are three small boats available for hire.*

accessible • *This information is accessible on the internet.*

at hand • *Having the right equipment at hand will be enormously useful.*

at someone's disposal • *Do you have all the facts at your disposal?*

free • *There was only one seat free on the train.*

handy • *Keep your keys handy so you can get into your car quickly.*

to hand • *Keep your insurance details to hand when driving.*

ANTONYM:

• unavailable

average ① ADJECTIVE

standard or normal • *the average American teenager*

normal • *I am now back to leading a perfectly normal life.*

regular • *He's just a regular guy.*

standard • *the standard price of milk*

typical • *A typical day begins at 8.30.*

usual • *This isn't the usual kind of mail-order catalogue.*

average ② : **on average** ADVERB

for the most part • *Men are, on average, taller than women.*

as a rule • *As a rule, the fee is roughly equal to the savings you have made.*

generally • *Organic food generally costs more to produce.*

normally • *Normally, the transport system carries 50,000 passengers a day.*

typically • *In America, estate agents typically charge 5–6% of the sale price.*

usually • *In good condition, these models usually fetch up to 300 dollars at auction.*

A

avoid ① VERB
to make an effort not to do
something • *We economists
always try to avoid giving a
straight answer.*
dodge • *dodging games by
feigning illness*
duck out of (INFORMAL)
• *ducking out of the post-match
press conference*
fight shy of • *She fought shy of
confronting her critics.*
refrain from • *Mrs Hardie
refrained from making any
comment.*
shirk • *We won't shirk our
responsibility.*

avoid ② VERB
to keep away from someone
or something • *She thought he
was trying to avoid her.*
dodge • *He refuses to dodge his
critics.*
elude • *an attempt to elude
photographers*
eschew (FORMAL) • *He
eschewed publicity and avoided
nightclubs.*
evade • *He managed to evade
the police.*
shun • *Everybody shunned
him.*
sidestep • *Rarely does he
sidestep a question.*
steer clear of • *It would be best
to steer clear of her.*

aware ① : **aware of**
ADJECTIVE
conscious of something • *She
was acutely aware of the noise of
the city.*

acquainted with • *He was
well acquainted with American
literature.*
conscious of • *She was very
conscious of Max studying her.*
familiar with • *I am not
familiar with your work.*
mindful of • *Everyone should be
mindful of the dangers.*
ANTONYM:
• unaware

aware ② ADJECTIVE
knowing about something
• *Keep me aware of any
developments.*
informed • *the importance of
keeping the public properly
informed*
in the picture • *He's always
kept me in the picture.*
knowledgeable • *He's very
knowledgeable about new
technology.*

awful ADJECTIVE
very unpleasant or very bad
• *the same awful jokes*
appalling • *living under the
most appalling conditions*
dreadful • *They told us the
dreadful news.*
frightful (OLD-FASHIONED)
• *a frightful ordeal*
ghastly • *It was a ghastly week
– the worst of my life.*
horrendous • *The violence used
was horrendous.*
terrible • *Her French is terrible.*

Bb

babble VERB
to talk in an excited way • *He babbled on and on.*
burble • *He burbles on about the goals he has scored.*
chatter • *Jane chattered about the children.*
gabble • *I started to gabble in the interview.*
prattle • *Alan is prattling on again.*

baby NOUN
a very young child • *I've had this birthmark since I was a baby.*
ankle-biter (AUSTRALIAN AND NEW ZEALAND; SLANG) • *I knew him when he was just an ankle-biter.*
bairn (SCOTTISH) • *My wife's expecting a bairn.*
child • *They celebrated the birth of their first child.*
infant • *young mums with infants in prams*

back ① NOUN
the part that is behind the front • *the back of a postcard*
end • *the end of the queue*
rear • *the rear of the building*
reverse • *the reverse of the sheet*
stern • *the stern of a boat*

ANTONYM:
• front

back ② VERB
to support a person or organisation • *His friends are backing him.*
advocate • *Mr Jones advocates longer school days.*
encourage • *The government is encouraging better child care.*
endorse • *Do you endorse his opinion?*
favour • *I favour a different approach.*
promote • *Ann is promoting Alan's ideas.*
support • *We supported his political campaign.*
ANTONYM:
• oppose

background NOUN
where you come from • *a rich background*
culture • *people from different cultures*
environment • *the environment I grew up in*
history • *She has an interesting history.*
upbringing • *a strict upbringing*

bad ① ADJECTIVE
harmful, unpleasant or upsetting • *I have some bad news.*
▶ see Word Study **bad**, page 702
ANTONYM:
• good

bad ② ADJECTIVE
of poor quality • *bad roads*

B

▶ see Word Study **bad**, page 702

ANTONYM:
• satisfactory

bad ③ ADJECTIVE
evil in character • a bad person
▶ see Word Study **bad**, page 702

ANTONYM:
• good

badly ① ADVERB
in an inferior way • This essay is
badly written.

inadequately • He had been
inadequately trained for the job.
ineptly • a department which is
run ineptly
poorly • The event had been
poorly organised.
shoddily • housing which is
ugly and shoddily built
unsatisfactorily • an
unsatisfactorily regulated system

ANTONYM:
• well

badly ② ADVERB
seriously • She was badly hurt in
a fall.

deeply • I was deeply hurt by
these comments.
desperately • Felicity looked
desperately unhappy.
gravely (FORMAL) • He was
gravely ill before his heart
operation.
seriously • Four people have
been seriously injured.

ANTONYM:
• slightly

badly ③ ADVERB
in a cruel manner • He treated
his dog badly.

brutally • The words came out
more brutally than I had intended.
callously • She taunted her
sister callously.
cruelly • He was cruelly
tormented by his older brothers.
savagely • savagely beaten by
thugs
viciously • He struck me
viciously across the face.

ANTONYM:
• well

bait NOUN
something used to tempt
someone • Charles isn't taking
the bait.

bribe • a politician who took bribes
decoy • He acted as a decoy to
trap the murderer.
inducement • financial
inducements to talk to the
newspapers
lure • the lure of a huge salary
temptation • the temptation
of easy money

balance ① VERB
to make or remain steady
• Balancing on one leg is difficult.

level • House prices have levelled.
stabilise • attempts to stabilise
the economy
steady • He steadied himself
and shot at goal.

balance ② NOUN
a stable relationship between
things • the chemical balance of
the brain

equilibrium • the political
equilibrium of Europe
equity • plans for greater equity
of incomes

parity • *She won pay parity with male colleagues.*

ball NOUN
a round object • *a ball of wool*
drop • *a drop of blood*
globe • *the globe of the eyeball*
pellet • *an airgun pellet*
sphere • *a sphere the size of the earth*

ban ① VERB
to disallow something • *I am banned from taking part.*
bar • *The press will be barred from the talks.*
disqualify • *He was disqualified from driving.*
exclude • *They were excluded from the maths class.*
forbid • *The rules forbid the use of force.*
outlaw • *regulations outlawing child labour*
prohibit • *a law that prohibits alcohol*
ANTONYM:
• permit

ban ② NOUN
a rule disallowing something • *a ban on junk food advertising*
disqualification • *a four-year disqualification from athletics*
embargo • *an embargo on trade with the country*
prohibition • *a prohibition on tobacco*
suppression • *the suppression of anti-government protests*
ANTONYM:
• permit

band ① NOUN
a group of musicians who play together • *a singer in a rock and roll band*
group • *They formed the group while they were still at school.*
orchestra • *the National Youth Orchestra*

band ② NOUN
a group of people who share a common purpose • *a band of rebels*
bunch • *A bunch of protesters were picketing the factory.*
company • *a company of actors*
crowd • *A small crowd of onlookers had gathered.*
gang • *a gang of criminals*
party • *a party of sightseers*
troupe • *She toured with a professional dance troupe.*

bang ① VERB
to hit or put something down hard, with a loud noise • *a toddler banging a saucepan with a wooden spoon*
beat • *They sat in a circle, beating small drums.*
hammer • *The supporters hammered on the windows of the bus.*
hit • *They were hitting the sides of the van with sticks.*
knock • *I knocked on the door for ages, but no-one answered.*
pound • *We pounded on the walls.*
slam • *I slammed down the receiver.*
thump • *The children cheered and thumped on their desks.*

bang ② NOUN
a sudden, short, loud noise
• *The TV exploded with a bang.*
blast • *the ear-splitting blast of a cannon*
boom • *There was a boom and a cloud of smoke.*
crack • *the crack of a pistol shot*
detonation • *We heard several loud detonations coming from the building.*
explosion • *the deafening explosion of gunshots*
thump • *She dropped her case to the floor with a loud thump.*

bang ③ NOUN
a hard or painful bump against something • *I got a nasty bang on the elbow.*
blow • *a blow to the side of the head*
clout (INFORMAL) • *She gave him a swift clout on the ear.*
knock • *Knocks like this can cause damage to the spine.*
thump • *Ralph got a thump on the chest.*
whack (INFORMAL) • *She gave the horse a whack on the rump.*

banish ① VERB
to exile someone • *She banished him from the house.*
deport • *Many fans are being deported from Italy.*
eject • *He was ejected from the club.*
evict • *Police evicted ten families from the building.*
exile • *He was exiled from Russia.*
expel • *She was expelled from the university.*

transport • *He was transported to a prison camp.*

banish ② VERB
to get rid of something or someone • *to banish illness*
discard • *Read the instructions before discarding the box.*
dismiss • *I dismissed the idea from my mind.*
dispel • *The myths are being dispelled.*
eliminate • *They eliminated him from their enquiries.*
eradicate • *projects to eradicate certain diseases*
remove • *talks to remove the last obstacles to the deal*

bank ① NOUN
a store of something • *a blood bank*
fund • *a pension fund*
hoard • *a hoard of treasure*
reserve • *the world's oil reserves*
stock • *stocks of paper and ink*
store • *a secret store of sweets*

bank ② NOUN
the edge of a river or lake • *He sat fishing on the bank.*
brink • *orchards near the brink of the sea cliffs*
edge • *She stood too close to the edge and fell in.*
shore • *He swam towards the shore.*
side • *a picnic by the side of the river*

bar ① NOUN
a piece of metal • *bars across the windows*
pole • *He was tied to a pole.*

rail • *a curtain rail*
rod • *a fishing rod*
shaft • *the shaft of a spear*

bar ② VERB
to stop someone • *His bodyguards barred the way.*
obstruct • *Vehicles have obstructed the entrance.*
prevent • *A fence prevents people from entering.*

bare ① ADJECTIVE
not covered • *bare legs*
exposed • *His whole back is exposed.*
uncovered • *His arms were uncovered.*
ANTONYM:
• covered

bare ② ADJECTIVE
with nothing on top or inside • *a small bare office*
empty • *an empty room*
open • *open country*
spartan • *spartan accommodation*

barely ADVERB
only just • *She is barely sixteen.*
almost • *I almost didn't make it.*
hardly • *I could hardly believe it.*
just • *They only just won.*
scarcely • *I can scarcely hear her.*

barren ADJECTIVE
with nothing growing on it • *a barren desert*
arid • *the arid lands of Botswana*
desert • *desert regions*
desolate • *a desolate place*
dry • *poor, dry countries*
empty • *the empty desert*
waste • *waste land*

ANTONYM:
• fertile

barrier ① NOUN
something preventing entry • *Demonstrators broke through the barriers.*
barricade • *a barricade of vehicles*
fence • *a garden fence*
obstruction • *Check the exhaust pipe is clear of obstructions.*
wall • *the huge city walls*

barrier ② NOUN
something that prevents progress • *plans to reduce the barriers to trade*
handicap • *It is a handicap not knowing a foreign language.*
hindrance • *a potential hindrance to the peace process*
hurdle • *the first hurdle in a job search*
impediment • *a serious impediment to progess*
obstacle • *the main obstacle to victory*

base ① NOUN
the lowest part of something • *the base of the cliffs*
bed • *the river bed*
bottom • *the bottom of the lake*
foot • *the foot of the mountain*
foundation • *They have laid the foundations for the new building.*
pedestal • *The statue is back on its pedestal.*
stand • *a microphone stand*
ANTONYM:
• top

base ② NOUN
the place you work from • *a military base*
camp • *refugee camps*
centre • *a health centre*
headquarters • *army headquarters in Colombo*
post • *a military post in the capital*
station • *the police station*

base ③ VERB
to use as a foundation • *The film is based on a true story.*
build • *a reputation built on lies*
derive • *The name is derived from a Greek word.*
found • *My hopes were founded on a mistake.*
ground • *I like a film to be grounded in reality.*
hinge • *The whole play hinges on one character.*

basic ADJECTIVE
most necessary • *the basic requirements for the job*
elementary • *elementary computer training*
essential • *essential reading and writing skills*
fundamental • *fundamental rights*
key • *key skills such as communication and teamwork*
necessary • *They lack the necessary resources.*
vital • *vital supplies*

basis NOUN
the main principle of something • *The same theme is the basis of several poems.*
core • *the core of the country's problems*

fundamental • *the fundamentals of road safety*
heart • *the heart of the matter*
premise • *the premise of his argument*
principle • *the principles of Buddhism*

bay ① NOUN
a curve in a coastline • *the Bay of Biscay*
cove • *a sandy cove with white cliffs*
gulf • *the Gulf of Mexico*
inlet • *a deep inlet on the west coast*
sound • *streams that run into the sound*

bay ② VERB
to make a howling noise • *wolves baying in the moonlight*
bark • *a small dog barking at a seagull*
cry • *I heard animals cry in the forest.*
howl • *distant coyotes howling in the night*
yelp • *A dog snapped and yelped at them.*

beach NOUN
an area beside the sea • *making sandcastles on the beach*
coast • *a day at the coast*
sands • *the long white sands of Goa*
seashore • *walks along the seashore*
seaside • *trips to the seaside*
shore • *He swam out from the shore.*
strand • *collecting shells on the strand*

bear ① VERB
to carry something • *The ice wasn't thick enough to bear their weight.*
carry • *He always carried a gun.*
convey (FORMAL) • *The taxi conveyed us to the centre.*
hold • *She held the baby in her arms.*
support • *Thick wooden posts support the ceiling.*
take • *You'd better take an umbrella.*

bear ② VERB
to have or show something • *The room bore the signs of neglect.*
exhibit • *He began to exhibit symptoms of the disease.*
harbour • *She still harbours feelings of resentment.*
have • *I have a grudge against her.*

bear ③ VERB
to accept something • *He can't bear to talk about it.*
abide • *I can't abide arrogant people.*
endure • *The pain was hard to endure.*
stand • *I can't stand the cold weather.*
stomach • *He could not stomach violence.*
suffer • *I had to suffer his company all day.*
tolerate • *The ability to tolerate pain varies from person to person.*

beat ① VERB
to hit someone or something hard • *The rain was beating on the windowpanes.*

batter • *The waves kept battering the life raft.*
buffet • *Their plane was buffeted by storms.*
hit • *He hit me on the head.*
pound • *Someone was pounding on the door.*
strike • *She struck him across the mouth.*
thrash • *My friends thrashed tunelessly at their guitars.*

beat ② VERB
to defeat • *She was easily beaten in the race.*
defeat • *The team hasn't been defeated all year.*
outdo • *One man was trying to outdo the other.*
outstrip • *The company is outstripping its rivals.*
overcome • *Molly had overcome her fear of flying.*
overwhelm • *One attack could overwhelm the enemy.*
vanquish (LITERARY) • *the man who helped vanquish Napoleon*

beat ③ NOUN
a rhythm • *the thumping beat of rock music*
cadence • *the pulsing cadences of his music*
metre • *the strict metre of the poem*
rhythm • *His foot tapped a rhythm on the floor.*
stress • *differences of stress in speech*
time • *a song written in waltz time*

beautiful ADJECTIVE
attractive or pleasing • *beautiful music*

attractive • *an attractive woman*
delightful • *The perfume is delightful.*
fine • *a fine summer's day*
gorgeous • *a gorgeous man*
lovely • *You look lovely.*
pleasing • *a pleasing appearance*
ANTONYM:
• ugly

beauty ① NOUN
the quality of being beautiful
• *an area of outstanding beauty*
attractiveness • *the attractiveness of the region*
charm • *a woman of great charm*
elegance • *the elegance of the overall design*
loveliness • *the loveliness of the scene*
ANTONYM:
• ugliness

beauty ② NOUN
an attractive feature • *The beauty of the fund is its simplicity.*
advantage • *the advantages of the new system over the old one*
asset • *The one asset the job provided was contacts.*
attraction • *The main attraction of the place is the monument.*
benefit • *Every age has its benefits.*

because CONJUNCTION
for the reason that • *I went home because I was tired.*

as • *Don't cook for me as I'll be home late.*
since • *Since you didn't listen, I'll repeat that.*

before ADVERB
at a previous time • *Have you been to Greece before?*
earlier • *Here is a cake I made earlier.*
formerly • *He had formerly been in the army.*
in advance • *We booked the room well in advance.*
previously • *Previously she had little time to work.*
sooner • *I wish I'd arrived sooner.*
ANTONYM:
• after

RELATED WORDS:
• PREFIXES ante-, fore-, pre-

beg VERB
to ask anxiously for something
• *I begged him to leave me alone.*
beseech (LITERARY) • *He beseeched the queen to show mercy.*
implore • *I implore you not to say anything.*
petition • *He petitioned the Court to let him go free.*
plead • *She was pleading with me to stay.*

begin VERB
to start or cause to start • *She began to move around the room.*
commence (FORMAL) • *He commenced his journey.*
inaugurate (FORMAL) • *The committee was inaugurated ten days ago.*

initiate • *They wanted to initiate a discussion.*
originate • *Mankind may have originated in Africa.*
set about • *He set about tackling his problems.*
start • *The meeting starts at 10 o'clock.*
ANTONYM:
• end

beginner NOUN
someone learning to do something • *a beginner's course*
apprentice • *an apprentice in a law firm*
learner • *young learners of French*
novice • *a complete novice at competitive cycling*
starter • *new starters at school*
trainee • *a trainee in a newspaper office*
ANTONYM:
• expert

beginning NOUN
where something starts • *the beginning of the city*
birth • *the birth of modern art*
commencement (FORMAL) • *a date for the commencement of talks*
opening • *the opening of the trial*
origin • *the origins of civilisation*
outset • *There were lots of problems from the outset.*
start • *the start of all the trouble*
ANTONYM:
• end

behave VERB
to act in a certain way • *They were behaving badly.*
act • *He is acting like a spoilt child.*
function • *They are functioning as a team.*
operate • *I know how Graham operates.*
work • *My mind is working well today.*

belief ① NOUN
the certainty something is true • *belief in reincarnation*
confidence • *I have every confidence that you'll do well.*
conviction • *She speaks with conviction.*
judgment • *My judgment is that he should leave.*
opinion • *Robert has strong opinions.*
trust • *She has complete trust that you'll help her.*
view • *In my view, he is wrong.*

belief ② NOUN
a principle of a religion or system • *the culture and beliefs of ancient times*
creed • *people of every race and creed*
doctrine • *Christian doctrine*
dogma • *religious dogma*
faith • *Do you practise any faith?*
ideology • *different political ideologies*
principle • *the principles of Jewish faith*
tenet (FORMAL) • *the fundamental tenets of Islam*

believable ADJECTIVE
possible or likely to be the case
• The book is full of believable
characters.
credible • credible witnesses
imaginable • It is scarcely
imaginable that it happened
here.
likely • It's more likely that she
forgot.
plausible • a plausible
explanation
possible • It's quite possible
that I'm wrong.
probable • the most probable
outcome
ANTONYM:
• unbelievable

believe VERB
to accept something is true
• Don't believe everything you
read in the papers.
accept • He can't accept that he
is wrong.
assume • I assume these eggs
are fresh.
presume • The missing person
is presumed to be dead.
swallow (INFORMAL) • I found
their story hard to swallow.
trust • I trust that you will
manage.
ANTONYM:
• doubt

belittle VERB
to make someone or
something seem less
important • He belittles my
opinions.
deride (FORMAL) • He is derided
as weak and incompetent.

detract from • Her sour
comments detracted from Meg's
happiness.
downgrade • I fear failure, but I
downgrade my successes.
scorn • Eleanor scorns the work
of others.
undervalue • We must never
undervalue freedom.
ANTONYM:
• praise

beloved ADJECTIVE
dearly loved • his beloved wife
adored • an adored father
cherished • his most cherished
possession
darling • our darling child
dearest • my dearest Maria
precious • I love my precious
cat.
treasured • treasured
memories
ANTONYM:
• despised

below PREPOSITION or
ADVERB
lower down • six centimetres
below soil level
beneath • She hid the letter
beneath her mattress.
down • I fell down to the
bottom.
lower • The price will fall lower
than this.
under • tunnels under the
ground
underneath • He crawled
underneath the table.
ANTONYM:
• above

bend ① VERB
to make or become curved
• Bend the bar into a horseshoe.
buckle • A wave buckled the ship's deck.
curve • The wall curves to the left.
turn • The road turns right at the end.
twist • glass twisted into elaborate patterns
warp • The wood had started to warp.

bend ② VERB
to move forwards and downwards • I bent over and kissed her cheek.
arch • Don't arch your back!
bow • He turned and bowed to her.
crouch • We were crouching in the bushes.
incline • The woman inclined her head to one side.
lean • She leant out of the window.
stoop • Stooping down, he picked up a stone.

bend ③ NOUN
a curve in something • a bend in the road
arc • the full arc of a rainbow
corner • He drove round the corner.
curve • the curve of the stream
loop • The river curves in a loop.
turn • a turn in the path

beneficial ADJECTIVE
giving some benefit • Regular exercise is beneficial to health.
advantageous • an advantageous arrangement

good for you • Most vegetables are good for you.
healthy • trying to switch to a healthy lifestyle
helpful • This treatment is particularly helpful to hay fever sufferers.
useful • a useful addition to your first aid kit
wholesome • food made with good, wholesome ingredients

benefit ① NOUN
an advantage • the benefits of relaxation
advantage • The advantages of the new system far outweigh its disadvantages.
asset • A second language is an asset in this job.
boon • a great boon for busy people
gain • He used the knowledge for his personal gain.
good • Study for your own good!
help • It's no help to know I was right.
profit • the profits of working hard
use • His training was of no use to him.

ANTONYM:
• disadvantage

benefit ② VERB
to help in something • The experience will benefit you.
aid • measures to aid working mothers
assist • The extra money will assist you.
enhance • His injury does not enhance our chances.

B

further • *His support will further our cause.*

help • *The new laws won't help the environment.*

profit • *It won't profit us to complain.*

ANTONYM:
• harm

benevolent ADJECTIVE
kind and helpful • *a benevolent ruler*

benign • *a benign and loveable man*

charitable • *charitable organisations*

compassionate • *my compassionate friends*

humane • *humane treatment of prisoners*

kind • *You have been kind and helpful to us.*

beside PREPOSITION
next to • *I stood beside my father and my uncle.*

adjacent to • *a hotel adjacent to the beach*

alongside • *a house alongside the river*

close to • *The restaurant is close to their home.*

near • *He stood very near the front door.*

next to • *She sat down next to him.*

best ① ADJECTIVE
of the highest standard • *the best film I have seen in a long time*

finest • *the finest foods available*

first-rate • *a first-rate musical performance*

foremost • *the foremost painter of his generation*

greatest • *the greatest film ever made*

leading • *He has established himself as one of Britain's leading actors.*

outstanding • *one of England's outstanding tennis players*

pre-eminent • *her status as the pre-eminent pop act of her day*

principal • *London's principal publishing houses*

superlative • *companies that offer superlative products*

supreme • *the supreme achievement of his career*

top • *one of the country's top athletes*

ANTONYM:
• worst

best ② ADJECTIVE
most desirable • *the best thing you could have said*

correct • *the correct thing to do in the circumstances*

most fitting • *the most fitting location for a house*

right • *Are you the right person for the job?*

ANTONYM:
• worst

best ③ NOUN
the preferred thing • *Of all my presents, this is the best.*

cream • *a showcase for the cream of Scottish artists*

elite • *the elite of the sporting world*

finest • *the finest of all film comedians*

pick • *the pick of the crop*

ANTONYM:
• worst

betray ① VERB
to do someone harm • *I was betrayed by someone I had thought a friend.*
break your promise • *I broke my promise to help her.*
double-cross (INFORMAL) • *I was angry that he double-crossed me.*
inform on • *people who inform on their colleagues*

betray ② VERB
to show feelings • *Jeremy's voice betrayed little emotion.*
expose • *She never exposed her hostile feelings.*
manifest (FORMAL) • *Fear can manifest itself in many ways.*
reveal • *Her expression revealed nothing.*
show • *His eyes showed his unhappiness.*

better ① ADJECTIVE
of more worth than another • *Today was much better than yesterday.*
finer • *There is no finer place to live.*
grander • *moving to a much grander house*
greater • *Their eyes are now set on a greater prize.*
higher-quality • *We are trying to provide a higher-quality service.*
nicer • *This is a much nicer room than mine.*
preferable • *Owning property is preferable to renting.*

superior • *His work is far superior to yours.*
surpassing • *a film of surpassing quality*
worthier • *You should save your energies for a worthier cause.*

ANTONYM:
• inferior

better ② ADJECTIVE
well after being ill • *I hope you feel better soon.*
cured • *I used to have insomnia but now I'm cured.*
fitter • *I'm a lot fitter now I've started jogging.*
fully recovered • *He had a back injury but now he's fully recovered.*
healthier • *My grandad's much healthier since he gave up smoking.*
improving • *His symptoms are improving since the treatment.*
on the mend (INFORMAL) • *She's on the mend now.*
recovering • *She's recovering after an attack of appendicitis.*
stronger • *He's slowly getting stronger after his accident.*
well • *I hope you're feeling well again soon.*

ANTONYM:
• worse

beware VERB
to be cautious • *Beware of the dog.*
be careful • *Be careful what you say to him.*
be cautious • *Doctors are cautious about using the treatment.*

b

bias

be wary • *The cat is wary of strangers.*
guard against • *We have to guard against thieves.*
look out • *Look out, there's a train coming.*
watch out • *Watch out for fog and ice.*

bias NOUN
prejudice for or against a person or group • *bias against women*
bigotry • *religious bigotry*
favouritism • *His promotion was due to favouritism.*
prejudice • *racial prejudice*

biased ADJECTIVE
showing prejudice • *biased attitudes*
one-eyed (AUSTRALIAN AND NEW ZEALAND) • *I may be a bit one-eyed because of the family connection.*
one-sided • *a one-sided argument*
partial • *a very partial view of the situation*
prejudiced • *Don't be prejudiced by what you read.*
slanted • *a slanted newspaper article*
weighted • *a scheme weighted towards those in need*
ANTONYM:
• neutral

big ① ADJECTIVE
of a large size • *a big house*
▶ see Word Study **big**, page 704
ANTONYM:
• small

big ② ADJECTIVE
of great importance • *a big name*
▶ see Word Study **big**, page 704
ANTONYM:
• unimportant

bill NOUN
a statement of how much is owed • *a huge restaurant bill*
account • *Please charge it to my account.*
charges • *charges for eye tests*
invoice • *They sent an invoice for the damage.*
statement • *a credit card statement*

bit NOUN
a small amount • *a bit of coal*
crumb • *a crumb of comfort*
fragment • *glittering fragments of broken glass*
grain • *His story contains a grain of truth.*
part • *part of the problem*
piece • *The vase was smashed to pieces.*
scrap • *a scrap of evidence*

bite VERB
to cut into something with your teeth • *His cat bit me when I tried to pat it.*
chew • *The puppy was chewing a pair of slippers.*
gnaw • *The bones had been gnawed by wild animals.*
nibble • *She nibbled a biscuit.*
nip • *There were blotches where the mosquitoes had nipped him.*

bitter ① ADJECTIVE
angry and resentful • *a bitter row*

acrimonious (FORMAL) • *an acrimonious discussion*
begrudging • *He gave me begrudging thanks.*
embittered • *an embittered former employee*
rancorous (FORMAL) • *the issue that has led to rancorous disputes*
resentful • *She is resentful of others' success.*
sour • *a sour expression*

bitter ② ADJECTIVE
tasting or smelling sharp • *bitter lemons*
acid • *the acid smell of sweat*
acrid • *clouds of acrid smoke*
astringent • *astringent disinfectant*
sharp • *a clean, sharp taste*
sour • *a rich, sour stew*
tart • *the tart qualities of citrus fruit*

ANTONYM:
• sweet

bizarre ADJECTIVE
very strange or eccentric • *the bizarre behaviour of the team's manager*
curious • *a curious mixture of ancient and modern*
eccentric • *Her eccentric behaviour was beginning to attract attention.*
extraordinary • *What an extraordinary character he is!*
odd • *a series of very odd coincidences*
outlandish • *her outlandish style of dressing*
peculiar • *a peculiar combination of flavours*

queer (OLD-FASHIONED) • *A very queer thing happened to me tonight.*
strange • *She's been behaving in a very strange way lately.*
weird • *his weird theories about UFOs*

ANTONYM:
• ordinary

black NOUN or ADJECTIVE
SHADES OF BLACK
coal-black
ebony
inky
jet
jet-black
pitch-black
raven
sable
sooty

blame ① VERB
to believe someone caused something • *Don't blame me for this trouble.*
accuse • *She accused him of causing the fire.*
charge • *He will be charged with murder.*
hold responsible • *I hold you responsible for this mess.*

blame ② NOUN
the responsibility for something bad • *I'm not going to take the blame for that!*
accountability • *He escaped accountability for his crimes.*
fault • *The fault was all yours.*
guilt • *the sole guilt for the outbreak of war*

liability • He admitted liability for the crash.
rap (SLANG) • A maid took the rap for stealing the letters.
responsibility • responsibility for the murder

blank ① ADJECTIVE
with nothing on it • a blank card
bare • bare walls
clean • a clean sheet of paper
clear • a clear patch of floor
empty • an empty page
plain • a plain envelope
unmarked • an unmarked board

blank ② ADJECTIVE
showing no feeling • John just looked blank.
deadpan • a deadpan expression
dull • a dull stare
empty • She saw the empty look in his eyes.
impassive • her impassive smile
vacant • the vacant expression on his face

blend ① VERB
to mix things so as to form a single item or substance
• Blend the butter with the sugar.
combine • Combine the ingredients in a large bowl.
merge • how to merge the graphics with the text
mingle • the mingled smells of flowers and wood smoke
mix • Mix the two liquids together with a whisk.

ANTONYM:
• separate

blend ② VERB
to combine in a pleasing way
• The colours blend with the rest of the decor.
go well • a sauce which goes well with fish
harmonise • shades which harmonise with most skin tones

blend ③ NOUN
a mixture or combination of things • a blend of Asian and European culture
alloy • an alloy of copper and tin
amalgamation • Bartók's rich amalgamation of musical styles
combination • a fantastic combination of colours
compound • a compound of water, sugar and enzymes
fusion • a fusion of cooking styles
mix • a delicious mix of exotic spices
mixture • a sticky mixture of flour and water

bless VERB
to ask God's protection • The bishop blessed the congregation.
anoint • The priest anointed the child with oil.
consecrate • ground that has been consecrated
dedicate • The well was dedicated to saints.
hallow • A building could be hallowed by prayer.

ANTONYM:
• curse

blessing ① NOUN
something good • Good health is a blessing.

benefit • *the benefits of technology*
boon • *Subtitles are a boon for deaf people.*
gift • *A cheerful nature is a gift.*
godsend • *The extra twenty dollars was a godsend.*
help • *The counselling sessions have been a real help.*

ANTONYM:
• disadvantage

blessing ② NOUN
approval or permission to do something • *He got married with his parents' blessing.*
approval • *Does this plan have your approval?*
backing • *We can't do anything without his backing.*
consent • *He gave his consent to the article.*
leave • *She gave us leave to start.*
permission • *You have my permission to go.*
support • *My manager has given his full support to my project.*

ANTONYM:
• disapproval

blob NOUN
a small amount of a thick or sticky substance • *He had a blob of chocolate mousse on his tie.*
bead • *Beads of blood spattered the counter.*
dab • *You've got a dab of glue on your nose.*
drop • *a few thick drops of fluid*
droplet • *droplets of congealed fat*

block ① NOUN
a large piece • *a block of wood*
bar • *a bar of soap*
brick • *concrete bricks*
chunk • *chunks of meat*
ingot • *a gold ingot*
lump • *lumps of metal*
piece • *a big piece of cake*

block ② VERB
to close by putting something across • *A ship had run aground and was blocking the entrance to the harbour.*
choke • *The town was choked with cars.*
clog • *Dishes clogged the sink.*
obstruct • *The crash obstructed the road.*
plug • *Did you plug the leaks?*

ANTONYM:
• unblock

block ③ VERB
to prevent something happening • *The council blocked his plans.*
bar • *He was barred from entering.*
check • *a policy to check population growth*
halt • *attempts to halt the spread of disease*
obstruct • *Lack of funds obstructed our progress.*
stop • *measures to stop the rising crime rate*
thwart • *My plans were thwarted by Taylor.*

blockage NOUN
a thing that clogs something • *a blockage in the pipe*

block • *a block in the blood vessel*
obstruction • *an obstruction on the track*
stoppage • *We have to clear the stoppage.*

blow ① VERB
to move or cause to move in the wind • *The wind blew his papers away.*
buffet • *The ship was buffeted by gales.*
drive • *The strong wind drove us forward.*
flutter • *The flags are fluttering.*
sweep • *A sudden blast swept away the cloth.*
waft • *His hair wafted in the breeze.*
whirl • *The fallen leaves whirled around.*

blow ② NOUN
a hit from something • *a blow to the head*
bang • *He suffered some bangs and bumps.*
clout (INFORMAL) • *a clout on the head*
knock • *Knocks can cause damage to the spine.*
smack • *She gave the child a smack.*
thump • *Ralph got a thump on the chest.*
whack (INFORMAL) • *The horse got a whack from its rider.*

blow ③ NOUN
something disappointing or upsetting • *Marc's death was a terrible blow.*
bombshell • *His departure was a bombshell for the team.*

disappointment • *My exam results were a real disappointment.*
misfortune • *a series of misfortunes*
setback • *We faced many setbacks before we got the house.*
shock • *The news came as a shock.*
upset • *The defeat caused an upset.*

blue NOUN or ADJECTIVE
SHADES OF BLUE
aqua
aquamarine
azure
cerulean
cobalt
cyan
duck-egg blue
electric blue
gentian
indigo
lapis lazuli
midnight blue
navy
Nile blue
peacock blue
periwinkle
petrol blue
royal blue
sapphire
saxe blue
sky blue
teal
turquoise
ultramarine

blunt ① ADJECTIVE
having rounded edges • *blunt scissors*
dull • *a dull knife*
rounded • *rounded edges*

unsharpened • *an unsharpened pencil*

ANTONYM:
• sharp

blunt ② ADJECTIVE
saying what you think • *a blunt speaker*
bluff • *He writes with bluff good humour.*
brusque • *His response was brusque.*
forthright • *a forthright reply*
frank • *I'll be frank with you.*
outspoken • *an outspoken critic*
straightforward • *She has a straightforward manner.*

ANTONYM:
• tactful

blush ① VERB
to go red in the face • *I felt myself blushing.*
colour • *I found myself colouring as I spoke.*
flush • *I saw her face flush.*
go red • *His face went red as a beetroot.*
turn crimson • *He looked at her and she turned crimson.*
turn red • *He turned red with embarrassment.*
turn scarlet • *She turned scarlet with humiliation.*

blush ② NOUN
a red colour • *Ann took the gift with a blush.*
colour • *The walk will bring colour to your cheeks.*
flush • *A slow flush spread over the man's face.*
glow • *a healthy glow*

boast VERB
to talk proudly • *Carol boasted about her costume.*
brag • *I don't mind bragging about my talents.*
crow (INFORMAL) • *Stop crowing about your success.*
skite (AUSTRALIAN AND NEW ZEALAND; INFORMAL) • *That's nothing to skite about.*

boastful ADJECTIVE
tending to brag about things • *a boastful liar*
bragging • *bragging stories about his time in the navy*
cocky • *The boxer is cocky and brash.*
conceited • *I thought her overconfident and conceited.*
crowing • *crowing remarks*
egotistical • *egotistical fibs*
swaggering • *He has a swaggering arrogance.*

ANTONYM:
• modest

body ① NOUN
all your physical parts • *My whole body hurt.*
build • *He is of medium build.*
figure • *Janet has a nice figure.*
form • *clothes that flatter your form*
frame • *their bony frames*
physique • *a powerful physique*
shape • *his trim shape*

RELATED WORDS:
• ADJECTIVES corporal, physical

body ② NOUN
a dead body • *Police found a body hidden in the forest.*

carcass • *a sheep's carcass*
corpse • *the corpse of a young man*
dead body • *He'd never seen a dead body.*
remains • *human remains*

body ③ NOUN
an organised group of people • *local voluntary bodies*
association • *the Football Association*
band • *a band of rebels*
company • *the Royal Shakespeare Company*
confederation • *a confederation of workers*
organisation • *student organisations*
society • *I joined the local opera society.*

boil ① VERB
to bubble • *The water is boiling.*
bubble • *Potatoes bubbled in the pot.*
fizz • *The liquid fizzed and bubbled.*
foam • *When the butter foams, add the onions.*
froth • *The milk frothed over in the pan.*

boil ② NOUN
a swelling on the skin • *five boils on his face*
blister • *a blister on my index finger*
swelling • *a swelling under the eye*
tumour • *The tumours had all disappeared.*

bold ① ADJECTIVE
confident and not shy • *a bold question*

brash • *a brash young sergeant*
brazen • *They were brazen enough to ask for the day off.*
cheeky • *a cheeky grin*
confident • *I felt confident confronting him.*
forward • *It was forward of you to ask him.*
impudent • *an impudent child*
ANTONYM:
• shy

bold ② ADJECTIVE
unafraid of risk or danger • *a bold attempt*
adventurous • *an adventurous spirit*
brave • *a brave woman*
courageous • *courageous firefighters*
daring • *daring feats*
fearless • *a fearless warrior*
intrepid • *an intrepid explorer*
ANTONYM:
• cowardly

bold ③ ADJECTIVE
clear and noticeable • *bold colours*
bright • *bright light*
flashy • *flashy clothes*
loud • *a loud tie*
striking • *a striking tartan pattern*
strong • *dressed in strong reds and yellows*
vivid • *vivid green and purple*
ANTONYM:
• dull

bolt VERB
to escape or run away • *I bolted towards the exit.*

dash • *He dashed out of the room in a panic.*

escape • *They escaped across the frontier.*

flee • *We fled before the police arrived.*

fly • *She flew down the stairs with her sister in hot pursuit.*

run away • *I called to him but he just ran away.*

run off • *The children ran off when they spotted me.*

rush • *They all rushed away as we approached.*

bomb ① NOUN
an explosive device • *The bomb exploded in the centre of the city.*

device • *Experts defused the device.*

explosive • *a block of plastic explosive*

missile • *long-range missiles*

rocket • *a rocket launcher*

shell • *Shells began to fall.*

torpedo • *The torpedo struck the ship.*

bomb ② VERB
to attack with bombs • *His house was bombed.*

attack • *We are being attacked!*

blow up • *He attempted to blow up the building.*

bombard • *Warships began to bombard the coast.*

destroy • *Helicopters destroyed his village.*

shell • *They shelled the troops.*

torpedo • *His ship was torpedoed.*

bond ① NOUN
a close relationship • *a special bond between us*

attachment • *Mother and child form a close attachment.*

connection • *a family connection*

link • *the links of friendship*

relation • *the relation between husband and wife*

tie • *the ties of blood*

union • *the union of father and son*

bond ② NOUN
an obligation to do something • *the social bonds of community*

agreement • *He has broken our agreement.*

contract • *He signed a two-year contract.*

obligation • *your obligation to your father*

pledge • *a pledge of support*

promise • *You must keep your promises.*

word • *I give you my word.*

bond ③ VERB
to attach separate things • *Strips of wood are bonded together.*

bind • *Tape was used to bind the files.*

fasten • *I fastened the picture to the wall.*

fuse • *The pieces to be joined are melted and fused together.*

glue • *Glue the pieces together.*

paste • *He pasted posters to the wall.*

book ① NOUN
a number of pages in a cover • *I'm reading a great book just now.*

publication • *publications about job hunting*

textbook • *He wrote a textbook on law.*

volume • *small volumes of poetry*

work • *my favourite work by this author*

TYPES OF BOOK

anthology
atlas
autobiography
biography
dictionary
directory
encyclopedia
gazetteer
glossary
guidebook
manual
novel
phrasebook
thesaurus

PARTS OF A BOOK

appendix
bibliography
blurb
caption
chapter
contents
cover
epilogue
footnote
foreword
glossary
heading
illustration
index
introduction
jacket
layout
line
page
preface

prologue
title

RELIGIOUS BOOKS

Bible (CHRISTIANITY)
Book of Mormon (MORMON CHURCH)
Diamond Scriptures (ZEN BUDDHISM)
Guru Granth or Adi Granth (SIKHISM)
I Ching (CONFUCIANISM AND TAOISM)
Mahabharata (HINDUISM)
Qu'ran or Koran (ISLAM)
Ramayana (HINDUISM)
Sutras (BUDDHISM AND HINDUISM)
Talmud (JUDAISM)
Tao-te-Ching (TAOISM)
Torah (JUDAISM)
Tripitaka (BUDDHISM)
Veda (HINDUISM)

book ② VERB

to arrange to have or use • *The tickets are booked.*

charter • *A plane was chartered for them.*

engage • *We engaged the services of a plumber.*

organise • *I have organised our flights.*

reserve • *Hotel rooms have been reserved.*

schedule • *A meeting is scheduled for Monday.*

border ① NOUN

a dividing line between things or places • *the border between two countries*

borderline • *the borderline between health and sickness*

boundary • *national boundaries*
frontier • *the American frontier*
line • *the line between fact and fiction*

border ② NOUN
an edge of something • *plain tiles with a bright border*
bounds • *the bounds of good taste*
edge • *the edge of town*
limits • *the city limits*
margin • *the western margins of the island*
rim • *the rim of the lake*

border ③ VERB
to form an edge • *Tall trees bordered the fields.*
edge • *the woods that edge the lake*
fringe • *Street lights fringe the bay.*
hem • *dresses hemmed with feathers*
rim • *the restaurants rimming the harbour*
trim • *coats trimmed with fur*

bored ADJECTIVE
impatient and not interested in something • *I am bored with this business.*
fed up • *He is fed up with this country.*
tired • *I am tired of this music.*
uninterested • *He seems uninterested in politics.*
wearied • *He spoke in a wearied voice.*
ANTONYM:
• interested

boredom NOUN
a lack of interest • *the boredom of long trips*
apathy • *political apathy*
dullness • *a period of dullness*
flatness • *a feeling of flatness*
monotony • *the monotony of winter*
tedium • *the tedium of unemployment*
weariness • *a sense of weariness*
ANTONYM:
• interest

boring ADJECTIVE
dull and uninteresting • *a boring job*
dull • *dull tasks*
flat • *a flat performance*
humdrum • *humdrum lives*
monotonous • *the monotonous prison routine*
tedious • *The work is tedious.*
tiresome • *a tiresome wait*
ANTONYM:
• interesting

boss NOUN
a person in charge of something • *He can't stand his boss.*
chief • *the police chief*
director • *the directors of the bank*
employer • *He was sent to Rome by his employer.*
head • *Heads of government met in New York.*
leader • *The party's leader has resigned.*
manager • *the company's marketing manager*

bossy ADJECTIVE (INFORMAL)
telling people what to do • *a rather bossy little girl*
authoritarian • *an authoritarian approach to parenthood*
dictatorial • *a dictatorial management style*
domineering • *She is domineering and ruthless.*
imperious • *He has an imperious manner.*
overbearing • *an impatient, sometimes overbearing personality*

botch VERB (INFORMAL)
to do something badly • *a botched operation*
bungle (INFORMAL) • *inefficient people who bungled the job*
mar • *She marred her exit by twisting her ankle.*
mess up • *He manages to mess up his life.*

bother ① VERB
to cause worry or concern • *His lack of money bothers him.*
annoy • *the things that annoy me*
concern • *The future concerns me.*
disturb • *It disturbs me to see you unhappy.*
get on someone's nerves (INFORMAL) • *This place gets on my nerves.*
trouble • *Are you troubled by nightmares?*
worry • *I'm worried by his lack of concentration.*

bother ② NOUN
trouble and difficulty • *I hate the bother of shopping.*
annoyance • *Snoring can be an annoyance.*
difficulty • *The strikes are causing difficulties for commuters.*
inconvenience • *a minor inconvenience*
irritation • *Noise is an irritation.*
trouble • *You've caused me a lot of trouble.*
worry • *It was a time of worry for us.*

bottom ① NOUN
the lowest part of something • *the bottom of the stairs*
base • *the base of the spine*
bed • *the river bed*
depths • *the depths of the earth*
floor • *the ocean floor*
foot • *the foot of the bed*
ANTONYM:
• top

bottom ② ADJECTIVE
in the lowest place or position • *the bottom drawer*
base • *the base edge of the curtain*
basement • *a basement flat*
ground • *ground level*
lowest • *the lowest part of the brain*
ANTONYM:
• highest

bounce ① VERB
to spring back after hitting something • *The ball bounced off the wall.*

rebound • *The car rebounded into the opposite carriageway.*
ricochet • *The bullets ricocheted off the jeep.*

bounce ② VERB
to move up and down • *He bounced across the floor.*
bob • *The raft bobbed along.*
bound • *He bounded up the stairway.*
bump • *My bicycle bumped along the rough ground.*
jump • *They jumped up and down to keep warm.*

box NOUN
a container with a firm base and sides • *All her possessions were packed in boxes.*
carton • *cartons full of books*
case • *It is still in its original case.*
chest • *She kept her heirlooms in a carved wooden chest.*
container • *substances kept in heavy metal containers*
trunk • *a trunk full of toys*

boy NOUN
a male child • *I knew him when he was a boy.*
kid (INFORMAL) • *He seems like a nice kid.*
lad (INFORMAL) • *I remember being a lad his age.*
schoolboy • *a group of schoolboys*
youngster • *I was only a youngster in 1970.*
youth • *gangs of youths who cause trouble*

brag VERB
to boast about something

• *I hate people who brag about their achievements.*
boast • *She kept boasting about how good she was at football.*
crow (INFORMAL) • *Stop crowing about your victory.*
skite (AUSTRALIAN AND NEW ZEALAND; INFORMAL) • *That's nothing to skite about.*

braggart NOUN
a person who boasts • *He was a braggart and a liar.*
bigmouth (SLANG) • *He's nothing but a bigmouth.*
boaster • *an idle boaster looking for the main chance*
bragger • *She was quite a bragger.*
show-off • *I've always been a show-off.*
skite or **skiter** (AUSTRALIAN AND NEW ZEALAND; INFORMAL) • *a bit of a skite*

brave ① ADJECTIVE
willing to do dangerous things • *a brave attempt to stop the attack*
bold • *Amrita became a bold rebel.*
courageous • *a courageous decision*
fearless • *his fearless campaigning for justice*
heroic • *The heroic sergeant risked his life.*
plucky • *The plucky schoolgirl amazed the doctors.*
valiant • *a valiant attempt to keep going*
ANTONYM:
• cowardly

b

B

brave ② VERB
to face something without
fear • *Fans braved the rain to
hear him sing.*
face • *I can't face another three
years of this.*
stand up to • *I have managed
to stand up to the bullies.*

bravery NOUN
the quality of being
courageous • *He deserves praise
for his bravery.*
boldness • *an outward display
of boldness*
courage • *They do not have the
courage to apologise.*
fortitude • *He suffered with
tremendous fortitude.*
heroism • *acts of heroism*
pluck • *He has pluck and
presence of mind.*
valour • *She won a medal for
valour.*
ANTONYM:
• cowardice

breach ① NOUN
a breaking of an agreement or
law • *a breach of contract*
infringement • *an
infringement of the rules*
offence • *criminal offences*
trespass • *a campaign of
trespasses and demonstrations*
violation • *a violation of the
peace agreement*

breach ② NOUN
a gap in something • *a breach
in the sea wall*
crack • *a large crack in the ice*
gap • *a narrow gap in the curtains*

hole • *We cut holes in the fabric.*
opening • *an opening in the
fence*
rift • *The earthquake caused a
deep rift.*
split • *There's a split in my
mattress.*

break ① VERB
to separate into pieces • *I broke
a plate.*
▶ see Word Study **break**, page 705

break ② VERB
to fail to keep a rule or promise
• *He broke his promise to attend.*
breach • *The company breached
safety rules.*
contravene • *Her behaviour
contravenes our code of conduct.*
infringe • *The judge ruled that
he had infringed no rules.*
violate • *They violated the
peace agreement.*

break ③ NOUN
a short period of rest or
change • *I took a five-minute
break from work.*
interlude • *a happy interlude in
my life*
interval • *a long interval when
no-one spoke*
pause • *After a pause Alex
spoke.*
recess • *The court adjourned for
a recess.*
respite • *They have had no
respite from bombing.*
rest • *I'll start again after a rest.*

breed ① NOUN
a type of animal • *rare breeds
of cattle*

kind • *What kind of horse is that?*

species • *Pandas are an endangered species.*

stock • *cattle of Highland stock*

strain • *a special strain of rat*

type • *What type of dog should we get?*

variety • *many varieties of birds*

breed ② VERB
to produce and look after • *He breeds dogs for the police.*

cultivate • *She cultivates fruit and vegetables.*

develop • *A new variety of potato is being developed.*

keep • *He keeps guinea pigs.*

nurture • *trimming and nurturing plants and saplings*

raise • *He raises birds of prey as a hobby.*

rear • *the difficulties of rearing children*

breed ③ VERB
to produce offspring • *Frogs can breed in most ponds.*

multiply • *Rats multiply quickly.*

produce • *She produced a son.*

propagate • *This plant is difficult to propagate.*

reproduce • *the instinct to reproduce*

brief ① ADJECTIVE
lasting for a short time • *a brief appearance on television*

fleeting • *a fleeting glimpse*

momentary • *There was a momentary silence.*

quick • *a quick look at the newspaper*

short • *a short holiday*

swift • *a swift glance at John's face*

ANTONYM:
• long

brief ② VERB
to give necessary information • *A spokesman briefed reporters.*

advise • *I must advise you of my decision to retire.*

fill in (INFORMAL) • *Can you fill me in on Wilbur's visit?*

inform • *They would inform him of their progress.*

instruct • *He instructed us in first aid.*

prepare • *I will prepare you for this exam.*

prime • *Arnold primed him for his duties.*

bright ① ADJECTIVE
strong and startling • *a bright light*

brilliant • *brilliant green eyes*

dazzling • *a dazzling white shirt*

glowing • *the glowing windows of the Cathedral*

luminous • *a luminous star*

radiant • *eyes as radiant as sapphires*

vivid • *strong, vivid colours*

ANTONYM:
• dull

bright ② ADJECTIVE
clever and alert • *my brightest student*

brainy (INFORMAL) • *I don't consider myself brainy.*

brilliant • *She has a brilliant mind.*

clever • *a clever child*

ingenious • *an ingenious idea*
intelligent • *Dolphins are an intelligent species.*
smart • *He thinks he's as smart as Sarah.*
ANTONYM:
• dim

bright ③ ADJECTIVE
cheerful and lively • *a bright smile*
cheerful • *Jack sounded quite cheerful about the idea.*
happy • *a confident, happy child*
jolly • *a jolly nature*
light-hearted • *They are light-hearted and enjoy life.*
lively • *He has a lively personality.*
merry • *bursts of merry laughter*

brilliant ① ADJECTIVE
very bright • *a brilliant light*
bright • *a bright star*
dazzling • *a dazzling white shirt*
gleaming • *gleaming headlights*
glowing • *glowing colours*
luminous • *luminous orange paint*
radiant • *a figure surrounded by a radiant glow*
sparkling • *a choker of sparkling jewels*
vivid • *the vivid hues of tropical flowers*
ANTONYM:
• dull

brilliant ② ADJECTIVE
very clever • *a brilliant pupil*
acute • *His relaxed exterior hides an acute mind.*

brainy (INFORMAL) • *You don't have to be too brainy to work that one out.*
bright • *an exceptionally bright child*
clever • *What a clever idea!*
intelligent • *a lively and extremely intelligent person*
perceptive • *a perceptive analysis of the situation*
sharp • *a sharp intellect*
smart • *She's the smartest student we've ever had.*
ANTONYM:
• stupid

brilliant ③ ADJECTIVE
wonderful or superb • *It's a brilliant film.*
first-class • *a first-class violinist*
great • *one of the greatest novels of the century*
magnificent • *a magnificent display*
marvellous • *I've had a marvellous time.*
outstanding • *He's an outstanding actor.*
superb • *a superb artist*
tremendous • *a tremendous performance*
wonderful • *the most wonderful music I've ever heard*
ANTONYM:
• terrible

bring ① VERB
to take somewhere • *Bring a friend to the party.*
bear • *They bore the box into the kitchen.*
carry • *She carried her son to the car.*

convey (FORMAL) • *Emergency supplies were conveyed by truck.*
lead • *She led him into the house.*
take • *He took cakes to the party.*
transport • *The troops were transported to Moscow.*

bring ② VERB
to cause to happen • *Bring the vegetables to the boil.*
cause • *My mistake caused me some worry.*
create • *The new factory will create more jobs.*
inflict • *The attack inflicted heavy casualties.*
produce • *The drug produces side effects.*
result in • *Many accidents result in serious injuries.*
wreak • *Violent storms wreaked havoc.*

bring about VERB
to cause something to happen • *It was his arrogance that brought about his downfall.*
cause • *This may cause delays.*
create • *The new scheme will create even more confusion.*
generate • *the excitement generated by this film*
make happen • *If you want change, you have to make it happen yourself.*
produce • *His comments produced a furious response.*
provoke • *a move that has provoked a storm of protest*

broad ① ADJECTIVE
large, especially from side to side • *His shoulders were broad and his waist narrow.*

expansive • *There are also several swing sets and an expansive grassy play area.*
extensive • *The palace grounds were more extensive than the town itself.*
large • *He was a large man with a thick square head.*
thick • *a finger as thick as a sausage*
vast • *rich families who own vast stretches of land*
wide • *a sunhat with a wide brim*

ANTONYM:
• narrow

broad ② ADJECTIVE
including or affecting many different things or people • *A broad range of issues was discussed.*
comprehensive • *This book is a comprehensive guide to the region.*
extensive • *extensive research into public attitudes to science*
general • *The project should raise general awareness about bullying.*
sweeping • *sweeping economic reforms*
universal • *the universal problem of pollution*
wide • *a major event which brought together a wide range of interest groups*
wide-ranging • *The aims of our campaign are wide-ranging but simple.*

broad ③ ADJECTIVE
general rather than detailed

• These documents provided a broad outline of the Society's development.

approximate • They did not have even an approximate idea of what the word meant.

general • The figures represent a general decline in employment.

non-specific • I intend to use these terms in a deliberately non-specific way.

rough • I've got a rough idea of what he looks like.

sweeping • a sweeping statement about young people

vague • They have only a vague idea of the amount of water available.

broadcast ① NOUN

a programme on radio or television • this morning's broadcast on Radio 4

podcast • a podcast devoted to snowmobiling

programme • Did you see that programme about child geniuses?

show • my favourite television show

transmission • The radio transmission continued all night long.

webcast • a live webcast from the Wimbledon final

broadcast ② VERB

to send out so that it can be seen or heard • Dean and his band are broadcasting live from Brighton.

air • The show airs at 9 o'clock every Thursday.

show • The television station refused to show the documentary.

stream • All four matches will be streamed live.

transmit • The concert will be transmitted on radio and television.

broadcast ③ VERB

to make known publicly • You don't need to broadcast your feelings to the entire world.

advertise • If you're going on holiday, don't advertise the fact with an uncut lawn.

announce • Are you going to announce your engagement tonight?

make public • The terms of the agreement were not made public for many years.

proclaim • I happily proclaim my ignorance on this one.

tweet • She tweeted that her boyfriend had proposed to her.

broken ① ADJECTIVE

in pieces • a broken window

burst • a burst pipe

demolished • a demolished house

fractured • He suffered a fractured skull.

fragmented • fragmented images

shattered • shattered glass

smashed • smashed windows

broken ② ADJECTIVE

not kept • a broken promise

infringed • a case of infringed human rights

violated • a series of violated agreements

brown NOUN or ADJECTIVE

SHADES OF BROWN

auburn
bay
beige
bronze
brunette
buff
burnt sienna
burnt umber
café au lait
camel
chestnut
chocolate
cinnamon
coffee
dun
fawn
ginger
hazel
khaki
mahogany
mocha
oatmeal
ochre
putty
russet
rust
sandy
sepia
tan
taupe
tawny
terracotta
umber

build ① VERB
to make something • *The house was built last year.*
assemble • *Workers were assembling planes.*
construct • *plans to construct a temple on the site*
erect • *The building was erected in 1900.*
fabricate • *All the tools are fabricated from steel.*
form • *hotels formed from cheap cement*
make • *a wall made of bricks*
ANTONYM:
• dismantle

build ② VERB
to develop gradually • *I want to build a relationship with them.*
develop • *These battles could develop into war.*
extend • *Three new products extend the range.*
increase • *The population continues to increase.*
intensify • *The conflict is bound to intensify.*
strengthen • *Cycling strengthens the muscles.*

build ③ NOUN
the size of a body • *He is of medium build.*
body • *a body of average size*
figure • *Janet has a nice figure.*
form • *clothes that flatter your form*
frame • *their bony frames*
physique • *a powerful physique*
shape • *his trim shape*

building NOUN
a structure with walls • *a glass building*
edifice • *historic edifices in the area*
structure • *The museum is an impressive structure.*

bulge ① VERB

to swell out • *Veins bulged out of his neck.*

expand • *The pipes expanded in the heat.*

protrude (FORMAL) • *Her blue eyes protruded from her head.*

stick out • *His stomach stuck out under his jacket.*

swell • *My ankles swelled.*

bulge ② NOUN

a lump in something • *My purse made a bulge in my pocket.*

bump • *a bump in the road*

hump • *a camel's hump*

lump • *itchy red lumps on the skin*

protrusion • *a strange protrusion on his forehead*

swelling • *a swelling on my foot*

bully ① NOUN

someone who tries to frighten or hurt others • *I was confronted by the class bully.*

oppressor • *They were powerless against their oppressors.*

persecutor • *Eventually he stood up to his persecutors.*

bully ② VERB

to try to frighten or hurt other people • *I wasn't going to let him bully me.*

intimidate • *Jones had set out to intimidate and dominate Paul.*

oppress • *people who try to dominate and oppress others*

persecute • *Tom was persecuted by his sisters.*

pick on • *I don't like to see you pick on younger children.*

tease • *The boys in the village had set on him, teasing him.*

torment • *My older brother and sister used to torment me.*

bully ③ VERB

to make someone do something by using force • *She used to bully me into doing my schoolwork.*

force • *I cannot force you in this. You must decide.*

intimidate • *attempts to intimidate people into voting for the governing party*

pressurise • *Do not be pressurised into making your decision immediately.*

bump ① VERB

to hit something • *He bumped his head on the wall.*

bang • *I banged my shin on the edge of the table.*

collide • *The car collided with a tree.*

hit • *She hit the last barrier and fell.*

jolt • *He jolted my elbow.*

knock • *He knocked on the door.*

strike • *His head struck the windscreen.*

bump ② NOUN

a dull noise • *He heard a bump outside.*

bang • *I heard four or five loud bangs.*

knock • *They heard a knock at the door.*

thud • *She tripped and fell with a thud.*

thump • *There was a loud thump against the house.*

bump ③ NOUN

a raised part of something • *a bump in the road*

bulge • *My purse made a bulge in my pocket.*

hump • *a camel's hump*

knob • *a hairbrush with knobs on the bristles*

lump • *itchy red lumps on the skin*

swelling • *a swelling on my foot*

bunch ① NOUN

a group of people • *The players were a great bunch.*

band • *Bands of criminals have been roaming some neighbourhoods.*

crowd • *All the old crowd have come out for this occasion.*

gaggle • *A gaggle of journalists sit in a hotel foyer waiting impatiently.*

gang • *Come on over – we've got lots of the old gang here.*

group • *The trouble involved a small group of football supporters.*

lot • *Future generations are going to think that we were a pretty boring lot.*

multitude • *surrounded by a noisy multitude*

bunch ② NOUN

several cut flowers held together • *He had left a huge bunch of flowers in her hotel room.*

bouquet • *She laid a bouquet on his grave.*

posy • *a posy of wild flowers*

spray • *a small spray of freesias*

bunch ③ NOUN

a group of things • *George took out a bunch of keys and went to work on the lock.*

batch • *She brought a large batch of newspaper cuttings.*

bundle • *a bundle of sticks tied together with string*

cluster • *a cluster of shops, cabins and motels*

heap • *a heap of old boxes for the bonfire*

load • *His people came up with a load of embarrassing stories.*

pile • *I've got a pile of questions afterwards for you.*

set • *Only she and Mr Cohen had complete sets of keys to the shop.*

burden ① NOUN

a load that is carried • *My wet clothes were an added burden.*

load • *a big load of hay*

weight • *straining to lift heavy weights*

burden ② NOUN

something that worries you • *the burden of looking after others*

anxiety • *He expressed his anxieties to me.*

care • *Forget all the cares of the day.*

strain • *I find the travelling a strain.*

stress • *the stress of exams*

trouble • *The Sullivans have money troubles.*

worry • *My son is a worry to me.*

RELATED WORD:

• ADJECTIVE onerous

bureaucracy NOUN
complex rules and procedures
• *Is there too much bureaucracy in government?*
administration • *high administration costs*
officialdom • *Officialdom is against us.*
red tape (INFORMAL) • *Our application was delayed by red tape.*
regulations • *absurd regulations about opening hours*

burn ① VERB
to be on fire • *a fire burning in the fireplace*
be ablaze • *The houses were ablaze.*
be on fire • *The ship was on fire.*
blaze • *The wreckage blazed.*
flame • *We watched as the house flamed.*
flare • *The match flared in the dark.*
flicker • *The fire flickered and crackled.*

burn ② VERB
to destroy with fire • *They burned the house down.*
char • *charred bodies*
incinerate • *Hospitals incinerate waste.*
scorch • *The bonfire scorched the grass.*
shrivel • *The papers shrivelled in the flames.*
singe • *Her hair was singed and her coat burnt.*

burst ① VERB
to split apart • *The balloon burst.*
break • *He broke the box open.*

crack • *A water pipe had cracked.*
explode • *The glass exploded.*
puncture • *The nail punctured the tyre.*
rupture • *His appendix ruptured.*
split • *The seam of my dress split.*

burst ② VERB
to enter suddenly • *She burst into the kitchen.*
barge • *He barged into the room.*
rush • *Water rushed out of the hole.*

burst ③ VERB
to happen or come suddenly
• *to burst into flames*
break • *Her face broke into a smile.*
erupt • *Violence could erupt soon.*

burst ④ NOUN
a short period of something
• *a burst of energy*
fit • *a fit of rage*
outbreak • *an outbreak of violence*
rush • *a sudden rush of excitement*
spate • *a spate of burglaries*
surge • *a surge of emotion*
torrent • *a torrent of words*

business ① NOUN
the buying and selling of goods • *a career in business*
commerce • *commerce between Europe and South America*
dealings • *All dealings with the company were suspended.*
industry • *the American car industry*

trade • *French trade with the West Indies*

trading • *trading between the two countries*

transaction • *We settled the transaction over lunch.*

business ② NOUN

an organisation selling goods or services • *a family business*

company • *the Ford Motor Company*

corporation • *international corporations*

enterprise • *small industrial enterprises*

establishment • *shops and other commercial establishments*

firm • *a firm of engineers*

organisation • *a well-run organisation*

business ③ NOUN

any event or situation • *This business has upset me.*

affair • *He handled the affair badly.*

issue • *What is your view on this issue?*

matter • *This is a matter for the police.*

problem • *solutions to the problem of homelessness*

question • *the whole question of TV censorship*

subject • *He raised the subject of money.*

bustle ① VERB

to move hurriedly • *My mother bustled about the room.*

dash • *We dashed about purposefully.*

fuss • *Waiters were fussing round the table.*

hurry • *Claire hurried along the road.*

rush • *I'm rushing to finish the cooking.*

scurry • *rats scurrying around*

scuttle • *Crabs scuttle along the bank.*

bustle ② NOUN

busy and noisy activity • *the bustle of modern life*

activity • *a burst of activity in the building*

commotion • *He heard a commotion outside.*

excitement • *The news created great excitement.*

flurry • *a flurry of activity*

fuss • *He works without any fuss.*

hurry • *the hurry and excitement of the city*

ANTONYM:
• peace

busy ① ADJECTIVE

doing something • *What is it? I'm busy.*

active • *He is active in local politics.*

employed • *He was employed helping me.*

engaged • *He was engaged in conversation.*

engrossed • *She is engrossed in her work.*

occupied • *He is occupied with the packing.*

working • *I am working on a novel.*

ANTONYM:
• idle

busy ② ADJECTIVE
full of activity • *a busy tourist resort*
active • *an active, independent country*
full • *a full life*
hectic • *my hectic work schedule*
lively • *a lively restaurant*
restless • *a restless mind*

busy ③ VERB
to occupy or keep busy • *Dad busied himself in the kitchen.*
absorb • *Her career absorbed her completely.*
employ • *You'd be better employed helping me.*
engage • *He was engaged in a meeting when I called.*
immerse • *She immersed herself in her book.*
occupy • *Try to occupy yourself with something.*

but ① CONJUNCTION
although • *Heat the cider until it is very hot but not boiling.*
although • *He was in love with her, although he had not yet admitted it to himself.*
though • *He's very attractive, though not exactly handsome.*
while • *The first two services are free, while the third costs £35.*
yet • *It is completely waterproof, yet light and comfortable.*

but ② PREPOSITION
with the exception of • *The crew gave them nothing but bread to eat.*
except • *I don't like any hot drinks except tea.*

except for • *No-one has complained except for you.*
other than • *This route is not recommended to anyone other than the most experienced cyclist.*
save • *The people had no water at all save that brought up from bore holes.*

buy VERB
to obtain with money • *I'd like to buy him lunch.*
acquire • *I have acquired a new car.*
get • *She went to get a ticket.*
invest in • *I invested in a house.*
pay for • *He let me pay for his drink.*
procure • *attempts to procure more food*
purchase • *He purchased a sandwich for lunch.*

ANTONYM:
• sell

Cc

calculate VERB
to work out a number or amount • *how to calculate the cost of setting up a business*
count • *Shareholders are counting the cost of the slump.*
determine • *calculations to determine the rate of tax*
reckon • *an amount reckoned at 140 billion euros*
work out • *Work out the distance of the journey.*

calculated ADJECTIVE
deliberately planned • *Everything they said was calculated to wound.*
aimed • *The restructuring is aimed at reducing costs.*
designed • *a scheme designed to help families*
intended • *the intended effect of the revised guidelines*
planned • *a carefully planned campaign*
ANTONYM:
• unplanned

call ① VERB
to give a name • *a man called Jeffrey*
christen • *He decided to christen his first-born son Arthur.*

designate • *The wood was designated an "area of natural beauty".*
dub • *the woman dubbed "the world's greatest living singer"*
name • *They named their child Anthony.*

call ② VERB
to telephone • *He called me at my office.*
contact • *Contact us immediately if you have any new information.*
phone • *Phone me as soon as you get home.*
ring • *I'll ring you tomorrow.*
telephone • *Please telephone to make an appointment.*

call ③ VERB
to say loudly • *I heard someone calling my name.*
announce • *"Dinner is served," he announced.*
cry • *"Run, Forrest!" she cried.*
cry out • *She cried out to us as she disappeared from view.*
shout • *He shouted to me from across the room.*
yell • *"Ahoy there!" the captain yelled over to us.*

call ④ NOUN
an instance of someone shouting out • *a call for help*
cry • *the cry of a seagull*
shout • *I heard a distant shout.*
yell • *He let out a yell.*

callous ADJECTIVE
not concerned about other people • *his callous disregard for human life*

calm

cold • What a cold, unfeeling woman she was.
heartless • It was a heartless thing to do.
indifferent • indifferent to the suffering of others
insensitive • insensitive remarks
ANTONYM:
• caring

calm ① ADJECTIVE
not worried or excited • Try to keep calm.
collected • She was cool and collected during her interrogation.
composed • a very composed, businesslike woman
cool • We have to keep a cool head in this situation.
impassive • He remained impassive as his sentence was passed.
relaxed • a relaxed manner
ANTONYM:
• worried

calm ② ADJECTIVE
still because there is no wind • Tuesday was a fine, clear, and calm day.
balmy • balmy summer evenings
mild • a mild winter climate
still • The air was still.
tranquil • a tranquil lake
ANTONYM:
• rough

calm ③ NOUN
the state of being peaceful • He liked the calm of the evening.
calmness • an aura of calmness
peace • a wonderful feeling of peace

peacefulness • the peacefulness of the gardens
quiet • I need quiet to work.
serenity • the peace and serenity of a tropical sunset
stillness • the stillness of the summer night

calm ④ VERB
to make less upset or excited • We were trying to calm him.
quieten • trying to quieten the restless horses
relax • This music is supposed to relax you.
soothe • I think a bath may soothe me.

campaign NOUN
actions planned to get a certain result • a campaign to educate people
crusade • a crusade against injustice
movement • the human rights movement
operation • a full-scale military operation
push • an all-out push to promote the show

cancel ① VERB
to stop something from happening • We're going to have to cancel our picnic.
abandon • He had to abandon his holiday plans.
call off • The union has called off the strike.

cancel ② VERB
to stop something from being valid • They were forced to cancel their contract.

annul • *The marriage was annulled.*

quash • *His jail sentence was quashed when new evidence came to light.*

repeal • *The new law was repealed within the year.*

revoke • *His licence was immediately revoked.*

candid ADJECTIVE
honest and frank • *a candid interview*

blunt • *She is blunt about his faults.*

frank • *They had a frank discussion about the issue.*

honest • *What is your honest opinion?*

open • *He had always been open with her and she would know if he lied.*

straightforward • *I was impressed by his straightforward manner.*

truthful • *We've all learnt to be fairly truthful about our personal lives.*

candidate NOUN
a person being considered for a position • *a candidate for the presidency*

applicant • *one of thirty applicants for the manager's post*

competitor • *several competitors for the contract*

contender • *a strong contender for the chairmanship*

capable ADJECTIVE
able to do something well • *a capable leader*

able • *a very able businessman*

accomplished • *an accomplished painter*

adept • *an adept diplomat*

competent • *a competent and careful driver*

efficient • *efficient administration*

proficient • *proficient with computers*

skilful • *the country's most skilful politician*

ANTONYM:

• incompetent

capacity ① NOUN
the maximum amount that something holds or produces • *the vehicle's fuel capacity*

dimensions • *a car of compact dimensions*

room • *There wasn't enough room in the baggage compartment for all the gear.*

size • *My bedroom is half the size of yours.*

space • *There is space in the back for two people.*

volume • *a container with a volume of two litres*

capacity ② NOUN
a person's power or ability to do something • *Our capacity for giving care, love and attention is limited.*

ability • *The public never had faith in his ability to handle the job.*

capability • *a country with the capability of launching a nuclear attack*

facility • *Humans have lost the facility to use their sense of smell properly.*

gift • *As a youth he discovered a gift for making people laugh.*
potential • *the economic potentials of Eastern and Western Europe*
power • *Human societies have the power to solve the problems confronting them.*

capture ① VERB
to take prisoner • *He was captured by rebels.*
apprehend • *Police have not yet apprehended the killer.*
arrest • *Seven people were arrested.*
catch • *The thief was caught and the money was returned.*
seize • *seized by armed police*
take • *An army unit took the town.*
ANTONYM:
• release

capture ② NOUN
the act of capturing • *He evaded capture for eight years.*
arrest • *Police made two arrests.*
seizure • *the seizure of territory*
taking • *the taking of hostages*
trapping • *The trapping of these animals is illegal.*

car NOUN
a vehicle for carrying a few people • *I finally left the car at the garage.*
automobile (AMERICAN) • *the Japanese automobile manufacturer, Nissan*
motor (OLD-FASHIONED) • *Patricia's new motor*
vehicle • *She managed to scramble out of the vehicle.*

care ① VERB
to be concerned about something • *a company that cares about the environment*
be bothered • *I am not bothered what others think about me.*
be concerned • *We are concerned about the problem.*
be interested • *He's not interested in what anyone else says.*
mind • *I do not mind who wins.*

care ② NOUN
something that causes you to worry • *without a care in the world*
anxiety • *anxieties about money*
concern • *Their main concern is unemployment.*
stress • *the stresses of modern life*
trouble • *She has had her share of troubles.*
woe • *They blame the government for all their woes.*
worry • *My biggest worry is how I will cope on my own.*

care ③ NOUN
close attention when doing something • *We took great care in choosing a location.*
attention • *medical attention*
caution • *Proceed with caution.*
pains • *She takes great pains with her work.*

careful ① ADJECTIVE
acting with care • *Be careful what you say to him.*
cautious • *a cautious approach*

prudent • *prudent management*

ANTONYM:
• careless

careful ② ADJECTIVE
complete and well done • *It needs careful planning.*
meticulous • *meticulous attention to detail*
painstaking • *a painstaking search*
precise • *precise instructions*
thorough • *a thorough examination*

ANTONYM:
• careless

careless ① ADJECTIVE
not taking enough care
• *careless driving*
irresponsible • *an irresponsible attitude*
neglectful • *neglectful managers*
sloppy (INFORMAL) • *sloppy work*

ANTONYM:
• careful

careless ② ADJECTIVE
relaxed and unconcerned
• *careless laughter*
casual • *a casual remark*
nonchalant • *a nonchalant attitude*
offhand • *his usual offhand way*

carry VERB
to hold and take something somewhere • *He was carrying a briefcase.*
bear • *He arrived bearing gifts.*
convey (FORMAL) • *The minibus conveyed us to the station.*

lug • *lugging boxes of books around*
take • *Don't forget to take your camera.*
transport • *goods being transported abroad*

carry out VERB
to do and complete something • *the surgeon who carried out the operation*
accomplish • *the desire to accomplish a task*
achieve • *We have achieved our objective.*
fulfil • *to fulfil a promise*
perform • *people who have performed acts of bravery*

carve VERB
to make something by cutting • *He carves his figures from pine.*
chisel • *the mason chiselling his stone*
cut • *a figure cut from marble*
engrave • *an engraved crystal goblet*
inscribe • *the words inscribed on his monument*
sculpt • *a sculpted clay figure*

case ① NOUN
a particular situation or example • *a case of mistaken identity*
example • *an example of what can go wrong*
illustration • *a clear illustration of this point*
instance • *a serious instance of corruption*
occasion • *the last occasion on which he appeared*

occurrence • *a frequent occurrence*

case ② NOUN
a container for holding something • *a spectacle case*
box • *a chocolate box*
container • *a huge plastic container*

case ③ NOUN
a trial or inquiry • *a libel case*
action • *a civil action for damages*
lawsuit • *the rising cost of defending a lawsuit*
proceedings • *criminal proceedings against the former leader*
trial • *The date of the trial was set.*

casual ① ADJECTIVE
happening by chance • *a casual remark*
accidental • *insured against accidental damage*
chance • *a chance meeting*
incidental • *an incidental effect*
ANTONYM:
• deliberate

casual ② ADJECTIVE
showing no concern or interest • *a casual look over his shoulder*
careless • *careless remarks*
cursory • *a cursory glance*
nonchalant • *his nonchalant attitude to life*
offhand • *a deceptively offhand style*
relaxed • *a relaxed manner*
ANTONYM:
• concerned

cat NOUN
a small animal kept as a pet • *sharing his flat with four cats*
feline (FORMAL) • *Even the most cuddly feline has claws.*
kitty (INFORMAL) • *a kitty stuck up a tree*
moggy or **moggie** (BRITISH AND NEW ZEALAND; SLANG) • *a grey, long-haired moggy*
pussy or **puss** or **pussycat** (INFORMAL) • *a fluffy little pussycat*

RELATED WORDS:
• ADJECTIVE feline
• MALE tom
• FEMALE queen
• YOUNG kitten

catch ① VERB
to capture an animal or fish • *We still haven't caught any tuna.*
capture • *Poachers had captured a gorilla.*
snare • *He'd snared a rabbit.*
trap • *Their aim was to trap a tiger.*

catch ② VERB
to capture a person • *another technique for catching criminals*
apprehend • *the force necessary to apprehend a suspect*
arrest • *Police arrested the gunman.*

catch ③ NOUN
a device that fastens something • *windows fitted with safety catches*
bolt • *the sound of a bolt being slid open*

clasp • the clasp of her handbag

clip • She took the clip out of her hair.

latch • You left the latch off the gate.

catch ④ NOUN

a hidden difficulty • The catch is that you have to fly via Paris.

disadvantage • The disadvantage is that this plant needs frequent watering.

drawback • The flat's only drawback was its size.

snag • The snag is that you have to pay in advance.

category NOUN

a set of things with something in common • The items were organised into six different categories.

class • dividing the stars into six classes of brightness

classification • There are various classifications of genres or types of book.

group • She is one of the most promising players in her age group.

set • Pupils are divided into sets according to ability.

sort • What sort of school did you go to?

type • The majority of complaints received are of this type.

cause ① NOUN

what makes something happen • the most common cause of back pain

origin • the origin of the present war

root • We need to get to the root of the problem.

source • the source of the leak

cause ② NOUN

an aim supported by a group • dedication to the cause of peace

aim • political aims

ideal • religious ideals

movement • the women's movement

cause ③ NOUN

the reason for something • They gave us no cause to believe that.

basis • There is no basis for this assumption.

grounds • discrimination on the grounds of race or religion

justification • There was no justification for what he was doing.

motivation • the motivation for his actions

motive • Police have ruled out robbery as a motive.

reason • You have no reason to cry.

cause ④ VERB

to make something happen • This may cause delays.

bring about • We must try to bring about a better world.

create • The scheme may create even more confusion.

generate • the excitement generated by this film

produce • His comments produced a furious response.

provoke • a move that has provoked a storm of protest

caution ① NOUN

great care taken in order to avoid danger • *Drivers are urged to exercise extreme caution in icy weather.*

care • *Scissors can be safe for young children if used with care.*

prudence • *A lack of prudence may lead to problems.*

caution ② VERB

to scold or warn someone against doing something • *The two men were cautioned but they will not be charged.*

reprimand • *He was reprimanded by a teacher for talking in the corridor.*

tick off (INFORMAL) • *Traffic police ticked off the driver for jumping a red light.*

warn • *My mother warned me not to talk to strangers.*

cautious ADJECTIVE

acting very carefully to avoid danger • *a cautious approach*

careful • *Be extremely careful when travelling.*

guarded • *a guarded response*

tentative • *a tentative agreement to end the war*

wary • *small firms remain wary of committing themselves to debt*

ANTONYM:
• daring

cease ① VERB

to stop happening • *Almost miraculously, the noise ceased.*

be over • *The captured planes will be kept until the war is over.*

come to an end • *The strike came to an end.*

die away • *The sound died away and silence reigned.*

end • *The college year ends in March.*

finish • *The teaching day finished at around four o'clock.*

stop • *The rain had stopped.*

ANTONYM:
• begin

cease ② VERB

to stop doing something • *A small number of firms have ceased trading.*

desist from • *I never desisted from trying to change his mind.*

discontinue • *Do not discontinue the treatment without consulting your doctor.*

finish • *As soon as he'd finished eating, he excused himself.*

give up • *smokers who give up the habit*

stop • *Stop throwing those stones!*

suspend • *The union suspended strike action this week.*

ANTONYM:
• start

celebrate VERB

to do something special to mark an event • *I was in a mood to celebrate.*

commemorate • *The anniversary of the composer's death was commemorated with a concert.*

party • *It's your birthday – let's party!*

rejoice • *My family rejoiced in the happy outcome to events.*

ANTONYM:
• mourn

celebration NOUN
an event in honour of a special
occasion • *his eightieth birthday
celebrations*
festival • *a religious festival*
festivity • *the wedding
festivities*
gala • *the opening gala of the
London Film Festival*
party • *a housewarming party*

celebrity NOUN
a famous person • *At the age of
twelve, he was already a
celebrity.*
big name • *all the big names in
rock and pop*
name • *some of the most
famous names in modelling and
show business*
personality • *a well-known
radio and television personality*
star • *her favourite football
stars*
superstar • *a Hollywood
superstar*
VIP • *such VIPs as Prince Charles
and the former US President*

censure ① NOUN (FORMAL)
strong disapproval • *a
controversial policy which has
attracted international censure*
blame • *I'm the one who'll get
the blame if things go wrong.*
condemnation • *There was
widespread condemnation of the
kidnappings.*
criticism • *This policy had
repeatedly come under strong
criticism.*

disapproval • *His action had
been greeted with almost
universal disapproval.*
reproach • *Those in public life
should be beyond reproach.*

censure ② VERB (FORMAL)
to criticise severely • *I would
not presume to censure him for
his views.*
condemn • *He condemned the
players for lack of ability and
application.*
criticise • *The regime has been
harshly criticised for its human
rights violations.*
denounce • *The letter called for
civil rights, but did not openly
denounce the regime.*
reproach • *She had not even
reproached him for breaking his
promise.*

centre ① NOUN
the middle of something • *the
centre of the room*
core • *the earth's core*
focus • *Children's welfare is the
main focus of the plan.*
heart • *the heart of the problem*
hub • *The kitchen is the hub of
most households.*
middle • *in the middle of the
back row*
ANTONYM:
• edge

centre ② VERB
to have as the main subject
• *All his thoughts were centred
around himself.*
concentrate • *Scientists are
concentrating their efforts on
finding a cure.*

focus • *Attention is likely to focus on sales growth.*
revolve • *Since childhood, her life has revolved around tennis.*

ceremony ① NOUN

formal actions done for a special occasion • *his recent coronation ceremony*
observance • *a Memorial Day observance*
pomp • *His departure was celebrated with suitable pomp.*
rite • *a marriage rite*
ritual • *a Summer Solstice ritual*
service • *The President attended the morning service.*

ceremony ② NOUN

formal and polite behaviour • *He hung up without ceremony.*
decorum • *a responsibility to behave with decorum*
etiquette • *the rules of diplomatic etiquette*
formality • *his lack of stuffy formality*
niceties • *social niceties*
protocol • *minor breaches of protocol*

certain ① ADJECTIVE

definite or reliable • *One thing is certain – they respect each other.*
definite • *It's too soon to give a definite answer.*
established • *an established medical fact*
guaranteed • *Success is not guaranteed.*
inevitable • *If she wins her case, it is inevitable that other people will sue the company.*

known • *It is not known when the bomb was planted.*
sure • *Sharpe's leg began to ache, a sure sign of rain.*
undeniable • *undeniable proof of guilt*

ANTONYM:
• uncertain

certain ② ADJECTIVE

having no doubt in your mind • *She's absolutely certain she's going to succeed.*
clear • *It is important to be clear about what you are doing.*
confident • *I am confident that everything will come out right.*
convinced • *He was convinced that I was part of the problem.*
definite • *Mary is very definite about this fact.*
positive • *I'm as positive as I can be about it.*
satisfied • *People must be satisfied that the treatment is safe.*
sure • *She was no longer sure how she felt about him.*

ANTONYM:
• uncertain

certainly ADVERB

without any doubt • *I'll certainly do all I can to help.*
definitely • *Something should definitely be done.*
undeniably • *Bringing up a baby is undeniably hard work.*
undoubtedly • *He is undoubtedly a great player.*
unquestionably • *He is unquestionably a star.*

without doubt • *The refugees are, without doubt, extremely vulnerable.*

challenge ① NOUN

a suggestion to try something • *They issued a challenge to their rivals.*

dare • *He'd do almost anything for a dare.*

challenge ② VERB

to give someone a challenge • *He challenged his rival to a duel.*

dare • *I dare you to ask him.*

defy • *He looked at me as if he was defying me to argue.*

challenge ③ VERB

to question the truth or value of something • *challenging the authority of the state*

dispute • *He disputed the charge.*

question • *questioning the jury's verdict*

champion ① NOUN

a person who wins a competition • *He became a world chess champion.*

hero • *the goal-scoring hero of the British hockey team*

title holder • *She became the youngest world title holder at the age of 22.*

victor • *the British Grand Prix victors*

winner • *The winner was a horse called Baby Face.*

champion ② NOUN

someone who supports a group, cause or principle • *He received acclaim as a champion of the oppressed.*

advocate • *He was a staunch advocate of free trade.*

defender • *a strong defender of human rights*

guardian • *The party wants to be seen as a guardian of traditional values.*

protector • *She was seen as a protector and provider.*

champion ③ VERB

to support a group, cause or principle • *She passionately championed these.*

defend • *his courage in defending religious and civil rights*

fight for • *Our Government should be fighting for an end to child poverty.*

promote • *You don't have to sacrifice the environment to promote economic growth.*

stick up for (INFORMAL) • *He has shown courage in sticking up for civil liberties.*

support • *The vice president has always supported the people of New York.*

uphold • *upholding the artist's right to creative freedom*

chance ① NOUN

a possibility of something happening • *a good chance of success*

likelihood • *the likelihood of infection*

odds • *What are the odds of that happening?*

possibility • *the possibility of pay cuts*

probability • *a probability of victory*

prospect • There is little prospect of peace.

chance ② NOUN

an opportunity to do something • He didn't give me a chance to explain.

occasion • I had no occasion to speak to her that day.

opening • an opening for finding a peaceful outcome to the conflict

opportunity • an opportunity to go abroad to study

time • There was no time to think.

chance ③ NOUN

the way things happen without being planned • events which were merely the result of chance

accident • a strange accident of fate

coincidence • It was no coincidence that she arrived just then.

fortune • a change of fortune

luck • His injury was just bad luck.

RELATED WORD:
• ADJECTIVE fortuitous

change ① NOUN

an alteration in something • a change in her attitude

alteration • some alterations in your diet

difference • a noticeable difference in his behaviour

modification • Some minor modifications were required.

transformation • the transformation of a wilderness into a garden

change ② VERB

to make or become different • Her views have changed since then.

alter • There is no prospect of the decision being altered.

convert • a plan to convert his spare room into an office

moderate • They persuaded him to moderate his views.

modify • He refused to modify his behaviour.

reform • his plans to reform the economy

transform • The landscape has been transformed.

change ③ VERB

to exchange one thing for another • Can I change this sweater for one a size bigger?

barter • bartering wheat for cotton and timber

exchange • the chance to sell back or exchange goods

interchange • Meat can be interchanged with pulses as a source of protein.

replace • His smile was replaced by a frown.

substitute • You can substitute honey for the sugar.

swap • Let's swap places.

trade • They traded land for goods and money.

changeable ADJECTIVE

likely to change all the time • changeable weather

erratic • erratic driving

fickle • Fashion is a fickle business.

irregular • an irregular heartbeat

unpredictable • *unpredictable behaviour*
unstable • *The political situation is unstable.*
variable • *a variable rate of interest*
volatile • *a volatile atmosphere*
ANTONYM:
• constant

character ① NOUN
the qualities of a person • *He has a dark side to his character.*
make-up • *Determination has always been a part of his make-up.*
nature • *a sunny nature*
personality • *an outgoing personality*
temperament • *his impulsive temperament*

character ② NOUN
an honourable nature • *She showed real character in her attempt to win over the crowd.*
honour • *He has acted with honour.*
integrity • *a man of integrity*
strength • *He had the strength to turn down the offer.*

characteristic ① NOUN
a typical quality • *His chief characteristic is honesty.*
attribute • *a normal attribute of human behaviour*
feature • *a feature of the local culture*
property • *This liquid has many unique properties.*
quality • *leadership qualities*
trait • *personality traits*

characteristic ② ADJECTIVE
typical of a person or thing
• *She responded with characteristic generosity.*
distinctive • *a distinctive voice*
distinguishing • *no distinguishing marks*
typical • *He spoke with typical modesty.*

ANTONYM:
• uncharacteristic

charge ① VERB
to ask someone for money as a payment • *The majority of producers charged a fair price.*
ask (for) • *The artist was asking £6,000 for each painting.*
bill • *Are you going to bill me for this?*
levy • *Taxes should not be levied without the authority of Parliament.*

charge ② VERB
to rush forward, often to attack someone • *He charged into the room.*
dash • *She dashed in from the garden.*
rush • *A schoolgirl rushed into the burning flat to help an elderly man.*
stampede • *The crowd stampeded.*
storm • *He stormed into the shop, demanding to see the manager.*

charge ③ NOUN
the price you have to pay for something • *We can arrange this for a small charge.*

cost • Badges are available at a cost of £2.50.
fee • Pay your solicitor's fees.
payment • I'll do it in return for a small payment.
price • We negotiated a price for the service.

charm ① NOUN

an attractive quality • a man of great personal charm
allure • the allure of Egypt
appeal • confident of his appeal to young voters
attraction • the attractions of living by the sea
fascination • It is hard to explain the fascination of this place.
magnetism • a woman of enormous magnetism

charm ② VERB

to use charm to please someone • He charmed his 2,000-strong audience.
bewitch • bewitched by her beauty
captivate • The crowd was captivated by her honesty.
delight • a style of music that has delighted audiences
entrance • entranced by his smile

chase ① VERB

to try to catch someone or something • She chased the thief for a hundred yards.
hunt • He fled to Portugal after being hunted by police.
pursue • She pursued the man who had snatched her bag.

chase ② VERB

to force to go somewhere • Angry demonstrators chased him away.
drive • The troops drove the rebels into the jungle.
hound • He was hounded out of his job.

chat ① NOUN

a friendly talk • We sat around and had a chat.
conversation • a telephone conversation
gossip • Don't you enjoy a good gossip?
natter (INFORMAL) • Let's get together for a natter some time.
talk • We will have a talk about it later.

chat ② VERB

to talk in a friendly way • He was chatting to his father.
gossip • We gossiped into the night.
natter (INFORMAL) • His mother would natter to anyone.
talk • She's very easy to talk to.

cheap ① ADJECTIVE

costing very little • Cheap flights are available.
bargain • selling at bargain prices
economical • These cars are very economical to run.
inexpensive • an inexpensive holiday
reasonable • His fees were quite reasonable.
ANTONYM:
• expensive

cheap ② ADJECTIVE
inexpensive but of poor quality • *a suit of some cheap material*
inferior • *an inferior imitation*
second-rate • *second-rate equipment*
tawdry • *tawdry souvenirs*

cheat VERB
to get something from someone dishonestly • *the people he cheated out of their life savings*
con (INFORMAL) • *He conned his way into a job.*
deceive • *Investors were deceived by a scam.*
defraud • *charges of conspiracy to defraud the government*
dupe • *Stamp collectors were duped into buying fakes.*
fleece • *He fleeced her out of thousands of pounds.*
rip off (SLANG) • *ticket touts ripping off soccer fans*
swindle • *two executives who swindled their employer*

check ① VERB
to examine something • *Check all the details first.*
check out • *Check out the financial figures.*
examine • *He examined her passport and stamped it.*
inspect • *the right to inspect company files*
test • *The drug must be tested in clinical trials.*

check ② VERB
to reduce or stop something • *a policy to check fast population growth*
control • *a measure to control illegal mining*
curb • *reforms which aim to curb spending*
halt • *an attempt to halt the spread of the disease*
inhibit • *factors which inhibit growth*
restrain • *the need to restrain wage rises*
stop • *measures to stop the trade in ivory*

check ③ NOUN
an examination • *a thorough check of the equipment*
examination • *a medical examination*
inspection • *a routine inspection of the premises*
test • *a test for cancer*

cheek NOUN
speech or behaviour that is rude or disrespectful • *I'm amazed they had the cheek to ask in the first place.*
audacity • *I was shocked at the audacity of the gangsters.*
gall • *She had the gall to claim she had been cheated.*
impudence • *My sister had the impudence to go out wearing my clothes.*
insolence • *The pupil was excluded for insolence.*
nerve • *He had the nerve to ask me to prove who I was.*
rudeness • *Mother was cross at Tom's rudeness.*

cheeky ADJECTIVE
rude and disrespectful • *cheeky humour*

impertinent • *an impertinent question*
impudent • *his rude and impudent behaviour*
insolent • *a defiant, almost insolent look*
rude • *She was often rude to her mother.*
ANTONYM:
• polite

cheerful ADJECTIVE
in a happy mood • *She was very cheerful despite her illness.*
bright • *"May I help you?" said a bright voice.*
buoyant • *in a buoyant mood*
cheery • *a cheery nature*
happy • *a confident, happy child*
jaunty • *a jaunty tune*
jolly • *a jolly, easy-going man*
light-hearted • *They were light-hearted and enjoyed life.*
merry • *a burst of merry laughter*
ANTONYM:
• miserable

cheery ADJECTIVE
happy and cheerful • *He is loved by everyone for his cheery disposition.*
cheerful • *They are both very cheerful in spite of their circumstances.*
chirpy • *She sounded quite chirpy on the phone.*
good-humoured • *Charles was brave and remarkably good-humoured.*
happy • *Marina was a confident, happy child.*
jolly • *She was a jolly, kind-hearted woman.*

sunny • *a nice lad with a sunny disposition*
upbeat • *Neil's colleagues said he was in a joking, upbeat mood.*
ANTONYM:
• gloomy

chew VERB
to break food up with the teeth • *Eat slowly and chew your food properly.*
crunch • *She crunched the ice cube loudly.*
gnaw • *He sat and gnawed at an apple.*
munch • *Sheep were munching the leaves.*

chief ① NOUN
the leader of a group or organisation • *the deputy chief of the territory's defence force*
boss • *He cannot stand his boss.*
chieftain • *the legendary British chieftain, King Arthur*
director • *the financial director of the company*
governor • *The incident was reported to the prison governor.*
head • *heads of government from 100 countries*
leader • *the leader of the Conservative Party*
manager • *a retired bank manager*

chief ② ADJECTIVE
most important • *The job went to one of his chief rivals.*
foremost • *one of the world's foremost scholars of ancient Indian culture*
key • *He is expected to be the key witness at the trial.*

main • *one of the main tourist areas of Amsterdam*
prevailing • *the prevailing attitude towards women in this society*
primary • *His language difficulties were the primary cause of his other problems.*
prime • *The police will see me as the prime suspect!*
principal • *The principal reason for my change of mind is this.*

child NOUN
a young person • *I lived in France as a child.*
ankle-biter (AUSTRALIAN AND NEW ZEALAND; SLANG) • *I knew him when he was just an ankle-biter.*
baby • *She took care of me when I was a baby.*
bairn (SCOTTISH) • *a two-year-old bairn*
infant • *young parents with infants in prams*
juvenile (FORMAL) • *a prison for juveniles*
kid (INFORMAL) • *They've got three kids.*
minor (FORMAL) • *Edgar became king while he was still a minor.*
offspring • *parents choosing shoes for their offspring*
toddler • *a toddler in a pushchair*
tot (INFORMAL) • *The tot was too young to know what was happening.*
youngster • *I was only a youngster in 1985.*

ANTONYM:
• adult

RELATED WORDS:
• ADJECTIVE filial
• PREFIX paedo-

childish ADJECTIVE
immature and foolish • *I don't have time for this childish behaviour.*
immature • *emotionally immature*
infantile • *infantile jokes*
juvenile • *juvenile behaviour*
puerile • *a puerile sense of humour*

ANTONYM:
• mature

china NOUN (BRITISH AND SOUTH AFRICAN; INFORMAL)
a friend • *How are you, my old china?*
buddy (INFORMAL) • *We've been buddies since we were kids.*
chum (INFORMAL) • *He went on holiday with his two best chums.*
crony (OLD-FASHIONED) • *She is always surrounded by her cronies.*
friend • *lifelong friends*
mate (INFORMAL) • *Come on, mate, things aren't that bad.*
pal (INFORMAL) • *He'd never let a pal down.*

choice ① NOUN
a range of things to choose from • *available in a choice of colours*
range • *a range of sun-care products*

selection • *an interesting selection of recipes*
variety • *a variety of candidates from which to choose*

choice ② NOUN
the power to choose • *They had little choice in the matter.*
alternative • *He said he could not see any alternative.*
option • *He was given the option of going to jail or paying a fine.*
say • *We don't have a say in the company's decisions.*

choose VERB
to decide to have or do something • *a number of foods to choose from*
opt for • *He opted for early retirement.*
pick • *She was picked for the debating team.*
select • *She paused to select another cookie from the box.*
take • *She took the option he offered her.*

chop VERB
to cut down or into pieces • *I heard him chopping wood in the yard.*
cut • *Cut the vegetables up.*
fell • *43,000 square miles of tropical forest are felled each year.*
hack • *They hacked away at the undergrowth.*
lop • *Somebody had lopped the heads off our tulips.*

circulate VERB
to pass around • *He circulated rumours about everyone.*

distribute • *distributing leaflets*
propagate • *They propagated their political ideas.*
spread • *spreading malicious gossip*

city NOUN
a large town • *the city of London*
metropolis • *a busy metropolis*
town • *the oldest town in Europe*
RELATED WORD:
• ADJECTIVE CIVIC

civilised ADJECTIVE
having an advanced society • *a highly civilised country*
cultured • *a mature and cultured nation*
enlightened • *this enlightened century*

claim ① VERB
to say something is the case • *He claims to have lived here all his life.*
allege • *He is alleged to have lied under oath.*
assert • *The defendants continued to assert their innocence.*
hold • *He holds that these measures are unnecessary.*
insist • *They insisted that they had no money.*
maintain • *I still maintain that I am not guilty.*
profess • *She professed to hate her nickname.*

claim ② NOUN
a statement that something is the case • *He rejected claims that he had taken bribes.*
allegation • *allegations of theft*

assertion • *his assertion that he did not plan to remarry*

clash ① VERB
to fight or argue with another person • *A group of 400 demonstrators clashed with police.*

battle • *The armies battled into the night.*

fight • *two rival gangs fighting in the streets*

quarrel • *My brother quarrelled with my father.*

wrangle • *Delegates wrangled over the future of the organisation.*

clash ② VERB
of two things: to be so different that they do not go together • *Don't make policy decisions which clash with company thinking.*

conflict • *He held opinions which sometimes conflicted with my own.*

contradict • *Cutbacks like these surely contradict the Government's commitment to education.*

differ • *The two leaders differed on several issues.*

disagree • *Our managers disagreed on several policy issues.*

go against • *Changes are being made which go against my principles.*

jar • *They had always been good together and their temperaments seldom jarred.*

clash ③ NOUN
a fight or argument • *a number of clashes between rival parties*

battle • *an army general who never won a battle*

conflict • *attempts to prevent a conflict between workers and management*

confrontation • *This issue could lead to a military confrontation.*

fight • *He had had a fight with Smith and bloodied his nose.*

skirmish • *Border skirmishes between the two countries were common.*

squabble • *There have been minor squabbles about phone bills.*

struggle • *a struggle between competing political factions*

clasp ① VERB
to hold something tightly • *Mary clasped the children to her desperately.*

clutch • *She was clutching a photograph.*

embrace • *People were crying for joy and embracing each other.*

grip • *She gripped the rope.*

hold • *He held the pencil in his right hand.*

hug • *She hugged her legs tight to her chest.*

press • *I pressed the child closer to my heart and prayed.*

squeeze • *He longed to just scoop her up and squeeze her.*

clasp ② NOUN
a fastening such as a hook or catch • *She undid the clasp of her hooded cloak.*

buckle • *He wore a belt with a large brass buckle.*

catch • She fiddled with the catch of her bag.

clip • She took the clip out of her hair.

fastener • a product range which includes nails, woodscrews and fasteners

fastening • The sundress has a neat back zip fastening.

class ① NOUN

a group of a particular type • a new class of vehicle

category • different categories of taxpayer

genre • films of the horror genre

grade • the lowest grade of paper

group • a plan to help people in this group

kind • the biggest prize of its kind in the world

set • The fashionable set all go to this club.

sort • several articles of this sort

type • various types of vegetable

class ② VERB

to regard as being in a particular group • They are officially classed as visitors.

categorise • His films are hard to categorise.

classify • Tomatoes are also classified as a fruit.

designate • The house is designated as a national monument.

grade • This ski-run is graded as easy.

rank • She is ranked in the world's top 50 players.

rate • He rates the film highly.

classify VERB

to arrange similar things in groups • We can classify the differences into three groups.

arrange • Arrange the books in neat piles.

categorise • This film is hard to categorise.

grade • musical pieces graded according to difficulty

rank • He was ranked among Britain's best-known millionaires.

sort • sorting the material into folders

clean ① ADJECTIVE

free from dirt or marks • clean shoes

immaculate • immaculate white flannels

impeccable • dressed in an impeccable trouser suit

laundered • freshly laundered shirts

spotless • The kitchen was spotless.

washed • newly washed hair

ANTONYM:
• dirty

clean ② ADJECTIVE

free from germs or infection • a lack of clean water and sanitation

antiseptic • an antiseptic hospital room

hygienic • a hygienic kitchen

purified • Only purified water is used.

sterilised • sterilised milk

uncontaminated • uncontaminated air

unpolluted • *unpolluted beaches*
ANTONYM:
• contaminated

clean ③ VERB
to remove dirt from • *She cleaned the house from top to bottom.*
cleanse • *a lotion to cleanse the skin*
dust • *I vacuumed, dusted and polished the living room.*
scour • *He scoured the sink.*
scrub • *I started to scrub off the dirt.*
sponge • *Sponge your face and body.*
swab • *a cleaner swabbing the floor*
wash • *He got a job washing dishes in a restaurant.*
wipe • *He wiped the sweat from his face.*
ANTONYM:
• soil

clear ① ADJECTIVE
easy to see or understand • *He made it clear he did not want to talk.*
apparent • *There is no apparent reason for the crime.*
blatant • *a blatant piece of cheating*
conspicuous • *one conspicuous difference*
definite • *a definite advantage*
evident • *He ate with evident enjoyment.*
explicit • *He was very explicit about his intentions.*
obvious • *There are obvious dangers.*
plain • *The results are plain to see.*

clear ② ADJECTIVE
easy to see through • *a clear liquid*
crystalline • *crystalline green waters*
glassy • *The water was a deep glassy blue.*
translucent • *translucent stones*
transparent • *transparent glass walls*
ANTONYM:
• cloudy

clear ③ VERB
to prove someone is not guilty • *She was cleared of any wrongdoing.*
absolve • *He was absolved of all charges.*
acquit • *acquitted of disorderly conduct*
ANTONYM:
• convict

clever ADJECTIVE
very intelligent • *My sister was always a lot cleverer than I was.*
brainy (INFORMAL) • *I don't consider myself to be especially brainy.*
bright • *an exceptionally bright child*
intelligent • *a lively and intelligent woman*
shrewd • *a shrewd businessman*
smart • *a very smart move*
ANTONYM:
• stupid

climb VERB
to move upwards over something • *Climbing the first hill took half an hour.*

ascend • *He ascended the ladder into the loft.*
clamber • *They clambered up the stone walls.*
mount • *He mounted the steps.*
scale • *the first British woman to scale Everest*

close ① VERB
to shut something • *Close the gate behind you.*
secure • *The shed was secured by a padlock.*
shut • *Someone had forgotten to shut the door.*
ANTONYM:
• open

close ② VERB
to block so that nothing can pass • *All the roads out are closed.*
bar • *Protesters barred the way to his car.*
block • *The road was blocked by debris.*
obstruct • *parked cars obstructing the pavement*
seal • *Soldiers had sealed the border.*

close ③ ADJECTIVE
near to something • *a restaurant close to their home*
adjacent • *The fire spread to adjacent buildings.*
adjoining • *the smell of hamburgers from the adjoining stall*
at hand • *Don't worry, help is at hand.*
handy • *Keep a pencil and paper handy.*
near • *The station is quite near.*

nearby • *I dashed into a nearby shop.*
neighbouring • *a man sitting at a neighbouring table*
ANTONYM:
• distant

close ④ ADJECTIVE
friendly and loving • *We became close friends.*
attached • *We've got very attached to one another over the years.*
dear • *a dear and valued companion*
devoted • *My parents were a deeply devoted couple.*
friendly • *We gradually became very friendly.*
intimate • *one of my most intimate friends*
loving • *They forged a loving relationship.*
ANTONYM:
• distant

cloth NOUN
woven or knitted fabric • *a piece of red cloth*
fabric • *waterproof fabric*
material • *This material shrinks badly.*
textile • *a trader in clothes and textiles*

clothes PLURAL NOUN
the things people wear • *I'm fed up wearing these old clothes.*
attire (FORMAL) • *suitable attire*
clothing • *men's clothing*
costume • *national costume*
dress • *traditional dress*

garments • *winter garments*
gear (INFORMAL) • *trendy gear*
outfit • *a stunning scarlet outfit*
wardrobe • *next summer's wardrobe*
wear • *evening wear*

cloud ① NOUN
a mass of vapour or smoke
• *The sky was dark with clouds.*
billow • *billows of smoke*
fog • *The sun streamed through a fog of dust.*
haze • *a haze of exhaust fumes*
mist • *The valley was wrapped in thick mist.*
vapour • *warm vapour rising from the ground*

cloud ② VERB
to make something confusing
• *Anger has clouded his judgement.*
confuse • *You're just confusing the matter by bringing politics into it.*
distort • *a distorted memory*
muddle • *The question muddles two separate issues.*

cloudy ① ADJECTIVE
full of clouds • *a cloudy sky*
dull • *It's always dull and wet here.*
gloomy • *gloomy weather*
leaden • *leaden skies*
overcast • *a damp, overcast morning*
ANTONYM:
• clear

cloudy ② ADJECTIVE
difficult to see through • *a glass of cloudy liquid*
muddy • *a muddy duck pond*

murky • *murky waters*
opaque • *an opaque glass jar*
ANTONYM:
• clear

club ① NOUN
an organisation for people with a special interest • *a swimming club*
association • *the Women's Tennis Association*
circle • *a local painting circle*
group • *an environmental group*
guild • *The Screen Writers' Guild*
society • *a historical society*
union • *the International Astronomical Union*

club ② NOUN
a heavy stick • *armed with knives and clubs*
bat • *a baseball bat*
stick • *a crowd carrying sticks and stones*
truncheon • *a police officer's truncheon*

clue NOUN
something that helps to solve a problem or mystery • *a vital clue to the thief's identity*
hint • *There is a hint to the story's ending in its title.*
indication • *There was no indication that anyone had been in the house.*
lead • *The police had no leads to follow about who carried out the attack.*

clumsiness NOUN
awkwardness of movement
• *The accident was entirely the result of his own clumsiness.*

c

clumsy

awkwardness • *They moved with the awkwardness of mechanical dolls.*

ungainliness • *his physical ungainliness*

clumsy ADJECTIVE
moving awkwardly • *He is big and clumsy in his movements.*

awkward • *an awkward gesture*

gauche • *He makes me feel stupid and gauche.*

lumbering • *a big, lumbering man*

uncoordinated • *an uncoordinated dancer*

ungainly • *As a girl she was lanky and ungainly.*

ANTONYM:
• graceful

coast NOUN
the land next to the sea • *a holiday by the coast*

beach • *a beautiful sandy beach*

border • *the border of the Black Sea*

coastline • *the stunning Caribbean coastline*

seaside • *a day at the seaside*

shore • *a bleak and rocky shore*

strand • *boats fishing from the strand*

coat NOUN
an animal's fur or hair • *She gave the dog's coat a brush.*

fleece • *a blanket of lamb's fleece*

fur • *a kitten with black fur*

hair • *He's allergic to cat hair.*

hide • *rhino hide*

pelt • *a wolf pelt*

skin • *convicted of attempting to sell the skin of a Siberian tiger*

wool • *Lanolin comes from sheep's wool.*

coating NOUN
a layer of something • *a thin coating of ice*

coat • *a coat of paint*

covering • *a covering of dust*

layer • *a layer of dead leaves*

coax VERB
to persuade gently • *We coaxed her into coming with us.*

cajole • *Her sister cajoled her into playing.*

persuade • *My husband persuaded me to come.*

talk into • *They've talked him into getting a new car.*

cocky ① ADJECTIVE
cheeky or too self-confident • *He was a bit cocky because he was winning all the time.*

arrogant • *an air of arrogant indifference*

brash • *On stage she seems hard and brash.*

conceited • *I thought him conceited.*

overconfident • *She had met many overconfident city boys.*

cocky ② NOUN (AUSTRALIAN AND NEW ZEALAND)
a farmer, especially one whose farm is small • *He got some work with the cane cockies on Maroochy River.*

crofter (SCOTTISH) • *the financial plight of crofters in the islands*

farmer • *He was a simple farmer scratching a living from the soil.*

coil VERB
to wind in loops • *a coiled spring*
curl • *dark, curling hair*
loop • *A rope was looped between his hands.*
spiral • *vines spiralling up towards the roof*
twine • *This lily produces twining stems.*
twist • *She twisted her hair into a bun.*
wind • *a rope wound round her waist*

cold ① ADJECTIVE
having a low temperature • *the coldest winter for ten years*
arctic • *arctic conditions*
biting • *a biting wind*
bitter • *driven inside by the bitter cold*
bleak • *The weather can be bleak on the coast.*
chilly • *It's chilly for June.*
freezing • *This house is freezing.*
icy • *the icy north wind*
raw • *a raw December morning*
wintry • *wintry showers*
ANTONYM:
• hot

cold ② ADJECTIVE
not showing affection • *a cold, unfeeling woman*
aloof • *He seemed aloof and detached.*
distant • *She was polite but distant.*
frigid • *a frigid smile*
lukewarm • *a lukewarm response*
reserved • *emotionally reserved*
stony • *He gave me a stony look.*

ANTONYM:
• warm

collapse ① VERB
to fall down • *The whole building is about to collapse.*
fall down • *The ceiling fell down.*
give way • *The bridge gave way beneath him.*

collapse ② VERB
to fail • *50,000 small businesses collapsed last year.*
fail • *His hotel business has failed.*
fold • *We were laid off when the company folded.*
founder • *a foundering radio station*

collapse ③ NOUN
the failure of something • *the collapse of her business empire*
downfall • *the downfall of the government*
failure • *the failure of the whole venture*

colleague NOUN
a person someone works with • *I'll have to consult my colleagues.*
associate • *business associates*
co-worker • *She gets on well with her co-workers.*
partner • *her business partner*
workmate • *the nickname his workmates gave him*

collect VERB
to gather together • *collecting signatures for a petition*
accumulate • *Most children enjoy accumulating knowledge.*

collection

assemble • *trying to assemble a team*
gather • *gathering information*
raise • *They've raised over £100 for charity.*

ANTONYM:
• scatter

collection NOUN
a group of things collected together • *a collection of paintings*
assortment • *an assortment of pets*
group • *a group of songs*
store • *a vast store of knowledge*

colloquial ADJECTIVE
used in conversation • *a colloquial expression*
conversational • *a conversational style*
everyday • *He used plain, everyday English.*
informal • *an informal expression*

colony ① NOUN
a country controlled by another country • *an American colony*
dependency • *the tiny British dependency of Montserrat*
dominion • *The Republic is a dominion of Brazil.*
territory • *disputed territories under UN control*

colony ② NOUN
a group of settlers in a place • *a colony of Scots*
community • *the Sikh community in Britain*
outpost • *a remote outpost*

settlement • *a Muslim settlement*

colossal ADJECTIVE
very large indeed • *a colossal statue*
enormous • *The main bedroom is enormous.*
gigantic • *a gigantic task*
huge • *They are making huge profits.*
immense • *an immense cloud of smoke*
mammoth • *This mammoth undertaking was completed in 18 months.*
massive • *a massive steam boat*
vast • *farmers who own vast stretches of land*

ANTONYM:
• tiny

colour ① NOUN
a shade or hue • *Her favourite colour is blue.*
hue • *delicate pastel hues*
pigmentation • *skin pigmentation*
shade • *walls painted in two shades of green*
tint • *a distinct orange tint*

colour ② NOUN
a substance used to give colour • *food colour*
dye • *hair dye*
paint • *a pot of red paint*
pigment • *a layer of blue pigment*

colour ③ VERB
to give something a colour • *Many people colour their hair.*
dye • *Only dye clean garments.*

paint • *She paints her toenails red.*
stain • *Some foods can stain the teeth.*
tint • *tinted glass*

colour ④ VERB
to affect the way you think
• *Her upbringing has coloured her view of family.*
bias • *a biased opinion*
distort • *The shock of the accident distorted my judgement.*
prejudice • *Criticism will prejudice the Government's decision.*
slant • *deliberately slanted news coverage*

colourful ① ADJECTIVE
full of colour • *colourful clothes*
bright • *a bright green dress*
brilliant • *The garden has burst into brilliant flower.*
intense • *an intense shade of blue*
jazzy (INFORMAL) • *a jazzy tie*
rich • *a rich blue glass bowl*
vibrant • *vibrant orange shades*
vivid • *vivid hues*
ANTONYM:
• dull

colourful ② ADJECTIVE
interesting or exciting • *a colourful character*
graphic • *a graphic account of his career*
interesting • *He has had an interesting life.*
lively • *a lively imagination*
rich • *the rich history of the island*
vivid • *a vivid description*

ANTONYM:
• dull

combination NOUN
a mixture of things • *a combination of charm and skill*
amalgamation • *an amalgamation of two organisations*
blend • *a blend of fruit juice and spring water*
mix • *a mix of fantasy and reality*
mixture • *a mixture of horror, envy and awe*

combine VERB
to join or mix together • *trying to combine hobbies with homework*
amalgamate • *a plan to amalgamate the two parties*
blend • *The band blends jazz and folk music.*
fuse • *a performer who fuses magic and dance*
integrate • *integrating various styles of art*
merge • *The two countries have merged into one.*
mix • *mixing business with pleasure*
unite • *people uniting to fight racism*

ANTONYM:
• separate

come ① VERB
to move or arrive somewhere • *Two men came into the room.*
appear • *He appeared at about 9 o'clock.*
arrive • *My brother has just arrived.*
enter • *The class fell silent as the teacher entered.*

materialise • *The car just materialised from nowhere.*
show up (INFORMAL) • *He showed up over an hour late.*
turn up (INFORMAL) • *I'll call you when she turns up.*

come ② VERB
to happen or take place
• *Christmas only comes once a year.*

happen • *Nothing ever happens in this town.*
occur • *How did the accident occur?*
take place • *The meeting never took place.*

comfort ① NOUN
a state of ease • *He settled back in comfort.*

ease • *a life of ease*
luxury • *brought up in an atmosphere of luxury*
wellbeing • *a wonderful sense of wellbeing*

comfort ② NOUN
relief from worry or unhappiness • *Her words gave him some comfort.*

consolation • *He knew he was right, but it was no consolation.*
help • *Just talking to you has been a great help.*
relief • *temporary relief from the pain*
satisfaction • *At least I have the satisfaction of knowing I tried.*
support • *His family were a great support to him.*

comfort ③ VERB
to give someone comfort

• *trying to comfort the screaming child*

cheer • *The thought did nothing to cheer him.*
console • *"Never mind," he consoled me.*
reassure • *He did his best to reassure her.*
soothe • *She took him in her arms and soothed him.*

comfortable ① ADJECTIVE
physically relaxing • *a comfortable chair*

cosy • *a cosy living room*
homely • *a homely atmosphere*
relaxing • *a relaxing holiday*
restful • *a restful scene*

ANTONYM:
• uncomfortable

comfortable ② ADJECTIVE
feeling at ease • *I don't feel comfortable around him.*

at ease • *He is not at ease in company.*
at home • *We soon felt quite at home.*
contented • *a contented life*
happy • *I'm not very happy with that idea.*
relaxed • *a relaxed attitude*

ANTONYM:
• uneasy

command ① VERB
to order someone to do something • *She commanded me to lie down.*

bid • *The soldiers bade us turn and go back.*
demand • *They demanded that he leave.*

direct • *His doctor has directed him to rest.*
order • *He ordered his men to cease fire.*

command ② VERB
to be in charge of • *the general who commanded the UN troops*
control • *She now controls the whole company.*
head • *Who heads the firm?*
lead • *He led the country between 2010 and 2015.*
manage • *I manage a small team of workers.*
supervise • *He supervised more than 400 volunteers.*

command ③ NOUN
an order to do something • *The operation was carried out at his command.*
bidding • *They refused to leave at his bidding.*
decree • *a presidential decree*
directive • *a government directive*
injunction (FORMAL) • *He left her with the injunction to go to sleep.*
instruction • *They were just following instructions.*
order • *I don't take orders from you.*

command ④ NOUN
knowledge and ability • *a good command of English*
grasp • *a good grasp of foreign languages*
knowledge • *He has no knowledge of law.*
mastery • *a mastery of grammar*

commemorate VERB
to do something in memory of • *concerts to commemorate the anniversary of his death*
celebrate • *celebrating their golden wedding*
honour • *celebrations to honour his memory*

comment ① VERB
to make a remark • *He refused to comment on the rumours.*
mention • *I mentioned that I didn't like jazz.*
note • *He noted that some issues remained to be settled.*
observe • *"You're very pale," he observed.*
point out • *I should point out that these figures are approximate.*
remark • *Everyone had remarked on her new hairstyle.*
say • *"Well done," he said.*

comment ② NOUN
something you say • *sarcastic comments*
observation • *a few general observations*
remark • *snide remarks*
statement • *That statement puzzled me.*

commit VERB
to do something • *A crime has been committed.*
carry out • *attacks carried out by terrorists*
do • *They have done a lot of damage.*
perform • *people who have performed acts of bravery*
perpetrate • *A fraud has been perpetrated.*

common ① ADJECTIVE
of many people • *a common complaint*

general • *the general opinion*
popular • *a popular belief*
prevailing • *the prevailing atmosphere*
prevalent • *a style of art that became prevalent in the 1980s*
universal • *The book has received universal acclaim.*
widespread • *widespread support*

ANTONYM:
• rare

common ② ADJECTIVE
not special • *the common man*

average • *the average teenager*
commonplace • *a commonplace observation*
everyday • *your everyday routine*
ordinary • *an ordinary day*
plain • *My parents were just plain ordinary folks.*
standard • *standard practice*
usual • *In a usual week I watch about 15 hours of television.*

ANTONYM:
• special

common ③ ADJECTIVE
having bad taste or manners • *a common, rude woman*

coarse • *coarse humour*
rude • *It's rude to stare.*
vulgar • *vulgar remarks*

ANTONYM:
• refined

common sense NOUN
the ability to make good judgments • *Use your common sense.*

good sense • *He had the good sense to call me at once.*
judgment • *I respect your judgment.*
level-headedness • *He prides himself on his level-headedness.*
prudence • *His lack of prudence led to financial problems.*
wit • *They don't have the wit to realise what's happening.*

communicate ① VERB
to be in touch with someone • *We communicate mainly by email.*

be in contact • *I'll be in contact with him next week.*
be in touch • *He hasn't been in touch with me yet.*
correspond • *We correspond regularly.*

communicate ② VERB
to pass on information • *The results will be communicated by post.*

convey (FORMAL) • *They have conveyed their views to the government.*
impart (FORMAL) • *the ability to impart knowledge*
inform • *Will you inform me of any changes?*
pass on • *I'll pass on your good wishes.*
spread • *She has spread the news to everyone.*
transmit • *He transmitted his enjoyment to the audience.*
tweet • *He has been tweeting his comments all through the match.*

companion NOUN
someone you travel with or spend time with • *He has been her constant companion for the last six years.*
comrade • *Unlike so many of his comrades he survived the war.*
crony (OLD-FASHIONED) • *a round of golf with his business cronies*
friend • *Sara's old friend, Charles*
mate (INFORMAL) • *A mate of mine used to play soccer for Liverpool.*
pal (INFORMAL) • *We've been pals for years.*
partner • *a partner in crime*

company ① NOUN
a business • *a publishing company*
business • *a family business*
corporation • *multinational corporations*
establishment • *a commercial establishment*
firm • *a firm of engineers*
house • *the world's top fashion houses*

company ② NOUN
a group of people • *the Royal Shakespeare Company*
assembly • *an assembly of citizens*
band • *bands of rebels*
circle • *a large circle of friends*
community • *a community of believers*
crowd • *I don't go around with that crowd.*
ensemble • *an ensemble of young musicians*
group • *an environmental group*

party • *a party of sightseers*
troupe • *a troupe of actors*

company ③ NOUN
the act of spending time with someone • *I could do with some company.*
companionship • *He keeps a dog for companionship.*
presence • *Your presence is not welcome here.*

compare VERB
to look at things for similarities or differences • *Compare these two illustrations.*
contrast • *In this section we contrast four possible approaches.*
juxtapose • *art juxtaposed with reality*
weigh up • *She weighed up her options.*

compartment NOUN
one of the separate parts of an object • *the freezer compartment of the fridge*
bay • *the cargo bays of the aircraft*
chamber • *the chambers of the heart*
division • *Each was further split into several divisions.*
section • *a toolbox with sections for various items*

compassionate ADJECTIVE
feeling or showing sympathy and pity for others • *My father was a deeply compassionate man.*
caring • *He is a lovely boy, very gentle and caring.*

humane • She began to campaign for humane treatment of prisoners and their families.
kind • I must thank you for being so kind to me.
kind-hearted • He was a warm, generous and kind-hearted man.
merciful • a merciful God
sympathetic • She was very sympathetic to their problems.
tender • Her voice was tender, full of pity.

compatible ① ADJECTIVE
having similar opinions and interests • Lifelong partners should be compatible.
congenial • congenial company
harmonious • a harmonious partnership

ANTONYM:
• incompatible

compatible ② ADJECTIVE
able to exist together successfully • Physics and religion are quite compatible.
consistent • injuries consistent with a car crash
in keeping • This behaviour was in keeping with his character.

ANTONYM:
• incompatible

compensate ① VERB
to repay someone for loss or damage • You will be properly compensated for your loss.
atone • He felt he had atoned for what he had done.

refund • The company will refund the full cost.
repay • collateral with which to repay swindled investors
reward • Their patience was finally rewarded.

compensate ② VERB
to cancel out • His lack of skill was compensated for by his enthusiasm.
balance • The pros balance the cons.
cancel out • The two influences cancel each other out.
counteract • pills to counteract high blood pressure
make up for • I'll make up for what I've done.
offset • The loss is being offset by a new tax.

compensation NOUN
something that makes up for loss or damage • compensation for his injuries
amends • an attempt to make amends for his crime
atonement • an act of atonement for our sins
damages • damages for libel
payment • a redundancy payment

compete VERB
to try to win • companies competing for business
contend • two groups contending for power
contest • the candidates contesting in the election
fight • rivals fighting for supremacy

vie • *The contestants vied to finish first.*

competition ① NOUN
an attempt to win • *There's a lot of competition for places.*
contention • *contention for the gold medal*
contest • *the contest between the government and the opposition*
opposition • *They are in direct opposition for the job.*
rivalry • *the rivalry between the two leaders*
struggle • *a power struggle*

competition ② NOUN
a contest to find the winner in something • *a surfing competition*
championship • *a swimming championship*
contest • *a talent contest*
event • *major sporting events*
tournament • *a judo tournament*

competitor NOUN
a person who competes for something • *one of the youngest competitors in the event*
adversary • *his political adversaries*
challenger • *20 seconds faster than the nearest challenger*
competition • *staying ahead of the competition*
contestant • *contestants in TV quiz shows*
opponent • *the best opponent I've played all season*
opposition • *They can outplay the opposition.*

rival • *a business rival*

complain VERB
to express dissatisfaction • *He came round to complain about the noise.*
carp • *His instructor is constantly carping at him.*
find fault • *He's always finding fault with my work.*
grouse • *You're always grousing about something.*
grumble • *It's not in her nature to grumble.*
kick up a fuss (INFORMAL) • *He kicks up a fuss whenever she goes out.*
moan • *moaning about the weather*
whine • *whining children*
whinge (INFORMAL) • *Stop whingeing and get on with it.*

complaint NOUN
an instance of complaining about something • *There have been a number of complaints about the standard of service.*
criticism • *The criticism that we do not try hard enough to learn other languages was voiced.*
grievance • *They had a legitimate grievance against the company.*
grumble • *Her main grumble is over the long hours she has to work.*
objection • *I have no objections about the way I have been treated.*
protest • *Despite our protests, they went ahead anyway.*

complete ① ADJECTIVE
to the greatest degree
possible • *a complete
transformation*
absolute • *absolute nonsense*
consummate • *a consummate
professional*
outright • *an outright
victory*
perfect • *a perfect stranger*
thorough • *a thorough snob*
total • *a total failure*
utter • *an utter shambles*

complete ② ADJECTIVE
with nothing missing • *a
complete set of tools*
entire • *the entire plot*
full • *a full report*
intact • *the few buildings which
have survived intact*
undivided • *I want your
undivided attention.*
whole • *I told him the whole
story.*
ANTONYM:
• incomplete

complete ③ VERB
to finish • *He has just completed
his first novel.*
conclude • *The judge concluded
his summing-up.*
end • *The crowd was in tears as
he ended his speech.*
finish • *I'll finish my report this
week.*

complex ① ADJECTIVE
having many different parts
• *complex issues*
complicated • *a very
complicated voting system*

difficult • *Adoption can be a
long and difficult process.*
intricate • *intricate patterns*
involved • *a long, involved
explanation*
tangled • *His personal life has
become more tangled than ever.*
ANTONYM:
• simple

complex ② NOUN
an emotional problem • *I have
never had a complex about my
weight.*
fixation • *She has a fixation
with her favourite TV show.*
obsession • *95% of patients
know their obsessions are
irrational.*
phobia • *The man had a phobia
about flying.*
preoccupation • *his total
preoccupation with neatness*
problem • *an eating problem*
thing • *He's got this thing about
wearing a lucky charm.*

complicated ADJECTIVE
complex and difficult • *a
complicated situation*
complex • *a complex issue*
convoluted • *a convoluted
plot*
elaborate • *an elaborate theory*
intricate • *an intricate process*
involved • *a long, involved
explanation*
ANTONYM:
• simple

compose VERB
to create or write • *He has
composed a symphony.*

create • *He has created a new ballet.*

devise • *a play devised by the drama company*

invent • *the woman who invented a new musical form*

produce • *He has produced a book about the city.*

write • *I've never been able to write poetry.*

comprehend VERB
to understand or appreciate something • *I just cannot comprehend your attitude.*

appreciate • *She has never really appreciated the scale of the problem.*

fathom • *I really couldn't fathom what Steiner was talking about.*

grasp • *The Government has not yet grasped the seriousness of the crisis.*

see • *I don't see why you're complaining.*

take in • *I try to explain, but you can tell he's not taking it in.*

understand • *They are too young to understand what's going on.*

work out • *It took me some time to work out what was causing the problem.*

compulsory ADJECTIVE
required by law • *School attendance is compulsory.*

mandatory • *the mandatory retirement age*

obligatory • *an obligatory medical examination*

required • *the required reading for this course*

requisite • *the requisite documents*

ANTONYM:
• voluntary

computer NOUN
an electronic machine that stores and processes data • *The computer calculates the position of each vehicle.*

laptop • *sensitive information found on stolen laptops*

PC • *a PC equipped with everything you might need*

tablet • *This tablet features all the latest software.*

con ① VERB
to trick someone into doing or believing something • *He claimed that the salesman conned him out of his life savings.*

cheat • *a deliberate attempt to cheat the referee*

deceive • *She deceived us into giving her a job.*

mislead • *Ministers must not knowingly mislead the public.*

swindle • *A City businessman swindled investors out of millions of pounds.*

trick • *They tricked him into thinking he'd become a star.*

con ② NOUN
a trick intended to mislead or disadvantage someone • *Slimming snacks that offer miraculous weight loss are a con.*

bluff • *The letter was a bluff.*

deception • *You've been the victim of a rather cruel deception.*

fraud • *an investigation into fraud in the world of horseracing*

swindle • *a tax swindle*
trick • *a cheap trick to encourage people to spend their money*

conceit NOUN
excessive pride • *his insufferable conceit*
egotism • *typical showbiz egotism*
pride • *a blow to his pride*
self-importance • *his bad manners and self-importance*
vanity • *her vanity about her long hair*

conceited ADJECTIVE
too proud • *a conceited young idiot*
bigheaded (INFORMAL) • *an arrogant, bigheaded man*
cocky • *I was very cocky as a youngster.*
egotistical • *an egotistical show-off*
self-important • *self-important pop stars*
vain • *a shallow, vain woman*
ANTONYM:
modest

concentrate ① VERB
to give something all your attention • *Concentrate on your studies.*
be engrossed in • *He was engrossed in his work.*
focus your attention on • *focusing his attention on the race*
give your attention to • *I gave my attention to the question.*
put your mind to • *You could do it if you put your mind to it.*

concentrate ② VERB
to be found in one place • *They are mostly concentrated in the urban areas.*
accumulate • *Cholesterol accumulates in the arteries.*
collect • *dust collecting in the corners*
gather • *residents gathered in huddles*

concern ① NOUN
a feeling of worry • *public concern about violence*
anxiety • *anxiety about the economy*
apprehension • *apprehension about the future*
disquiet • *a growing sense of disquiet*
worry • *She has no worries about his health.*

concern ② NOUN
someone's duty or responsibility • *His private life is not my concern.*
affair • *If you want to go, that's your affair.*
business • *This is none of my business.*
responsibility • *He's not my responsibility.*

concern ③ VERB
to make someone worried • *It concerns me that he doesn't want to go.*
bother • *Nothing bothers me.*
distress • *They are distressed by the accusations.*
disturb • *disturbed by the news*
trouble • *Is anything troubling you?*

worry • *an issue that had worried him for some time*

concern ④ VERB
to affect or involve • *This concerns all of us.*
affect • *The illness affects the lives of thousands of people.*
apply to • *This rule does not apply to us.*
be relevant to • *These documents are relevant to the case.*
involve • *meetings which involve most of the staff*

concise ADJECTIVE
using no unnecessary words • *a concise guide*
brief • *a brief description*
short • *a short speech*
succinct • *a succinct explanation*
terse • *a terse statement*
ANTONYM:
• long

conclude ① VERB
to decide something • *He concluded that she had been right.*
decide • *I decided he must be ill.*
deduce • *She deduced that I had written the letter.*
infer • *His feelings were easily inferred from his reply.*
judge • *The doctor judged that he was not fit enough to play.*
reckon (INFORMAL) • *I reckon we should wait a while.*
suppose • *There's no reason to suppose he'll be there.*

surmise (FORMAL) • *It is surmised that he must have known.*

conclude ② VERB
to finish something • *He concluded the letter with a postscript.*
close • *They closed the show with a song.*
end • *His speech ended with a prayer for peace.*
finish • *We finished the evening with a walk on the beach.*
round off • *This rounded the afternoon off perfectly.*
wind up • *She quickly wound up her conversation.*
ANTONYM:
• begin

conclusion ① NOUN
a decision made after thinking carefully about something • *I've come to the conclusion that she was lying.*
deduction • *a shrewd deduction about what was going on*
inference • *There were two inferences to be drawn from her letter.*
judgment • *My judgment is that things are going to get worse.*
verdict • *The doctor's verdict was that he was fine.*

conclusion ② NOUN
the finish or ending of something • *the conclusion of the programme*
close • *bringing the talks to a close*

end • *The war is coming to an end.*

ending • *a dramatic ending*

finish • *The finish of the race*

termination (FORMAL) • *the termination of her contract*

ANTONYM:
• beginning

condemn ① VERB

to say that something is bad or unacceptable • *He was condemned for his arrogance.*

blame • *He blames video games for the rise in violence.*

censure (FORMAL) • *a motion censuring the government*

criticise • *He was criticised for his failure to act.*

damn • *The report damns the government's handling of the affair.*

denounce • *He was denounced as a traitor.*

condemn ② VERB

to give a punishment • *condemned to life imprisonment*

damn • *She said sinners were damned to eternal torment.*

doom • *doomed to die for his crime*

sentence • *sentenced to ten years in prison*

condition ① NOUN

the state of something • *The house is in good condition.*

form • *The team are not in good form this season.*

shape • *He's in great shape for his age.*

state • *Look at the state of my car!*

condition ② NOUN

something required for something else to be possible • *terms and conditions of the contract*

prerequisite • *A science background is a prerequisite for the job.*

provision • *a provision in his will forbidding the sale of the house*

proviso • *The answer is yes, with one proviso.*

qualification • *He agreed, but with some qualifications.*

requirement • *The product meets all legal requirements.*

requisite • *the main requisite for membership*

stipulation • *The only dress stipulation was "no jeans".*

term • *the terms of the agreement*

conduct ① VERB

to carry out an activity or task • *to conduct an experiment*

carry out • *to carry out a survey*

direct • *Christopher will direct day-to-day operations.*

do • *I'm doing a piece of important research right now.*

manage • *his ability to manage the business*

organise • *The initial mobilisation was well organised.*

perform • *She performed the task with great skill.*

run • *Each teacher will run a different workshop.*

conduct ② NOUN
the way someone behaves
• Other people judge you by your
conduct.
attitude • His attitude made
me angry.
behaviour • Make sure that
good behaviour is rewarded.
manners • He dressed well and
had impeccable manners.
ways • I urged him to alter his
ways.

conduct yourself VERB
to behave in a particular way
• The way he conducts himself
reflects on the school.
act • Did you notice anyone who
may have been acting
suspiciously?
behave • He'd behaved badly.

conference NOUN
a meeting for discussion • a
conference on education
congress • a congress of coal
miners
convention • the Geneva
convention
discussion • a round of formal
discussions
forum • a forum for trade
negotiations
meeting • a meeting of
shareholders

confess VERB
to admit to something • Your
son has confessed to his crimes.
acknowledge • He
acknowledged that he was a
cheat.
admit • I admit to feeling
jealous.

own up • The headmaster is
waiting for someone to own up.
ANTONYM:
• deny

confession NOUN
the act of confessing • a
confession of wrongdoing
acknowledgment • an
acknowledgment of his
mistakes
admission • an admission of
guilt

confidence ① NOUN
a feeling of trust • I have
complete confidence in you.
belief • his belief in his partner
faith • He has great faith in her
judgment.
reliance • I don't put much
reliance on that idea.
trust • He destroyed my trust in
people.
ANTONYM:
• distrust

confidence ② NOUN
sureness of yourself • I've never
had much confidence.
aplomb • She handled the
interview with aplomb.
assurance • He led the
orchestra with great assurance.
self-assurance • his supreme
self-assurance
self-possession • an air of
self-possession
ANTONYM:
• shyness

confident ① ADJECTIVE
sure about something
• confident of success

confident | 114

confident ① adjective

certain • *certain of getting a place on the team*
convinced • *He is convinced it's your fault.*
positive • *I'm positive it will happen.*
satisfied • *We must be satisfied that the treatment is safe.*
secure • *secure about his job prospects*
sure • *I'm not sure I understand.*

ANTONYM:
• uncertain

confident ② adjective

sure of yourself • *a confident attitude*
assured • *His playing became more assured.*
self-assured • *a self-assured young man*
self-possessed • *a self-possessed woman*

ANTONYM:
• shy

confine ① verb

to limit to something specified • *They confined themselves to talking about the weather.*
limit • *Don't limit yourself to one activity.*
restrict • *The patient was restricted to a meagre diet.*

confine ② verb

to prevent from leaving • *confined to bed for two days*
hem in • *hemmed in by spectators*
imprison • *imprisoned in a tiny cell*

restrict • *We were restricted to the building.*
shut up • *He can't stand being shut up in the house.*

confirm ① verb

to say or show that something is true • *Police confirmed that they had received a call.*
bear out • *The figures bear out his words.*
endorse • *This theory has been endorsed by research.*
prove • *The results prove his point.*
substantiate • *no evidence to substantiate the claims*
validate • *It is difficult to validate this belief.*
verify • *I was asked to verify this statement.*

confirm ② verb

to make something definite • *Can we confirm the arrangements for tomorrow?*
fix • *The date for the election was fixed.*
settle • *I've settled a time to see him.*

conflict ① noun

disagreement and argument • *conflict between workers and management*
antagonism • *antagonism within the team*
disagreement • *The meeting ended in disagreement.*
discord • *public discord*
friction • *friction between him and his father*
hostility • *hostility between political parties*

opposition • *a wave of opposition*
strife • *a cause of strife in many relationships*

conflict ② NOUN
a war or battle • *conflicts in the Gulf*
battle • *a battle between two gangs*
combat • *men who died in combat*
fighting • *Villagers have left their homes to avoid the fighting.*
strife • *civil strife*
war • *the decision to join the war*

conflict ③ VERB
to differ or disagree • *conflicting ideas*
be at variance • *His statements are at variance with the facts.*
be incompatible • *These two principles are incompatible.*
clash • *a decision which clashes with official policy*
differ • *The two leaders differ on several issues.*
disagree • *Governments disagree over the need for action.*

confuse ① VERB
to mix two things up • *confusing fact with fiction*
mistake • *I mistook you for someone else.*
mix up • *He sometimes mixes up his words.*
muddle up • *I keep muddling him up with his brother.*

confuse ② VERB
to puzzle or bewilder • *This response confused me.*
baffle • *Police are baffled by the murder.*
bewilder • *His silence bewildered her.*
mystify • *I was mystified by his attitude.*
puzzle • *One thing still puzzles me.*

confused ① ADJECTIVE
puzzled or bewildered • *confused about health risks*
baffled • *He stared in baffled amazement.*
bewildered • *bewildered holidaymakers*
muddled • *She was muddled about the date.*
perplexed • *perplexed by recent events*
puzzled • *a puzzled expression*

confused ② ADJECTIVE
in an untidy mess • *They lay in a confused heap.*
chaotic • *the chaotic mess on his desk*
disordered • *a disordered pile of papers*
disorganised • *a disorganised lifestyle*
untidy • *an untidy room*
ANTONYM:
• tidy

confusing ADJECTIVE
puzzling or bewildering • *a confusing situation*
baffling • *a baffling statement*

bewildering • *a bewildering choice of products*
complicated • *a complicated voting system*
puzzling • *a puzzling problem*

confusion NOUN

an untidy mess • *My life is in confusion.*
chaos • *economic chaos*
disarray • *The nation is in disarray.*
disorder • *The hospital ward was in disorder.*
disorganisation • *scenes of chaos and disorganisation*
mess • *He always leaves the bathroom in a mess.*
ANTONYM:
• order

connect ① VERB

to join together • *Connect the pipe to the tap.*
affix • *His name was affixed to his cubicle.*
attach • *Attach the curtains to the rods with hooks.*
couple • *The engine is coupled to a gearbox.*
fasten • *A hatchet was fastened to his belt.*
join • *two springs joined together*
link • *the Channel Tunnel linking Britain with France*
ANTONYM:
• separate

connect ② VERB

to associate one thing with another • *evidence connecting him with the robberies*

ally • *The new government is allied with the military.*
associate • *symptoms associated with migraine headaches*
link • *Detectives said the crimes could be linked.*
relate • *the denial that global warming is related to human activity*

connection ① NOUN

a link or relationship • *a connection between sugary drinks and tooth decay*
affiliation • *He has no affiliation with any political party.*
association • *the association between the two companies*
bond • *the bond between a mother and child*
correlation • *the correlation between diet and athletic performance*
correspondence • *the correspondence between Eastern and Western religions*
link • *There has been a link between our families for many years.*
relation • *This theory bears no relation to reality.*
relationship • *the relationship between humans and their environment*

connection ② NOUN

a point where things are joined • *The fault was just a loose connection.*
coupling • *The coupling between the railway carriages snapped.*

fastening • *a zip fastening*
junction • *the junction between nerve and muscle*
link • *a link between the city and the motorway*

conscience NOUN
a sense of right and wrong
• *He had a guilty conscience.*
principles • *It's against my principles to eat meat.*
scruples • *a man with no moral scruples*
sense of right and wrong
• *people with no sense of right and wrong*

conservative ADJECTIVE
unwilling to change
• *Conservative people may not like the new approach.*
conventional • *conventional tastes*
traditional • *a traditional school*
ANTONYM:
• *radical*

consider ① VERB
to think of someone or something as • *They do not consider him a suitable candidate.*
believe • *I believe him to be innocent.*
judge • *His work was judged unsatisfactory.*
rate • *The film was rated excellent.*
regard as • *They regard the tax as unfair.*
think • *Many people think him arrogant.*

consider ② VERB
to think carefully • *I will consider your offer.*
contemplate • *He contemplated his fate.*
deliberate • *The jury deliberated for three days.*
meditate • *He meditated on the problem.*
muse • *She sat musing on how unfair life was.*
ponder • *pondering how to improve the team*
reflect • *I reflected on the child's future.*
think about • *I've been thinking about what you said.*

consider ③ VERB
to take into account • *We should consider her feelings.*
bear in mind • *There are a few points to bear in mind.*
make allowances for
• *Remember to make allowances for delays.*
respect • *We will respect your wishes.*
take into account • *another factor to be taken into account*
think about • *more important things to think about*

consideration ① NOUN
careful thought about something • *a decision requiring careful consideration*
attention • *I gave the question all my attention.*
contemplation • *The problem deserves serious contemplation.*
deliberation • *After much deliberation, he called the police.*

study • *The proposals need careful study.*

thought • *I've given the matter a great deal of thought.*

consideration ② NOUN
concern for someone • *Show some consideration for other passengers.*

concern • *concern for the homeless*

kindness • *We have been treated with great kindness.*

respect • *no respect for wildlife*

tact • *a master of tact and diplomacy*

consideration ③ NOUN
something to be taken into account • *Safety is a major consideration.*

factor • *an important factor in buying a house*

issue • *Price is not the only issue.*

point • *There is another point to remember.*

consist: consist of VERB
to be made up of • *The brain consists of millions of nerve cells.*

be composed of • *The committee is composed of ten people.*

be made up of • *The bouquet was made up of roses and carnations.*

comprise • *The show comprises 50 paintings and sketches.*

conspicuous ADJECTIVE
easy to see or notice • *Her conspicuous lack of warmth confirmed her disapproval.*

apparent • *It has been apparent that someone has been stealing.*

blatant • *a blatant disregard for rules*

evident • *He spoke with evident emotion about his ordeal.*

noticeable • *the most noticeable effect of these changes*

obvious • *an obvious injustice*

perceptible • *a perceptible air of neglect*

constant ① ADJECTIVE
going on all the time • *a city under constant attack*

continual • *continual pain*

continuous • *continuous gunfire*

eternal • *an eternal hum in the background*

nonstop • *nonstop music*

perpetual • *her perpetual complaints*

relentless • *relentless pressure*

ANTONYM:
• periodic

constant ② ADJECTIVE
staying the same • *a constant temperature*

even • *an even level of sound*

fixed • *a fixed salary*

regular • *a regular beat*

stable • *a stable condition*

steady • *travelling at a steady 50 miles per hour*

uniform • *a uniform thickness*

ANTONYM:
• changeable

construct VERB
to build or make something

• The boxes are constructed from rough-sawn timber.

assemble • She had been trying to assemble a model railway.

build • Workers at the plant build the F-16 jet fighter.

create • We created a makeshift platform for him to stand on.

erect • The building was erected in 1900.

make • The company now makes cars at two plants in Europe.

put together • the mechanic whose job was to put together looms within the plant

put up • He was putting up a new fence.

consult VERB

to go to for advice • Consult your doctor before undertaking exercise.

ask for advice • Ask your bank manager for advice on mortgages.

confer with • He is conferring with his lawyers.

refer to • I had to refer to the manual.

contact ① NOUN

the state of being in touch with someone • We must keep in contact.

communication • The leaders were in constant communication.

touch • I've lost touch with her over the years.

contact ② NOUN

someone you know • a contact in the music business

acquaintance • We met through a mutual acquaintance.

connection • She had a connection in England.

contact ③ VERB

to get in touch with • We contacted the company to complain.

approach • A journalist has approached me for a story.

communicate with • I rarely communicate with my cousins.

get hold of • I've been trying to get hold of you all week.

get in touch with • I will get in touch with my solicitors.

reach • Where can I reach you in an emergency?

contain ① VERB

to include as a part of • Fruit contains sugar.

comprise • The band comprises two singers and two guitarists.

include • The price includes VAT.

contain ② VERB

to keep under control • efforts to contain the disease

control • He could hardly control his rage.

curb • measures to curb inflation

repress • people who repress their emotions

restrain • unable to restrain her anger

stifle • stifling the urge to scream

container NOUN

something which holds things • a plastic container for food

holder • a document holder

vessel • storage vessels

contemplate ① VERB
to think carefully about
something • He cried as he
contemplated his future.
consider • She paused to
consider her options.
examine • I have examined all
the possible alternatives.
muse on • Many of the papers
muse on the fate of the President.
ponder • He didn't waste time
pondering the question.
reflect on • I reflected on the
child's future.
think about • Think about how
you can improve the situation.

contemplate ② VERB
to consider doing something
• He contemplated a career as a
doctor.
consider • Watersports
enthusiasts should consider
hiring a wetsuit.
envisage • He had never
envisaged spending the whole of
his life in that job.
plan • I had been planning a trip
to the West Coast.
think of • Martin was thinking
of taking legal action against his
employers.

contempt NOUN
complete lack of respect • I
shall treat that remark with the
contempt it deserves.
derision • He was greeted with
shouts of derision.
disdain • Janet looked at him
with disdain.
disregard • total disregard for
the safety of the public

disrespect • complete
disrespect for authority
scorn • They greeted the
proposal with scorn.
ANTONYM:
• respect

contest ① NOUN
a competition or game • Few
contests in the history of sport
have been as thrilling.
competition • a surfing
competition
game • the first game of the
season
match • He was watching a
football match.
tournament • Here is a player
capable of winning a world
tournament.

contest ② NOUN
a struggle for power • a bitter
contest over who should control
the state's future
battle • the eternal battle
between good and evil
fight • the fight for the US
Presidency
struggle • locked in a power
struggle with his Prime Minister

contest ③ VERB
to object formally to a
statement or decision • Your
former employer has 14 days to
contest the case.
challenge • The move was
immediately challenged.
dispute • He disputed the
allegations.
oppose • Many individuals
oppose bilingual education in
schools.

question • *It never occurs to them to question the doctor's decisions.*

ANTONYM:
• accept

continual ① ADJECTIVE
happening all the time without stopping • *Despite continual pain, he refused all treatment.*
constant • *They were under constant pressure to increase sales.*
endless • *her endless demands for attention*
eternal • *In the background was that eternal hum.*
nagging • *a nagging pain between his shoulder blades*
perpetual • *the perpetual thump of music from the flat downstairs*
uninterrupted • *five years of uninterrupted growth*

continual ② ADJECTIVE
happening again and again • *I was tired of their continual arguments.*
frequent • *He is prone to frequent tantrums.*
recurrent • *buildings in which staff suffer recurrent illness*
regular • *He is a regular visitor to our house.*
repeated • *Mr Smith did not return the money, despite repeated reminders.*

ANTONYM:
• occasional

continue ① VERB
to keep doing something

• *He continued working until he was 75.*
carry on • *The assistant carried on talking.*
go on • *Unemployment is likely to go on rising.*
keep on • *He kept on trying.*
persist • *She persists in using his nickname.*

continue ② VERB
to go on existing • *The fighting continued after they'd left.*
carry on • *My work will carry on after I'm gone.*
endure • *Their friendship has endured for 30 years.*
last • *Nothing lasts forever.*
persist • *The problem persists.*
remain • *The building remains to this day.*
survive • *companies which survived after the recession*

continue ③ VERB
to start doing again • *After a moment, she continued speaking.*
carry on • *He took a deep breath, then carried on.*
recommence • *He recommenced work on his novel.*
resume • *Police will resume the search today.*

continuous ADJECTIVE
going on without stopping • *continuous growth*
constant • *under constant pressure*
continued • *a continued improvement*
extended • *conflict over an extended period*
prolonged • *a prolonged drought*

c

uninterrupted • *uninterrupted rule*
ANTONYM:
• *periodic*

control ① NOUN
power over something • *He was forced to give up control of the company.*
authority • *You have no authority here.*
command • *He was in command of the ceremony.*
direction • *The team worked well under his direction.*
government • *The entire country is under the government of one man.*
management • *the day-to-day management of the business*
power • *a position of great power*
rule • *15 years of Communist rule*
supremacy • *The party has re-established its supremacy.*

control ② VERB
to be in charge of • *companies fighting to control the market*
administer • *the authorities who administer the island*
be in charge of • *She is in charge of the project.*
command • *the general who commanded the troops*
direct • *He will direct day-to-day operations.*
govern • *his ability to govern France*
have power over • *He believes head teachers should have total power over school discipline.*

manage • *the government's ability to manage the economy*
rule • *the dynasty which ruled China*

convenient ADJECTIVE
helpful or easy to use • *a convenient mode of transport*
handy • *Credit cards can be handy.*
helpful • *a helpful fact sheet*
useful • *a useful invention*
user-friendly • *Other user-friendly features include remote control.*
ANTONYM:
• *inconvenient*

convention ① NOUN
an accepted way of behaving or doing something • *It's a social convention to shake hands when meeting.*
code • *the code of the Shaolin monks*
custom • *The custom of lighting the Olympic flame goes back centuries.*
etiquette • *the rules of diplomatic etiquette*
practice • *It is normal practice to display the menu outside the restaurant.*
tradition • *different cultural traditions from ours*

convention ② NOUN
a large meeting of an organisation or group • *the annual convention of the Parapsychological Association*
assembly • *an assembly of Olympic gold-medal winners*
conference • *a conference attended by 450 delegates*

congress • *A lot changed after the party congress.*

meeting • *the annual meeting of company shareholders*

conventional ① ADJECTIVE
having or relating to a very ordinary lifestyle • *conventional opinions*

conformist • *He may have to become more conformist if he is to prosper.*

conservative • *The girl was dressed in a rather conservative style.*

unadventurous • *He was a strong player, but rather unadventurous.*

conventional ② ADJECTIVE
familiar, or usually used • *I can only manage 23 miles an hour on a conventional machine.*

customary • *the customary one minute's silence*

ordinary • *It has 25 per cent less fat than ordinary ice cream.*

orthodox • *Many of these ideas are being incorporated into orthodox medical treatment.*

regular • *This product looks and tastes like regular margarine.*

standard • *It was standard practice for untrained clerks to deal with serious cases.*

traditional • *traditional teaching methods*

convey VERB (FORMAL)
to cause information or ideas to be known • *I tried to convey the wonder of the experience to my husband.*

communicate • *They successfully communicate their knowledge to others.*

express • *She did her best to express wordless disapproval by scowling.*

get across • *I wanted to get my message across.*

impart (FORMAL) • *the ability to impart knowledge*

convince VERB
to persuade that something is true • *I convinced him of my innocence.*

assure • *She assured me that there was nothing wrong.*

persuade • *I had to persuade him of the advantages.*

satisfy • *He had to satisfy the doctors that he was fit to play.*

convincing ADJECTIVE
persuasive • *a convincing argument*

conclusive • *conclusive proof*

effective • *an effective speaker*

persuasive • *persuasive reasons*

plausible • *a plausible explanation*

powerful • *a powerful speech*

telling • *a telling criticism*

ANTONYM:
• unconvincing

cook VERB
to prepare food for eating by heating it in some way • *I enjoy cooking for friends.*

bake • *a machine for baking bread*

barbecue • *a Korean method of barbecuing meat*

C

boil • *Boil the fruit and syrup together for half an hour.*

fry • *Garnish the rice with thinly sliced onion.*

grill • *Grill the fish for five minutes.*

microwave • *Microwaved vegetables have a fresher flavour.*

poach • *I had ordered poached eggs on toast for breakfast.*

roast • *Roast the aubergine in the oven for about one hour until soft.*

steam • *mussels on a bed of steamed cabbage*

stew • *You can stew the vegetables in oil.*

toast • *This currant loaf is delicious either fresh or toasted.*

cool ① ADJECTIVE
having a low temperature • *a gust of cool air*

chilled • *a chilled drink*

chilly • *a chilly afternoon*

cold • *Your dinner's getting cold.*

refreshing • *a refreshing breeze*

ANTONYM:
• warm

cool ② ADJECTIVE
staying calm • *He kept cool through the whole thing.*

calm • *Try to stay calm.*

collected • *She was cool and collected throughout the interview.*

composed • *a composed player*

level-headed • *Simon is level-headed and practical.*

relaxed • *a relaxed manner*

serene • *a serene smile*

ANTONYM:
• nervous

cool ③ VERB
to make or become cool • *Put the cookies on a wire rack to cool.*

chill • *Leave them to chill in the fridge.*

cool off • *Dip the carrots in water to cool them off.*

freeze • *Make double the quantity and freeze half for later.*

refrigerate • *Refrigerate the dough overnight.*

ANTONYM:
• heat

cooperate VERB
to work together • *The family cooperated with the author of the book.*

collaborate • *They collaborated on an album.*

join forces • *The two political parties are joining forces.*

pull together • *The staff and management pull together.*

work together • *industry and government working together*

copy ① NOUN
something made to look like something else • *He had kept a copy of the letter.*

counterfeit • *This credit card is a counterfeit.*

duplicate • *I lost my key and had to get a duplicate made.*

fake • *How do I know this painting isn't a fake?*

forgery • *The letter was a forgery.*

imitation • *Beware of cheap imitations.*

replica • *a replica of the Statue of Liberty*

reproduction • *a reproduction of a famous painting*

copy ② VERB
to do the same thing as someone else • *My little brother copies everything I do.*

ape • *Generations of artists have aped his style.*

emulate • *Younger siblings often try to emulate older brothers and sisters.*

follow • *She followed her mother and became a teacher.*

imitate • *Children imitate what they see on TV.*

mimic • *He mimicked her accent.*

copy ③ VERB
to make a copy of • *documents copied by hand*

counterfeit • *These banknotes are very easy to counterfeit.*

duplicate • *DVDs are being illicitly duplicated all over the country.*

reproduce • *a new method of reproducing oil paintings*

corny ADJECTIVE
unoriginal or sentimental • *corny old love songs*

banal • *banal dialogue*

hackneyed • *a hackneyed plot*

maudlin • *a maudlin film*

sentimental • *a sentimental ballad*

stale • *stale ideas*

stereotyped • *a stereotyped image of Britain*

trite • *a trite ending*

correct ① ADJECTIVE
without mistakes • *a correct diagnosis*

accurate • *an accurate description*

exact • *an exact copy*

faultless • *Hans's English was faultless.*

flawless • *a flawless performance*

precise • *precise calculations*

right • *That clock never shows the right time.*

true • *a true account*

correct ② ADJECTIVE
socially acceptable • *correct behaviour*

acceptable • *Such lavish entertainment is less acceptable today.*

appropriate • *appropriate dress*

fitting • *behaving in a manner not fitting for a diplomat*

okay or **OK** (INFORMAL) • *Is it okay if I bring a friend with me?*

proper • *In those days it was not proper for women to go on the stage.*

seemly (OLD-FASHIONED) • *It is not seemly to joke about such things.*

ANTONYM:
• wrong

correct ③ VERB
to make right • *trying to correct his faults*

amend • *They want to amend the current system.*

cure • *an operation to cure his limp*

improve • *We must improve the situation.*
rectify • *attempts to rectify the problem*
reform • *He promised to reform his wicked ways.*
remedy • *What is needed to remedy these deficiencies?*
right • *I intend to right these wrongs.*

correction NOUN
the act of making something right • *the correction of obvious mistakes*
adjustment • *My car needs a brake adjustment.*
amendment • *He has made lots of amendments to the script.*
righting • *the righting of the country's domestic troubles*

correspond VERB
to be similar to or connected to something else • *The two maps correspond closely.*
agree • *His statement agrees with those of other witnesses.*
be related • *These philosophical problems are closely related.*
coincide • *He was delighted to find that her feelings coincided with his own.*
correlate • *Obesity correlates with increased risk for diabetes.*
fit • *The punishment must always fit the crime.*
match • *Our value system does not match with theirs.*
tally • *This description did not tally with what we saw.*

corrupt ① ADJECTIVE
acting dishonestly or illegally • *corrupt politicians*
crooked • *a crooked cop*
dishonest • *a dishonest scheme*
fraudulent • *fraudulent trading*
shady (INFORMAL) • *shady deals*
unscrupulous • *unscrupulous landlords*

ANTONYM:
• honest

corrupt ② VERB
to make dishonest • *Organised crime has corrupted local government.*
bribe • *accused of bribing officials*
buy off • *Police were bought off by local criminals.*
fix (INFORMAL) • *He fixed the match by bribing the players.*

corruption NOUN
dishonest and illegal behaviour • *charges of corruption*
bribery • *on trial for bribery*
dishonesty • *She accused the government of dishonesty and incompetence.*
fraud • *jailed for fraud*

cost ① NOUN
the amount of money needed • *The cost of petrol has increased.*
charge • *We can arrange this for a small charge.*
expense • *household expenses*
outlay • *Buying the materials in bulk is well worth the outlay.*

payment • *an initial payment of just $100*
price • *House prices are expected to rise.*
rate • *specially reduced rates*

cost ② NOUN
loss or damage • *the total cost in human misery*
detriment • *These changes are to the detriment of staff morale.*
expense • *He supported his brother's career at the expense of his own.*
penalty • *paying the penalty for someone else's mistakes*

cost ③ VERB
to involve a cost of • *The air fares were going to cost a lot.*
come to • *Lunch came to nearly $15.*
sell at • *The books are selling at £10 per copy.*
set someone back (INFORMAL) • *This wedding will set us back thousands of pounds.*

cosy ① ADJECTIVE
warm and comfortable • *Guests can relax in the cosy lounge.*
comfortable • *a comfortable fireside chair*
snug • *a snug log cabin*
warm • *warm blankets*

cosy ② ADJECTIVE
pleasant and friendly • *a cosy chat between friends*
friendly • *a friendly little get-together*
informal • *The house has an informal atmosphere.*

intimate • *an intimate candlelit dinner for two*
relaxed • *a relaxed evening in*

council NOUN
a governing group of people • *the city council*
assembly • *the National Assembly*
board • *the Pakistan Cricket Board*
committee • *the management committee*
panel • *a panel of judges*

count ① VERB
to add up • *I counted the money.*
add up • *Add up the sales figures.*
calculate • *First, calculate your monthly living expenses.*
tally • *Computers now tally the votes.*

count ② VERB
to be important • *Our opinions don't count.*
carry weight • *a politician whose words carry weight*
matter • *It doesn't matter what she thinks.*
rate • *This does not rate as one of my main concerns.*
signify • *His absence does not signify much.*
weigh • *This evidence did not weigh with the jury.*

count ③ NOUN
a counting or number counted • *The count revealed that our party had the majority.*
calculation • *I did a quick calculation in my head.*

reckoning • *By my reckoning we were about two miles from camp.*

sum • *I've never been good at sums.*

tally • *They keep a tally of visitors to the castle.*

counteract VERB
to reduce the effect of something • *pills to counteract high blood pressure*

act against • *The immune system acts against infection.*

offset • *The slump was offset by a surge in exports.*

countless ADJECTIVE
too many to count • *the star of countless films*

infinite • *an infinite number of atoms*

innumerable • *innumerable problems*

myriad • *pop music in all its myriad forms*

untold • *untold wealth*

country ① NOUN
a political area • *the boundary between the two countries*

kingdom • *The kingdom's power declined.*

land • *This is a land of opportunity*

state • *a communist state*

country ② NOUN
land away from towns and cities • *He lives right out in the country.*

bush (AUSTRALIAN, NEW ZEALAND AND SOUTH AFRICAN) • *a trip out to the bush*

countryside • *surrounded by beautiful countryside*

outback (AUSTRALIAN AND NEW ZEALAND) • *nostalgic paintings of the outback*

outdoors • *He loves the great outdoors.*

RELATED WORDS:
• ADJECTIVES pastoral, rural

courage NOUN
lack of fear • *Her courage impressed everyone.*

bravery • *an act of bravery*

daring • *tales of daring and adventure*

guts (INFORMAL) • *He didn't have the guts to admit he was wrong.*

heroism • *the young soldier's heroism*

nerve • *I didn't have the nerve to complain.*

pluck • *You have to admire her pluck.*

valour • *He was decorated for valour in the war.*

ANTONYM:
• fear

course ① NOUN
a series of lessons • *a course in computing*

classes • *I go to dance classes.*

curriculum • *the history curriculum*

course ② NOUN
a policy of action • *He took the only course left open to him.*

plan • *Your best plan is to see your doctor.*

policy • *She decided the best policy was to wait.*

procedure • *He did not follow the correct procedure.*

course ③ NOUN
a way taken to get somewhere • *She sensed the plane had changed course.*
direction • *He went off in the opposite direction.*
line • *the birds' line of flight*
path • *the path of an oncoming car*
route • *the most direct route*
trajectory • *the trajectory of the missile*
way • *What way do you go home?*

court ① NOUN
a place where legal matters are decided • *He ended up in court for theft.*
bench • *He was brought before the bench.*
law court • *prisoners tried by a law court*
tribunal • *The claim was thrown out by a European tribunal.*

court ② VERB (OLD-FASHIONED)
to intend to marry • *I was courting Billy at 19 and married him at 21.*
go steady • *They've been going steady for six months now.*
woo • *He wooed and married his first love.*

courtesy NOUN
polite and considerate behaviour • *a lack of courtesy to other drivers*

civility • *Handle customers with tact and civility.*
courteousness • *his courteousness and kindness*
gallantry • *He treated me with old-fashioned gallantry.*
good manners • *the rules of good manners*
grace • *He didn't even have the grace to apologise.*
graciousness • *The team displayed graciousness in defeat.*
politeness • *basic standards of politeness*

cover ① VERB
to protect or hide • *He covered his face.*
cloak • *a land cloaked in mist*
conceal • *The hat concealed her unwashed hair.*
cover up • *I covered him up with a blanket.*
hide • *His sunglasses hid his eyes.*
mask • *A cloud masked the sun.*
obscure • *One wall was obscured by a huge banner.*
screen • *The road was screened by a block of flats.*
shade • *shading his eyes from the glare*
ANTONYM:
• reveal

cover ② VERB
to form a layer over • *Tears covered his face.*
coat • *Coat the fish with batter.*
overlay • *The floor was overlaid with rugs.*

cover ③ NOUN
something which protects or hides • *a duvet cover*

case • *a spectacle case*
coating • *steel with a coating of zinc*
covering • *a plastic covering*
jacket • *the jacket of a book*
mask • *a surgical mask*
screen • *They put a screen round me.*
wrapper • *Take the product from its sealed wrapper.*

COW NOUN
a farm animal kept for milk or meat • *a herd of dairy cows*
bovine (FORMAL) • *a herd of deranged bovines*
cattle • *fields where cattle graze*

coward NOUN
someone who is easily scared • *I was too much of a coward to introduce myself.*
chicken (SLANG) • *We called her a chicken.*
wimp (INFORMAL) • *He seems like a wimp to me.*

cowardly ADJECTIVE
easily scared • *too cowardly to tell the truth*
chicken (SLANG) • *I was too chicken to complain.*
faint-hearted • *This is no time to be faint-hearted.*
gutless (INFORMAL) • *a gutless coward*
sookie (NEW ZEALAND) • *a sookie thing to do*
ANTONYM:
• brave

cower VERB
to bend down with fear • *The hostages cowered in their seats.*

cringe • *I cringed in horror.*
quail • *She quailed at the sight.*
shrink • *He shrank back in terror.*

crack ① VERB
to become damaged, with lines on the surface • *A gas main has cracked.*
break • *She broke her leg playing rounders.*
fracture • *You've fractured a rib.*
snap • *The mast snapped like a dry twig.*

crack ② VERB
to find the answer to something • *We've managed to crack the problem.*
decipher • *trying to decipher the code*
solve • *attempts to solve the mystery*
work out • *I've worked out where I'm going wrong.*

crack ③ NOUN
a line or gap caused by damage • *a large crack in the wall*
break • *a train crash caused by a break in the rails*
cleft • *a cleft in the rocks*
crevice • *a crevice in the cliff-face*
fracture • *a hip fracture*

crafty ADJECTIVE
clever and rather dishonest • *That crafty devil has taken us for a ride.*
artful • *the smiles and schemes of an artful woman*

cunning • I have a cunning plan to get us out of this mess.

devious • By devious means she obtained the address.

scheming • You're a scheming little devil, aren't you?

slippery • a slippery customer

sly • He is a sly operator if ever there was one.

wily • the wily manoeuvring of the President

cram VERB
to stuff something into a container or place • She crammed her mouth with nuts.

jam • The place was jammed with people.

pack • The drawers were packed with clothes.

squeeze • The two of us were squeezed into one seat.

stuff • wallets stuffed with dollars

crash ① NOUN
an accident involving a moving vehicle • a plane crash

accident • a serious car accident

bump (INFORMAL) • I had a bump in the car park.

collision • a head-on collision

pile-up (INFORMAL) • a 54-car pile-up

smash (INFORMAL) • He was hurt in a car smash.

crash ② NOUN
a loud noise • There was a sudden crash outside.

bang • The door slammed with a bang.

clash • the clash of cymbals

din • the din of battle

smash • the smash of falling crockery

crash ③ NOUN
the failure of a business • a stock market crash

bankruptcy • Many firms are now facing bankruptcy.

collapse • The economy is on the edge of collapse.

depression • the Great Depression of the 1930s

failure • a major cause of business failure

ruin • Inflation has driven them to the brink of ruin.

crash ④ VERB
to have an accident • His car crashed into the rear of a van.

bump (INFORMAL) • I've just bumped my car.

collide • Two trains collided in London today.

drive into • He drove his car into a tree.

have an accident • My brother's had an accident on his moped.

plough into (INFORMAL) • The plane had ploughed into the mountainside.

wreck • He's wrecked his van.

crawl VERB (INFORMAL)
to be full of • The place is crawling with armed militia.

be alive with • The river was alive with frogs.

be full of • The place was full of insects.

be overrun • The area is overrun with tourists.

swarm • *The wood was swarming with police officers.*
teem • *ponds teeming with fish*

craze NOUN
a brief enthusiasm for something • *the latest fitness craze*
fad • *a new-age fad*
fashion • *the fashion for Seventies toys*
trend • *the latest trend among film stars*
vogue • *a vogue for so-called health drinks*

crazy ① ADJECTIVE
(INFORMAL)
very strange or foolish • *People thought we were crazy when we told them our plans.*
foolish • *It is foolish to risk sunburn for the sake of a tan.*
insane • *If you want my opinion, I think your idea is completely insane.*
mad • *You'd be mad to work with him again.*
ridiculous • *It was an absolutely ridiculous decision.*
wild • *all sorts of wild ideas*
zany • *zany humour*
ANTONYM:
• sensible

crazy ② ADJECTIVE
(INFORMAL)
very keen on something • *He's crazy about football.*
fanatical • *fanatical about computer games*
mad • *She's not as mad about sport as I am.*

obsessed • *He was obsessed with American gangster movies.*
passionate • *He is passionate about the project.*
smitten • *They were totally smitten with each other.*
wild • *I'm just wild about Peter.*

create ① VERB
to make something happen • *His reaction created a bad atmosphere.*
bring about • *helping to bring about peace*
cause • *Sugar causes dental decay.*
lead to • *The takeover led to widespread redundancies.*
occasion (FORMAL) • *the distress occasioned by her dismissal*

create ② VERB
to invent something • *creating a new style of painting*
coin • *the man who coined the term "virtual reality"*
compose • *Vivaldi composed many concertos.*
devise • *We devised a scheme to help him.*
formulate • *He formulated his plan for escape.*
invent • *He invented the first electric clock.*
originate • *the designer who originated platform shoes*

creative ADJECTIVE
able to invent • *her creative talents*
fertile • *a fertile imagination*
imaginative • *an imaginative writer*

inspired • *his inspired use of colour*
inventive • *an inventive storyline*

credit NOUN
praise for something • *He took all the credit for my idea.*
commendation • *Both teams deserve commendation.*
glory • *basking in reflected glory*
praise • *Praise is due to all concerned.*
recognition • *She got no recognition for her work.*
thanks • *He received no thanks for his efforts.*
ANTONYM:
• disgrace

creepy ADJECTIVE (INFORMAL)
strange and frightening • *This place is really creepy at night.*
disturbing • *There was something about the tale she found disturbing.*
eerie • *I walked down the eerie dark path.*
macabre • *macabre stories*
scary (INFORMAL) • *We watched scary movies.*
sinister • *There was something sinister about him.*
spooky • *The whole place has a slightly spooky atmosphere.*
unnatural • *The altered landscape looks unnatural and weird.*

crime NOUN
an act that breaks the law • *the problem of organised crime*
misdemeanour • *a financial misdemeanour*

offence • *a serious offence*
violation • *tax law violations*
wrong • *I intend to right that wrong.*

criminal ① NOUN
someone who has committed a crime • *the country's most dangerous criminals*
crook (INFORMAL) • *The man is a crook and a liar.*
culprit • *the true culprit's identity*
delinquent • *juvenile delinquents*
offender • *a first-time offender*
skelm (SOUTH AFRICAN) • *a skelm from the city*
villain • *He tackled an armed villain single-handed.*

criminal ② ADJECTIVE
involving crime • *criminal activities*
corrupt • *corrupt practices*
crooked • *crooked business deals*
illegal • *an illegal action*
illicit • *illicit dealings*
unlawful • *unlawful entry*
ANTONYM:
• legal

cripple VERB
to prevent from working • *The crisis may cripple the Irish economy.*
bring to a standstill • *The strike brought France to a standstill.*
impair • *Their actions will impair Britain's national interests.*
put out of action • *The port has been put out of action.*

critical ① ADJECTIVE

very important • *a critical point in history*

crucial • *a crucial election campaign*

deciding • *Price was a deciding factor.*

decisive • *a decisive moment in my life*

momentous • *a momentous decision*

pivotal • *He played a pivotal role in the match.*

vital • *vital information*

ANTONYM:
• unimportant

critical ② ADJECTIVE

very serious • *a critical illness*

grave (FORMAL) • *grave danger*

precarious • *a precarious financial situation*

serious • *His condition is said to be serious.*

critical ③ ADJECTIVE

finding fault with something or someone • *critical remarks*

carping • *carping comments*

derogatory • *derogatory references to women*

disapproving • *a disapproving look*

disparaging • *He spoke in disparaging tones.*

scathing • *a scathing attack*

ANTONYM:
• complimentary

criticise VERB

to find fault • *The regime has been harshly criticised.*

censure (FORMAL) • *a decision for which she was censured*

condemn • *He refused to condemn their behaviour.*

find fault with • *She keeps finding fault with my work.*

knock (INFORMAL) • *Don't knock it till you've tried it.*

pan (INFORMAL) • *Critics panned the show.*

put down (INFORMAL) • *She's always putting me down in front of others.*

ANTONYM:
• praise

criticism NOUN

expression of disapproval • *public criticism of his actions*

censure (FORMAL) • *They deserve praise rather than censure.*

disapproval • *a chorus of disapproval*

disparagement • *their disparagement of this book*

fault-finding • *her friend's constant fault-finding*

flak (INFORMAL) • *I got a lot of flak for that idea.*

panning (INFORMAL) • *a panning from the critics*

ANTONYM:
• praise

crook ① NOUN (INFORMAL)

a criminal • *The man is a crook and a liar.*

cheat • *a rotten cheat*

rogue • *Mr Scott wasn't a rogue at all.*

scoundrel (OLD-FASHIONED) • *He is a lying scoundrel!*

shark (INFORMAL) • *Beware the sharks when you are deciding how to invest.*

swindler • *Swindlers have cheated investors out of £12 million.*

thief • *The thieves snatched the camera.*

villain • *As a copper, I've spent my life putting villains behind bars.*

crook ② ADJECTIVE
(AUSTRALIAN AND NEW ZEALAND; INFORMAL)
ill • *He admitted to feeling a bit crook.*

ill • *I was feeling ill.*

nauseous • *The drugs may make the patient feel nauseous.*

poorly (BRITISH; INFORMAL) • *Julie's still poorly.*

queasy • *He was very prone to seasickness and already felt queasy.*

sick • *The very thought of food made him feel sick.*

under the weather (INFORMAL) • *I was still feeling a bit under the weather.*

unwell • *He felt unwell as he was travelling home this afternoon.*

crooked ① ADJECTIVE
bent or twisted • *a crooked tree*

bent • *a bent back*

deformed • *born with a deformed right leg*

distorted • *a distorted image*

irregular • *irregular and discoloured teeth*

out of shape • *The wires were bent out of shape.*

twisted • *bits of twisted metal*

warped • *warped wooden shutters*

ANTONYM:
• straight

crooked ② ADJECTIVE
dishonest or illegal • *crooked business practices*

corrupt • *corrupt politicians*

criminal • *criminal activities*

dishonest • *dishonest behaviour*

fraudulent • *a fraudulent claim*

illegal • *illegal trading*

shady (INFORMAL) • *shady deals*

ANTONYM:
• honest

cross ① VERB
to go across • *the bridge which crosses the river*

ford • *trying to find a safe place to ford the stream*

go across • *going across the road*

span • *the iron bridge spanning the railway*

traverse • *a valley traversed by streams*

cross ② VERB
to meet and go across • *the intersection where the roads cross*

crisscross • *Phone wires crisscross the street.*

intersect • *The circles intersect in two places.*

cross ③ NOUN
a mixture of two things • *a cross between a collie and a retriever*

blend • *a blend of the old and the new*
combination • *a combination of fear and anger*
mixture • *a mixture of two factors*

cross ④ ADJECTIVE
rather angry • *I'm very cross with him.*
angry • *Are you angry with me?*
annoyed • *I'm annoyed with myself for being so stupid.*
fractious • *The children were getting fractious.*
fretful • *the fretful expression on her face*
grumpy • *Some passengers got grumpy when the train was delayed.*
in a bad mood • *He's in a bad mood about something.*
irritable • *She had been restless and irritable all day.*

crouch VERB
to squat down • *A man was crouching behind the car.*
bend down • *I bent down and touched the grass.*
squat • *He squatted on his heels to talk to the children.*

crowd ① NOUN
a large group of people • *A huge crowd gathered in the square.*
horde • *hordes of tourists*
host • *a host of fans*
mass • *a heaving mass of people*
mob • *a mob of demonstrators*
multitude • *surrounded by a noisy multitude*
swarm • *swarms of visitors*

throng • *An official pushed through the throng.*

crowd ② VERB
to gather close together • *Hundreds of fans crowded into the hall.*
congregate • *A large crowd congregated outside the stadium.*
gather • *Dozens of people gathered to watch.*
swarm • *Police swarmed into the area.*
throng • *The crowds thronged into the mall.*

crowded ADJECTIVE
full of people • *a crowded room*
congested • *congested cities*
full • *The train was full.*
overflowing • *buildings overflowing with students*
packed • *By 10.30 the shop was packed.*

crucial ADJECTIVE
very important • *a crucial moment in his career*
central • *central to the whole process*
critical • *a critical point in the campaign*
decisive • *ready to strike at the decisive moment*
momentous • *a momentous event*
pivotal • *He played a pivotal role in the match.*
vital • *vital information*

crude ① ADJECTIVE
rough and simple • *a crude weapon*

primitive • *They managed to make a primitive harness.*
rough • *a rough sketch*
rudimentary • *some form of rudimentary heating*
simple • *a simple stringed instrument*

crude ② ADJECTIVE
rude and offensive • *a crude sense of humour*
coarse • *coarse speech*
tasteless • *a tasteless remark*
vulgar • *a vulgar phrase*
ANTONYM:
• refined

cruel ADJECTIVE
deliberately causing hurt • *I hate people who are cruel to animals.*
barbarous • *a barbarous attack*
brutal • *a brutal murder*
callous • *callous treatment*
cold-blooded • *a cold-blooded killer*
heartless • *It was a heartless thing to do.*
inhumane • *He was kept under inhumane conditions.*
sadistic • *mistreated by sadistic guards*
savage • *a savage beating*
vicious • *a vicious blow*
ANTONYMS:
• compassionate, kind

cruelty NOUN
cruel behaviour • *an act of unbelievable cruelty*
barbarity • *the barbarity of war*
brutality • *the brutality of their words*

callousness • *the callousness of his murder*
inhumanity • *man's inhumanity to man*
savagery • *scenes of unimaginable savagery*
viciousness • *the viciousness of the attacks*
ANTONYMS:
• compassion, kindness

crumple VERB
to squash and wrinkle • *She crumpled the paper in her hand.*
crease • *Don't crease the material.*
crush • *Andrew crushed his empty can.*
screw up • *He screwed the letter up in anger.*
wrinkle • *trying not to wrinkle her silk skirt*

crush ① VERB
to destroy the shape of by squeezing • *The car was crushed in a compactor.*
crumble • *Crumble the stock cubes into a jar.*
crumple • *She crumpled the note up and threw it away.*
mash • *Mash the bananas with a fork.*
squash • *She squashed the wasp under her heel.*

crush ② VERB
to defeat completely • *his bid to crush the uprising*
overcome • *working to overcome the enemy forces*
put down • *Soldiers moved in to put down the rebellion.*
quell • *Troops eventually quelled the unrest.*

stamp out • *steps to stamp out bullying in schools*
vanquish (LITERARY) • *his vanquished foe*

cry ① VERB

to have tears coming from your eyes • *Stop crying and tell me what's wrong.*
▶ see Word Study **cry**, page 706

cry ② VERB

to call out loudly • *"See you soon!" they cried.*
call • *She called to me across the square.*
exclaim • *"You must be mad!" she exclaimed.*
shout • *"Over here!" they shouted.*
yell • *He yelled out of the window.*

cry ③ NOUN

a loud or high shout • *a cry of pain*
call • *the call of a seagull*
exclamation • *an exclamation of surprise*
shout • *I heard a distant shout.*
yell • *Bob let out a yell.*

cunning ① ADJECTIVE

clever and deceitful • *a cunning and ruthless businessman*
artful • *an artful scheme*
crafty • *a crafty plan*
devious • *a devious mind*
sly • *a sly trick*
wily • *a wily politician*
ANTONYM:
• open

cunning ② NOUN

cleverness and deceit • *the cunning of today's criminals*

deviousness • *the deviousness of online scammers*
guile • *She was without guile or pretence.*

curb ① VERB

to keep something within limits • *He must learn to curb that temper of his.*
check • *an attempt to check the spread of the disease*
contain • *A hundred firefighters are still trying to contain the fire.*
control • *the need to control environmental pollution*
limit • *He limited payments to the country's foreign debt.*
restrain • *efforts to restrain corruption*
suppress • *The Government is suppressing inflation by devastating the economy.*

curb ② NOUN

an attempt to keep something within limits • *He called for stricter curbs on immigration.*
brake • *Illness had put a brake on his progress.*
control • *price controls*
limit • *limits on government spending*
limitation • *We need a limitation on the powers of the government.*
restraint • *new restraints on trade unions*

cure ① VERB

to make well • *a treatment which cures eczema*
heal • *plants used to heal wounds*

remedy • *an operation to remedy the effects of the illness*

cure ② NOUN
something that makes an illness better • *a cure for cancer*
medicine • *herbal medicines*
remedy • *a remedy for colds and flu*
treatment • *the most effective treatment for malaria*

curiosity ① NOUN
the desire to know • *a curiosity about the past*
inquisitiveness • *the inquisitiveness of children*
interest • *a lively interest in current affairs*

curiosity ② NOUN
something unusual • *a museum displaying relics and curiosities*
freak • *a freak of nature*
marvel • *a marvel of science*
novelty • *in the days when a motor car was a novelty*
oddity • *Tourists are still something of an oddity here.*
rarity • *Mexican restaurants are a rarity here.*

curious ① ADJECTIVE
wanting to know • *He was curious about my family.*
inquiring • *He gave me an inquiring look.*
inquisitive • *Cats are very inquisitive.*
interested • *A crowd of interested villagers gathered.*
nosy (INFORMAL) • *nosy neighbours*

ANTONYM:
• incurious

curious ② ADJECTIVE
strange and unusual • *a curious mixture of the old and the new*
bizarre • *his bizarre behaviour*
extraordinary • *an extraordinary story*
odd • *an odd coincidence*
peculiar • *a peculiar smell*
singular • *a singular talent*
strange • *a strange taste*
unusual • *an unusual name*

ANTONYM:
• ordinary

current ① NOUN
a strong continuous movement of water • *swept away by the strong current*
flow • *the quiet flow of the olive-green water*
tide • *We will sail with the tide.*
undertow • *Dangerous undertows make swimming unsafe along the coastline.*

current ② ADJECTIVE
happening, being done, or being used now • *current trends*
contemporary • *He has adopted a more contemporary style.*
fashionable • *the fashionable theory about this issue*
ongoing • *an ongoing debate on inner city problems*
present • *skilfully renovated by the present owners*
present-day • *Even by present-day standards these are large aircraft.*

c

today's • In today's America, health care is big business.
up-to-the-minute • up-to-the-minute information on sales and stocks
ANTONYM:
• past

curve ① NOUN
a bending line • a curve in the road
arc • The ball rose in an arc.
bend • a bend in the river
trajectory • the trajectory of an artillery shell
turn • every turn in the road
RELATED WORD:
• ADJECTIVE sinuous

curve ② VERB
to move in a curve • The road curved sharply to the left.
arc • A rainbow arced over the town.
arch • a domed ceiling arching overhead
bend • The path bent to the right.
swerve • His car swerved off the road.

custom ① NOUN
a traditional activity • an ancient Chinese custom
convention • the conventions of Western art
practice • an old Jewish practice
ritual • an ancient Shintoist ritual
tradition • different cultural traditions

custom ② NOUN
something a person always

does • It was his custom to start work at 8.30.
habit • his habit of making tactless remarks
practice • her usual practice of attending church
routine • his daily routine
wont (FORMAL) • Paul woke early, as was his wont.

customer NOUN
someone who buys something • The shop was filled with customers.
buyer • show homes to tempt potential buyers
client • a solicitor and his client
consumer • the increasing demands of consumers
patron • the restaurant's patrons
purchaser • a prospective purchaser
shopper • late-night shoppers on their way home

cut ① VERB
to mark, injure or remove part of (something or someone) with something sharp • The thieves cut a hole in the fence.
▶ see Word Study cut, page 707

cut ② VERB
to reduce something • The department's first priority is to cut costs.
cut back • The Government has decided to cut back on defence spending.
decrease • calls to decrease income tax
lower • The Central Bank has lowered interest rates.

reduce • *Gradually reduce the dosage.*
slash • *Holiday prices have been slashed.*
ANTONYM:
• increase

cut ③ NOUN
a mark or injury made by cutting • *a cut on his left eyebrow*
gash • *There was a deep gash across his forehead.*
incision • *a tiny incision in the skin*
slash • *jeans with slashes in the knees*
slit • *Make a slit along the stem.*

cut ④ NOUN
a reduction in something • *another cut in interest rates*
cutback • *cutbacks in funding*
decrease • *a decrease in foreign investment*
lowering • *the lowering of taxes*
reduction • *reductions in staff*
saving • *household savings on energy use*
ANTONYM:
• increase

cute ADJECTIVE
pretty or attractive • *You were such a cute baby!*
appealing • *an appealing kitten*
attractive • *I thought he was very attractive.*
charming • *a charming little cottage*
dear • *Look at their dear little faces!*

good-looking • *Cassandra noticed him because he was so good-looking.*
gorgeous • *All the girls think Ryan's gorgeous.*
pretty • *She's a very pretty girl.*
ANTONYM:
• ugly

cynical ADJECTIVE
always thinking the worst of people • *a cynical attitude*
distrustful • *distrustful of all politicians*
sceptical • *a sceptical response*

Dd

daft ADJECTIVE (BRITISH;
INFORMAL)
extremely silly • *Now there's a
daft suggestion!*

crazy (INFORMAL) • *He has this
crazy idea about his neighbours.*
foolish • *It would be foolish to
raise his hopes unnecessarily.*
ludicrous • *It was ludicrous to
suggest that the visit could be
kept a secret.*
preposterous • *their
preposterous claim that they had
discovered a plot*
ridiculous • *It was an
absolutely ridiculous decision.*
silly • *That's a silly question.*
stupid • *I made a stupid
mistake.*

ANTONYM:
• sensible

damage ① VERB
to cause harm to something
• *A fire had severely damaged the
school.*

harm • *a warning that the
product may harm the
environment*
hurt • *He had hurt his back in an
accident.*
injure • *Several police officers
were injured in the clashes.*

damage ② NOUN
harm that is done to something
• *The bomb caused extensive
damage to the restaurant.*

harm • *She didn't mean any
harm by what she said.*
injury • *He escaped without
injury.*

damp ① ADJECTIVE
slightly wet • *a damp towel*
clammy • *clammy hands*
dank • *The kitchen was dank
and cheerless.*
humid • *Visitors can expect hot
and humid conditions.*
moist • *The soil is reasonably
moist after the September rain.*
sodden • *I slipped on the sodden
grass.*
soggy • *soggy cheese
sandwiches*
wet • *My hair was still wet.*

damp ② NOUN
slight wetness • *There was
damp all over the walls.*
dampness • *I could see big circles
of dampness under each arm.*
humidity • *The heat and
humidity were intolerable.*
moisture • *Compost helps the
soil retain moisture.*

danger NOUN
the possibility of harm • *Your
life is in danger.*
hazard • *a health hazard*
jeopardy • *A series of setbacks
have put the whole project in
jeopardy.*
menace • *In my view you are a
menace to the public.*
peril • *the perils of the sea*

risk • There is a small risk of infection.
threat • Dogs that are let off the lead can pose a threat to livestock.

ANTONYM:
• safety

dangerous ADJECTIVE

likely to cause harm • It's dangerous to drive when you're tired.
hazardous • They have no way to dispose of the hazardous waste they produce.
perilous • a perilous journey across the war-zone
risky • Investing is risky.
treacherous • Blizzards had made the roads treacherous.

ANTONYM:
• safe

dare ① VERB

to challenge someone to do something • I dare you to ask him his name.
challenge • He left a note at the scene of the crime, challenging detectives to catch him.
defy • I defy you to watch it on your own.
throw down the gauntlet
• The heavyweight champion has thrown down the gauntlet to his rival.

dare ② VERB

to have the courage to do something • Nobody dared to complain.
risk • The skipper was not willing to risk taking his ship through the straits.

venture • the few Europeans who had ventured beyond the Himalayas

daring ① ADJECTIVE

willing to take risks • a daring escape by helicopter
adventurous • an adventurous skier
audacious • an audacious plan to win the presidency
bold • bold economic reforms
brave • He was not brave enough to report the loss of the documents.
fearless • They were young and strong and fearless.

ANTONYM:
• cautious

daring ② NOUN

the courage to take risks • His daring may have cost him his life.
audacity • He had the audacity to make a 200–1 bet on himself to win.
boldness • the boldness of his economic programme
bravery • He deserves the highest praise for his bravery.
courage • She impressed everyone with her personal courage.
guts (INFORMAL) • I haven't got the guts to tell him.
nerve (INFORMAL) • He didn't have the nerve to meet me.

ANTONYM:
• caution

dark ① ADJECTIVE

lacking light • It was too dark to see what was happening.
cloudy • a cloudy sky

dim • *the dim outline of a small boat*

dingy • *a dingy bedsit*

murky • *the murky waters of the loch*

overcast • *a cold, windy, overcast afternoon*

shadowy • *a shadowy corner*

ANTONYM:
• light

dark ② ADJECTIVE
dull in colour • *a dark suit*

black • *a black leather coat*

swarthy • *a broad swarthy face*

dark ③ NOUN
lack of light • *I've always been afraid of the dark.*

darkness • *The room was plunged into darkness.*

dimness • *I squinted to adjust my eyes to the dimness.*

dusk • *She disappeared into the dusk.*

gloom • *the gloom of a foggy November morning*

ANTONYM:
• light

dash ① VERB
to rush somewhere • *Suddenly she dashed out into the garden.*

bolt • *I bolted for the exit.*

fly • *She flew downstairs.*

race • *The hares raced away out of sight.*

run • *The trespassers ran off into the woods.*

rush • *Someone rushed out of the building.*

sprint • *Sergeant Greene sprinted to the car.*

tear • *He tore off down the road.*

dash ② VERB
to throw or be thrown violently against something • *The waves dashed against the rocks.*

break • *Danny listened to the waves breaking against the shore.*

crash • *The door swung inwards and crashed against a cupboard behind it.*

hurl • *He hurled the vase to the ground in rage.*

slam • *They slammed me on to the ground.*

smash • *smashing the bottle against a wall*

dash ③ VERB
to ruin or frustrate someone's hopes or ambitions • *They had their hopes raised and dashed.*

crush • *My dreams of becoming an actor have been crushed.*

destroy • *Even the most gifted can have their confidence destroyed by the wrong teacher.*

disappoint • *His hopes have been disappointed many times before.*

foil • *Our idea of building a water garden was foiled by the planning authorities.*

frustrate • *The government has deliberately frustrated his efforts.*

shatter • *A failure would shatter all our hopes.*

thwart • *Her ambition to be an artist was thwarted by failing eyesight.*

dash ④ NOUN
a sudden movement or rush
• *a 160-mile dash to the hospital*
bolt • *He made a bolt for the door.*
race • *a race for the finishing line*
run • *One of the gang made a run for it.*
rush • *the mad rush not to be late for school*
sprint • *a last-minute sprint to catch the bus*
stampede • *There was a stampede for the exit.*

dash ⑤ NOUN
a small quantity of something
• *a dash of balsamic vinegar*
drop • *I'll have a drop of that milk in my tea.*
pinch • *a pinch of salt*
splash • *add a splash of lemon juice*
sprinkling • *a light sprinkling of sugar*

daydream ① NOUN
a series of pleasant thoughts
• *He learnt to escape into daydreams.*
dream • *My dream is to have a house in the country.*
fantasy • *fantasies of exotic holidays*

daydream ② VERB
to think about pleasant things
• *He daydreams of being a famous journalist.*
dream • *She used to dream of becoming an actor.*
fantasise • *I fantasised about writing music.*

dazed ADJECTIVE
unable to think clearly • *At the end of the interview I was dazed and exhausted.*
bewildered • *Some shoppers looked bewildered by the sheer variety.*
confused • *Things were happening too quickly and Brian was confused.*
dizzy • *Her head hurt and she felt dizzy.*
light-headed • *If you miss breakfast, you may feel light-headed.*
numbed • *I'm so numbed with shock that I can hardly think.*
stunned • *a stunned silence*

dead ① ADJECTIVE
no longer alive • *My husband's been dead a year now.*
deceased (FORMAL) • *his recently deceased mother*
departed • *my dear departed father*
extinct • *the bones of extinct animals*
late • *my late wife*
ANTONYM:
• alive

dead ② ADJECTIVE
no longer functioning • *a dead language*
defunct • *the now defunct Social Democratic Party*
not working • *The radio is not working.*

deadly ADJECTIVE
causing death • *a deadly disease*

D

destructive • *the destructive power of nuclear weapons*
fatal • *a fatal heart attack*
lethal • *a lethal dose of sleeping pills*
mortal • *Our lives were in mortal danger.*

deal VERB

to cope successfully with something • *He must learn to deal with stress.*
attend to • *We have business to attend to first.*
cope with • *She has had to cope with losing all her money.*
handle • *I have learned how to handle pressure.*
manage • *As time passed I learned to manage my grief.*
see to • *Sarah saw to the packing while Jim fetched the car.*
take care of • *Malcolm took care of all the arrangements.*

dear ① NOUN

a person for whom you have affection • *What's the matter, dear?*
angel • *Be an angel and fetch my bag.*
beloved (OLD-FASHIONED) • *He took his beloved into his arms.*
darling • *Thank you, darling.*
treasure (INFORMAL) • *Charlie? Oh, he's a treasure.*

dear ② ADJECTIVE

much loved • *a dear friend of mine*
beloved • *his beloved wife*
cherished • *his most cherished possession*
darling • *his darling daughter*

esteemed • *my esteemed colleagues*
precious • *Her family's support is very precious to her.*
prized • *one of the gallery's most prized possessions*
treasured • *one of my most treasured memories*

dear ③ ADJECTIVE

costing a lot • *They're too dear.*
costly • *Having curtains professionally made can be costly.*
expensive • *Property is so expensive in this country.*
pricey (INFORMAL) • *Medical insurance is very pricey.*

deceive VERB

to make someone believe something untrue • *I was really hurt that he had deceived me.*
con (INFORMAL) • *The British motorist has been conned by the government.*
double-cross • *They were frightened of being double-crossed.*
dupe • *a plot to dupe stamp collectors into buying fake rarities*
fool • *They tried to fool you into coming after us.*
mislead • *He was furious with his doctors for having misled him.*
take in • *I wasn't taken in for one moment.*
trick • *His family tricked him into signing the document.*

decent ① ADJECTIVE

of an acceptable standard • *He gets a decent pension.*
adequate • *an adequate diet*

passable • *She speaks passable French.*

reasonable • *He couldn't make a reasonable living from his writing.*

respectable • *investments that offer respectable rates of return*

satisfactory • *I never got a satisfactory answer.*

tolerable • *to make life more tolerable*

decent ② ADJECTIVE

correct and respectable • *the decent thing to do*

proper • *It is right and proper to do this.*

respectable • *He came from a perfectly respectable middle-class family.*

ANTONYM:
• improper

deceptive ADJECTIVE

likely to make people believe something untrue • *First impressions can be deceptive.*

false • *"Thank you," she said with false enthusiasm.*

fraudulent • *fraudulent claims about being a nurse*

illusory • *They argue that freedom is illusory.*

misleading • *It would be misleading to say that we were friends.*

unreliable • *His account is quite unreliable.*

decide VERB

to choose to do something • *She decided to do a secretarial course.*

choose • *The council chose to inform the public about the risks.*

come to a decision • *Have you come to a decision about where you're going tonight?*

determine (FORMAL) • *He determined to rescue his two countrymen.*

elect (FORMAL) • *I have elected to stay.*

make up your mind • *He simply can't make his mind up whether he should stay.*

reach a decision • *He demanded to know all the facts before reaching any decision.*

resolve (FORMAL) • *She resolved to report the matter to the authorities.*

decision NOUN

a judgment about something • *The editor's decision is final.*

conclusion • *I've come to the conclusion that she's a great musician.*

finding • *It is the finding of this court that you are guilty.*

judgment • *a landmark judgment by the Court of Appeal*

resolution • *a resolution condemning violence*

ruling • *He tried to have the court ruling overturned.*

verdict • *The judges will deliver their verdict in October.*

declaration NOUN

a forceful or official announcement • *a declaration of war*

affirmation • *her first public affirmation of her decision*

protestation (FORMAL) • *his protestations of innocence*

statement • *He made a formal statement to the police.*
testimony • *His testimony was an important element in the case.*

declare VERB

to state something forcefully or officially • *He declared that he was going to be famous.*
affirm • *a speech in which he affirmed a commitment to lower taxes*
announce • *She was planning to announce her engagement.*
assert • *He asserted his innocence.*
certify • *The president certified that the project would receive $650m.*
proclaim • *He still proclaims himself a believer in the Revolution.*
profess (FORMAL) • *Why do organisations profess that they care?*
pronounce • *The authorities took time to pronounce their verdict.*
state • *Please state your name.*

decline ① VERB

to become smaller or weaker • *a declining birth rate*
decrease • *The number of independent firms decreased from 198 to 96.*
diminish • *The threat of war has diminished.*
drop • *His blood pressure had dropped.*
fall • *Output will fall by six per cent.*
go down • *Crime has gone down 70 per cent.*

plummet • *The Prime Minister's popularity has plummeted to an all-time low.*
reduce • *The number of students learning Latin has been steadily reducing.*

ANTONYM:
• increase

decline ② VERB

to refuse politely to accept or do something • *He declined their invitation.*
abstain (FORMAL) • *I will abstain from voting in the ballot.*
excuse yourself • *I was invited, but I excused myself.*
refuse • *He refused to comment after the trial.*
turn down • *I thanked him for the offer but turned it down.*

ANTONYM:
• accept

decline ③ NOUN

a gradual weakening or decrease • *economic decline*
decrease • *a decrease in the number of young people out of work*
downturn • *a sharp downturn in the industry*
drop • *a drop in the number of participants*
fall • *a sharp fall in the value of the pound*
recession • *pull the economy out of recession*
shrinkage • *a shrinkage in industrial output*
slump • *a slump in property prices*

ANTONYM:
• increase

decorate ① VERB
to make more attractive • *He decorated his room with pictures.*
adorn • *Several oil paintings adorn the walls.*
deck • *The house was decked with flowers.*
ornament • *a high ceiling, ornamented with plaster fruits and flowers*

decorate ② VERB
to put paint or wallpaper on • *when they came to decorate the bedroom*
do up (INFORMAL) • *He spent the summer doing up the barn.*
renovate • *The couple spent thousands renovating the house.*

decrease ① VERB
to become or make less • *Population growth is decreasing by 1.4% each year.*
cut down • *He cut down his coffee intake.*
decline • *The number of staff has declined.*
diminish • *The threat of war has diminished.*
drop • *Temperatures can drop to freezing at night.*
dwindle • *his dwindling authority*
lessen • *changes to their diet that would lessen the risk of disease*
lower • *The Central Bank has lowered interest rates.*
reduce • *Exercise reduces stress and improves wellbeing.*
shrink • *The forests have shrunk to half their size.*
ANTONYM:
• increase

decrease ② NOUN
a lessening in the amount of something • *a decrease in the number of unemployed*
cutback • *cutbacks in defence spending*
decline • *the rate of decline in milk consumption*
drop • *a drop in temperature*
lessening • *a lessening of tension*
reduction • *dramatic reductions in staff*
ANTONYM:
• increase

deep ① ADJECTIVE
having a long way to the bottom • *a deep hole*
bottomless • *a bottomless pit*
yawning • *a yawning chasm*
ANTONYM:
• shallow

deep ② ADJECTIVE
great or intense • *his deep love of his homeland*
extreme • *extreme poverty*
grave (FORMAL) • *a grave crisis*
great • *the great gulf between the two teams*
intense • *The pain was intense.*
profound • *discoveries which had a profound effect on medicine*
serious • *a serious problem*

deep ③ ADJECTIVE
low in sound • *a deep voice*
bass • *a beautiful bass voice*
low • *He's good at singing the low notes.*
ANTONYM:
• high

d

defeat ① VERB

to win a victory over someone
• His guerrillas defeated the colonial army in 1954.

beat • the team that beat us in the final

conquer • During 1936, Mussolini conquered Abyssinia.

crush • in his bid to crush the rebels

rout • the battle at which the Norman army routed the English

trounce • Australia trounced France by 60 points to 4.

vanquish (LITERARY) • after the hero had vanquished the dragon

defeat ② NOUN

a failure to win • a 2–1 defeat by Sweden

conquest • He had led the conquest of southern Poland.

debacle (FORMAL) • It will be hard for them to recover from this debacle.

rout • The retreat turned into a rout.

trouncing • after a 6–2 trouncing on Sunday

ANTONYM:
• victory

defect NOUN

a fault or flaw • A defect in the aircraft caused the crash.

deficiency • There is a deficiency in their approach to protecting the environment.

failing • She blamed the country's failings on its culture of greed.

fault • a minor technical fault

flaw • The only flaw in his character is a short temper.

imperfection • my physical imperfections

shortcoming • The book has its shortcomings.

weakness • His only weakness is his laziness.

defence ① NOUN

action to protect something
• The flat land offered no scope for defence.

cover • They could not provide adequate air cover for ground operations.

protection • The bus shelter gave us some protection from the wind and rain.

resistance • Most people have a natural resistance to the disease.

safeguard • legislation that offers safeguards against discrimination

security • Airport security was tightened.

defence ② NOUN

an argument in support of something • Chomsky's defence of his approach

argument • There's a strong argument for lowering the price.

excuse • There's no excuse for behaviour like that.

explanation • The authorities have given no explanation for his arrest.

justification • There was no justification for what he was doing.

plea • a plea of insanity

defend ① VERB

to protect from harm • They would have hurt him if he hadn't defended himself.

cover • *travel insurance covering you against theft*
guard • *A few men were left outside to guard her.*
protect • *What can people do to protect themselves from heart disease?*
safeguard • *action to safeguard the ozone layer*
shelter • *a wooden house, sheltered by a low roof*
shield • *He shielded his head from the sun with an old sack.*

defend ② VERB
to argue in support of • *I can't defend what he did.*
endorse • *I can endorse their opinion wholeheartedly.*
justify • *No argument can justify a war.*
stick up for (INFORMAL) • *Why do you always stick up for her?*
support • *Would you support such a move?*
uphold • *upholding the artist's right to creative freedom*

defender NOUN
a person who argues in support of something • *a committed defender of human rights*
advocate • *a strong advocate of free market policies*
champion • *a champion of women's causes*
supporter • *a major supporter of the tax reform*

deficiency NOUN
a lack of something • *signs of vitamin deficiency*
deficit • *a staffing deficit*

deprivation • *sleep deprivation*
inadequacy • *the inadequacies of the current system*
lack • *a lack of people wanting to start new businesses*
want (FORMAL) • *a want of manners and charm*
ANTONYM:
• abundance

deficient ADJECTIVE
lacking in something • *a diet deficient in vitamins*
inadequate • *inadequate staffing*
lacking • *Why was military intelligence so lacking?*
poor • *soil that is poor in zinc*
short • *The proposals were short on detail.*
wanting • *He analysed his game and found it wanting.*

definite ① ADJECTIVE
unlikely to be changed • *It's too soon to give a definite answer.*
assured • *Victory was still not assured.*
certain • *Very little in life is certain.*
decided • *Is anything decided yet?*
fixed • *a world without fixed laws*
guaranteed • *Success is not guaranteed.*
settled • *Nothing is settled yet.*

definite ② ADJECTIVE
certainly true • *The police had nothing definite against her.*
clear • *It was a clear case of homicide.*
positive • *We have positive proof that he was a blackmailer.*

deformed ADJECTIVE
abnormally shaped • *a deformed right leg*
disfigured • *the scarred, disfigured face*
distorted • *the distorted image caused by the projector*

degrade VERB
to humiliate someone • *The story strikes at the heart of our society and degrades us all.*
demean • *I wasn't going to demean myself by reacting to the criticism.*
humiliate • *He enjoyed humiliating me.*

delay ① VERB
to put something off until later • *the decision to delay the launch until tomorrow*
defer • *Customers often defer payment for as long as possible.*
postpone • *The visit has been postponed indefinitely.*
put off • *He keeps putting off his driving test.*
shelve • *The project has now been shelved.*
suspend • *Relief convoys will be suspended until the fighting stops.*

delay ② VERB
to slow or hinder something • *Various setbacks delayed production.*
check • *a policy to check fast population growth*
hinder • *Further investigation was hindered by the loss of all documentation.*
impede • *Fallen rocks are impeding the progress of rescue workers.*

obstruct • *The authorities are obstructing a UN investigation.*
set back • *public protests that could set back reforms*
ANTONYM:
• hurry

delay ③ NOUN
a time when something is delayed • *a 7-hour stoppage that caused delays on most flights*
interruption • *interruptions in the supply of food*
obstruction • *Obstruction of justice is a criminal offence.*
setback • *a setback for the peace process*

delete VERB
to remove something written • *The word "exploded" had been deleted.*
cross out • *He crossed out the first sentence and wrote it again.*
erase • *It was unfortunate that she had erased the message.*
rub out • *She rubbed out the marks in the margin.*

deliberate ① ADJECTIVE
done on purpose • *a deliberate act of sabotage*
calculated • *a calculated attempt to cover up her crime*
conscious • *I made a conscious decision not to hide.*
intentional • *The kick was intentional.*
premeditated • *a premeditated attack*
studied • *"It's an interesting match," he said with studied understatement.*

ANTONYM:
• accidental

deliberate ② ADJECTIVE
careful and not hurried • *His movements were gentle and deliberate.*
careful • *The trip needs careful planning.*
cautious • *a cautious approach*
measured • *walking at the same measured pace*
methodical • *Da Vinci was methodical in his research.*

ANTONYM:
• casual

deliberate ③ VERB
to think carefully about something • *The jury deliberated for five days before reaching a verdict.*
debate • *He was debating whether or not he should tell her.*
meditate • *She meditated on the uncertainties of his future.*
mull over • *McLaren had been mulling over an idea to make a movie.*
ponder • *He was pondering the problem when Phillipson drove up.*
reflect • *I reflected on the child's future.*

delicious ADJECTIVE
tasting very nice • *a wide selection of delicious meals*
appetising • *the appetising smell of freshly baked bread*
delectable • *a delectable treat*
luscious • *luscious fruit*
tasty • *The food was very tasty.*

delight ① NOUN
great pleasure or joy • *To my great delight, it worked.*
glee • *His victory was greeted with glee by his supporters.*
happiness • *Our happiness at being reunited knew no bounds.*
joy • *the joys of being a parent*
pleasure • *the pleasure of seeing her face*
rapture • *gasps of rapture*
satisfaction • *I felt a glow of satisfaction at my achievement.*

delight ② VERB
to give someone great pleasure • *The report has delighted environmentalists.*
amuse • *a selection of toys to amuse your baby*
captivate • *She captivated the world with her radiant looks.*
charm • *He charmed his landlady with his good manners.*
enchant • *Dena was enchanted by the house.*
please • *It pleased him to talk to her.*
thrill • *The electric atmosphere thrilled him.*

demand VERB
to need or require something • *This situation demands hard work.*
involve • *Running a kitchen involves a great deal of discipline.*
need • *a problem that needs careful handling*
require • *Then he'll know what's required of him.*
take • *Walking across the room took all her strength.*

d

want • *The windows wanted cleaning.*

deny ① VERB
to say that something is untrue • *She denied both accusations.*
contradict • *Her version contradicted the Government's claim.*
refute • *He angrily refutes the charge.*
ANTONYM:
• admit

deny ② VERB
to refuse to believe something • *He denied the existence of God.*
reject • *people who rejected their parents' religious beliefs*
renounce • *after she renounced terrorism*

deny ③ VERB
to refuse to give something • *They were denied access to the stadium.*
refuse • *The council had refused permission for the march.*
withhold • *Financial aid for Russia has been withheld.*

department NOUN
a section of an organisation • *the marketing department*
division • *the bank's Latin American division*
office • *Contact your local tax office.*
section • *a top-secret section of the Foreign Office*
unit • *the health services research unit*

depend ① VERB
to rely on • *You can depend on me.*

bank on • *The government is banking on the Olympics to make money for the city.*
count on • *I can always count on you to cheer me up.*
rely on • *They can always be relied on to turn up.*
trust • *I knew I could trust him to meet a tight deadline.*

depend ② VERB
to be affected by • *Success depends on the quality of the workforce.*
be determined by • *Their decision will be determined by the test results.*
hinge on • *Victory or defeat hinged on her final putt.*

deposit VERB
to put down or leave somewhere • *She deposited the case at the left luggage office.*
drop • *He dropped me outside the hotel.*
lay • *The table was spread with a cloth, and the box was laid on top.*
leave • *Leave your key with a neighbour.*
place • *I placed the book on the counter.*
put down • *Mishka put down her heavy shopping bag.*

derelict ADJECTIVE
abandoned and in poor condition • *a derelict warehouse*
abandoned • *a network of abandoned mines*
dilapidated • *a dilapidated castle*
neglected • *a neglected garden*
ruined • *a ruined church*

descend VERB

to move downwards • *as we descend to the cellar*

dip • *The sun dipped below the horizon.*

dive • *The shark dived down and under the boat.*

fall • *Bombs fell in the town.*

go down • *after the sun has gone down*

plummet • *as the plane plummeted through the air*

sink • *A fresh egg will sink and an old egg will float.*

ANTONYM:

• ascend

describe VERB

to give an account of something • *We asked her to describe what she did in her spare time.*

define • *Culture can be defined in many ways.*

depict • *a novel depicting a gloomy, futuristic America*

portray • *a writer who accurately portrays provincial life*

deserve VERB

to have a right to something • *He deserves a rest.*

be entitled to • *She is entitled to feel proud.*

be worthy of • *The bank might think you're worthy of a loan.*

earn • *You've earned this holiday.*

justify • *The decision was fully justified by economic conditions.*

merit • *Such ideas merit careful consideration.*

warrant • *no evidence to warrant a fuller investigation*

design ① VERB

to make a plan of something • *They wanted to design a machine that was both attractive and practical.*

draft • *The legislation was drafted by Democrats.*

draw up • *a working party to draw up a formal agreement*

plan • *when we plan road construction*

design ② NOUN

a plan or drawing • *his design for a new office*

model • *an architect's model of a wooden house*

plan • *when you have drawn a plan of the garden*

design ③ NOUN

the shape or style of something • *a new design of clock*

form • *the form of the human body*

pattern • *a pattern of coloured dots*

shape • *a kidney shape*

style • *Several styles of hat were available.*

desire ① VERB

to want something • *We can stay longer if you desire.*

crave • *I crave her approval.*

fancy • *She fancied living in Canada.*

long for • *He longed for the winter to be over.*

want • *I want a drink.*

wish • *We wished to return.*

yearn • *He yearned to sleep.*

d

desire ② NOUN

a feeling of wanting something • I had a strong desire to help people.

appetite • She had lost her appetite for air travel.
craving • a craving for sugar
hankering • a hankering to be an actor
longing • her longing to return home
wish • Her wish is to be in films.
yearning • a yearning to be with his family
yen (INFORMAL) • Mike had a yen to try cycling.

despair ① NOUN

a loss of hope • feelings of despair

dejection • There was an air of dejection about her.
despondency • There's a mood of despondency in the country.
gloom • the deepening gloom over the economy
hopelessness • She had a feeling of hopelessness about the future.

despair ② VERB

to lose hope • I despair at the attitude with which their work is received.

feel dejected • Everyone has days when they feel dejected.
feel despondent • John often felt despondent about losing his job.
lose heart • He appealed to his countrymen not to lose heart.
lose hope • You mustn't lose hope.

despite PREPOSITION

in spite of • He fell asleep despite all the coffee he'd drunk.

in spite of • In spite of all the gossip, Virginia stayed behind.
notwithstanding (FORMAL) • Notwithstanding his age, Sikorski had an important job.
regardless of • He led from the front, regardless of the danger.

destroy VERB

to ruin something completely • The building was completely destroyed.

annihilate • The lava annihilates everything in its path.
demolish • A storm moved over the island, demolishing buildings.
devastate • A fire had devastated large parts of Windsor castle.
obliterate • Whole villages were obliterated by fire.
raze • The town was razed to the ground during the occupation.
ruin • My wife was ruining her health through worry.
wreck • the injuries which nearly wrecked his career

destruction NOUN

the act of destroying something • the destruction of the ozone layer

annihilation • Leaders fear the annihilation of their society.
demolition • the demolition of an old bridge
devastation • A huge bomb blast brought chaos and devastation.

obliteration • *the obliteration of three rainforests*

detail NOUN
an individual feature of something • *We discussed every detail of the performance.*
aspect • *Climate affects every aspect of our lives.*
element • *one of the key elements of the peace plan*
particular • *You will find all the particulars in Chapter 9.*
point • *Many of the points in the report are correct.*
respect • *At least in this respect we are equals.*

determination NOUN
a firm decision to do something • *the government's determination to beat inflation*
perseverance • *Adam's perseverance proved worthwhile.*
persistence • *She was determined to be a doctor and her persistence paid off.*
resolution • *She acted with resolution and courage.*
resolve (FORMAL) • *the American public's resolve to go to war if necessary*
tenacity • *Hard work and sheer tenacity are crucial to career success.*

determine ① VERB
to cause or control a situation or result • *The size of the chicken pieces will determine the cooking time.*
control • *Scientists may soon be able to control the ageing process.*
decide • *The results will decide if*

he will win a place on the course.
dictate • *A number of factors will dictate how long the tree will survive.*
govern • *the rules governing eligibility for scholarship programmes*
shape • *the role of key leaders in shaping the future of Europe*

determine ② VERB
to decide or settle something firmly • *The final wording had not yet been determined.*
arrange • *It was arranged that the party would gather in the Royal Garden Hotel.*
choose • *Houston was chosen as the site for the convention.*
decide • *Her age would be taken into account when deciding her sentence.*
fix • *The date of the election was fixed.*
resolve • *She resolved to report the matter to the authorities.*
settle • *That's settled then. We'll do it tomorrow.*

determine ③ VERB
to find out the facts about something • *The investigation will determine what really happened.*
ascertain (FORMAL) • *We need to ascertain the true facts.*
confirm • *X-rays have confirmed that he has not broken any bones.*
discover • *It was difficult for us to discover the reason for the decision.*
establish • *an inquiry to establish the cause of the accident*

find out • *one family's campaign to find out the truth*
verify • *A clerk verifies that the payment and invoice amount match.*

determined ADJECTIVE
firmly decided • *She was determined not to repeat her error.*
bent on • *They seem bent on destroying the city.*
dogged • *dogged persistence*
intent on • *He is intent on repeating his victory.*
persistent • *He phoned again this morning. He's very persistent.*
purposeful • *She had a purposeful air.*
resolute (FORMAL) • *a decisive and resolute leader*
single-minded • *a single-minded determination to win*
tenacious • *a tenacious and persistent interviewer*

develop ① VERB
to grow or become more advanced • *Children develop at different rates.*
advance • *tracing how medical technology has advanced to its present state*
evolve • *As scientific knowledge evolves, beliefs change.*
grow • *The boys grew into men.*
mature • *Other changes occur as the child matures physically.*
progress • *His disease progressed quickly.*
result • *Ignore the warnings and illness could result.*

spring • *The inspiration for the song sprang from a conversation.*

develop ② VERB
to become affected by an illness or fault • *He developed pneumonia.*
catch • *to catch a cold*
contract (FORMAL) • *He contracted a rare blood disease.*
fall ill with • *She fell ill with measles.*
get • *When I was five I got mumps.*
go down with • *Three members of the band went down with flu.*
pick up • *They've picked up an infection from something they've eaten.*
succumb to (FORMAL) • *I was determined not to succumb to the virus.*

devious ADJECTIVE
getting what you want by sly methods • *a devious politician*
calculating • *a calculating businesswoman*
scheming • *He was branded a "scheming liar".*
underhand • *She used underhand tactics to win the election.*
wily • *a wily old statesman*

devoted ADJECTIVE
very loving and loyal • *a devoted father*
constant • *her constant companion*
dedicated • *dedicated follower of classical music*
doting • *His doting parents bought him a racing bike.*

faithful • *I'm very faithful when I love someone.*
loving • *Jim was a loving husband.*
loyal • *a loyal friend*
true • *David was true to the cause.*

dictionary NOUN
PARTS OF A DICTIONARY OR THESAURUS
antonym
definition
entry
example
headword
homonym
homophone
inflection
label
pronunciation
root word
synonym
word class
word derivation

die ① VERB
to stop living • *My hamster died of old age.*
cark it (AUSTRALIAN AND NEW ZEALAND; INFORMAL) • *You think you're about to cark it.*
expire (FORMAL) • *before he finally expired*
pass away • *He passed away last year.*
pass on • *My great-grandmother passed on four years ago.*
perish (FORMAL) • *the ferry disaster in which 193 passengers perished*

die ② VERB
to fade away • *My love for you will never die.*
fade away • *With time, they said, the pain will fade away.*
fade out • *Thanks to supermarkets, the corner shop is gradually fading out.*
peter out • *The six-month strike seemed to be petering out.*

die out VERB
to cease to exist • *That custom has died out now.*
disappear • *Huge areas of the countryside are disappearing.*
fade • *Prospects for peace had already started to fade.*
vanish • *those species which have vanished*

difference ① NOUN
a lack of similarity between things • *the vast difference in size*
contrast • *the real contrast between the two poems*
discrepancy • *discrepancies between their statements*
disparity • *disparities between poor and wealthy districts*
distinction • *a distinction between the body and the soul*
divergence • *There's a substantial divergence of opinion within the party.*
variation • *a wide variation in the prices charged*
ANTONYM:
• similarity

difference ② NOUN
the amount by which two

quantities differ • *The difference is 8532.*
balance • *They were due to pay the balance on delivery.*
remainder • *They own a 75% stake. The remainder is owned by the bank.*

different ① ADJECTIVE
unlike something else • *We have totally different views.*
contrasting • *painted in contrasting colours*
disparate (FORMAL) • *The republics are very disparate in size and wealth.*
dissimilar • *His methods were not dissimilar to those used by Freud.*
divergent (FORMAL)
• *divergent opinions*
opposed • *two opposed ideologies*
unlike • *This was a foreign country, so unlike San Jose.*
ANTONYM:
• similar

different ② ADJECTIVE
unusual and out of the ordinary • *The result is interesting and different.*
special • *a special variety of strawberry*
unique • *Each person's signature is unique.*

different ③ ADJECTIVE
distinct and separate • *Our school supports a different charity each year.*
another • *Her doctor referred her to another therapist.*
discrete (FORMAL) • *two discrete sets of nerves*
distinct • *A word may have two quite distinct meanings.*
individual • *Each family needs individual attention.*
separate • *The word "quarter" has two completely separate meanings.*

difficult ① ADJECTIVE
not easy to do or solve • *a difficult decision to make*
arduous • *a long, arduous journey*
demanding • *a demanding job*
hard • *He found it hard to get work.*
intractable (FORMAL) • *an intractable problem*
laborious • *a laborious task*
uphill • *an uphill battle*
ANTONYM:
• easy

difficult ② ADJECTIVE
not easy to deal with • *I hope she isn't going to be difficult.*
demanding • *a demanding child*
troublesome • *a troublesome teenager*
trying • *The whole business has been very trying.*

difficulty ① NOUN
a problem • *The central difficulty is its stubbornness.*
complication • *An added complication is the growing concern for the environment.*
hassle (INFORMAL) • *all the usual hassles at the airport*
hurdle • *preparing a CV, the first hurdle in a job search*
obstacle • *To succeed, you must learn to overcome obstacles.*

pitfall • *the pitfalls of working abroad*
problem • *He left home because of family problems.*
snag • *The only snag was that he had no transport.*
trouble • *What seems to be the trouble?*

difficulty ② NOUN
the quality of being difficult • *the difficulty of the problem*
hardship • *economic hardship*
strain • *the stresses and strains of a busy career*
tribulation (FORMAL) • *the trials and tribulations of everyday life*

dig ① VERB
to break up soil or sand • *He dug a hole in the ground.*
burrow • *The larvae burrow into cracks in the floor.*
excavate • *A contractor was hired to excavate soil from the area.*
gouge • *quarries which have gouged great holes in the hills*
hollow out • *They hollowed out crude dwellings from the soft rock.*
quarry • *The caves are quarried for cement.*
till • *freshly tilled fields*
tunnel • *The rebels tunnelled out of jail.*

dig ② VERB
to push something in • *He could feel the beads digging into his palm.*
jab • *A needle was jabbed into my arm.*

poke • *She poked a fork into the turkey skin.*
thrust • *She thrust her hand into the sticky mess.*

dig ③ NOUN
a push or poke • *She silenced him with a dig in the ribs.*
jab • *a swift jab in the stomach*
poke • *a playful poke in the arm*
prod • *He gave the donkey a prod in the backside.*
thrust • *sword thrusts*

dim ① ADJECTIVE
not bright or well-lit • *a dim outline of a small boat*
dark • *a dark corridor*
dull • *The stamp was a dark, dull blue.*
grey • *a grey, wet, April Sunday*
murky • *one murky November afternoon*
poorly lit • *a poorly lit road*
shadowy • *a shadowy corner*

dim ② ADJECTIVE
vague or unclear • *a dim memory*
faint • *a faint recollection*
hazy • *Many details remain hazy.*
indistinct • *the indistinct murmur of voices*
obscure • *The origin of the custom is obscure.*
shadowy • *the shadowy world of spies*
vague • *I have a vague memory of shots being fired.*
ANTONYM:
• clear

dim ③ ADJECTIVE (INFORMAL)
slow to understand • *He is rather dim.*

dumb (INFORMAL) • *I've met a lot of dumb people.*
obtuse (FORMAL) • *I've really been very obtuse.*
slow • *She can be a bit slow.*
stupid • *How could I have been so stupid?*
thick (INFORMAL) • *I must have seemed incredibly thick.*

ANTONYM:
• bright

diminish VERB
to reduce or become reduced • *The threat of war has diminished.*
contract • *Output fell last year and is expected to contract further.*
decrease • *Gradually decrease the amount of vitamin C you are taking.*
lessen • *The attention he gets will lessen when the new baby is born.*
lower • *This drug lowers cholesterol levels.*
reduce • *It reduces the risk of heart disease.*
shrink • *the entertainment giant's intention to shrink its interest in the venture*
weaken • *The Prime Minister's authority has been fatally weakened.*

dinkum ADJECTIVE
(AUSTRALIAN AND NEW ZEALAND; INFORMAL)
genuine or right • *a fair dinkum bloke with no pretensions*
genuine • *If this offer is genuine I will gladly accept.*

guileless • *She was so guileless that he had to believe her.*
honest • *My dad was the most honest man I ever met.*
sincere • *a sincere desire to reform*

direct ① ADJECTIVE
in a straight line or by the shortest route • *the direct route*
straight • *Keep the boat in a straight line.*
uninterrupted • *an uninterrupted view*

ANTONYM:
• indirect

direct ② ADJECTIVE
open and honest • *He can be very direct sometimes.*
blunt • *She is blunt about her personal life.*
candid • *I haven't been completely candid with you.*
forthright • *forthright language*
frank • *She is always very frank.*
straight • *He never gives you a straight answer.*
straightforward • *his straightforward manner*

ANTONYM:
• devious

direct ③ ADJECTIVE
without anyone or anything intervening • *direct control*
first-hand • *She has little first-hand knowledge of Quebec.*
immediate • *his immediate superior*
personal • *I have no personal experience of this.*

ANTONYM:
• indirect

direct ④ VERB

to control and guide
something • *Christopher will
direct day-to-day operations.*
control • *She now controls the
entire company.*
guide • *He should have let his
instinct guide him.*
lead • *He led the country
between 1949 and 1984.*
manage • *Within two years he
was managing the store.*
oversee • *an architect to
oversee the work*
run • *Is this any way to run a
country?*
supervise • *I supervise the
packing of all mail orders.*

direction ① NOUN

the line in which something is
moving • *ten miles in the
opposite direction*
course • *The captain altered
course.*
path • *He stepped into the path
of a reversing car.*
route • *We took the wrong
route.*
way • *Does anybody know the
way to the station?*

direction ② NOUN

control and guidance of
something • *He was chopping
vegetables under the chef's
direction.*
charge • *A few years ago he took
charge of the company.*
command • *In 1942 he took
command of 108 Squadron.*

control • *The restructuring
involves Ronson giving up control
of the company.*
guidance • *the reports which
were produced under his
guidance*
leadership • *The agency
doubled in size under his
leadership.*
management • *The zoo needed
better management.*

dirt ① NOUN

dust or mud • *I started to scrub
off the dirt.*
dust • *The furniture was covered
in dust.*
filth • *tons of filth and sewage*
grime • *Kelly got the grime off
his hands.*
muck • *This congealed muck
was interfering with the filter.*
mud • *Their lorry got stuck in the
mud.*

dirt ② NOUN

earth or soil • *He drew a circle in
the dirt with the stick.*
earth • *a huge pile of earth*
soil • *an area with very good soil*

dirty ① ADJECTIVE

marked with dirt • *The kids
have got their clothes dirty.*
filthy • *a pair of filthy jeans*
grimy • *a grimy industrial city*
grubby • *kids with grubby faces*
mucky • *a mucky floor*
muddy • *his muddy boots*
soiled • *a soiled white apron*
unclean • *unclean water*

ANTONYM:
• clean

dirty ② ADJECTIVE
unfair or dishonest • *a dirty fight*

corrupt • *corrupt practices*
crooked • *crooked business deals*
ANTONYM:
• honest

disable VERB
to stop something working
• *You need to disable the alarm before you enter.*

deactivate • *The Escape key usually deactivates the screensaver.*
defuse • *to defuse a bomb*
immobilise • *a car alarm that immobilises the engine*

disadvantage NOUN
an unfavourable circumstance
• *the advantages and disadvantages of social media*

drawback • *The apartment's only drawback was that it was too small.*
handicap • *Their refusal to work together has been a handicap to the team.*
minus • *The pluses and minuses were about equal.*
weakness • *the strengths and weaknesses of the argument*
ANTONYM:
• advantage

disagree ① VERB
to have a different opinion
• *They can communicate even when they disagree.*

differ • *They differ on lots of issues.*
dispute • *Nobody disputed that Davey was clever.*

dissent • *dissenting views*
ANTONYM:
• agree

disagree ② VERB
to think that something is wrong • *I disagree with the board's proposal.*

object • *We objected strongly but were outvoted.*
oppose • *protesters opposing nuclear tests*
take issue with • *I take issue with much of what he said.*

disagreeable ADJECTIVE
unpleasant in some way • *a disagreeable odour*

horrible • *a horrible, snarling cat*
horrid (OLD-FASHIONED) • *What a horrid smell!*
nasty • *What a nasty little snob you are!*
objectionable • *an objectionable, stuck-up individual*
obnoxious • *One of the parents was a most obnoxious character.*
unfriendly • *She spoke in a loud, rather unfriendly voice.*
unpleasant • *The side-effects can be unpleasant.*
ANTONYM:
• agreeable

disagreement ① NOUN
a dispute about something
• *My driving instructor and I had a brief disagreement.*

altercation (FORMAL) • *an altercation with the referee*
argument • *an argument about money*

difference • *We have our differences but we get along.*
dispute • *a pay dispute*
quarrel • *I had a terrible quarrel with my brother.*
row • *a major diplomatic row*
squabble • *minor squabbles about phone bills*
tiff • *a lovers' tiff*

ANTONYM:
• agreement

disagreement ② NOUN

an objection to something • *Britain and France have expressed some disagreement with the proposal.*
dissent • *voices of dissent*
objection • *I have no objection to banks making money.*
opposition • *their opposition to the scheme*

disappear ① VERB

to go out of sight • *The aircraft disappeared off the radar.*
be lost to view • *They observed the comet for 70 days before it was lost to view.*
drop out of sight • *After his first film he dropped out of sight.*
fade • *We watched the harbour fade into the mist.*
recede • *Luke receded into the distance.*
vanish • *My car keys have vanished.*

ANTONYM:
• appear

disappear ② VERB

to stop existing • *The pain has finally disappeared.*

cease (FORMAL) • *At 1 o'clock the rain ceased.*
die out • *How did the dinosaurs die out?*
go away • *All she wanted was for the pain to go away.*
melt away • *His anger melted away.*
pass • *He told her the fear would pass.*
vanish • *species which have vanished*

disappointed ADJECTIVE

sad because something has not happened • *I was disappointed that Kluge was not there.*
dejected • *Her refusal left him feeling dejected.*
despondent • *After the interview John was despondent.*
disenchanted • *She has become very disenchanted with her job.*
disillusioned • *I've become very disillusioned with politics.*
downcast • *After his defeat Mr Rabin looked downcast.*
saddened • *He is saddened that they did not win anything.*

ANTONYM:
• satisfied

disappointment ① NOUN

a feeling of being disappointed • *Book early to avoid disappointment.*
dejection • *There was an air of dejection about her.*
despondency • *a mood of gloom and despondency*
regret • *my one great regret in life*

disappointment ② NOUN

something that disappoints you • *The reunion was a bitter disappointment.*

blow • *It was a terrible blow when he was made redundant.*

setback • *a setback for the peace process*

disapproval NOUN

the belief that something is wrong • *his mother's disapproval of his choice of career*

censure (FORMAL) • *He deserves support, not censure.*

condemnation • *the universal condemnation of French nuclear tests*

criticism • *actions which have attracted fierce criticism*

ANTONYM:
• approval

disapprove VERB

to think that something is wrong • *Everyone disapproved of the closure of the youth club.*

condemn • *Political leaders condemned the speech.*

deplore (FORMAL) • *He deplores violence.*

dislike • *Her father seemed to dislike all her friends.*

find unacceptable • *I find such behaviour totally unacceptable.*

take a dim view of • *They took a dim view of local trade unionists.*

ANTONYM:
• approve

disaster NOUN

an occasion where there is serious damage or harm • *another air disaster*

calamity (FORMAL) • *It could only end in calamity.*

catastrophe • *War would be a catastrophe.*

misfortune • *She seemed to enjoy the misfortunes of others.*

tragedy • *They have suffered an enormous personal tragedy.*

discard VERB

to get rid of something • *Read the instructions before discarding the box.*

cast aside • *The concerns of the local community must not be cast aside.*

dispose of • *how he disposed of the weapon*

dump (INFORMAL) • *The getaway car was dumped near the motorway.*

jettison • *The crew jettisoned excess fuel.*

shed • *a snake that has shed its skin*

throw away • *I never throw anything away.*

throw out • *Why don't you throw out all those old magazines?*

discern VERB (FORMAL)

to notice or understand something clearly • *trying to discern a pattern in his behaviour*

detect • *Arnold could detect a certain sadness in the man's face.*

make out • *I could just make out a shadowy figure through the mist.*

notice • *Mrs Shedden noticed a bird sitting on the garage roof.*

observe • *In 1664 Hooke observed a reddish spot on the planet's surface.*

perceive • *Get pupils to perceive the relationship between success and effort.*

see • *Supporters saw in him a champion of the oppressed.*

spot • *I've spotted an error in your calculations.*

discharge ① VERB
to send something out • *The resulting salty water will be discharged at sea.*

emit • *the amount of greenhouse gases emitted*

empty • *companies which empty toxic by-products into rivers*

expel • *Poisonous gas is expelled into the atmosphere.*

flush • *Flush out all the sewage.*

give off • *natural gas, which gives off less carbon dioxide than coal*

release • *a weapon which releases toxic nerve gas*

discharge ② VERB
to allow someone to leave hospital or prison • *He has a broken nose but may be discharged today.*

free • *The country is set to free more prisoners.*

let go • *They held him for three hours and then let him go.*

liberate • *They promised to liberate prisoners held in detention camps.*

release • *He was released on bail.*

set free • *More than ninety prisoners have been set free.*

discharge ③ VERB
to dismiss someone from a job • *He was discharged from the military.*

dismiss • *The military commander has been dismissed.*

eject • *He was ejected from his first job for persistent latecoming.*

fire (INFORMAL) • *If he wasn't so good at his job, I'd fire him.*

sack (INFORMAL) • *The teacher was sacked for slapping a schoolboy.*

discharge ④ NOUN
a sending away from a job or institution • *They face a dishonourable discharge from the Army.*

dismissal • *shock at the director's dismissal from his post*

ejection • *These actions led to his ejection from office.*

expulsion • *his expulsion from the party in 2015*

the sack (INFORMAL) • *People who make mistakes can be given the sack.*

discourage VERB
to make someone lose enthusiasm • *Don't let these problems discourage you.*

daunt • *He was not the type of man to be daunted by adversity.*

deter • *Tougher sentences would do nothing to deter crime.*

dissuade • *He considered emigrating, but his family managed to dissuade him.*

put off • I wouldn't let it put you off applying.

ANTONYM:
• encourage

discover VERB
to find something or find out about something • He discovered that his ancestors came from Norway.

come across • He came across the jawbone of a carnivorous dinosaur.

find • The police also found a pistol.

find out • Watch the next episode to find out what happens.

learn • The Admiral, on learning who I was, wanted to meet me.

realise • As soon as we realised something was wrong, we took action.

stumble on or **stumble across** • They stumbled on a magnificent waterfall.

unearth • Researchers have unearthed documents implicating her in the crime.

discuss VERB
to talk about something • I will be discussing the situation with colleagues tomorrow.

debate • The UN Security Council will debate the issue today.

exchange views on • They exchanged views on a wide range of subjects.

go into • We didn't go into that.

talk about • What did you talk about?

discussion NOUN
a talk about something
• informal discussions

consultation • consultations between lawyers

conversation • I struck up a conversation with him.

debate • There has been a lot of debate among scholars about this.

dialogue • a direct dialogue between the two nations

discourse • a long tradition of political discourse

talk • We had a long talk about it.

disgrace ① NOUN
lack of respect • She has brought disgrace upon the whole team.

scandal • They kept quiet about the deal for fear of scandal.

shame • I don't want to bring shame on the family name.

ANTONYM:
• credit

disgrace ② VERB
to bring shame upon • I have disgraced my family's name.

discredit • He said such methods discredited the movement worldwide.

shame • I wouldn't shame my father by doing that.

disgraceful ADJECTIVE
deserving of shame
• disgraceful behaviour

scandalous • a scandalous waste of money

shameful • the most shameful episode in US naval history

shocking • *a shocking invasion of privacy*

disgust ① NOUN
a strong feeling of dislike • *his disgust at the incident*
loathing • *She looked at him with loathing.*
repulsion • *a shudder of repulsion*
revulsion • *They expressed their shock and revulsion.*

disgust ② VERB
to cause someone to feel disgust • *He disgusted many with his behaviour.*
repel • *an idea that frightened and repelled her*
revolt • *The smell revolted him.*
sicken • *What he saw there sickened him.*

disgusting ADJECTIVE
very unpleasant or unacceptable • *one of the most disgusting sights I had ever seen*
foul • *a foul stench*
gross • *Don't be so gross!*
obnoxious • *a most obnoxious character*
repellent • *a very large, repellent toad*
revolting • *The smell was revolting.*
sickening • *a sickening attack*
vile • *a vile odour*

dishonest ADJECTIVE
not truthful • *It would be dishonest to mislead people.*
corrupt • *corrupt politicians*
crooked • *crooked business deals*

deceitful • *The ambassador called the report deceitful and misleading.*
fraudulent • *fraudulent claims about being a nurse*
lying • *He called her "a lying little twit".*
ANTONYM:
• honest

dishonesty NOUN
dishonest behaviour • *She accused the government of dishonesty.*
cheating • *He was accused of cheating.*
corruption • *The President faces 54 charges of corruption.*
deceit • *the deceit and lies of the past*
trickery • *They resorted to trickery in order to impress their clients.*
ANTONYM:
• honesty

disintegrate VERB
to break into many pieces • *At 420 mph the windscreen disintegrated.*
break up • *There was a danger of the ship breaking up completely.*
crumble • *The flint crumbled into fragments.*
fall apart • *Bit by bit the building fell apart.*
fall to pieces • *The radio handset fell to pieces.*
fragment • *The clouds fragmented and out came the sun.*

d

D

dislike ① VERB
to consider something
unpleasant • We don't serve it
often because many people
dislike it.
abhor (FORMAL) • a man who
abhorred violence
be averse to • He's not averse
to a little publicity.
detest • Jean detested being
photographed.
hate • Most people hate him.
loathe • a play loathed by the
critics
not be able to abide • I can't
abide liars.
not be able to bear • I can't
bear people who speak like that.
not be able to stand • He can't
stand the sound of her voice.
ANTONYM:
• like

dislike ② NOUN
a feeling of not liking
something • She looked at him
with dislike.
animosity • The animosity
between the two men grew.
antipathy (FORMAL) • their
antipathy towards the media
aversion • I've always had an
aversion to being part of a group.
distaste • Roger looked at her
with distaste.
hatred • her hatred of authority
hostility • hostility to minority
groups
loathing • He made no secret of
his loathing of her.
ANTONYM:
• liking

disobey VERB
to deliberately refuse to
follow instructions • He was
forever disobeying the rules.
break • drivers breaking speed
limits
defy • the first time that I dared
to defy my mother
flout • illegal campers who
persist in flouting the law
infringe • He was adamant that
he had infringed no rules.
violate • They violated the
ceasefire agreement.
ANTONYM:
• obey

disorder ① NOUN
a state of untidiness • Inside,
all was disorder.
clutter • She prefers the
worktop to be free of clutter.
disarray • Her clothes were in
disarray.
muddle • a general muddle of
pencils and boxes
ANTONYM:
• order

disorder ② NOUN
a lack of organisation • The
men fled in disorder.
chaos • Their concerts often
ended in chaos.
confusion • There was
confusion when a fight broke out.
disarray • The nation is in
disarray following rioting.
turmoil • political turmoil

disorder ③ NOUN
a disease or illness • a rare
nerve disorder

affliction • *an affliction which can ruin a young person's life*
complaint • *a common skin complaint*
condition • *a heart condition*
disease • *heart disease*
illness • *serious illness*

dispose of VERB
to get rid of something • *Fold up the nappy and dispose of it.*
discard • *Read the instructions before discarding the box.*
dispense with • *He dispensed with his notes after the talk.*
dump • *The government declared that it did not dump radioactive waste at sea.*
get rid of • *The owner needs to get rid of the car for financial reasons.*
jettison • *The crew jettisoned excess fuel and made an emergency landing.*
throw away • *I never throw anything away.*

disprove VERB
to show that something is not true • *the statistics that will prove or disprove the hypothesis*
discredit • *There would be difficulties in discrediting the evidence.*
give the lie to • *This survey gives the lie to the idea that the economy is recovering.*
invalidate • *Some of the other criticisms were invalidated years ago.*
prove false • *It is hard to prove such claims false.*

refute • *the kind of rumour that is impossible to refute*
ANTONYM:
• prove

dispute ① NOUN
an argument • *The dispute between them is settled.*
argument • *a heated argument*
clash • *the clash between trade union leaders and the government*
conflict • *Avoid any conflict between yourself and your siblings.*
disagreement • *disagreements among the member states*
feud • *a bitter feud between the state government and the villagers*
row • *a major diplomatic row with France*
wrangle • *a legal wrangle*

dispute ② VERB
to question something's truth or wisdom • *He disputed the allegations.*
challenge • *I challenge the wisdom of this decision.*
contest • *Your former employer wants to contest the case.*
contradict • *Her version contradicted the Government's claim.*
deny • *She denied both accusations.*
query • *No one queried my decision.*
question • *It never occurred to me to question the doctor's diagnosis.*
ANTONYM:
• accept

d

distant ① ADJECTIVE
far away in space or time • *a distant land*
far • *Is it very far?*
outlying • *outlying districts*
out-of-the-way • *an out-of-the-way spot*
remote • *a remote village*
ANTONYM:
• close

distant ② ADJECTIVE
cold and unfriendly • *He is polite but distant.*
aloof • *He seemed aloof and detached.*
detached • *He observed me with a detached curiosity.*
reserved • *She's quite a reserved person.*
withdrawn • *Her sister had become withdrawn and moody.*
ANTONYM:
• friendly

distinguish ① VERB
to see the difference between things • *Could he distinguish right from wrong?*
differentiate • *At this age your baby cannot differentiate one person from another.*
discriminate • *He is unable to discriminate a good idea from a terrible one.*
tell • *How do you tell one from another?*
tell apart • *I can only tell them apart by the colour of their shoes.*
tell the difference • *I can't tell the difference between their policies and ours.*

distinguish ② VERB
to recognise something • *I heard shouting but was unable to distinguish the words.*
discern • *We could just discern a narrow ditch.*
make out • *He couldn't make out what she was saying.*
pick out • *Through my binoculars I picked out a group of figures.*
recognise • *He did not think she could recognise his car in the snow.*

distract VERB
to stop someone from concentrating • *Playing online games distracts him from his homework.*
divert • *They want to divert our attention from the real issues.*
draw away • *to draw attention away from the crime*

distress ① NOUN
great suffering • *Jealousy causes distress and painful emotions.*
heartache • *the heartache of her divorce*
pain • *eyes that seemed filled with pain*
sorrow • *a time of great sorrow*
suffering • *to put an end to his suffering*

distress ② NOUN
the state of needing help • *The ship might be in distress.*
difficulty • *rumours about banks being in difficulty*
need • *When you were in need, I loaned you money.*

straits • *The company's closure left them in desperate financial straits.*

trouble • *a charity that helps young people in trouble*

distress ③ VERB
to cause someone unhappiness • *Her departure had profoundly distressed me.*

bother • *It bothered me that nobody wanted to listen to me.*

disturb • *dreams so vivid that they disturb me for days*

grieve • *It grieved her to be separated from her son.*

pain • *It pains me to think of you struggling all alone.*

sadden • *The cruelty in the world saddens me deeply.*

trouble • *He was troubled by the lifestyle of his son.*

upset • *I'm sorry if I've upset you.*

worry • *I didn't want to worry you.*

distribute ① VERB
to hand something out • *They publish and distribute brochures.*

circulate • *He has circulated a discussion document.*

hand out • *One of my jobs was to hand out the prizes.*

pass around • *Sweets were being passed around.*

pass round • *She passed her holiday photos round.*

distribute ② VERB
to spread something through an area • *Distribute the topping evenly over the fruit.*

diffuse • *Interest in books is more widely diffused than ever.*

disperse • *The leaflets were dispersed throughout the country.*

scatter • *She scattered the petals down the aisle.*

spread • *A thick layer of wax was spread over the surface.*

distribute ③ VERB
to divide and share something • *Distribute chores evenly among all family members.*

allocate • *funds allocated for nursery education*

allot • *The seats are allotted to the candidates who have won the most votes.*

dispense (FORMAL) • *The Union had already dispensed £400 in grants.*

divide • *Paul divides his spare time between the bedroom and the study.*

dole out • *I got out my wallet and began to dole out the money.*

share out • *You could share out the food a bit more equally.*

disturb ① VERB
to intrude on someone's peace • *She slept in a separate room so as not to disturb him.*

bother • *I'm sorry to bother you.*

disrupt • *Protesters disrupted the debate.*

intrude on • *I don't want to intrude on your parents.*

disturb ② VERB
to upset or worry someone • *Some scenes may disturb you.*

agitate • *The thought agitated her.*

distress • *Her departure had profoundly distressed me.*

d

shake • Well, it shook me quite a bit.

trouble • He was troubled by the lifestyle of his son.

unsettle • The presence of the two police officers unsettled her.

upset • I'm sorry if I've upset you.

worry • I didn't want to worry you.

dive VERB
to jump or fall into water • She was standing by the pool, about to dive in.

jump • He ran along the board and jumped in.

leap • as she leapt into the water

submerge • Hippos are unable to submerge in the few remaining water holes.

divide ① VERB
to split something up • The idea is to divide the country into four sectors.

cut up • Halve the tomatoes, then cut them up.

partition • a plan to partition the country

segregate • Police were used to segregate the two rival camps.

separate • Fluff the rice with a fork to separate the grains.

split • Split the chicken in half.

split up • He split up the company.

ANTONYM:
• join

divide ② VERB
to form a barrier between things • the frontier dividing Mexico from the USA

bisect • The main street bisects the town.

separate • the fence that separated the yard from the paddock

divide ③ VERB
to cause people to disagree • the enormous differences that still divide them

come between • It's difficult to imagine anything coming between them.

set against one another • The case has set neighbours against one another in the village.

split • The issue is in danger of splitting the church.

division ① NOUN
separation into parts • the unification of Germany after its division into two states

partition • fighting which followed the partition of India

separation • the separation of church and state

division ② NOUN
a disagreement • There were divisions in the Party on economic policy.

breach • a serious breach in relations between the two countries

difference of opinion • Was there a difference of opinion over what to do with the money?

rupture • a rupture of the family unit

split • They accused both sides of trying to provoke a split in the party.

division ③ NOUN
a section of something • the Research Division

department • *the company's chemicals department*
section • *a top-secret section of the Foreign Office*
sector • *the nation's manufacturing sector*

dizzy ADJECTIVE
about to lose your balance • *He kept getting dizzy spells.*
giddy • *She felt slightly giddy.*
light-headed • *If you skip breakfast, you may feel light-headed.*

do ① VERB
to carry out a task • *He just didn't want to do any work.*
carry out • *Police believe the attacks were carried out by a rival gang.*
execute (FORMAL) • *The landing was skilfully executed.*
perform • *people who have performed outstanding acts of bravery*
undertake • *She undertook the arduous task of monitoring the elections.*

do ② VERB
to be sufficient • *Home-made stock is best, but cubes will do.*
be adequate • *A simple supper should be perfectly adequate for most people.*
be sufficient • *One teaspoon of sugar should be sufficient.*
suffice (FORMAL) • *Often a far shorter letter will suffice.*

do ③ VERB
to perform well or badly • *Connie did well at school.*

fare • *Some later expeditions fared better.*
get on • *I asked him how he had got on.*
manage • *How did your mother manage to juggle work and family commitments?*

dodge ① VERB
to move out of the way • *We dodged behind a pillar out of sight of the tourists.*
duck • *I wanted to duck down and slip past but they saw me.*
swerve • *He swerved to avoid a truck.*

dodge ② VERB
to avoid doing something • *dodging military service by feigning illness*
avoid • *They managed to avoid paying their fares.*
elude • *He eluded the police for 13 years.*
evade • *by evading taxes*
get out of • *He'll do almost anything to get out of paying his share.*
shirk • *We can't shirk our responsibility.*
sidestep • *Rarely, if ever, does he sidestep a question.*

dog NOUN
an animal often kept as a pet • *a children's book about dogs*
brak (SOUTH AFRICAN) • *a rabid brak*
canine (FORMAL) • *A new canine was needed.*
mongrel • *a rescued mongrel called Chips*

mutt (SLANG) • *the most famous mutts in the western world*

pooch (SLANG) • *Julian's pet pooch*

RELATED WORDS:
• ADJECTIVE canine
• FEMALE bitch
• YOUNG pup, puppy

doomed ADJECTIVE

certain to fail • *Shackleton led a doomed mission to the Antarctic.*

condemned • *Many people are condemned to poverty.*

hopeless • *I don't believe your situation is as hopeless as you think.*

ill-fated • *his ill-fated attempt on the world record*

double ① ADJECTIVE

twice the usual size • *a double portion*

twice • *Unemployment in the county is twice the national average.*

twofold • *a twofold risk*

double ② ADJECTIVE

consisting of two parts • *a double album*

dual • *dual nationality*

twin • *twin beds*

twofold • *Their concern was twofold: personal and political.*

doubt ① NOUN

a feeling of uncertainty • *This raises doubts about the point of advertising.*

misgiving • *I had misgivings about his methods.*

qualm • *I have no qualms about recommending this approach.*

scepticism • *The report has been greeted with scepticism.*

uncertainty • *the uncertainties regarding the future funding of the company*

ANTONYM:
• certainty

doubt ② VERB

to feel uncertain about something • *No one doubted his ability.*

be dubious • *I was dubious about the entire proposition.*

be sceptical • *Other archaeologists are sceptical about his findings.*

query • *No one queried my decision.*

question • *It never occurs to them to question the doctor's decisions.*

ANTONYM:
• believe

doubtful ADJECTIVE

unlikely or uncertain • *It is doubtful whether he will appear again.*

debatable • *Whether the Bank of England would do any better is highly debatable.*

dubious • *This claim seems to us rather dubious.*

questionable • *It is questionable whether the expenditure is justified.*

uncertain • *It's uncertain whether they will accept the plan.*

ANTONYM:
• certain

down ① ADVERB
towards the ground, or in a lower place • *We went down in the lift.*

downwards • *She gazed downwards.*

downstairs • *Denise went downstairs and made some tea.*

ANTONYM:
• up

down ② ADJECTIVE
depressed • *He sounded really down.*

dejected • *Everyone has days when they feel dejected.*

depressed • *She's been very depressed about this situation.*

dispirited • *I left feeling utterly dispirited.*

fed up (INFORMAL) • *I'm just fed up and I don't know what to do.*

glum • *She was very glum and was missing her children.*

melancholy (LITERARY) • *It was in the afternoon that Tom felt most melancholy.*

miserable • *My work was making me really miserable.*

downfall NOUN
the failure of a person or thing • *His lack of experience had led to his downfall.*

collapse • *The medical system is facing collapse.*

fall • *the fall of the military dictator*

ruin • *Inflation has driven them to the brink of ruin.*

drab ADJECTIVE
dull and unattractive • *the same drab grey dress*

dingy • *his rather dingy office*

dismal • *a dark dismal day*

dreary • *a dreary little town*

gloomy • *the gloomy days of winter*

grey • *a New Year that will be grey and cheerless*

sombre • *a worried official in sombre black*

ANTONYM:
• bright

drag VERB
to pull something along the ground • *He dragged his chair towards the table.*

draw • *He drew his chair nearer the fire.*

haul • *A crane was used to haul the car out of the stream.*

lug • *Nobody wants to lug around huge suitcases.*

tow • *They threatened to tow away my car.*

trail • *She came down the stairs slowly, trailing the coat behind her.*

drain ① VERB
to cause a liquid to flow somewhere • *Miners built the tunnel to drain water out of the lakes.*

draw off • *The fluid can be drawn off with a syringe.*

pump • *to get rid of raw sewage by pumping it out to sea*

drain ② VERB
to flow somewhere • *rivers that drain into lakes*

discharge • *Blood was discharging from its nostrils.*

empty • *The Washougal empties into the Columbia River.*

flow • The waters of Lake Erie now flow into the Niagara River.

seep • Radioactive water has seeped into underground reservoirs.

drain ③ VERB

to use something up • The prolonged boardroom battle drained him of energy and money.

consume • plans which will consume hours of time

exhaust • People are now living longer and exhausting natural resources.

sap • The illness sapped his strength.

tax • Overcrowding has taxed the city's ability to deal with waste.

use up • They aren't the ones who use up the world's resources.

drastic ADJECTIVE

severe and urgent • It's time for drastic action.

extreme • His response was rather extreme.

harsh • harsh new measures to combat drink-driving

radical • radical economic reforms

severe • a severe shortage of drinking water

draw ① VERB

to make a picture • He starts a painting by drawing simplified shapes.

paint • She is painting a huge volcano.

sketch • He sketched a map on the back of a menu.

trace • She learned to draw by tracing pictures out of old storybooks.

draw ② VERB

to move somewhere • as the car drew away

move • She moved away from the window.

pull • He pulled into the driveway.

draw ③ VERB

to pull something • He drew his chair nearer the fire.

drag • He dragged his chair towards the table.

haul • A crane was used to haul the car out of the stream.

pull • a freight train pulling waggons

drawback NOUN

a problem that makes something less than perfect • The only drawback was that the apartment was too small.

difficulty • There is only one difficulty - I don't have the key.

hitch • It's a great idea but I can see a serious hitch.

problem • The main problem with the house is its inaccessibility.

snag • It's a great school – the snag is the fees are £15,000 a year.

trouble • The trouble is that he might not agree with our plans.

dreadful ADJECTIVE

very bad or unpleasant • He told us the dreadful news

appalling • living under the most appalling conditions

atrocious • The food here is atrocious.

awful • Jeans look awful on me.

frightful (OLD-FASHIONED) • *The war had been so frightful he couldn't talk about it.*

ghastly • *a ghastly pair of shoes*

horrendous • *the most horrendous experience of his life*

terrible • *Thousands more people suffered terrible injuries.*

ANTONYM:
• wonderful

dream ① NOUN
mental pictures while sleeping • *He had a dream about Claire.*

hallucination • *The illness left him feverish and experiencing hallucinations.*

trance • *She seemed to be in a trance.*

vision • *seeing his late grandmother in a vision*

dream ② NOUN
something that you want very much • *his dream of winning the lottery*

ambition • *His ambition is to sail round the world.*

aspiration • *one of his greatest aspirations*

daydream • *He learned to escape into daydreams of becoming a writer.*

fantasy • *fantasies of travelling the world*

dreary ADJECTIVE
dull or boring • *the dreary winter months*

boring • *a boring job*

drab • *The rest of the day's activities often seem drab.*

dull • *There was scarcely a dull moment.*

humdrum • *The new government seemed rather humdrum.*

monotonous • *It's monotonous work, like most factory jobs.*

tedious • *Such lists are tedious to read.*

uneventful • *her dull, uneventful life*

ANTONYM:
• exciting

dress ① NOUN
a piece of clothing • *a black dress*

frock • *a party frock*

gown • *wedding gowns*

robe • *a fur-lined robe*

dress ② NOUN
clothing in general • *evening dress*

attire (FORMAL) • *women dressed in their finest attire*

clothes • *casual clothes*

clothing • *protective clothing*

costume • *women in traditional costume*

garb (FORMAL) • *his usual garb of a dark suit*

dress ③ VERB
to put on clothes • *a tall woman dressed in black*

attire (FORMAL) • *He was attired in a smart blue suit.*

clothe • *He lay down on the bed fully clothed.*

garb (FORMAL) • *He was garbed in sweater, jacket and boots.*

ANTONYM:
• undress

drink ① VERB
to swallow liquid • *He drank some tea.*
gulp • *She quickly gulped her coffee.*
guzzle • *She guzzled a glass of lemonade.*
sip • *She sipped from her coffee mug.*
swig (INFORMAL) • *I swigged down two glasses of the stuff.*

drink ② NOUN
an amount of liquid suitable for drinking • *a drink of water*
draught • *She had a draught of the hot coffee.*
sip • *Harry took a sip of juice.*

drip ① VERB
to fall in small drops • *Rain dripped from the brim of his cap.* **dribble** • *Sweat dribbled down his face.*
splash • *Tears splashed into her hands.*
trickle • *A tear trickled down the man's cheek.*

drip ② NOUN
a small amount of a liquid • *drips of water*
bead • *beads of sweat*
drop • *a drop of blue ink*
droplet • *water droplets*

drive ① VERB
to operate or power a machine or vehicle • *Don't drive a car or operate heavy machinery after taking this medication.*
operate • *A rock fall trapped the men as they operated a tunnelling machine.*

pilot • *He piloted his own plane to Washington.*
power • *The flywheel's battery could be used to power an electric car.*
propel • *Attached is a tiny rocket designed to propel the spacecraft towards Mars.*
run • *It costs a lot to run a car of this size.*
steer • *What is it like to steer a ship this size?*
work • *I learned how to work the forklift.*

drive ② VERB
to force someone to do something • *Bankruptcy drove him to flee the country.*
compel • *He felt compelled to speak out against their actions.*
force • *A back injury forced her to withdraw from the tournament.*
lead • *His abhorrence of racism led him to write his first book.*
motivate • *What motivates people to behave like this?*
prompt • *The recession prompted consumers to cut back on spending.*
push • *James did not push her into stealing the money.*
spur • *What spurs these fishermen to take such risks?*

drive ③ VERB
to force something pointed into a surface • *I used the sledgehammer to drive the pegs in.*
hammer • *Hammer a wooden peg into the hole.*

knock • *He knocked a couple of nails into the wall.*

ram • *He rammed the stake with all his strength into the creature's heart.*

sink • *He sinks the needle into my arm.*

thrust • *thrusting a knife into the cabbage*

drive ④ NOUN
a journey in a vehicle • *We might go for a drive on Sunday.*

excursion • *an excursion to a local vineyard*

jaunt • *Let's take a jaunt down to the beach.*

journey • *The journey from Manchester to Plymouth took a few hours.*

ride • *We took some friends for a ride in the family car.*

run • *We went for a run in the new car to try it out.*

spin (INFORMAL) • *I was thinking about going for a spin.*

trip • *We went on a coach trip to the seaside.*

drive ⑤ NOUN
energy and determination • *He is best remembered for his drive and enthusiasm.*

ambition • *When I was young I never had any ambition.*

determination • *her natural determination to succeed*

energy • *At 84 years old, her energy is magnificent.*

enterprise • *the group's lack of enterprise*

initiative • *We were disappointed by his lack of initiative.*

motivation • *His poor performance may be attributed to lack of motivation.*

vigour • *He played with great vigour.*

drop ① VERB
to fall downwards • *She let her head drop.*

descend • *as the aircraft descended*

fall • *Bombs fell in the town.*

plummet • *His parachute failed to open and he plummeted to the ground.*

sink • *She sank to her knees.*

tumble • *The gun tumbled out of his hand.*

drop ② VERB
to become less • *Temperatures can drop to freezing at night.*

decline • *The number of staff has declined.*

decrease • *Population growth is decreasing by 1.4% each year.*

diminish • *diminishing resources*

fall • *Her weight fell to under seven stone.*

plummet • *Share prices have plummeted.*

sink • *Pay increases have sunk to around 7%.*

slump • *Net profits slumped by 41%.*

tumble • *House prices have tumbled by almost 30%.*

ANTONYM:
• rise

drop ③ NOUN
a small amount of a liquid • *a drop of blue ink*

bead • *beads of sweat*

drip • *drips of water*
droplet • *water droplets*

drowsy ADJECTIVE
tired and sleepy • *The medicine made him drowsy.*
lethargic • *He felt too lethargic to get dressed.*
sluggish • *feeling sluggish after a big meal*

drug ① NOUN
a treatment for disease • *a new drug to help cancer patients*
medication • *She is not on any medication.*
medicine • *herbal medicines*
RELATED WORD:
• COMBINING FORM
pharmaco-

drug ② NOUN
an illegal substance • *She was sure Leo was taking drugs.*
narcotic • *He was indicted for dealing in narcotics.*
stimulant • *the use of stimulants in sport*

drunk ADJECTIVE
having consumed too much alcohol • *She said she wasn't drunk.*
babalas (SOUTH AFRICAN) • *He was babalas again last night.*
intoxicated (FORMAL) • *He appeared intoxicated.*
tipsy • *I'm feeling a bit tipsy.*
ANTONYM:
• sober

dry ① ADJECTIVE
without any liquid • *The path was dry after the sunshine.*

arid • *arid conditions*
dried-up • *a dried-up river bed*
parched • *parched brown grass*
ANTONYM:
• wet

dry ② VERB
to remove liquid from something • *Wash and dry the lettuce.*
dehydrate • *Avoid alcohol, which dehydrates the body.*
drain • *The authorities have mobilised vast numbers of people to drain flooded land.*
ANTONYM:
• moisten

dubious ① ADJECTIVE
not entirely honest or reliable • *a rather dubious claim*
crooked • *expose his crooked business deals*
dishonest • *He had become rich by dishonest means.*
questionable • *allegations of questionable business practices*
suspect • *The whole affair is highly suspect.*
suspicious • *two characters who looked suspicious*
unreliable • *a notoriously unreliable source of information*

dubious ② ADJECTIVE
doubtful about something • *My parents were a bit dubious about it all.*
doubtful • *I was still very doubtful about our chances for success.*

nervous • *The party has become nervous about its prospects of winning.*

sceptical • *Other archaeologists are sceptical about his findings.*

suspicious • *I'm a little suspicious about his motives.*

unconvinced • *Most consumers seem unconvinced that the recession is over.*

undecided • *After university she was still undecided as to what career she wanted.*

unsure • *Fifty-two per cent were unsure about the idea.*

dull ① ADJECTIVE
not interesting • *I found him rather dull.*

boring • *a boring job*

drab • *The rest of the day's activities often seem drab.*

humdrum • *The new government seemed rather humdrum.*

monotonous • *It's monotonous work, like most factory jobs.*

tedious • *Such lists are tedious to read.*

uninteresting • *Their media has a reputation for being dull and uninteresting.*

ANTONYM:
• interesting

dull ② ADJECTIVE
not bright or clear • *a dark, dull blue colour*

drab • *the same drab grey dress*

gloomy • *Inside it's gloomy after all that sunshine.*

muted • *He likes sombre, muted colours.*

sombre • *an official in sombre black*

subdued • *subdued lighting*

ANTONYM:
• bright

dull ③ ADJECTIVE
covered with clouds • *It's always dull and raining.*

cloudy • *In the morning it was cloudy.*

leaden • *a leaden sky*

murky • *one murky November afternoon*

overcast • *For three days it was overcast.*

ANTONYM:
• bright

dumb ① ADJECTIVE
unable to speak • *We were all struck dumb for a minute.*

mute • *a mute look of appeal*

silent • *Suddenly they both fell silent.*

speechless • *Alex was almost speechless with rage.*

dumb ② ADJECTIVE
(INFORMAL)
slow to understand • *I've met a lot of pretty dumb people.*

dim • *He is rather dim.*

obtuse (FORMAL) • *I've really been very obtuse.*

stupid • *How could I have been so stupid?*

thick (INFORMAL) • *I must have seemed incredibly thick.*

ANTONYM:
• smart

dump ① VERB

to get rid of something • The getaway car was dumped near the motorway.

discharge • The resulting salty water will eventually be discharged at sea.

dispose of • how he disposed of the weapon

get rid of • I need to get rid of these empty boxes.

jettison • The crew jettisoned their excess fuel.

throw away • You should have thrown the letter away.

throw out • You ought to throw out those empty bottles.

dump ② VERB

to put something down • We dumped our bags at the hotel and went for a walk.

deposit • Imagine if you were suddenly deposited on a desert island.

drop • Many children had been dropped outside the stadium by their parents.

dupe VERB

to trick someone • Some of the offenders duped the psychologists.

cheat • Many brokers were charged with cheating customers.

con (INFORMAL) • The British people have been conned by the government.

deceive • He has deceived us all.

delude • Television deludes you into thinking you are experiencing reality.

fool • Art forgers fool a lot of people.

play a trick on • She realised he had played a trick on her.

trick • He'll be upset when he finds out you tricked him.

duty ① NOUN

something that you ought to do • We have a duty as adults to listen to children.

obligation • He had not felt an obligation to help save his old friend.

responsibility • work and family responsibilities

duty ② NOUN

a task associated with a job • My main duty as librarian was the acquisition of books.

assignment • dangerous assignments

job • One of my jobs was to make the tea.

responsibility • He handled his responsibilities as a counsellor very well.

role • Both sides had important roles to play.

duty ③ NOUN

tax paid to the government • customs duties

excise • These products are excused VAT and excise.

levy (FORMAL) • An annual motorway levy is imposed on all drivers.

tariff • America wants to eliminate tariffs on such items as electronics.

tax • the tax on new cars and motorcycles

dying: be dying for VERB
to want something very much
• I'm dying for a breath of fresh air.
ache for • She still ached for a
place of her own.
be hungry for • Jules was
hungry for adventure.
long for • He longed for the
winter to be over.
pine for • I pine for the
countryside.
yearn for • He yearned for
freedom.

Ee

eager ADJECTIVE
wanting very much to do or
have something • Robert is
eager to earn some extra money.
anxious • She was anxious to
leave early.
ardent • one of the government's
most ardent supporters
avid • He's always been an avid
reader.
enthusiastic • Tom usually
seems very enthusiastic.
keen • Kirsty has always been a
keen swimmer.
raring to go (INFORMAL)
• They're all ready and raring to go.

early ① ADJECTIVE
before the arranged or expected
time • You're not late – I'm early!
advance • We got an advance
copy of her new book.
premature • The injury put a
premature end to his sporting
career.
untimely • her untimely death
at the age of 21
ANTONYM:
• late

early ② ADJECTIVE
happening or existing a
very long time ago • early
British history

primeval • *These insects first appeared in the primeval forests of Europe.*

primitive • *We found a fossil of a primitive bird-like creature.*

early ③ ADVERB

before the arranged or expected time • *We left early so we wouldn't have to queue.*

ahead of time • *The bus always arrives ahead of time.*

beforehand • *If you'd let me know beforehand, you could have come with us.*

in advance • *You need to book in advance to get a good seat.*

in good time • *We arrived at the airport in good time.*

prematurely • *men who go prematurely bald*

earn ① VERB

to get money in return for doing work • *He earns a lot more than I do.*

bring in • *My job brings in just enough to pay the bills.*

draw • *I draw a salary, so I can afford to run a car.*

get • *How much do you get if you're a lorry driver?*

make • *She makes a lot of money.*

obtain • *the profits obtained from buying and selling shares*

earn ② VERB

to receive something that you deserve • *He earned the respect of his troops.*

acquire • *She has acquired a reputation as a liar and a cheat.*

attain (FORMAL) • *He finally attained his pilot's licence.*

win • *She won the admiration of all her colleagues.*

earth ① NOUN

the planet on which we live • *the tallest mountain on earth*

globe • *from every corner of the globe*

planet • *the effects of pollution on the atmosphere of our planet*

world • *the first person to cycle round the world*

RELATED WORD:
• ADJECTIVE terrestrial

earth ② NOUN

soil from the ground • *He filled a pot with earth and popped the seeds in it.*

clay • *lumps of clay that stuck to his boots*

dirt • *kneeling in the dirt*

ground • *digging potatoes out of the ground*

soil • *We planted some bulbs in the soil around the pond.*

ease ① NOUN

lack of difficulty or worry • *He passed his driving test with ease.*

leisure • *living a life of leisure*

relaxation • *The town has a feeling of relaxation and tranquillity about it.*

simplicity • *The simplicity of the new scheme has made it popular with motorists.*

ease ② VERB

to make or become less severe or intense • *The doctor gave him another injection to ease the pain*

abate • *By morning the storms had abated.*

calm • *The government is taking steps to calm the situation.*

relax • *He relaxed his grip on the axe and smiled.*

relieve • *The pills will help relieve the pain for a while.*

slacken • *Her grip on the rope slackened and she fell back.*

ease ③ VERB

to move slowly or carefully • *He eased the door open and peered outside.*

creep • *The car crept down the ramp.*

edge • *I edged the van slowly back into the garage.*

guide • *Bob guided the plane out onto the tarmac.*

inch • *The ambulance inched its way through the crowds of shoppers.*

lower • *He lowered himself into the armchair.*

manoeuvre • *We attempted to manoeuvre his canoe towards the shore.*

squeeze • *They squeezed him into his seat and strapped him in.*

easy ① ADJECTIVE

able to be done without difficulty • *The software is very easy to install.*

light • *a few light exercises to warm up*

painless • *Finding somewhere to stay was pretty painless in the end.*

simple • *All you have to do is answer a few simple questions.*

smooth • *a smooth changeover to the new system*

straightforward • *The route is fairly straightforward so you shouldn't need a map.*

ANTONYM:
• hard

easy ② ADJECTIVE

comfortable and without worries • *He has not had an easy life.*

carefree • *a carefree summer spent on the beach*

comfortable • *a comfortable teaching job at a small private school*

leisurely • *a leisurely weekend spent with a few close friends*

quiet • *a quiet weekend in the sun*

relaxed • *It's very relaxed here, you can do what you like.*

eat ① VERB

to chew and swallow food • *For lunch he ate a cheese sandwich.*

▶ see Word Study **eat**, page 708

eat ② VERB

to have a meal • *We like to eat early.*

breakfast (FORMAL) • *Some hotel guests like to breakfast in their rooms.*

dine (FORMAL) • *We usually dine at about six.*

feed • *Leopards only feed when they are hungry.*

have a meal • *We could have a meal at Pizza Palace after the film.*

lunch (FORMAL) • *We lunched at El Greco's.*

picnic • *After our walk, we picnicked by the river.*

eat away VERB

to destroy something slowly
• The front of the car had been eaten away by rust.
corrode • buildings corroded by acid rain
destroy • Areas of the coast are being destroyed by the sea.
dissolve • Chemicals in the water are dissolving the bridge.
erode • the floods that erode the dry, loose soil
rot • Too many sweets will rot your teeth.
wear away • The weather soon wears away the paintwork.

eccentric ① ADJECTIVE

regarded as odd or peculiar
• His maths teacher was considered a bit eccentric.
bizarre • He's quite a bizarre character.
outlandish • His outlandish behaviour sometimes put people off.
quirky • a quirky, delightful film that is full of surprises
strange • his strange views about UFOs
weird • His taste in music is a bit weird.
whimsical • a whimsical elderly gentleman

eccentric ② NOUN

someone who is regarded as odd or peculiar • He's always been regarded as a bit of an eccentric.
character (INFORMAL) • a well-known character who lived in Johnson Street

crank • People regarded vegetarians as cranks in those days.

economic ① ADJECTIVE

concerning the way money is managed • the need for economic reforms
budgetary • a summit meeting to discuss various budgetary matters
commercial • a purely commercial decision
financial • The financial pressures on the government are mounting.

economic ② ADJECTIVE

making a profit • goods that happen to be economic to produce
productive • the need to make these industries more productive
profitable • a new venture that has proved highly profitable
viable • businesses that are no longer viable

economical ① ADJECTIVE

cheap to use and saving you money • Our car may not be fast, but it's very economical.
cheap • This isn't a very cheap way of buying stationery.
cost-effective • the most cost-effective way of shopping
economic • the most economic way to see the museum
inexpensive • There are several good inexpensive restaurants in town.

economical ② ADJECTIVE

careful and sensible with money or materials • He's neve

been very economical about
housekeeping.
careful • She's very careful with
her pocket money.
frugal • his frugal lifestyle
prudent • the prudent use of
precious natural resources
thrifty • My mother was very
thrifty because she had so little
spare cash.

economy NOUN
the careful use of things to
save money • improvements in
the fuel economy of new cars
frugality (FORMAL) • We must
live with strict frugality if we are
to survive.
prudence • A lack of prudence
could seriously affect his
finances.
restraint • We need to exercise
some restraint in our spending.
thrift • He was widely praised
for his thrift and imagination.

ecstasy NOUN
extreme happiness • his feeling
of ecstasy after winning the
medal
bliss • husband and wife living
together in bliss and harmony
delight • He squealed with
delight when we told him.
elation • His supporters reacted
to the news with elation.
euphoria • There was a sense of
euphoria after our election
victory.
exaltation • the mood of
exaltation that affected everyone
joy • her joy at finding him after
so long

rapture • His speech was
received with rapture by a huge
crowd.

edge ① NOUN
the place where something
ends or meets something else
• on the edge of the forest
border • a pillowcase with a lace
border
boundary • The area beyond
the western boundary belongs to
Denmark.
brim • He kept climbing until he
reached the brim of the crater.
fringe • the rundown areas on
the fringes of the city
lip • The lip of the jug was badly
cracked.
margin • standing on the
margin of the land where it met
the water
rim • a large round mirror with a
gold rim
ANTONYM:
• centre

edge ② VERB
to move somewhere slowly
• He edged towards the phone,
ready to grab it if it rang.
creep • The car crept forward a
few feet, then stopped.
inch • The ambulance inched its
way through the crowds.
sidle • A man sidled up to him
and tried to sell him a ticket.

educated ADJECTIVE
having a high standard of
learning • He is an educated,
tolerant and reasonable man.
cultivated • His mother was an
elegant, cultivated woman.

E

cultured • *a cultured man with a wide circle of friends*
intellectual • *He is the intellectual type.*
learned • *He was a scholar, a very learned man.*

education NOUN

the process of learning or teaching • *the importance of a good education*
coaching • *extra coaching to help him pass his exams*
e-learning • *The company wants to encourage staff to take e-learning courses.*
instruction • *All instruction is provided by qualified experts.*
schooling • *He began to wish he'd paid more attention to his schooling.*
training • *His military training was no use to him here.*
tuition • *personal tuition in the basics of photography*

effect NOUN

a direct result of something • *the effect that nutrition has on children*
consequence • *aware of the consequences of their actions*
end result • *The end result of this process is still unclear.*
fruit • *The new software is the fruit of three years' hard work.*
result • *The result of all this uncertainty is that no-one is happy.*
upshot • *The upshot is that we have a very unhappy workforce.*

efficient ADJECTIVE

able to work well without wasting time or energy • *The new hatchback has a much more efficient engine.*
businesslike • *a highly businesslike approach that impressed everyone*
competent • *an extremely competent piece of work*
economic • *The new system is much more economic, and will save millions.*
effective • *effective use of the time we have left*
organised • *Tony seemed very organised, and completely in control of the situation.*
productive • *the need to make farmers much more productive*
ANTONYM:
• inefficient

effort ① NOUN

physical or mental energy • *It took a lot of effort, but we managed in the end.*
application • *His talent, application and energy are a credit to the school.*
energy • *He decided to devote his energy to writing another book.*
exertion • *Is it really worth all the exertion?*
trouble • *It's not worth the trouble.*
work • *All the work I put in has now been wasted!*

effort ② NOUN

an attempt or struggle • *an unsuccessful effort to save the local library*
attempt • *an attempt to obtain an interview with the President*

bid • *a last-minute bid to stop the trial going ahead*

stab (INFORMAL) • *his latest stab at acting*

struggle • *his struggle to clear his name*

elaborate ① ADJECTIVE
having many different parts • *an elaborate research project*

complex • *a complex explanation*

complicated • *a complicated plan of the building's security system*

detailed • *the detailed plans that have been drawn up*

intricate • *an intricate system of levers and pulleys*

involved • *a very involved operation, lasting many hours*

ANTONYM:
• simple

elaborate ② ADJECTIVE
highly decorated • *elaborate wooden carvings*

fancy • *the fancy plasterwork on the ceiling*

fussy • *a rather fussy design*

ornate • *an ornate wrought-iron staircase*

elaborate ③ VERB
to add more information about something • *He promised to elaborate on what had been said last night.*

develop • *Maybe we should develop this idea.*

enlarge • *He was enlarging on proposals made earlier.*

expand • *a view that I will expand on later*

eliminate ① VERB
to get rid of someone or something • *We've eliminated two of the four options so far.*

cut out • *His guilty plea cut out the need for a long, costly trial.*

do away with • *the attempt to do away with nuclear weapons altogether*

eradicate • *Efforts to eradicate malaria seem to be failing.*

get rid of • *Why don't we just get rid of the middlemen altogether?*

remove • *You should try and remove these fatty foods from your diet.*

stamp out • *We need to stamp out this disgusting practice.*

eliminate ② VERB
to beat someone in a competition • *His team was eliminated in the first round.*

knock out • *We were knocked out by the Dutch champions.*

put out • *Decker finally put her fellow American out in the quarter final.*

embarrass VERB
to make someone feel ashamed or awkward • *You always embarrass me in front of my friends!*

disconcert • *The way Anderson was smirking disconcerted her.*

fluster • *Nothing could fluster him.*

humiliate • *How dare you humiliate me like that!*

shame • *Her son's behaviour had upset and shamed her.*

embarrassed ADJECTIVE
ashamed and awkward • *I'm not embarrassed by my early paintings.*
ashamed • *I felt so ashamed I wanted to die.*
awkward • *It was a very awkward occasion.*
humiliated • *A humiliated Mr Stevens admitted that the concert had been cancelled.*
red-faced • *Red-faced executives had to explain this fact.*
self-conscious • *I always feel self-conscious when I'm having my picture taken.*
sheepish • *He looked very sheepish when he finally appeared.*

embarrassment NOUN
shame and awkwardness • *I laughed loudly to cover my embarrassment.*
awkwardness • *the awkwardness of our first meeting*
bashfulness • *Overcome with bashfulness, he lowered his voice.*
humiliation • *the humiliation of having to ask for money*
self-consciousness • *her painful self-consciousness*
shame • *the shame he felt at having let her down*

emergency NOUN
an unexpected and difficult situation • *This is an emergency!*
crisis • *the economic crisis affecting parts of the continent*
pinch • *I don't mind working late in a pinch.*

emit VERB
to give out or release something • *Polly blinked and emitted a long sigh.*
exude • *a plant that exudes an extremely unpleasant smell*
give off • *The fumes it gives off are poisonous, so watch out.*
give out • *The alarm gave out a series of bleeps, then stopped.*
release • *The factory is still releasing toxic fumes.*
send out • *The volcano has been sending out smoke for weeks.*
utter • *He uttered a loud snort and continued eating.*

emphasis NOUN
special or extra importance • *too much emphasis on commercialism*
accent • *In the new government the accent will be on co-operation.*
importance • *There's not enough importance being given to environmental issues.*
prominence • *Crime prevention has to be given more prominence.*
weight • *This adds more weight to the government's case.*

emphasise VERB
to make something seem specially important or obvious • *He emphasised the need for everyone to remain calm.*
accent • *a white dress accented by a coloured scarf*
accentuate • *His shaven head accentuates his round face.*

highlight • *This disaster has highlighted the difficulty faced by the government.*

play up • *He played up his bad-boy image.*

stress • *I would like to stress that we are in complete agreement.*

underline • *This underlines how important the new trade deal really is.*

employ ① VERB

to pay someone to work for you • *Mollison was employed by Mr Darnley as a bodyguard.*

appoint • *We need to appoint a successor to Mr Stevens.*

commission • *He has been commissioned to design a new bridge.*

engage (FORMAL) • *They have finally engaged a suitable nanny.*

hire • *I was hired as a gardener on the estate.*

take on • *the need to take on more workers for the summer*

employ ② VERB

to use something • *the tactics employed by the police*

bring to bear • *We can bring two very different techniques to bear on this.*

make use of • *He makes use of some very long and colourful words.*

use • *the methods used in the investigation*

utilise • *Engineers will utilise a range of techniques to improve the signal.*

employee NOUN

someone who is paid to work

for someone else • *the way they look after their employees*

hand • *He's been working as a farm hand down south.*

worker • *Workers at the plant have been laid off.*

workman • *A council workman finally arrived to fix the door.*

employer NOUN

someone that other people work for • *a meeting with her employer to discuss the issue*

boss • *My boss has always been very fair.*

gaffer (INFORMAL) • *You'll need to speak to the gaffer about that.*

employment NOUN

the fact of employing people • *the employment of children to work in shops*

engagement • *the engagement of suitable staff*

enlistment • *Enlistment in the armed forces is falling.*

hiring • *The hiring of new staff is our top priority.*

recruitment • *new policies on recruitment and training*

taking on • *The taking on of extra staff would make life a lot easier.*

empty ① ADJECTIVE

having no people or things in it • *The roads were empty.*

bare • *When she got there, the cupboard was bare.*

blank • *all the blank pages in his diary*

clear • *The runway must be kept clear at all times.*

deserted • *By nightfall, the square was deserted.*

unfurnished • *The flat was unfurnished when we moved in.*
uninhabited • *The house has remained uninhabited since she moved out.*
vacant • *two vacant lots on the industrial estate*

ANTONYM:
• full

empty ② ADJECTIVE
boring or without value or meaning • *My life is empty without him.*
inane • *a series of inane remarks*
meaningless • *the feeling that his existence was meaningless*
worthless • *a worthless film with nothing to say about anything*

empty ③ VERB
to remove people or things • *He emptied all the cupboards before Tony arrived.*
clear • *The police cleared the building just in time.*
drain • *She drained the bottles and washed them out.*
evacuate • *Fortunately the building had been evacuated.*
unload • *It only took twenty minutes to unload the van.*

ANTONYM:
• fill

enclose VERB
to surround a thing or place completely • *The book arrived enclosed in a red plastic bag.*
encircle • *The area had been encircled by barbed wire.*
fence off • *We decided to fence off the land.*

hem in • *We were hemmed in by walls and hedges.*
surround • *the low wall that surrounded the rose garden*
wrap • *Wrap the chicken in foil and bake it in a medium oven.*

encourage ① VERB
to give someone confidence • *We were very encouraged by the response.*
cheer • *This news cheered us all and helped us keep going.*
hearten • *I am heartened to hear that.*
reassure • *He always reassures me when I'm feeling down.*

ANTONYM:
• discourage

encourage ② VERB
to support a person or activity • *the need to encourage people to be sensible*
aid • *I tried to aid his creative efforts.*
boost • *Efforts to boost investment seem to be succeeding.*
favour • *conditions which favour growth in the economy*
help • *policies aimed at helping small businesses*
incite • *He incited his followers to break the law.*
support • *Rowe will support me in this campaign.*

end ① NOUN
the last part of a period or event • *the end of the 20th century*
climax • *the dramatic climax of the trial*

close • *the close of the festival*
conclusion • *the conclusion of this fascinating tale*
culmination • *the remarkable culmination of a glittering career*
ending • *the ending of a great era*
expiry • *the expiry of his period of training*
finale • *a grand finale to the week-long celebrations*
finish • *a disappointing finish to our adventures*

ANTONYM:
• beginning

RELATED WORDS:
• ADJECTIVES final, terminal, ultimate

end ② NOUN
the furthest point of something • *the room at the end of the corridor*
boundary • *We worked along the boundaries of the paths.*
bounds • *the landscape beyond the bounds of London*
edge • *the edge of the cliff*
extremity • *the western extremity of the continent*
limit • *an area outside the official city limits*
margin • *agricultural regions well beyond the forest margin*

end ③ NOUN
the purpose for which something is done • *The factory was closed down for political ends.*
aim • *groups united by a common aim*
goal • *We're all working towards the same goal.*

intention • *He concealed his real intentions.*
object • *the stated object of the mission*
objective • *the objective of all this effort*
purpose • *the true purpose of their visit*
reason • *Are you here on holiday, or for business reasons?*

end ④ VERB
to come or bring to a finish • *talks being held to end the fighting*
bring to an end • *The treaty brought to an end fifty years of conflict.*
cease • *By one o'clock the storm had ceased.*
conclude • *The evening concluded with the usual speeches.*
finish • *waiting for the film to finish*
stop • *When is it all going to stop?*
terminate (FORMAL) • *the decision to terminate their contract*

ANTONYM:
• begin

endanger VERB
to put someone or something in danger • *a dispute that could endanger the peace talks*
compromise • *We will not allow safety to be compromised.*
jeopardise • *a scandal that could jeopardise his government*
put at risk • *those who were put at risk by her stupidity*

risk • He is risking the lives of others.

threaten • A breakdown in this system could threaten the whole project.

endure ① VERB
to experience something difficult • He had to endure hours of discomfort.

cope with • We've had a lot to cope with in the last few weeks.

experience • The company has experienced heavy financial losses.

go through • having to go through the public humiliation of a court case

stand • I don't know how he stood it for so long.

suffer • Steven has suffered years of pain from arthritis.

endure ② VERB
to continue to exist • Our friendship has endured through everything.

last • a car that is built to last

live on • His name will live on as an inspiration to others.

remain • When all the rest is forgotten, this fact will remain.

survive • the few traces of their civilisation that have survived

enemy NOUN
someone who is against you • She has many enemies in the government.

adversary • face to face with his old adversary

antagonist • He killed his antagonist in a duel.

foe • He plays Dracula's foe, Dr. Van Helsing.

opponent • Her political opponents will be delighted at this news.

ANTONYM:
• friend

energetic ADJECTIVE
full of energy • an able, energetic and very determined politician

animated • an animated conversation about politics and sport

dynamic • a dynamic and ambitious businessman

indefatigable • trying to keep up with their indefatigable boss

spirited • a spirited defence of his new tax proposals

tireless • a tireless campaigner for the homeless

vigorous • a vigorous campaign

energy NOUN
the ability and strength to do things • I'm saving my energy for tomorrow.

drive • a man with immense drive and enthusiasm

life • At 96, she's still as full of life as ever.

spirit • Despite trailing 6-2, they played with a lot of spirit.

strength • She put all her strength into finding a new job.

vigour • They returned to their work with renewed vigour.

vitality • a woman with considerable charm and endless vitality

enjoy VERB
to find pleasure in something • I haven't enjoyed a film as much as that in ages!

appreciate • *people who don't appreciate classical music*

delight in • *He delights in playing practical jokes.*

like • *Kirsty likes scuba diving.*

love • *He loves skiing.*

relish • *She relished the opportunity to get back at him.*

revel in • *Stevens was revelling in the attention.*

take pleasure from • *He took no pleasure from the knowledge that he had won.*

take pleasure in • *She seemed to take pleasure in my discomfort.*

enlarge VERB

to make something larger
• *plans to enlarge the 30,000-seat stadium*

add to • *We've decided to add to this house rather than move again.*

expand • *If we want to stay in business, we need to expand.*

extend • *They extended the house by adding a conservatory.*

increase • *They have increased the peace-keeping force to 2000.*

magnify • *A more powerful lens will magnify the image.*

enlarge on VERB

to give more information about something • *I'd like you to enlarge on that last point.*

develop • *Maybe I should develop this idea a little bit further.*

elaborate on • *He refused to elaborate on what he had said earlier.*

expand on • *an idea that I will expand on later*

enormous ADJECTIVE

very large in size or amount
• *an enormous dust cloud*

colossal • *a colossal waste of public money*

gigantic • *The road is bordered by gigantic rocks.*

huge • *Several painters were working on a huge piece of canvas.*

immense • *an immense cloud of smoke*

massive • *The scale of the problem is massive.*

tremendous • *I felt a tremendous pressure on my chest.*

vast • *vast stretches of land*

ANTONYM:
• tiny

ensure VERB

to make sure about something • *We must ensure that this never happens again.*

guarantee • *Further investment should guarantee that profits will rise.*

make certain • *to make certain that he'll get there*

make sure • *I will personally make sure that the job gets done.*

enterprise ① NOUN

a business or company • *a small enterprise with a high turnover*

business • *a medium-sized business*

company • *a company that was doing very well*

concern • *It's not a large concern, but it makes a profit.*
establishment • *a modest establishment dedicated to sailing*
firm • *a clothing firm*
operation • *a one-man operation*

enterprise ② NOUN
a project or task • *a risky enterprise such as horse breeding*
effort • *her latest fund-raising effort for cancer research*
endeavour • *an endeavour that was bound to end in failure*
operation • *He'd set up a small mining operation.*
project • *a project that will attract a lot of media attention*
undertaking • *This undertaking will rely on the hard work of our volunteers.*
venture • *a venture that few were willing to invest in*

entertain VERB
to keep people amused or interested • *things that might entertain children in the school holidays*
amuse • *She amused us all evening, singing and telling jokes.*
charm • *He charmed Mrs Nisbet with his tales of life on the road.*
delight • *a routine that will delight everyone*
enthral • *She enthralled audiences all over Europe.*
please • *He certainly knows how to please a crowd.*

entertainment NOUN
enjoyable activities • *Their main form of entertainment is the TV.*

amusement • *looking for some amusement on a Saturday night*
enjoyment • *We need a bit of enjoyment to cheer us up.*
fun • *It's not really my idea of family fun.*
pleasure • *Hours of pleasure can be had with a pack of cards.*
recreation • *a healthy and enjoyable form of recreation*

enthusiasm NOUN
eagerness and enjoyment in something • *We were disappointed by their lack of enthusiasm.*
eagerness • *He could barely contain his eagerness.*
excitement • *Her excitement got the better of her.*
interest • *He doesn't show much interest in football.*
keenness • *I don't doubt his keenness, it's his ability that worries me.*
warmth • *He greeted us with his usual warmth and affection.*

enthusiastic ADJECTIVE
showing great excitement and eagerness for something • *He was very enthusiastic about the new scheme.*
ardent • *one of the government's most ardent supporters*
avid • *an avid reader*
devoted • *a devoted Star Trek fan*
eager • *He is eager to learn more about computers.*
excited • *We are very excited about getting a new dog.*

keen • *Dave is a keen angler.*

passionate • *a passionate opponent of the government*

ANTONYM:
• apathetic

entrance ① NOUN
the way into a particular place • *I met Barry at the entrance to the station.*

door • *She was waiting by the front door.*

doorway • *the mass of people blocking the doorway*

entry • *Kevin had been hanging round the back entry for hours.*

gate • *the security guard at the main gate*

way in • *Is this the way in to the hospital?*

entrance ② NOUN
a person's arrival somewhere • *She had failed to notice her father's entrance.*

appearance • *She had timed her appearance at the dinner to perfection.*

arrival • *journalists awaiting the arrival of the team*

entry • *He was arrested on his entry into Mexico.*

entrance ③ NOUN
the right to enter somewhere • *He gained entrance to the hotel where the band were staying.*

access • *We were denied access to the stadium.*

admission • *no admission without a ticket*

entry • *I was unable to gain entry to the meeting.*

entrance ④ VERB
to amaze and delight someone • *The audience was entranced by her voice.*

bewitch • *Young Gordon's smile bewitched everyone.*

captivate • *I was captivated by her piercing blue eyes.*

charm • *He charmed Mr Darnley and made him feel young again.*

delight • *a new album that will delight her many fans*

enthral • *Audiences were enthralled by his spectacular stage act.*

fascinate • *She never failed to fascinate him.*

entry ① NOUN
a person's arrival somewhere • *her dramatic entry*

appearance • *She made her appearance to tumultuous applause.*

arrival • *He apologised for his late arrival.*

entrance • *My entrance was spoiled when I tripped over the carpet.*

entry ② NOUN
the way into a particular place • *He was hanging around at the entry to the station.*

door • *I'll meet you at the front door.*

doorway • *A bicycle was blocking the doorway.*

entrance • *The parcel had been left outside the entrance to the building.*

gate • *Guards were posted at the main gate.*

way in • *I can't find the way in.*

e

E

entry ③ NOUN

something that has been written down • *the final entry in his journal*

item • *A number of interesting items appear in his diary.*

note • *He grunted and made a note in his pocket book.*

record • *There is no record for 13 October in the log book.*

envy ① NOUN

a feeling of resentment about what someone else has • *his feelings of envy towards Kevin*

jealousy • *the jealousy people felt towards him because of his money*

resentment • *All the anger, bitterness and resentment suddenly melted away.*

envy ② VERB

to want something that someone else has • *I don't envy you one bit.*

be envious • *people who were envious of her good fortune*

begrudge • *Surely you don't begrudge me one night out.*

be jealous • *I couldn't help being jealous when I knew he had won.*

covet • *She coveted his job.*

resent • *Anyone with money was resented and ignored.*

equal ① ADJECTIVE

the same in size, amount or value • *equal numbers of men and women*

equivalent • *A kilogram is equivalent to 2.2 pounds.*

identical • *glasses containing identical amounts of water*

the same • *different areas of research that have the same importance*

equal ②: equal to ADJECTIVE

having the necessary ability for something • *She was equal to any task they gave her.*

capable of • *I'm no longer capable of this kind of work.*

up to • *He said he wasn't up to a long walk.*

equal ③ VERB

to be as good as something else • *a time that equalled the European record*

be equal to • *The final score is equal to his personal best.*

match • *able to match her previous time for the 100m*

equip VERB

to supply someone with something • *The boat was equipped with an outboard motor.*

arm • *The children arrived armed with a range of gardening tools.*

endow • *The male bird is endowed with a vicious-looking beak.*

fit out • *the amount spent on fitting out their offices*

provide • *We provided them with waterproofs and sandwiches.*

supply • *They supplied us with camping gear and a stove.*

equipment NOUN

the things you need for a particular job • *a shed full of gardening equipment*

apparatus • *All the firefighters were wearing breathing apparatus.*
gear (INFORMAL) • *Police in riot gear have sealed off the area.*
paraphernalia • *all the paraphernalia of the courtroom*
stuff • *The builders had left all their stuff in the garden.*
tackle • *Martin kept all his fishing tackle in the spare room.*

erode VERB
to wear something away and destroy it • *The cliffs were being eroded by the constant pounding of the sea.*
corrode • *buildings corroded by acid rain*
destroy • *ancient monuments destroyed by pollution*
deteriorate • *The tapestry had deteriorated badly where the roof was leaking.*
disintegrate • *Once they were exposed to light the documents rapidly disintegrated.*

err VERB
to make a mistake • *The builders had erred considerably in their original estimate.*
blunder • *Fletcher had obviously blundered.*
go wrong • *We must have gone wrong somewhere in our calculations.*
make a mistake • *Okay, I made a mistake, I'm only human.*
miscalculate • *They miscalculated, and now they're in deep trouble.*

error NOUN
a mistake • *a mathematical error*

blunder • *He made a tactical blunder by announcing his intentions.*
fault • *It is a fault to think you can learn how to manage people in business school.*
lapse • *a serious security lapse*
mistake • *spelling mistakes*
slip • *We must be careful – we can't afford any slips.*

escape ① VERB
to manage to get away • *Three prisoners who escaped have given themselves up.*
break free • *He was handcuffed to his bed, but somehow managed to break free.*
break out • *two prisoners who broke out of the maximum security wing*
get away • *She got away from her guards.*
make your escape • *We made our escape down a drainpipe using knotted sheets.*
run away • *I called him but he just ran away.*
run off • *The children ran off when they spotted me.*

escape ② VERB
to manage to avoid something • *He was lucky to escape injury.*
avoid • *She has managed to avoid arrest so far.*
dodge • *He dodged his military service by pretending to be ill.*
duck • *a pathetic attempt to duck her responsibilities*
elude • *He managed to elude the police for 13 years.*

escape • *He has now been charged with evading tax.*

escape ③ NOUN
something that distracts you from something unpleasant • *Cycling gives me an escape from the routine of work.*
distraction • *a distraction from his troubles*
diversion • *a pleasant diversion from my studies*
relief • *The piano provides relief from all the stress.*

essence ① NOUN
the most basic and important part of something • *The essence of good management is the ability to listen.*
core • *the need to get to the core of the problem*
heart • *a problem that reaches to the very heart of the party*
nature • *the nature of what it is to be European*
soul • *a song that captures the soul of this proud nation*
spirit • *the spirit of modern manhood*

essence ② NOUN
a concentrated liquid • *vanilla essence*
concentrate • *orange concentrate*
extract • *lemon extract*

essential ① ADJECTIVE
extremely important • *Good ventilation is essential in a greenhouse.*
crucial • *Her speech was a crucial part of the campaign.*

indispensable • *She has become indispensable to the department.*
vital • *a vital aspect of the plans that everyone has overlooked*

essential ② ADJECTIVE
basic • *an essential part of any child's development*
basic • *the basic laws of physics*
cardinal • *He had broken one of the cardinal rules of business.*
fundamental • *the fundamental principles of democracy*
key • *Mollison had a key role to play in the negotiations.*
main • *an attempt to analyse the main points of his theory*
principal • *the principal idea that underpins their argument*

essentials PLURAL NOUN
the things that are most important • *We only had enough money for the essentials.*
basics • *We need to get back to basics.*
fundamentals • *the fundamentals of road safety*
necessities • *Water, food and shelter are the necessities of life.*
prerequisites • *Self-confidence is one of the prerequisites for a happy life.*
rudiments • *teaching him the rudiments of car maintenance*

esteem NOUN
admiration and respect for another person • *He is held in high esteem by his colleagues.*
admiration • *I have always had the greatest admiration for her.*

estimation • *He has gone down in my estimation.*
regard • *I had a very high regard for him and his work.*
respect • *I have tremendous respect for Dean.*
reverence • *She is still spoken of with reverence by those who knew her.*

estimate NOUN
a guess at an amount, quantity or outcome • *This figure is five times the original estimate.*
appraisal • *an appraisal of your financial standing*
assessment • *assessments of mortgaged property*
estimation • *The first group were correct in their estimation of the man's height.*
guess • *He examined her and made a guess at her temperature.*
quote • *Never agree to a job without getting a quote first.*
reckoning • *By my reckoning we were seven kilometres from the town.*
valuation • *The valuations reflect prices at the end of the fiscal year.*

eternal ADJECTIVE
lasting forever • *the secret of eternal life*
everlasting • *everlasting love*
immortal • *your immortal soul*
unchanging • *the unchanging laws of the cosmos*

even ① ADJECTIVE
flat and level • *I need an even surface to write on.*

flat • *a small hut with a flat roof*
horizontal • *He drew a series of horizontal lines on the paper.*
level • *checking the floor to make sure it was level*
smooth • *the smooth marble floor tiles*
ANTONYM:
• uneven

even ② ADJECTIVE
without changing or varying • *an even flow of liquid*
constant • *The temperature remained more or less constant.*
regular • *her quiet, regular breathing*
smooth • *He caught the ball and passed it in one smooth motion.*
steady • *a steady stream of people*
uniform • *The price rises are not uniform across the country.*

even ③ ADJECTIVE
the same • *At half-time the scores were still even.*
equal • *The two teams shared equal points into the second round.*
identical • *At the end of the contest, our scores were identical.*
level • *The scores were level at half-time.*
neck and neck • *They're still neck and neck with two minutes to go.*

event ① NOUN
something that happens • *still amazed at the events of last week*
affair • *He preferred to forget the whole affair.*

business • *Do you remember that business with Jim?*
circumstance • *due to circumstances beyond our control*
episode • *a rather embarrassing episode at Yvonne's wedding*
experience • *an experience that changed his mind about going to university*
incident • *the incident in the restaurant*
matter • *She doesn't seem to be taking this matter seriously.*

event ② NOUN
a competition • *The next event is the long jump.*
bout • *This is his fifth heavyweight bout in three months.*
competition • *the first competition of the afternoon*
contest • *She's out of the contest for good.*

everyday ADJECTIVE
usual or ordinary • *the drudgery of everyday life*
common • *a common occurrence*
daily • *In our daily life we follow predictable patterns of behaviour.*
day-to-day • *I use a lot of spices in my day-to-day cooking.*
mundane • *the mundane realities of life*
ordinary • *ordinary tableware*
routine • *routine maintenance of the machine*

evident ADJECTIVE
easily noticed or understood • *He spoke with evident emotion about his ordeal.*

apparent • *He spoke with apparent nonchalance about his experience.*
clear • *It became clear that I hadn't convinced Mike.*
noticeable • *a noticeable effect*
obvious • *It's obvious that he doesn't like me.*
palpable • *The tension between Jim and Amy is palpable.*
plain • *It was plain to him that she was destined for great things.*
visible • *the most visible sign of her distress*

evil ① NOUN
the force that causes bad things to happen • *the conflict between good and evil*
badness • *behaving that way out of sheer badness*
immorality • *the immorality that is typical of the arms trade*
sin • *The whole town is a den of sin and corruption.*
vice • *a place long associated with vice and immorality*
wickedness • *the wickedness of his behaviour*
ANTONYM:
• good

evil ② NOUN
something unpleasant or harmful • *a lecture on the evils of overpopulation*
affliction • *Hay fever is an affliction that affects thousands.*
ill • *Many of the nation's ills are his responsibility.*
misery • *the misery of unemployment*

sorrow • *the joys and sorrows of family life*

evil ③ ADJECTIVE
morally wrong or bad • *an utterly evil man*
bad • *He's not a bad man, he's just very unhappy.*
depraved • *a throughly depraved film*
malevolent • *a malevolent influence on the whole school*
sinful • *He is a good person in a sinful world.*
vile • *vile acts of brutality*
wicked • *a senseless and wicked attack*
ANTONYM:
• good

exact ① ADJECTIVE
correct in every detail • *It's an exact reproduction of the first steam engine.*
accurate • *an accurate description of the man*
authentic • *authentic Elizabethan costumes*
faithful • *faithful copies of ancient stone tools*
faultless • *She spoke with a faultless French accent.*
precise • *It's difficult to give a precise date for the painting.*
true • *Is this a true picture of life in the Middle Ages?*
ANTONYM:
• approximate

exact ② VERB (FORMAL)
to demand and obtain something • *They are certain to*
exact a high price for their cooperation.
command • *an excellent surgeon who commanded the respect of all his colleagues*
extract • *to extract the maximum political advantage from this situation*
impose • *the first council to impose a fine for dropping litter*
insist on • *She insisted on conducting all the interviews herself.*
insist upon • *He insists upon good service.*
wring • *attempts to wring concessions from the government*

exactly ① ADVERB
with complete accuracy and precision • *He arrived at exactly five o'clock.*
accurately • *We cannot accurately predict where the missile will land.*
faithfully • *I translated the play as faithfully as I could.*
just • *There are no statistics about just how many people won't win.*
on the dot • *At nine o'clock on the dot, they have breakfast.*
precisely • *No-one knows precisely how many people are in the camp.*
quite • *That wasn't quite what I meant.*
ANTONYM:
• approximately

exactly ② INTERJECTION
an expression implying total agreement • *"We'll never know*

the answer."—"Exactly. So let's stop speculating."
absolutely • "It's worrying, isn't it?"—"Absolutely."
indeed • "That's a topic that's getting a lot of media coverage."—"Indeed."
precisely • "So, you're suggesting we do away with these laws?"—"Precisely."
quite • "It's your choice, isn't it?"—"Quite."

exaggerate VERB
to make things seem worse than they are • He thinks I'm exaggerating, but I'm not!
overdo • I think he's overdoing it a bit when he complains like that.
overestimate • I think we're overestimating their desire to cooperate.
overstate • It's impossible to overstate the seriousness of this situation.

exam NOUN
a test to find out how much you know • a maths exam
examination • a three-hour written examination
oral • I got good marks for my French oral.
test • I failed my history test again.

examination ① NOUN
a careful inspection of something • The Navy is carrying out an examination of the wreck.
analysis • An analysis of the ash revealed traces of lead oxide.

inspection • The police inspection of the vehicle found no fingerprints.
study • A study of the wreckage has thrown new light on the crash.

examination ② NOUN
a check carried out on someone by a doctor • The doctor suggested an immediate examination of his ear.
check • a quick check just to make sure everything's working properly
checkup • my annual checkup at the clinic
medical • He had a medical before leaving England.

examine ① VERB
to look at something very carefully • Police scientists are examining the scene of the crash.
analyse • We haven't had time to analyse all the samples yet.
go over • I'll go over your report tomorrow.
go through • We went through his belongings and found a notebook.
inspect • Customs officials inspected the vehicle.
look over • Once we've looked the house over we should know what caused the fire.
study • Experts are studying the frozen remains of a mammoth.

examine ② VERB
to give someone a medical examination • I was examined by several specialists.
check • Dr Mollison checked my nose and throat.

inspect • *I was inspected twice by Dr Stevens.*
look at • *He said he wanted to look at my chest again just to make sure.*
test • *They tested my eyes but my vision was fine.*

example ① NOUN
something that represents a group of things • *some examples of medieval wood carving*
illustration • *Lo's success is an illustration of how well China is doing.*
sample • *This drawing is a sample of his early work.*
specimen • *I had to submit a specimen of my handwriting for analysis.*

example ② NOUN
something that people can imitate • *His dedication is an example to us all.*
ideal • *a woman who was the American ideal of beauty*
model • *His conduct at the talks was a model of dignity.*
paragon • *She is a paragon of neatness and efficiency.*
prototype • *He was the prototype of the English gentleman.*

excellent ADJECTIVE
extremely good • *It's an excellent book, one of my favourites.*
beaut (AUSTRALIAN AND NEW ZEALAND; INFORMAL) • *a beaut spot to live*
brilliant • *What a brilliant film!*

cracking (BRITISH, AUSTRALIAN AND NEW ZEALAND; INFORMAL) • *You've done a cracking job in the garden!*
fine • *There's a fine view from the bedroom window.*
first-class • *a first-class effort*
great • *He's a great player and we'll be sorry to lose him.*
outstanding • *an outstanding performance*
superb • *a superb craftsman*
ANTONYM:
• terrible

except PREPOSITION
apart from • *I've never been abroad, except for one trip to Paris.*
apart from • *The room was empty apart from one man seated by the fire.*
but • *He didn't speak anything but Greek.*
other than • *She makes no reference to any research other than her own.*
save (FORMAL) • *We had almost nothing to eat, save the few berries and nuts we could find.*
with the exception of
• *Yesterday was a day off for everybody, with the exception of Tom.*

exceptional ① ADJECTIVE
unusually excellent, talented or clever • *Her piano playing is exceptional.*
excellent • *The recording quality is excellent.*
extraordinary • *She is an extraordinary musician.*

outstanding • *an outstanding athlete*
phenomenal • *The performances have been absolutely phenomenal.*
remarkable • *a remarkable achievement*
talented • *He is a talented violinist.*
ANTONYM:
• mediocre

exceptional ② ADJECTIVE
unusual and likely to happen very rarely • *The courts hold that this case is exceptional.*
isolated • *They said the allegations related to an isolated case.*
out of the ordinary • *I've noticed nothing out of the ordinary.*
rare • *those rare occasions when he did eat alone*
special • *In special cases, an exception to this rule may be made.*
unheard-of • *White bread was an unheard-of luxury at that time.*
unusual • *To be appreciated as a parent is unusual.*
ANTONYM:
• common

excess ① NOUN
behaviour that goes beyond what is acceptable • *a life of excess*
extravagance • *Examples of her extravagance were everywhere.*
indulgence • *a moment of sheer indulgence*

excess ② NOUN
a larger amount than necessary • *An excess of houseplants made the room look like a jungle.*
glut • *the current glut of dairy products in Europe*
overdose • *An overdose of sun can lead to skin problems later.*
surfeit • *A surfeit of rich food did not help his digestive problems.*
surplus • *Germany suffers from a surplus of teachers at the moment.*
ANTONYM:
• shortage

excess ③ ADJECTIVE
more than is needed • *problems associated with excess weight*
extra • *Pour any extra liquid into a bowl and set aside.*
superfluous • *all our superfluous belongings, things we don't need*
surplus • *Farmers have to sell off their surplus stock cheap.*

excessive ADJECTIVE
too great • *an excessive reliance on government funding*
exaggerated • *the exaggerated claims made by their supporters*
undue • *the need to avoid undue expense*
unreasonable • *unreasonable increases in the price of petrol*

exchange ① VERB
to give something in return for something else • *We exchanged phone numbers.*

barter • *Traders came from everywhere to barter in the markets.*

change • *Can you change euros for pounds?*

swap • *I wouldn't swap places with her for anything!*

switch • *They switched cars and were away before the alarm was raised.*

trade • *a secret deal to trade arms for hostages*

exchange ② NOUN

the act of giving something for something else • *a ceasefire to allow the exchange of prisoners*

interchange • *a meeting at which the interchange of ideas was encouraged*

swap • *They agreed to a swap and made the necessary arrangements.*

switch • *The switch went ahead as planned.*

trade • *I am willing to make a trade with you.*

excite ① VERB

to make someone feel enthusiastic or nervous • *The idea of visiting America really excited the kids.*

agitate • *I've no idea what has agitated him.*

animate • *There was plenty about this match to animate the capacity crowd.*

thrill • *The reception he got at the meeting thrilled him.*

titillate • *a meal that will titillate the taste buds of every gourmet*

excite ② VERB

to cause a particular feeling or reaction • *The meeting failed to excite strong feelings in anyone.*

arouse • *a move that has aroused deep public anger*

elicit • *His proposal elicited a storm of protest.*

evoke • *The film has evoked a sense of nostalgia in many older people.*

incite • *a few radicals who want to incite trouble*

inspire • *The handling of the new car quickly inspires confidence.*

provoke • *The suggestion has provoked anger.*

stir up • *He's just trying to stir up trouble.*

excited ADJECTIVE

happy and unable to relax • *We are very excited about getting a new dog.*

agitated • *in an excited and agitated state*

enthusiastic • *Tom usually seems very enthusiastic.*

feverish • *a state of feverish anticipation*

high (INFORMAL) • *I was feeling really high after Lorraine's party.*

thrilled • *The children were thrilled when the snow came.*

ANTONYM:
• bored

excitement NOUN

interest and enthusiasm • *The release of his latest film has caused great excitement.*

activity • *a scene of frenzied activity*

adventure • *setting off in search of adventure*

agitation • *He reacted to the news with considerable agitation.*

commotion • *We decided to find out what all the commotion was about.*

enthusiasm • *They greeted our arrival with enthusiasm.*

thrill • *the thrill of scuba diving*

exciting ADJECTIVE
making you feel happy and enthusiastic • *the most exciting race I've ever seen*

dramatic • *Their arrival was dramatic and exciting.*

electrifying • *It was an electrifying performance.*

exhilarating • *an exhilarating walk along the cliff tops*

rousing • *a rousing speech*

stimulating • *It's a stimulating book, full of ideas.*

thrilling • *a thrilling opportunity to watch the lions as they feed*

ANTONYM:
• boring

exclude ① VERB
to decide not to include something • *We cannot exclude this possibility altogether.*

eliminate • *We can eliminate Mr Darnley from our list of suspects.*

ignore • *We cannot afford to ignore this option.*

leave out • *We can narrow it down by leaving out everywhere that's too expensive.*

omit • *His name seems to have been omitted from the list.*

rule out • *The police have already ruled out a retrial.*

ANTONYM:
• include

exclude ② VERB
to stop someone going somewhere or doing something • *The university used to exclude women from all lectures.*

ban • *Tony was banned from driving for three years.*

bar • *She was barred from the tennis club.*

forbid • *Carver was forbidden to attend any of the society's meetings.*

keep out • *We need to keep out troublemakers.*

exclusive ADJECTIVE
available only to a few rich people • *one of Britain's most exclusive golf clubs*

chic • *a chic nightclub in Monaco*

classy • *a very classy restaurant*

posh (INFORMAL) • *She took me to a posh hotel to celebrate.*

select • *a very lavish and very select party*

up-market • *The area is much more up-market than it used to be.*

excuse ① NOUN
a reason or explanation • *Stop making excuses and get on with it!*

explanation • *You'd better have a good explanation for your conduct.*

justification • *What possible justification can there be for this?*
pretext • *His pretext for leaving early was an upset stomach.*
reason • *This gave me the perfect reason for visiting London.*

excuse ② VERB
to forgive someone or someone's behaviour • *Please excuse my late arrival.*
forgive • *Forgive me, I'm so sorry.*
overlook • *the need to overlook each other's failings*
pardon • *Pardon my ignorance, but who is Cliff Hanley?*
turn a blind eye to • *We can't be expected to turn a blind eye to this behaviour.*

exempt ADJECTIVE
excused from a duty or rule • *Teachers were exempt from military service.*
excused • *Some MPs will have been officially excused attendance.*
immune • *Members of the parliament are immune from prosecution.*
not liable • *They are not liable to pay income tax.*

exercise NOUN
activity that keeps you fit • *I need to get more exercise.*
activity • *a bit of physical activity to get the heart going*
exertion • *I'm tired out by all this exertion.*
training • *He needs to do a bit more training before the match.*

work • *I'm doing a lot more work at the gym now I'm feeling better.*

exhaust ① VERB
to make very tired • *I mustn't exhaust myself as I did last time.*
drain • *My emotional turmoil had drained me.*
fatigue • *He is easily fatigued.*
tire out • *a great new job that tires me out*
wear out • *Living out of a suitcase wears you out.*

exhaust ② VERB
to use something up completely • *She has exhausted all my patience.*
consume • *plans which will consume hours of time*
deplete • *chemicals that deplete the earth's protective ozone shield*
run through • *The project ran through its funds in months.*
use up • *The gas has all been used up.*

expand VERB
to make or become larger • *The rails expanded and buckled in the fierce heat.*
develop • *We need to develop the company's engineering division.*
enlarge • *Plans to enlarge the stadium have been approved.*
extend • *We're trying to extend our range of sports wear.*
fill out • *The balloon had filled out and was already almost airborne.*
grow • *The Japanese share of the market has grown dramatically.*

expand on

increase • We will need to increase our overseas operations.
swell • The river had swollen rapidly.
ANTONYM:
• decrease

expand on VERB
to give more information about something • an idea that I will expand on later
develop • You should develop this theme a little bit further.
elaborate on • He refused to elaborate on what he had said earlier.
enlarge on • I'd like you to enlarge on that last point.

expect ① VERB
to believe that something is going to happen • The trial is expected to last several weeks.
anticipate • We do not anticipate any problems.
assume • He assumed that they would wait for him.
believe • Experts believe the comet will pass close to the earth.
imagine • The meal cost more than we had imagined.
presume • I presume they'll be along shortly.
reckon (INFORMAL) • We reckon it'll be a fairly quick journey.
think • I thought the concert would be cancelled.

expect ② VERB
to believe that something is your right • I was expecting to have a bit of time to myself.

demand • a job that demands a lot of time and money
rely on • I'm relying on you to help me.
require • They require a lot of her, maybe too much.

expensive ADJECTIVE
costing a lot of money • a very expensive Italian suit
costly • a costly court case
dear • Those trainers are far too dear.
pricey (INFORMAL) • Medical insurance can be very pricey.
ANTONYM:
• cheap

experience ① NOUN
knowledge or skill in a particular activity • We're looking for someone with engineering experience.
expertise • They lack the expertise to deal with such a complex case.
know-how • Her technical know-how was invaluable.
knowledge • We need someone with knowledge of computing.
training • His military training made the difference between life and death.
understanding • someone with considerable understanding of the law

experience ② NOUN
something that happens to you • a terrifying experience that she still talks about
adventure • a series of hair-raising adventures during the war

affair • *He seemed keen to forget the affair and never discussed it.*
encounter • *his first encounter with poetry*
episode • *The episode has proved deeply embarrassing for her.*
incident • *an incident he would rather forget*
ordeal • *a painful ordeal that is now over*

experience ③ VERB
to have something happen to you • *We are experiencing a few technical problems.*
encounter • *The storms were the worst they had ever encountered.*
have • *We're having a few difficulties with the computer.*
meet • *The next time you meet a situation like this, be careful.*
undergo • *The market is now undergoing a severe recession.*

experienced ADJECTIVE
very skilful as a result of practice • *an experienced diver*
expert • *an expert pilot*
knowledgeable • *He's very knowledgeable in this field.*
practised • *a practised and accomplished surgeon*
seasoned • *a seasoned climber*
well-versed • *He is well-versed in many styles of jazz.*
ANTONYM:
• inexperienced

expert ① NOUN
a skilled or knowledgeable person • *A team of experts will be on hand to offer advice.*

ace (INFORMAL) • *former motor-racing ace Alain Prost*
authority • *an authority on ancient Egypt*
buff (INFORMAL) • *Cliff is a bit of a film buff.*
geek (INFORMAL) • *a new site designed by dog-loving computer geeks*
guru • *fashion gurus who predicted a 70's revival*
master • *He is a master in the art of office politics.*
professional • *He's widely respected in the theatre as a true professional.*
specialist • *a specialist in tropical diseases*
wizard • *a financial wizard who made millions*
ANTONYM:
• beginner

expert ② ADJECTIVE
skilled and knowledgeable • *Mollison's expert approach impressed everyone.*
able • *an able and dedicated surgeon*
adept • *She's an adept guitar player.*
experienced • *She was an experienced traveller and knew the area well.*
knowledgeable • *He's very knowledgeable about Chinese pottery.*
proficient • *Jackson is proficient in several European languages.*
skilful • *the skilful use of light in his early paintings*

skilled • *Ian is a highly skilled photographer.*

explain VERB

to give extra information about something • *He explained to us how the system worked.*

define • *Can you define what you mean by "excessive"?*

describe • *an attempt to describe the whole process*

illustrate • *Let me illustrate this point with an example.*

explanation NOUN

a helpful or clear description • *his lucid explanation of Einstein's theories*

clarification • *Her clarification has done little to help matters.*

definition • *a definition of what we actually mean by "symbolism"*

description • *a fascinating description of how the pyramids were built*

exposition • *the fullest available exposition of Coleridge's ideas*

explode ① VERB

to burst or cause to burst loudly • *the sound of a bomb exploding nearby*

blow up • *Their boat blew up as they slept.*

burst • *Joey blew up the balloon until it burst.*

detonate • *Troops managed to detonate the mine safely.*

go off • *The bomb went off without any warning.*

set off • *No-one knows who planted the bomb, or how it was set off.*

explode ② VERB

to become angry suddenly • *I asked him if he'd finished and he just exploded.*

blow up • *When she finally told him, he blew up and walked out.*

go berserk • *She'll go berserk if she ever finds out.*

go mad • *He went mad when I mentioned the money.*

explode ③ VERB

to increase suddenly and rapidly • *Online sales have exploded.*

rocket • *Inflation has rocketed in the last few months.*

shoot up • *Prices shot up and the shelves were soon empty.*

soar • *Demand for shares in his new company has soared.*

explosion NOUN

a violent burst of energy • *The explosion shattered windows all along the street.*

bang • *A loud bang made me run for cover.*

blast • *Three people were killed in the blast.*

expose ① VERB

to make something visible • *The wreck was exposed by the action of the tide.*

reveal • *The sun rose and revealed a beautiful landscape.*

show • *Replays showed the full extent of her athleticism.*

uncover • *She removed her scar and uncovered her head.*

expose ② VERB

to tell the truth about someone

or something • *He has been exposed as a liar and a cheat.*
bring to light • *The truth will be brought to light eventually.*
reveal • *an investigation that revealed widespread corruption*
show up • *She was finally shown up as a hypocrite.*
uncover • *We uncovered evidence of fraud.*
unearth • *Investigators have unearthed new evidence.*

express ① VERB
to say what you think • *She expressed interest in the plans for the new dam.*
communicate • *People must learn to communicate their feelings.*
couch • *Their demands, though extreme, are couched in moderate language.*
phrase • *It sounds fine, but I would have phrased it differently.*
put • *Absolutely - I couldn't have put it better.*
put across • *the need to put across your message without offending anyone*
voice • *Local people have voiced their concern over plans for a bypass.*

express ② ADJECTIVE
very fast • *a special express delivery service*
direct • *There's also a direct train.*
fast • *delays due to an accident in the fast lane*
high-speed • *the high-speed rail link between London and Paris*

nonstop • *the new nonstop service to New York*

expression ① NOUN
the look on your face that shows your feelings • *an aggrieved expression*
countenance (FORMAL) • *the beaming countenance of the prime minister*
face • *Why are you all wearing such long faces?*

expression ② NOUN
a word or phrase used to communicate • *a good old American expression*
idiom • *the old idiom about carrying coals to Newcastle*
phrase • *What is the origin of the phrase?*
remark • *her passing remark to the camera*
term • *a derogatory term*

extend ① VERB
to have a particular size or position • *The region will extend way beyond the capital.*
continue • *The caves continue for miles beneath the hills.*
hang • *The branches hang down to the ground.*
reach • *a long shirt that reached to her knees*
stretch • *an area of forest stretching as far as the eye could see*

extend ② VERB
to stick out • *a brass peg that extended from the end of the mast*
jut out • *The tip of the island juts out like a finger into the sea.*

project • *the ruins of a fort which projected from the mud*
protrude (FORMAL) • *a huge rock protruding from the surface of the lake*
stick out • *pieces of rough metal that stuck out like spikes*

extend ③ VERB
to make something larger
• *We'd like to extend the house and build a conservatory.*
add to • *They will be adding to their range of children's wear.*
develop • *He developed the US arm of the company.*
enlarge • *plans to enlarge the conference centre*
expand • *an unsuccessful attempt to expand the store's range of footwear*
widen • *the need to widen the appeal of the scheme*

extensive ① ADJECTIVE
covering a large area • *a manor house set in extensive grounds*
broad • *a broad expanse of green lawn*
expansive • *an expansive grassy play area*
large • *a large country estate*
spacious • *a spacious dining area*
sweeping • *The sweeping curve of the bay*
vast • *vast stretches of land*
wide • *Worktops should be wide enough to allow food preparation.*

extensive ② ADJECTIVE
very great in effect • *The blast caused extensive damage.*

comprehensive • *comprehensive television coverage of last week's events*
considerable • *He has considerable powers within the party.*
far-reaching • *a decision with far-reaching consequences*
great • *great changes in British society*
pervasive • *the pervasive influence of the army in national life*
untold • *This might do untold damage to his health.*
widespread • *There is widespread support for the proposals.*

extent NOUN
the length, area or size of something • *The full extent of the losses was revealed yesterday.*
degree • *To what degree were you in control of these events?*
level • *the level of public concern over this issue*
measure • *The full measure of the government's dilemma has become apparent.*
scale • *He underestimates the scale of the problem.*
size • *the size of the task*

extra ① ADJECTIVE
more than is usual or expected • *The company is taking on extra staff for the summer.*
added • *The Tandoori Cottage has the added advantage of being cheap.*
additional • *the need for additional funding*

excess • *If there's any excess sauce, you can freeze it.*
further • *the introduction of further restrictions*
more • *We need three more places at the table.*
new • *the burden of new legislation on top of all the recent changes*
spare • *There are spare blankets in the cupboard.*

extra ② NOUN
something that is not included with other things • *Air conditioning is an optional extra.*
accessory • *the accessories you have to buy to make the place look good*
addition • *the latest addition to the team*
bonus • *The view from the hotel was an added bonus.*

extract ① VERB
to take or get something out of somewhere • *Citric acid can be extracted from orange juice.*
draw • *Villagers still have to draw their water from wells.*
mine • *the finest gems, mined from all corners of the world*
obtain • *Linseed oil is obtained from flax.*
pull out • *I can pull that information out of the database for you.*
remove • *Three bullets were removed from his wounds.*
take out • *I got an abscess so he took the tooth out.*

extract ② VERB
to get information from someone • *He tried to extract further information from the witness.*
draw • *They finally drew a confession from him.*
elicit (FORMAL) • *the question of how far to go to elicit a confession*
get • *How did you get an admission like that out of her?*
glean • *We're gleaning information from all sources.*
obtain • *Police have obtained statements from several witnesses.*

extract ③ NOUN
a small section of music or writing • *an extract from her latest novel*
excerpt • *an excerpt from Tchaikovsky's Nutcracker*
passage • *He read out a passage from his diary.*
reading • *The author treated us to a reading from her latest novel.*
section • *Let's study a section of the text in more detail.*
snatch • *We played them a snatch of a violin concerto.*
snippet • *snippets of popular classical music*

extraordinary ADJECTIVE
unusual or surprising • *He really is an extraordinary man.*
amazing • *What an amazing coincidence!*
bizarre • *It's such a bizarre thing to happen.*
odd • *It's an odd combination of colours.*

singular • *Cathy gave me a smile of singular sweetness.*
strange • *It's a strange piece of music.*
surprising • *A surprising number of candidates turned up late for their interviews.*
unusual • *It's a most unusual way to spend your holiday.*

ANTONYM:
• ordinary

extreme ① ADJECTIVE
very great in degree or intensity
• *those people living in extreme poverty*
acute • *a mistake that caused acute embarrassment for everyone concerned*
deep • *a decision that caused deep resentment*
dire • *He is in dire need of hospital treatment.*
great • *a change in the law that could cause many people great hardship*
intense • *A number of people collapsed in the intense heat that day.*
profound • *feelings of profound shock and anger*
severe • *a business with severe financial problems*

extreme ② ADJECTIVE
unusual or unreasonable
• *I think that's rather an extreme reaction.*
drastic • *Let's not do anything too drastic.*
exceptional • *I think this is an exceptional case.*

excessive • *He was driving at excessive speed.*
extravagant • *All that money being spent on hospitality seemed a bit extravagant.*
radical • *The government is introducing a series of radical economic reforms.*
unreasonable • *I don't think she's being the least bit unreasonable.*

extreme ③ NOUN
the highest or furthest degree or point • *We're just going from one extreme to the other.*
boundary • *the boundaries of artistic freedom*
depth • *the beauty of the countryside in the depths of winter*
end • *There are extremist groups at both ends of the political spectrum.*
height • *His behaviour was the height of bad manners.*
limit • *The ordeal tested the limits of their endurance.*
ultimate • *A Rolls-Royce is the ultimate in luxury.*

Ff

overlook • *The pretty room overlooks a beautiful garden.*

fact NOUN

a piece of information that is true • *a statement of verifiable fact*

certainty • *A general election became a certainty three weeks ago.*

reality • *Fiction and reality became increasingly blurred.*

truth • *In the town, very few know the whole truth.*

ANTONYM:

• lie

factor NOUN

something that helps to cause a result • *Physical activity is an important factor in maintaining fitness.*

aspect • *Exam results illustrate only one aspect of a school's success.*

cause • *Smoking is the biggest preventable cause of death and disease.*

consideration • *Money was also a consideration.*

element • *Fitness has now become an important element in our lives.*

influence • *Van Gogh was a major influence on the development of modern painting.*

part • *Respect is a very important part of any relationship.*

factory NOUN

a building where goods are made • *He owned furniture factories in several areas.*

face ① NOUN

the front part of the head • *A strong wind was blowing in my face.*

countenance (FORMAL) • *He met each enquiry with an impassive countenance.*

features • *Her features were strongly defined.*

mug (SLANG) • *He managed to get his ugly mug on the telly.*

face ② NOUN

a surface or side of something • *the north face of Everest*

aspect • *The house had a south-west aspect.*

exterior • *The exterior of the building was made of brick.*

front • *There was a large veranda at the front of the house.*

side • *narrow valleys with steep sides*

surface • *tiny waves on the surface of the water*

face ③ VERB

to look towards something or someone • *a room that faces on to the street*

be opposite • *I was opposite her at the breakfast table.*

look at • *She turned to look at the person who was speaking.*

mill • *a textile mill*
plant • *The plant produces most of the company's output.*
works • *the steel works*

fade VERB

to make or become less intense • *The fabric had faded in the bright sunlight.*
die away • *The sound died away gradually.*
dim • *The house lights dimmed.*
discolour • *Exposure to bright light can cause wallpaper to discolour.*
dull • *Repeated washing had dulled the bright finish.*
wash out • *This dye won't wash out.*

fail ① VERB

to be unsuccessful • *He failed in his attempt to take over the company.*
be defeated • *The vote to change the law was defeated.*
be in vain • *It became clear that his efforts had been in vain.*
be unsuccessful • *My job application was unsuccessful.*
come to grief • *She realised that all her careful plans had come to grief.*
fall through • *Negotiations with business leaders fell through last night.*
flunk (INFORMAL) • *He flunked all his exams.*
ANTONYM:
• succeed

fail ② VERB

to omit to do something • *They failed to phone her.*

neglect • *They never neglect their duties.*
omit • *He had omitted to tell her of the change in his plans.*

fail ③ VERB

to stop working properly • *The car's brakes had failed.*
crash • *My computer keeps crashing.*
give out • *All machines give out eventually.*
stop working • *The boat came to a halt when the engine stopped working.*

fail ④ VERB

to become gradually less effective • *His eyesight began to fail.*
decline • *His power declined as he grew older.*
deteriorate • *Her health started to deteriorate.*
weaken • *The storm eventually weakened.*

failure ① NOUN

a lack of success • *to end in failure*
breakdown • *a breakdown of the talks between the parties*
collapse • *the collapse of her business empire*
defeat • *It is important not to admit defeat.*
downfall • *people wishing to see the downfall of the government*
ANTONYM:
• success

failure ② NOUN

an unsuccessful person or

thing • *The venture was a complete failure.*

disappointment • *a disappointment to his family*

fiasco • *The evening was a total fiasco.*

flop (INFORMAL) • *The play turned out to be a flop.*

loser (INFORMAL) • *He had always been a loser.*

no-hoper (INFORMAL) • *hanging around a group of no-hopers*

failure ③ NOUN
a weakness in something • *a failure in the insurance system*

deficiency • *a serious deficiency in their defence system*

shortcoming • *The book has many shortcomings.*

faint ① ADJECTIVE
lacking in intensity • *a faint smell of disinfectant*

dim • *dim lighting*

faded • *a faded sign on the side of the building*

indistinct • *The lettering was worn and indistinct.*

low • *She spoke in a low voice.*

muted • *some muted cheers from the gallery*

vague • *a vague memory*

ANTONYM:
• strong

faint ② ADJECTIVE
feeling dizzy and unsteady • *Feeling faint is one of the symptoms.*

dizzy • *suffering from dizzy spells*

giddy • *He felt giddy after the ride.*

light-headed • *She felt light-headed because she hadn't eaten.*

faint ③ VERB
to lose consciousness temporarily • *to faint from shock*

black out • *The blood drained from his head and he blacked out.*

collapse • *I collapsed when I heard the news.*

pass out • *to pass out with pain*

swoon (LITERARY) • *Women in the 1920s swooned over Valentino.*

fair ① ADJECTIVE
reasonable and just • *a fair trial*

equal • *the commitment to equal opportunities*

equitable • *an equitable allocation of resources*

impartial • *an impartial observer*

legitimate • *a legitimate claim to the money*

proper • *It's right and proper that he should be here.*

upright • *an upright and trustworthy man*

ANTONYM:
• unfair

fair ② ADJECTIVE
having light-coloured hair or pale skin • *long fair hair*

blonde or **blond** • *She had blonde tresses.*

light • *He had a light complexion and blue eyes.*

ANTONYM:
• dark

fair ③ NOUN

an outdoor entertainment • *a country fair*

bazaar • *a fundraising bazaar*
carnival • *the annual Antigua Carnival*
exhibition • *an international trade exhibition*
festival • *a rock festival*
fete • *The church fete was a popular attraction.*
show • *an agricultural show*

faith ① NOUN

trust in a thing or a person • *to have great faith in something*
confidence • *He had no confidence in himself at all.*
trust • *His trust in them was misplaced.*

faith ② NOUN

a person's or community's religion • *They believed in the old faith.*
belief • *united by belief*
creed • *open to all, regardless of creed*
persuasion • *people of all religious persuasions*
religion • *Forgiveness is a central idea in most religions.*

faithful ① ADJECTIVE

loyal to someone or something • *a faithful dog*
devoted • *They are devoted to each other.*
loyal • *a sign of true and loyal friendship*
staunch • *a staunch member of the party*
true • *a true believer*

ANTONYM:
• unfaithful

faithful ② ADJECTIVE

accurate and truthful • *The film was faithful to the novel.*
accurate • *an accurate description of the event*
exact • *an exact copy of the original*
strict • *We demand strict adherence to the rules.*
true • *The film was quite true to life.*

fake ① NOUN

a deceitful imitation of a thing or person • *These paintings are fakes.*
copy • *It wasn't real, just a copy.*
forgery • *The signature was a forgery.*
fraud • *Many psychics are frauds.*
imitation • *The "antique" chair is in fact a clever imitation.*
reproduction • *a reproduction of a famous painting*
sham • *The election was denounced as a sham.*

fake ② ADJECTIVE

imitation and not genuine • *fake fur*
artificial • *It's made with artificial sweeteners.*
counterfeit • *a large number o counterfeit documents*
false • *a false passport*
imitation • *bound in imitation leather*
phoney or **phony** (INFORMAL) • *He used a phoney accent.*

ANTONYM:
• real

RELATED WORD:
• PREFIX pseudo-

fake ③ VERB
to pretend to experience
something • *He faked his own
death.*
feign • *to feign illness*
pretend • *Todd shrugged with
pretended indifference.*
simulate • *writhing around in
simulated agony*

fall ① VERB
to descend towards the
ground • *The tile fell from the
roof.*
collapse • *The bridge collapsed
on to the road.*
drop • *hailstones dropping from
the sky*
plunge • *A bus plunged into the
river.*
topple • *He toppled slowly
backwards.*
trip • *She tripped and broke her
leg.*

ANTONYM:
• rise

fall ② VERB
to become lower or less
• *Output fell by more than half.*
decline • *a declining birth rate*
decrease • *The number of
bankruptcies decreased last year.*
diminish • *Resources are
diminishing steadily.*
dwindle • *his dwindling authority*
plummet • *plummeting share
prices*

subside • *The flood waters have
subsided.*

ANTONYM:
• increase

fall ③ NOUN
a reduction in amount • *a fall
in the exchange rate*
decline • *signs of economic
decline*
decrease • *an overall decrease
of 10%*
drop • *the sharp drop in export
sales*
reduction • *The bank announced
a reduction in interest rates.*
slump • *a slump in property prices*

ANTONYM:
• rise

false ① ADJECTIVE
not true or correct • *He gave a
false name and address.*
erroneous (FORMAL) • *to
arrive at an erroneous conclusion*
fictitious • *the source of the
fictitious rumours*
incorrect • *a decision based on
incorrect information*
mistaken • *I had a mistaken
view of what had happened.*
untrue • *The remarks were
completely untrue.*

ANTONYM:
• true

false ② ADJECTIVE
not genuine but intended to
seem so • *false hair*
artificial • *an artificial limb*
bogus • *their bogus insurance
claim*
fake • *a fake tan*

forged • *They crossed the frontier using forged documents.*
simulated • *a simulated display of affection*
ANTONYM:
• genuine
RELATED WORD:
• PREFIX pseudo-

false ③ ADJECTIVE
unfaithful and deceitful • *They turned out to be false friends.*
deceitful • *deceitful and misleading remarks*
disloyal • *He was accused of being disloyal to the company.*
insincere • *A lot of actors are insincere.*
unfaithful • *his unfaithful servant*

fame NOUN
the state of being very well-known • *The film brought him international fame.*
eminence • *to achieve eminence as a politician*
glory • *my moment of glory*
prominence • *He came to prominence with his bestselling novel.*
renown • *a singer of great renown*
reputation • *the city's reputation as a place of romance*

familiar ADJECTIVE
knowing something well • *Most children are familiar with the stories.*
acquainted with • *Peter was well acquainted with Wordsworth.*
aware of • *aware of the dangers of smoking*
knowledgeable about • *They were very knowledgeable about gardening.*
versed in • *She was well versed in company law.*
ANTONYM:
• unfamiliar

family ① NOUN
a group of relatives • *My family are always supportive of me.*
descendants • *Their descendants lived there for centuries.*
relations • *friends and relations*
relatives • *She had relatives in many countries.*
RELATED WORD:
• ADJECTIVE familial

family ② NOUN
a group of related species • *Tigers are members of the cat family.*
class • *several classes of butterflies*
classification • *The classification includes conifers.*
kind • *different kinds of roses*

famous ADJECTIVE
very well-known • *the most famous woman of her time*
celebrated • *his most celebrated film*
distinguished • *a distinguished academic family*
illustrious • *the most illustrious scientists of the century*
legendary • *His skills are legendary.*
noted • *He is noted for his generosity.*

renowned • *The area is renowned for its cuisine.*
ANTONYM:
• unknown

fan NOUN
an enthusiast about something or someone • *a fan of the new band*
adherent (FORMAL) • *The movement was gaining adherents everywhere.*
admirer • *one of her many admirers*
devotee • *a devotee of chamber music*
geek (INFORMAL) • *a real football geek*
lover • *an art lover*
supporter • *rival football supporters*
zealot • *a religious zealot*

fanatic NOUN
someone who is extremely enthusiastic about something • *a football fanatic*
activist • *political activists*
devotee • *a devotee of the movement*
extremist • *groups of religious extremists*
militant • *The militants took over the organisation.*
zealot • *He was a supporter but not a zealot.*

fanatical ADJECTIVE
showing extreme support for something • *a fanatical patriot*
fervent • *a fervent supporter*
obsessive • *obsessive about motor racing*

passionate • *a passionate interest*
rabid • *a rabid warmonger*
wild • *I am wild about this band.*

fancy ① VERB
to want to have or do something • *He fancied a sandwich.*
be attracted to • *I am attracted to the idea of emigrating.*
hanker after • *to hanker after a bigger car*
have a yen for • *She had a yen for some new clothes.*
would like • *I would really like some ice cream.*

fancy ② ADJECTIVE
special and elaborate • *dressed up in fancy clothes*
decorated • *She preferred decorated surfaces to plain ones.*
elaborate • *his elaborate costume ideas*
extravagant • *the extravagant frescoes in the upper church*
intricate • *covered with intricate patterns*
ornate • *an ornate picture frame*
ANTONYM:
• plain

far ① ADVERB
at a great distance from something • *The sea was far below us.*
afar • *seen from afar*
a great distance • *They travelled a great distance.*
a long way • *The guy's lonely and a long way from home.*
deep • *deep into the jungle*
miles • *He lived miles away.*

f

far ② ADVERB
to a great extent or degree
• *far better than the others*
considerably • *The dinners were considerably less formal than before.*
incomparably • *This is an incomparably better book than her first novel.*
much • *I feel much better now.*
very much • *Things got very much worse.*

far ③ ADJECTIVE
very distant • *in the far south of the country*
distant • *the distant horizon*
long • *a long distance from here*
outlying • *The outlying areas are accessible only by air.*
remote • *a cottage in a remote village*
ANTONYM:
• near

fascinate VERB
to be of intense interest to someone • *He was fascinated by the new discovery.*
absorb • *totally absorbed by her career*
bewitch • *Bill was bewitched by her charm.*
captivate • *Her looks captivated the whole world.*
enthral • *She sat enthralled by the actors.*
intrigue • *Her story intrigued them.*

fashion ① NOUN
a popular style of dress or

behaviour • *changing fashions in clothing*
craze • *the latest health craze*
fad • *just a passing fad*
style • *a revival of an old style*
trend • *the current trend in footwear*
vogue • *a vogue for fitness training*

fashion ② NOUN
a manner or way of doing something • *It works in a similar fashion.*
manner • *in a friendly manner*
method • *He did it by his usual method.*
mode • *a different mode of life*
way • *in her usual resourceful way*

fashion ③ VERB
to make and shape something
• *fashioned from rough wood*
construct • *an inner frame constructed from timber*
create • *It was created from odds and ends.*
make • *a doll made from fabric*
mould • *They moulded the cups from clay.*
shape • *Shape the dough into a loaf.*
work • *a machine for working the stone*

fashionable ADJECTIVE
very popular • *a fashionable restaurant*
current • *the current thinking on the subject*
in (INFORMAL) • *Jogging was the in thing.*
latest • *all the latest hairstyles*
popular • *the most popular move*

prevailing • contrary to prevailing attitudes

ANTONYM:
• old-fashioned

fast ① ADJECTIVE
moving at great speed • a fast train

accelerated • at an accelerated pace

hurried • He ate a hurried breakfast.

quick • a quick learner

rapid • a rapid rise through the company

speedy • best wishes for a speedy recovery

swift • as swift as an arrow

ANTONYM:
• slow

fast ② ADVERB
quickly and without delay • You'll have to move fast.

hastily • sheltering in hastily erected tents

hurriedly • students hurriedly taking notes

quickly • She worked quickly and methodically.

rapidly • moving rapidly across the field

swiftly • They had to act swiftly to save him.

ANTONYM:
• slowly

fast ③ ADVERB
firmly and strongly • She held fast to the rail.

firmly • with windows firmly shut

securely • The door was securely locked.

tightly • held tightly in his arms

fasten VERB
to close or attach something • Fasten your seat belts.

attach • He attached a label to the plant.

fix • It was fixed on the wall.

join • joined together by string

lock • a locked door

secure • The chest was secured with a lock and chain.

tie • Tie your shoelaces.

fat ADJECTIVE
weighing too much • a fat man

obese • Avoid becoming obese.

overweight • I'm a bit overweight.

plump • a plump little baby

portly • a portly gentleman

ANTONYM:
• thin

fatal ① ADJECTIVE
causing death • fatal injuries

deadly • a deadly disease

incurable • It was regarded as an incurable illness.

lethal • a lethal dose of poison

mortal • They were in mortal danger.

terminal • terminal illness

fatal ② ADJECTIVE
having an undesirable effect • The mistake was fatal to my plans.

calamitous • a calamitous air crash

catastrophic • The water shortage is potentially catastrophic.

f

disastrous • *This could have disastrous consequences for industry.*

lethal • *a lethal left hook*

fate NOUN
a power believed to control events • *the fickleness of fate*

chance • *a victim of chance*

destiny • *We are masters of our own destiny.*

fortune • *Remember, fortune favours the brave.*

providence • *His death was an act of providence.*

fault ① NOUN
something for which someone is responsible • *It was all my fault.*

blame • *They put the blame on her.*

liability • *The company was forced to admit liability.*

responsibility • *He accepted full responsibility for the error.*

fault ② NOUN
a defective quality in something • *a minor technical fault*

blemish • *a blemish on an otherwise outstanding career*

defect • *a manufacturing defect*

deficiency • *serious deficiencies in the system*

drawback • *The plan had one major drawback.*

failing • *the country's many failings*

flaw • *serious character flaws*

imperfection • *small imperfections on the surface*

weakness • *his one weakness*

ANTONYM:
• strength

fault ③ VERB
to find reasons to be critical of someone • *Her conduct cannot be faulted.*

blame • *I don't blame him.*

censure (FORMAL) • *He was censured by the committee.*

criticise • *The minister criticised the police.*

faulty ADJECTIVE
containing flaws or errors • *Faulty goods should be sent back.*

defective • *a lorry with defective brakes*

flawed • *The test results were seriously flawed.*

imperfect • *an imperfect specimen*

invalid • *That's an invalid argument.*

unsound • *a building that is structurally unsound*

favour ① NOUN
a liking or approval of something • *The proposals met with favour.*

approval • *to gain his father's approval*

esteem • *in high esteem*

grace • *to fall from grace*

support • *They gave us their full support.*

ANTONYM:
• disapproval

favour ② NOUN
a kind and helpful action • *Can you do me a favour?*

courtesy • *the courtesy of a personal response*
good turn • *to do someone a good turn*
kindness • *She did me the kindness of calling.*
service • *a service to your country*

ANTONYM:
• wrong

favour ③ VERB
to prefer something or someone • *They favoured the eldest child.*
prefer • *the preferred candidate*
single out • *He is always being singled out for special treatment.*

favourable ① ADJECTIVE
of advantage and benefit to someone • *favourable conditions*
advantageous • *the most advantageous course of action*
beneficial • *a beneficial effect on our health*
good • *He got a very good deal.*
opportune • *an opportune moment to attack*
suitable • *Conditions were not suitable for life to flourish.*

ANTONYM:
• unfavourable

favourable ② ADJECTIVE
positive and expressing approval • *a favourable response*
affirmative • *to give an affirmative answer*
amicable • *amicable discussions*
approving • *a warm, approving glance*
friendly • *The proposal was given a friendly reception.*

positive • *a positive effect on the situation*
sympathetic • *He got a sympathetic hearing.*
welcoming • *a welcoming atmosphere*

ANTONYM:
• unfavourable

favourite ① ADJECTIVE
being someone's best-liked person or thing • *my favourite hotel*
best-loved • *our best-loved music*
dearest • *Her dearest wish was fulfilled.*
favoured • *the favoured child of elderly parents*
preferred • *his preferred method of exercise*

favourite ② NOUN
the thing or person someone likes best • *The youngest was always her favourite.*
darling • *the spoilt darling of the family*
idol • *the idol of his fans*
pet • *the teacher's pet*
pick • *the pick of the bunch*

favouritism NOUN
unfair favour shown to a person or group • *There was never a hint of favouritism.*
bias • *political bias in broadcasting*
one-sidedness • *The committee must show no one-sidedness.*

ANTONYM:
• impartiality

fear ① NOUN

an unpleasant feeling of danger • *shivering with fear*
alarm • *I looked at him with growing alarm.*
awe • *in awe of his great powers*
dread • *She thought with dread of the coming storm.*
fright • *He jumped with fright at the noise.*
panic • *a moment of panic*
terror • *to shake with terror*

fear ② VERB

to feel frightened of something • *There is nothing to fear.*
be afraid • *The dog was afraid of him.*
be frightened • *I am frightened of thunder.*
be scared • *Are you scared of snakes?*
dread • *He dreaded angry scenes.*
take fright • *The horse took fright at the sudden noise.*

feature ① NOUN

a particular characteristic of something • *an unusual feature of the room*
aspect • *every aspect of our lives*
attribute • *a normal attribute of human behaviour*
characteristic • *their physical characteristics*
mark • *distinguishing marks*
property • *the magnetic properties of iron*
quality • *skills and personal qualities*

feature ② NOUN

a special article or programme • *a news feature*

article • *a travel article*
column • *the advice column*
item • *an item about chemical waste*
piece • *a specially-written piece*
report • *a film report on the scandal*
story • *front-page news stories*

feature ③ VERB

to include and draw attention to something • *featuring an interview with the president*
emphasise • *to emphasise their differences*
give prominence to • *The Times is alone in giving prominence to the visit.*
spotlight • *a book spotlighting female singers*
star • *starring a major Australian actor*

feel ① VERB

to experience emotionally • *I felt enormous happiness.*
experience • *They seem to experience more distress than the others.*
suffer • *suffering from pangs of conscience*
undergo • *to undergo a change of heart*

feel ② VERB

to believe that something is the case • *She feels she is in control of her life.*
believe • *I believe they are right.*
consider • *We consider them to be our friends.*
deem • *I deemed it best to cancel the party.*

judge • *She was judged to be capable of anything.*
think • *I think I am very lucky.*

feel ③ VERB
to touch something physically • *Feel this lovely material!*
finger • *He was fingering the coins in his pocket.*
fondle • *She fondled the dog's ears.*
stroke • *I stroked the smooth wooden surface.*
touch • *He touched my face.*

feeling ① NOUN
an emotional reaction to something • *He spoke with real feeling.*
emotion • *trembling with emotion*
fervour • *religious fervour*
heat • *He spoke with some heat about his experiences.*
passion • *She argued with great passion.*

feeling ② NOUN
a physical sensation • *a feeling of pain*
sensation • *a very pleasant sensation*
sense • *a slight sense of heat at the back of my throat*

feeling ③ NOUN
an opinion on something • *strong feelings on politics*
inclination • *neither the time nor the inclination*
opinion • *a consensus of opinion*
point of view • *an unusual point of view on the subject*
sentiment • *I'm afraid I don't share your sentiments.*

view • *Make your views known.*

fellowship ① NOUN
a feeling of friendliness within a group • *a sense of community and fellowship*
brotherhood • *a symbolic act of brotherhood*
camaraderie • *the camaraderie among soldiers*
companionship • *the companionship between old friends*

fellowship ② NOUN
a group of people with a common interest • *a fellowship of writers*
association • *a trade association*
brotherhood • *a secret international brotherhood*
club • *a youth club*
league • *the League of Nations*
society • *the historical society*

female ADJECTIVE
relating to women and girls • *the world's greatest female distance runner*
feminine • *the traditional feminine role*
womanly • *a womanly shape*
ANTONYM:
• male

fertile ADJECTIVE
capable of producing plants or offspring • *fertile soil*
fruitful • *The fruitful earth gave forth its treasures.*
productive • *the most productive vineyards*
prolific • *Chinchillas are prolific breeders.*

rich • *This plant grows in moist rich ground.*

ANTONYM:
• barren

fervent ADJECTIVE
showing sincere and enthusiastic feeling • *a fervent admirer of her work*
ardent • *one of the most ardent supporters of the policy*
committed • *a committed socialist*
devout • *She was a devout Christian.*
enthusiastic • *a huge and enthusiastic crowd*
impassioned • *an impassioned appeal for peace*
passionate • *I'm a passionate believer in public art.*
zealous • *He was a recent convert, and very zealous.*

festival ① NOUN
an organised series of events • *an arts festival*
carnival • *The carnival lasted for three days.*
entertainment • *theatrical entertainments*
fair • *The book fair attracted many visitors.*
fete • *a church fete*
gala • *the May Day gala*

festival ② NOUN
a day or period of religious celebration • *open except on days of religious festivals*
anniversary • *The anniversary is celebrated each spring.*
holiday • *the Easter holiday*

CHRISTIAN FESTIVALS
Advent
Ascension Day
Ash Wednesday
Candlemas
Christmas
Corpus Christi
Easter
Epiphany
Good Friday
Lent
Maundy Thursday
Michaelmas
Palm Sunday
Pentecost
Quadragesima
Shrove Tuesday
Trinity
Whitsun

JEWISH FESTIVALS
Feast of Tabernacles
Hanukkah, Hanukah or Chanukah
Passover or Pesach
Purim
Rosh Hashanah
Shavuot, Shabuoth or Pentecost
Sukkoth or Succoth
Yom Kippur or Day of Atonement

HINDU FESTIVALS
Diwali
Durga-puja
Dussehra
Ganesh Chaturthi
Holi
Janmashtami
Navaratri
Raksha Bandhan
Ramanavami
Sarasvati-puja

MUSLIM FESTIVALS
Al Hijrah
Ashura
Eid-ul-Adha or Id-ul-Adha
Eid-ul-Fitr or Id-ul-Fitr
Lailat-ul-Isra' wa'l Mi'raj
Lailat-ul-Qadr
Mawlid al-Nabi
Ramadan

SIKH FESTIVALS
Baisakhi Mela
Diwali Mela
Hola Mohalla Mela
the Gurpurabs

BUDDHIST FESTIVALS
Wesak

few ADJECTIVE
small in number • *a few moments ago*
infrequent • *at infrequent intervals*
meagre • *a society with meagre resources*
not many • *Not many people attended the meeting.*
scanty • *Records are scanty but these documents help build a picture of his life.*
scarce • *Resources are scarce.*
sparse • *a bare landscape with sparse trees*
ANTONYM:
• many

fidget VERB
to move and change position restlessly • *fidgeting in his seat*
fiddle (INFORMAL) • *She fiddled with her pencil.*
jiggle • *He's jiggling his keys.*
squirm • *He squirmed and wriggled with impatience.*

twitch • *Everybody twitched in their seats.*

field ① NOUN
an area of farm land • *a field full of sheep*
green • *on the village green*
meadow • *a grassy meadow*
pasture • *cows grazing in the pasture*

field ② NOUN
a particular subject or interest • *a breakthrough in the field of physics*
area • *a politically sensitive area*
department • *Health care isn't my department.*
domain • *in the domain of art*
province • *This is the province of a different section.*
speciality • *His speciality was mythology.*
territory • *an expert in his own territory of history*

fierce ① ADJECTIVE
wild and aggressive • *a fierce lion*
aggressive • *encouraging aggressive behaviour in later life*
dangerous • *These birds are dangerous.*
ferocious • *two and a half days of ferocious violence*
murderous • *a murderous attack*
ANTONYM:
• gentle

fierce ② ADJECTIVE
very intense • *a fierce contest*
intense • *We found ourselves standing in intense heat.*

keen • *a keen interest in cars*
relentless • *The pressure was relentless.*
strong • *a strong dislike*

fight ① VERB
to take part in a battle or contest • *He fought the world champion.*
battle • *The group had to battle for equal treatment.*
brawl • *young people brawling in the street*
grapple • *grappling with an alligator*
struggle • *He was struggling to pull himself free.*

fight ② NOUN
an aggressive struggle • *a fight to the death*
action • *wounded in action*
battle • *a gun battle*
bout • *a wrestling bout*
combat • *the end of a long combat*
duel • *He was killed in a duel.*
skirmish • *a minor border skirmish*

fight ③ NOUN
an angry disagreement • *a fight with my mother*
argument • *an argument over a boyfriend*
blue (AUSTRALIAN; SLANG) • *a bloke I'd had a blue with years ago*
dispute • *a dispute over ticket allocation*
row • *Maxine and I had a terrible row.*
squabble • *a family squabble over Sunday lunch*

fighter NOUN
someone who physically fights another person • *a tough street fighter*
soldier • *well-equipped soldiers*
warrior • *a brave warrior*

figure ① NOUN
a number, or amount represented by a number • *No one really knows the true figures.*
amount • *Postal money orders are available in amounts up to $700.*
digit • *a code made up of letters and digits*
number • *A lot of marriages end in divorce, but we don't know the exact number.*
numeral • *the numeral six*
statistic • *Official statistics show wages declining by 24%.*
total • *Then he added everything together to arrive at the final total.*

figure ② NOUN
a shape, or the shape of someone's body • *A figure appeared in the doorway.*
body • *A longer skirt gives the illusion of a taller and slimmer body.*
build • *a tall woman with a naturally slim build*
form • *The shadowy form receded into the darkness.*
physique • *He has the physique and energy of a man half his age.*
shape • *tall, dark shapes moving in the mist*
silhouette • *Tuck the shirt in to give yourself a streamlined silhouette.*

figure ③ NOUN
a person • *international political figures*
character • *What a smart character that Nigel is.*
dignitary • *a visiting dignitary of great importance*
person • *My grandfather was a person of some influence.*
personality • *The event was attended by many showbiz personalities.*
player • *a key player in the negotiations*

figure ④ VERB (INFORMAL)
to guess or conclude something • *I figure I'll learn from experience.*
expect • *I expect you're just tired.*
guess • *I guess he's right.*
reckon (INFORMAL) • *Toni reckoned that it must be about three o'clock.*
suppose • *What do you suppose he's up to?*

fill VERB
to make something full • *Fill it up with water.*
cram • *Mourners crammed the small church.*
gorge • *gorged with food*
pack • *a lorry packed with explosives*
stock • *a lake stocked with carp*
stuff • *Stuff the pillow with feathers.*
ANTONYM:
• empty

final ① ADJECTIVE
being the last one in a series
• *the fifth and final day*

closing • *in the closing stages of the race*
concluding • *the concluding part of the serial*
eventual • *the eventual aim of their policies*
last • *his last chance*
ultimate • *The ultimate outcome will be different.*
ANTONYM:
• first

final ② ADJECTIVE
unable to be changed or questioned • *The judges' decision is final.*
absolute • *absolute authority*
conclusive • *conclusive proof*
definite • *too soon to give a definite answer*
definitive • *the definitive account of the war*

finally ① ADVERB
happening after a long time
• *It finally arrived.*
at last • *He came at last.*
at the last moment • *They changed their minds at the last moment.*
eventually • *The flight eventually left.*
in the end • *It all turned out right in the end.*
in the long run • *a success in the long run*

finally ② ADVERB
in conclusion of something
• *Finally, I'd like to talk about safety measures.*
in conclusion • *In conclusion, we have to agree.*

in summary • *It was, in summary, a satisfactory outcome.*
lastly • *Lastly, I would like to thank my agent.*

finance ① VERB
to provide the money for something • *financed by the government*
back • *a fund backed by local businesses*
fund • *The scheme is funded by the banks.*
pay for • *He paid for his trip out of his savings.*
support • *She supported herself through university.*

finance ② NOUN
the managing of money and investments • *the world of high finance*
banking • *the international banking system*
budgeting • *We must exercise caution in our budgeting this year.*
commerce • *industry and commerce*
economics • *the economics of the third world*
investment • *tax incentives to encourage investment*

financial ADJECTIVE
relating to money • *financial difficulties*
economic • *an economic crisis*
fiscal • *the long-term fiscal policy of this country*
money • *on the money markets*

find ① VERB
to discover something • *I can't find my notes.*

come across • *He came across the book by chance.*
discover • *They discovered the bag in the bushes.*
locate • *locating the position of the gene*
track down • *to track down her parents*
turn up • *They failed to turn up any evidence.*
unearth • *to unearth the missing copy*
ANTONYM:
• lose

find ② VERB
to realise or learn something • *We found that we got on well.*
become aware • *I became aware of his work last year.*
detect • *I detected a note of envy in her voice.*
discover • *It was discovered that the goods were missing.*
learn • *I flew from New York on learning of his death.*
realise • *They realised too late that it was wrong.*

fine ① ADJECTIVE
very good and admirable • *fine clothes*
admirable • *with many admirable qualities*
beautiful • *a beautiful view of the river*
excellent • *inns with excellent cuisine*
magnificent • *his magnificent country house*
outstanding • *an area of outstanding natural beauty*

splendid • *a splendid collection of cartoons*

fine ② ADJECTIVE
small in size or thickness • *powder with very fine particles*

delicate • *delicate curtains to let in the light*

lightweight • *certain lightweight fabrics*

powdery • *soft powdery dust*

sheer • *a sheer chiffon shirt*

small • *netting with a small mesh*

fine ③ ADJECTIVE
subtle and precise • *the fine details*

fastidious • *fastidious attention to detail*

keen • *a keen eye for a bargain*

precise • *a gauge with precise adjustment*

refined • *a woman of refined tastes*

sensitive • *The radio had very sensitive tuning.*

subtle • *a very subtle distinction*

finish ① VERB
to complete something • *to finish a report*

close • *They have closed the deal.*

complete • *She completed her first novel.*

conclude • *He concluded his speech.*

end • *That ended our discussion.*

finalise • *to finalise an agreement*

ANTONYM:
• start

finish ② NOUN
the last part of something • *to see it through to the finish*

close • *to bring to a close*

completion • *The project is nearing completion.*

conclusion • *at the conclusion of the programme*

end • *the end of the race*

ending • *The film had an unexpected ending.*

finale • *the grand finale of the evening*

ANTONYM:
• start

finish ③ NOUN
the surface appearance of something • *a glossy finish*

grain • *the smooth grain of the wood*

lustre • *a similar lustre to silk*

polish • *The bodywork had a high polish.*

shine • *It gives a beautiful shine to the hair.*

surface • *a polished surface*

texture • *paper with a linen-like texture*

fire ① NOUN
the flames produced when something burns • *a ball of fire*

blaze • *The firefighters were hurt in the blaze.*

combustion • *Energy is released by combustion.*

flames • *rescued from the flames*

inferno • *The building was an inferno.*

fire ② VERB
to shoot or detonate something
• *to fire a cannon*
detonate • *to detonate an explosive device*
explode • *They exploded a bomb.*
launch • *The protesters launched the missile from a boat.*
set off • *the largest nuclear explosion ever set off on earth*
shoot • *people shooting guns in all directions*

fire ③ VERB (INFORMAL)
to dismiss someone from a job
• *She was fired yesterday.*
discharge • *A trooper has been discharged from the army.*
dismiss • *He was dismissed by the bank.*
make redundant • *Many people were made redundant.*
sack (INFORMAL) • *Jones was sacked for disciplinary reasons.*

firm ① ADJECTIVE
solid and not soft • *Leave the ice cream until it is firm.*
compressed • *compressed wood pulp made into cardboard*
congealed • *a bowl of congealed grease*
hard • *The snow was hard and slippery.*
rigid • *Pour the mixture into a rigid plastic container.*
set • *The glue wasn't completely set.*
solid • *a block of solid wax*
stiff • *egg whites beaten until stiff*
ANTONYM:
• soft

firm ② ADJECTIVE
resolute and determined • *The department needs a firm manager.*
adamant • *He was adamant that he would not resign.*
determined • *She was determined to finish the game.*
inflexible • *his inflexible routine*
resolute • *a willingness to take resolute action*
staunch • *many staunch supporters*
unshakable • *an unshakable belief in democracy*

firm ③ NOUN
a commercial organisation
• *a firm of builders*
business • *a stockbroking business*
company • *his software development company*
corporation • *one of the leading banking corporations*
enterprise • *small business enterprises*
organisation • *a multinational organisation*

first ① ADJECTIVE
done or in existence before anything else • *the first moon landing*
earliest • *The earliest settlers lived there.*
initial • *our initial meeting*
opening • *There was a standing ovation on opening night.*
original • *She was one of the original cast.*
primeval • *the primeval forests of Europe*

ANTONYM:
• last

first ② ADVERB
done or occurring before
anything else • You must do
that first.
beforehand • Bill had prepared
beforehand.
earlier • I did that one earlier.
firstly • Firstly, I'd like to thank
you all for coming.
initially • not as bad as they
initially predicted
to begin with • To begin with,
we must prepare the soil.

first ③ ADJECTIVE
more important than
anything else • our first
responsibility
chief • the chief pilot
foremost • one of our foremost
thinkers
leading • the team's leading
scorer
main • the main tourist area of
Copenhagen
prime • He was the prime
suspect.
principal • the principal reason

first-rate ADJECTIVE
excellent • They were dealing
with a first-rate professional.
excellent • She does an
excellent job as my personal
assistant.
exceptional • Her piano
playing is exceptional.
first-class • The food was
first-class.
marvellous • He certainly is a
marvellous actor.

outstanding • an outstanding
athlete
splendid • We had a splendid
meal.
superb • a superb 18-hole golf
course

fissure NOUN
a deep crack in rock or the
ground • There was a rumbling,
and a fissure opened up.
cleft • a narrow cleft in the rocks
crack • The building developed
large cracks in walls and ceilings.
crevice • a huge boulder with
ferns growing in every crevice
fault • the San Andreas Fault
rift • In the open bog are many
rifts and potholes.
split • The slate has a few small
splits around the edges.

fit ① VERB
to be the right shape or size
• made to fit a child
belong • I just didn't belong
there.
correspond • The two angles
didn't correspond exactly.
dovetail • The movement's
interests dovetailed with her
own.
go • small enough to go in your
pocket
match • Match the pegs with
the holes.

fit ② VERB
to place something in position
• a fitted carpet
adapt • shelves adapted to suit
the smaller books
arrange • Arrange the pieces to
form a picture.

place • *Place the card in the slots.*

position • *plants which are carefully positioned in the alcove*

fit ③ ADJECTIVE
in good physical condition • *a reasonably fit person*

healthy • *a healthy mind in a healthy body*

in good condition • *in good condition for his age*

robust • *a strong, robust man*

trim • *a trim figure*

well • *Alison was looking well.*

ANTONYM:
• unfit

fitting ① ADJECTIVE
appropriate and suitable for something • *a fitting end*

appropriate • *an appropriate outfit for the occasion*

correct • *the correct thing to say*

proper • *It isn't proper that she should be here.*

right • *He always said just the right thing.*

suitable • *some hymns suitable for a wedding*

fitting ② NOUN
a part attached to something else • *fixtures and fittings*

accessory • *bathroom accessories*

attachment • *a wide range of attachments*

component • *special components*

part • *Extra parts can be added later.*

unit • *The unit plugs into any TV set.*

fix ① VERB
to attach or secure something • *fixed to the wall*

attach • *The label was attached with glue.*

bind • *sticks bound together with string*

fasten • *Fasten the two parts securely.*

secure • *firmly secured by strong nails*

stick • *She stuck the pictures into the book.*

fix ② VERB
to repair something broken • *The bike is fixed now.*

correct • *to correct our mistakes*

mend • *They finally got round to mending the roof.*

patch up • *Patch up those holes.*

repair • *I had my shoes repaired.*

fix ③ NOUN (INFORMAL)
a difficult situation • *in a bit of a fix*

difficulty • *He was in real difficulties with money.*

mess • *Their economy was in a mess.*

predicament • *a tricky predicament*

quandary • *in a quandary about what to do*

flabby ADJECTIVE
fat and with loose flesh • *a flabby stomach*

sagging • *a sagging double chin*

slack • *The skin around her eyelids is now slack and baggy.*

ANTONYM:
• taut

flash ① NOUN
a sudden short burst of light
• *a flash of lightning*
burst • *a burst of fire*
flare • *the sudden flare of a match*
sparkle • *sparkles from her sequinned dress*

flash ② VERB
to shine briefly and often repeatedly • *They signalled by flashing a light.*
flare • *matches flaring in the darkness*
glint • *the low sun glinting off the windscreens*
glitter • *the glittering crown on his head*
sparkle • *Diamonds sparkled on her wrists.*
twinkle • *stars twinkling in the night sky*

flashy ADJECTIVE
showy in a vulgar way • *flashy clothes*
flamboyant • *an unsuitably flamboyant outfit*
garish • *curtains in garish colours*
showy • *an expensive and showy watch*
tacky (INFORMAL) • *tacky red sunglasses*
tasteless • *a house with tasteless decor*
ANTONYM:
• modest

flat ① NOUN
a set of rooms for living in • *a two-bedroomed flat*

apartment • *a huge apartment overlooking the park*
rooms • *We shared rooms while we were students.*

flat ② ADJECTIVE
level and smooth • *a flat surface*
horizontal • *horizontal with the ground*
level • *a completely level base*
levelled • *The floor must be levelled before you start.*
smooth • *a smooth marble top*
unbroken • *the unbroken surface of the sea*
ANTONYM:
• uneven

flat ③ ADJECTIVE
without emotion or interest
• *a dreadfully flat speech*
boring • *a boring menu*
dull • *He told some really dull stories.*
insipid • *an insipid performance*
monotonous • *an interesting story expressed in a monotonous voice*
weak • *A weak ending spoiled the story.*

flatter ① VERB
to praise someone insincerely
• *flattering remarks*
compliment • *She was often complimented for her wit.*
fawn • *surrounded by fawning attendants*

flatter ② VERB
to make more attractive
• *clothes that flatter your figure*
enhance • *tinted lenses which enhance your natural eye colour*

f

set off • Blue sets off the colour of your eyes.
suit • That shade really suits your skin tone.

flattery NOUN
flattering words and behaviour • susceptible to flattery
adulation • received with adulation by the critics
fawning • the constant fawning of her courtiers

flaw NOUN
an imperfection in something • The program contained serious flaws.
blemish • A small blemish spoiled the surface.
defect • a manufacturing defect
fault • a fault in the engine
imperfection • slight imperfections in the weave

flee VERB
to run away from something • to flee the country
bolt • He bolted for the exit.
escape • They escaped across the frontier.
fly • to fly from war
leave • to leave the scene of the crime
run away • to run away from the police
take flight • 250,000 took flight from the floods.

flexible ① ADJECTIVE
able to bend or be bent easily • long flexible bristles
elastic • an elastic rope
lithe • lithe and graceful movements

pliable • baskets made from pliable cane
supple • exercises to keep you supple

flexible ② ADJECTIVE
able to adapt or change • flexible working hours
adaptable • an adaptable attitude to work
discretionary • the discretionary powers of the courts
open • an open mind

flinch VERB
to move suddenly with fear or pain • The sharp pain made her flinch.
cringe • to cringe in terror
shrink • She shrank from the flames.
start • They started at the sudden noise.
wince • I could see him wincing with pain.

float ① VERB
to be supported by water • leaves floating on the river
be on the surface • The oil is on the surface of the sea.
bob • toys bobbing in the bath
drift • to drift in on the tide
lie on the surface • The boat lay on the surface of the lake.
stay afloat • They could stay afloat without swimming.
ANTONYM:
• sink

float ② VERB
to be carried on the air • floating on the breeze

drift • *The music drifted in through the window.*

glide • *eagles gliding above us*

hang • *A haze of perfume hung in the room.*

hover • *Butterflies hovered above the flowers.*

flood ① NOUN
a large amount of water coming suddenly • *Many people were drowned in the floods.*

deluge • *houses overwhelmed by the deluge*

downpour • *a downpour of torrential rain*

spate • *The river was in spate.*

torrent • *Torrents of water gushed into the reservoir.*

flood ② NOUN
a sudden large amount of something • *a flood of angry letters*

rush • *a sudden rush of panic*

stream • *a stream of inspired songs*

torrent • *a torrent of criticism*

flood ③ VERB
to overflow with water • *The river flooded its banks.*

deluge • *Heavy rain deluged the capital.*

drown • *a drowned village*

overflow • *an overflowing bath*

submerge • *to prevent water submerging the cobbled streets*

swamp • *His small boat was swamped by the waves.*

flourish ① VERB
to develop or function successfully or healthily • *Business was flourishing.*

bloom • *Not many economies bloomed during that period.*

boom • *Sales are booming.*

come on • *He is coming on very well at his new school.*

do well • *Online stores are doing well.*

prosper • *The farm grew and prospered.*

succeed • *the qualities needed in small businesses to succeed*

thrive • *Today the company continues to thrive.*

ANTONYM:
• fail

flourish ② VERB
to wave or display something • *He flourished his glass.*

brandish (LITERARY) • *He appeared brandishing a sword.*

display • *She proudly displayed the letter and began to read.*

hold aloft • *He held the cup aloft.*

wave • *Crowds were waving flags and applauding.*

flourish ③ NOUN
a bold sweeping or waving movement • *with a flourish of his hand*

flick • *a flick of the whip*

sweep • *With one sweep of her hand she threw back the sheets.*

wave • *Steve stopped him with a wave of the hand.*

flow ① VERB
to move or happen in a continuous stream • *a river flowing gently down into the valley*

flow

circulate • *to circulate round the entire house*

glide • *models gliding down the catwalk*

roll • *rolling gently to the sea*

run • *A stream ran beside the road.*

slide • *Tears slid down her cheeks.*

flow ② NOUN

a continuous movement of something • *traffic flow*

current • *currents of air*

drift • *the drift towards the cities*

flood • *a flood of complaints*

stream • *a constant stream of visitors*

tide • *to slow the tide of change*

fluent ADJECTIVE

expressing yourself easily and without hesitation • *a fluent speaker of French*

articulate • *an articulate young woman*

easy • *the easy flow of his argument*

effortless • *He spoke with effortless ease.*

flowing • *a smooth, flowing presentation*

ready • *a ready answer*

ANTONYM:

• hesitant

fly ① VERB

to move through the air • *to fly to Paris*

flit • *butterflies flitting among the flowers*

flutter • *The birds fluttered on to the feeder.*

sail • *a kite sailing above the trees*

soar • *eagles soaring in the sky*

fly ② VERB

to move very quickly • *She flew down the stairs.*

dart • *She darted to the window.*

dash • *We had to dash.*

hurry • *They hurried to catch the train.*

race • *I had to race round the shops.*

rush • *rushing off to work*

speed • *The car sped off.*

tear • *He tore off down the road.*

foam ① NOUN

a mass of tiny bubbles • *waves tipped with foam*

bubbles • *She liked to have bubbles in the bath.*

froth • *Yeast swells up to form a froth.*

lather • *It took a lot of shampoo to get a good lather.*

foam ② VERB

to swell and form bubbles • *a foaming river*

bubble • *The boiling liquid bubbled up.*

fizz • *a drink fizzing in the glass*

froth • *It frothed up over the top.*

focus ① VERB

to concentrate your vision on something • *His eyes began to focus.*

aim • *Astronomers aimed optical telescopes in their direction.*

concentrate • *concentrating his gaze on a line of ants*

direct • *He directed the light on to the roof.*

fix • *Their radar was fixed on the enemy ship.*

focus ② NOUN
the centre of attention • *the focus of the conversation*
centre • *She was the centre of an admiring crowd.*
focal point • *the focal point of the whole room*
hub • *the hub of the financial world*
target • *the target of the attack*

foil ① VERB
to prevent something from happening • *The police foiled an armed robbery.*
check • *to check the rise in crime*
counter • *countering the threat of strike action*
defeat • *an important role in defeating the rebellion*
frustrate • *a frustrated attempt*
thwart • *to thwart someone's plans*

foil ② NOUN
a contrast to something • *a perfect foil for his temperament*
antithesis • *the antithesis of his extrovert brother*
background • *a fitting background for her beauty*
complement • *the perfect complement to the antique furniture*
contrast • *The green woodwork is a stunning contrast to the black walls.*

fold ① VERB
to bend something • *He folded the paper carefully.*
bend • *Bend the top towards you.*
crease • *Crease along the dotted line.*

crumple • *He crumpled the note and put it in his pocket.*
tuck • *Tuck in the top and bottom.*
turn under • *The end was turned under.*

fold ② NOUN
a crease in something • *lying in folds*
bend • *There was a bend in the photograph.*
crease • *sharp creases in his shirt*
pleat • *a skirt with pleats*
wrinkle • *all the little wrinkles on Paul's face*

follow ① VERB
to pursue someone • *We were being followed.*
hound • *constantly hounded by photographers*
pursue • *He was pursued across several countries.*
stalk • *The tiger stalked its prey.*
track • *They tracked him to his home.*

follow ② VERB
to come after someone or something • *Night follows day.*
come after • *Summer comes after spring.*
succeed • *He was succeeded by his son.*
supersede • *Horses were superseded by cars.*

ANTONYM:
• precede

follow ③ VERB
to act in accordance with something • *Follow the instructions carefully.*

comply • *in order to comply with EU regulations*
conform • *conforming to the new safety requirements*
obey • *You must obey the law.*
observe • *The army was observing a ceasefire.*

follower NOUN
a supporter of a person or belief • *a loyal follower of the movement*
believer • *many devout believers in the faith*
disciple • *one of his disciples*
fan • *football fans*
henchman • *always surrounded by his henchmen*
supporter • *He was a major supporter of the plan.*
ANTONYM:
• leader

fond ① ADJECTIVE
feeling affection or liking • *a fond father*
adoring • *an adoring husband*
affectionate • *an affectionate smile*
devoted • *a devoted couple*
doting • *doting grandparents*
having a liking for • *She had a great liking for chocolate.*
loving • *a loving son*

fond ② ADJECTIVE
unlikely to happen or be fulfilled • *fond wishes for a better life*
deluded • *a deluded belief in future improvement*
empty • *empty promises of full employment*
foolish • *What foolish dreams we have!*

naive • *her naive belief in others' goodness*
vain • *the vain hope that he might lose weight*

food NOUN
things eaten to provide nourishment • *our favourite food*
diet • *a healthy balanced diet*
fare • *traditional regional fare*
foodstuffs • *basic foodstuffs*
grub (INFORMAL) • *Get yourself some grub.*
kai (NEW ZEALAND; INFORMAL) • *There's no kai in the house.*
nourishment • *unable to take nourishment*
provisions • *provisions for two weeks*
refreshment • *Refreshments will be provided.*
tucker (AUSTRALIAN AND NEW ZEALAND; INFORMAL) • *some of the cheapest pub tucker in town*
RELATED WORDS:
• ADJECTIVE alimentary
• NOUN gastronomy

fool ① NOUN
an unintelligent person • *What a stupid fool he is!*
dope (INFORMAL) • *He felt such a dope.*
dunce • *I was a complete dunce at chemistry.*
idiot • *acting like an idiot*
ignoramus • *the ignoramus of the group*

fool ② VERB
to trick someone • *Don't let him fool you.*

con (INFORMAL) • *conned out of all his money*
deceive • *deceiving the audience*
dupe • *in order to dupe the medical staff*
mislead • *a deliberately misleading statement*
trick • *They tricked him into believing it.*

foolish ADJECTIVE
silly and unwise • *feeling foolish*
inane • *an inane remark*
nonsensical • *a nonsensical thing to say*
senseless • *It would be senseless to stop her.*
silly • *a silly thing to say*
unintelligent • *a weak and unintelligent man*
unwise • *He had made some unwise investments.*
ANTONYM:
• wise

forbid VERB
to order someone not to do something • *forbidden to go out*
ban • *banned from driving*
exclude • *She was excluded from the classes.*
outlaw • *the outlawed political parties*
prohibit • *Fishing is prohibited.*
veto • *Their application was vetoed.*
ANTONYM:
• allow

force ① VERB
to compel someone to do something • *We were forced to turn right.*
compel • *I felt compelled to act.*
drive • *They are driving the company into bankruptcy.*
make • *They made me do it.*
oblige • *We were obliged to abandon the car.*
pressurise • *trying to pressurise them*

force ② NOUN
a pressure to do something • *They made him agree by force.*
compulsion • *a compulsion to write*
duress • *carried out under duress*
pressure • *under pressure to resign*

force ③ NOUN
the strength of something • *the force of the explosion*
impact • *the impact of the blast*
might • *the full might of the army*
power • *the great power of the mind*
pressure • *the pressure of work*
strength • *The storm was gaining strength.*

foreign ADJECTIVE
relating to other countries • *foreign travel*
distant • *in that distant land*
exotic • *filmed in an exotic location*
overseas • *a long overseas trip*

foremost ADJECTIVE
most important or best • *one of the world's foremost scholars*

best • *She was the best player in the world.*

chief • *my chief reason for objecting to the plan*

first • *The first priority is to defeat inflation.*

greatest • *one of the West Indies' greatest cricketers*

leading • *the leading researchers in this area*

most important • *the country's most important politicians and philosophers*

prime • *I regard this as my prime duty.*

principal • *one of the country's principal publishing houses*

top • *The prime minister met with her top military advisers.*

forest NOUN

TYPES OF FOREST

bush
coppice
copse
grove
jungle
spinney
thicket
wood
woodland

forget VERB

to fail to remember something • *I forgot to lock the door.*

fail to remember • *He failed to remember my name.*

omit • *omitting to mention the details*

overlook • *to overlook an important fact*

ANTONYM:
• remember

forgive VERB

to stop blaming someone for something • *Can you ever forgive me?*

absolve • *The verdict absolved him from blame.*

condone • *We cannot condone violence.*

excuse • *Please excuse our bad behaviour.*

pardon • *Relatives had begged the authorities to pardon him.*

ANTONYM:
• blame

forgiveness NOUN

the act of forgiving • *I ask for your forgiveness.*

mercy • *to beg for mercy*

pardon • *a presidential pardon*

form ① NOUN

a type or kind • *He has a rare form of memory disorder.*

class • *a new class of nuclear-powered submarine*

kind • *a new kind of leadership*

sort • *Try to do some sort of exercise every day.*

type • *There are various types of this disease.*

variant • *The quagga was a beautiful variant of the zebra.*

variety • *an unusual variety of this common garden flower*

form ② NOUN

the shape or pattern of something • *Valleys often take the form of deep canyons.*

contours • *the contours of the body*

layout • *He tried to recall the layout of the farmhouse.*
outline • *I could just see the outline of a building in the mist.*
shape • *little pens in the shape of baseball bats*
structure • *the chemical structure of this molecule*

form ③ VERB
to be the elements that something consists of • *the articles that formed the basis of his book*
compose • *The force would be composed of troops from NATO countries.*
constitute • *The country's ethnic minorities constitute about 7% of its total population.*
make up • *Women officers make up 13 per cent of the police force.*
serve as • *an arrangement of bricks and planks that served as a bookshelf*

form ④ VERB
to organise, create or come into existence • *The bowl was formed out of clay.*
assemble • *a model assembled entirely from matchsticks*
create • *These patterns were created by the action of water.*
develop • *We must develop closer ties with Germany.*
draw up • *We've drawn up a plan of action.*
establish • *The school was established in 1989 by an Italian professor.*

fashion • *Stone Age settlers fashioned necklaces from animals' teeth.*
make • *The organic waste decomposes to make compost.*

formal ① ADJECTIVE
in accordance with convention • *a formal dinner*
conventional • *a conventional style of dress*
correct • *polite and correct behaviour*
precise • *They spoke very precise English.*
stiff • *his stiff manner and lack of humour*
ANTONYM:
• informal

formal ② ADJECTIVE
official and publicly recognised • *No formal announcement has been made.*
approved • *A legally approved method of dealing with these*
legal • *They have a legal responsibility.*
official • *according to the official figures*
prescribed • *There is a prescribed procedure for situations like this.*
regular • *through the regular channels*

former ADJECTIVE
existing in the past • *a former tennis champion*
ancient • *the ancient civilisations*
bygone • *memories of a bygone age*
old • *our old school*
past • *a long list of past winners*

formidable ADJECTIVE
difficult to overcome • They
faced formidable obstacles.
challenging • a more
challenging job
daunting • a daunting prospect
difficult • A difficult task lay
ahead.
intimidating • She was an
intimidating opponent.
mammoth • a mammoth
undertaking
onerous • onerous
responsibilities

fort NOUN
a building for defence and
shelter • They had to abandon
the fort.
castle • a heavily-guarded
castle
citadel • The citadel towered
above the river.
fortification • fortifications
along the border
fortress • an ancient fortress

fossick VERB (AUSTRALIAN
AND NEW ZEALAND)
to search for something • If
you fossick around in some
specialist music stores, you may
find a copy.
forage • They were forced to
forage for clothing and fuel.
hunt • A forensic team was
hunting for clues.
look • I've looked through all my
drawers and I can't find it
anywhere.
rummage • He rummaged
around the post room and found
the document.

search • We've searched
through the whole house for the
keys.

fragile ADJECTIVE
easily broken or damaged
• fragile china
breakable • Anything
breakable or sharp had to be
removed.
dainty • a dainty Japanese tea
service
delicate • a delicate instrument
flimsy • packed in a flimsy box
frail • a frail shell
ANTONYM:
• tough

fragrance NOUN
a pleasant smell • the fragrance
of the roses
aroma • the aroma of fresh
bread
perfume • enjoying the perfume
of the lemon trees
scent • flowers chosen for their
scent
smell • a sweet smell of pine

fragrant ADJECTIVE
having a pleasant smell
• fragrant oils
aromatic • a plant with
aromatic leaves
perfumed • perfumed body
cream
sweet-smelling • posies of
sweet-smelling flowers
ANTONYM:
• smelly

frank ADJECTIVE
open and straightforward
• a frank discussion

F

blunt • *his blunt approach*
candid • *She was completely candid with me.*
honest • *my honest opinion*
open • *an open, trusting nature*
plain • *plain talking*
straightforward • *spoken in a straightforward manner*

fraud ① NOUN
the act of deceiving someone
• *electoral fraud*
deceit • *deliberate deceit*
deception • *obtaining money by deception*
guile • *children's lack of guile*
trickery • *They had to resort to trickery.*

fraud ② NOUN
something that deceives you
• *The whole story was an elaborate fraud.*
fake • *The painting was a fake.*
forgery • *just a clever forgery*
hoax • *a bomb hoax*

fraud ③ NOUN
someone who is not what they claim to be • *Many psychics are frauds.*
charlatan • *exposed as a charlatan*
cheat • *Cheats will be disqualified.*
imposter • *an imposter with false documents*
quack • *He tried all sorts of quacks.*

free ① ADJECTIVE
not being held prisoner • *a free man*
at large • *Three prisoners are at large.*

at liberty • *the last member of the gang still at liberty*
liberated • *newly liberated slaves*
loose • *He broke loose from his bonds.*

ANTONYM:
• captive

free ② ADJECTIVE
available without payment • *a free brochure*
complimentary
• *complimentary tickets*
gratis • *The meal was gratis.*
unpaid • *unpaid voluntary work*
without charge • *They mended it without charge.*

free ③ VERB
to release from captivity • *to free the slaves*
discharge • *discharged from prison*
liberate • *liberated under the terms of the amnesty*
release • *The hostages were soon released.*
set at liberty • *He was set at liberty after ten years.*
set loose • *The animals were set loose after treatment.*

ANTONYM:
• imprison

freedom ① NOUN
the ability to choose • *freedom of action*
discretion • *Use your own discretion.*
latitude • *There is more latitude for personal opinions.*
leeway • *granted more leeway to pass reforms*

licence • *a licence to kill*
scope • *plenty of scope for improvement*

freedom ② NOUN
the state of being free or being set free • *gaining their freedom after months of captivity*
emancipation • *the emancipation of the slaves*
liberty • *three months' loss of liberty*
release • *the immediate release of the captives*
ANTONYM:
• captivity

freedom ③ NOUN
the absence of something unpleasant • *freedom from pain*
exemption • *granted exemption from all taxes*
immunity • *information in exchange for immunity from prosecution*

frenzy NOUN
wild and uncontrolled behaviour • *gripped by a frenzy of nationalism*
agitation • *in a state of intense agitation*
fury • *He stalked out in a fury.*
hysteria • *mass hysteria*
madness • *a moment of madness*
rage • *She flew into a rage.*

frequent ① ADJECTIVE
happening often • *his frequent visits*
common • *a common occurrence*

continual • *continual demands for money*
everyday • *an everyday event*
habitual • *a habitual daydreamer*
recurrent • *a recurrent theme in her work*
repeated • *His parents made repeated attempts to visit.*
ANTONYM:
• rare

frequent ② VERB
to go somewhere often • *a restaurant which he frequents*
attend • *He often attends their meetings.*
haunt • *She haunted their house.*
patronise • *to patronise a hotel*
visit • *a place we often visit*
ANTONYM:
• avoid

friend NOUN
a person you know and like • *lifelong friends*
buddy (INFORMAL) • *We've been buddies for a long time.*
china (BRITISH AND SOUTH AFRICAN; INFORMAL) • *having a laugh with his chinas*
chum (INFORMAL) • *She went on holiday with two chums.*
companion • *my constant companion*
confidant or **confidante** • *her only confidant*
crony (OLD-FASHIONED) • *surrounded by her cronies*
mate (BRITISH; INFORMAL) • *going out with his mates*

pal (INFORMAL) • *We are great pals.*

ANTONYM:
• enemy

friendly ADJECTIVE
kind and pleasant • *a very friendly crowd*
affectionate • *on affectionate terms*
amiable • *He was very amiable company.*
close • *The two were very close.*
cordial • *a most cordial welcome*
genial • *a genial host*
welcoming • *a welcoming house*

ANTONYM:
• unfriendly

friendship NOUN
a state of being friendly with someone • *I value our friendship.*
affection • *to win their affection*
attachment • *the deep attachment between them*
closeness • *her closeness to her sister*
goodwill • *as a gesture of goodwill*

ANTONYM:
• hostility

frighten VERB
to make someone afraid • *trying to frighten us*
alarm • *alarmed by the noise*
intimidate • *I am intimidated by my boss.*
scare • *You aren't scared of mice, are you?*
startle • *I didn't mean to startle you.*
terrify • *Heights terrified him.*
terrorise • *The gunmen terrorised the villagers.*
unnerve • *an unnerving silence*

frightened ADJECTIVE
having feelings of fear about something • *frightened of thunder*
afraid • *She was afraid of the other children.*
alarmed • *Don't be alarmed.*
petrified • *petrified of wasps*
scared • *scared of being alone in the house*
startled • *a startled animal*
terrified • *a terrified look*

frightening ADJECTIVE
causing someone to feel fear • *a frightening experience*
alarming • *an alarming increase*
hair-raising • *at hair-raising speed*
intimidating • *threatening and intimidating behaviour*
menacing • *a menacing glance*
terrifying • *one of the most terrifying diseases*

frivolous ADJECTIVE
not serious or sensible • *a frivolous young person*
flippant • *a flippant comment*
foolish • *saying foolish and inappropriate things*
juvenile • *juvenile behaviour*
puerile • *your puerile sense of humour*
silly • *making silly jokes*

ANTONYM:
• serious

front ① NOUN

the part that faces forward
• *the front of the house*
facade • *the cleaning of the temple's facade*
face • *the face of the building*
frontage • *a restaurant with a river frontage*

ANTONYM:
• back

front ② NOUN

the outward appearance of something • *a respectable front*
appearance • *the appearance of fair treatment*
exterior • *his tough exterior*
facade • *a cheerful facade*
face • *a brave face*
show • *a convincing show of affection*

front ③ : in front of

PREPOSITION
further forward than • *too close to the car in front of us*
ahead of • *ahead of the rest of the field*
before • *I'm before you.*

frown VERB

to draw the eyebrows together • *She frowned in concentration.*
glare • *The woman glared angrily at him.*
glower • *She glowered but said nothing.*
knit your brows • *He knitted his brows in concentration.*
scowl • *He scowled at the waiter.*

frozen ADJECTIVE

extremely cold • *frozen to the bone*
arctic • *arctic weather conditions*
chilled • *chilled to the marrow*
frigid • *frigid temperatures*
icy • *an icy wind*
numb • *numb with cold*

frustrate VERB

to prevent something from happening • *His efforts were frustrated.*
block • *They are blocking the peace process.*
check • *to check the spread of the virus*
foil • *They foiled all my plans.*
thwart • *his way to thwart your club's ambitions*

fulfil VERB

to carry out or achieve something • *He decided to fulfil his dream and go to college.*
accomplish • *If they all work together they can accomplish their goal.*
achieve • *We will strive to achieve these goals.*
carry out • *They seem to have very little intention of carrying out their commitments.*
perform • *Each component performs a different function.*
realise • *The question is, will our hopes ever be realised?*
satisfy • *The procedures should satisfy certain basic requirement*

full ① ADJECTIVE

filled with something • *full of books*

filled • *filled up to the top*
loaded • *The van was loaded with furniture.*
packed • *The train was packed.*
saturated • *completely saturated with liquid*
ANTONYM:
• empty

full ② ADJECTIVE
missing nothing out • *I want a full account of what happened.*
comprehensive • *a comprehensive guide to the area*
detailed • *a detailed description*
exhaustive • *an exhaustive treatment of the subject*
extensive • *extensive coverage of the earthquake*
maximum • *the way to take maximum advantage of pay TV*
thorough • *a thorough search*

full ③ ADJECTIVE
loose-fitting • *a full skirt*
baggy • *a baggy sweater*
loose • *hidden under his loose shirt*
voluminous • *voluminous sleeves*

fun ① NOUN
an enjoyable activity • *It was great fun.*
amusement • *There is no amusement for teenagers in the village.*
enjoyment • *It gave us much enjoyment.*
entertainment • *little opportunity for entertainment*
pleasure • *to mix business and pleasure*
recreation • *time for recreation*

fun ② : **make fun of** VERB
to tease someone • *Don't make fun of him.*
deride (FORMAL) • *This theory is widely derided.*
laugh at • *They laughed at his hat.*
mock • *He was often mocked by his classmates.*
ridicule • *She allowed them to ridicule her.*
taunt • *a fellow pupil who had taunted him about his height*
tease • *They used to tease me about my unusual name.*

function ① NOUN
the useful thing that something or someone does • *The main function of merchant banks is to raise capital.*
duty • *My duty is to look after the animals.*
job • *Their main job is to keep us healthy.*
purpose • *The purpose of the occasion was to raise money for charity.*
remit • *The centre's remit is to advise businesses.*
responsibility • *He handled his responsibilities as a counsellor in an intelligent fashion.*
role • *information about the drug's role in preventing infection*

function ② NOUN
a large formal dinner, reception or party • *We were going down to a function in London.*
dinner • *a series of official dinners*

gathering • *I'm always shy at formal gatherings like that.*
party • *They met at a party.*
reception • *At the reception they served smoked salmon.*

function ③ VERB
to operate or work • *The heater was not functioning properly.*
go • *My car won't go in fog.*
operate • *Ceiling and wall lights can operate independently.*
perform • *When there's snow, how is this car going to perform?*
run • *The system is now running smoothly.*
work • *Is the telephone working today?*

fund ① NOUN
an amount of money • *the pension fund*
capital • *difficulty in raising capital*
foundation • *money from a research foundation*
pool • *a reserve pool of cash*
reserve • *a drain on the cash reserves*
supply • *to curb money supply and inflation*

fund ② NOUN
a large amount of something • *an extraordinary fund of energy*
hoard • *his hoard of supplies*
mine • *a mine of information*
reserve • *oil reserves*
reservoir • *the body's short-term reservoir of energy*
store • *a store of fuel*

fund ③ VERB
to provide the money for

something • *to raise money to fund research into cancer*
finance • *big projects financed by foreign aid*
pay for • *His parents paid for his holiday.*
subsidise • *heavily subsidised by the government*
support • *He is supporting himself through college.*

fundi NOUN (SOUTH AFRICAN)
an expert • *The local fundis are wonderfully adept and have created a car for hunting.*
expert • *our team of experts*
geek (INFORMAL) • *a new site designed by dog-loving computer geeks*
guru • *Fashion gurus dictate some crazy ideas.*
master • *a master of the English language*
specialist • *a specialist in diseases of the nervous system*
virtuoso • *He was gaining a reputation as a piano virtuoso.*

funny ① ADJECTIVE
being strange or odd • *They heard a funny noise.*
mysterious • *in mysterious circumstances*
odd • *There was something odd about her.*
peculiar • *It tasted very peculiar.*
puzzling • *a puzzling development*
strange • *A strange thing happened.*
unusual • *a most unusual man*
weird • *That guy is really weird*

funny ② ADJECTIVE
causing amusement • *a funny story*
amusing • *a most amusing lecturer*
comic • *comic moments*
comical • *the comical expression on his face*
hilarious • *We thought it was hilarious.*
humorous • *a humorous magazine*
witty • *a very witty speech*
ANTONYM:
• serious

furious ① ADJECTIVE
extremely angry • *He is furious at the way his wife has been treated.*
enraged • *I got more and more enraged at my father.*
fuming • *He was still fuming over the remark.*
infuriated • *He knew how infuriated the conversation had made me.*
livid • *She was absolutely livid about it.*
mad • *I'm pretty mad about this, I can tell you.*
raging • *Inside, Sally was raging.*

furious ② ADJECTIVE
involving great energy, effort or speed • *a furious battle*
breakneck • *Jack drove to Mayfair at breakneck speed.*
fierce • *Competition has been fierce between the rival groups.*
frantic • *There was frantic activity behind the scenes.*

frenzied • *the frenzied run-up to the general election*
intense • *The military on both sides are involved in intense activity.*
manic • *Preparations continued at a manic pace.*

fuss ① NOUN
anxious or excited behaviour • *What's all the fuss about?*
agitation • *in a state of intense agitation*
bother • *I don't want any bother.*
commotion • *a commotion in the market*
confusion • *in the confusion after an ammunition dump blew up*
stir • *The play caused a stir here.*
to-do (INFORMAL) • *a big to-do*

fuss ② VERB
to behave in a nervous or restless way • *Waiters fussed around the table.*
bustle • *shoppers bustling around the store*
fidget • *He was fidgeting with his tie.*
fret • *Stop fretting about the details.*

fussy ADJECTIVE
difficult to please • *fussy about his food*
choosy (INFORMAL) • *Cats can be choosy about what they eat.*
discriminating • *a discriminating visitor*
exacting • *She failed to meet his exacting standards.*
fastidious • *Disney was also fastidious about cleanliness.*

particular • *very particular about the colours he used*

futile ADJECTIVE
having no chance of success
• *a futile effort to run away*
abortive • *the abortive coup attempt*
forlorn • *forlorn hopes of future improvement*
unsuccessful • *an unsuccessful bid for independence*
useless • *It was useless to even try.*
vain • *in the vain hope of success*
ANTONYM:
• successful

future ADJECTIVE
relating to a time after the present • *to predict future growth*
approaching • *concerned about the approaching winter*
coming • *in the coming months*
forthcoming • *candidates for the forthcoming elections*
impending • *her impending marriage*
later • *We'll discuss it at a later date.*
prospective • *my prospective employers*
ANTONYM:
• past

Gg

gadget NOUN
a small machine or tool
• *kitchen gadgets such as toasters and kettles*
appliance • *Switch off all electrical appliances when they're not in use.*
device • *a device that warns you when the batteries need changing*
machine • *a machine for slicing vegetables*
tool • *a tool for cutting wood, metal or plastic*

gain ① VERB
to get something gradually
• *Students can gain valuable experience by working.*
achieve • *Achieving our goals makes us feel good.*
acquire • *Companies should reward workers for acquiring more skills.*
earn • *She has earned the respect of the world's top cyclists*
obtain • *You would need to obtain permission to copy the design.*
secure (FORMAL) • *He failed to secure enough votes for outright victory.*
win • *The long-term aim is to win promotion.*

gain ② VERB
to get an advantage • Would
any areas of the world actually
gain from global warming?
benefit • Both sides have
benefited from the talks.
profit • Frankie is now profiting
from his crimes.

gain ③ NOUN
an increase or improvement in
something • The Party has
made substantial gains in local
elections.
advance • advances in
computer technology
growth • The area has seen a
rapid population growth.
improvement • a major
improvement in standards
increase • an increase of 7% in
visitors to the UK
rise • a 3% rise in electricity
prices

gamble ① VERB
to bet money on something
• John gambled heavily on the
horses.
back • I backed Germany to win
1–0.
bet • He bet them £500 they
would lose.

gamble ② VERB
to take a risk • Few firms will be
willing to gamble on new
products.
chance • Armstrong chanced a
gallop to the water.
risk • One of his daughters risked
everything to join him in exile.
stake • He has staked his
reputation on the outcome.

gamble ③ NOUN
a risk that someone takes • We
are taking a gamble on a young
player.
chance • You take a chance on
the weather when you holiday in
the UK.
lottery • Robinson described
the final as a bit of a lottery.
risk • How much risk are you
prepared to take?

game NOUN
an occasion on which people
compete • South Africa's first
game of the season
clash • the clash between
Australia and the West Indies
contest • The rain spoiled a
good contest.
match • a football match

gap ① NOUN
a space or a hole in something
• They squeezed through a gap in
the fence.
break • stars twinkling between
the breaks in the clouds
chink • All the walls have wide
chinks in them.
crack • a crack in the curtains
hole • a hole in the wall
opening • an opening in the
trees
space • the space between their
car and the one in front

gap ② NOUN
a period of time • After a gap of
nearly a decade, Manley was
back.
hiatus (FORMAL) • The shop
is open again after a two-year
hiatus.

g

interlude • *a happy interlude in the Kents' life*
interval • *There was a long interval of silence.*
lull • *a lull in the conversation*
pause • *Then, after a pause, he goes on.*

gap ③ NOUN
a difference between people or things • *the gap between rich and poor*
difference • *He denied there were any major differences between them.*
disparity (FORMAL)
• *disparities between poor and wealthy school districts*
inconsistency • *There were major inconsistencies in his evidence.*

garbage ① NOUN
things that people do not want • *piles of garbage*
debris • *screws, bolts and other debris from a scrapyard*
junk (INFORMAL) • *What are you going to do with all that junk?*
litter • *If you see litter in the corridor, pick it up.*
refuse (FORMAL) • *refuse collection and street cleaning*
rubbish • *household rubbish*
trash • *I forgot to take out the trash.*
waste • *industrial waste*

garbage ② NOUN
(INFORMAL)
ideas and opinions that are untrue or unimportant • *I personally think this is complete garbage.*

drivel • *What absolute drivel!*
gibberish • *a politician talking gibberish*
nonsense • *all that poetic nonsense about love*
rubbish • *He's talking rubbish.*

garbled ADJECTIVE
confused or incorrect • *A garbled message awaited us at the desk.*
confused • *the latest twist in a murky and confused story*
distorted • *a distorted version of what was said*
incomprehensible • *Her speech was incomprehensible.*
jumbled • *his jumbled account of how Jack had been hired*
unintelligible • *He muttered something unintelligible.*

gasp ① VERB
to breathe in quickly through your mouth • *She gasped for air.*
choke • *People began to choke as smoke filled the air.*
gulp • *She gulped air into her lungs.*
pant • *Amy climbed rapidly until she was panting with the effort.*
puff • *I could see he was unfit because he was puffing.*

gasp ② NOUN
a short quick breath of air • *An audible gasp went round the court.*
gulp • *I took in a large gulp of air*
pant • *Her breath came in pant*
puff • *He blew out a little puff of air.*

gather ① VERB
to come together in a group
• *We gathered around the fireplace.*
assemble • *a place for students to assemble between classes*
congregate • *Youngsters love to congregate here in the evenings.*
flock • *The criticisms will not stop people flocking to see the film.*
mass • *The General was massing his troops for a counterattack.*
round up • *The police rounded up a number of suspects.*
ANTONYM:
• scatter

gather ② VERB
to bring things together • *I suggest we gather enough firewood to last the night.*
accumulate • *In five years it has accumulated a huge debt.*
amass • *She has amassed a personal fortune of $38 million.*
collect • *1.5 million signatures have been collected.*
hoard • *They've begun to hoard food and gasoline.*
stockpile • *People are stockpiling food for the coming winter.*

gather ③ VERB
to learn or believe something
• *"He speaks English."—"I gathered that."*
assume • *I assume the eggs are fresh.*
conclude • *He concluded that Oswald was somewhat untypical.*

hear • *I heard that he was forced to resign.*
learn • *She wasn't surprised to learn that he was involved.*
understand • *I understand that he's just taken early retirement.*

gathering NOUN
a meeting with a purpose
• *polite social gatherings*
assembly • *an assembly of party members*
congregation • *The congregation sang hymns and said prayers.*
get-together (INFORMAL)
• *family get-togethers*
meeting • *Can we have a meeting to discuss that?*
rally • *a pre-election rally*

gaudy ADJECTIVE
colourful in a vulgar way
• *gaudy fake jewellery*
bright • *fake fur, dyed in bright colours*
flashy • *women in flashy satin suits*
garish • *They climbed the garish purple-carpeted stairs.*
loud • *a loud checked shirt*
showy • *He favoured large showy flowers.*
tacky (INFORMAL) • *tacky red sunglasses*
vulgar • *I think it's a very vulgar house.*

general ① ADJECTIVE
relating to the whole of something • *a general decline in employment*
broad • *a broad outline of the Society's development*

comprehensive • *a comprehensive guide to the region*
overall • *The overall quality of pupils' work had shown a marked improvement.*

ANTONYM:
• specific

general ② ADJECTIVE
widely true, suitable or relevant • *The project should raise general awareness about bullying.*
accepted • *the accepted version of events*
broad • *a film with broad appeal*
common • *Such behaviour is common among young people.*
universal • *Music and sports programmes have a universal appeal.*
widespread • *The proposals have attracted widespread support.*

ANTONYM:
• special

generosity NOUN
willingness to give money, time or help • *She is well known for her generosity.*
benevolence • *Banks are not known for their benevolence.*
charity • *private acts of charity*
kindness • *We have been treated with such kindness by everybody.*

ANTONYM:
• meanness

generous ① ADJECTIVE
willing to give money, time or help • *The gift is generous by any standards.*
charitable • *Individuals can be charitable and help their neighbours.*
hospitable • *He was very hospitable to me when I came to New York.*
kind • *She is warm-hearted and kind to everyone.*
lavish • *The Princess received a number of lavish gifts from her hosts.*
liberal • *Don't be too liberal with your spending.*

ANTONYM:
• mean

generous ② ADJECTIVE
very large • *a generous portion of spaghetti*
abundant • *an abundant supply of hot food*
ample • *There is ample space for a good-sized kitchen.*
plentiful • *a plentiful supply of water*

ANTONYM:
• meagre

genius ① NOUN
a very clever or talented person • *a mathematical genius*
brain • *the financial brain behind the company*
master • *Spiro Rosakis is a master of his craft.*
mastermind • *the mastermind behind the opening ceremony*
virtuoso • *The man is a virtuoso of pop music.*

genius ② NOUN
extraordinary ability or talent
• *a poet of genius*
brains • *She has the brains needed for the job.*
brilliance • *his brilliance as a director*
intellect • *people of great intellect*

gentle ADJECTIVE
not violent or rough • *a quiet and gentle man*
benign • *a good-looking chap with a benign expression*
kind • *I fell in love with him because of his kind nature.*
kindly • *a kindly old gentleman*
meek • *He was a meek, mild-mannered fellow.*
mild • *Alexis was quiet, mild and happy-go-lucky.*
placid • *a look of impatience on her normally placid face*
soft • *She had a very soft heart.*
tender • *Her voice was tender.*
ANTONYM:
• cruel

genuine ADJECTIVE
not false or pretend • *They're convinced the picture is genuine.*
authentic • *an authentic French recipe*
bona fide • *We are happy to donate to bona fide charities.*
dinkum (AUSTRALIAN AND NEW ZEALAND; INFORMAL)
• *They are all dinkum stolen bank notes.*
real • *a real Rembrandt*
ANTONYM:
• fake

get ① VERB
to fetch or receive something
• *I'll get us all a cup of coffee.*
acquire • *I have recently acquired a new camera.*
fetch • *Sylvia fetched a towel from the bathroom.*
obtain • *Evans was trying to obtain a false passport.*
procure (FORMAL) • *It remained very difficult to procure food.*
receive • *I received your letter of November 7.*
secure (FORMAL) • *He failed to secure enough votes for outright victory.*

get ② VERB
to change from one state to another • *People draw the curtains once it gets dark.*
become • *The wind became stronger.*
grow • *He grew to love his work.*
turn • *The leaves have turned golden-brown.*

get on VERB
to enjoy someone's company
• *I get on very well with his wife.*
be compatible • *Mary and I are very compatible.*
hit it off (INFORMAL) • *They hit it off straight away.*

ghost NOUN
the spirit of a dead person
• *the ghost of the drowned sailor*
apparition • *She felt as if she were seeing a ghostly apparition.*
phantom • *She was relentlessly pursued by a grossly disfigured phantom.*

g

spectre • *The Tower is said to be haunted by the spectre of Anne Boleyn.*

spirit • *the spirits of our dead ancestors*

RELATED WORD:
• ADJECTIVE spectral

gidday or **g'day**
INTERJECTION (AUSTRALIAN AND NEW ZEALAND)
hello • *Gidday, mate!*

good afternoon (FORMAL)
• *Good afternoon, Miss Bates.*

good morning (FORMAL)
• *Good morning, class.*

good evening (FORMAL)
• *Good evening, ladies and gentlemen!*

hello • *Hello, Trish. Glad you could make it.*

hi (INFORMAL) • *Hi, how are you doing?*

gift ① NOUN
something you give someone • *He showered her with gifts.*

bequest (FORMAL) • *They received a bequest of $310,000.*

bonsela (SOUTH AFRICAN) • *a generous bonsela*

contribution • *companies that make charitable contributions*

donation • *donations of food and clothing for victims of the hurricane*

legacy • *What about the legacy from your uncle?*

present • *This book would make a great Christmas present.*

gift ② NOUN
a natural skill or ability • *a gift for comedy*

ability • *It's obvious he has an exceptional ability.*

aptitude • *She realised she had an aptitude for writing.*

flair • *Tony found he had a real flair for design.*

talent • *Both her children have a talent for music.*

give ① VERB
to provide someone with something • *I gave her a DVD.*

award • *The Mayor awarded him a medal.*

deliver • *The Canadians plan to deliver more food to southern Somalia.*

donate • *Others donated second-hand clothes.*

grant • *Permission was granted a few weeks ago.*

hand • *Isabel handed me a glass of orange juice.*

present • *The Queen presented the prizes.*

provide • *The government was not in a position to provide them with food.*

supply • *a contract to supply radar equipment to the Philippines*

ANTONYM:
• take

give ② VERB
to collapse or break under pressure • *My knees gave under me.*

buckle • *His left wrist buckled under the strain.*

cave in • *Half the ceiling caved in.*

collapse • *The roof supports had collapsed.*

give way • *He fell when a ledge gave way beneath him.*
yield • *The handle yielded to her grasp.*

give in VERB
to admit that you are defeated • *The minister said he would not give in to the strikers.*
capitulate • *Cohen capitulated to virtually every demand.*
concede • *Mr Pyke is not prepared to concede defeat.*
submit • *Mrs Jones submitted to an operation on her right knee.*
succumb (FORMAL) • *The Minister said his country would never succumb to pressure.*
surrender • *He surrendered to American troops.*
yield (FORMAL) • *an enemy who had shown no desire to yield*

glad ADJECTIVE
happy about something • *They'll be glad to get away from it all.*
delighted • *Frank will be delighted to see you.*
happy • *Jacques is very happy that you are here.*
joyful • *a joyful reunion with his mother*
overjoyed • *Shelley was overjoyed to see me.*
pleased • *They're pleased to be going home.*
ANTONYM:
• sorry

glance ① NOUN
a brief look at something • *The boys exchanged glances.*
glimpse • *They caught a glimpse of their hero.*

look • *Lucille took a last look in the mirror.*
peek • *Could I just have another quick peek at the bedroom?*
peep • *Would you take a peep out of the window?*

glance ② VERB
to look at something quickly • *He glanced at his watch.*
glimpse • *I soon glimpsed the doctor in his garden.*
look • *Bethan looked quickly at the elegant people around her.*
peek • *She had peeked at him through a crack in the wall.*
peep • *Now and then she peeped to see if he was noticing her.*
scan • *She scanned the advertisement pages of the newspaper.*

glance ③ VERB
to hit something quickly and bounce away • *The ball glanced off the edge of the hoop.*
bounce • *The ball bounced off the opposite post.*
brush • *She brushed her fingers over the photograph.*
skim • *pebbles skimming across the water*

glare ① VERB
to look angrily at someone • *Joe glared at his brother.*
frown • *She looked up to see Vic frowning at her.*
glower • *He glowered at me but said nothing.*
scowl • *Robert scowled, and slammed the door behind him.*

glare ② NOUN
an angry look • *The waiter lowered his eyes to avoid Harold's furious glare.*
frown • *There was a deep frown on the boy's face.*
scowl • *Chris met the remark with a scowl.*

glare ③ NOUN
very bright light • *the glare of the headlights*
blaze • *There was a sudden blaze of light.*
glow • *the glow of the fire*

gloomy ① ADJECTIVE
feeling very sad • *They are gloomy about their chances of success.*
dejected • *Everyone has days when they feel dejected.*
down • *The elderly man sounded really down.*
glum • *What on earth are you looking so glum about?*
miserable • *She went to bed, miserable and depressed.*
sad • *You must feel sad about what's happened.*
ANTONYM:
• cheerful

gloomy ② ADJECTIVE
dark and depressing • *a gloomy house on the edge of Phoenix Park*
dark • *The house looked dark and unwelcoming.*
dismal • *damp and dismal weather*
dreary • *a dreary, industrial city*
dull • *It's always dull and raining.*

ANTONYM:
• sunny

glory ① NOUN
fame and admiration that someone gets • *It was her moment of glory.*
fame • *The film earned him international fame.*
honour • *the honour of captaining one's country*
immortality • *Some people want to achieve immortality through their work.*
praise • *Holbrooke deserves full praise for his efforts.*
prestige • *I'm not in this job for the prestige.*
ANTONYM:
• disgrace

glory ② NOUN
magnificence or great beauty • *Spring arrived in all its glory.*
grandeur • *the grandeur of the country mansion*
magnificence • *the magnificence of the sunset*
majesty • *the majesty of Niagara Falls*
splendour • *the splendour of the palace of Versailles*

glory ③ VERB
to enjoy something very much • *The workers were glorying in their new-found freedom.*
gloat • *Their rivals were gloating over their triumph.*
relish • *He relished the idea of getting some cash.*
revel • *a jumped-up official who revels in his power*

G

gloss NOUN
a bright shine on a surface
• *aluminium foil with a high gloss surface*
brilliance • *ceramic tiles of great brilliance*
gleam • *the gleam of brass*
polish • *His boots had a high polish.*
sheen • *The carpet had a silvery sheen to it.*
shine • *This gel gives a beautiful shine to the hair.*

glossy ADJECTIVE
smooth and shiny • *The leaves were dark and glossy.*
bright • *Her eyes were bright with excitement.*
brilliant • *The woman had brilliant green eyes.*
polished • *a highly polished floor*
shiny • *a shiny new sports car*
sleek • *sleek black hair*

glow ① NOUN
a dull steady light • *the glow of the fire*
gleam • *the first gleam of dawn*
glimmer • *In the east there was the slightest glimmer of light.*
light • *the light of the evening sun*

glow ② VERB
to shine with a dull steady light • *A light glowed behind the curtains.*
gleam • *Lights gleamed in the deepening mist.*
glimmer • *A few stars still glimmered.*
shine • *Scattered lights shone on the horizon.*

smoulder • *A very small fire was smouldering in the grate.*

glue VERB
to stick things together • *Glue the two halves together.*
fix • *Fix the fabric to the roller.*
paste • *The children were busy pasting gold stars on a chart.*
seal • *He sealed the envelope and put on a stamp.*
stick • *I stuck the notice on the board.*

go ① VERB
to move or travel somewhere
• *I went home at the weekend.*
advance • *Rebel forces are advancing on the capital.*
drive • *My husband and I drove to Liverpool to see my mum.*
fly • *He flew to Los Angeles.*
journey (FORMAL) • *They intended to journey up the Amazon.*
leave • *What time are you leaving?*
proceed (FORMAL) • *The taxi proceeded along a lonely road.*
set off • *He set off for the station.*
travel • *Students often travel hundreds of miles to get here.*

go ② VERB
to work properly • *stuck on the motorway with a car that won't go*
function • *All the instruments functioned properly.*
work • *The pump doesn't work and we have no running water.*

g

go ③ NOUN
an attempt to do something
• I always wanted to have a go at waterskiing.
attempt • one of his rare attempts at humour
shot (INFORMAL) • a shot at winning a brand new car
stab (INFORMAL) • Several sports stars have had a stab at acting and singing.
try • After a few tries, Patrick had given up.

goal NOUN
something that a person hopes to achieve • The goal is to make as much money as possible.
aim • The aim of the festival is to raise awareness of this issue.
end • This is another policy designed to achieve the same end.
intention • He announced his intention of standing for parliament.
object • The object of the exercise is to raise money for charity.
objective • His objective was to play golf and win.
purpose • His purpose was to make a profit.
target • She failed to achieve her target of losing 20 pounds.

gobble VERB
to eat food very quickly • Pete gobbled all the beef stew.
bolt • Being under stress can cause you to bolt your food.
devour • She devoured two bars of chocolate.
wolf • Pitt wolfed down a peanut butter sandwich.

good ① ADJECTIVE
pleasant, acceptable or satisfactory • We had a really good time.
▶ see Word Study **good**, page 709
ANTONYM:
• bad

good ② ADJECTIVE
skilful or successful • I'm not very good at art.
▶ see Word Study **good**, page 709
ANTONYM:
• incompetent

good ③ ADJECTIVE
kind, thoughtful and loving
• You are so good to me.
▶ see Word Study **good**, page 709
ANTONYM:
• unkind

goodwill NOUN
kindness and helpfulness towards other people
• I invited them to dinner as a gesture of goodwill.
benevolence • He chuckles often and radiates benevolence.
favour • in order to gain the favour of whoever is in power
friendliness • Visitors remarked on the friendliness of the people.
friendship • The two countries signed treaties of friendship.

gossip NOUN
informal conversation about other people • Don't you like a good gossip?
dirt (INFORMAL) • the latest dirt on the other candidates

hearsay • *They have had only hearsay and rumour to go on.*

go through VERB
to experience an unpleasant event • *I was going through a very difficult time.*
endure • *He'd endured years of pain and sleepless nights.*
experience • *British business was experiencing a severe recession.*
undergo • *Magee underwent emergency surgery.*

grab VERB
to take hold of something roughly • *I grabbed him by the neck.*
clutch • *Michelle clutched my arm.*
grasp • *He grasped both my hands.*
seize • *She seized a fork and started to eat.*
snatch • *Mick snatched the cards from Archie's hand.*

grace NOUN
an elegant way of moving • *He moved with the grace of a trained boxer.*
elegance • *She is elegance personified.*
poise • *Ballet classes are important for poise and grace.*
ANTONYM:
• clumsiness

grade VERB
to arrange things according to quality • *The oil is tasted and graded according to quality.*

class • *They are officially classed as visitors.*
classify • *Rocks can be classified according to their origin.*
group • *The fact sheets are grouped into seven sections.*
rate • *He was rated as one of the country's top young players.*
sort • *The students are sorted into three ability groups.*

gradual ADJECTIVE
happening or changing slowly • *the gradual improvement in communications*
continuous • *Our policy is one of continuous improvement.*
progressive • *a progressive decline in the number of pupils studying Latin*
slow • *The distribution of passports has been a slow process.*
steady • *a steady rise in sales*
ANTONYM:
• sudden

grammar NOUN
GRAMMAR WORDS
active
aspect
comparative
passive
person
plural
possessive
singular
superlative
tense
voice

g

grand ① ADJECTIVE

very impressive in size or appearance • *a grand building in the centre of town*

imposing • *the imposing gates at the entrance to the estate*

impressive • *The old boat presented an impressive sight.*

magnificent • *magnificent views over the San Fernando valley*

majestic • *a stupendous vista of majestic peaks*

monumental • *a monumental sculpture of a human face*

splendid • *a splendid Victorian mansion*

grand ② ADJECTIVE (INFORMAL)

pleasant or enjoyable • *It was a grand day.*

brilliant • *I've had a brilliant time.*

fantastic (INFORMAL) • *That was a fantastic holiday.*

great (INFORMAL) • *I had a great time at university.*

marvellous • *It was a marvellous day and we were all so happy.*

terrific • *Everybody there was having a terrific time.*

tremendous • *I thought it was a tremendous book.*

wonderful • *It was a wonderful experience.*

grant ① NOUN

a money award given for a particular purpose • *My application for a grant has been accepted.*

allocation • *The aid allocation for that country is under review.*

allowance • *She gets an allowance for looking after Lillian.*

award • *a study award worth £2,000*

handout • *a cash handout of six thousand rupees*

subsidy • *state subsidies to public transport companies*

grant ② VERB

to allow someone to have something • *France has agreed to grant him political asylum.*

allocate • *The budget allocated $7 billion for development programmes.*

allow • *Children should be allowed the occasional treat.*

award • *A High Court judge awarded him £6 million damages.*

give • *We have been given permission to attend the meeting.*

permit • *The doorman said he could not permit them entry to the film.*

ANTONYM:
• deny

grant ③ VERB

to admit that something is true • *I grant that you had some justification for your actions.*

accept • *I do not accept that there is a crisis in British science.*

acknowledge • *He acknowledged that he had been partly to blame.*

admit • *I admit that I do make mistakes.*

allow • *He allows that capitalist development may result in social inequality.*

concede • *Bess finally conceded that Nancy was right.*

ANTONYM:
• deny

grasp ① VERB

to hold something firmly • *He grasped both my hands.*

clutch • *I staggered and had to clutch at a chair for support.*

grab • *I grabbed him by the hand.*

grip • *She gripped the rope.*

hold • *He held the pencil tightly in his right hand.*

seize • *He seized my arm to hold me back.*

snatch • *I snatched at a hanging branch and pulled myself up.*

grasp ② VERB

to understand an idea • *The Government has not yet grasped the seriousness of the crisis.*

absorb • *He only absorbed about half the information we gave him.*

appreciate • *She never really appreciated the bitterness of the conflict.*

assimilate • *My mind could only assimilate one concept at a time.*

realise • *People don't realise how serious this recession has been.*

take in • *She listens to the explanation, but you can see she's not taking it in.*

understand • *They are too young to understand what is going on.*

grasp ③ NOUN

a firm hold • *She slipped her hand from his grasp.*

clasp • *He gripped my hand in a strong clasp.*

embrace • *He held her in an embrace.*

grip • *His strong hand eased the bag from her grip.*

hold • *He released his hold on the camera.*

grasp ④ NOUN

a person's understanding of something • *They have a good grasp of foreign languages.*

awareness • *The children demonstrated their awareness of green issues.*

comprehension (FORMAL) • *This was utterly beyond her comprehension.*

grip • *He has lost his grip on reality.*

knowledge • *She has a good knowledge of these processes.*

understanding • *a basic understanding of how the mind works*

grateful ADJECTIVE

pleased and wanting to thank someone • *I am grateful to you for your help.*

appreciative • *We have been very appreciative of their support.*

indebted • *I am deeply indebted to him for his help.*

thankful • *I'm just thankful that I've got a job.*

ANTONYM:
• ungrateful

gratitude NOUN
the feeling of being grateful • *I wish to express my gratitude to Kathy Davis for her help.*

appreciation • *their appreciation of his efforts*

recognition • *an honour given in recognition of his help to the college*

thanks • *They accepted their certificates with words of thanks.*

ANTONYM:
• ingratitude

grave ① NOUN
a place where a corpse is buried • *They visited her grave twice a year.*

mausoleum • *the great mausoleum at the top of the hill*

pit • *The bodies were buried in a shallow pit.*

sepulchre (LITERARY) • *Death holds him in his sepulchre.*

tomb • *the tomb of the Unknown Soldier*

RELATED WORD:
• ADJECTIVE sepulchral

grave ② ADJECTIVE (FORMAL)
very worrying • *The situation in his country is very grave.*

acute • *The report has caused acute embarrassment to the government.*

critical • *Its finances are in a critical state.*

heavy (INFORMAL) • *Things were just starting to get heavy when the police arrived.*

serious • *The government faces very serious difficulties.*

grave ③ ADJECTIVE (FORMAL)
having a quiet and serious manner • *The doctor had a grave expression.*

sober • *a room filled with sad, sober faces*

solemn • *His solemn little face broke into smiles.*

sombre • *His expression became increasingly sombre.*

graze ① VERB
to slightly injure your skin • *He fell heavily and grazed his left arm.*

scrape • *She stumbled and fell, scraping her palms and knees.*

scratch • *The branches scratched my hands and face.*

skin • *He fell and skinned both his knees.*

graze ② NOUN
a slight injury to your skin • *He just has a slight graze.*

abrasion (FORMAL) • *He had severe abrasions to his right cheek.*

scratch • *She had scratches to her face.*

great ① ADJECTIVE
very large in size • *great columns of ice*

big • *He lives in a big house.*

colossal • *a colossal tomb*

huge • *a huge marquee in the grounds*

large • *a large pile of logs*

enormous • *They entered an enormous hall.*

extensive • *an extensive range of stock*

gigantic • *a gigantic theme park*

immense • *an immense building*

massive • *a massive surge in popularity*

stupendous • *a stupendous sum of money*

tremendous • *It's a tremendous challenge*

vast • *The fire destroyed a vast area of forest.*

ANTONYM:
• small

great ② ADJECTIVE
important or famous • *the great novels of the nineteenth century*

celebrated • *the celebrated author of "Lord of the Rings"*

chief • *one of our chief problems*

distinguished • *a distinguished baritone*

eminent • *two eminent French scientists*

famed • *the famed Australian actor*

famous • *a famous artist*

illustrious • *some of the world's most illustrious ballerinas*

important • *an important question*

main • *our main competitor*

major • *a major issue in the next election*

momentous • *a momentous occasion*

notable • *a notable chess player*

principal • *our principal aim*

prominent • *Scotland's most prominent historian*

renowned • *the renowned heart surgeon*

serious • *a serious deficiency in the system*

significant • *This is a significant step towards peace.*

g

great ③ ADJECTIVE
(INFORMAL)
very good • *I thought it was a great idea.*

beaut (AUSTRALIAN AND NEW ZEALAND; INFORMAL) • *a beaut place to live*

excellent • *an excellent pasta sauce*

fantastic (INFORMAL) • *a fantastic firework display*

fine • *The young actors put in a fine performance.*

first-rate • *They pride themselves on their first-rate service.*

marvellous • *a marvellous rooftop restaurant*

outstanding • *outstanding works of art*

superb • *a superb staircase made from oak*

terrific • *It was a terrific party.*

tremendous • *You've done a tremendous job.*

wonderful • *I've had a wonderful time.*

ANTONYM:
• terrible

greedy ADJECTIVE
wanting more than you
need • *greedy bosses who
award themselves huge pay
rises*
materialistic • *I think Britain
has become a very materialistic
society.*
snoep (SOUTH AFRICAN;
INFORMAL) • *a bunch of snoep
businessmen*

green ADJECTIVE
concerned with
environmental issues
• *Children and adolescents are
now aware of green issues.*
conservationist • *a chorus of
protest from conservationist
groups*
ecological • *shared interest in
ecological issues*

SHADES OF GREEN
apple green
avocado
bottle green
chartreuse
eau de nil
emerald
grass green
jade
khaki
lime
Lincoln green
olive
pea green
pistachio
sage
sea green
turquoise

RELATED WORD:
• ADJECTIVE verdant

greet VERB
to say hello to someone when
they arrive • *The president was
greeted by local political leaders.*
meet • *A nurse met me at the
entrance.*
receive (FORMAL) • *250 guests
were received by the bride and
bridegroom.*
welcome • *She was there to
welcome him home.*

grey NOUN or ADJECTIVE
SHADES OF GREY
ash
charcoal
gunmetal
pewter
platinum
silver
slate
steel grey
stone
taupe

grief NOUN
a feeling of extreme sadness
• *a huge outpouring of national
grief*
distress • *the intense distress
they were causing my family*
heartache • *She has suffered
more heartache than anyone
deserves.*
misery • *All that money brought
nothing but misery.*
sadness • *It is with a mixture of
sadness and joy that I say
farewell.*
sorrow • *a time of great sorrow*
unhappiness • *There was a lot
of unhappiness in my
adolescence.*

ANTONYM:
• happiness

grieve ① VERB
to feel extremely sad • *He still grieves for his wife.*
lament • *All who knew Spender will lament his death.*
mourn • *The whole nation mourns the death of their great leader.*

grieve ② VERB
to make someone feel extremely sad • *It grieved Elaine to be separated from her son.*
distress • *It distresses me that the President has not tackled crime.*
pain • *It pains me to think of you struggling all alone.*
sadden • *The cruelty in the world saddens me.*
upset • *The news upset me.*
ANTONYM:
• cheer

grim ADJECTIVE
looking very serious • *Her face was grim.*
grave (FORMAL) • *Mrs Williams was looking very grave.*
severe • *He leaned towards me, a severe expression on his face.*
solemn • *What a solemn-faced kid he had been.*
stern • *Michael gave the dog a stern look.*

grip ① NOUN
a firm hold on something • *His strong hand eased the bag from her grip.*

clasp • *With one last clasp of his hand, she left him.*
grasp • *The spade slipped from her grasp and fell to the ground.*
hold • *He released his hold on the camera.*

grip ② NOUN
someone's control over something • *The president maintains an iron grip on his country.*
clutches • *She fell into the clutches of the wrong sort of person.*
control • *The port area is under the control of rebel forces.*
influence • *Alexandra fell under the influence of Grigori Rasputin.*
power • *I was really in the power of my mother.*

grip ③ VERB
to hold something firmly • *Alison gripped the steering wheel and stared straight ahead.*
clutch • *Michelle clutched my arm.*
grasp • *He grasped both my hands.*
hold • *He was struggling to hold on to the rope.*

ground NOUN
the surface of the earth • *We slid down the roof and dropped to the ground.*
dirt • *They sat on the dirt in the shade of a tree.*
earth • *The road winds for miles through parched earth.*
land • *800 acres of agricultural land*

g

soil • *In Southern India the soil is fertile.*

terrain • *Farms give way to hilly terrain.*

grounds ① PLURAL NOUN

the land surrounding a building • *the grounds of the university*

estate • *Lord Wyville's estate in Yorkshire*

gardens • *an elegant Regency house set in beautiful gardens*

land • *Their home is on his father's land.*

grounds ② PLURAL NOUN

the reason for doing or thinking something • *Owen was against it on the grounds of expense.*

basis • *Could you tell me on what basis the fee is calculated?*

cause • *No one had cause to get angry or unpleasant.*

excuse • *There's no excuse for behaviour like that.*

justification • *There was no justification for what I was doing.*

reason • *Who would have a reason to want to harm her?*

group ① NOUN

a number of people or things • *a group of football supporters*

band • *a band of rebels*

bunch • *They're a nice bunch of lads.*

collection • *a collection of essays from foreign affairs experts*

crowd • *A small crowd of onlookers has gathered.*

gang • *a gang of teenagers*

pack • *a pack of cards*

party • *a party of sightseers*

set • *Different sets of people often use the same buildings.*

group ② VERB

to link people or things together • *Their responses are grouped into 11 categories.*

arrange • *He started to arrange the books in piles.*

class • *They are officially classed as visitors.*

classify • *Rocks can be classified according to their origin.*

organise • *I was organising the vast array of junk we had collected.*

sort • *The students are sorted into three ability groups.*

grow ① VERB

to increase in size or amount • *Bacteria grow more quickly once food is contaminated.*

develop • *These clashes could develop into open warfare.*

expand • *Will the universe continue to expand forever?*

increase • *Industrial output increased by 2%.*

multiply • *Her new job multiplied the demands on her time.*

ANTONYM:

• shrink

grow ② VERB

to be alive or exist • *Trees and bushes grew down to the water's edge.*

flourish • *The plant flourishes in slightly harsher climates.*

germinate • *Heat will encourage seeds to germinate.*
sprout • *It only takes a few days for beans to sprout.*

grow ③ VERB
to pass gradually into a particular state • *I grew a little afraid of the guy next door.*
become • *The wind became stronger.*
get • *The boys were getting bored.*
turn • *In October it turned cold.*

growth NOUN
the act of getting bigger • *the growth of the fishing industry*
development • *What are your plans for the development of your company?*
enlargement • *the enlargement of the European Union*
expansion • *a new period of economic expansion*
increase • *a sharp increase in the number of homeless people*

grumble ① VERB
to complain in a bad-tempered way • *"This is very inconvenient," he grumbled.*
carp • *the man whom other actors love to carp about*
complain • *They complained about the high cost of visiting Europe.*
groan • *parents groaning about the price of college tuition*
moan • *moaning about the weather*
mutter • *She could hear the woman muttering about missing the bus.*

whine • *children who whine that they are bored*
whinge • *All she ever does is whinge.*

grumble ② NOUN
a bad-tempered complaint • *I didn't hear any grumbles from anyone at the time.*
complaint • *I get nothing but complaints about my cooking.*
moan • *Sometimes it helps to have a good old moan.*
murmur • *She paid without a murmur.*
objection • *If you have any objections, please raise them now.*
protest • *Despite our protests, they went ahead with the plan.*
whinge • *It's depressing listening to everybody's whinges.*

grumpy ADJECTIVE
bad-tempered and annoyed • *Some passengers got grumpy when the train was delayed.*
irritable • *He had missed his dinner and grew irritable.*
sulky • *I was quite sulky, so I didn't take part in games.*
sullen • *Several leading players have maintained a sullen silence.*
surly • *They were surly, sometimes downright rude to me.*

guarantee ① NOUN
something that makes another thing certain • *The package offered a guarantee of job security.*
assurance • *a written assurance that he would start work at once*

g

pledge • *a pledge of support from the Ministry of Culture*

promise • *I'd made him a promise that I'd write a book for him.*

undertaking • *She gave an undertaking not to repeat the allegations.*

word • *He simply cannot be trusted to keep his word.*

guarantee ② VERB
to make it certain that something will happen • *Reports of this kind are guaranteed to cause anxiety.*

ensure • *We need to ensure that every student has basic literacy skills.*

pledge • *Both sides pledged that a nuclear war would never be fought.*

promise • *He promised that the rich would not get preferential treatment.*

guard ① VERB
to protect someone • *Police were guarding his home yesterday.*

defend • *He and his friends defended themselves against racist thugs.*

protect • *What can people do to protect themselves from heart disease?*

safeguard • *measures to safeguard their forces from chemical weapons*

shelter • *A neighbour sheltered the boy for several days.*

shield • *She had shielded him from the terrible truth.*

watch over • *two police officers to watch over him*

guard ② VERB
to stop someone making trouble or escaping • *The soldiers had been guarding paramilitary prisoners.*

patrol • *Prison officers continued to patrol the grounds.*

police • *It is extremely difficult to police the border.*

supervise • *Only two staff were supervising over 100 prisoners.*

guard ③ NOUN
someone who guards people or places • *The prisoners overpowered their guards and locked them in a cell.*

sentry • *We can sneak past the sentries.*

warden • *The siege began when the prisoners seized three wardens.*

guess ① VERB
to form an idea or opinion about something • *Wood guessed that he was a very successful banker.*

estimate • *It's difficult to estimate how much money is involved.*

imagine • *"Was she meeting someone?"—"I imagine so."*

reckon (INFORMAL) • *Toni reckoned that it must be about three o'clock.*

speculate • *The reader can speculate what will happen next.*

suppose • *I supposed you would have a meal somewhere.*

suspect • *I suspect they were right.*

think • *Nora thought he was seventeen years old.*

guess ② NOUN
an attempt to give the right answer • My guess is that the answer will be negative.
feeling • My feeling is that everything will come right for us.
reckoning • By my reckoning, 50% of the team will be available.
speculation • speculations about the future of the universe

guide ① VERB
to lead someone somewhere • He took Elliott by the arm and guided him out.
accompany • We accompanied Joe to the magazine's midtown offices.
direct • Officials directed him to the wrong airport.
escort • I escorted him to the door.
lead • The nurse led me to a large room.

guide ② VERB
to influence someone • He should have let his instinct guide him.
counsel (FORMAL) • Green was counselled not to talk to reporters.
govern • Our thinking is as much governed by habit as by behaviour.
influence • My dad influenced me to do electronics.

guilty ① ADJECTIVE
having done something wrong • They were found guilty of murder.
convicted • a convicted drug dealer

criminal • He had a criminal record for petty theft.
ANTONYM:
• innocent

guilty ② ADJECTIVE
unhappy because you have done something bad • When she saw me she looked guilty.
ashamed • Zumel said he was not ashamed of what he had done.
regretful • Surprisingly, she didn't feel regretful about her actions.
remorseful (FORMAL) • He felt remorseful for what he had done.
sorry • She was very sorry about all the trouble she'd caused.

gullible ADJECTIVE
easily tricked • I'm so gullible I would have believed him.
naive • It would be naive to believe Mr Gonzalez's statement.
trusting • She has an open, trusting nature.
ANTONYM:
• suspicious

gush VERB
to flow in large quantities • Piping-hot water gushed out.
flow • Tears flowed down his cheeks.
pour • Blood was pouring from his broken nose.
spurt • a fountain that spurts water nine stories high
stream • water streaming from the pipes

Hh

habit NOUN
something that is done
regularly • *his habit of smiling at
everyone he saw*
convention • *It's a social
convention to shake hands when
meeting.*
custom • *an ancient Japanese
custom*
practice • *the practice of
clocking in at work*
routine • *my daily routine*
tradition • *a family tradition at
Christmas*

habitat NOUN
the natural home of a plant or
animal • *the habitat of the
spotted owl*
environment • *a safe
environment for marine mammals*
territory • *a bird's territory*

hackneyed ADJECTIVE
used too often to be
meaningful • *hackneyed
postcard snaps of lochs and glens*
banal • *banal lyrics*
clichéd • *clichéd slogans*
stale • *Her writing style has
become stale.*
tired • *a tired excuse*
trite • *The film is teeming with
trite ideas.*

ANTONYM:
• original

hail ① NOUN
a lot of things falling together
• *a hail of bullets*
barrage • *a barrage of angry
questions*
bombardment • *the sound of
heavy aerial bombardment*
shower • *a shower of rose petals*
storm • *The announcement
provoked a storm of protest.*
volley • *A volley of shots rang
out.*

hail ② VERB
to attract someone's
attention • *He hailed me from
across the street.*
call • *He called me over the PA
system.*
signal to • *The lollipop lady
signalled to me to stop.*
wave down • *I ran on to the
road and waved down a taxi.*

halt ① VERB
to come or bring to a stop • *She
held her hand out to halt him.*
draw up • *The car drew up
outside the house.*
pull up • *The cab pulled up, and
the driver jumped out.*
stop • *The event literally stopped
the traffic.*

halt ② VERB
to bring something to an end
• *Production was halted.*
cease • *A small number of firms
have ceased trading.*
check • *measures to check the
spread of the disease*

curb • *efforts to curb the spread of nuclear weapons*
cut short • *They had to cut short a holiday abroad.*
end • *They decided to end the ceasefire.*
terminate (FORMAL) • *His contract has been terminated.*
ANTONYM:
• begin

halt ③ NOUN
an interruption or end to something • *He brought the car to a halt.*
close • *The musical was brought to a close.*
end • *The war came to an end.*
pause • *There was a pause before he replied.*
standstill • *The country was brought to a standstill by strikes.*
stop • *He slowed the car almost to a stop.*
stoppage • *Air and ground crew are staging a 24-hour stoppage today.*

hamper VERB
to make movement or progress difficult for someone • *I was hampered by a lack of information.*
frustrate • *His attempt was frustrated by the weather.*
hinder • *A thigh injury hindered her mobility.*
impede • *Their work was being impeded by shortages of supplies.*
obstruct • *charged with obstructing the course of justice*
restrict • *Her life is restricted by asthma.*

hand down VERB
to pass from one generation to another • *Recipes are handed down from parent to child.*
bequeath • *He bequeathed all his silver to his children.*
give • *a necklace given to me by my grandmother*
pass down • *an heirloom passed down from generation to generation*
pass on • *My parents passed on their love of classical music to me.*

handicap ① NOUN
something that makes progress difficult • *Being a foreigner was not a handicap.*
barrier • *Taxes are the most obvious barrier to free trade.*
disadvantage • *the disadvantage of unemployment*
drawback • *The flat's only drawback was that it was too small.*
hindrance • *She was a help rather than a hindrance to my work.*
impediment • *an impediment to economic development*
obstacle • *the main obstacle to the deal*

handicap ② VERB
to make something difficult for someone • *Greater levels of stress may seriously handicap some students.*
burden • *We decided not to burden him with the news.*
hamper • *I was hampered by a lack of information.*

h

hinder • A thigh injury hindered her mobility.
impede • Fallen rocks impeded the progress of the rescue workers.
restrict • laws to restrict foreign imports

handle ① NOUN

the part of an object by which it is held • a broom handle
grip • He fitted new grips to his golf clubs.
hilt • the hilt of the small, sharp knife

handle ② VERB

to hold or move with the hands • Wear rubber gloves when handling cat litter.
feel • The doctor felt her arm.
finger • He fingered the few coins in his pocket.
grasp • Grasp the end firmly.
hold • Hold it by the edge.
touch • She touched his hand reassuringly.

handle ③ VERB

to deal with or control something • She handled the travel arrangements.
administer • The project is administered by the World Bank.
conduct • This is no way to conduct a business.
deal with • The matter has been dealt with by the school.
manage • Within two years he was managing the store.
supervise • I supervise the packing of all mail orders.
take care of • He took care of the catering arrangements.

handsome ① ADJECTIVE

very attractive in appearance • a handsome man
attractive • an attractive woman
good-looking • good-looking actors
ANTONYM:
• ugly

handsome ② ADJECTIVE

large and generous • a handsome profit
ample • ample space for a good-sized kitchen
considerable • his considerable wealth
generous • a generous gift
liberal • a liberal donation
plentiful • a plentiful supply of vegetables
sizable or **sizeable** • He inherited the house and a sizeable chunk of land.
ANTONYM:
• small

handy ① ADJECTIVE

conveniently near • Keep a pencil and paper handy.
at hand • Having the right equipment at hand will be enormously useful.
at your fingertips • Firms need information at their fingertips.
close • a secluded area close to her home
convenient • Martin drove along until he found a convenient parking space.
nearby • He tossed the match into a nearby wastepaper bin.

on hand • *Experts are on hand to offer advice.*

handy ② ADJECTIVE
easy to handle or use • *handy hints on looking after indoor plants*
convenient • *a convenient way of paying*
easy to use • *This ice cream maker is cheap and easy to use.*
helpful • *helpful instructions*
neat • *It had been such a neat, clever plan.*
practical • *the most practical way of preventing crime*
useful • *useful information*
user-friendly • *Other user-friendly features include remote control.*

hang ① VERB
to be attached at the top with the lower part free • *His jacket hung from a hook behind the door.*
dangle • *A gold bracelet dangled from his left wrist.*
droop • *Pale wilting roses drooped from a vase.*

hang ② VERB
to fasten something to another thing by its top • *I hung the clothes on the line.*
attach • *He attached the picture to the wall with a nail.*
drape • *He draped the coat round his shoulders.*
fasten • *stirrups fastened to the saddle*
fix • *He fixed a pirate flag to the mast.*
suspend • *The TV is suspended from the ceiling on brackets.*

happen VERB
to take place • *The accident happened on Wednesday.*
come about • *It came about almost by accident.*
follow • *He was arrested in the confusion which followed.*
occur • *The crash occurred on a sharp bend.*
result • *Ignore the early warnings and illness could result.*
take place • *The festival took place last September.*

happiness NOUN
a feeling of great pleasure • *Money can't buy happiness.*
delight • *To my delight, it worked perfectly.*
ecstasy • *a state of ecstasy*
elation • *His supporters reacted to the news with elation.*
joy • *tears of joy*
pleasure • *I get a lot of pleasure from music.*
satisfaction • *job satisfaction*
ANTONYM:
• sadness

happy ① ADJECTIVE
feeling or causing joy • *a happy atmosphere*
▶ see Word Study **happy**, page 711
ANTONYM:
• sad

happy ② ADJECTIVE
fortunate or lucky • *a happy coincidence*
auspicious • *It was not an auspicious start to his new job.*
convenient • *a convenient outcome for all concerned*

favourable • *a favourable result*
fortunate • *We're in a very fortunate situation.*
lucky • *It was a lucky chance that you were here.*
opportune • *It was hardly an opportune moment to bring the subject up.*
timely • *his timely arrival*
ANTONYM:
• unlucky

hard ① ADJECTIVE

firm, solid or rigid • *a hard piece of cheese*
firm • *a firm mattress*
rigid • *rigid plastic containers*
solid • *solid rock*
stiff • *stiff metal wires*
strong • *It has a strong casing which won't crack or chip.*
tough • *dark brown beans with a rather tough outer skin*
ANTONYM:
• soft

hard ② ADJECTIVE

requiring a lot of effort • *hard work*
arduous • *a long, arduous journey*
exhausting • *It's a pretty exhausting job.*
laborious • *Keeping the garden tidy can be a laborious task.*
rigorous • *rigorous military training*
strenuous • *Avoid strenuous exercise in the evening.*
tough • *Change is often tough to deal with.*
ANTONYM:
• easy

hard ③ ADJECTIVE

difficult to understand • *That's a very hard question.*
baffling • *a baffling remark*
complex • *a complex problem*
complicated • *a complicated system of voting*
difficult • *It was a very difficult decision to make.*
puzzling • *Some of this book is rather puzzling.*
ANTONYM:
• simple

harden VERB

to make or become stiff or firm • *Give the cardboard two coats of varnish to harden it.*
bake • *The soil had been baked solid by the heatwave.*
cake • *The blood had begun to cake and turn brown.*
freeze • *The lake freezes in winter.*
set • *Lower the heat and allow the omelette to set.*
stiffen • *paper that had been stiffened with paste*
ANTONYM:
• soften

hardly ADVERB

almost not or not quite • *I could hardly believe what I was seeing.*
barely • *His voice was barely audible.*
just • *Her hand was just visible under her coat.*
only just • *For centuries farmers there have only just managed to survive.*
scarcely • *He could scarcely breathe.*

hardship NOUN

difficult circumstances • Many people are suffering economic hardship.

adversity • They manage to enjoy life despite adversity.

destitution • a life of poverty and destitution

difficulty • Many new golf clubs are in serious financial difficulty.

misfortune • She seemed to enjoy the misfortunes of others.

want • They were fighting for freedom of speech and freedom from want.

harm ① VERB

to injure someone or damage something • The hijackers seemed anxious not to harm anyone.

abuse • Animals are still being exploited and abused.

damage • He damaged his knee during training.

hurt • He fell and hurt his back.

ill-treat • They thought he had been ill-treating his pets.

ruin • My wife was ruining her health through worry.

wound • The bomb wounded five people.

harm ② NOUN

injury or damage • the harm caused by lies and deceit

abuse • The abuse of animals is inexcusable.

damage • The bomb caused extensive damage.

hurt • an evil desire to cause hurt and damage

injury • The two other passengers escaped serious injury.

harmful ADJECTIVE

having a bad effect on something • Whilst most stress is harmful, some is beneficial.

damaging • damaging allegations about his business dealings

destructive • the awesome destructive power of nuclear weapons

detrimental • levels of radioactivity which are detrimental to public health

hurtful • Her comments can only be hurtful to the family.

pernicious • the pernicious influence of secret societies

ANTONYM:
• harmless

harmless ADJECTIVE

safe to use or be near • This experiment was harmless to the animals.

innocuous • Both mushrooms look innocuous but are in fact deadly.

nontoxic • a cheap and nontoxic method of cleaning up our water

not dangerous • The tests are not dangerous to the environment.

safe • The doll is safe for children.

ANTONYM:
• harmful

harsh ADJECTIVE

severe, difficult and unpleasant • harsh weather conditions

austere • The life of the troops was still comparatively austere.

h

cruel • *an unusually cruel winter*
hard • *He had a hard life.*
ruthless • *the ruthless treatment of staff*
severe • *My boss gave me a severe reprimand.*
stern • *a stern warning*
ANTONYM:
• mild

hassle ① NOUN (INFORMAL)
something that is difficult or causes trouble • *It's not worth the hassle.*
bother • *I buy sliced bread – it's less bother.*
effort • *This chore is well worth the effort.*
inconvenience • *the expense and inconvenience of having central heating installed*
trouble • *You've caused us a lot of trouble.*
upheaval • *Moving house is always a big upheaval.*

hassle ② VERB (INFORMAL)
to annoy someone by nagging or making demands • *My boss started hassling me.*
badger • *They kept badgering me to go back.*
bother • *Go away and don't bother me about all that just now.*
go on at • *She's always going on at me to have a go back.*
harass • *The woman was harassed by her neighbours.*
nag • *He was nagging me about cleaning the car.*
pester • *He gets fed up with people pestering him for money.*

hasty ADJECTIVE
done or happening suddenly and quickly • *The signs of their hasty departure could be seen everywhere.*
brisk • *a brisk walk*
hurried • *a hurried breakfast*
prompt • *It is not too late, but prompt action is needed.*
rapid • *a rapid retreat*
swift • *my swift departure*

hate ① VERB
to have a strong dislike for something or someone • *Most people hate him, but they don't care to say so.*
abhor (FORMAL) • *He abhorred violence.*
be sick of • *We're sick of being ripped off.*
despise • *A lot of people despise and loathe what I do.*
detest • *Jean detested being photographed.*
dislike • *those who dislike change*
loathe • *a play universally loathed by the critics*
ANTONYM:
• love

hate ② NOUN
a strong dislike • *a violent bully destructive and full of hate*
animosity • *The animosity between the two men grew.*
aversion • *I've always had an aversion to being part of a group*
dislike • *Consider what your likes and dislikes are about your job.*
hatred • *her hatred of authority*

hostility • *He looked at her with open hostility.*
loathing • *Critics are united in their unmitigated loathing of the band.*

ANTONYM:
• love

hateful ADJECTIVE
extremely unpleasant • *It was a hateful thing to say.*
abhorrent (FORMAL)
• *Discrimination is abhorrent to my council and our staff.*
despicable • *a despicable crime*
horrible • *a horrible, snarling cat*
loathsome • *the loathsome spectacle we were obliged to witness*
obnoxious • *He was a most obnoxious character. No-one liked him.*
offensive • *an offensive remark*

hatred NOUN
an extremely strong feeling of dislike • *her hatred of authority*
animosity • *The animosity between the two men grew.*
antipathy (FORMAL) • *public antipathy towards politicians*
aversion • *my aversion to housework*
dislike • *his dislike of modern buildings*
hate • *These people are so full of hate.*
revulsion • *They expressed their revulsion at events.*

ANTONYM:
• love

haughty ADJECTIVE
showing excessive pride • *He spoke in a haughty tone.*
arrogant • *an air of arrogant indifference*
conceited • *They had grown too conceited and pleased with themselves.*
disdainful • *She cast a disdainful glance at me.*
proud • *She was said to be proud and arrogant.*
snobbish • *They had a snobbish dislike for their intellectual inferiors.*
stuck-up (INFORMAL) • *She was a famous actor, but she wasn't a bit stuck-up.*

ANTONYM:
• humble

have ① VERB
to own something • *We have two tickets for the concert.*
hold • *He does not hold a firearm certificate.*
keep • *We keep chickens.*
own • *His father owns a local pub.*
possess • *He is said to possess a fortune.*

have ② VERB
to experience something • *He had a marvellous time.*
endure • *The company endured heavy losses.*
enjoy • *The average German will enjoy 40 days' paid holiday this year.*
experience • *We are experiencing a few technical problems.*

feel • *I felt a sharp pain in my shoulder.*
sustain • *He had sustained a cut on his left eyebrow.*
undergo • *He recently underwent brain surgery.*

head ① NOUN
a person's mind and mental abilities • *I don't have a head for business.*
aptitude • *an aptitude for accountancy*
brain • *If you stop using your brain you'll go stale.*
common sense • *Use your common sense.*
intelligence • *Try to use your intelligence to solve the puzzle – don't just guess.*
mind • *I'm trying to clear my mind of all this.*
wits • *She has used her wits to get where she is today.*

head ② NOUN
the top, front or start of something • *the head of the queue*
beginning • *the beginning of this chapter*
front • *Stand at the front of the line.*
source • *the source of this great river*
start • *Go back to the start of this section.*
top • *the top of the stairs*
ANTONYM:
• tail

head ③ NOUN
the person in charge of something • *heads of government*

boss • *the boss of the new company*
chief • *the President's chief of security*
director • *the director of the Edinburgh Festival*
leader • *the leader of the Conservative Party*
manager • *the manager of our division*
president • *the president of the medical commission*
principal • *the principal of the school*

head ④ VERB
to be in charge of something • *He heads the department.*
be in charge of • *She's in charge of the overseas division.*
control • *He controls the largest fast food empire in the world.*
direct • *Christopher will direct day-to-day operations.*
lead • *leading a campaign to save the rainforest*
manage • *Within two years he was managing the store.*
run • *Each teacher will run a different workshop.*

health ① NOUN
the condition of your body • *Smoking is bad for your health.*
condition • *He remains in a critical condition in hospital.*
constitution • *He must have an extremely strong constitution*
shape • *He is in great shape for his age.*

health ② NOUN
a state in which a person is

feeling well • *In hospital they nursed me back to health.*
fitness • *He has fitness problems.*
good condition • *She is in good condition despite her recent illness.*
wellbeing • *Singing can create a sense of wellbeing.*

ANTONYM:
• illness

healthy ① ADJECTIVE
having good health • *She was a very healthy child.*
fit • *A short, physically fit man of 61.*
in good shape (INFORMAL) • *I kept myself in good shape by swimming.*
robust • *a robust and vibrant young man*
strong • *a strong constitution*
well • *I'm not very well today.*

ANTONYM:
• ill

healthy ② ADJECTIVE
producing good health • *a healthy diet*
beneficial • *beneficial natural herbs*
bracing • *a bracing walk*
good for you • *Regular, moderate exercise is good for you.*
nourishing • *sensible, nourishing food*
nutritious • *a hot, nutritious meal*
wholesome • *fresh, wholesome ingredients*

ANTONYM:
• unhealthy

heap ① NOUN
a pile of things • *a heap of rubble*
hoard • *a hoard of silver and jewels*
mass • *a mass of flowers*
mound • *The bulldozers piled up huge mounds of dirt.*
pile • *a pile of discarded socks*
stack • *stacks of books on the bedside table*

heap ② VERB
to pile things up • *She heaped vegetables onto his plate.*
pile • *He was piling clothes into the suitcase.*
stack • *They stacked up pillows behind his back.*

heaps PLURAL NOUN
(INFORMAL)
plenty of something • *heaps of energy*
loads (INFORMAL) • *I've got loads of money.*
lots (INFORMAL) • *lots of fun*
plenty • *We've got plenty of time before the bus comes.*
stacks (INFORMAL) • *She has stacks of friends.*
tons (INFORMAL) • *I've got tons of work to do.*

hear ① VERB
to listen to something • *I heard the sound of gunfire.*
catch • *Sorry, I didn't catch your name.*
eavesdrop • *The government illegally eavesdropped on his phone conversations.*
heed • *Few at the conference heeded his warning.*
listen in • *Secret agents listened in on his phone calls.*

listen to • *He spent his time listening to the radio.*
overhear • *I overheard two doctors discussing my case.*

hear ② VERB
to learn about something • *I heard that he was forced to resign.*
ascertain • *They had ascertained that he was not a spy.*
discover • *She discovered that they'd escaped.*
find out • *As soon as we found this out, we closed the ward.*
gather • *I gather the report is critical of the judge.*
learn • *She wasn't surprised to learn that he was involved.*
understand • *I understand that she's just taken early retirement.*

heat ① NOUN
the quality of being warm or hot • *the heat of the sun*
high temperature • *The suffering caused by the high temperature has been great.*
warmth • *the warmth of the sand between her toes*
ANTONYM:
• cold
RELATED WORD:
• ADJECTIVE thermal

heat ② NOUN
a state of strong emotion • *in the heat of the election campaign*
excitement • *in a state of great excitement*
fervour • *religious fervour*
intensity • *the intensity of feeling about this issue*

passion • *He spoke with great passion.*
vehemence • *I was surprised by the vehemence of his criticism.*

heat ③ VERB
to raise the temperature of something • *Heat the oil in a frying pan.*
reheat • *Reheat the soup to a gentle simmer.*
warm up • *Just before serving, warm up the tomato sauce.*
ANTONYM:
• cool

heaven ① NOUN
the place where good people are believed to go when they die • *She told them their mother was now in heaven.*
next world • *He said, "We will see each other again in the next world."*
paradise • *They believed they would go to paradise if they died in battle.*
ANTONYM:
• hell

heaven ② NOUN
a place or situation liked very much • *I was in cinematic heaven*
bliss • *a scene of domestic bliss*
ecstasy • *the ecstasy of being in love*
paradise • *The Algarve is a golfer's paradise.*
rapture • *the sheer rapture of listening to Bach's music*

heavy ① ADJECTIVE
great in weight or force • *a heavy frying pan*

bulky • *a bulky grey sweater*
massive • *a massive blue whale*
ANTONYM:
• light

heavy ② ADJECTIVE
serious or important • *a heavy speech*
deep • *a period of deep personal crisis*
grave (FORMAL) • *the grave crisis facing the country*
profound • *Anna's patriotism was profound.*
serious • *It was a question which deserved serious consideration.*
solemn • *a simple, solemn ceremony*
weighty • *Surely such weighty matters merit a higher level of debate.*
ANTONYM:
• trivial

heed ① VERB
to pay attention to someone's advice • *Few at the conference heeded his warning.*
follow • *If you are not going to follow my advice, we are both wasting our time.*
listen to • *They won't listen to my advice.*
pay attention to • *The food industry is now paying attention to young consumers.*
take notice of • *We want the government to take notice of what we think.*

heed ② NOUN
careful attention • *He pays too much heed to her.*

attention • *He never paid much attention to his audience.*
notice • *So do they take any notice of public opinion?*

hell ① NOUN
the place where souls of evil people are believed to go after death • *Milton's Satan would rather "reign in Hell, than serve in Heaven".*
abyss • *Satan rules over the dark abyss.*
inferno • *an inferno described in loving detail by Dante*
ANTONYM:
• heaven

hell ② NOUN (INFORMAL)
an unpleasant situation or place • *His feelings of guilt made his life hell.*
agony • *the agony of divorce*
anguish • *the anguish of families unable to trace relatives who've disappeared*
misery • *All that money brought nothing but sadness and misery.*
nightmare • *The years in prison were a nightmare.*
ordeal • *the painful ordeal of the last year*

hello INTERJECTION
a greeting • *I popped my head in to say hello.*
gidday (AUSTRALIAN AND NEW ZEALAND) • *Gidday, mate! How you doing?*
good afternoon (FORMAL) • *Good afternoon. Won't you sit down?*
good evening (FORMAL) • *Good evening, and welcome!*

h

H

good morning (FORMAL)
• Good morning, everyone.
hi (INFORMAL) • She smiled and
said, "Hi."
how do you do? (FORMAL)
• "How do you do, Mrs Brown?"
Sam said, holding out his hand.
ANTONYM:
• goodbye

help ① VERB
to make something easier or
better for someone • He began
to help with the chores.
aid • a software system to aid
managers
assist • information to assist you
lend a hand • I'd be glad to lend
a hand.
support • He thanked everyone
who had supported the
campaign.

help ② NOUN
assistance or support • The
books were not much help.
advice • He has given me lots of
good advice in my time here.
aid • millions of dollars of aid
assistance • I would be grateful
for any assistance.
guidance • the reports which
were produced under his
guidance
helping hand • Students
sometimes need a helping hand.
support • Only 60 clubs pledged
their support for the scheme.

helper NOUN
a person who gives assistance
• There is an adult helper for every
two children.
aide • a presidential aide

assistant • a research assistant
deputy • I can't make it so I'll
send my deputy.
henchman • Adolf Eichmann,
Hitler's notorious henchman
right-hand man • He was the
perfect right-hand man for the
president.
supporter • the Prime Minister
and his supporters

helpful ① ADJECTIVE
giving assistance or advice
• The staff in the office are very
helpful.
accommodating • Paul
seemed a nice, accommodating
colleague.
cooperative • I made every
effort to be cooperative.
kind • I must thank you for being
so kind to me.
supportive • Her boss was very
supportive.
ANTONYM:
• unhelpful

helpful ② ADJECTIVE
making a situation better
• Having the right equipment will
be enormously helpful.
advantageous • an
advantageous arrangement
beneficial • beneficial changes
in the tax system
constructive • constructive
criticism
profitable • a profitable
exchange of ideas
useful • useful information

helpless ADJECTIVE
weak or unable to cope • a
helpless baby

defenceless • *a savage attack on a defenceless person*
powerless • *He was powerless to help.*
unprotected • *She felt unprotected and defenceless.*
vulnerable • *the most vulnerable members of society*
weak • *taking ruthless advantage of a weak man*

hesitant ADJECTIVE
uncertain about something • *At first he was hesitant to accept the role.*
diffident • *John was as outgoing as Helen was diffident.*
doubtful • *I was very doubtful about the chances for success.*
reluctant • *She was reluctant to get involved.*
unsure • *He made her feel awkward and unsure of herself.*
wavering • *wavering voters*

hesitate VERB
to pause or show uncertainty • *She hesitated before replying.*
dither • *We're still dithering over whether to marry.*
pause • *The crowd paused for a minute, wondering what to do next.*
waver • *Louise never wavered in her determination to take up the post.*

hide ① VERB
to put something where it cannot be seen • *She hid her face in her hands.*
cache • *He has £289 million cached away.*

conceal • *The hat concealed her hair.*
secrete • *She secreted the letter in the kitchen cabinet.*
stash (INFORMAL) • *He had stashed money away in a secret offshore account.*

hide ② NOUN
the skin of a large animal • *the process of tanning hides*
pelt • *a bed covered with beaver pelts*
skin • *a leopard-skin coat*

high ① ADJECTIVE
tall or a long way above the ground • *a high tower*
elevated • *an apartment in an elevated position overlooking the docks*
lofty • *lofty towers and spires*
soaring • *a 14th-century church with a soaring spire*
steep • *the steep hill leading up to their house*
tall • *a garden screened by tall walls*
towering • *towering red sandstone cliffs*
ANTONYM:
• low

high ② ADJECTIVE
great in degree, quantity or intensity • *There is a high risk of heart disease.*
acute • *a state of acute anxiety*
excessive • *He was driving at excessive speed.*
extraordinary • *an extraordinary number of people*
extreme • *acting under extreme emotional pressure*

h

great • *These products created a great level of interest.*

severe • *There are severe penalties for drug smuggling.*

ANTONYM:
• low

hill NOUN

TYPES OF HILL
brae (SCOTTISH)
down
dune
elevation
fell
foothill
height
hillock
hummock
knoll
kopje (SOUTH AFRICAN)
mound
prominence
tor

hinder VERB
to get in the way of someone or something • *A thigh injury hindered her mobility.*

block • *The President is blocking the release of the two men.*

check • *We have managed to check the spread of terrorism.*

delay • *Various problems have delayed production.*

frustrate • *They have frustrated his efforts to gain a work permit.*

hamper • *I was hampered by a lack of information.*

impede • *Fallen rocks are impeding the progress of rescue workers.*

hint ① NOUN
an indirect suggestion • *He gave a strong hint that there would be*

a referendum sooner rather than later.

clue • *How a man shaves may be a telling clue to his age.*

indication • *He gave no indication that he was ready to compromise.*

intimation • *I did not have any intimation that he was going to resign.*

suggestion • *We reject any suggestion that the law needs amending.*

hint ② NOUN
a helpful piece of advice • *I hope to get some fashion hints.*

advice • *Don't be afraid to ask for advice.*

pointer • *Here are a few pointers to help you make your choice.*

suggestion • *Can I give you a few suggestions?*

tip • *tips for busy managers*

hint ③ VERB
to suggest something indirectly • *Criticism is hinted at but never made explicit.*

imply • *The report implied that his death was inevitable.*

indicate • *She has indicated that she may resign.*

insinuate • *an article which insinuated that he was lying*

intimate • *He intimated that he was contemplating a shake-up of the company.*

suggest • *Are you suggesting that I need to lose some weight?*

hire ① VERB
to pay money to use something • *She hired the car for three days.*

charter • *They chartered a jet to fly her home.*
lease • *He went to Toronto, where he leased an apartment.*
rent • *She rents a house with three other girls.*

hire ② VERB
to employ the services of someone • *The staff have been hired on short-term contracts.*
appoint • *The Prime Minister has appointed a civilian as defence minister.*
commission • *You can commission her to paint something especially for you.*
employ • *They employed me as a nanny.*
engage • *We engaged the services of a recognised engineer.*
sign up • *He persuaded the company to sign her up.*

hit ① VERB
to strike someone or something forcefully • *They were hitting the sides of the van with sticks.*
▶ see Word Study **hit**, page 712

hit ② VERB
to collide with something • *The car had apparently hit a traffic sign.*
bang into • *She fell after another skier banged into her.*
bump • *The boat bumped against something.*
collide with • *He almost collided with Daisy.*
meet head-on • *Their cars met head-on down a narrow alleyway.*

run into • *The mail train ran into a derailed goods train at 75mph.*
smash into • *The car plunged down a cliff and smashed into a tree.*

hit ③ NOUN
the action of hitting something • *Give it a good hard hit with the hammer.*
blow • *He went to hospital after a blow to the face.*
knock • *a painful knock on the knee*
rap • *There was a rap on the door.*
slap • *She reached forward and gave him a slap.*
smack • *a smack with a ruler*
stroke • *six strokes of the cane*

hoard ① VERB
to store for future use • *People have begun to hoard food and petrol.*
save • *Save some fuel in case of emergencies.*
stockpile • *People are stockpiling food for the coming winter.*
store • *It's perfect for storing eggs or vegetables.*

hoard ② NOUN
a store of things • *a hoard of silver and jewels*
cache • *a cache of weapons and explosives*
fund • *a scholarship fund for engineering students*
reserve • *the world's oil reserves*
stockpile • *stockpiles of nuclear warheads*

h

store • *I have a store of food and water here.*
supply • *food supplies*

hoarse ADJECTIVE
rough and unclear • *Nick's voice was hoarse with screaming.*
croaky • *He sounds a bit croaky today.*
gruff • *his gruff Scottish growl*
husky • *Her deep husky voice was her trademark.*
rasping • *Both men sang in a deep rasping tone.*
ANTONYM:
• clear

hobby NOUN
an enjoyable activity pursued in your spare time • *My hobbies are music and photography.*
diversion • *Finger painting is very messy but an excellent diversion.*
leisure activity • *America's top leisure activity is watching television.*
leisure pursuit • *His main leisure pursuit is hill walking.*
pastime • *His favourite pastime is golf.*

hold ① VERB
to carry or support something • *Hold the baby while I load the car.*
carry • *He was carrying a briefcase.*
clasp • *She clasped the children to her.*
clutch • *He was clutching a photograph.*
embrace • *The couple in the corridor were embracing each other.*

grasp • *He grasped both my hands.*
grip • *They gripped the rope tightly.*

hold ② NOUN
power or control over someone or something • *The party has a considerable hold over its own leader.*
control • *He will have to give up his control of the company.*
dominance • *the gang's dominance of the London underworld*
sway • *ideas that held sway for centuries*

hold ③ NOUN
the act or a way of holding something • *He grabbed the rope and got a hold on it.*
grasp • *His hand was taken in a warm, firm grasp.*
grip • *His strong hand eased the bag from her grip.*

hole ① NOUN
an opening or hollow in something • *The builders had cut holes into the stone.*
gap • *The wind was tearing through gaps in the window frames.*
hollow • *Water gathers in a hollow and forms a pond.*
opening • *He squeezed through a narrow opening in the fence.*
pit • *He lost his footing and began to slide into the pit.*
split • *The seat has a few small splits around the corners.*
tear • *I peered through a tear in the van's curtains.*

hole ② NOUN
a weakness in a theory or
argument • There are some
holes in that theory.
defect • A defect in the aircraft
caused the crash.
error • NASA discovered an error
in its calculations.
fault • There is a fault in the
computer program.
flaw • Almost all of these studies
have serious flaws.
loophole • They exploited a
loophole in the law.

hole ③ NOUN (INFORMAL)
a difficult situation • He
admitted that the government
was in a hole.
fix (INFORMAL) • This will put
homeowners in a fix.
hot water (INFORMAL) • They
have already been in hot water
over high prices this year.
mess • the many reasons why
the economy is in such a mess
predicament • the once
great club's current
predicament
tight spot (INFORMAL) • This
was one tight spot he couldn't get
out of.

holiday NOUN
time spent away from home
for enjoyment • I'm exhausted
– I really need a holiday.
break • They are currently
taking a short break in Spain.
leave • Why don't you take a few
days' leave?
recess • Parliament returns
today after its summer recess.

staycation (INFORMAL) • The
recession made the staycation
very popular.
time off • He took time off to go
sailing with his wife.
vacation • We went on vacation
to Puerto Rico.

holy ① ADJECTIVE
relating to God or a particular
religion • Muslims consider this
a holy place.
blessed • Blessed are the
peacemakers, for they shall be
called the children of God.
consecrated • the consecrated
bread from the Eucharist
hallowed • hallowed ground
sacred • sacred music
sacrosanct • For him the
Sabbath was sacrosanct.
venerated (FORMAL) • the
nation's most venerated shrine

holy ② ADJECTIVE
religious and leading a good life
• He was considered a holy man,
a combination of doctor and priest.
devout • She is a devout believer.
pious • He was brought up by
pious relatives.
religious • They are both very
religious.
saintly • his saintly mother
virtuous • a virtuous family man
ANTONYM:
• wicked

home ① NOUN
the building in which someone
lives • They stayed at home and
watched TV.
abode (OLD-FASHIONED) • a
luxurious abode

h

dwelling (FORMAL) • *One thousand new dwellings are planned for the area.*

house • *our new house*

residence (FORMAL) • *the Royal Family's private residence*

home ② ADJECTIVE
involving your own country • *the home news pages of this newspaper*

domestic • *over 100 domestic flights a day to 15 UK destinations*

internal • *The government stepped up internal security.*

national • *major national and international issues*

native • *He was glad to be back on his native soil.*

ANTONYM:
• foreign

homely ADJECTIVE
simple, ordinary and comfortable • *The room was small and homely.*

comfortable • *A home should be warm and comfortable.*

cosy • *Guests can relax in the cosy lounge.*

modest • *the modest home of a family who lived off the land*

simple • *They held the service in a simple chapel.*

welcoming • *The restaurant is small and very welcoming.*

ANTONYM:
• grand

honest ADJECTIVE
truthful and trustworthy • *He is a very honest, decent man.*

law-abiding • *law-abiding citizens*

reputable • *a reputable car dealer*

trustworthy • *She is a trustworthy and level-headed leader.*

truthful • *She could not give him a truthful answer.*

virtuous • *a virtuous family man*

ANTONYM:
• dishonest

honour ① NOUN
personal integrity • *I can no longer serve with honour in your government.*

decency • *No-one had the decency to tell me to my face.*

goodness • *He retains a faith in human goodness.*

honesty • *Her reputation for honesty and integrity is second to none.*

integrity • *He was praised for his fairness and high integrity.*

ANTONYM:
• dishonour

honour ② NOUN
an award or mark of respect • *He was showered with honours – among them an Oscar.*

accolade • *the ultimate international accolade, the Nobel Peace prize*

commendation • *The officer received a commendation for brave conduct.*

homage • *films that pay homage to our literary heritage*

praise • *He had won consistently high praise for his theatre work.*

recognition • *At last, her father's work has received popular recognition.*

tribute • *He paid tribute to the organising committee.*

honour ③ VERB
to give someone special praise • *He was honoured by the French government with the Légion d'Honneur.*

commemorate • *a plaque commemorating the servicemen who died*

commend • *I commended her for that action.*

decorate • *He was decorated for his gallantry by the General.*

glorify • *His aim in life was to glorify God.*

praise • *She praised their excellent work.*

hooligan NOUN
a destructive and violent young person • *Two buses were badly damaged by hooligans.*

delinquent • *a nine-year-old delinquent*

hoon (AUSTRALIAN AND NEW ZEALAND; INFORMAL) • *the rocks hurled by hoons*

lout • *He was attacked by stone-throwing louts.*

vandal • *The Scout hut was burnt down by vandals.*

yob (BRITISH AND AUSTRALIAN; SLANG) • *drunken yobs chanting football songs*

hope NOUN
a wish or feeling of desire and expectation • *There was little hope of recovery.*

ambition • *His ambition is to sail around the world.*

dream • *his dream of becoming a pilot*

expectation • *The hotel was being renovated in expectation of a tourist boom.*

hopeless ① ADJECTIVE
certain to fail or be unsuccessful • *Our situation is hopeless.*

forlorn • *the forlorn hope of finding a better life*

futile • *their futile attempts to avoid publicity*

impossible • *The tax is impossible to administer.*

pointless • *a pointless exercise that would only waste more time*

useless • *She knew it was useless to protest.*

vain • *a vain attempt to sign a goalkeeper*

hopeless ② ADJECTIVE
bad or inadequate • *I don't drive and the buses are hopeless.*

inadequate • *The problem lies with inadequate staffing.*

pathetic • *the pathetic state of the rail network*

poor • *The flat was in a poor state of repair.*

useless (INFORMAL) • *I am useless at games.*

horrible ① ADJECTIVE
disagreeable or unpleasant • *a horrible, snarling cat*

awful • *I had an awful time.*

disagreeable • *a disagreeable odour*

horrid (OLD-FASHIONED) • *My brothers are horrid to each other.*

h

horrible

mean • *Why are you always so mean to me?*

nasty • *This match could turn nasty.*

unpleasant • *He's a very unpleasant man.*

horrible ② ADJECTIVE
causing shock, fear or disgust • *horrible crimes*

appalling • *They have been living under the most appalling conditions.*

dreadful • *She told me the dreadful news.*

grim • *a grim discovery*

gruesome • *gruesome murders*

terrifying • *a terrifying experience*

horrify VERB
to cause to feel horror or shock • *a crime trend that will horrify parents*

appal • *I was appalled by her behaviour.*

disgust • *He disgusted everyone with his boorish behaviour.*

dismay • *He was deeply dismayed by the decision.*

outrage • *Human rights campaigners were outraged by the execution.*

shock • *Pictures of emaciated prisoners shocked the world.*

sicken • *What he saw at the accident sickened him.*

horror ① NOUN
a strong feeling of alarm or disgust • *He gazed in horror at the knife.*

alarm • *She sat up in alarm.*

dread • *She thought with dread of the cold winter to come.*

fear • *I stood there crying and shaking with fear.*

fright • *He uttered a shriek and jumped with fright.*

panic • *He felt a sudden rush of panic at the thought.*

terror • *She shook with terror.*

horror ② NOUN
a strong fear of something • *his horror of death*

abhorrence (FORMAL) • *their abhorrence of racism*

aversion • *Many people have a natural aversion to insects.*

disgust • *I threw the book aside in disgust.*

hatred • *My hatred for him is intense.*

loathing • *She looked at him with loathing.*

revulsion • *They expressed their revulsion at his violent death.*

horse NOUN
an animal kept for riding • *a fall from a horse*

brumby (AUSTRALIAN AND NEW ZEALAND) • *There's a mob of about 30 brumbies up there.*

equine (FORMAL) • *the history and uses of equines*

moke (AUSTRALIAN AND NEW ZEALAND; SLANG) • *a tired old moke*

nag (INFORMAL) • *He unhitched his sorry-looking nag from a nearby post.*

pony • *Peter trotted about on the fat pony he had been given.*

RELATED WORDS:
• ADJECTIVES equestrian, equine, horsey

• NOUN equitation
• MALE stallion
• FEMALE mare
• YOUNG colt, filly, foal

hostile ADJECTIVE
unfriendly, aggressive and
unpleasant • *The Governor
faced hostile crowds.*
antagonistic • *They were
nearly all antagonistic to the
idea.*
belligerent • *a belligerent war
of words between India and
Pakistan*
malevolent • *He fixed our
photographer with a malevolent
stare.*
unkind • *All last summer he'd
been unkind to her.*
ANTONYM:
• friendly

hostility NOUN
aggressive or unfriendly
behaviour towards someone
or something • *She looked at me
with open hostility.*
animosity • *The animosity
between the two men grew.*
antagonism • *a history of
antagonism between the two sides*
hatred • *her lifelong hatred of
authority*
ill will • *He didn't bear anyone
any ill will.*
malice • *There was no malice in
her voice.*
resentment • *There is growing
resentment against newcomers.*
ANTONYM:
• friendship

hot ① ADJECTIVE
having a high temperature
• *a hot climate*
boiling • *It's boiling in here.*
heated • *a heated swimming
pool*
scalding • *Her son was burned
by scalding tea.*
scorching • *It was a scorching
hot day.*
warm • *a warm, dry summer*
ANTONYM:
• cold

hot ② ADJECTIVE
very spicy • *a hot, aromatic Thai
red curry*
peppery • *a rich, peppery extra
virgin olive oil*
spicy • *a spicy Cajun sauce*
ANTONYM:
• bland

house NOUN
a building where a person or
family lives • *They live in a large
house with eight rooms.*
abode (OLD-FASHIONED) • *I
went round the streets and found
his new abode.*
building • *Their flat was on the
first floor of the building.*
dwelling (FORMAL) • *One
thousand new dwellings are
planned for the area.*
home • *One in four people are
without adequate homes.*
residence (FORMAL) • *the
Royal Family's private residence*

hug ① VERB
to hold someone close to you
• *Lynn and I hugged each other.*

h

clasp • *She clasped the children to her.*

cuddle • *They used to kiss and cuddle in front of everyone.*

embrace • *The couple in the corridor were embracing each other.*

squeeze • *He kissed her on the cheek and squeezed her tight.*

hug ② NOUN

the act of holding someone close to you • *She gave him a hug.*

cuddle • *He asked his mother for a cuddle.*

embrace • *a young couple locked in an embrace*

huge ADJECTIVE

extremely large in amount, size or degree • *a huge crowd*

colossal • *a colossal waste of money*

enormous • *The main bedroom is enormous.*

giant • *a giant statue*

immense • *He wielded immense power.*

massive • *a massive surge in popularity*

vast • *this vast area of northern Canada*

ANTONYM:
• tiny

hui NOUN (NEW ZEALAND)

a meeting • *He arranged a hui which called together a broad span of Maori tribes.*

assembly • *an assembly of prizewinning journalists*

conference • *a conference attended by 280 delegates*

congress • *a congress of coal miners*

convention • *the annual convention of the Society of Professional Journalists*

gathering • *the annual gathering of the South Pacific Forum*

meeting • *Can we have a meeting to discuss this?*

rally • *They held a rally to mark International Human Rights Day.*

humane ADJECTIVE

showing kindness and sympathy towards others • *a more just and humane society*

benevolent • *a most benevolent employer*

caring • *a very caring boy*

charitable • *charitable work*

compassionate • *a deeply compassionate man*

kind • *She is warmhearted and kind.*

merciful • *a merciful ruler*

thoughtful • *a very thoughtful gesture*

humble ① ADJECTIVE

not vain or boastful • *He gave a great performance, but he was very humble.*

meek • *He was a meek, mild-mannered fellow.*

modest • *He's modest, as well as being a great player.*

unassuming • *She has a gentle, unassuming manner.*

ANTONYM:
• haughty

humble ② ADJECTIVE

ordinary or unimportant • *A few*

well-chosen herbs will transform a humble casserole.

lowly • *He was irked by his lowly status.*

modest • *his modest beginnings*

ordinary • *It was just an ordinary weekend.*

simple • *a simple dinner of rice and beans*

humble ③ VERB
to make someone feel humiliated • *the little car company that humbled the industry giants*

disgrace • *I have disgraced the family's name.*

humiliate • *His teacher continually humiliates him in maths lessons.*

humid ADJECTIVE
damp and hot • *a hot, humid Italian summer*

clammy • *My shirt was clammy with sweat.*

muggy • *The weather was muggy and overcast.*

steamy • *The air was hot and steamy from the heat of a hundred bodies.*

sticky • *four hot, sticky days in the middle of August*

humiliate VERB
to hurt someone's pride • *He enjoyed humiliating me.*

disgrace • *I have disgraced my family.*

embarrass • *It embarrassed him that he had no idea of what was going on.*

humble • *The champion was humbled by the unseeded qualifier.*

put down • *I know that I do put people down occasionally.*

shame • *Her son's behaviour had shamed her.*

humour ① NOUN
something which is thought to be funny • *The film's humour contains a serious message.*

comedy • *his career in comedy*

wit • *She was known for her biting wit.*

humour ② NOUN
the mood someone is in • *He hasn't been in a good humour lately.*

frame of mind • *Clearly, she was not in the right frame of mind to continue.*

mood • *Lily was in one of her aggressive moods.*

spirits • *He was in very low spirits.*

temper • *Lee stormed off the field in a furious temper.*

humour ③ VERB
to please someone so that they will not become upset • *I nodded, partly to humour him.*

flatter • *I knew she was just flattering me.*

indulge • *He did not agree with indulging children.*

mollify • *The investigation was undertaken primarily to mollify pressure groups.*

pander to • *politicians who pander to big business*

hungry ADJECTIVE
wanting to eat • *I didn't have any lunch, so I'm really hungry.*

h

famished • *Isn't dinner ready? I'm famished.*
ravenous • *a pack of ravenous animals*
starving • *starving refugees*

hurry ① VERB
to move or do something as quickly as possible • *She hurried through the empty streets.*
dash • *He dashed upstairs.*
fly • *I must fly or I'll miss my train.*
get a move on (INFORMAL) • *Get a move on because my car's on a double yellow line.*
rush • *I've got to rush. I've got a meeting in a few minutes.*
scurry • *Reporters scurried to find telephones.*

hurry ② VERB
to make something happen more quickly • *his attempt to hurry the process of independence*
accelerate • *They must now accelerate the development of their new car.*
hasten • *This will hasten the closure of small post offices.*
quicken • *He quickened his pace a little.*
speed up • *an effort to speed up the negotiations*
ANTONYM:
• slow down

hurt ① VERB
to cause someone to feel pain • *I didn't mean to hurt her.*
harm • *The hijackers seemed anxious not to harm anyone.*
injure • *He was injured in a road accident.*

wound • *The bomb wounded five people.*

hurt ② VERB
to upset someone or something • *What you said really hurt me.*
distress • *I did not want to frighten or distress the horse.*
sadden • *He is saddened that they did not win anything.*
upset • *I'm sorry if I've upset you.*
wound • *My relatives have wounded me in the past.*

hurt ③ ADJECTIVE
upset or offended • *He felt hurt by all the lies.*
aggrieved • *He felt aggrieved at what happened.*
offended • *He was offended at being left out.*
upset • *I'm upset by your attitude.*
wounded • *I think she feels desperately wounded and unloved.*

hygiene NOUN
the principles and practice of health and cleanliness • *Be extra careful about personal hygiene.*
cleanliness • *Many of the beaches fail to meet minimum standards of cleanliness.*
sanitation • *the hazards of contaminated water and poor sanitation*

hypnotise VERB
to put someone into a state in which they seem to be asleep

but can respond to suggestions • She will hypnotise you and you will feel nothing.

put in a trance • A stage hypnotist put her in a trance.

put to sleep • First the hypnotist will put you to sleep.

hysterical ① ADJECTIVE

in a state of uncontrolled excitement or panic • Calm down. Don't get hysterical.

frantic • A bird had been locked in and was by now quite frantic.

frenzied • her frenzied attempts to get free

overwrought • One overwrought man had to be restrained by friends.

raving • He looked at her as if she were a raving lunatic.

hysterical ② ADJECTIVE

(INFORMAL)

extremely funny • His stand-up routine was hysterical.

comical • Her expression is almost comical.

hilarious • He had a fund of hilarious jokes on the subject.

icon NOUN

a picture that represents a person or thing • Click on the icon to start the program.

avatar • This game lets you create your own avatar.

representation • an ancient representation of a spear

thumbnail • You can make thumbnails of your photographs with this application.

idea ① NOUN

a plan or suggestion for something • She said she'd had a brilliant idea.

plan • I have a cunning plan.

recommendation • a range of recommendations for change

scheme • a proposed scheme

solution • He came up with a solution to the problem.

suggestion • Do you have a better suggestion?

idea ② NOUN

an opinion or belief about something • old-fashioned ideas about technology

belief • my religious beliefs

conviction • a firm conviction that things have improved

impression • your first impressions of college

notion • *I have a notion of what he is like.*

opinion • *a favourable opinion of our neighbours*

view • *Make your views known to local politicians.*

idea ③ NOUN
what you know about something • *They had no idea where they were.*

clue • *I don't have a clue what you mean.*

guess • *My guess is he went east.*

hint • *He gave no hint about where he was.*

inkling • *We had an inkling that something was happening.*

notion • *I have a notion how it is done.*

suspicion • *I have a strong suspicion they are lying.*

ideal ① NOUN
a principle or idea you try to achieve • *I don't live up to my ideal of myself.*

principle • *acts that go against your principles*

standard • *My father has high moral standards.*

value • *the values of liberty and equality*

ideal ② NOUN
the best example of something • *She remains his feminine ideal.*

epitome • *The hotel was the epitome of luxury.*

example • *He was held up as an example of courage.*

model • *a model of good manners*

paragon • *You are not a paragon of virtue.*

prototype • *He was the prototype of a strong leader.*

standard • *the standard by which we are compared*

ideal ③ ADJECTIVE
being the best example of something • *the ideal person for the job*

classic • *a classic example of hypocrisy*

complete • *She is the complete athlete.*

consummate • *a consummate politician*

model • *She is a model pupil.*

perfect • *He is the perfect husband for her.*

supreme • *a supreme method of cooking vegetables*

identify ① VERB
to recognise or name someone or something • *I tried to identify her perfume.*

diagnose • *This illness is easily diagnosed.*

label • *Poisonous substances should be labelled as such.*

name • *The winners of the award have been named.*

pinpoint • *They could not pinpoint the cause of death.*

place • *The man was familiar, but I couldn't place him.*

recognise • *a man I recognised as Luke's father*

identify ②: identify with VERB
to understand someone's

feelings • *I can't identify with the characters.*

associate with • *I associate myself with the green movement.*

empathise with • *I empathise with the people who live here.*

feel for • *I pitied and felt for him.*

relate to • *We have difficulty relating to each other.*

respond to • *She responded to his pain.*

idiot NOUN

a stupid person • *You're an idiot!*

fool • *He'd been a fool to get involved.*

galah (AUSTRALIAN; INFORMAL) • *sounding like an illiterate galah*

imbecile • *I don't want to deal with these imbeciles.*

oaf • *You clumsy oaf!*

twit (INFORMAL) • *I feel such a twit.*

idiotic ADJECTIVE

extremely foolish or silly • *an idiotic thing to do*

crazy (INFORMAL) • *You were crazy to leave then.*

daft (BRITISH; INFORMAL) • *He's not so daft as to listen to them.*

dumb (INFORMAL) • *I've met a lot of dumb people.*

foolish • *It is foolish to risk injury.*

senseless • *acts of senseless violence*

stupid • *stupid ideas*

idle ADJECTIVE

doing nothing • *a popular occupation for idle, wealthy young women*

jobless • *One in four people are now jobless.*

redundant • *redundant workers*

unemployed • *jobs for unemployed people*

ANTONYM:

• busy

ignorant ① ADJECTIVE

not knowing about something • *He was completely ignorant of the rules.*

inexperienced • *I am inexperienced at decorating.*

innocent • *Like a young child, she's innocent about the world.*

oblivious • *John appeared oblivious to his surroundings.*

unaware • *She was unaware that she was being filmed.*

unconscious • *He was unconscious of his failure.*

ignorant ② ADJECTIVE

not knowledgeable about things • *People are afraid to appear ignorant.*

green (INFORMAL) • *The new boy is very green and immature.*

naive • *a shy, naive man*

unaware • *Young children are fairly unaware.*

ignore VERB

to take no notice of someone or something • *Her husband ignored her.*

blank (SLANG) • *The crowd blanked her for the first four songs.*

discount • *They simply discounted his feelings.*

disregard • *He disregarded his father's advice.*

neglect • They never neglect their duties.
overlook • a fact that we all tend to overlook

ill ADJECTIVE
unhealthy or sick • Payne was seriously ill with pneumonia.
ailing • The President is said to be ailing.
poorly (BRITISH; INFORMAL) • Julie is still poorly.
queasy • I feel queasy on boats.
sick • He's very sick and he needs treatment.
unhealthy • an unhealthy-looking fellow
unwell • She felt unwell back at the office.
ANTONYM:
• healthy

illegal ADJECTIVE
forbidden by the law • an illegal organisation
banned • banned substances
criminal • a criminal offence
illicit • illicit payments to officials
outlawed • a place where hunting is outlawed
prohibited • Lighting fires is prohibited here.
unlawful • unlawful acts
ANTONYM:
• legal

illness NOUN
a particular disease • a mystery illness
affliction • a severe hereditary affliction
ailment • common ailments

complaint • a skin complaint
disease • He has been cured of the disease.
disorder • a rare nervous disorder
lurgy (BRITISH, AUSTRALIAN AND NEW ZEALAND; INFORMAL) • It's only a matter of days before Joan gets the lurgy as well.
sickness • radiation sickness

illusion ① NOUN
a thing that you think you can see • Painters create the illusion of space.
hallucination • Perhaps the footprint was a hallucination.
mirage • I began to see mirages.
semblance • A semblance of normality has been restored.

illusion ② NOUN
a false belief • Their hopes proved to be an illusion.
delusion • I was under the delusion that I could win.
fallacy • It's a fallacy that the rich are generous.
fancy • childhood fancies
misconception • There are many misconceptions about school.

imaginary ADJECTIVE
existing in your mind but not in real life • an imaginary friend
fictional • a fictional character
fictitious • a fictitious illness
hypothetical • a hypothetical situation
ideal • in an ideal world
illusory • Freedom is illusory.
invented • distorted or invented stories

mythological • *mythological creatures*

ANTONYM:
• real

imagination NOUN
the ability to form new ideas • *a girl who lacks imagination*
creativity • *She paints with great creativity.*
ingenuity • *the ingenuity of engineers*
inventiveness • *the artistic inventiveness of Mozart*
originality • *a composer of great originality*
vision • *a leader with vision*

imagine ① VERB
to have an idea of something • *He could not imagine a more peaceful scene.*
conceive • *I can't even conceive of that much money.*
envisage • *I envisage them staying together.*
fantasise • *I fantasised about writing music.*
picture • *I tried to picture the place.*
visualise • *He could not visualise her as old.*

imagine ② VERB
to believe that something is the case • *I imagine you're talking about my brother.*
assume • *Don't assume we are similar.*
believe • *I believe you have my pen.*
gather • *I gather that his mother was Scottish.*

guess (INFORMAL) • *I guess he's right.*
suppose • *He supposed I would be back at school.*
suspect • *Susan suspected that things would get worse.*

imitate VERB
to copy someone or something • *She imitated her parents.*
ape • *She is aping her sister's style.*
copy • *I used to copy everything my big brother did.*
emulate • *Sons are expected to emulate their fathers.*
impersonate • *He could impersonate all the other students.*
mimic • *He mimicked her accent.*
simulate • *a machine which simulates natural sounds*

immediate ① ADJECTIVE
happening or done without delay • *My immediate reaction was fear.*
instant • *He took an instant dislike to Mark.*
instantaneous • *The applause was instantaneous.*

immediate ② ADJECTIVE
most closely connected to you • *my immediate family*
close • *I have a few close friends.*
direct • *your direct descendants*
near • *near relatives*

immediately ① ADVERB
right away • *Ingrid answered Peter's letter immediately.*

at once • *You must come at once.*

directly • *He will be there directly.*

instantly • *She'd been knocked down in the street and died almost instantly.*

now • *Get out, now!*

promptly • *The telephone was answered promptly.*

right away • *You'd better tell them right away.*

straight away • *I'd like to see you straight away.*

immediately ② ADVERB

very near in time or position • *immediately behind the house*

closely • *He rushed out, closely followed by Kemp.*

directly • *James stopped directly under the window.*

right • *He stood right behind me.*

immense ADJECTIVE

very large or huge • *an immense cloud of smoke*

colossal • *a colossal waste of money*

enormous • *The main bedroom is enormous.*

giant • *a giant oak table*

gigantic • *a gigantic task*

huge • *Several painters were working on a huge piece of canvas.*

massive • *a massive cruise liner*

vast • *a vast expanse of water*

ANTONYM:
• tiny

imminent ADJECTIVE

going to happen very soon • *my sister's imminent arrival*

close • *My birthday is quite close.*

coming • *the coming dawn*

forthcoming • *their forthcoming marriage*

impending • *impending doom*

looming • *My exams are looming.*

near • *in the near future*

upcoming • *the upcoming elections*

immune ADJECTIVE

not subject to or affected by something • *He seems immune to pressure.*

exempt • *She is exempt from blame.*

free • *He was not completely free of guilt.*

protected • *He is protected from the law.*

resistant • *crops that are resistant to disease*

safe • *I was safe from punishment.*

unaffected • *She is unaffected by the sight of blood.*

impatient ① ADJECTIVE

easily annoyed • *You are too impatient with others.*

brusque • *a brusque manner*

curt • *He had spoken in a very curt tone of voice.*

irritable • *Brian was nervous and irritable with her.*

ANTONYM:
• patient

impatient ② ADJECTIVE

eager to do something • *He was impatient to leave.*

eager • *Children are eager to learn*

restless • *The kids were bored and restless.*

impede VERB
to make someone's or
something's progress difficult
• *Fallen rocks are impeding the
progress of rescue workers.*
block • *The country has been
trying to block these imports.*
delay • *Various setbacks delayed
production.*
disrupt • *The drought has
severely disrupted agricultural
production.*
get in the way • *She had a job
which never got in the way of her
hobbies.*
hamper • *The bad weather
hampered rescue operations.*
hinder • *The investigation was
hindered by the loss of vital
documents.*
obstruct • *The authorities are
obstructing the inquiry.*

imperfect ADJECTIVE
having faults or problems • *We
live in an imperfect world.*
broken • *broken toys*
damaged • *damaged goods*
defective • *defective eyesight*
faulty • *a car with faulty brakes*
flawed • *a flawed character*
ANTONYM:
• perfect

impersonal ADJECTIVE
not concerned with people
and their feelings • *I found him
strangely distant and impersonal.*
aloof • *His manner was aloof.*
cold • *Sharon was very cold
with me.*
detached • *He felt emotionally
detached from the victims.*

formal • *Business relationships
are usually formal.*
neutral • *He told me the news in
a neutral manner.*
remote • *She was beautiful but
remote.*

implore VERB
to beg someone to do
something • *"Tell me what to
do!" she implored him.*
beg • *I begged him to come with
me.*
beseech (LITERARY) • *I beseech
you to show him mercy.*
plead with • *The woman
pleaded with her daughter to
come home.*

important ① ADJECTIVE
necessary or significant • *Her
sons are the most important
thing to her.*
momentous • *the momentous
decision to go to war*
serious • *a serious matter*
significant • *a significant
discovery*
weighty • *We discussed
weighty matters.*
ANTONYM:
• unimportant

important ② ADJECTIVE
having great influence or
power • *the most important
person in the country*
eminent • *an eminent scientist*
foremost • *the foremost expert
in American history*
influential • *one of the most
influential books ever written*
leading • *a leading nation in
world politics*

notable • *notable celebrities*
powerful • *large, powerful countries*

impose ① VERB

to force something on someone • *Fines were imposed on the culprits.*
dictate • *The policy is dictated from the top.*
enforce • *It is a difficult law to enforce.*
inflict • *Inflicting punishment to stop crime is not the answer.*
levy • *a tax levied on imported goods*
ordain • *the task of trying to ordain parliamentary behaviour*

impose ②: impose on VERB

to take advantage of someone • *I should stop imposing on your hospitality.*
abuse • *They abused my hospitality by eating everything.*
take advantage of • *He took advantage of her generosity.*
use • *She's just using you.*

impossible ADJECTIVE

unable to happen or be believed • *You shouldn't promise impossible things.*
absurd • *absurd claims to have met big stars*
hopeless • *a hopeless task*
inconceivable • *It's inconceivable that people can still be living in those conditions.*
ludicrous • *his ludicrous plan to build a house*
out of the question • *Is a pay increase out of the question?*

unthinkable • *The idea of splitting up is unthinkable.*
ANTONYM:
• possible

impression ① NOUN

the way someone or something seems to you • *your first impressions of college*
feeling • *the feeling that she was wasting her life*
hunch • *Was your hunch right or wrong?*
idea • *I had my own ideas about what had happened.*
notion • *I have a notion of what he is like.*
sense • *She had the sense that she was in trouble.*

impression ②: make an impression VERB

to have a strong effect on people • *He certainly made an impression on his teachers.*
cause a stir • *News of her death caused a stir.*
influence • *You can't do anything to influence him.*
make an impact • *Events can make an impact on our lives.*

impressionable ADJECTIVE

easy to influence
• *impressionable teenagers*
gullible • *I'm so gullible I'd have believed him.*
open • *an open, trusting nature*
receptive • *moulding their young, receptive minds*
sensitive • *Ouija boards can be dangerous, especially to sensitive minds.*

susceptible • *Children can be susceptible to advertisements.*
vulnerable • *vulnerable elderly people*

impressive ADJECTIVE
tending to impress • *an impressive achievement*
awesome • *awesome mountains, deserts and lakes*
exciting • *He tells the most exciting stories.*
grand • *a grand old building*
powerful • *a powerful image*
stirring • *stirring music*
striking • *her striking personality*

imprison VERB
to lock someone up • *He was imprisoned for murder.*
confine • *Keep your dog confined to the house.*
detain • *They'll be detained and charged.*
incarcerate • *Prisoners were incarcerated in terrible conditions.*
jail • *An innocent man was jailed.*
lock up • *You people should be locked up!*
send to prison • *The judge sent him to prison for life.*
ANTONYM:
• free

improbable ADJECTIVE
unlikely or unbelievable • *improbable stories*
doubtful • *It was doubtful if they would arrive on time.*
dubious • *dubious evidence*
far-fetched • *This all sounds a bit far-fetched.*

implausible • *a film with an implausible ending*
unbelievable • *an unbelievable storyline*
unlikely • *It is unlikely that he is alive.*
ANTONYM:
• probable

improve VERB
to get or make better • *He improved their house.*
advance • *Medical technology has advanced.*
better • *They tried to better their working conditions.*
enhance • *Good jewellery enhances your outfits.*
look up (INFORMAL) • *Things are looking up for me now.*
progress • *Jack's condition is progressing well.*
upgrade • *You'll have to upgrade your image.*
ANTONYM:
• worsen

improvement NOUN
the fact or process of getting better • *dramatic improvements in conditions*
advance • *the advances in air safety*
development • *monitoring her language development*
enhancement • *the enhancement of the human condition*
progress • *The doctors are pleased with her progress.*
upturn • *an upturn in the economy*

impudence NOUN

disrespectful talk or behaviour towards someone • *Have you ever heard such impudence?*

audacity • *He had the audacity to speak up.*

boldness • *I was amazed at her boldness towards him.*

cheek (INFORMAL) • *I can't believe he had the cheek to complain.*

chutzpah (AMERICAN; INFORMAL) • *He had the chutzpah to ask us to leave.*

gall • *the most presumptuous question any interviewer has ever had the gall to ask*

impertinence • *His words sounded like impertinence.*

insolence • *I got punished for insolence.*

nerve • *You've got a nerve coming round here after what you've done.*

inability NOUN

a lack of ability to do something • *an inability to concentrate*

impotence • *a sense of impotence in the situation*

inadequacy • *my inadequacy as a gardener*

incompetence • *the incompetence of government officials*

ineptitude • *political ineptitude*

ANTONYM:
• ability

inadequate ① ADJECTIVE

not enough in quantity • *Supplies of medicine are inadequate.*

insufficient • *insufficient evidence to justify criminal proceedings*

lacking • *Why was military intelligence so lacking?*

poor • *poor wages*

scarce • *the region's scarce supplies of water*

short • *Deliveries are unreliable and food is short.*

ANTONYM:
• adequate

inadequate ② ADJECTIVE

not good enough • *She felt painfully inadequate in the crisis.*

deficient • *He made me feel deficient as a mother.*

incapable • *an incapable leader*

incompetent • *the power to sack incompetent doctors*

inept • *He was inept and lacked the intelligence to govern.*

pathetic • *She made some pathetic excuse.*

useless (INFORMAL) • *I'm useless around the house.*

inappropriate ADJECTIVE

not suitable for a purpose or occasion • *This behaviour is inappropriate.*

improper • *the improper use of resources*

incongruous • *an incongruous assortment of clothes*

unfit • *houses that are unfit for living in*

unseemly • *He thought crying was unseemly.*

unsuitable • *food that is unsuitable for children*

untimely • *their unjustified and untimely interference*

ANTONYM:
• *appropriate*

incentive NOUN
something that encourages you to do something • *the incentive to work*

bait • *He added some bait to make the agreement sweeter.*

encouragement • *She didn't get much encouragement to do anything.*

inducement • *Are gangster films an inducement to crime?*

motivation • *Money is my motivation.*

stimulus • *He needed all the stimulus he could get.*

incident NOUN
an event • *Little incidents can shape our lives.*

circumstance • *This is a fortunate circumstance.*

episode • *I'm glad this episode is over.*

event • *recent events in Europe*

happening • *the latest happenings in sport*

occasion • *I remember that occasion fondly.*

occurrence • *Nancy wondered about the strange occurrence.*

incite VERB
to excite someone into doing something • *The comments incited a huge row.*

agitate for • *Workers agitated for better conditions.*

goad • *He tried to goad me into a response.*

instigate • *The protest was instigated by a few people.*

provoke • *I provoked him into doing something stupid.*

whip up • *an attempt to whip up public hostility to the president*

include VERB
to have as a part • *A British breakfast always includes sausages.*

contain • *This sheet contains a list of names.*

cover • *The books covers many topics.*

embrace • *a small county embracing two cities*

encompass • *classes which encompass a wide range of activities*

incorporate • *The new cars incorporate many improvements.*

involve • *a high-energy workout which involves nearly every muscle*

ANTONYM:
• *exclude*

income NOUN
the money someone or something earns • *families on low incomes*

earnings • *his earnings as an accountant*

pay • *We complained about our pay.*

profits • *The bank made profits of millions of dollars.*

salary • *The lawyer was paid a good salary.*

takings • *The shop had huge takings that week.*

wages • *His wages have gone up.*

incomparable ADJECTIVE
too good to be compared with
anything else • *an area of
incomparable beauty*
inimitable • *his inimitable style*
peerless (LITERARY) • *He gave
a peerless performance.*
superlative • *The hotel has
superlative views.*
supreme • *the supreme piece of
writing about the war*
unparalleled • *unparalleled
happiness*
unrivalled • *an unrivalled
knowledge of music*

incompetent ADJECTIVE
lacking the ability to do
something properly • *You are
incompetent, and you know it.*
bungling • *a bungling amateur*
cowboy (BRITISH; INFORMAL)
• *cowboy builders*
incapable • *an incapable leader*
inept • *an inept performance*
unable • *He felt unable to
handle the situation.*
useless (INFORMAL) • *I felt
useless and a failure.*

ANTONYM:
• competent

incomplete ADJECTIVE
not finished or whole • *an
incomplete book*
deficient • *a deficient diet*
half-pie (NEW ZEALAND;
INFORMAL) • *His report was
half-pie.*
insufficient • *insufficient
information*
partial • *The concert was a
partial success.*

ANTONYM:
• complete

increase ① VERB
to make or become larger in
amount • *The population
continues to increase.*
enlarge • *They are trying to
enlarge their customer base.*
expand • *We will expand the
size of the picture.*
extend • *She plans to extend her
stay.*
grow • *The sound grew in
volume.*
multiply • *viruses which can
multiply rapidly in the human
body*
swell • *His anger swelled within
him.*

ANTONYM:
• decrease

increase ② NOUN
a rise in the amount of
something • *a pay increase*
gain • *a gain in speed*
growth • *the growth of
unemployment*
increment • *tiny increments of
movement*
rise • *a rise in prices*
upsurge • *an upsurge of interest
in books*

ANTONYM:
• decrease

incredible ① ADJECTIVE
totally amazing • *a champion
with incredible skill*
amazing • *an amazing success*
astonishing • *an astonishing
piece of good luck*

astounding • *an astounding discovery*

extraordinary • *extraordinary beauty*

marvellous • *a marvellous thing to do*

sensational (INFORMAL) • *a sensational performance*

incredible ② ADJECTIVE
impossible to believe • *the incredible stories of some children*

absurd • *absurd ideas*

far-fetched • *This all sounds very far-fetched to me.*

improbable • *highly improbable claims*

unbelievable • *The film has an unbelievable plot.*

unimaginable • *unimaginable wealth*

unthinkable • *It's unthinkable that Tom forgot your birthday.*

indecent ADJECTIVE
shocking or rude • *indecent lyrics*

crude • *crude pictures*

improper • *improper behaviour*

rude • *a rude gesture*

vulgar • *vulgar language*

independent ① ADJECTIVE
separate from other people or things • *an independent political party*

autonomous • *an autonomous country*

free • *Do we have a free press?*

separate • *We live separate lives.*

unrelated • *two unrelated incidents*

independent ② ADJECTIVE
not needing other people's help • *a fiercely independent woman*

individualistic • *individualistic behaviour*

liberated • *a genuinely liberated woman*

self-sufficient • *I am quite self-sufficient.*

unaided • *his first unaided walk through the park*

indicate VERB
to show something • *a gesture which indicates his relief*

denote • *Messy writing denotes a messy mind.*

reveal • *His diary revealed his disturbed state of mind.*

show • *I would like to show my appreciation.*

signal • *Ted signalled that everything was all right.*

signify • *A white flag signifies surrender.*

indication NOUN
a sign of something • *He gave no indication that he had heard me.*

clue • *Did she give any clue as to how she was feeling?*

hint • *The Minister gave a strong hint that she intended to resign.*

sign • *Your blood will be checked for any sign of kidney failure.*

signal • *They saw the visit as an important signal of support.*

suggestion • *There is no suggestion that the two sides are any closer to agreeing.*

warning • *a warning of impending doom*

indirect ADJECTIVE

not done or going directly but
by another way • the indirect
effects of smoking

meandering • the meandering
course of the river

oblique • oblique threats

rambling • In a rambling
answer, he denied the charge.

roundabout • a roundabout
way of getting information

tortuous • a tortuous path

wandering • a wandering route
through the woods

ANTONYM:

• direct

individual ① ADJECTIVE

relating to separate people or
things • individual dishes of trifle

discrete (FORMAL) • breaking
down the job into discrete steps

independent • two
independent studies

separate • Use separate
chopping boards for different foods.

single • every single house in the
street

individual ② ADJECTIVE

different and unusual
• Develop your own individual
writing style.

characteristic • a characteristic
feature

distinctive • His voice was very
distinctive.

idiosyncratic • a highly
idiosyncratic personality

original • a chef with an original
touch

personal • his own personal
method of playing

special • her own special way of
doing things

unique • Each person's
signature is unique.

individual ③ NOUN

a person, different from any
other person • the rights of the
individual

character • a remarkable
character

party • Who is the guilty party?

person • One person died and
several others were injured.

soul • He's a jolly soul.

industrious ADJECTIVE

tending to work hard
• industrious groups of students

busy • an exceptionally busy
man

conscientious • Sherry was
slow but conscientious.

diligent • Williams was diligent
in the writing of letters.

hard-working • an
exceptionally disciplined and
hard-working young man

tireless • a tireless and willing
worker

ANTONYM:

• lazy

inefficient ADJECTIVE

badly organised and slow • an
inefficient government

disorganised • My boss is
completely disorganised.

incapable • If he fails he will be
considered incapable.

incompetent • an incompetent
officer

inept • an inept use of power

sloppy • sloppy management

ANTONYM:
• efficient

inexperienced ADJECTIVE
lacking experience of a
situation or activity
• *inexperienced drivers*
green (INFORMAL) • *He was a
young lad, and very green.*
new • *a new mother*
raw • *raw talent*
unaccustomed • *Kate is
unaccustomed to being on TV.*

ANTONYM:
• experienced

infect VERB
to cause disease in something
• *One mosquito can infect many
people.*
affect • *Neil has been affected
by the virus.*
blight • *trees blighted by
pollution*
contaminate • *These
substances can contaminate fish.*
taint • *water that had been
tainted with chemicals*

infectious ADJECTIVE
spreading from one person to
another • *infectious diseases*
catching • *There is no
suggestion that multiple
sclerosis is catching.*
contagious • *a highly
contagious disease of the lungs*
spreading • *The spreading virus
is threatening the population.*

inferior ① ADJECTIVE
having a lower position than
something or someone else
• *Women were given inferior status.*

lesser • *the work of lesser writers*
lower • *lower animals*
minor • *a minor celebrity*
secondary • *He was relegated
to a secondary position.*
second-class • *second-class
citizens*
subordinate • *His subordinate
officers followed his example.*

ANTONYM:
• superior

inferior ② ADJECTIVE
of low quality • *work of inferior
quality*
mediocre • *mediocre music*
poor • *a poor standard of service*
second-class • *a second-class
education*
second-rate • *second-rate
restaurants*
shoddy • *Customers no longer
tolerate shoddy goods.*

ANTONYM:
• superior

inferior ③ NOUN
a person in a lower position
than another • *You must still be
polite to your inferiors.*
junior • *the office junior*
menial • *menials in poorly paid
jobs*
subordinate • *All her
subordinates adored her.*
underling • *Every underling
feared him.*

ANTONYM:
• superior

infinite ADJECTIVE
without any limit or end • *an
infinite number of possibilities*

boundless • *boundless energy*
endless • *a seemingly endless war*
eternal • *the secret of eternal youth*
everlasting • *our everlasting friendship*
inexhaustible • *an inexhaustible supply of ideas*
perpetual • *a perpetual source of worry*

influence ① NOUN
power over other people • *He has quite a lot of influence.*
authority • *You have no authority over me.*
control • *I don't have a lot of control over what I can do.*
importance • *a politician of great importance*
power • *a position of power*
sway • *My mother holds sway at home.*

influence ② NOUN
an effect that someone or something has • *the influence of environment on human behaviour*
effect • *Your age has an effect on your views.*
hold • *He is losing his hold on the public.*
magnetism • *a man of great personal magnetism*
spell • *under the spell of one of his teachers*
weight • *the weight of the law*

influence ③ VERB
to have an effect on someone or something • *I never try to influence my children.*

affect • *He will not let personal preference affect his choice.*
control • *I can't control him.*
direct • *I don't need you directing my life.*
guide • *Let your instinct guide you.*
manipulate • *I hate the way she manipulates people.*
sway • *efforts to sway voters*

inform VERB
to tell someone about something • *Please inform me of your progress.*
advise (FORMAL) • *I can advise you of his whereabouts.*
enlighten • *a history lesson which enlightens you*
notify • *Ann was notified of her sister's illness.*
tell • *Tell me what is going on.*

informal ADJECTIVE
relaxed and casual • *His manner was informal and relaxed.*
casual • *a casual attitude towards money*
colloquial • *colloquial language*
easy • *easy conversation*
familiar • *John was too familiar towards his teacher.*
natural • *Beth was friendly and natural with us.*
relaxed • *a relaxed atmosphere in class*

ANTONYM:
• *formal*

information NOUN
the details you know about something • *Pat would not give any information about Sarah.*

data • *The survey provided valuable data.*

drum (AUSTRALIAN; INFORMAL) • *I don't have the drum on this yet.*

facts • *Pass on all the facts to the police.*

material • *highly secret material*

news • *We have news of your brother.*

notice • *advance notice of the event*

word • *I received word that the guests had arrived.*

inform on VERB
to tell the police about someone who has committed a crime • *Somebody must have informed on the thieves.*

betray • *They betrayed their associates to the police.*

denounce • *He was denounced as a dangerous rebel.*

grass on (BRITISH; SLANG) • *He grassed on the members of his own gang.*

tell on (INFORMAL) • *It's all right, I won't tell on you.*

ingredient NOUN
a thing that something is made from • *Place all the ingredients in a pan.*

component • *the components of hamburgers*

constituent • *the main constituent of fish oil*

element • *the various elements in a picture*

inhabit VERB
to live in a place • *the people who inhabit these islands*

dwell (FORMAL) • *the people who dwell in the forest*

live • *She has lived here for ten years.*

lodge • *Some people lodged permanently in the hallway.*

occupy • *Forty tenants occupy the block.*

populate • *a swamp populated by huge birds*

reside (FORMAL) • *He resides in the country.*

inhabitant NOUN
someone who lives in a place • *an inhabitant of Norway*

citizen • *American citizens*

inmate • *prison inmates*

native • *Dr Brown is a native of New Zealand.*

occupant • *the previous occupant of the house*

resident • *the residents of the retirement home*

inheritance NOUN
something that is passed on • *The house would be his son's inheritance.*

bequest • *His aunt left a bequest for him in her will.*

heritage • *This building is part of our heritage.*

legacy • *His politeness was the legacy of his upbringing.*

injure VERB
to damage part of someone's body • *A bomb exploded, injuring five people.*

harm • *The hijackers did not harm anyone.*

hurt • *He hurt his back in an accident.*

maim • *landmines that maim and kill civilians*

wound • *wounded by shrapnel*

injury NOUN

damage to part of the body • *He sustained serious injuries in the accident.*

damage • *brain damage*

harm • *Dogs can do harm to human beings.*

wound • *a head wound*

injustice NOUN

unfairness and lack of justice • *the injustice of the system*

bias • *He shows bias against women.*

discrimination • *racial discrimination*

inequality • *people concerned about social inequality*

prejudice • *prejudice against workers over 45*

unfairness • *the unfairness of the decision*

wrong • *I intend to right past wrongs.*

ANTONYM:

• justice

innocence NOUN

inexperience of evil or unpleasant things • *the innocence of babies*

gullibility • *I'm paying for my gullibility back then.*

inexperience • *their inexperience of the real world*

naivety • *There was a youthful naivety to his honesty.*

simplicity • *She prayed with childlike simplicity.*

innocent ① ADJECTIVE

not guilty of a crime • *the arrest of innocent suspects*

blameless • *I have led a blameless life.*

clear • *He was clear of blame for the accident.*

not guilty • *Both men were found not guilty.*

ANTONYM:

• guilty

innocent ② ADJECTIVE

without experience of evil or unpleasant things • *They seem so young and innocent.*

childlike • *childlike trust*

guileless • *Her eyes were as guileless as a doll's.*

naive • *I was young and naive when I left home.*

pure • *She had led a pure life.*

spotless • *a spotless, pure child*

insane ADJECTIVE

very foolish • *This is an insane thing to do.*

crazy (INFORMAL) • *People thought they were crazy to try it.*

foolhardy • *Some described the act as foolhardy.*

foolish • *It would be foolish to raise hopes unnecessarily.*

mad • *He'd be mad to refuse.*

insert VERB

to put something into something else • *He inserted the key into the lock.*

enter • *Enter your name in the box.*

implant • *a device implanted in the arm*

introduce • *Scientists introduced new genes into mice.*
place • *Cover the casserole tightly and place in the oven.*
put • *She put a coin in the slot.*
set • *diamonds set in gold*

inside ADJECTIVE
surrounded by the main part and often hidden • *We booked an inside cabin.*
inner • *the inner ear*
innermost • *the innermost parts of the galaxy*
interior • *a car with plenty of interior space*
internal • *your internal organs*
ANTONYM:
• outside

insides PLURAL NOUN
(INFORMAL)
the parts inside your body • *My insides ached from eating too much.*
entrails • *chicken entrails*
guts • *fish guts*
innards • *the innards of a human body*
internal organs • *damage to internal organs*

insignificant ADJECTIVE
small and unimportant • *a small, insignificant village*
irrelevant • *irrelevant details*
little • *It seems such a little thing to get upset over.*
minor • *Western officials say the problem is minor.*
petty • *Rows can start over petty things.*
trifling • *These difficulties may seem trifling to you.*

trivial • *He tried to wave aside these issues as trivial matters.*
unimportant • *The age difference seemed unimportant.*
ANTONYM:
• significant

insincere ADJECTIVE
saying things you do not mean • *an apology that seems insincere*
deceitful • *deceitful and misleading remarks*
dishonest • *dishonest salespeople*
false • *a false confession*
two-faced • *the most two-faced politicians in the world*
ANTONYM:
• sincere

insist VERB
to demand something forcefully • *My family insisted I should not give in.*
demand • *The teacher demanded an explanation.*
press • *She is pressing for improvements to education.*
urge • *We urge vigorous action be taken immediately.*

inspect VERB
to examine something carefully • *the right to inspect company files*
check • *Check each item for obvious flaws.*
examine • *He examined her passport and stamped it.*
eye • *We eyed each other thoughtfully.*

investigate • Police are
investigating the scene of the
crime.
scan • The officer scanned the
room.
survey • He surveyed the ruins
of the building.

instant ① NOUN
a short period of time • The
pain disappeared in an instant.
flash • It was all over in a flash.
minute • I'll see you in a minute.
moment • In a moment he was
gone.
second • Seconds later,
firefighters reached his door.
split second • Her gaze met
Michael's for a split second.
trice • She was back in a trice.

instant ② ADJECTIVE
immediate and without delay
• He had taken an instant dislike
to her.
immediate • We need an
immediate reply.
instantaneous • Technology
gives us instantaneous access to
information.
prompt • Prompt action is needed.

instinct NOUN
a natural tendency to do
something • My first instinct
was to protect myself.
feeling • You seem to have a
feeling for drawing.
impulse • Peter resisted an
impulse to smile.
intuition • You should trust
your intuition.
sixth sense • Some sixth sense
told him to keep going.

urge • He fought the urge to
panic.

instruct ① VERB
to tell someone to do
something • They have
instructed solicitors to sue.
command • He commanded his
troops to attack.
direct • They have been directed
to give attention to this problem.
order • Williams ordered him to
leave.
tell • A passer-by told him to
move his car.
ANTONYM:
• forbid

instruct ② VERB
to teach someone about a
subject or skill • He instructs
therapists in relaxation
techniques.
coach • He coached me in
French.
educate • We need to educate
people about the destructive
effects of alcohol.
school • She's been schooling
her kids herself.
teach • She taught children
French.
train • We train them in a range
of building techniques.
tutor • He was tutoring her in
the stringed instruments.

insufficient ADJECTIVE
not enough for a particular
purpose • insufficient
information
deficient • a deficient diet
inadequate • The problem lies
with inadequate staffing.

lacking • *My confidence is lacking.*
scant • *Gareth paid scant attention to what was going on.*
short • *She was short of breath.*

ANTONYM:
• sufficient

insult ① VERB
to offend someone by being rude to them • *I did not mean to insult you.*
abuse • *footballers abusing referees*
affront • *He pretended to be affronted by what I said.*
offend • *I had no intention of offending the community.*
put down • *They seemed to delight in putting me down.*
slag off (BRITISH; INFORMAL) • *He's always slagging me off in front of his mates.*
slight • *They felt slighted by not being consulted.*
snub • *He snubbed her in public and made her feel foolish.*

ANTONYM:
• compliment

insult ② NOUN
a rude remark that offends someone • *The two men exchanged insults.*
abuse • *Raft hurled verbal abuse at his co-star.*
affront • *She took my words as a personal affront.*
offence • *I meant no offence to Mr Hardy.*
slight • *She is very sensitive to slights.*
snub • *This was a deliberate snub to me.*

ANTONYM:
• compliment

intelligence NOUN
the ability to understand and learn things • *students of high intelligence*
cleverness • *Her cleverness gets in the way of her emotions.*
comprehension • *an idea beyond human comprehension*
intellect • *Lucy's lack of intellect disappointed her father.*
perception • *You have brilliant perception and insight.*
sense • *They have the sense to seek help.*
understanding • *I've got no sense, no understanding.*
wit • *He had the wit to see this was a good idea.*

intelligent ADJECTIVE
able to understand and learn things • *Dolphins are an intelligent species.*
acute • *His relaxed exterior hides a very acute mind.*
brainy (INFORMAL) • *I don't consider myself brainy.*
bright • *an exceptionally bright child*
clever • *a clever girl*
quick • *His quick mind soon grasped the situation.*
sharp • *a very sharp intellect*
smart • *He thinks he's as smart as Sarah.*

ANTONYM:
• stupid

intend ① VERB
to decide or plan to do

something • She intended to move back to Cape Town.
aim • We aim to raise funds for charity.
be determined • Kate was determined to enjoy the day.
mean • I didn't mean any harm.
plan • He planned to leave Adelaide on Monday.
propose • Where do you propose building such a huge thing?
resolve • She resolved to report the matter.

intend ② VERB
to mean for a certain use • a book intended for serious students
aim • children's games aimed at developing quickness
design • The house had been designed for a large family.
earmark • That money was earmarked for house repairs.
mean • I was not meant for domestic life.

intense ① ADJECTIVE
very great in strength or amount • intense heat
acute • an acute shortage of accommodation
deep • He felt a deep sense of relief.
extreme • Proceed with extreme caution.
fierce • There was fierce competition for the job.
great • Dawes felt a great pain and weakness.
powerful • I had a powerful urge to scream at him.
profound • The book had a profound effect in the USA.
severe • I had severe problems.

intense ② ADJECTIVE
tending to have strong feelings • He was dark-haired and intense.
ardent • one of his most ardent supporters
earnest • Ella was a pious, earnest woman.
fervent • a fervent admirer of Beethoven's music
fierce • fierce loyalty to his friends
impassioned • He made an impassioned appeal for peace.
passionate • He is very passionate about the project.
vehement • a vehement critic of the plan

intention NOUN
a plan to do something • He announced his intention of retiring.
aim • The aim of this book is to inform you.
goal • The goal is to raise a lot of money.
idea • I bought books with the idea of reading them.
object • It was his object in life to find the island.
objective • His objective was to play golf and win.
purpose • He did not know the purpose of Vincent's visit.

interest ① NOUN
a feeling of wanting to know about something • I have a great interest in that period of history.
attention • The book attracted considerable attention.

concern • How it happened is of little concern to me.
curiosity • His reply satisfied our curiosity.
fascination • a lifelong fascination with the sea

interest ② NOUN
a hobby • He has a wide range of sporting interests.
activity • I enjoy outdoor activities like canoeing and climbing.
hobby • My hobbies are football, photography and tennis.
pastime • His favourite pastime is golf.
pursuit • his favourite childhood pursuits

interest ③ VERB
to attract someone's attention and curiosity • This part of the book interests me most.
appeal • The bright colours seem to appeal to children.
captivate • this author's ability to captivate young minds
fascinate • Politics fascinated my father.
intrigue • The situation intrigued him.
stimulate • Bill was stimulated by the challenge.
ANTONYM:
• bore

interesting ADJECTIVE
making you want to know, learn or hear more • an interesting hobby
▶ see Word Study **interesting**, page 714

ANTONYM:
• boring

interfere ① VERB
to try to influence a situation • Stop interfering and leave me alone.
butt in • I butted in where I didn't belong.
intervene • Soldiers don't like civilians intervening in their affairs.
intrude • I don't want to intrude on your meeting.
meddle • Scientists should not meddle in such matters.
tamper • the price we pay for tampering with the environment

interfere ② VERB
to have a damaging effect on a situation • His problems interfered with his work.
conflict • an evening that conflicted with my work schedule
disrupt • Strikes disrupted air traffic in Italy.

internet NOUN
a worldwide network of computers • He is always posting photos on the internet.
blogosphere • an event that set the blogosphere buzzing
cloud • downloading software from the cloud
cyberspace • The volume of business which takes place in cyberspace is growing.
net • comments on the net
web • one of the biggest sites on the web
world wide web • articles published on the world wide web

interrogate VERB
to question someone thoroughly • I interrogated everyone involved.

examine • Lawyers examined the witnesses.

grill (INFORMAL) • The police grilled Jenkins for over an hour.

question • He was questioned by police.

quiz • She quizzed me quite closely for a while.

interrupt ① VERB
to start talking when someone else is talking • He tried to speak, but she interrupted him.

butt in • Mirella butted in without a greeting.

heckle • It is easy to heckle from the safety of the audience.

interrupt ② VERB
to stop a process or activity for a time • The match was interrupted by torrential rain.

break • allowing passengers to break their journey in Fiji

discontinue • Do not discontinue the treatment without seeing your doctor.

suspend • Relief convoys will be suspended until the fighting stops.

interval NOUN
a period of time between two moments or dates • There was a long interval of silence as we thought about what had been said.

break • a short break from work

gap • the gap between school terms

hiatus (FORMAL) • There was a momentary hiatus in the sounds.

interlude • It was a happy interlude in the Kents' life.

intermission • There will be a short intermission between acts.

pause • a pause between two periods of intense activity

intervene VERB
to step in to prevent conflict • I relied on them to intervene if anything happened.

arbitrate • A committee was set up to arbitrate in the dispute.

mediate • efforts to mediate between the two communities

introduction ① NOUN
the act of presenting someone or something new • the introduction of a single European currency

establishment • the establishment of a democratic system

inauguration (FORMAL) • the inauguration of the President

initiation • your initiation into adulthood

institution • the institution of new laws

launch • the launch of this popular author's new book

introduction ② NOUN
a piece of writing at the beginning of a book • The book contains a new introduction by the author.

foreword • I am happy to write the foreword to this collection.

preface • I read through the preface quickly.

prologue • *the General Prologue to The Canterbury Tales*

intrude VERB
to disturb someone or something • *I don't want to intrude on your parents.*
butt in • *I butted in where I didn't belong.*
encroach • *Does your work encroach on your private life?*
infringe • *She promised not to infringe on his space.*
interrupt • *Georgina interrupted his thoughts.*
trespass • *I don't like to trespass on your time.*
violate • *These men were violating her family's privacy.*

invade VERB
to enter a country by force • *The allies invaded the Italian mainland at Anzio.*
attack • *Government planes attacked the town.*
enter • *The troops entered the capital.*
occupy • *Soldiers occupied the town within a few minutes.*
violate • *A helicopter violated Greek territory yesterday.*

invent ① VERB
to be the first person to think of a device or idea • *He invented the first electric clock.*
coin • *Lanier coined the term "virtual reality".*
come up with (INFORMAL) • *He came up with a gadget to relieve hay fever.*
conceive • *He conceived the first portable computer.*

create • *The company decided to create a new perfume.*
formulate • *He formulated his plan for escape.*
originate • *the designer who originated platform shoes*

invent ② VERB
to make up a story or excuse • *I tried to invent a plausible excuse.*
concoct • *A newspaper concocted an imaginary interview.*
fabricate • *The evidence against them was fabricated.*
make up • *Donna was known for making up stories about herself.*
manufacture • *The children manufactured an elaborate tale.*

investigate VERB
to find out all the facts about something • *Police are still investigating the incidents.*
examine • *I have examined all the possible alternatives.*
explore • *a book which explores the history of technology*
probe • *He probed into her private life.*
research • *I'm researching for an article on New England.*
sift • *I sifted the evidence for conclusions.*
study • *Experts are studying the security in the building.*

invincible ADJECTIVE
unable to be defeated • *When Woods is on form he is invincible.*
impregnable • *an impregnable fortress*

indomitable • *the indomitable spirit of the Polish people*
unbeatable • *a performance record that is unbeatable*

invisible ADJECTIVE
unable to be seen • *His face was invisible beneath his hat.*
concealed • *a concealed weapon*
disguised • *a disguised panel in the wall*
hidden • *a hidden camera*
inconspicuous • *She tried to make herself inconspicuous.*
unseen • *His work was guided by an unseen hand.*
ANTONYM:
• visible

involve VERB
to have as a necessary part • *Running a kitchen involves a great deal of discipline.*
incorporate • *The program incorporates a range of activities.*
require • *Caring for a baby requires special skills.*
take in • *This study takes in a number of areas.*

irrational ADJECTIVE
not based on logical reasons • *irrational fears*
absurd • *It was an absurd over-reaction.*
crazy (INFORMAL) • *crazy ideas*
illogical • *his completely illogical arguments*
nonsensical • *Such an idea sounds paradoxical, if not downright nonsensical.*
unsound • *The thinking is good-hearted, but muddled and unsound.*

irregular ① ADJECTIVE
not smooth or even • *an irregular surface*
asymmetrical • *She has asymmetrical features.*
bumpy • *bumpy roads*
jagged • *jagged fragments of stained glass*
lopsided • *his lopsided smile*
ragged • *the ragged edges of a tear*
uneven • *uneven teeth*
ANTONYM:
• regular

irregular ② ADJECTIVE
not forming a regular pattern • *He worked irregular hours.*
erratic • *a planet with an erratic orbit*
haphazard • *a haphazard system*
occasional • *occasional rain showers*
patchy • *Her career has been patchy.*
random • *The stock market is random and unpredictable.*
variable • *a variable rate of interest*
ANTONYM:
• regular

irresponsible ADJECTIVE
not concerned with the consequences of your actions • *an irresponsible attitude*
careless • *a careless driver*
reckless • *reckless spending*
thoughtless • *a thoughtless remark*
wild • *a night of wild celebrations*
ANTONYM:
• responsible

irritable ADJECTIVE
easily annoyed • *Nicol was unusually tense and irritable.*
bad-tempered • *You're very bad-tempered today.*
cantankerous • *a cantankerous man*
petulant • *He was like a petulant child.*
ratty (BRITISH AND NEW ZEALAND; INFORMAL) • *There's no need to get ratty.*

irritate VERB
to annoy someone • *Their attitude irritates me.*
anger • *This article angered me.*
annoy • *It just annoyed me to hear him going on.*
bother • *Nothing bothers me.*
exasperate • *Bertha was exasperated by the delay.*
needle (INFORMAL) • *If her remark needled him, he didn't show it.*
ruffle • *He doesn't get ruffled by anything.*

issue ① NOUN
a subject that people are talking about • *important issues of the day*
concern • *Political concerns continue to dominate the news.*
matter • *He touched on many matters in his speech.*
problem • *the energy problem*
question • *The whole question of aid is a tricky one.*
subject • *the president's views on the subject*
topic • *the main topic for discussion*

issue ② NOUN
a particular edition of a newspaper or magazine • *the latest issue of the Lancet*
copy • *a copy of "USA Today"*
edition • *There's an article about the film in next month's edition.*
instalment • *a magazine published in monthly instalments*

issue ③ VERB
to make a formal statement • *They have issued a statement denying the allegations.*
deliver • *He delivered a speech to his fellow union members.*
give • *The minister gave a warning that war should be avoided at all costs.*
make • *He says he was angry when he made the statement.*
pronounce • *The authorities took time to pronounce their verdicts.*
read out • *She read out an announcement outside the court.*
release • *The police are not releasing any more details about the attack.*
ANTONYM:
• withdraw

issue ④ VERB
to give something officially • *Staff will be issued with badges.*
equip • *plans to equip the reserve army with guns*
furnish (FORMAL) • *They will furnish you with the necessary items.*
give out • *The prizes were given out by a local dignitary.*

provide • *The government was unable to provide them with food.*
supply • *an agreement not to supply these countries with chemical weapons*

item ① NOUN
one of a collection or list of things • *an item on the agenda*
article • *articles of clothing*
matter • *He dealt with a variety of matters.*
point • *Many of the points in the report are correct.*
thing • *Big things are paid for by the government.*

item ② NOUN
a newspaper or magazine article • *There was an item in the paper about him.*
article • *a short article in one of the papers*
feature • *The magazine contained a special feature on the project.*
notice • *notices in today's national newspapers*
piece • *I disagree with your recent piece about Australia.*
report • *a film report on the scandal*

Jj

jagged ADJECTIVE
sharp and spiky • *jagged black cliffs*
barbed • *barbed wire*
craggy • *craggy mountains*
rough • *the rough surface of the rock*
serrated • *a serrated knife*
ANTONYM:
• smooth

jail ① NOUN
a place where prisoners are held • *sentenced to 18 months in jail*
nick (BRITISH, AUSTRALIAN AND NEW ZEALAND; SLANG) • *He spent seven years in the nick.*
prison • *his release from prison*

jail ② VERB
to put in prison • *He was jailed for twenty years.*
detain • *Police can detain a suspect for 48 hours.*
imprison • *imprisoned for 18 months on charges of theft*
incarcerate • *They have been incarcerated as political prisoners.*

jam ① NOUN
a crowded mass of people or things • *stuck in a jam on the motorway*
crowd • *elbowing his way through the crowd*

crush • *We got separated in the crush.*

mass • *a mass of excited fans*

mob • *a growing mob of demonstrators*

multitude • *surrounded by a noisy multitude*

throng • *An official pushed through the throng.*

jam ② NOUN (INFORMAL)
a difficult situation • *We're in a real jam now.*

dilemma • *faced with a dilemma*

fix (INFORMAL) • *a difficult economic fix*

hole (SLANG) • *He admitted that the government was in a hole.*

plight • *the plight of the Third World countries*

predicament • *a way out of our predicament*

quandary • *We're in a quandary over our holiday plans.*

trouble • *You are in serious trouble.*

jam ③ VERB
to push something somewhere roughly • *He jammed his hat on to his head.*

cram • *He crammed the bank notes into his pocket.*

force • *I forced the key into the ignition.*

ram • *He rammed the pole into the ground.*

stuff • *She stuffed the newspaper into a litter bin.*

jam ④ VERB
to become stuck • *The second time he fired, his gun jammed.*

stall • *The engine stalled.*

stick • *She tried to open the window but it was stuck.*

jealous ADJECTIVE
wanting to have something which someone else has • *She was jealous of his success.*

envious • *envious of the attention his brother was getting*

resentful • *resentful of her friend's new job*

job ① NOUN
the work someone does to earn money • *I'm still looking for a job.*

employment • *unable to find employment*

occupation • *his occupation as a carpenter*

position • *He's leaving to take up a position abroad.*

post • *She has resigned her post as his assistant.*

profession • *She chose teaching as her profession.*

trade • *her trade as a jeweller*

job ② NOUN
a duty or responsibility • *It's your job to find out what's going on.*

concern • *The technical aspects are the concern of the engineers.*

duty • *I consider it my duty to write and thank you.*

function • *an important function to fill*

responsibility • *It's not my responsibility to look after your mother.*

role • *Our role is to keep the peace.*

task • *She had the task of breaking the bad news.*

j

join ① VERB
to become a member of something • *He joined the Army five years ago.*

enlist • *He was 18 when he enlisted in the US Navy.*

enrol • *She has enrolled in an acting class.*

sign up • *I've signed up as a member.*

ANTONYM:
• resign

join ② VERB
to fasten two things together • *two parcels joined together with string*

attach • *The gadget can be attached to any surface.*

connect • *two rooms connected by a passage*

couple • *an engine coupled to a gearbox*

fasten • *a wooden bench fastened to the floor*

link • *tree houses linked by ropes*

tie • *He tied the dog to a post by its leash.*

ANTONYM:
• separate

joke ① NOUN
something that makes people laugh • *I heard a great joke today.*

gag (INFORMAL) • *a gag about unscrupulous lawyers*

jest • *It was only intended as a jest.*

lark • *They just did it for a lark.*

prank • *an end-of-term prank*

quip • *a famous quip by Groucho Marx*

wisecrack (INFORMAL) • *She was tempted to make a wisecrack.*

witticism • *laughing at each other's witticisms*

joke ② VERB
to say something funny • *She was always joking about her appearance.*

banter • *He played trick shots and bantered with the crowd.*

jest • *laughing and jesting with his cronies*

kid (INFORMAL) • *Don't worry, I'm only kidding.*

quip • *"You'll have to go on a diet," he quipped.*

tease • *"You must be in love," she teased.*

journey ① NOUN
the act of travelling from one place to another • *the journey from Paris to Bordeaux*

excursion • *The trip includes an excursion to Zermatt.*

expedition • *an expedition to the South Pole*

passage • *a 10-hour passage from Swansea*

tour • *a two-month tour of Europe*

trek • *a trek through the Gobi desert*

trip • *a business trip*

voyage • *the first space shuttle voyage*

journey ② VERB
to travel from one place to another • *She journeyed through Turkey and Africa.*

go • *We went from Glasgow to London in six hours.*

proceed (FORMAL) • *proceeding along the road in the wrong direction*

tour • *He toured China last year.*

travel • *Gran travelled down by train.*

trek • *trekking through the jungle*

voyage • *They voyaged as far as Spain.*

joy NOUN
great happiness • *Her face shone with joy.*

bliss • *an expression of pure bliss*

delight • *He let out a yell of delight.*

ecstasy • *Her eyes closed in ecstasy.*

elation • *He felt a surge of elation at the news.*

rapture • *His speech was received with rapture.*

ANTONYM:
• misery

joyful ADJECTIVE
extremely happy • *a joyful smile*

delighted • *I'm delighted to be here.*

elated • *the elated faces of the freed hostages*

jubilant • *the jubilant crowds*

over the moon (INFORMAL) • *I was over the moon to hear about your promotion.*

judge ① NOUN
the person in charge of a law court • *The judge awarded him £2000 in damages.*

justice • *his appointment as a Justice of the High Court*

magistrate • *defendants appearing before a magistrate*

RELATED WORD:
• ADJECTIVE judicial

judge ② NOUN
someone who picks the winner or keeps control of a competition • *A panel of judges are selecting the finalists.*

referee • *The referee awarded a free kick against Rourke.*

umpire • *The umpire's decision is final.*

judge ③ VERB
to form an opinion about someone or something • *Don't judge people by their looks.*

appraise • *The teachers are appraised by an official.*

assess • *It is too early to assess the impact of the change.*

consider • *We consider him to be dangerous.*

estimate • *The cost of the damage is estimated at over a million dollars.*

evaluate • *a test to evaluate a candidate's potential*

rate • *The film was rated a hit.*

judge ④ VERB
to pick the winner or keep control in a competition • *Entrants will be judged in two age categories.*

referee • *He has refereed in two World Cups.*

umpire • *He umpired baseball games.*

judgment NOUN
an opinion or decision based on evidence • *It's hard to form a judgment without all the facts.*

appraisal • *a calm appraisal of the situation*
assessment • *my own personal assessment of our position*
conclusion • *I've come to the conclusion that she knows what she's talking about.*
opinion • *Seek a medical opinion before you travel.*
ruling • *a High Court ruling*
verdict • *The doctor's verdict was that he was entirely healthy.*
view • *In my view, things aren't going to get any better.*

jump ① VERB
to leap up or over something
• *I jumped over the fence.*
bound • *He bounded up the steps.*
clear • *The horse cleared the gate by inches.*
hurdle • *He crossed the lawn and hurdled the fence.*
leap • *He had leapt from a window and escaped.*
spring • *The lion roared once and sprang.*
vault • *Ned vaulted over a fallen tree.*

jump ② VERB
to increase suddenly • *Sales jumped by 25% last year.*
escalate • *Costs escalated dramatically.*
increase • *Trading has increased by 20% this month.*
rise • *Unemployment is rising rapidly.*
surge • *The party's share of the vote surged from 10% to 17%.*

jump ③ NOUN
a leap into the air • *the longest ever jump by a man*
bound • *With one bound Jack was free.*
leap • *Smith took the gold medal with a leap of 2.37 metres.*
vault • *She regained the record with a vault of 3.80 metres.*

junior ADJECTIVE
having a relatively low position compared to others
• *a junior minister*
inferior • *inferior status*
lesser • *He resigned to take a lesser position and a cut in wages.*
lower • *the lower ranks of council officers*
subordinate • *sixty of his subordinate officers*
ANTONYM:
• senior

junk NOUN (INFORMAL)
old articles that people usually throw away • *What are you going to do with all that junk?*
clutter • *She likes her worktops to be clear of clutter.*
odds and ends • *My handbag's full of useless odds and ends.*
refuse (FORMAL) • *a weekly collection of refuse*
rubbish • *They piled most of their rubbish into skips.*
scrap • *a small yard containing a heap of scrap*
trash • *cluttered with trash*

justice ① NOUN
fairness in the way that people

are treated • *He wants freedom, justice and equality.*
equity • *Income should be distributed with some sense of equity.*
fairness • *concern about the fairness of the election campaign*
impartiality • *a system lacking impartiality*
ANTONYM:
• injustice

justice ② NOUN
the person in charge of a law court • *his appointment as a Justice of the High Court*
judge • *The judge awarded him £2000 in damages.*
magistrate • *defendants appearing before a magistrate*

justify VERB
to show that something is reasonable or necessary • *How can you justify what you've done?*
defend • *Her conduct is hard to defend.*
excuse • *That still doesn't excuse his behaviour.*
explain • *She left a note explaining her actions.*
vindicate • *Ministers are confident their decision will be vindicated.*
warrant • *These allegations warrant an investigation.*

Kk

kai NOUN (NEW ZEALAND; INFORMAL)
food • *I'm starving – let's have some kai.*
food • *Enjoy your food.*
grub (INFORMAL) • *Get yourself some grub.*
provisions • *enough provisions for two weeks*
rations • *The soldiers sampled the officers' rations.*
tucker (AUSTRALIAN AND NEW ZEALAND; INFORMAL) • *I haven't had any decent tucker for days.*

keen ① ADJECTIVE
showing eagerness and enthusiasm for something • *a keen amateur photographer*
ardent • *one of his most ardent supporters*
avid • *an avid reader*
eager • *We're eager to have another go at it.*
enthusiastic • *Tom was very enthusiastic about the place.*
fond of • *Are you fond of Chinese cuisine?*
into (INFORMAL) • *I'm really into football.*

keen ② ADJECTIVE
quick to notice or understand things • *a keen intellect*

astute • *an astute judge of character*

brilliant • *She had a brilliant mind.*

perceptive • *a perceptive gaze*

quick • *His quick mind soon grasped the situation.*

shrewd • *Her questions showed a shrewd perception.*

keep ① VERB

to have and look after something • *His father keeps a small shop.*

care for • *vintage cars lovingly cared for by their owners*

maintain • *The house costs a fortune to maintain.*

preserve • *the need to preserve the rainforest*

keep ② VERB

to store something • *She kept her money under the mattress.*

deposit • *You are advised to deposit your valuables in the hotel safe.*

hold • *Our stock is held in a warehouse.*

store • *Store the cookies in an airtight tin.*

keep ③ VERB

to do what you said you would do • *I always keep my promises.*

carry out • *He carried out his threat.*

fulfil • *He fulfilled all his responsibilities.*

honour • *The two sides have agreed to honour a new ceasefire.*

kidnap VERB

to take someone away by force

• *Four tourists have been kidnapped by rebels.*

abduct • *people claiming to have been abducted by aliens*

capture • *The guerrillas shot down one plane and captured the pilot.*

seize • *hostages seized by terrorists*

kill VERB

to make someone or something die • *The earthquake killed 62 people.*

assassinate • *the plot to assassinate Martin Luther King*

butcher • *The guards butchered hundreds of prisoners.*

destroy • *The jockey was unhurt but his horse had to be destroyed.*

execute • *He was executed for treason.*

exterminate • *an effort to exterminate all the rats*

massacre • *300 civilians have been massacred by the rebels.*

murder • *the widow of the murdered leader*

slaughter • *Whales are being slaughtered for commercial gain.*

slay (LITERARY) • *a painting of Saint George slaying the dragon*

kin PLURAL NOUN

the people who are related to you • *She has gone to live with her husband's kin.*

family • *There's a history of heart disease in our family.*

kindred • *his loyalty to his friends and kindred*

people • *She was reunited with her people.*

relations • *I was staying with relations in Atlanta.*
relatives • *On Sundays his relatives come to visit.*

kind ① NOUN

a particular type of person or thing • *I don't like that kind of film.*

brand • *his favourite brand of toothpaste*
breed • *a rare breed of cattle*
category • *Cereal bars are the fastest-growing category of breakfast products.*
class • *a better class of restaurant*
classification • *the cost of coverage for different classifications of motorcycle*
genre • *a writer who does not confine himself to one particular genre*
grade • *an improved grade of fertiliser*
sort • *a dozen trees of various sorts*
species • *a rare species of moth*
type • *What type of cat are they?*
variety • *a new variety of rose*

kind ② ADJECTIVE

considerate towards other people • *Thank you for being so kind to me.*

benevolent • *a very benevolent employer*
benign • *a benign ruler*
charitable • *a charitable nature*
compassionate • *My father was a deeply compassionate man.*
considerate • *a caring and considerate husband*

good • *a good man driven to a desperate act*
humane • *the humane treatment of prisoners*
kind-hearted • *Meera was kind-hearted, generous and loved life.*
kindly • *a kindly aunt and uncle*
thoughtful • *a thoughtful gesture*
unselfish • *his generous and unselfish attitude towards others*

ANTONYM:
• cruel

kindness NOUN

the quality of being considerate towards other people • *Everyone has treated me with great kindness.*

benevolence • *an act of selfless benevolence*
charity • *Ms Rubens writes with warmth and charity.*
compassion • *He showed no compassion to his victim.*
gentleness • *the gentleness with which she treated her mother*
humanity • *Her speech showed great maturity and humanity.*

ANTONYM:
• cruelty

king NOUN

a man who is the head of a royal family • *the king and queen of Spain*

monarch • *the coronation of the new monarch*
sovereign • *the first British sovereign to visit the country*

RELATED WORDS:
• ADJECTIVES royal, regal, monarchical

k

know ① VERB

to understand or be aware of
something • *I don't know
anything about cars.*

apprehend • *It is impossible to
apprehend the whole painting at
once.*

be aware of • *Smokers are
aware of the risks they run.*

comprehend • *They do not
comprehend the nature of the
problem.*

perceive • *the world as we
perceive it*

see • *Don't you see what he's up
to?*

understand • *too young to
understand what was happening*

know ② VERB

to be familiar with a person or
thing • *I believe you two already
know each other.*

be acquainted with • *Are you
acquainted with my husband?*

be familiar with • *I am
familiar with his work.*

recognise • *She recognised him
at once.*

knowledge NOUN

all you know about something
• *She had no knowledge of
French.*

education • *a man with little
education*

learning • *people of great
learning*

scholarship • *a lifetime of
scholarship*

wisdom • *a source of wisdom
and knowledge*

Ll

label ① NOUN

a piece of paper or plastic
attached to something for
information • *He peered at the
label on the bottle.*

sticker • *There's a sticker on the
box showing the price.*

tag • *a name tag*

ticket • *a price ticket*

label ② VERB

to put a label on something
• *The produce was labelled "Made
in China".*

flag • *Flag the pages which need
corrections.*

sticker • *products stickered at a
special price*

tag • *The pigeon was tagged
with a numbered band.*

labour ① NOUN

very hard work • *the labour of
weeding and digging*

effort • *legs aching with the
effort of the climb*

exertion • *She felt dizzy with
the exertion of walking.*

industry • *At last his industry
was rewarded.*

toil • *their day's toil in the
fields*

work • *All our work is starting
to pay off.*

labour ② NOUN
the workforce of a country or industry • *unskilled labour*
employees • *Only a third of all employees are union members.*
workers • *Thousands of workers have been laid off.*
workforce • *a country where half the workforce is unemployed*

labour ③ VERB
to work very hard • *peasants labouring in the fields*
slave • *We've been slaving half the night to finish this.*
toil • *workers toiling in wretched conditions*
work • *He works twelve hours a day.*
ANTONYM:
• relax

lack ① NOUN
the shortage or absence of something which is needed • *a lack of funds*
absence • *an absence of evidence*
deficiency • *tests for vitamin deficiency*
scarcity • *a scarcity of water*
shortage • *a food shortage*
want • *becoming weak from want of rest*
ANTONYM:
• abundance

lack ② VERB
to be without something that is needed • *She lacks confidence.*
be deficient in • *Your diet is deficient in vitamins.*
be short of • *I'm short of cash.*

miss • *Your jacket is missing a button.*

lag VERB
to make slower progress than other people or things • *He is now lagging 10 points behind the champion.*
fall behind • *The city is falling behind in attracting tourists.*
trail • *The party is trailing badly in the opinion polls.*

lake NOUN
TYPES OF LAKE
lagoon
loch (SCOTTISH)
lough (IRISH)
mere
reservoir
tarn

lame ADJECTIVE
weak or unconvincing • *a lame excuse*
feeble • *his feeble attempt at humour*
flimsy • *MPs condemned his evidence as flimsy.*
pathetic • *a pathetic attempt at humour*
poor • *a poor effort*
unconvincing • *an unconvincing argument*
weak • *a weak performance*

lament ① VERB
to express sorrow or regret over something • *She lamented the decisions she had made.*
grieve • *grieving over his wife and son*
mourn • *We mourned the loss of our home.*

lament | 342

wail • *a child wailing for her lost toy*

weep • *She wept for her lost love.*

lament ② NOUN
something you say to express sorrow or regret • *a lament for a vanished age*

moan • *a moan of sorrow*

wail • *wails of grief*

land ① NOUN
an area of ground which someone owns • *a dispute over land*

estate • *a shooting party on his estate in Yorkshire*

grounds • *the palace grounds*

property • *people who camped on his property*

land ② NOUN
a region or country • *This is a land of opportunity.*

country • *the boundary between the two countries*

nation • *the nation's financial crisis*

province • *The Algarve is Portugal's southernmost province.*

region • *the region of Tuscany*

territory • *the disputed territory on the border*

land ③ VERB
to arrive on the ground after flying or sailing • *We landed in New York around noon.*

alight • *A thrush alighted on a nearby branch.*

dock • *The ship docked in Le Havre.*

touch down • *The plane touched down in Barbados.*

language ① NOUN
the system of words people use to communicate • *She speaks four languages.*

dialect • *the Cantonese dialect*

idiom • *the Australian idiom*

jargon • *scientific jargon*

lingo (INFORMAL) • *I don't speak the lingo.*

tongue • *The French feel passionately about their native tongue.*

vernacular • *an Indian vernacular derived from Sanskrit*

vocabulary • *a new word in the German vocabulary*

language ② NOUN
the style in which you speak or write • *He explained the process in plain language.*

phrasing • *The phrasing of this report is confusing.*

style • *a simple writing style*

wording • *The wording of the contract was ambiguous.*

large ADJECTIVE
of a greater size or amount than usual • *a large room*

big • *Her husband was a big man.*

colossal • *a colossal task*

enormous • *an enormous house*

giant • *a giant bird*

gigantic • *a gigantic spider*

great • *a great hall as long as a church*

huge • *huge profits*

immense • *an immense chamber*

massive • *a massive ship*

vast • *a vast desert*

L

ANTONYM:
• small

last ① ADJECTIVE
the most recent • *last year*
latest • *his latest thriller*
most recent • *her most recent film*
preceding • *The bank's turnover had risen during the preceding year.*
previous • *his previous marriage*

ANTONYM:
• first

last ② ADJECTIVE
happening or remaining after all the others of its kind • *the last three chapters of the book*
closing • *the closing years of the century*
concluding • *the concluding scene of the film*
final • *This is your final chance.*
ultimate • *the ultimate result of the move*

ANTONYM:
• first

last ③ VERB
to continue to exist or happen • *The film lasted for two and a half hours.*
carry on • *The situation can't carry on like this.*
continue • *The exhibition continues till 25 November.*
endure • *Somehow their friendship endures.*
persist • *The problem persists.*
remain • *The building remains to this day.*

survive • *companies which survived the recession*

late ① ADJECTIVE
after the expected time • *The train was late.*
behind • *I've got behind with my payments.*
behind time • *Hurry up. We're behind time already.*
belated • *a belated birthday card*
delayed • *The kick-off was delayed by 10 minutes.*
last-minute • *buying some last-minute Christmas presents*
overdue • *The birth is two weeks overdue.*

ANTONYM:
• early

late ② ADJECTIVE
dead, especially recently • *my late husband*
dead • *He has been dead for a year now.*
deceased (FORMAL) • *his recently deceased mother*
departed • *memories of departed friends*

laugh ① VERB
to make a noise which shows you are amused or happy • *You never laugh at my jokes.*
▶ see Word Study **laugh**, page 715

laugh ② NOUN
the noise you make when amused or happy • *She has a very infectious laugh.*
chortle • *"That's what you think," he said with a chortle.*
chuckle • *We had a quiet chuckle at his mistake.*

giggle • *She gave a nervous giggle.*

guffaw • *He let out a huge guffaw of amusement.*

snigger • *barely able to stifle a snigger*

titter • *A titter went round the room.*

law ① NOUN

a country's system of rules • *The use of this drug is against the law.*

charter • *a citizen's charter for France*

code • *a code of conduct*

constitution • *proposed changes to the constitution*

• ADJECTIVES: legal, judicial

law ② NOUN

one of the rules of a country • *Laws against fox-hunting were introduced in 2005.*

act • *A new act has been passed by Parliament.*

code • *a code designed to protect the rights of children*

decree • *a decree lifting the state of emergency*

regulation • *regulations outlawing child labour*

rule • *a rule that was imposed in 1962*

statute • *a practice regulated by statute*

lawyer NOUN

someone who advises people about the law • *I'm discussing the matter with my lawyers.*

advocate • *A public advocate will be appointed to represent you.*

attorney • *a prosecuting attorney*

barrister • *The author is a practising barrister.*

counsel • *His counsel advised him to appeal against the verdict.*

solicitor • *She took advice from a solicitor.*

lay ① VERB

to put something somewhere • *Lay a sheet of newspaper on the floor.*

place • *She placed a mug of coffee in front of him.*

put • *He put the photograph on the desk.*

set • *He set his briefcase on the floor.*

set down • *I set the glasses down on the table.*

settle • *He settled his coat over my shoulders.*

spread • *She spread a towel over the sand and lay down.*

lay ② VERB

to arrange or set something out • *A man came to lay the carpet.*

arrange • *He started to arrange the books in piles.*

set out • *The flower garden was set out with large beds of roses.*

layer NOUN

something that covers a surface or comes between two other things • *A fresh layer of snow covered the street.*

blanket • *a blanket of fog*

coat • *a coat of paint*

coating • *a crisp chocolate coating*

L

covering • *a thin covering of dust*
film • *a film of plastic*
sheet • *a sheet of ice*
stratum • *the correct geological stratum*

layout NOUN
the way in which something is arranged • *the layout of the garden*
arrangement • *the arrangement of a room*
design • *the design of the museum*
format • *the format of the book*
plan • *a detailed plan of the house*

laze VERB
to relax and do no work • *We spent a few days lazing around by the pool.*
idle • *We spent hours idling in one of the cafés.*
loaf • *loafing around the house all day*
lounge • *They lounged in the shade.*
ANTONYM:
• work

lazy ADJECTIVE
not willing to work • *a lazy and incompetent employee*
idle • *an idle young layabout*
slack • *Many workers have simply become too slack.*
ANTONYM:
• industrious

lead ① VERB
to guide or take someone somewhere • *She led him into the house.*

conduct (FORMAL) • *He asked if he might conduct us to the ball.*
escort • *They were escorted by police to their plane.*
guide • *He took me by the arm and guided me out.*
steer • *Nick steered them towards the door.*
usher • *I ushered him into the office.*

lead ② VERB
to be in charge of • *He led the country between 1949 and 1984.*
command • *the general who commanded the troops*
direct • *He will direct day-to-day operations.*
govern • *her ability to govern the country*
head • *Who heads the firm?*
manage • *I manage a small team of workers.*
supervise • *She supervised more than 400 volunteers.*

lead ③ NOUN
a clue which may help solve a crime • *The police are following up several leads.*
clue • *a vital clue to the killer's identity*
indication • *All the indications suggest that he is the murderer.*
trace • *No traces of violence were found at the scene.*

leader NOUN
the person in charge of something • *the leader of the Republican Party*
boss • *Who's the boss around here?*
captain • *the captain of the team*

chief • *the chief of police*
commander • *a commander in the Royal Navy*
director • *the director of the film*
head • *Heads of government met in New York.*
principal • *the principal of the school*
ringleader • *the ringleader of the gang*
ANTONYM:
• follower

leading ADJECTIVE
particularly important, respected or advanced • *a leading industrial nation*
chief • *one of his chief rivals*
eminent • *an eminent surgeon*
key • *the key witness at the trial*
main • *one of the main tourist areas of Amsterdam*
major • *Exercise has a major part to play in preventing disease.*
principal • *one of the principal figures in politics today*
prominent • *a prominent member of the Law Society*
top • *a top model*

lead to VERB
to cause something to happen • *Poor posture can lead to back pain.*
cause • *Knocks can cause damage to the spine.*
contribute to • *problems which contributed to their defeat*
produce • *The drug produces side effects.*

leaflet NOUN
a piece of paper with information about a subject • *Protesters were handing out leaflets in the street.*
booklet • *He handed out an A4 booklet.*
brochure • *a travel brochure*
circular • *A circular was sent out to shareholders.*
pamphlet • *Mary was still working on the pamphlet.*

leak ① VERB
to escape from a container or other object • *The gas had leaked from a cylinder.*
escape • *A vent was opened to let some air escape.*
ooze • *Blood was oozing from the wound.*
seep • *Radioactive water has seeped into underground reservoirs.*
spill • *70,000 tonnes of oil spilled from the tanker.*

leak ② NOUN
a hole which lets gas or liquid escape • *Have you plugged the leaks?*
chink • *A mist rose from the chinks in the pavement.*
crack • *The lava oozed through cracks in the rock.*
fissure • *Water trickled out of fissures in the limestone.*
hole • *The sea was flowing in through the hole in the ship's hull.*
puncture • *My tyre has a slow puncture.*

leap ① VERB
to jump a great distance or height • *The deer leapt into the air*

bounce • *She bounced up and down on the spot, looking for attention.*
bound • *The dog came bounding up the stairs.*
jump • *I jumped over the fence.*
spring • *He sprang to his feet.*
vault • *He could easily vault the wall.*

leap ② NOUN
a jump of great distance or height • *a leap of 2.37 metres*
bound • *With one bound, Jack was free.*
jump • *the longest jumps by a man and a woman*
spring • *The cheetah gave a great spring into the air.*

learn ① VERB
to gain knowledge by studying or training • *I am trying to learn French.*
grasp • *The basics of the language are easy to grasp.*
master • *He's having trouble mastering the piano.*
pick up • *You'll soon pick up enough German to get by.*

earn ② VERB
to find out about something • *On learning who she was, I asked to meet her.*
ascertain • *They had ascertained that he was not a spy.*
determine • *calculations to determine the rate of tax*
discover • *She discovered that they'd escaped.*
find out • *As soon as we found this out, we closed the ward.*

gather • *I gather the report is critical of the judge.*
hear • *I heard he had moved away.*
understand • *I understand that she's just taken early retirement.*

learned ADJECTIVE
having gained a lot of knowledge by studying • *a very learned man*
academic • *I feel intimidated by academic people.*
erudite • *a witty and erudite leader*
intellectual • *an artistic and intellectual couple*
literate • *a literate and educated readership*
scholarly • *a scholarly researcher*

least ADJECTIVE
as small or few as possible • *Stick to foods with the least fat.*
fewest • *Which product has the fewest calories?*
lowest • *the lowest temperatures on record for this time of year*
minimum • *a minimum age limit*
slightest • *He showed only the slightest hint of emotion.*
smallest • *the smallest measurable unit of light*
ANTONYM:
• most

leave ① VERB
to go away from a person or place • *He is not allowed to leave the country.*

abandon • *a charity for pets that have been abandoned*
depart • *A number of staff departed during his time as director.*
desert • *a soldier who had deserted his post*
forsake • *I would never forsake my children.*
go • *Let me know when you're ready to go.*
quit • *He quit his job to concentrate on music.*
withdraw • *Troops withdrew from the country last month.*

leave ② NOUN
a period of time off work • *Why don't you take a few days' leave?*
holiday • *I still have several days' holiday to take.*
time off • *He took time off to go sailing with his wife.*
vacation • *We went on vacation to Puerto Rico.*

lecture ① NOUN
a formal talk about a particular subject • *In his lecture he covered several topics.*
address • *an address to the American people*
discourse • *a lengthy discourse on market strategy*
presentation • *a business presentation*
sermon • *his first sermon as a bishop*
speech • *He delivered his speech in French.*
talk • *a brief talk on the history of the site*

lecture ② NOUN
a talk intended to tell someone off • *The police gave us a stern lecture on safety.*
reprimand • *He has been given a severe reprimand.*
scolding • *given a scolding for offending his opponents*
telling-off (INFORMAL) • *I got a severe telling-off for not phoning him.*
warning • *He was given a severe warning from the referee.*

lecture ③ VERB
to teach by giving formal talks to audiences • *She has lectured all over the world.*
give a talk • *He set about campaigning, giving talks and fund-raising.*
speak • *He's been invited to speak at the Democratic Convention.*
talk • *Today, I plan to talk about the issues of education and nursery care.*
teach • *She has taught at the university for 34 years.*

left-wing ADJECTIVE
believing in socialist policies • *a left-wing demonstration*
leftist • *three leftist groups*
liberal • *a politician with liberal views*
socialist • *a socialist state*

legacy NOUN
property someone leaves you when they die • *He left his sons a generous legacy.*
bequest • *He made a bequest to his favourite charity.*

estate • *documents concerning the estate*
heirloom • *a family heirloom*
inheritance • *She was worried she'd lose her inheritance to her stepmother.*

legal ① ADJECTIVE
relating to the law • *the Dutch legal system*
forensic • *the forensic skill of a good barrister*
judicial • *a judicial review*
judiciary • *various levels of the judiciary system*

legal ② ADJECTIVE
allowed by the law • *The strike was perfectly legal.*
authorised • *an authorised procedure*
lawful • *What I did was lawful and proper.*
legitimate • *a legitimate business*
permissible • *the current permissible levels of pesticide in food*
rightful • *the rightful owner of the property*
valid • *a valid passport*
ANTONYM:
• illegal

leisure NOUN
time when you can relax • *There wasn't a lot of time for leisure.*
free time • *He played piano in his free time.*
recreation • *Saturday afternoons are for recreation.*
relaxation • *Make time for a bit of relaxation.*

time off • *I haven't had any time off all day.*
ANTONYM:
• work

leisurely ADJECTIVE
unhurried or calm • *a leisurely walk along the beach*
comfortable • *going at a comfortable speed*
easy • *an easy pace*
gentle • *His movements were gentle and deliberate.*
relaxed • *a relaxed meal*
unhurried • *an unhurried way of life*
ANTONYM:
• hasty

lekker ADJECTIVE (SOUTH AFRICAN; SLANG)
pleasant or tasty • *We had a really lekker meal.*
delectable • *delectable chocolates*
delicious • *a wide selection of delicious desserts*
luscious • *luscious fruit*
pleasant • *a pleasant dinner*
tasty • *Try this tasty dish for supper.*

length ① NOUN
the distance from one end of something to the other • *The fish was about a metre in length.*
distance • *Work out the distance of the journey.*
extent • *the extent of the rain forest*
span • *a butterfly with a two-inch wing span*

length ② NOUN

the amount of time
something lasts for • *The film is
over two hours in length.*

duration • *The duration of the
course is one year.*

period • *for a limited period only*

space • *A dramatic change takes
place in the space of a few
minutes.*

span • *The batteries have a life
span of six hours.*

term • *a 12-month term of
service*

lengthen VERB

to make something longer
• *The runway had to be
lengthened.*

extend • *They have extended the
deadline.*

make longer • *You can make
your hair longer by using
extensions.*

prolong • *a move which will
prolong the strike*

stretch • *Take care not to
stretch the fabric.*

ANTONYM:
• shorten

lessen VERB

to decrease in size or amount
• *changes to their diet that would
lessen the risk of disease*

abate • *The storm gradually
abated.*

decrease • *Population growth
is decreasing by 1.4% each year.*

diminish • *The threat of war
has diminished.*

dwindle • *his dwindling
authority*

lower • *The Central Bank has
lowered interest rates.*

minimise • *attempts to
minimise the risk of infection*

reduce • *Gradually reduce the
dosage.*

shrink • *The forests have shrunk
to half their size.*

ANTONYM:
• increase

lesson NOUN

a period of time for being
taught • *Johanna took piano
lessons.*

class • *I go to dance classes.*

coaching • *He needs extra
coaching in maths.*

lecture • *a series of lectures
on art*

period • *We get six periods of
French a week.*

tutoring • *a growing demand
for private tutoring*

let ① VERB

to allow someone to do
something • *The authorities
won't let her leave the country.*

allow • *I pleaded to be allowed
to go.*

give permission • *Who gave
you permission to come here?*

permit • *Permit me to express
my opinion.*

sanction • *He may now be ready
to sanction the use of force.*

ANTONYM:
• forbid

let ② VERB

to let someone use your
property for money • *She*

always lets her house for the summer.

hire out • *The machines are hired out to farmers.*

lease • *She plans to lease the building to students.*

rent • *He rents rooms to backpackers.*

level ① ADJECTIVE

completely flat • *a plateau of level ground*

flat • *Cricket should be played on a totally flat field.*

horizontal • *Every horizontal surface was covered with plants.*

ANTONYM:
• uneven

level ② VERB

to make something flat • *We levelled the ground.*

flatten • *Flatten the dough and cut it into four pieces.*

plane • *planing the surface of the wood*

smooth • *He smoothed his hair.*

level ③ NOUN

a point on a scale which measures something • *Crime levels have started to decline.*

grade • *the lowest grade of staff*

rank • *He rose to the rank of captain.*

stage • *an early stage of development*

standard • *a decent standard of living*

status • *She has reached the status of "national treasure".*

lie ① VERB

to rest somewhere horizontally

• *The injured man was lying on his back.*

loll • *He was lolling on the sofa.*

lounge • *We lounged on the beach all day.*

recline • *She reclined on the couch.*

sprawl • *They sprawled in a lawn chair, snoozing.*

lie ② VERB

to say something that is not true • *She always lies about her age.*

fib (INFORMAL) • *He fibbed when she asked him where he'd been.*

perjure yourself • *All of the witnesses perjured themselves.*

tell a lie • *He could never tell a lie or do anything devious.*

lie ③ NOUN

something you say which is not true • *His whole story was a lie.*

deceit • *the deceits of political leaders*

fabrication • *She described the magazine interview as "a complete fabrication".*

falsehood • *He accused them of spreading falsehoods about him.*

fib (INFORMAL) • *I caught him out in another fib.*

fiction • *His account of events is a complete fiction.*

life NOUN

the time during which you are alive • *a long and active life*

existence • *a very miserable existence*

life span • *This species of snake has a life span of up to 25 years.*

lifetime • *a lifetime devoted to service for others*

time • *If I had my time again, I would do things differently.*

RELATED WORDS:
• ADJECTIVES animate, vital

lift ① VERB
to move something to a higher position • *straining to lift heavy weights*

elevate • *a mechanism to elevate the platform*

hoist • *I hoisted my rucksack on to my shoulder.*

pick up • *Anthony picked up his case from the floor.*

raise • *He raised his hand to wave.*

ANTONYM:
• lower

lift ② VERB
to remove something such as a ban or law • *the decision to lift sanctions*

cancel • *The government has cancelled the state of emergency.*

end • *pressure to end the embargo*

relax • *an attempt to persuade the US Congress to relax the law*

remove • *an amendment to remove the ban on divorce*

light ① NOUN
brightness that enables you to see things • *Cracks of light filtered through the shutters.*

brightness • *the brightness of the full moon*

brilliance • *the brilliance of the noonday sun*

glare • *shading his eyes from the glare*

glow • *the red glow of the dying fire*

illumination • *The only illumination came from a small window.*

radiance • *The bedside lamp cast a soft radiance over her face.*

ANTONYM:
• dark

RELATED WORD:
• PREFIX photo-

light ② ADJECTIVE
pale in colour • *a light blue shirt*

bleached • *bleached pine tables*

blonde or **blond** • *blonde hair*

fair • *to protect my fair skin*

pale • *dressed in pale pink*

pastel • *delicate pastel shades*

ANTONYM:
• dark

light ③ ADJECTIVE
not weighing much • *working out with light weights*

flimsy • *a flimsy cardboard box*

lightweight • *They will carry lightweight skis on their backs.*

portable • *a portable television*

slight • *She is small and slight.*

ANTONYM:
• heavy

light ④ VERB
to make a place bright • *The room was lit by a single candle.*

brighten • *The late afternoon sun brightened the room.*

illuminate • *No streetlights illuminated the road.*

light up • *Fireworks lit up the sky*

ANTONYM:
• darken

light ⑤ VERB
to make a fire start burning • It's time to light the barbecue.
ignite • A stray spark ignited the fireworks.
kindle • I kindled a fire in the stove.

ANTONYM:
• extinguish

like ① PREPOSITION
similar to • He looks just like my father.
akin • She looked at me with something akin to hatred.
analogous • a process analogous to the curing of tobacco
parallel • Our situation is parallel to yours.
similar • a taste similar to that of celery

ANTONYM:
• unlike

like ② VERB
to find someone or something pleasant • I really like this music.
adore (INFORMAL) • All her employees adored her.
appreciate • I know you appreciate good food.
be fond of • Are you fond of Chinese cuisine?
be keen on • I'm not very keen on sport.
be partial to • I'm partial to apple juice.
enjoy • Most children enjoy cartoons.

go for • I always go for a starter rather than a dessert.
have a soft spot for • I've always had a soft spot for him.
have a weakness for • I have a weakness for slushy romantic novels.
love • She loves reading.
relish • He relished the idea of proving me wrong.
revel in • She appears to revel in being unpopular.

ANTONYM:
• dislike

likely ADJECTIVE
having a good chance of happening • It seems likely that he will come back.
anticipated • the anticipated result
expected • the expected response
liable • He is liable to be a nuisance.
possible • It's quite possible that I'm wrong.
probable • the probable outcome

ANTONYM:
• unlikely

limit ① NOUN
a point beyond which something cannot go • the speed limit
bounds • the bounds of good taste
deadline • We finished the job within the deadline.
maximum • He was given two years in prison, the maximum allowed for the charges.

ultimate • *This hotel is the ultimate in luxury.*

utmost • *His skills were tested to the utmost.*

limit ② VERB

to prevent something from going any further • *Don't limit yourself to one activity.*

confine • *Damage was confined to a small portion of the building.*

curb • *measures to curb inflation*

fix • *The mortgage rate is fixed at 8.5%.*

ration • *I'm rationing myself to one chocolate biscuit a day.*

restrict • *The patient was restricted to a meagre diet.*

limp ADJECTIVE

not stiff or firm • *a limp lettuce leaf*

drooping • *the drooping branches of a birch*

flabby • *a flabby stomach*

floppy • *She fondled the dog's floppy ears.*

slack • *a slack jaw*

soft • *a soft dough*

ANTONYM:
• stiff

line ① NOUN

a long thin mark on something • *Draw a line down the centre of the page.*

rule • *He drew a rule under the last name.*

score • *There was a long score on the car's bonnet.*

streak • *dark streaks on the surface of the moon*

stripe • *a green jogging suit with white stripes down the sides*

line ② NOUN

a row of people or things • *a line of spectators*

column • *a column of figures*

file • *A file of mourners walked behind the coffin.*

queue • *a long queue of angry motorists*

rank • *ranks of police in riot gear*

row • *a row of pretty little cottages*

line ③ NOUN

the route along which something moves • *the line of flight*

course • *the course of the river*

path • *The lava annihilates everything in its path.*

route • *the most direct route*

track • *a railway track*

trajectory • *the trajectory of the missile*

link ① NOUN

a connection between two things • *the link between sugary drinks and tooth decay*

affiliation • *He has no affiliation with any political party.*

association • *the association between the two companies*

attachment • *Mother and child form a close attachment.*

bond • *The experience created a bond between us.*

connection • *He has denied any connection to the crime.*

relationship • *the relationship between humans and their environment*

tie • *She has ties with this town.*

link ② VERB
to connect two things • *tree houses linked by ropes*
attach • *Attach the curtains to the rods with hooks.*
connect • *two rooms connected by a passage*
couple • *The engine is coupled to a gearbox.*
fasten • *a wooden bench fastened to the floor*
join • *the skin which joins the eye to the eyelid*
tie • *He tied the dog to the tree by its lead.*
ANTONYM:
• separate

liquid ① NOUN
a substance which is not solid and can be poured • *Drink plenty of liquids for the next few days.*
fluid • *The fluid can be removed with a syringe.*
liquor • *Pour the liquor off into the pan.*
solution • *a solution of honey and vinegar*

liquid ② ADJECTIVE
in the form of a liquid • *Wash in warm water with liquid detergent.*
fluid • *a fluid fertiliser*
molten • *molten metal*
runny • *a dessertspoon of runny honey*

list ① NOUN
a set of things written down one below the other • *There were six names on the list.*

catalogue • *a chronological catalogue of the Beatles' songs*
directory • *a telephone directory*
index • *The book includes a comprehensive subject index.*
inventory • *an inventory of stolen goods*
listing • *a listing of all the schools in the area*
record • *Keep a record of everything you eat and drink.*
register • *a register of births, deaths and marriages*

list ② VERB
to set things down in a list • *All the ingredients are listed on the label.*
catalogue • *I was cataloguing my stamp collection.*
index • *Most of the archive has been indexed.*
record • *400 species of fungi have been recorded.*
register • *a registered charity*

listen VERB
to hear and pay attention to something • *I'll repeat that for those of you who weren't listening.*
attend (FORMAL) • *Close your books and attend to me.*
hark (LITERARY) • *Hark! I hear the sound of footsteps.*
hear • *Will you hear me saying my lines?*
pay attention • *Pay attention or you won't know what to do.*

little ① ADJECTIVE
small in size or amount • *a little sailing boat*

dainty • *dainty sandwiches and cakes*

dwarf • *He grows dwarf tulips.*

meagre • *a meagre pay increase*

measly • *a measly ration of food*

mini • *a cat which resembles a mini leopard*

miniature • *a collection of miniature toy boats*

minute • *minute particles of soil*

paltry • *a boring job with a paltry salary*

pygmy • *a children's zoo with pygmy goats*

scant • *He paid scant attention to his colleagues.*

small • *They sat at a small table.*

tiny • *He tore the paper into tiny pieces.*

wee (SCOTTISH) • *Would you like a wee bit of cake?*

ANTONYM:
• large

little ② NOUN
a small amount or degree • *We offered her plenty to eat but she would only take a little.*

hardly any • *He's done hardly any work today.*

not much • *There's not much difference between them.*

live ① VERB
to have your home somewhere • *She has lived here for 20 years.*

dwell (FORMAL) • *the people who dwell in the forest*

inhabit • *the fish that inhabit the coral reefs*

reside (FORMAL) • *He used to reside in England.*

stay (SCOTTISH AND SOUTH AFRICAN) • *We've stayed in this house since we got married.*

live ② VERB
to be alive • *He will not live much longer.*

be alive • *You are lucky to be alive.*

exist • *the chances of finding life existing on Mars*

live ③ ADJECTIVE
not dead or artificial • *a live spider*

alive • *It is unlikely that he is still alive.*

animate • *an animate object*

living • *living tissue*

lively ADJECTIVE
full of life and enthusiasm • *a lively personality*

active • *an active youngster*

animated • *an animated discussion*

energetic • *She gave an energetic performance.*

perky • *He wasn't quite as perky as usual.*

sparkling • *I was enjoying a sparkling conversation.*

sprightly • *You're sprightly this morning.*

vivacious • *She is vivacious and charming.*

ANTONYM:
• dull

load ① NOUN
something being carried • *This truck can carry a load of up to 10 tons.*

cargo • *The boat was carrying its usual cargo of bananas.*

L

consignment • *The first consignment of food has been sent.*

freight • *Most of the freight was carried by rail.*

shipment • *a shipment of cranberry plants from Nova Scotia*

load ② VERB
to put a lot of things on or into • *The trucks were loaded with blankets and supplies.*

fill • *The van was filled with crates.*

pack • *helicopters packed with medical supplies*

pile • *Her trolley was piled with groceries.*

stack • *stalls stacked with wares*

loan ① NOUN
a sum of money that you borrow • *a small business loan*

advance • *She was paid a $100,000 advance on her next novel.*

credit • *He can't get credit to buy the equipment.*

mortgage • *I took out a second mortgage on the house.*

loan ② VERB
to lend something to someone • *He loaned us the painting for our exhibition.*

advance • *I advanced him some money till we got home.*

lend • *Will you lend me your jacket?*

local ① ADJECTIVE
belonging to the area where you live • *This is a local shop for local people.*

community • *the revival of family and community life*

district • *the district council*

neighbourhood • *a neighbourhood watch scheme*

parish • *the parish priest*

regional • *the regional elections*

local ② NOUN
a person who lives in a particular area • *That's what the locals call the place.*

inhabitant • *the inhabitants of Glasgow*

native • *She is proud to be a native of Sydney.*

resident • *a protest by residents of the village*

locate VERB
to find out where someone or something is • *We have been unable to locate him.*

find • *They can't find it on the map.*

pinpoint • *Computers pinpoint where the shells came from.*

track down • *She has spent years trying to track down her parents.*

located ADJECTIVE
existing or standing in a particular place • *The restaurant is located near the cathedral.*

placed • *The hotel is wonderfully placed right in the city centre.*

sited • *a castle romantically sited on a river estuary*

situated • *His hotel is situated in a lovely place.*

location NOUN
a place or position • *a house with a beautiful location*
place • *the place where the temple used to stand*
point • *a popular meeting point for tourists*
position • *The ship radioed its position to the coastguard.*
site • *the site of the battle*
situation • *The hotel has a superb isolated situation.*
spot • *Can you show me the spot where it happened?*
whereabouts • *His exact whereabouts are still not known.*

lock ① VERB
to close and fasten something with a key • *Are you sure you locked the door?*
latch • *He latched the gate.*
padlock • *The box has been padlocked shut.*
ANTONYM:
• unlock

lock ② NOUN
a device used to fasten something • *The lock had been burst open.*
latch • *A key clicked in the latch of the front door.*
padlock • *He put a padlock on the door of his flat.*

logical ① ADJECTIVE
using logic to work something out • *a logical argument*
consistent • *a consistent and well-presented theory*

rational • *a rational analysis*
reasoned • *a reasoned discussion*
sound • *His reasoning is sound, but he has missed the point.*
valid • *Both sides put forward valid points.*
ANTONYM:
• illogical

logical ② ADJECTIVE
sensible in the circumstances • *a logical deduction*
judicious (FORMAL) • *the judicious use of technology*
obvious • *I jumped to the obvious conclusion.*
plausible • *a plausible explanation*
reasonable • *a reasonable course of action*
sensible • *the sensible thing to do*
wise • *a wise decision*
ANTONYM:
• illogical

lonely ① ADJECTIVE
unhappy because of being alone • *She's lonely and just wants to talk.*
alone • *scared of being alone*
forlorn • *He looked a forlorn figure as he left the pitch.*
forsaken • *a forsaken and bitter man*
lonesome • *I'm lonesome without you.*

lonely ② ADJECTIVE
isolated and not visited by many people • *a lonely hillside*
deserted • *a deserted farmhous*

desolate • *a desolate place*
isolated • *Many of the villages are in isolated areas.*
remote • *a remote outpost*
secluded • *a secluded area close to her home*
uninhabited • *an uninhabited island*

long ① ADJECTIVE
continuing for a great amount of time • *a long interval when no-one spoke*
extended • *an extended period of unemployment*
interminable • *the interminable debate about GM foods*
lengthy • *a lengthy delay*
lingering • *the lingering pain of an injury*
long-drawn-out • *the effects of a long-drawn-out war*
prolonged • *Forecasters predict a prolonged period of good weather.*
protracted • *protracted negotiations over pay rises*
slow • *Writing music is a slow process.*
sustained • *a sustained run of bad luck*

ANTONYM:
• short

long ② ADJECTIVE
great in length or distance • *a long line of people*
elongated • *The catfish has an elongated body.*
extensive • *an extensive list of products*
lengthy • *lengthy queues*

ANTONYM:
• short

long ③ VERB
to want something very much
• *He longed for a holiday.*
ache • *She still ached for her homeland.*
covet • *She coveted his job.*
crave • *I crave her approval.*
hunger • *Jules hungered for adventure.*
lust • *She lusted after a designer kitchen.*
pine • *I pine for the countryside.*
yearn • *He yearned for freedom.*

longing NOUN
a strong wish for something
• *her longing to return home*
craving • *a craving for sugar*
desire • *her desire for a room of her own*
hankering • *a hankering to be an actor*
hunger • *a hunger for success*
thirst • *a thirst for adventure*
yearning • *a yearning to be part of a normal family*

look ① VERB
to turn your eyes towards something and see it • *She looked at me with something like hatred.*
▶ see Word Study **look**, page 716

look ② VERB
to appear or seem to be • *The buffet looks appetising.*
appear • *He appeared uncertain what to do.*
look like • *You look like you need a good night's sleep.*

seem • She seemed tense.
seem to be • They seem to be lacking in enthusiasm.

look ③ NOUN
the action of turning your eyes towards something • Lucy took a last look in the mirror.
gaze • her concentrated gaze
glance • a cursory glance
glimpse • a fleeting glimpse
peek • Give me a peek at his letter.

look ④ NOUN
the way someone or something appears • He had the look of a desperate man.
air • a nonchalant air
appearance • He was fastidious about his appearance.
bearing • a man of military bearing
expression • I saw his puzzled expression.
face • Why are you all wearing such long faces?
semblance • a semblance of normality

look after VERB
to take care of someone or something • Will you look after my cats when I go on holiday?
care for • vintage cars lovingly cared for by their owners
mind • Jim will mind the shop while I'm away.
nurse • My mother nursed him while he was ill.
take care of • I'll take care of the house for you.
tend • He tended his flower beds.
watch • My father will watch the kids while we're out.

lookalike NOUN
a person who looks like someone else • an Elvis lookalike
dead ringer (INFORMAL) • a dead ringer for his brother
double • He's the exact double of his father at that age.
spitting image (INFORMAL) • She is the spitting image of me.

look for VERB
to try to find a person or thing • I'm looking for my son.
forage • foraging for food
hunt • Police are hunting for clues.
search • Rescue teams are searching for the missing crew members.
seek • They have had to seek work as labourers.

loose ① ADJECTIVE
not firmly held or fixed • a loose tooth
free • She broke her fall with her free hand.
unsecured • corridors blocked by unsecured objects
wobbly • a wobbly bridge
ANTONYM:
• secure

loose ② ADJECTIVE
not fitting closely • Wear loose clothes for comfort.
baggy • a baggy black jumper
slack • Those trousers are very slack on you.
sloppy • wearing a sloppy t-shirt, jeans and trainers
ANTONYM:
• tight

loosen VERB
to make something looser
• He loosened his tie.
slacken • We slackened the
guy-ropes.
undo • She began to undo the
tiny buttons.
untie • He untied his shoes and
slipped them off.
ANTONYM:
• tighten

loot ① VERB
to steal from a place during a
riot or battle • Gangs began
breaking windows and looting
shops.
pillage • The bandits pillaged
the church.
plunder • They plundered and
burned the town.
raid • Rustlers have raided a
village in the region.
ransack • The three raiders
ransacked the house.

loot ② NOUN
stolen or illegal money or
goods • The loot was never
recovered.
booty • They divided the booty
between them.
haul • Police said the haul was
worth five thousand dollars.
plunder • pirates in search of
easy plunder
spoils • the spoils of war
swag (SLANG) • The thieves
carried the swag off in a stolen car.

lose ① VERB
to be unable to find • I've lost
my keys.

drop • She's dropped a contact
lens.
mislay • I seem to have mislaid
my glasses.
misplace • Somehow my
suitcase was misplaced.
ANTONYM:
• find

lose ② VERB
to be beaten • We lost the match.
be beaten • He was soundly
beaten in the election.
be defeated • They were
defeated in the final.
ANTONYM:
• win

lost ① ADJECTIVE
not knowing where you are
• I think we're lost.
adrift • two men adrift on a raft
in the middle of the sea
astray • I am lost and astray in
the world.
off course • After a while I
realised I was completely off
course.

lost ② ADJECTIVE
unable to be found • a child
wailing for her lost toy
mislaid • searching for his
mislaid keys
misplaced • I've found your
misplaced glasses.
missing • a missing person
vanished • unable to contact
the vanished convoy

lot ① : **a lot** or **lots** NOUN
a large amount of
something • Remember to
drink lots of water.

abundance • *an abundance of food*

a great deal • *I've spent a great deal of time on this project.*

masses (INFORMAL) • *There were masses of flowers at her funeral.*

piles (INFORMAL) • *He's got piles of money.*

plenty • *We've got plenty of time.*

quantities • *She drank quantities of hot, sweet tea.*

scores • *There were scores of witnesses.*

lot ② NOUN

an amount or number • *We've just sacked one lot of builders.*

batch • *a batch of cookies*

bunch (INFORMAL) • *My neighbours are a noisy bunch.*

crowd • *They're a real crowd of villains.*

group • *a small group of football supporters*

quantity • *a quantity of water*

set • *a set of photographs*

loud ① ADJECTIVE

having a high level of sound • *a loud explosion*

blaring • *a blaring television*

deafening • *a deafening roar*

noisy • *a noisy old car*

resounding • *a resounding slap*

strident • *her strident voice*

thunderous • *thunderous applause from the crowd*

ANTONYM:
• quiet

loud ② ADJECTIVE

too brightly coloured • *a loud tie*

flamboyant • *a flamboyant outfit*

flashy • *flashy clothes*

garish • *a garish three-piece suite*

gaudy • *a gaudy purple-and-orange hat*

lurid • *She painted her toenails a lurid pink.*

ANTONYM:
• dull

lovable ADJECTIVE

easy to love • *His vulnerability makes him very lovable.*

adorable • *an adorable black kitten*

charming • *a charming young Frenchman*

enchanting • *He was an enchanting baby.*

endearing • *one of his most endearing qualities*

sweet • *a sweet little girl*

ANTONYM:
• hateful

love ① VERB

to feel strong affection for someone • *I loved my husband very much.*

adore • *She adored her parents.*

cherish • *He genuinely loved and cherished her.*

worship • *She had worshipped him from afar for years.*

ANTONYM:
• hate

love ② VERB

to like something very much • *We both love fishing.*

appreciate • *I know you appreciate good food.*
enjoy • *Do you enjoy opera?*
like • *I've always liked horror films.*
relish • *I relish the challenge of dangerous sports.*
ANTONYM:
• hate

love ③ NOUN
a strong feeling of affection
• *a mother's love for her children*
adoration • *He had been used to adoration all his life.*
affection • *The thought of him with great affection.*
ardour • *an attempt to rekindle their lost ardour*
devotion • *At first she was flattered by his devotion.*
infatuation • *consumed with infatuation for her*
passion • *the object of her passion*
ANTONYM:
• hatred

love ④ NOUN
a strong liking for something
• *her love of animals*
devotion • *his devotion to literature*
fondness • *a fondness for modern art*
liking • *my liking for classical music*
weakness • *He had a weakness for cats.*
ANTONYM:
• hatred

lovely ADJECTIVE
very attractive and pleasant
• *You look lovely.*
attractive • *Polperro is an attractive harbour village.*
beautiful • *She's a very beautiful woman.*
delightful • *a delightful garden*
enjoyable • *I've had a very enjoyable time.*
pleasant • *a pleasant little apartment*
pretty • *a pretty room overlooking a beautiful garden*
ANTONYM:
• horrible

loving ADJECTIVE
feeling or showing love • *a loving husband and father*
affectionate • *openly affectionate with each other*
devoted • *a devoted couple*
doting • *a doting father*
fond • *She gave him a fond smile.*
tender • *Her voice was tender.*
warm • *a warm and loving mother*
ANTONYM:
• cold

low ① ADJECTIVE
short or not far above the ground • *The sun was low in the sky.*
little • *a little table*
short • *a short flight of steps*
small • *a small stool*
squat • *squat stone houses*
stunted • *stunted trees*
sunken • *a sunken garden*
ANTONYM:
• high

low ② ADJECTIVE

small in degree or quantity
• low prices

minimal • minimal expenditure

modest • a modest rate of unemployment

poor • working for poor wages

reduced • reduced customer demand

scant • scant stocks of fish

small • produced in small numbers

ANTONYM:
• high

low ③ ADJECTIVE

not considered respectable
• a man of low birth

common • She might be a little common, but at least she wasn't boring.

contemptible • He mixes with the most contemptible people in society.

despicable • a despicable wretch

disreputable • the company of some disreputable characters

lowly • his lowly status

vulgar • She considers herself to be above the vulgar rabble.

lower ① VERB

to move something downwards • They lowered a rope down the mine shaft.

drop • He dropped his plate into the sink.

let down • They let the barrier down.

take down • The pilot took the helicopter down.

ANTONYM:
• raise

lower ② VERB

to make something less in amount • a commitment to lower taxes

cut • The first priority is to cut costs.

decrease • The government plans to decrease interest rates.

diminish • to diminish the prestige of the monarchy

lessen • a diet that would lessen the risk of disease

minimise • attempts to minimise the risk of infection

reduce • Gradually reduce the dosage.

slash • We're slashing our prices.

ANTONYM:
• increase

loyal ADJECTIVE

firm in your friendship or support • a loyal friend

constant • I've lost my best friend and constant companion.

dependable • a cheerful, dependable mate

faithful • She remained faithful to the cause.

staunch • a staunch supporter

true • a true friend

trusty • a trusty ally

ANTONYM:
• treacherous

luck NOUN

something that happens by chance • It was just luck that we happened to meet.

accident • It came about almost by accident.

chance • We only met by chance.

destiny • *Is it destiny that brings people together?*
fate • *a simple twist of fate*
fortune • *smiled on by fortune*

lucky ① ADJECTIVE
having a lot of good luck • *He had always been lucky at cards.*

blessed • *blessed with an even temper*
charmed • *She seems to have a charmed life.*
fortunate • *He was extremely fortunate to survive.*

ANTONYM:
• unlucky

lucky ② ADJECTIVE
happening by chance with good consequences • *a lucky break*

fortuitous • *a fortuitous combination of circumstances*
fortunate • *a fortunate accident*
opportune • *I had arrived at an opportune moment.*
timely • *his timely intervention*

ANTONYM:
• unlucky

lump ① NOUN
a solid piece of something • *big lump of dough*

ball • *a ball of clay*
cake • *a cake of soap*
chunk • *a chunk of bread*
hunk • *a hunk of beef*
piece • *a piece of cake*
wedge • *a wedge of cheese*

lump ② NOUN
a bump on the surface of something • *I've got a big lump on my head.*

bulge • *My purse made a bulge in my pocket.*
bump • *a bump in the road*
hump • *a hump on his back*
swelling • *a swelling over one eye*

lure ① VERB
to attract someone somewhere or into doing something • *We are being lured into a trap.*

attract • *Warm weather attracts the fish close to the shore.*
beckon • *The mermaids beckoned the sailors towards the rocks.*
draw • *What drew him to the area was its proximity to London.*
entice • *Retailers will do anything to entice shoppers through their doors.*
tempt • *trying to tempt American tourists back to Britain*

lure ② NOUN
something that you find very attractive • *the lure of rural life*

attraction • *the attraction of living on the waterfront*
bait • *using cheap bread and milk as a bait to get people into the shop*
magnet • *The park is a magnet for dog walkers.*
pull • *feel the pull of the past*
temptation • *the many temptations to which they will be exposed*

lurk VERB

to wait hidden for someone or something • *He thought he saw someone lurking in the doorway.*

lie in wait • *Police lay in wait inside the house.*

loiter • *They loitered unseen in the alley.*

skulk • *skulking in the safety of the car*

luxurious ADJECTIVE

expensive and full of luxury • *a luxurious lifestyle*

de luxe • *de luxe cars*

lavish • *a lavish party*

opulent • *an opulent office*

plush (INFORMAL) • *a plush hotel*

sumptuous • *a sumptuous feast*

ANTONYM:
• plain

luxury ① NOUN

comfort in expensive surroundings • *a life of luxury*

affluence • *the trappings of affluence*

opulence • *the sheer opulence of her new life*

sumptuousness • *The hotel lobby was sumptuousness itself.*

luxury ② NOUN

something enjoyable which you do not have often • *This perfume is my favourite luxury.*

extra • *The car is a basic model with no extras.*

extravagance • *Eating out is an extravagance.*

indulgence • *This car is one of my few indulgences.*

treat • *I only eat cakes as a treat.*

lying ① NOUN

the action of telling lies • *I've had enough of your lying.*

deceit • *the deceits of political leaders*

dishonesty • *deliberate dishonesty*

fabrication • *His story is pure fabrication.*

fibbing • *Her fibbing eventually got her into trouble.*

perjury • *This witness has committed perjury.*

lying ② ADJECTIVE

telling lies • *The man is just a lying cheat.*

deceitful • *deceitful and misleading remarks*

dishonest • *a dishonest account of events*

false • *a false confession*

untruthful • *She unwittingly gave untruthful answers.*

ANTONYM:
• honest

Mm

machine NOUN
a piece of equipment • *a machine to pump water out of mines*
apparatus • *an apparatus for use in fires*
appliance • *electrical appliances*
contraption • *an interesting musical contraption called a Theremin*
device • *This device can measure minute quantities of matter.*
instrument • *navigation instruments*
mechanism • *the locking mechanism*

mad ① ADJECTIVE
very foolish or unwise • *He'd be mad to refuse.*
barmy (SLANG) • *a barmy idea*
crazy (INFORMAL) • *People thought they were crazy to try it.*
daft (BRITISH; INFORMAL) • *That's a daft question.*
foolhardy • *Some described the act as foolhardy.*
foolish • *It would be foolish to raise hopes unnecessarily.*
stupid • *It would be stupid to pretend otherwise.*

mad ② ADJECTIVE (INFORMAL)
angry about something • *They both got mad at me for interfering.*
angry • *She was angry at her husband.*
enraged • *I got more and more enraged at my father.*
fuming • *Mrs Vine was still fuming.*
furious • *He is furious at the way his wife has been treated.*
incensed • *Mum was incensed at his lack of compassion.*
infuriated • *He knew how infuriated this would make me.*
irate • *Bob was very irate, shouting and screaming about the flight delay.*
livid • *I am absolutely livid about it.*

magic NOUN
a special power • *They believe in magic.*
sorcery • *the use of sorcery to combat evil influences*
witchcraft • *people who practise witchcraft*

magical ADJECTIVE
wonderful and exciting • *Paris is a magical city.*
bewitching • *bewitching brown eyes*
enchanting • *an enchanting child*

main ADJECTIVE
most important • *the main reason*
cardinal • *one of the cardinal rules of movie reviewing*
chief • *one of his chief rivals*

m

foremost • *one of the foremost scholars on ancient Indian culture*

leading • *a leading industrial nation*

major • *one of the major causes of illness*

predominant • *Her predominant emotion was confusion.*

primary • *the primary source of water in the region*

prime • *the prime suspect*

principal • *the principal source of sodium in our diets*

mainly ADVERB

true in most cases • *The staff were mainly Russian.*

chiefly • *He painted chiefly portraits.*

generally • *It is generally true that the darker the fruit the higher its iron content.*

largely • *The early studies were done on men, largely by male researchers.*

mostly • *Cars are mostly metal.*

predominantly • *Business is conducted predominantly by phone.*

primarily • *The body is made up primarily of bone, muscle and fat.*

principally • *This is principally because the market is weak.*

major ADJECTIVE

very important or serious • *a major problem*

critical • *a critical factor*

crucial • *He took the crucial decisions himself.*

leading • *a leading industrial nation*

outstanding • *an outstanding contribution*

significant • *Her upbringing had a significant effect on her outlook.*

ANTONYM:
• minor

majority NOUN

more than half • *The majority of our cheeses are made with pasteurised milk.*

best part • *for the best part of 24 hours*

better part • *I spent the better part of £100 on her present.*

bulk • *the bulk of the world's great poetry*

mass • *the mass of the population*

most • *Most of the book is completely true.*

make ① VERB

to construct something • *Sheila makes all her own clothes.*

assemble • *Workers were assembling planes.*

build • *Workers at the site build the F-16 jet fighter.*

construct • *the campaign to construct a mall on the site*

create • *It's great for a radio producer to create a show like this.*

fabricate • *All the tools are fabricated from high quality steel*

fashion • *Stone Age settlers fashioned necklaces from sheep's teeth.*

form • *a figure formed from clay*
manufacture • *They manufacture plastics.*
produce • *We try to produce items that are the basics of a stylish wardrobe.*

make ② VERB
to force someone to do something • *Mary made him clean up the plate.*
compel • *legislation to compel cyclists to wear a helmet*
drive • *The desire to win drives sportspeople to train.*
force • *A back injury forced her to withdraw from the competition.*
oblige • *Finally I was obliged to abandon the car.*

make ③ NOUN
a particular type • *a certain make of phone*
brand • *a brand of washing powder*
model • *To keep the cost down, opt for a basic model.*

make up ① VERB
to form the parts of something • *Insects are made up of tens of thousands of proteins.*
compose • *The force would be composed of troops from NATO countries.*
comprise • *a crowd comprising the wives, husbands and children of scientists*
constitute • *Volunteers constitute 50% of the centre's staff.*
form • *Cereals form the staple diet.*

make up ② VERB
to invent a story • *It's very unkind of you to make up stories about him.*
concoct • *The prisoner concocted the story to get a lighter sentence.*
fabricate • *Officers fabricated evidence against them.*
invent • *I must invent something I can tell my mother.*

making ① NOUN
the act of creating something • *the making of this movie*
assembly • *the assembly of an explosive device*
building • *The building of the airport continues.*
construction • *boat construction*
creation • *the creation of large parks and forests*
fabrication • *the design and fabrication of the space shuttle*
manufacture • *the manufacture of nuclear weapons*
production • *These proteins stimulate the production of blood cells.*

making ②: **in the making**
ADJECTIVE
about to become something • *a captain in the making*
budding • *a budding author*
emergent • *an emergent state*
potential • *a potential champion*
up-and-coming • *an up-and-coming golfer*

m

male ADJECTIVE
relating to men and boys • *a deep male voice*
manly • *He was the ideal of manly beauty.*
masculine • *masculine characteristics like facial hair*
ANTONYM:
• female

malicious ADJECTIVE
having the intention of hurting someone • *She described the charges as malicious.*
cruel • *Children can be so cruel.*
malevolent (FORMAL) • *She gave me a malevolent stare.*
mean • *Someone's played a mean trick on you.*
spiteful • *spiteful telephone calls*
vicious • *a vicious attack on an innocent man's character*

man ① NOUN
an adult male human being • *a young man*
bloke (BRITISH, AUSTRALIAN AND NEW ZEALAND; INFORMAL) • *a really nice bloke*
chap (INFORMAL) • *I am a very lucky chap.*
gentleman • *It seems this gentleman was waiting for the doctor.*
guy (INFORMAL) • *a guy from Manchester*
male • *Some conditions affect more males than females.*
ANTONYM:
• woman

man ② NOUN
people in general • *Man is a social animal.*
humanity • *He has rendered a great service to humanity.*
human race • *Can the human race carry on expanding?*
mankind • *the evolution of mankind*

mana NOUN (NEW ZEALAND)
the authority and influence of an important person • *a leader of great mana*
authority • *figures of authority*
influence • *He denies using any political influence.*
power • *positions of great power*
standing • *The Prime Minister's standing was high in the US.*
stature • *his stature as the world's greatest cellist*
status • *the status of a national hero*

manage ① VERB
to succeed in doing something • *We managed to find somewhere to sit.*
cope with • *how my mother coped with bringing up three children*
succeed in • *We have succeeded in persuading cinemas to show the film.*

manage ② VERB
to be in charge of something • *Within two years he was managing the store.*
be in charge of • *Who's in charge of the canteen?*

command • *Who would command the troops in the event of war?*

control • *He now controls the largest retail development empire in southern California.*

direct • *Christopher will direct day-to-day operations.*

run • *Is this any way to run a country?*

management ① NOUN
the act of running an organisation • *The zoo needed better management.*

control • *The restructuring involves Mr Ronson giving up control of the company.*

direction • *Organisations need clear direction.*

running • *the day-to-day running of the clinic*

management ② NOUN
the people who run an organisation • *The management is doing its best.*

administration • *They would like the college administration to exert more control.*

board • *a recommendation which he wants to put before the board*

bosses • *a dispute between workers and bosses*

directors • *the board of directors of the company*

employers • *Employers are said to be considering the demand.*

manager NOUN
a person in charge of running an organisation • *the manager of our New York branch*

boss • *He cannot stand his boss.*

director • *the financial director of the company*

executive • *an advertising executive*

manifest ADJECTIVE
(FORMAL)
obvious or easily seen • *the manifest failure of the policy*

blatant • *a blatant attempt to spread the blame*

clear • *a clear case of discrimination*

conspicuous • *Politics has changed in a conspicuous way.*

glaring • *a glaring example of fraud*

obvious • *an obvious injustice*

patent • *This was patent nonsense.*

plain • *He's made it plain that he wants to be involved.*

manner ① NOUN
the way that you do something • *She smiled in a friendly manner.*

fashion • *another drug that works in a similar fashion*

mode • *He switched automatically into interview mode.*

style • *Kenny's writing style*

way • *He had a strange way of talking.*

manner ② NOUN
the way that someone behaves • *his kind manner*

bearing • *his military bearing*

behaviour • *her anti-social behaviour*

m

conduct • *principles of civilised conduct*

demeanour • *a cheerful demeanour*

manoeuvre ① VERB
to move something skilfully
• *It took expertise to manoeuvre the boat so close to the shore.*

guide • *He took Elliott by the arm and guided him out.*

navigate • *He attempted to navigate his way through the crowds.*

negotiate • *I negotiated my way out of the airport.*

steer • *I steered him towards the door.*

manoeuvre ② NOUN
a clever action • *manoeuvres to block the electoral process*

dodge • *a tax dodge*

ploy • *a cynical marketing ploy*

ruse • *This was a ruse to divide them.*

tactic • *The tactic paid off.*

manufacture ① VERB
to make goods in a factory
• *Several models are being manufactured here.*

assemble • *a factory where they assemble tractors*

fabricate • *a plant which fabricates aeroplane components*

make • *making cars at two plants in Europe*

mass-produce • *the invention of machinery to mass-produce footwear*

process • *The material will be processed into plastic pellets.*

produce • *The company produced computer parts.*

manufacture ② NOUN
the making of goods in a factory • *the manufacture of 3D printers*

assembly • *the assembly of cars by robots*

fabrication • *the design and fabrication of the shuttle*

making • *the steps that go into the making of a book*

mass production • *the mass production of baby food*

production • *We need to maintain the production of cars at last year's level.*

many ① ADJECTIVE
a large number • *Among his many hobbies was the breeding of fine horses.*

countless • *She brought joy to countless people.*

innumerable • *He has invented innumerable excuses.*

myriad • *the myriad other tasks we are trying to perform*

numerous • *I made numerous attempts to apologise to her.*

umpteen (INFORMAL) • *He has produced umpteen books.*

ANTONYM:
• few

many ② PRONOUN
a large number of people or things • *in many of these neighbourhoods*

a lot • *A lot of people would agree with you.*

a mass • *a mass of books and papers*

M

a multitude • *for a multitude of reasons*
large numbers • *Large numbers of people stayed away.*
lots (INFORMAL) • *lots of strange new animals*
plenty • *plenty of vegetables*
scores • *Scores of people were injured.*

ANTONYM:
• few

mark ① NOUN
a small stain • *I can't get this mark off the curtain.*
blot • *an ink blot*
line • *A line of dirt ran across his face like a scar.*
smudge • *a dirty smudge on his shirt*
spot • *He noticed a grease spot on his trousers.*
stain • *a stain on the front of her jacket*
streak • *A streak of mud smudged her cheek.*

mark ② VERB
to stain something • *to stop the pen from marking her shirt*
smudge • *Her face was smudged with dirt.*
stain • *His clothing was stained with mud.*
streak • *Rain had begun to streak the window-panes.*

market NOUN
a place to buy or sell things • *the fish market at Billingsgate*
bazaar • *an Eastern bazaar*
fair • *a craft fair*

marriage NOUN
the relationship between two people who are married • *six years of marriage*
matrimony (FORMAL) • *the bonds of matrimony*
wedlock (FORMAL) • *the blessings of wedlock*

RELATED WORDS:
• ADJECTIVES conjugal, connubial, marital, nuptial

marsh NOUN

TYPES OF MARSH

bog
fen
mire
morass
mudflats
quagmire
quicksands
saltmarsh
slough
swamp
wetland

marvellous ADJECTIVE
wonderful or excellent • *a marvellous actor*
brilliant • *a brilliant performance*
excellent • *He does an excellent job as club secretary.*
first-rate • *The service was absolutely first-rate.*
magnificent • *She was magnificent as Lady Macbeth.*
remarkable • *a remarkable achievement*
splendid • *splendid photographs*
superb • *a superb novel*

m

wonderful • *It's wonderful to see you.*

ANTONYM:
• terrible

mass ① NOUN
a large number or amount • *a mass of papers*
crowd • *A huge crowd of people gathered in the square.*
heap • *a heap of bricks*
load • *a load of kids*
lump • *a lump of clay*
mob • *a growing mob of demonstrators*
pile • *a pile of sand*
throng • *A shout went up from the throng of spectators.*

mass ② ADJECTIVE
involving a large number of people • *mass unemployment*
general • *We are trying to raise general awareness about this issue.*
popular • *popular anger at the decision*
universal • *universal health care*
widespread • *widespread support for the proposals*

mass ③ VERB
to gather together in a large group • *Police began to mass at the shipyard.*
assemble • *Thousands of people assembled in the stadium.*
congregate • *Youngsters congregate here in the evenings.*
gather • *In the evenings, we gathered round the fireplace.*
group • *The children grouped together under the trees.*

master ① NOUN
a male schoolteacher • *a retired maths master*
instructor • *a college instructor*
teacher • *her chemistry teacher*
tutor • *an adult education tutor in German*

master ② VERB
to learn how to do something • *She found it easy to master the piano.*
become proficient in • *He quickly became proficient in the language.*
get the hang of (INFORMAL) • *It's a bit tricky till you get the hang of it.*
grasp • *It took him a while to grasp the basics of the process.*
learn • *He enjoyed learning new skills.*

match ① NOUN
an organised game • *a football match*
competition • *a surfing competition*
contest • *one of the best contests in recent boxing history*
game • *England's first game of the new season*

match ② VERB
to be similar to • *The shoes matched her dress.*
agree • *Their statements do not agree.*
correspond • *The two maps correspond closely.*
fit • *The punishment must always fit the crime.*
go with • *The curtains didn't go with the carpet.*

suit • *the best package to suit your needs*

tally • *The figures didn't seem to tally.*

material ① NOUN
any type of cloth • *the thick material of her skirt*
cloth • *a piece of cloth*
fabric • *silk and other delicate fabrics*

material ② NOUN
a solid substance • *the materials to make red dye*
matter • *waste matter from industries*
stuff • *the stuff from which the universe is made*
substance • *a crumbly black substance*

matter ① NOUN
something that you have to deal with • *business matters*
affair • *The funeral was a sad affair.*
business • *This whole business has upset me.*
issue • *a major political issue*
question • *the difficult question of unemployment*
situation • *The situation is now under control.*
subject • *a difficult subject on which to reach a compromise*

matter ② NOUN
any substance • *the smallest divisible particle of matter*
material • *a conducting material such as metal*
stuff • *a dress made from some flimsy stuff*

substance • *a poisonous substance*

matter ③ VERB
to be important • *It does not matter how long their hair is.*
be of consequence • *Their choice of partner is of no consequence to anyone but themselves.*
count • *It's as if my opinions just don't count.*
make a difference • *Exercise makes all the difference.*

mature ① VERB
to become fully developed • *Some children mature earlier than others.*
come of age • *The money was held in trust until he came of age.*
grow up • *She grew up in Tokyo.*
reach adulthood • *She died before reaching adulthood.*

mature ② ADJECTIVE
fully developed • *He's very mature for his age.*
adult • *a pair of adult birds*
full-grown • *a full-grown male orang-utan*
fully-fledged • *She has developed into a fully-fledged adult.*
grown • *a grown man*
grown-up • *They have two grown-up children.*

maximum ① ADJECTIVE
being the most that is possible • *the maximum recommended intake*

m

top • *a top speed of 200 mph*
utmost • *a question of the utmost importance*

ANTONYM:
• minimum

maximum ② NOUN
the most that is possible • *a maximum of fifty men*
ceiling • *an agreement to put a ceiling on salaries*
height • *when emigration was at its height*
most • *The most he'll make is a hundred pounds.*
upper limit • *the need to put an upper limit on spending*
utmost • *He did his utmost to make her agree.*

ANTONYM:
• minimum

maybe ADVERB
it is possible that • *Maybe I should have done a bit more.*
conceivably • *The mission could conceivably be accomplished within a week.*
it could be • *It could be that's why he refused.*
perhaps • *Perhaps, in time, she'll understand.*
possibly • *Television is possibly to blame for this.*

meagre ADJECTIVE
very small and inadequate • *his meagre pension*
inadequate • *inadequate portions*
measly (INFORMAL) • *The average British bathroom measures a measly 3.5 square metres.*

paltry • *a paltry fine of £150*
scant • *She berated the police for paying scant attention to the theft.*
sparse • *sparse vegetation*

meal NOUN
an occasion when people eat • *She sat next to him throughout the meal.*
banquet • *a state banquet at Buckingham Palace*
dinner • *a series of official dinners*
feast • *the wedding feast*
kai (NEW ZEALAND; INFORMAL) • *a cheap kai in a local restaurant*

mean ① VERB
to convey a message • *The red signal means that you must stop.*
denote • *Red eyes denote strain and fatigue.*
indicate • *Today's vote indicates a change in policy.*
signify • *The raised flag signified the striker was offside.*

mean ② VERB
to intend to do something • *I meant to phone you, but didn't have time.*
aim • *I aim to arrive early.*
intend • *She intended to move back to France.*
plan • *They plan to marry in the summer.*

mean ③ ADJECTIVE
unwilling to spend money • *Don't be mean with the tip.*
miserly • *He is miserly with both his time and his money.*

snoep (SOUTH AFRICAN;
INFORMAL) • *Have you ever met
anyone as snoep as him?*

tight (INFORMAL) • *He was so
tight that he wouldn't even spend
three pounds.*

ANTONYM:
• generous

meaning NOUN
the idea expressed by
something • *the meaning of this
dream*

drift • *I was beginning to get his
drift.*

gist • *Grace could not get the
gist of their conversation.*

message • *the message of the
film*

significance • *The President's
visit is loaded with symbolic
significance.*

measure ① VERB
to check the size of something
• *We measured how tall he was.*

gauge • *He gauged the wind at
over 30 knots.*

survey • *geological experts who
surveyed the cliffs*

measure ② NOUN
an amount of something
• *There has been a measure of
agreement.*

amount • *a certain amount of
disappointment*

degree • *a degree of success*

portion • *I have spent a
considerable portion of my life
here.*

proportion • *A large proportion
of my time was spent abroad.*

measure ③ NOUN
an action in order to achieve
something • *Tough measures
are needed to maintain order.*

expedient • *I reduced my
spending by the simple expedient
of destroying my credit card.*

manoeuvre • *manoeuvres to
block the electoral process*

means • *The move is a means to
fight crime.*

procedure • *safety procedures*

step • *steps to discourage
careless driving*

medicine NOUN
something you take to make
you better • *They prevent the
food and medicine from reaching
its destination.*

drug • *Three new drugs recently
became available.*

medication • *some medication
for her ulcers*

muti (SOUTH AFRICAN;
INFORMAL) • *muti for treating a
fever*

remedy • *At the moment we are
trying a herbal remedy.*

medium ① ADJECTIVE
average in size • *He was of
medium height.*

average • *a ginger tomcat of
average size*

medium-sized • *a
medium-sized saucepan*

middling • *Small and middling
flats have increased in price much
more than luxury ones.*

medium ② NOUN
a means of communication
• *the medium of television*

m

channel • through diplomatic channels
vehicle • The play seemed an ideal vehicle for his music.

meek ADJECTIVE
quiet and timid • a meek, mild-mannered personality
deferential • his shy and deferential manner
docile • docile, obedient children
mild • a mild man
submissive • a submissive, unconfident character
timid • a timid child
unassuming • She's very polite and unassuming.
ANTONYM:
• bold

meet ① VERB
to be in the same place as someone • I met her quite by chance.
bump into (INFORMAL) • I bumped into a friend of yours today.
come across • where I came across a group of noisy children
come upon • We turned the corner and came upon a group of hikers.
encounter • the most gifted child he had ever encountered
run across • We ran across some old friends.
run into • You'll never guess who I ran into the other day.

meet ② VERB
to gather in a group • We meet for lunch once a week.

assemble • a convenient place for students to assemble between classes
congregate • Youngsters love to congregate here in the evening.
convene • Senior officials convened in October.
gather • We all gathered in the boardroom.
get together • the last time we all got together

meet ③ VERB
to fulfil a need • services intended to meet the needs of disabled people
answer • Would a new government answer their needs?
fulfil • All the requirements were fulfilled.
satisfy • Candidates must satisfy the general conditions for admission.

meeting ① NOUN
an event at which people come together for a purpose • a business meeting
audience • an audience with the Pope
conference • a conference on education
congress • a medical congress
convention • the annual convention of the World Boxing Council
gathering • a social gathering
get-together (INFORMAL) • a get-together I had at my home
reunion • a family reunion

meeting ② NOUN
an occasion when you meet someone • a chance meeting

assignation (FORMAL) • *She had an assignation with her boyfriend.*

encounter • *a remarkable encounter with a group of soldiers*

rendezvous • *Baxter arranged a six o'clock rendezvous.*

tryst (LITERARY) • *a lover's tryst*

melodramatic ADJECTIVE
behaving in an exaggerated way • *Don't you think you're being rather melodramatic?*

histrionic • *She let out a histrionic groan.*

sensational • *sensational tabloid newspaper reports*

theatrical • *In a theatrical gesture Glass clamped his hand over his eyes.*

melt ① VERB
to become liquid • *The snow had melted.*

dissolve • *Heat gently until the sugar dissolves.*

thaw • *It's so cold the snow doesn't get a chance to thaw.*

melt ② VERB
to disappear • *Her inhibitions melted.*

disappear • *The immediate threat has disappeared.*

disperse • *The crowd dispersed peacefully.*

dissolve • *His new-found optimism dissolved.*

evaporate • *My anger evaporated.*

vanish • *All her fears suddenly vanished.*

memorable ADJECTIVE
likely to be remembered • *a memorable victory*

catchy • *a catchy tune*

historic • *a historic meeting*

notable • *with a few notable exceptions*

striking • *the most striking feature of those statistics*

unforgettable • *an unforgettable experience*

memory NOUN
the ability to remember • *Every detail is fresh in my memory.*

recall • *a man blessed with total recall*

remembrance (FORMAL) • *My remembrance of the incident is somewhat hazy.*

mend VERB
to repair something broken • *I should have had the catch mended.*

darn • *a woman darning socks*

fix • *If something is broken, we get it fixed.*

patch • *They patched the barn roof.*

renovate • *The couple spent thousands renovating the house.*

repair • *to get her car repaired*

restore • *experts who specialise in restoring ancient parchments*

mention ① VERB
to talk about something briefly • *I may not have mentioned it to her.*

allude to • *She alluded to his absence in vague terms.*

bring up • *Why are you bringing it up now?*

m

broach • *I broached the subject of her early life.*

hint • *The President hinted that he might make some changes.*

intimate • *He did intimate that he is seeking legal action.*

refer to • *In his speech, he referred to a recent trip to Canada.*

touch on • *The film touches on these issues, but only superficially.*

touch upon • *I'd like to touch upon a more serious question now.*

mention ② NOUN

a brief comment about something • *There was no mention of elections.*

allusion • *She made an allusion to the events in Los Angeles.*

reference • *He made no reference to any agreement.*

merciful ① ADJECTIVE

showing kindness • *He is merciful and sympathetic to others.*

compassionate • *a deeply compassionate man*

humane • *the desire for a more humane society*

kind • *She is warm-hearted and kind to everyone.*

ANTONYM:
• merciless

merciful ② ADJECTIVE

showing forgiveness • *We can only hope the court is merciful.*

forgiving • *I don't think people are in a very forgiving mood.*

lenient • *He believes the government is already lenient with people who evade tax.*

ANTONYM:
• merciless

merciless ADJECTIVE

showing no kindness or forgiveness • *She was subjected to merciless teasing.*

callous • *his callous disregard for human life*

cruel • *Children can be so cruel.*

heartless • *I couldn't believe they were so heartless.*

implacable • *a powerful and implacable enemy*

ruthless • *his ruthless treatment of employees*

ANTONYM:
• merciful

mercy ① NOUN

the quality of kindness • *He showed no mercy.*

compassion • *his compassion for a helpless animal*

kindness • *He was treated with kindness by numerous officials.*

pity • *She saw no pity in their faces.*

mercy ② NOUN

the quality of forgiveness • *He threw himself upon the mercy of the court.*

forgiveness • *He fell to his knees begging for forgiveness.*

leniency • *He said he would show no leniency towards them.*

merit ① NOUN

worth or value • *Box-office*

success mattered more than artistic merit.

excellence • *the top US award for excellence in journalism*

value • *The value of this work experience should be underestimated.*

virtue • *There is little virtue in such an approach.*

worth • *people who had already proved their worth to their companies*

merit ② NOUN
a good quality that something has • *Whatever its merits, their work would never be used.*

advantage • *The great advantage of home-grown oranges is their flavour.*

asset • *Her leadership qualities were her greatest asset.*

strength • *The book's strength lay in its depiction of modern-day Tokyo.*

strong point • *Science was never my strong point at school.*

virtue • *Its other great virtue is its hard-wearing quality.*

merit ③ VERB
to deserve something • *Such ideas merit careful consideration.*

be entitled to • *She is entitled to feel proud.*

be worthy of • *The bank might think you're worthy of a loan.*

deserve • *He deserves a rest.*

earn • *Companies must earn a reputation for honesty.*

warrant • *no evidence to warrant a murder investigation*

mess ① NOUN
a state of untidiness • *I'll clear up the mess later.*

chaos • *Their concerts often ended in chaos.*

disarray • *He found the room in disarray.*

disorder • *Inside all was disorder.*

mess ② NOUN
a situation that is full of problems • *the reasons why the economy is in such a mess*

fix (INFORMAL) • *The government has really got itself into a fix.*

jam (INFORMAL) • *They were in a real jam.*

muddle • *Our finances are in a muddle.*

turmoil • *Her career was in turmoil.*

mess ③ or **mess up** VERB
to spoil something • *He had messed up his career.*

botch up (INFORMAL) • *I hate having builders botch up repairs on my house.*

bungle (INFORMAL) • *Two prisoners bungled an escape bid.*

make a hash of (INFORMAL) • *The government made a total hash of things.*

muck up (SLANG) • *He always seemed to muck everything up.*

message ① NOUN
a piece of information for someone • *He left a message on her phone.*

bulletin • *a news bulletin*

m

communication • *The ambassador brought a communication from the President.*

despatch or **dispatch** • *this dispatch from our West Africa correspondent*

memo • *office memos*

memorandum • *a memorandum from the Ministry of Defence*

note • *I'll have to leave a note for Karen.*

word • *There is no word from the authorities on the reported attack.*

message ② VERB

to send information to • *He messaged dozens of friends.*

email or **e-mail** • *Gwyn and I emailed each other every week.*

IM • *chatting and IMing online*

instant message • *We instant messaged each other before meeting.*

text • *He texted a journalist with his comments.*

messenger NOUN

someone who carries a message • *There will be a messenger at the airport to collect the photographs.*

courier • *a motorcycle courier*

envoy • *an envoy to the King*

runner • *a runner on a TV show*

method NOUN

a way of doing something • *the traditional method of making cheese*

approach • *different approaches to gathering information*

mode • *the capitalist mode of production*

procedure • *He did not follow the correct procedure.*

technique • *the techniques of modern agriculture*

way • *a way of making new friends*

middle ① NOUN

the part furthest from the edges • *in the middle of the room*

centre • *the centre of the table*

halfway point • *Postle was third fastest at the halfway point.*

midst • *a house in the midst of huge trees*

middle ② ADJECTIVE

furthest from the edges • *the middle house*

central • *central London*

halfway • *a point halfway between the two posts*

mild ① ADJECTIVE

not strong or powerful • *a mild shampoo*

insipid • *It tasted bland and insipid.*

weak • *weak tea*

ANTONYM:

• strong

mild ② ADJECTIVE

gentle and good-tempered • *a mild man*

gentle • *her gentle nature*

meek • *a meek, mild-mannered character*

placid • *a placid child who rarely cried*

mild ③ ADJECTIVE

warmer than usual • *The area*

is famous for its mild winter climate.

balmy • *balmy summer evenings*

temperate • *a temperate climate*

mind ① NOUN

your ability to think • *You have a very suspicious mind.*

brain • *Stretch your brain with these puzzles.*

head • *I can't get that song out of my head.*

imagination • *Africa was alive in my imagination.*

intellect • *good health and a lively intellect*

psyche • *disturbing elements of the human psyche*

RELATED WORD:
• ADJECTIVE **mental**

mind ② VERB

to be annoyed by something • *I don't mind what you do.*

be bothered • *I'm not bothered if he doesn't like me.*

care • *young men who did not care whether they lived or died*

object • *I don't object to his clothes.*

mind ③ VERB

to look after something • *My mother is minding the shop.*

keep an eye on • *She asked me to keep an eye on the children.*

look after • *I looked after the dogs while she was away.*

take care of • *There was no one else to take care of the children.*

watch • *She bought the tickets while I watched the bags.*

minimum ADJECTIVE

being the least possible • *a minimum age limit*

least possible • *I try to cause the least amount of trouble possible.*

minimal • *The aim is to incur minimal expense.*

ANTONYM:
• maximum

minor ADJECTIVE

less important • *a minor injury*

lesser • *They pleaded guilty to lesser charges.*

petty • *petty crime*

secondary • *matters of secondary importance*

slight • *We have a slight problem.*

trifling • *Outside California these difficulties may seem trifling.*

trivial • *trivial details*

ANTONYM:
• major

minute ① NOUN

a short period of time • *I'll be with you in just a minute.*

flash • *It was all over in a flash.*

instant • *For an instant, Catherine was tempted to flee.*

moment • *Stop for one moment and think about what you're doing!*

second • *Just a second. I'm coming.*

trice • *I'll be back in a trice.*

minute ② ADJECTIVE

extremely small • *Only a minute amount is needed.*

m

microscopic • *microscopic fibres*
negligible • *They are convinced the strike will have a negligible impact.*
slender • *We won the vote by a slender majority.*
small • *small particles of dust*
tiny • *a tiny fraction of US production*

ANTONYM:
• vast

miracle NOUN
a surprising and fortunate event • *the Italian economic miracle*
marvel • *a marvel of high technology*
wonder • *the wonders of science*

miserable ① ADJECTIVE
very unhappy • *a job which made me miserable*
dejected • *Everyone has days when they feel dejected.*
depressed • *He seemed somewhat depressed.*
down • *Try to support each other when one of you is feeling down.*
downcast • *She looked downcast when she failed the test.*
low • *"I didn't ask for this job," he tells friends when he is low.*
melancholy (LITERARY) • *It was in these hours that he felt most melancholy.*
mournful • *He looked mournful, even near to tears.*
sad • *It left me feeling sad and empty.*

unhappy • *She is desperately unhappy.*
wretched • *I feel really confused and wretched.*

ANTONYM:
• cheerful

miserable ② ADJECTIVE
causing unhappiness • *a miserable little flat*
gloomy • *The outlook for next year is gloomy.*
pathetic • *a pathetic sight*
sorry • *The fires have left the industry in a sorry state.*
wretched • *He died in wretched poverty.*

misery NOUN
great unhappiness • *All that money brought nothing but misery.*
despair • *feelings of despair*
grief • *her grief when her husband died*
melancholy (LITERARY) • *with an air of melancholy*
sadness • *with a mixture of sadness and joy*
sorrow • *a time of great sorrow*
unhappiness • *There was a lot of unhappiness in my adolescence.*
woe (FORMAL) • *a tale of woe*

ANTONYM:
• joy

misfortune NOUN
an unfortunate event • *I had the misfortune to fall off my bike*
adversity • *times of adversity*
bad luck • *He has had his share of bad luck.*

misrepresent VERB
to give a false account of
something • *Keynes deliberately
misrepresented the views of his
opponents.*
distort • *The minister said his
remarks had been distorted by
the press.*
falsify • *falsifying personal
details on his CV*
twist • *You're twisting my
words.*

miss ① VERB
to fail to notice • *It's on the
second floor. You can't miss it.*
fail to notice • *He failed to
notice that the lights had turned
red.*
mistake • *There's no mistaking
her sincerity.*
overlook • *a fact that we all
tend to overlook*

miss ② VERB
to feel the loss of • *The boys
miss their father.*
long for • *Steve longed for the
good old days.*
pine for • *Make sure your pet
won't pine for you while you're
away.*
yearn for • *He yearned for his
freedom.*

mistake ① NOUN
something that is wrong
• *spelling mistakes*
blunder • *It had been a
monumental blunder to give him
the assignment.*
error • *a mathematical error*
gaffe • *a social gaffe*

oversight • *By an unfortunate
oversight, full instructions do not
come with the product.*
slip • *There must be no slips.*

mistake ② VERB
to think one thing is another
thing • *I mistook him for the
owner of the house.*
confuse with • *I can't see how
anyone could confuse you with
your brother!*
misinterpret as • *She
misinterpreted his remarks as a
threat.*
mix up with • *People often mix
me up with other actors.*
take for • *She had taken him for
a journalist.*

mistreat VERB
to treat someone or
something badly • *The vet said
the horse had been mistreated.*
abuse • *those who abuse elderly
relatives*
ill-treat • *They thought he had
been ill-treating his pets.*

mix VERB
to combine things • *Mix the
ingredients together slowly.*
amalgamate • *a need to
amalgamate the two
companies*
blend • *Blend the butter with
the sugar.*
combine • *Combine the flour
with 3 tablespoons of water.*
merge • *how to merge the
graphic with text*
mingle • *the mingled smell of
flowers and wood smoke*

m

mixture NOUN

a combination of things • *a sticky mixture of flour and water*

alloy • *an alloy of copper and tin*

amalgamation • *an amalgamation of two organisations*

blend • *a blend of fruit juice and sparkling water*

combination • *a fantastic combination of colours*

compound • *a compound of water, sugar, vitamins and enzymes*

fusion • *fusions of jazz and pop*

medley • *We communicated in a medley of foreign words and gestures.*

mix up VERB

to confuse two things • *People often mix us up.*

confuse • *Great care is taken to avoid confusing the two projects.*

muddle • *Critics have begun to muddle the two names.*

mix-up NOUN

a mistake in something planned • *a mix-up with the bookings*

mistake • *There must be some mistake.*

misunderstanding • *Ensure that there is no misunderstanding about the instructions.*

muddle • *There's been a muddle about whose responsibility it is.*

moan ① VERB

to make a low sound • *Laura moaned in her sleep.*

groan • *He began to groan with pain.*

grunt • *The driver grunted, then let us board the bus.*

moan ② VERB

to complain about something • *Carol is always moaning about homework.*

complain • *People always complain that the big banks are unfriendly.*

groan • *His parents were beginning to groan about the price of college tuition.*

grumble • *A tourist grumbled that the waiter spoke too much Spanish.*

whine • *They come to me to whine about their troubles.*

whinge (INFORMAL) • *Stop whingeing and get on with it.*

moan ③ NOUN

a low sound • *She let out a faint moan.*

groan • *a groan of disappointment*

grunt • *grunts of disapproval*

mock ① VERB

to make fun of someone • *Don't mock me.*

deride (FORMAL) • *The theory is widely derided by scientists.*

laugh at • *I thought they were laughing at me because I tripped.*

make fun of • *Don't make fun of me.*

poke fun at • *She poked fun at people's shortcomings.*

ridicule • *Mr Goss ridiculed that suggestion.*

scoff at • Some people may scoff at the idea that animals communicate.

mock ② ADJECTIVE
not genuine • mock surprise
artificial • artificial limbs
bogus • their bogus insurance claim
counterfeit • counterfeit money
dummy • dummy weapons
fake • a fake fur
false • false teeth
feigned • with feigned indifference
imitation • imitation leather
phoney or **phony** (INFORMAL) • a phoney excuse
pretended • with pretended zeal
sham • sham marriages

mockery NOUN
the act of mocking someone • Was there a glint of mockery in his eyes?
derision • shouts of derision
jeering • there was a chorus of jeering, whistles and laughter
ridicule • Davis was subjected to public ridicule.

model ① NOUN
a copy of something • an architect's model of a wooden house
dummy • a tailor's dummy
replica • a replica of the Statue of Liberty
representation • a representation of a human figure

model ② NOUN
a perfect example of something • The essay is a model of clarity.
epitome • the epitome of good taste
example • He is an example to the younger lads.
ideal • the ideal of beauty
paragon • a paragon of virtue

model ③ VERB
to make something into a shape • clay modelled into the shape of a bear
carve • One of the prisoners had carved a wooden chess set.
fashion • Stone Age settlers fashioned necklaces from sheep's teeth.
form • figures formed from modelling clay
mould • We moulded a chair out of mud.
sculpt • An artist sculpted a full-size replica of her head.
shape • Shape each half into a loaf.

moderate ① ADJECTIVE
neither too much nor too little • moderate exercise
average • I was only average academically.
fair • Reimar had a fair command of English.
medium • a medium size
middling • The Beatles enjoyed only middling success until 1963.
reasonable • reasonable force

moderate ② VERB
to become or make less extreme • They are hoping he

m

can be persuaded to moderate his
views.
abate • *The storm had abated.*
curb • *You must curb your
extravagant tastes.*
ease • *Tensions had eased.*
relax • *Rules have been relaxed
recently.*
soften • *to soften the blow of
steep price rises*
temper • *He had to learn to
temper his enthusiasm.*
tone down • *He toned down his
statements after the meeting.*

modern ① ADJECTIVE
relating to the present time
• *modern society*
contemporary
• *contemporary music*
current • *the current situation*
present • *the government's
present economic difficulties*
present-day • *Even by
present-day standards these
were large aircraft.*
recent • *in recent years*

modern ② ADJECTIVE
new and involving the latest
ideas • *modern technology*
latest • *the latest fashions*
new • *new methods of treating
cancer*
up-to-date • *the most
up-to-date centres of research*
up-to-the-minute
• *up-to-the-minute information*
ANTONYM:
• old-fashioned

modest ① ADJECTIVE
small in size or amount • *a
modest improvement*

limited • *They may only have a
limited amount of time.*
middling • *After a few years of
middling success, her career
really took off.*
moderate • *moderate exercise*
small • *a relatively small problem*

modest ② ADJECTIVE
not boastful • *Dr Jones is
modest about her achievements.*
humble • *He gave a great
performance, but he was very
humble.*
unassuming • *She has a gentle,
unassuming manner.*
ANTONYM:
• conceited

moment ① NOUN
a short period of time • *He
paused for a moment.*
instant • *The pain disappeared
in an instant.*
minute • *See you in a minute.*
second • *Seconds later,
firefighters reached the door.*
split second • *Her gaze met
Michael's for a split second.*

moment ② NOUN
a point in time • *At that
moment, the doorbell rang.*
instant • *At that instant the
museum was plunged into
darkness.*
point • *At this point Diana
arrived.*
time • *It seemed like a good time
to tell her.*

money NOUN
coins or banknotes • *I needed
to earn some money.*

capital • *Companies are having difficulty in raising capital.*
cash • *We were desperately short of cash.*
dosh (BRITISH, AUSTRALIAN AND NEW ZEALAND; SLANG) • *They'll have the dosh to pay for a new sign.*
dough (INFORMAL) • *He worked hard for his dough.*
funds • *The concert will raise funds for research.*
RELATED WORD:
• ADJECTIVE pecuniary

mood NOUN
a state of mind • *She was in a really cheerful mood.*
frame of mind • *Lewis was not in the right frame of mind to continue.*
humour • *Could that have been the source of his good humour?*
spirits • *A bit of exercise will help lift his spirits.*
state of mind • *I want you to get into a whole new state of mind.*
temper • *I was in a bad temper last night.*

moody ① ADJECTIVE
depressed or unhappy • *Tony, despite his charm, could sulk and be moody.*
irritable • *He had missed his dinner, and grew irritable.*
morose • *She was morose and reticent.*
sulky • *I was quite sulky, so I didn't take part in games.*
sullen • *a sullen and resentful workforce*

389 | **motivate**

moody ② ADJECTIVE
liable to change your mood • *David was unstable and moody.*
temperamental • *He is very temperamental.*
volatile • *She has a volatile temper.*

more ADJECTIVE
greater than something else • *I've got more chips than you.*
added • *For added protection choose lipsticks with a sun screen.*
additional • *The US is sending additional troops to the region.*
extra • *Extra staff have been taken on.*
further • *There are likely to be further delays.*
ANTONYM:
• less

motivate VERB
to cause a particular behaviour • *How do you motivate people to work hard?*
drive • *The will to win drives athletes to train.*
inspire • *What inspired you to change your name?*
lead • *His abhorrence of racism led him to write the book.*
move • *The poverty she saw moved her to start an educational project.*
prompt • *Japan's recession prompted consumers to cut back on buying cars.*
provoke • *The destruction of the mosque has provoked much anger.*

mountain NOUN

TYPES OF MOUNTAIN
alp
ben (SCOTTISH)
elevation
height
mount
peak
precipice
range
ridge

move ① VERB
to change position • *The train began to move.*
▶ see Word Study **move**, page 718

move ② VERB
to change residence • *She had often considered moving to London.*
migrate • *People migrated to the cities to find work.*
move house • *They move house fairly frequently.*
relocate • *if the company was to relocate*

move ③ VERB
to cause a deep emotion • *Her story moved us to tears.*
affect • *Her loss still clearly affects him.*
touch • *Her enthusiasm touched me.*

movement ① NOUN
a change of position • *They monitor the movement of the fish going up river.*
flow • *the frantic flow of cars and buses along the street*
motion • *the wind from the car's motion*

movement ② NOUN
a group of people with similar aims • *the peace movement*
campaign • *the campaign against public smoking*
faction • *the leaders of the country's warring factions*
group • *members of an environmental group*
organisation • *the International Labour Organisation*

moving ADJECTIVE
causing deep emotion • *It was a moving moment.*
affecting • *one of the most affecting scenes in the film*
emotional • *an emotional reunion*
poignant • *a poignant love story*
stirring • *a stirring speech*
touching • *the touching tale of true friendship*

muddle ① NOUN
a state of disorder • *Our finances are in a muddle.*
chaos • *Their concerts often ended in chaos.*
confusion • *There was confusion when a fight broke out.*
disarray • *He found the room in disarray.*
disorder • *Inside all was disorder.*
disorganisation • *a state of complete disorganisation*
jumble • *a meaningless jumble of words*
mess • *the reasons why the economy is in such a mess*
tangle • *a tangle of wires*

M

muddle ② VERB
to mix things up • One or two critics have begun to muddle the two names.
confuse • Great care is taken to avoid confusing the two projects.
jumble • a pile of clothes all jumbled together
mix up • People often mix us up.

multiply VERB
to increase in number • The trip wore on and the hazards multiplied.
increase • The population continues to increase.
proliferate • New groups are proliferating by the day.
spread • Cholera is not spreading as quickly as it did in the past.

mumble VERB
to speak quietly • He mumbled a few words.
murmur • He murmured something to the professor.
mutter • He sat there muttering to himself.

murder ① NOUN
the act of killing someone • after being found guilty of murder
assassination • the assassination of John F. Kennedy
homicide • the scene of the homicide
killing • a brutal killing
manslaughter • She was found guilty of manslaughter.
slaughter • the army's slaughter of civilians

slaying (LITERARY) • a trail of motiveless slayings

murder ② VERB
to kill someone • a thriller about two men who murder a third
assassinate • Robert Kennedy was assassinated in 1968.
butcher • The guards butchered hundreds of prisoners.
kill • a man who killed his wife
slaughter • Thirty-four people were slaughtered while queueing up to cast their votes.
slay (LITERARY) • David slew Goliath with a stone.
take the life of • She admitted to taking the lives of two people.

mysterious ① ADJECTIVE
strange and not well understood • He died in mysterious circumstances.
arcane (FORMAL) • the arcane world of high finance
baffling • a baffling array of wires
cryptic • My father's notes are more cryptic here.
enigmatic • one of Orson Welles's most enigmatic films
mystifying • I find your attitude rather mystifying.

mysterious ② ADJECTIVE
secretive about something • Stop being so mysterious.
furtive • with a furtive glance over her shoulder
secretive • the secretive world of spying

m

mystery NOUN
something that is not
understood • *the mystery
surrounding his disappearance*
conundrum • *this theological
conundrum*
enigma • *The country remains
an enigma for the outside world.*
puzzle • *"Some people are a
puzzle," he said.*
riddle • *the answer to the riddle
of why it was never finished*

nag VERB
to keep complaining about
something to someone • *My
dad started nagging me about
cleaning the car.*
badger • *They kept badgering
me to go back.*
bother • *Go away and don't
bother me about all that just now.*
go on at • *She's always going on
at me to clear up.*
pester • *He gets fed up with the
kids pestering him for money.*

naked ADJECTIVE
openly displayed or shown
• *naked aggression*
blatant • *evidence of blatant
discrimination*
evident • *the party's evident
dislike of the president*
manifest (FORMAL) • *his
manifest enthusiasm*
open • *open opposition to the
government*
unmistakable • *with
unmistakable amusement in
his eyes*
ANTONYM:
• secret

name ① NOUN
a word that identifies a person
or thing • *My name is Joe.*

designation • *a level four alert, a designation reserved for very serious incidents*

epithet • *the common epithet for the Buddha*

nickname • *He's heard your nickname is Codfish.*

term • *I don't know the medical term for it.*

title • *Your actual title would be business manager.*

RELATED WORD:
• ADJECTIVE nominal

name ② NOUN
the opinion people have about someone • *to protect Janet's good name*

character • *a series of personal attacks on my character*

reputation • *I know Chris has a bad reputation.*

name ③ VERB
to give a name to someone or something • *a little girl named Betsy*

baptise • *She could be baptised Margaret.*

call • *in a town called Fishingpond*

christen • *He wanted to christen his son Arthur Albert.*

dub • *a girl aptly dubbed "Brains"*

style • *a character who styled himself the Memory Man*

term • *He had been termed a temporary employee.*

narrow ADJECTIVE
having a small distance from side to side • *a narrow stream*

fine • *the fine hairs on her arms*

slender • *long slender legs*

slim • *a slim volume of Auden's poems*

thin • *a thin layer of clay*

ANTONYM:
• wide

narrow-minded ADJECTIVE
unwilling to consider new ideas or other people's opinions • *their own narrow-minded view of the world*

biased • *a biased view*

bigoted • *bigoted opinions*

insular • *He was insular and difficult to get to know.*

opinionated • *the most opinionated rubbish I have read*

prejudiced • *a whole host of prejudiced and xenophobic ideas*

ANTONYM:
• tolerant

nasty ADJECTIVE
very unpleasant • *a nasty taste*

disagreeable • *a disagreeable experience*

disgusting • *the most disgusting behaviour*

foul • *They produce a foul smell of rotten eggs.*

horrible • *I've got a horrible feeling about this one.*

repellent • *a very large, very repellent toad*

unpleasant • *some unpleasant surprises*

vile • *All the food is vile.*

ANTONYM:
• pleasant

natural ① ADJECTIVE
normal and to be expected

n

• *the natural reaction to failing the exam*

common • *It is a common response.*

everyday • *the everyday drudgery of work*

normal • *Biting is normal for puppies when they are teething.*

ordinary • *The cottage looks quite ordinary from the road.*

typical • *typical symptoms of stress*

usual • *It is usual to tip waiters and taxi drivers.*

ANTONYM:
• unnatural

natural ② ADJECTIVE
not trying to pretend • *He was so natural with the children.*

candid • *rather candid about her lifestyle*

frank • *an unusually frank interview*

genuine • *He always seems so genuine.*

real • *She came across as a real person.*

unaffected • *She sang with unaffected simplicity.*

ANTONYM:
• false

natural ③ ADJECTIVE
existing from birth and not learned • *I never had much natural rhythm.*

inborn • *an inborn sense of optimism*

inherent • *the inherent goodness of people*

innate • *the innate conservatism of his predecessor*

instinctive • *an instinctive distrust of authority*

intuitive • *an intuitive understanding*

native • *He relies on his native wit to get him through.*

nature NOUN
someone's character • *It's not in my nature to sit still.*

character • *the funny side of his character*

make-up • *Compromise was never part of his make-up.*

personality • *his dominating personality*

naughty ADJECTIVE
tending to behave badly • *a naughty little boy*

bad • *the bad behaviour of their teenage children*

disobedient • *Lucy was similarly disobedient.*

impish • *a girl with an impish sense of humour*

mischievous • *a mischievous child*

wayward • *He tried to control his wayward son.*

ANTONYM:
• well-behaved

navigate VERB
to work out the direction in which a ship, plane or car should go • *She navigated the plane through the fog.*

guide • *He guided the car into the space.*

pilot • *Local fishermen piloted the boats.*

steer • *steering a large ship*

near ① PREPOSITION
not far from • He drew his chair nearer the fire.

adjacent to • a garden and maze adjacent to the castle

alongside • the huts set up alongside the river

close to • We parked close to the pavement.

next to • I realised someone was standing next to me.

not far from • a car park not far from the entrance

near ② ADJECTIVE
not far away in distance • The village is quite near.

adjacent • an adjacent room

adjoining • A phone rang in an adjoining office.

close • a close neighbour

nearby • the nearby village

ANTONYM:
• far

near ③ ADJECTIVE
not far away in time • The time of judgment is near.

approaching • the approaching deadline

forthcoming • the forthcoming football season

imminent • He is in imminent danger.

looming • The students are panicking due to the looming exams.

near at hand • His death is near at hand.

nigh • The end of the world is nigh.

upcoming • the upcoming elections

nearly ADVERB
not completely but almost • The beach was nearly empty.

almost • Over the past decade their wages have almost doubled.

as good as • The World Championship is as good as over.

just about • We are just about finished with this section.

practically • The house was practically a wreck.

virtually • Their country is virtually bankrupt.

neat ADJECTIVE
having everything arranged in a tidy way • The house was clean and neat.

orderly • an orderly office

smart • a smart navy blue suit

spruce • Mundo was looking spruce in a suit.

tidy • He always kept his bedroom tidy.

trim • a street of trim little villas

ANTONYM:
• untidy

necessary ① ADJECTIVE
needed so that something can happen • Make the necessary arrangements.

essential • It is essential that you visit a dentist.

imperative • It is imperative we end up with a win.

indispensable • Jordan is an indispensable part of the peace process.

required • That book is required reading.

vital • Bone marrow is vital for producing blood cells.

n

ANTONYM:
• unnecessary

necessary ② ADJECTIVE
(FORMAL)
certain to happen or exist • *a necessary consequence of war*
certain • *one certain outcome of the conference*
inevitable • *She now accepts that a divorce is inevitable.*
inexorable • *The growth in travel has been inexorable.*
unavoidable • *The union knows that job losses are unavoidable.*

need VERB
to believe you must have or do something • *You need some fresh air.*
demand • *The children demand her attention.*
require • *If you require further information, please telephone.*
want • *I want a glass of water.*

neglect ① VERB
to fail to look after someone or something • *unhappy and neglected children*
ignore • *They see the government ignoring poor people.*
overlook • *Pensioners feel they are being overlooked.*
turn your back on • *Do not turn your back on unemployed people.*

neglect ② VERB (FORMAL)
to fail to do something • *He had neglected to give her his address.*

fail • *I was shattered and I failed to tell her about the good bits.*
forget • *She forgot to lock her door.*
omit • *He omitted to mention his connection with the company.*

neglect ③ NOUN
lack of care • *Most of her plants died from neglect.*
disregard • *a callous disregard for his victims*
indifference • *Indifference to patients is rare in America.*
unconcern • *the government's unconcern for the environment*

nervous ADJECTIVE
worried about something • *She had been nervous before the match.*
anxious • *I was very anxious about her safety.*
apprehensive • *Their families are apprehensive about the trip.*
edgy • *I was edgy and tired.*
jittery (INFORMAL) • *She still feels jittery when she visits her sister.*
jumpy • *The Italians are getting jumpy after drawing against the Swiss.*
on edge • *Ever since their arrival she had felt on edge.*
tense • *too tense to sleep*
toey (AUSTRALIAN AND NEW ZEALAND; SLANG) • *Dad's getting a bit toey.*
worried • *You had me worried for a moment.*

ANTONYM:
• calm

neutral ADJECTIVE
not supporting either side

• We stayed neutral during the war.

disinterested • *a disinterested observer*

dispassionate • *a full and dispassionate account*

impartial • *How can he give impartial advice?*

nonaligned • *the politically nonaligned countries*

ANTONYM:
• biased

never ADVERB
at no time at all • *I never said I was leaving.*

at no time • *At no time did he see the helicopter.*

not ever • *The problem won't ever go away.*

new ADJECTIVE
recently created or discovered • *a new hotel*

advanced • *trial results of the company's most advanced drugs*

current • *all the current gossip on the stars*

fresh • *fresh footprints in the snow*

ground-breaking • *a ground-breaking discovery*

latest • *We review all the latest films.*

modern • *modern technology*

recent • *Lawson's most recent novel*

ultra-modern • *an ultra-modern shopping mall*

up-to-date • *the most up-to-date news*

up-to-the-minute • *up-to-the-minute information*

ANTONYM:
• old

news NOUN
information about things that have happened • *news about the civil war*

bulletin • *the main evening bulletin*

disclosure • *disclosures about his private life*

dispatch • *the latest dispatches from the war zone*

information • *up-to-date information on weather*

intelligence • *military intelligence from behind enemy lines*

latest (INFORMAL) • *the latest on the bomb explosion*

tidings (FORMAL) • *the bearer of bad tidings*

word • *There is no word about casualties.*

next ① ADJECTIVE
coming immediately after something else • *Their next child was a girl.*

ensuing • *the ensuing years of violence*

following • *The following day I went to work as usual.*

subsequent • *As subsequent events showed, he was wrong.*

succeeding • *succeeding generations of students*

next ② ADVERB
coming immediately after something else • *Steve arrived next.*

afterwards • *I felt dizzy afterwards and had to sit down.*

subsequently • *She was subsequently married to his cousin.*

n

next ③ ADJECTIVE
in a position nearest to
something • *in the next room*
adjacent • *I pulled into the
adjacent driveway.*
adjoining • *in adjoining streets*
closest • *Britain's closest
neighbours*
nearest • *the nearest Italian
restaurant*
neighbouring • *Liberians
fleeing to neighbouring countries*

nice ADJECTIVE
attractive or enjoyable • *Did
you have a nice time, dear?*
▶ see Word Study **nice**, page 720

no INTERJECTION
not at all • *"Any problems?"—
"No, everything's fine."*
absolutely not • *"Did they
consult you?"—"Absolutely not."*
certainly not • *"Perhaps it
would be better if I withdrew."—
"Certainly not!"*
definitely not • *"Are you going
to the party?"—"Definitely not."*
not at all • *"You're not upset, are
you?"—"Not at all."*
of course not • *"I'd like to talk
to the lads, if you don't
mind."—"Of course not, Chief."*
ANTONYM:
• yes

noble ① ADJECTIVE
deserving admiration because
of honesty, bravery and
unselfishness • *a good and
noble thing to do*
generous • *It reflects his
generous nature.*

honourable • *His colleagues
were honourable people.*
magnanimous • *Miss Balding
is magnanimous in victory.*
upright • *a very upright,
trustworthy man*
virtuous • *the virtuous Mrs
Friendall*
worthy • *less worthy members
of our profession*
ANTONYM:
• ignoble

noble ② NOUN
someone from the highest
social rank • *The Scottish nobles
were united.*
aristocrat • *All his sisters had
married German aristocrats.*
lord • *They assumed that Amy
was a snob because her father
was a lord.*
nobleman • *a Spanish
nobleman*
peer • *He was made a life peer in
1981.*
ANTONYM:
• peasant

noise NOUN
a loud or unpleasant sound
• *He is making an awful noise.*
commotion • *There was a
commotion in the corridor.*
din • *He'd never heard a din
like it.*
hubbub • *the hubbub of Paris in
the 1880s*
pandemonium • *There was
pandemonium in the classroom.*
racket • *There was a terrible
racket going on.*
row • *Whatever is that row?*

uproar • *The courtroom was in an uproar.*

ANTONYM:
• silence

noisy ADJECTIVE
making a lot of noise • *a noisy audience of schoolchildren*
deafening • *a deafening roar*
loud • *The music was a little too loud.*
piercing • *her piercing laugh*
strident • *the strident vocals of the lead singer*
tumultuous • *He took the field to tumultuous applause.*
vociferous • *vociferous support from the Scottish fans*

ANTONYM:
• quiet

nominate VERB
to suggest someone for a position • *The party refused to nominate him as its candidate.*
name • *He'll be naming a new captain.*
propose • *Cliff was proposed as chairman.*
recommend • *He recommended him as his successor at Boston.*
select • *no prospect of being selected to stand for Parliament*
submit • *Mr Heath submitted a list of 200 names.*
suggest • *Some commentators have suggested Clark for the job.*

nonsense NOUN
foolish words or behaviour • *I say the allegations are complete nonsense.*

drivel • *mindless drivel by a poor journalist*
garbage (INFORMAL) • *One source claimed the rumours were complete garbage.*
inanity • *the burbling inanities of the tabloids*
rot • *She is talking complete rot.*
rubbish • *complete and utter rubbish*
waffle (BRITISH; INFORMAL) • *He writes smug, sanctimonious waffle.*

normal ADJECTIVE
usual and ordinary • *my normal routine*
average • *What's your average day like?*
conventional • *conventional tastes*
habitual • *their country of habitual residence*
ordinary • *It was just an ordinary weekend.*
regular • *It looks like a regular house.*
routine • *a routine medical check*
standard • *standard practice*
typical • *A typical day begins at 8.30.*
usual • *She did not collect him at the usual time.*

ANTONYM:
• unusual

nosy ADJECTIVE
trying to find out about other people's business • *nosy neighbours watching us through the curtains*
curious • *surrounded by a group of curious villagers*

n

eavesdropping • *We don't want to be overheard by eavesdropping servants.*
inquisitive • *Bears are naturally inquisitive creatures.*
prying • *I hid it away, safe from prying eyes.*

note ① NOUN
a short letter • *I wrote him a note asking him to come round.*
communication (FORMAL) • *a communication from the President*
letter • *I have received a letter from a friend.*
memo • *a leaked memo to managers*
memorandum • *A memorandum has been sent to the members of the board.*
message • *He sent his mate round with a message for me.*
reminder • *We keep getting reminders from the garage to pay our bill.*

note ② NOUN
a written record that helps you remember something • *I made a note of his address.*
account • *Keep an account of all your outgoings.*
jotting • *Carry a notebook with you for your jottings.*
record • *Keep a record of all payments.*
register • *She kept a register of each child's progress.*

note ③ NOUN
an atmosphere, feeling or quality • *I detected a note of bitterness in his voice.*

hint • *Was there a hint of irony in that remark?*
tone • *He laughed again, this time with a cold, sharp tone.*
touch • *There is an unmistakable touch of pathos in his last film.*
trace • *He wrote on the subject without a trace of sensationalism.*

note ④ VERB
to become aware of or mention a fact • *I noted that the rain had stopped.*
mention • *I mentioned in passing that I liked her dress.*
notice • *Contact the police if you notice anything suspicious.*
observe • *Hooke observed a reddish spot on the surface of the planet.*
perceive • *He perceived a certain tension between them.*
register • *The sound was so familiar that she didn't register it.*
remark • *Everyone has remarked what a lovely person she is.*
see • *A lot of people saw what was happening but did nothing.*

notice ① VERB
to become aware of something • *Then I noticed Billy wasn't laughing.*
detect • *He detects signs of growing support for his plan.*
discern • *I did not discern any change in attitudes.*
note • *I noted that the rain had stopped.*

observe • *I've observed how hard she had to work.*
perceive • *gradually perceiving the possibilities*
see • *I saw that the lobby was swarming with police.*
spot • *Allen spotted me on the other side of the dance floor.*

notice ② NOUN
a written announcement • *a handwritten notice in the window*
advertisement • *one advertisement in a local paper*
bill • *students posting bills near the campus for a demo*
poster • *a poster advertising a charity concert*
sign • *a hand-written cardboard sign hung round his neck*

notice ③ NOUN
warning that something is going to happen • *She was transferred without notice.*
advance warning • *advance warning of the attack*
intimation • *He has given no intimation of an intention to resign.*
notification • *Official notification is expected to arrive today.*
warning • *I was sacked without warning.*

noticeable ADJECTIVE
obvious and easy to see • *a noticeable improvement*
conspicuous • *a conspicuous lack of sympathy*
evident • *He ate with evident enjoyment.*

obvious • *There are obvious dangers.*
perceptible • *Germany is showing a perceptible improvement.*
unmistakable • *a growing but unmistakable impatience*

notify VERB
to officially inform someone of something • *The skipper notified the coastguard of the tragedy.*
advise (FORMAL) • *I think it best that I advise you of my decision first.*
inform • *They would inform him of any progress they made.*
tell • *He told me I was on a final warning.*
warn • *They warned him of the dangers.*

notorious ADJECTIVE
well-known for something bad • *The district was notorious for violent crime.*
disreputable • *a low and disreputable character*
infamous • *an industry infamous for late payment of debts*
scandalous • *their scandalous behaviour at the party*

now ADVERB
at the present time or moment • *I need to talk to him now.*
at once • *I really must go at once.*
currently • *The vaccines are currently being tested.*
immediately • *Please come immediately.*

n

nowadays • *I don't see much of Tony nowadays.*
right now • *Stop that noise right now!*
straight away • *I think you should see a doctor straight away.*
without delay • *We'll come round without delay.*

nuisance NOUN
someone or something that is annoying • *Sorry to be a nuisance.*
annoyance • *Snoring can be an annoyance.*
bother • *Most men hate the bother of shaving.*
hassle (INFORMAL) • *Writing out a cheque is a hassle.*
inconvenience • *the inconvenience of a rail strike*
irritation • *He describes the tourists as "an irritation".*
pain (INFORMAL) • *She found dressing up for the occasion a real pain.*
pest • *I didn't want to be a cry baby or a pest.*

numb ① ADJECTIVE
unable to feel anything • *Your right arm goes numb.*
dead • *Hillier suffered a dead leg playing for the reserves.*
frozen • *a frozen shoulder*
insensitive • *The brain itself is insensitive to pain.*
paralysed • *He has been left with a paralysed arm.*

numb ② VERB
to make you unable to feel anything • *The cold numbed my fingers.*

dull • *morphine to dull the pain*
freeze • *an epidural to freeze the hip area*
paralyse • *people paralysed by illness or injury*
stun • *the gun used to stun the animals*

number ① NOUN
a word or symbol used for counting • *Pick a number between one and ten.*
digit • *a six-digit password*
figure • *a figure between a hundred and a thousand*
numeral • *Roman numerals*

number ② NOUN
a quantity of things or people • *Adrian has introduced me to a large number of people.*
collection • *a huge collection of books about Keats*
crowd • *a huge crowd of supporters*
horde • *a horde of angry protesters*
multitude • *Bands can play to multitudes of fans.*

numerous ADJECTIVE
existing or happening in large numbers • *on numerous occasions*
lots of • *I've got lots of photos of the kids.*
many • *I have met Imran many times.*
several • *He is fluent in several languages.*

Oo

oaf NOUN
a clumsy or aggressive person
• *You bungling oaf!*
brute • *The captain was an idiot and a brute.*
lout • *an ill-tempered lout*

oath NOUN
a formal promise • *He took an oath of loyalty to the government.*
pledge • *The meeting ended with a pledge to step up cooperation.*
promise • *If you make a promise, you should keep it.*
vow • *I made a silent vow to be more careful.*

obedient ADJECTIVE
tending to do what you are told • *He was always very obedient to his parents.*
law-abiding • *law-abiding citizens*
submissive • *a submissive, unconfident character*
subservient • *her willingness to be subservient to her children*
ANTONYM:
• disobedient

obey VERB
to do what you are told • *Most people obey the law.*

abide by • *They have got to abide by the rules.*
adhere to (FORMAL) • *All members adhere to a strict code of practice.*
comply with • *The army will comply with the ceasefire.*
follow • *Take care to follow the instructions carefully.*
observe • *forcing motorists to observe speed restrictions*
ANTONYM:
• disobey

object ① NOUN
anything solid and non-living
• *everyday objects such as wooden spoons*
article • *household articles*
thing • *What's that thing in the middle of the fountain?*

object ② NOUN
an aim or purpose • *The object of the exercise is to raise money for the charity.*
aim • *The aim of the festival is to increase awareness of local culture.*
goal • *The goal is to raise as much money as possible.*
idea • *The idea is to give children the freedom to explore.*
intention • *It is my intention to remain in my position.*
objective • *His objective was to win.*
purpose • *What is the purpose of your visit?*

object ③ VERB
to express disapproval • *A lot of people will object to the book.*

oppose • *Many individuals oppose bilingual education in schools.*

protest • *He picked up the cat before Rosa could protest.*

ANTONYM:
• approve

objection NOUN

disapproval of something
• *despite objections by the White House*

opposition • *Opposition to this plan has come from the media.*

protest • *protests against the government*

ANTONYM:
• support

obligatory ADJECTIVE

required by a rule or law
• *Physical education was made obligatory.*

compulsory • *School attendance is compulsory.*

forced • *a system of forced labour*

mandatory • *the mandatory retirement age*

required • *the required reading for this course*

requisite • *the requisite documents for travel abroad*

obscure ① ADJECTIVE

known by only a few people
• *an obscure Mongolian dialect*

little-known • *a little-known Austrian composer*

unknown • *an unknown writer*

ANTONYM:
• famous

obscure ② ADJECTIVE

difficult to understand • *The news was shrouded in obscure language.*

arcane (FORMAL) • *the arcane world of contemporary classical music*

cryptic • *cryptic comments*

opaque • *the opaque language of the inspector's reports*

ANTONYM:
• simple

obscure ③ VERB

to make something difficult to see • *His view was obscured by trees.*

cloak • *a land permanently cloaked in mist*

cloud • *Perhaps anger had clouded his vision.*

conceal • *The hat concealed her hair.*

hide • *The compound was hidden by trees and shrubs.*

mask • *A thick grey cloud masked the sun.*

screen • *Most of the road was screened by a block of flats.*

shroud • *Mist shrouded the outline of Buckingham Palace.*

ANTONYM:
• expose

observant ADJECTIVE

good at noticing things
• *Painting makes you really observant of things.*

attentive • *the attentive audience*

perceptive • *a perceptive remark*

vigilant • *He warned the public to be vigilant.*

watchful • *Keep a watchful eye on babies and toddlers.*

observe ① VERB
to watch something carefully
• He has spent years observing their behaviour.
monitor • I have been monitoring his progress carefully.
scrutinise • She scrutinised his features to see if he was telling the truth.
study • Debbie studied her friend's face for a moment.
survey • He surveys American politics from an interesting standpoint.
view • You can view the lesson from the gallery.
watch • A man was watching him from across the square.

observe ② VERB
to notice something • I observed a number of strange phenomena.
discover • They discovered that they were being watched.
note • People noted how much care she took over her work.
notice • Contact the police if you notice anything unusual.
see • I saw a man coming towards me.
spot • Moments later, smoke was spotted coming out of the kitchen.
witness • Anyone who witnessed the attack should call the police.

observe ③ VERB
to make a comment about something • "You've had your hair cut," he observed.
comment • Stuart commented that this was true.

mention • I mentioned that I didn't like contemporary music.
remark • "Some people have more money than sense," he remarked.
say • She said that I looked tired.
state • He stated that this was, indeed, the case.

obsession NOUN
a compulsion to think about something • her obsession with video games
complex • I have never had a complex about my height.
fixation • the country's fixation on the war
mania • a mania for horror films
preoccupation • today's preoccupation with royal misdeeds
thing (INFORMAL) • He's got this thing about ties.

obstacle NOUN
something which makes it difficult to go forward • a large obstacle to improving housing conditions
barrier • Taxes are the most obvious barrier to free trade.
difficulty • the difficulties ahead
hindrance • The higher rates have been a hindrance to economic recovery.
hurdle • the first hurdle for many women returning to work
impediment • There was no legal impediment to the marriage.
obstruction • an obstruction in the road

o

obstinate ADJECTIVE

unwilling to change your mind • *He is obstinate and will not give up.*

dogged • *her dogged insistence on their rights*

headstrong • *He's young and very headstrong.*

inflexible • *His opponents viewed him as dogmatic and inflexible.*

intractable • *He protested but Wright was intractable.*

stubborn • *a stubborn character who is used to getting her own way*

wilful • *a wilful child*

ANTONYM:
• flexible

obstruct VERB

to block a road or path • *Lorries obstructed the road.*

bar • *He stood there, barring her way.*

block • *Some students blocked the highway.*

choke • *The roads are choked with cars.*

clog • *The traffic clogged the Thames bridges.*

obtain VERB

to get something • *He tried to obtain a false passport*

acquire • *I recently acquired a beautiful old lamp.*

get • *trying to get enough food to live*

get hold of • *For more information get hold of one of the books mentioned.*

get your hands on (INFORMAL) • *reading everything she could get her hands on*

procure (FORMAL) • *It became hard to procure fuel.*

secure (FORMAL) • *continuing their efforts to secure a ceasefire*

obvious ADJECTIVE

easy to see or understand • *an obvious injustice*

apparent • *It was apparent that he had lost interest.*

blatant • *a blatant foul*

clear • *a clear breach of the rules*

evident • *His love of nature is evident in his paintings.*

overt • *parents who showed us no overt affection*

palpable • *The tension between them is palpable.*

plain • *It was plain to her that I was unhappy.*

self-evident • *The implications for this country are self-evident.*

occasion ① NOUN

an important event • *The launch of a ship was a big occasion.*

affair • *The visit was to be a purely private affair.*

event • *A new book by James is always an event.*

occasion ② NOUN

an opportunity to do something • *an important occasion for setting out government policy*

chance • *the chance to practise medicine in British hospitals*

opportunity • *I had an opportunity to go to New York.*

time • *This was no time to make a speech.*

ccasion ③ VERB (FORMAL)
to cause something • *damage occasioned by fire*
bring about • *the only way to bring about peace*
give rise to • *The judge's decision gave rise to practical problems.*
induce • *an economic crisis induced by high oil prices*
produce • *The drug is known to produce side-effects.*
prompt • *The demonstration prompted fears of more violence.*
provoke • *The incident has provoked outrage in Okinawa.*

ccasional ADJECTIVE
happening sometimes • *an occasional outing*
intermittent • *after three hours of intermittent rain*
odd • *at odd moments*
periodic • *periodic bouts of illness*
sporadic • *a year of sporadic fighting*

ANTONYM:
• frequent

ccur ① VERB
to happen or exist • *The disease occurs mainly in winter.*
appear • *a test to reveal infection before symptoms appear*
arise • *We will leave when the opportunity arises.*
be present • *This vitamin is present in breast milk.*
exist • *A conflict of interest may exist in such situations.*

happen • *The accident happened close to Martha's Vineyard.*
take place • *Elections will take place on the second of November.*

occur ② VERB
to come into your mind • *It didn't occur to me to check.*
cross your mind • *The possibility of failure did cross my mind.*
dawn on • *It dawned on me that I shouldn't give up without a fight.*
strike • *A thought struck her.*

odd ADJECTIVE
strange or unusual • *an odd coincidence*
bizarre • *his bizarre behaviour*
curious • *a curious mixture of the ancient and modern*
funny • *There's something funny about him.*
peculiar • *Rachel thought it tasted peculiar.*
queer (OLD-FASHIONED)
• *There's something a bit queer going on.*
singular (FORMAL) • *Where he got that singular notion I just can't think.*
strange • *Then a strange thing happened.*
weird • *That first day was weird.*

ANTONYM:
• ordinary

offend VERB
to upset or embarrass someone
• *He says he had no intention of offending the community.*

affront • *She pretended to be affronted, but inwardly she was pleased.*

insult • *Buchanan says he was insulted by the judge's remarks.*

outrage • *Many people have been outraged by what was said.*

ANTONYM:
• please

offensive ADJECTIVE
rude and upsetting • *offensive behaviour*

abusive • *abusive language*

insulting • *an insulting remark*

objectionable • *I find your tone highly objectionable.*

offer ① VERB
to ask if someone wants something • *Rhys offered him an apple.*

hold out • *I held out my ticket for him to check.*

tender • *She has tendered her resignation.*

offer ② NOUN
something that someone offers you • *He had refused several excellent job offers.*

proposition • *I made her a proposition.*

tender • *a tender for a public contract*

official ① ADJECTIVE
approved by someone in authority • *the official figures*

authorised • *the authorised biography*

certified • *a certified accountant*

formal • *No formal announcement has been made.*

licensed • *a licensed doctor*

ANTONYM:
• unofficial

official ② NOUN
someone in authority • *a senior UN official*

executive • *a senior bank executive*

officer • *a local authority education officer*

representative • *trade union representatives*

often ADVERB
happening many times • *They often spent Christmas at Prescott Hill.*

frequently • *They miss school fairly frequently.*

repeatedly • *Both men have repeatedly denied the allegations.*

okay or **OK** ADJECTIVE
(INFORMAL)
acceptable or satisfactory • *Is it okay if I come by myself?*

acceptable • *Such lavish entertainment is less acceptable today.*

all right • *if it's all right with you*

old ① ADJECTIVE
having lived for a long time • *an old woman*
▶ see Word Study **old**, page 722

ANTONYM:
• young

old ② ADJECTIVE
in the past • *my old art teacher*
▶ see Word Study **old**, page 722

ANTONYM:
• new

old-fashioned ADJECTIVE
no longer fashionable
• old-fashioned shoes
antiquated • an antiquated system
archaic • archaic practices such as these
dated • Some of the language sounds quite dated.
obsolete • So much equipment becomes obsolete almost as soon as it's made.
outdated • outdated attitudes
outmoded • toiling in outmoded factories
out of date • a make of car that is now out of date
passé • Punk is passé.

ANTONYM:
• fashionable

omen NOUN
a sign of what will happen
• Her appearance at this moment is an omen of disaster.
sign • people who look to the skies for signs
warning • a warning of trouble to come

ominous ADJECTIVE
suggesting that something bad will happen • an ominous silence
sinister • a sinister message
threatening • a threatening sky

omit VERB
to not include something
• Omit the salt in this recipe.
exclude • Women felt excluded from the workplace.

leave out • The Spaniard has been left out of the team.
miss out • What about Sally? You've missed her out!
skip • It is all too easy to skip meals.

only ① ADVERB
involving one person or thing
• Only Keith knows whether he will continue.
just • It's not just a financial matter.
merely • Watson was far from being merely a furniture expert.
purely • a racing machine, designed purely for speed
simply • Most of the damage was simply because of fallen trees.
solely • decisions based solely upon what we see in magazines

only ② ADJECTIVE
having no other examples
• their only hit single
one • My one aim is to look after the horses well.
sole • Our sole intention is to reunite her with her baby.

open ① VERB
to cause something not to be closed • She opened the door.
uncover • When the seedlings sprout, uncover the tray.
undo • I managed secretly to undo a corner of the parcel.
unlock • She unlocked the case.

ANTONYM:
• shut

open ② ADJECTIVE
not closed • an open box of chocolates

ajar • He left the door ajar.
uncovered • The uncovered bucket in the corner stank.
undone • Your shirt was undone and you looked a mess.
unlocked • an unlocked room

ANTONYM:
• shut

open ③ ADJECTIVE

not trying to deceive someone • He had always been open with her.
candid • I haven't been completely candid with him.
frank • My client has been less than frank with me.
honest • He had been honest with her and she had tricked him!

opening ① ADJECTIVE

coming first • the opening day of the season
first • the first night of the play
inaugural (FORMAL) • his inaugural address
initial • the aim of this initial meeting
introductory • an introductory offer

opening ② NOUN

the first part of something • the opening of the film
beginning • the beginning of the book
commencement (FORMAL) • at the commencement of the course
start • four years after the start of the Great War

ANTONYM:
• conclusion

opening ③ NOUN

a hole or gap • a narrow opening in the fence
chink • a chink in the wall
cleft • a narrow cleft in the rocks
crack • Kathryn had seen him through a crack in the curtains.
gap • the wind tearing through gaps in the window frames
hole • a hole in the wall
slot • a slot in which to insert a coin
space • a half-inch space between the curtains
vent • Steam escaped from the vent at the front of the machine.

opinion NOUN

a belief or view • I wasn't asking for your opinion.
assessment • What is your assessment of the situation?
belief • his religious beliefs
estimation • He has gone down considerably in my estimation.
judgment • In your judgment, what has changed?
point of view • Thanks for your point of view, John.
view • Make your views known to your local MP.
viewpoint • to include as many viewpoints as possible

oppose VERB

to disagree with something • protesters opposing planned nuclear tests
fight against • a lifetime fighting against racism
resist • They resisted our attempts to modernise.

speak out against • He spoke out strongly against some of the radical ideas.

ANTONYM:
• support

opposite ① ADJECTIVE
completely different to something • I take the opposite view to you.

conflicting • three powers with conflicting interests

contrary • He has a contrary opinion to mine.

contrasting • two men with completely contrasting backgrounds

opposed • This was a straight conflict of directly opposed aims.

reverse • The wrong attitude will have exactly the reverse effect.

opposite ② NOUN
a completely different person or thing • He was the complete opposite of Raymond.

antithesis (FORMAL) • They are the antithesis of the typical married couple.

contrary • There are no indications she will quit, quite the contrary.

converse • Don't you think that the converse might also be possible?

reverse • This didn't upset him at all, in fact quite the reverse.

opposition NOUN
disagreement about something • Much of the opposition to this plan has come from the media.

disapproval • His action had been greeted with almost universal disapproval.

hostility • There is hostility to this method among traditionalists.

resistance • Initially I met resistance from my own family.

ANTONYM:
• support

oppressed ADJECTIVE
treated cruelly or unfairly • a member of an oppressed minority

downtrodden • They made profit at the expense of downtrodden workers.

persecuted • the protection of persecuted peoples

oppression NOUN
cruel or unfair treatment • the oppression of black people throughout history

persecution • the persecution of minorities

tyranny • The 1930s was a decade of tyranny in Europe.

optimistic ADJECTIVE
hopeful about the future • an optimistic mood

buoyant • She was in a buoyant mood.

confident • I am confident that everything will come out right in time.

hopeful • I am hopeful this misunderstanding will be rectified.

positive • a positive frame of mind

sanguine • *They have begun to take a more sanguine view.*
ANTONYM:
• pessimistic

oral ADJECTIVE
spoken rather than written • *oral history*
spoken • *the spoken word*
verbal • *a verbal agreement*

orange NOUN or ADJECTIVE
SHADES OF ORANGE
amber
apricot
carrot
ochre
peach
tangerine

ordeal NOUN
a difficult and unpleasant experience • *the ordeal of being arrested*
hardship • *One of the worst hardships is having so little time.*
nightmare • *Taking my son Peter to a restaurant was a nightmare.*
torture • *Waiting for the result was torture.*
trial • *the trials of adolescence*
tribulation (FORMAL) • *the trials and tribulations of everyday life*

order ① NOUN
a command by someone in authority • *I don't take orders from him any more.*
command • *The tanker failed to respond to a command to stop.*

decree • *He issued a decree ordering all armed groups to disband.*
dictate • *to ensure that the dictates of the Party are followed*
directive • *a new EU directive*
instruction • *MPs defied a party instruction to vote against the Bill.*

order ② NOUN
a well-organised situation • *the wish to impose order upon confusion*
harmony • *the ordered harmony of the universe*
regularity • *the chessboard regularity of their fields*
symmetry • *the beauty and symmetry of a snowflake*
ANTONYM:
• disorder

order ③ VERB
to tell someone to do something • *He ordered his men to stop firing.*
command • *He commanded his troops to attack.*
decree • *The ruling decreed that women should receive equal pay.*
direct • *a court order directing the group to leave the land*
instruct • *The family has instructed solicitors to sue Thomson.*
ordain • *The council ordained that the demolition should go ahead.*
ANTONYM:
• forbid

orderly ADJECTIVE
well-organised or
well-arranged • *Their vehicles
were parked in orderly rows.*
neat • *She put her wet clothes in
a neat pile in the corner.*
regular • *regular rows of
wooden huts*
tidy • *a tidy desk*
ANTONYM:
• disorderly

ordinary ADJECTIVE
not special or different • *an
ordinary day*
conventional • *conventional
opinions*
normal • *He lives a normal life.*
regular • *the regular barman*
routine • *a routine procedure*
standard • *It was standard
practice.*
usual • *all the usual inner-city
problems*
ANTONYM:
• special

organisation ① NOUN
a group or business • *charitable
organisations*
association • *research
associations*
body • *the Chairman of the
police officers' representative
body*
company • *a shipping company*
confederation • *a
confederation of trade unions*
group • *an environmental group*
institution • *financial
institutions*
outfit (INFORMAL) • *We are a
professional outfit.*

organisation ② NOUN
the planning and arranging of
something • *He was involved in
the organisation of conferences
and seminars.*
organising • *His duties
involved the organising of
transport.*
planning • *The trip needs
careful planning.*
structuring • *improvements in
the structuring of courses*

organise VERB
to plan and arrange
something • *Organising a
wedding takes time.*
arrange • *The bank can arrange
a loan for students.*
establish • *How do you
establish a workable system?*
jack up (NEW ZEALAND;
INFORMAL) • *to jack up a
demonstration*
plan • *A team meeting was
planned for last night.*
set up • *This tribunal was set up
by the government.*

origin ① NOUN
the beginning or cause of
something • *the origins of the
custom*
derivation • *The derivation of
its name is obscure.*
root • *His sense of guilt had its
roots in his childhood.*
source • *the source of the problem*

origin ② NOUN
someone's family background
• *She was of Swedish origin.*
ancestry • *Noel can trace her
ancestry to the 11th century.*

o

descent • *All the contributors were of African descent.*
extraction • *a Malaysian citizen of Australian extraction*
lineage • *a respectable family of ancient lineage*
stock • *people of Mediterranean stock*

original ① ADJECTIVE
being the first example of something • *the original owner of the cottage*
first • *Her first reaction was disgust.*
initial • *His initial response was to disbelieve her.*

original ② ADJECTIVE
imaginative and clever • *a stunningly original idea*
fresh • *These designers are full of fresh ideas.*
new • *These proposals aren't new.*
novel • *a novel way of losing weight*

ANTONYM:
• unoriginal

ornament NOUN
an object that you display • *a shelf containing ornaments*
adornment • *a building without any adornments*
bauble • *a Christmas tree decorated with coloured baubles*
decoration • *The only wall decorations are candles.*
knick-knack (INFORMAL) • *Her flat is spilling over with knick-knacks.*
trinket • *She sold trinkets to tourists.*

ostentatious ADJECTIVE
intended to impress people with appearances • *an ostentatious lifestyle*
extravagant • *They make extravagant shows of generosity.*
flamboyant • *flamboyant clothes*
flashy • *a flashy sports car*
grandiose • *the grandiose building which housed the mayor's offices*
pretentious • *This hotel was smaller and less pretentious.*
showy • *large, showy flowers*

outbreak NOUN
a sudden occurrence of something • *the outbreak of war*
eruption • *this sudden eruption of violence*
explosion • *the global explosion of interest in rugby*

outdo VERB
to do something better than another person • *She would love to outdo her sister Manuela.*
go one better than • *You always have to go one better than anyone else.*
outshine • *Jesse has begun to outshine me in sports.*
surpass • *determined to surpass the achievements of his older brothers*
top • *How are you going to top that?*

outline ① VERB
to describe something in a general way • *The mayor outlined his plan to clean up the town's image.*

sketch • *The president sketched his vision of the country's future.*
summarise • *The article can be summarised in three sentences.*

outline ② NOUN
a general description of something • *an outline of the survey's findings*
rundown (INFORMAL) • *Here's a rundown of the options.*
summary • *a summary of the report*
synopsis • *a brief synopsis of the book*

outline ③ NOUN
the shape of something • *the hazy outline of the goalposts*
contours • *the contours of the face*
figure • *Alistair saw the dim figure of Rose in the chair.*
form • *She could discern his bulky form in the doorway.*
shape • *dark shapes of herons silhouetted against the moon*
silhouette • *the dark silhouette of the castle ruins*

outlook ① NOUN
your general attitude towards life • *I adopted a positive outlook on life.*
attitude • *Her negative attitude annoyed me.*
perspective • *It gave him a new perspective on life.*
view • *an optimistic view of the future*

outlook ② NOUN
the future prospects of something • *The economic*

outlook is one of rising unemployment.
future • *a conference on the country's political future*
prospects • *a detailed review of the company's prospects*

out of date ADJECTIVE
no longer useful • *The information is already out of date.*
antiquated • *an antiquated system*
archaic • *archaic practices such as these*
obsolete • *So much equipment becomes obsolete almost as soon as it's made.*
old-fashioned • *old-fashioned shoes*
outdated • *outdated attitudes*
outmoded • *toiling in outmoded factories*
ANTONYM:
• modern

outside ① NOUN
the outer part of something • *The moth was on the outside of the glass.*
exterior • *the exterior of the building*
facade • *the refurbishing of the cathedral's facade*
face • *the face of the watch*
surface • *the surface of the road*
ANTONYM:
• inside

outside ② ADJECTIVE
not inside • *an outside toilet*
exterior • *the oven's exterior surfaces*
external • *the external walls*

outdoor • *outdoor activities*
outer • *the outer suburbs of the city*
outward • *with no outward sign of injury*
surface • *Its total surface area was seven thousand square feet.*

ANTONYM:
• inside

outskirts PLURAL NOUN
the edges of an area • *the outskirts of New York*
edge • *We were on a hill, right on the edge of town.*
perimeter • *the perimeter of the airport*
periphery • *countries on the periphery of Europe*

outspan VERB (SOUTH AFRICAN)
to relax • *Let's take a break and just outspan for a while.*
laze • *Fred lazed in an easy chair.*
relax • *I ought to relax and stop worrying.*
rest • *He rested for a while before starting work again.*
take it easy • *Try to take it easy for a week or two.*

outstanding ① ADJECTIVE
extremely good • *an outstanding tennis player*
brilliant • *a brilliant performance*
excellent • *the recording quality is excellent.*
exceptional • *children with exceptional ability*
first-class • *first-class service*
first-rate • *The show was first-rate.*

great • *great cultural achievements*
superb • *a superb 18-hole golf course*

outstanding ② ADJECTIVE
still owed • *The total debt outstanding is $9 billion.*
due • *They sent me £100 and advised me that no further payment was due.*
overdue • *pay overdue salaries*
owing • *There is still some money owing for the rent.*
payable • *The amount payable is £175.*
unpaid • *a pile of unpaid bills*

over ① PREPOSITION
more than a particular amount • *It cost over a million dollars.*
above • *speeds above 50 mph*
exceeding • *a budget exceeding $700 million a year*
in excess of • *a fortune in excess of 150 million pounds*
more than • *The airport had been closed for more than a year.*

RELATED WORDS:
• PREFIXES hyper-, super-, supra-, sur-

over ② ADJECTIVE
completely finished • *I am glad it's all over.*
at an end • *The matter is now at an end.*
complete • *The work of restoring the farmhouse is complete.*
done • *When her deal is done, the client emerges with her purchase.*

finished • *once the season's finished*

gone • *Any chance of winning was now gone.*

past • *The time for loyalty is past.*

up • *when the six weeks were up*

overcome VERB

to manage to deal with something • *Molly had overcome her fear of flying.*

conquer • *He has never conquered his fear of speaking in public.*

get the better of • *She didn't allow her emotions to get the better of her.*

master • *His genius alone has mastered every crisis.*

surmount • *I realised I had to surmount the language barrier.*

triumph over • *a symbol of good triumphing over evil*

vanquish (LITERARY) • *the man who helped vanquish Napoleon*

overlook VERB

to ignore or fail to notice something • *We tend to overlook warning signals about our health.*

disregard • *Governments must not be allowed to disregard human rights.*

forget • *She never forgets his birthday.*

ignore • *For years her talents were ignored by the film industry.*

miss • *His searching eye never missed a detail.*

neglect • *She never neglects her duties.*

turn a blind eye to • *Are people turning a blind eye to these issues?*

overrule VERB

to reject a decision officially • *The Court of Appeal overruled this decision.*

overturn • *when the Russian parliament overturned his decision*

reverse • *They will not reverse the decision to increase prices.*

oversee VERB

to make sure a job is done properly • *Get a supervisor to oversee the work.*

be in charge of • *She is in charge of day-to-day operations.*

coordinate • *Government officials have been sent to coordinate the relief effort.*

direct • *his coolness in directing the rescue of the hostages*

manage • *Within two years, he was managing the project.*

preside • *Mr Brown will be presiding over the day's events.*

supervise • *He supervises the vineyards.*

overthrow VERB

to remove someone from power by force • *The government was overthrown in a military coup.*

bring down • *They brought down the government by withdrawing their support.*

depose • *He fled to Hawaii after being deposed as president.*

oust • *His opponents tried to oust him with a vote of no confidence.*

o

topple • *the revolution which toppled the regime*

overturn ① VERB
to knock something over • *Alex jumped up so violently that he overturned his glass.*

capsize • *I didn't count on his capsizing the raft.*

knock down • *Isabel rose so abruptly that she knocked down her chair.*

knock over • *Emma knocked over the box of cornflakes.*

tip over • *He tipped the table over in front of him.*

topple • *Winds and rain toppled trees and electricity lines.*

upset • *Don't upset the piles of sheets under the box.*

overturn ② VERB
to reject a decision officially • *when the Russian parliament overturned his decision*

overrule • *The Court of Appeal overruled this decision.*

reverse • *They will not reverse the decision to increase prices.*

overweight ADJECTIVE
too fat, and therefore unhealthy • *Being overweight increases your risk of heart problems.*

fat • *I could eat what I liked without getting fat.*

hefty • *She was quite a hefty woman.*

obese • *Obese people tend to have higher blood pressure than lean people.*

stout • *a stout man with grey hair*

own ① ADJECTIVE
belonging to a particular person or thing • *She stayed in her own house.*

personal • *That's my personal opinion.*

private • *76 bedrooms, all with private bathrooms*

own ② VERB
to have something that belongs to you • *His father owns a local pub.*

have • *They have a house in France.*

keep • *His father kept a village shop.*

possess • *I would give her everything I possess.*

own ③: on your own ADVERB
without other people • *I work best on my own.*

alone • *She lives alone.*

by yourself • *I didn't know if I could raise a child by myself.*

independently • *several people working independently*

unaided • *She brought us up completely unaided.*

owner NOUN
the person to whom something belongs • *the owner of the store*

possessor • *the proud possessor of a truly incredible voice*

proprietor • *the proprietor of a local restaurant*

Pp

pacify VERB
to calm down someone who is angry • *She shouted again, refusing to be pacified.*
appease • *The offer has not appeased separatists.*
calm • *A walk in the park helped calm her nerves.*
mollify • *The investigation was undertaken to mollify pressure groups.*
placate • *He went aboard to placate the angry passengers.*
soothe • *She took him in her arms and soothed him.*

pain ① NOUN
an unpleasant feeling of physical hurt • *I felt a sharp pain in my lower back.*
ache • *Poor posture can cause neck aches.*
discomfort • *Steve had some discomfort but no real pain.*
irritation • *These oils may cause irritation to sensitive skin.*
soreness • *The soreness lasted for about six weeks.*
trouble • *back trouble*
twinge • *He felt a slight twinge in his hamstring.*

pain ② NOUN
a feeling of deep unhappiness

• *the pain of rejection*
agony • *the agony of defeat*
anguish • *Mark looked at him in anguish.*
distress • *Jealousy causes distress and painful emotions.*
grief • *The grief soon gave way to anger.*
misery • *All that money brought nothing but sadness and misery.*

painful ① ADJECTIVE
causing emotional pain • *painful memories*
distressing • *one of the most distressing episodes in his life*
grievous • *Their loss would be a grievous blow to our industry.*
saddening • *a saddening experience*
unpleasant • *an unpleasant truth*

painful ② ADJECTIVE
causing physical pain • *a painful knock on the knee*
aching • *his aching joints*
excruciating • *an excruciating headache*
sore • *a sore throat*
tender • *My leg is very tender and sore.*

pale ADJECTIVE
rather white or without much colour • *Migrating birds filled the pale sky.*
ashen • *He fell back, shocked, his face ashen.*
colourless • *a colourless liquid*
faded • *a girl in faded jeans*
sallow • *His face was sallow and shiny with sweat.*
wan • *He looked wan and tired.*

P

panic

white • *He turned white and began to stammer.*

panic ① NOUN

a very strong feeling of fear or anxiety • *The earthquake caused panic among the population.*

alarm • *She sat up in alarm.*

dismay • *She discovered to her dismay that she was already too late.*

fear • *my fear of the dark*

fright • *To hide my fright I asked a question.*

hysteria • *mass hysteria*

terror • *She shook with terror.*

panic ② VERB

to become afraid or anxious • *Guests panicked when the doors wouldn't open.*

become hysterical • *I was scared, but my friend became hysterical.*

go to pieces • *England went to pieces when they conceded a goal.*

lose your nerve • *They lost their nerve and pulled out of the deal.*

parade NOUN

a line of people moving as a display • *A military parade marched through the streets.*

cavalcade • *a cavalcade of limousines and police motorcycles*

march • *Organisers expect 300,000 protesters to join the march.*

pageant • *a traditional Christmas pageant*

procession • *religious processions*

tattoo • *the world-famous Edinburgh military tattoo*

paragraph NOUN

PARTS OF A PARAGRAPH

clause
phrase
sentence
word

parent NOUN

your father or your mother • *I told my parents I was moving out.*

father • *Her father was furious.*

mother • *the mother of two girls*

old (AUSTRALIAN AND NEW ZEALAND; INFORMAL) • *a visit to the olds*

patriarch • *a domineering patriarch*

parody NOUN

an amusing imitation of someone else's style • *a parody of an American sitcom*

imitation • *I can do a pretty good imitation of him.*

satire • *a sharp satire on Australian family life*

spoof (INFORMAL) • *a spoof on Hollywood life*

takeoff (INFORMAL) • *She did a brilliant takeoff of the Queen.*

part ① NOUN

a piece or section of something • *I like that part of Edinburgh.*

bit • *a bit of paper*

fraction • *a fraction of a second*
fragment • *fragments of glass*
piece • *a piece of cheese*
portion • *Damage was confined to a small portion of the castle.*
section • *A large orchestra, with a vast percussion section*

part ② NOUN

a person's involvement in something • *He tried to conceal his part in the accident.*
capacity • *She has served the club in many capacities.*
duty • *My duty is to look after the animals.*
function • *Their main function is to raise capital for industry.*
involvement • *You have no proof of my involvement in anything.*
role • *the drug's role in preventing infection*

part ③ : take part in VERB

to do something with other people • *Thousands took part in the demonstrations.*
be instrumental in • *She was instrumental in solving the case.*
be involved in • *My grandparents were involved in the Methodist church.*
have a hand in • *He had a hand in three of the goals.*
join in • *I hope that everyone will be able to join in the fun.*
participate in • *They expected him to participate in the ceremony.*
play a part in • *He continued to play a part in their operations from prison.*

participate VERB

to take part in an activity
• *Over half the population participate in sport.*
be involved in • *HMS Cardiff was also involved in the exercise.*
engage in • *They have refused to engage in all-party talks.*
enter into • *We entered into discussions with them weeks ago.*
join in • *Their rivals refused to join in any price war.*
take part • *The oldest car taking part was built in 1907.*

particular ① ADJECTIVE

relating to only one thing or person • *That particular place is dangerous.*
distinct • *The book is divided into two distinct parts.*
exact • *Do you think I could get the exact thing I want?*
express • *Speed cameras were installed with the express purpose of preventing accidents.*
peculiar • *This is not a problem peculiar to London.*
precise • *the precise location of the ship*
specific • *There are several specific problems to be dealt with.*

particular ② ADJECTIVE

especially great or intense
• *Pay particular attention to the forehead.*
exceptional • *children with exceptional ability*
marked • *a marked increase in crime in the area*

P

notable • *Two other notable events took place last week.*
singular • *It was a goal of singular brilliance.*
special • *a special occasion*
uncommon • *Both are blessed with an uncommon ability to fix things.*

particular ③ ADJECTIVE
not easily satisfied • *Ted was very particular about the colours he used.*
choosy (INFORMAL) • *Skiers should be choosy about the insurance policy they buy.*
exacting • *exacting standards of craftsmanship*
fastidious • *He was fastidious about his appearance.*
fussy • *She is very fussy about her food.*
meticulous • *meticulous attention to detail*

partly ADVERB
to some extent but not completely • *This is partly my fault.*
in part (FORMAL) • *The levels of blood glucose depend in part on what you eat.*
in some measure (FORMAL) • *Power is in some measure an act of will.*
partially • *Jo is partially sighted.*
to some degree • *These statements are, to some degree, correct.*
to some extent • *Her concern is, to some extent, understandable.*

partner ① NOUN
either member of a couple in a relationship • *My partner moved in with me last year.*
husband • *Are husbands and wives included in the invitation?*
mate • *She has found her ideal mate.*
spouse • *Anything left to your spouse is free from inheritance tax.*
wife • *His wife is a lawyer.*

partner ② NOUN
the person someone is doing something with • *my tennis partner*
companion • *her travelling companion*
date • *Sam didn't bring a date to the wedding.*
plus-one (INFORMAL) • *Billy's going to be my plus-one at the party.*
team-mate • *his team-mate at Ferrari*

part of speech NOUN
PARTS OF SPEECH
adjective
adverb
conjunction
interjection
noun
plural noun
preposition
pronoun
reflexive verb
verb

party ① NOUN
a social event where people

enjoy themselves • *Most teenagers like to go to parties.*

celebration • *a New Year's Eve celebration*

function • *a charity function at the hotel*

gathering • *a gathering of friends and relatives*

get-together (INFORMAL) • *a family get-together*

hooley or **hoolie** (NEW ZEALAND, SCOTTISH AND IRISH) • *a hooley down on the beach*

reception • *a wedding reception*

party ② NOUN
an organisation for people with the same political beliefs • *his resignation as party leader*

alliance • *The two parties have agreed to form an electoral alliance.*

clique • *the clique attached to the Prime Minister*

coalition • *a coalition of right-wing and religious factions*

faction • *the party's small pro-European faction*

grouping • *two main political groupings pressing for independence*

party ③ NOUN
a group who are doing something together • *a research party of scientists*

band • *a small but dedicated band of supporters*

crew • *a ship's crew*

gang • *a gang of criminals*

squad • *the West Indies squad to tour Australia*

team • *He was examined by a team of doctors.*

unit • *the health services research unit*

pass ① VERB
to exceed or go past something • *She gave a triumphant wave as she passed the winning post.*

exceed • *The demand for places at some schools exceeds the supply.*

go beyond • *Her gaze went beyond him to the French windows.*

outdo • *The Colombian fans outdid the home supporters in fervour.*

outstrip • *Demand continues to outstrip supply.*

overtake • *He overtook the truck and pulled into the inside lane.*

surpass • *She was determined to surpass the achievements of her brothers.*

pass ② VERB
to be successful in a test • *Wendy has just passed her driving test.*

get through • *I got through my banking exams last year.*

graduate • *He graduated in engineering.*

qualify • *I qualified as a doctor.*

succeed • *the skills and qualities needed to succeed*

ANTONYM:
• fail

pass ③ NOUN
a document that allows you to

P

go somewhere • *Don't let any cars onto the land unless they've got a pass.*

identification • *Passport control asked me if I had any further identification.*

passport • *You should take your passport with you when changing money.*

ticket • *I'm not going to renew my season ticket.*

passage ① NOUN
a space that connects two places • *He cleared a passage for himself through the crammed streets.*

channel • *a drainage channel*

course • *the river's twisting course*

path • *A group of reporters blocked the path.*

road • *the road between Jerusalem and Bethlehem*

route • *the most direct route to the town centre*

way • *This is the way in.*

passage ② NOUN
a narrow space that connects one place with another • *up some stairs and along a narrow passage towards a door*

aisle • *the frozen food aisle*

corridor • *They sat crowded together in the hospital corridor.*

hall • *The lights were on in the hall and in the bedroom.*

lobby • *the cramped pitch-dark lobby*

passage ③ NOUN
a section of a book or piece of music • *a passage from the Bible*

excerpt • *an excerpt from her speech*

extract • *an extract from his new book*

quotation • *a favourite quotation from Shakespeare*

section • *a section from the first movement of Beethoven's "Eroica" symphony*

passing ADJECTIVE
lasting only for a short time • *a passing phase*

fleeting • *a fleeting glimpse*

momentary • *a momentary lapse*

short-lived • *Modelling is a short-lived career.*

transitory • *the transitory nature of political success*

passion NOUN
any strong emotion • *She spoke with great passion.*

emotion • *Her voice trembled with emotion.*

excitement • *I was in a state of great excitement.*

fire • *His speeches were full of fire.*

intensity • *His intensity alarmed me.*

warmth • *Jenny greeted us both with warmth and affection.*

zeal • *his zeal for teaching*

passionate ADJECTIVE
expressing very strong feelings about something • *I'm a passionate believer in public art.*

ardent • *ardent supporters of capital punishment*

emotional • *an emotional farewell*

heartfelt • *Our heartfelt thanks to all the staff at the hospital.*

impassioned • *He made an impassioned appeal for peace.*

intense • *intense hatred*

strong • *Many viewers have strong opinions about violence on TV.*

passive ADJECTIVE
submissive or not playing an active part • *His passive attitude made things easier for me.*

docile • *The grey nurse shark is a very docile sea creature.*

receptive • *The players seemed very receptive to his new ideas.*

resigned • *She was already resigned to losing her home.*

submissive • *The prisoners were required to be obedient and submissive.*

past ① : **the past** NOUN
the period of time before the present • *We would like to put the past behind us.*

antiquity • *famous monuments of classical antiquity*

days gone by • *This brings back memories of days gone by.*

former times • *In former times he would have been clapped in irons.*

long ago • *The old men told stories of long ago.*

past ② ADJECTIVE
happening or existing before the present • *details of his past activities*

ancient • *ancient history*

bygone • *a bygone era*

former • *Remember him as he was in his former years.*

olden • *We were talking about the olden days on his farm.*

previous • *She has a teenage daughter from a previous marriage.*

ANTONYM:
• future

past ③ PREPOSITION
situated on the other side of somewhere • *It's just past the church there.*

beyond • *Beyond the garden was a small orchard.*

by • *He walked by her house every day.*

over • *He lived in the house over the road.*

pastime NOUN
a hobby or something done for pleasure • *His favourite pastime is playing computer games.*

activity • *activities range from canoeing to birdwatching*

diversion • *Finger painting is very messy but an excellent diversion.*

hobby • *My hobbies are squash and swimming.*

recreation • *Saturday afternoon is for recreation and outings.*

path ① NOUN
a strip of ground for people to walk on • *We followed the paths along the clifftops.*

footpath • *It is accessible only by footpath.*

P

pathway • *a pathway leading towards the nearby river*
towpath • *He took a cycle trip along a canal towpath.*
track • *We set off over a rough mountain track.*
trail • *He was following a broad trail through the trees.*
way • *the Pennine Way*

path ② NOUN
the space ahead of someone as they move along • *A group of reporters stood in his path.*
course • *obstacles blocking our course*
direction • *St Andrews was 10 miles in the opposite direction.*
passage • *Two men elbowed a passage through the shoppers.*
route • *All escape routes were blocked by armed police.*
way • *Get out of my way!*

pathetic ① ADJECTIVE
causing someone to feel pity • *She was a pathetic little bundle of ragged fur.*
heartbreaking • *They suffered a heartbreaking defeat on penalties.*
sad • *He seemed a rather sad figure.*

pathetic ② ADJECTIVE
very poor or unsuccessful • *pathetic excuses*
feeble • *This is a particularly feeble argument.*
lamentable • *a lamentable display by the league leaders*
pitiful • *They are paid pitiful wages.*

poor • *The flat was in a poor state of repair.*
sorry • *Their oil industry is in a sorry state.*

patience NOUN
the ability to stay calm in a difficult situation • *It was exacting work and required all his patience.*
calmness • *calmness under pressure*
composure • *He regained his composure and went on to win the match.*
cool (SLANG) • *The big Irishman was on the verge of losing his cool.*
restraint • *They behaved with more restraint than I'd expected.*
tolerance • *a low tolerance of errors*

patient ① ADJECTIVE
staying calm in a difficult situation • *Please be patient – the money will arrive.*
calm • *She is usually calm and diplomatic.*
composed • *a composed and charming manner*
long-suffering • *long-suffering train commuters*
philosophical • *He is philosophical about the defeat.*
serene • *She looks dreamily into the distance, serene, calm and happy.*
ANTONYM:
• impatient

patient ② NOUN
a person receiving medical

treatment • *patients who wish to change their doctor*
case • *He is a suitable case for treatment.*
sick person • *a ward full of very sick people*

pattern ① NOUN
a decorative design of repeated shapes • *red and purple thread stitched into a pattern of flames*
design • *tableware decorated with a blackberry design*
motif • *a rose motif*

pattern ② NOUN
a diagram or shape used as a guide for making something • *sewing patterns*
design • *They drew up the design for the house in a week.*
diagram • *Follow the diagram on page 20.*
plan • *a plan of the garden*
stencil • *flower stencils*
template • *Make a paper template of the seat of the chair.*

pause ① VERB
to stop doing something for a short time • *On leaving, she paused for a moment at the door.*
break • *They broke for lunch.*
delay • *Various problems delayed the launch.*
halt • *Striking workers halted production at the plant.*
rest • *He rested briefly before pressing on.*
take a break • *He needs to take a break from work.*
wait • *I waited to see how she responded.*

pause ② NOUN
a short period when activity stops • *There was a pause while the waiter set down two plates.*
break • *Do you want to have a little break?*
halt • *Traffic was brought to a halt.*
interruption • *The sudden interruption stopped her in mid-flow.*
interval • *I had an ice cream during the interval.*
rest • *I think he's due for a rest now.*
stoppage • *Miners have voted for a one-day stoppage next month.*

pay ① VERB
to give money to someone to settle a debt • *You can pay by credit card.*
compensate • *Farmers could be compensated for their loss of subsidies.*
honour • *The bank refused to honour the cheque.*
settle • *I settled the bill for our meal.*

pay ② VERB
to give someone a benefit • *It pays to be honest.*
be advantageous • *It is easy to imagine cases where cheating is advantageous.*
be worthwhile • *He believed the operation had been worthwhile.*

pay ③ NOUN
money paid to someone for

p

work done • *their complaints about pay and conditions*
earnings • *her earnings as an accountant*
fee • *solicitors' fees*
income • *a modest income*
payment • *a redundancy payment*
salary • *The lawyer was paid a good salary.*
wages • *His wages have gone up.*

payment NOUN

an amount of money that is paid to someone • *mortgage payments*
advance • *She was paid a £100,000 advance for her next two novels.*
deposit • *A $50 deposit is required when ordering.*
instalment • *The first instalment is payable on application.*
premium • *higher insurance premiums*
remittance • *Please make your remittance payable in sterling.*

peace ① NOUN

a state of undisturbed calm and quiet • *They left me in peace to recover from the operation.*
calm • *the rural calm of Grand Rapids, Michigan*
quiet • *He wants some peace and quiet before his match.*
silence • *They stood in silence.*
stillness • *An explosion shattered the stillness of the night air.*
tranquillity • *The hotel is a haven of tranquillity.*

peace ② NOUN

freedom from war • *The people do not believe that the leaders want peace.*
armistice • *the armistice between the two countries*
cessation of hostilities • *a resolution calling for an immediate cessation of hostilities*
truce • *an uneasy truce between the two sides*

ANTONYM:
• war

peaceful ADJECTIVE

quiet and calm • *a peaceful house in the heart of the countryside*
calm • *a calm spot amid the bustle of the city*
placid • *the placid waters of Lake Erie*
quiet • *The street was unnaturally quiet.*
serene • *a beautiful, serene park*
still • *In the room it was very still.*
tranquil • *the tranquil paradise of his native Antigua*

peak ① NOUN

the point at which something is at its greatest or best • *the peak of the morning rush hour*
climax • *The tournament is building up to a dramatic climax.*
culmination • *The marriage was the culmination of an eight-month romance.*
high point • *The high point of his trip was a book signing with his favourite author.*

zenith • Her career is now at its zenith.

peak ② NOUN
the pointed top of a mountain • snow-covered peaks
brow • He overtook a car as he approached the brow of a hill.
crest • Burns was clear over the crest of the hill.
pinnacle • They reached the rocky pinnacle in under two hours of steady climbing.
summit • the first person to reach the summit of Mount Everest
top • the top of Mount Sinai

peak ③ VERB
to reach the highest point or greatest level • His career peaked during the early 2000s.
be at its height • when trade union power was at its height
climax • a tour that climaxed with a three-night stint at Wembley Arena
come to a head • The siege came to a head with the death of a marshal.
culminate • The celebration of the centenary will culminate with a dinner.
reach its highest point • The stock market reached its highest point since the 2008 crash.

peculiar ① ADJECTIVE
strange and perhaps unpleasant • a very peculiar sense of humour
bizarre • bizarre behaviour
curious • a curious mixture of the ancient and modern

funny • I had a funny feeling about the new teacher.
odd • Something odd began to happen.
queer (OLD-FASHIONED) • There's something queer going on.
strange • There was something strange about the flickering blue light.
weird • It must be weird to be so rich.

peculiar ② ADJECTIVE
associated with one particular person or thing • He has his own peculiar way of doing things.
distinctive • She has a very distinctive laugh.
distinguishing • Does he have any distinguishing features?
individual • all part of her very individual personality
personal • cultivating their own personal style
special • Everyone has their own special problems or fears.
unique • a feature unique to humans

peek ① VERB
to have a quick look at something • She peeked at him through a crack in the wall.
glance • He glanced at his watch.
peep • Children came to peep at him round the doorway.
snatch a glimpse • Spectators lined the route to snatch a glimpse of the Queen.

P

sneak a look • *We sneaked a look at his diary.*

peek ② NOUN

a quick look at something • *He took his first peek at the new course yesterday.*

glance • *Trevor and I exchanged a glance.*

glimpse • *Some people had waited all day to catch a glimpse of her.*

look • *She took a last look in the mirror.*

peep • *He took a peep at his watch.*

pent-up ADJECTIVE

held back for a long time without release • *She had a lot of pent-up anger to release.*

inhibited • *inhibited feelings*

repressed • *repressed hostility*

suppressed • *The classroom was ablaze with barely suppressed excitement.*

people ① PLURAL NOUN

men, women and children • *Millions of people have lost their homes.*

human beings • *The disease can be transmitted to human beings.*

humanity • *crimes against humanity*

humans • *millions of years before humans appeared on earth*

mankind • *the evolution of mankind*

people ② PLURAL NOUN

all the men, women and children of a particular place • *It's a triumph for the American people.*

citizens • *the citizens of New York City*

inhabitants • *the inhabitants of Hong Kong*

population • *Africa's rapidly rising population*

public • *the British public*

perceptive ADJECTIVE

good at noticing or realising things • *a perceptive account of the poet's life*

acute • *His relaxed exterior hides an extremely acute mind.*

astute • *She made a series of astute and brave decisions.*

aware • *They are politically very aware.*

penetrating • *He never stopped asking penetrating questions.*

sharp • *Melanie has a sharp eye and an excellent memory.*

perfect ① ADJECTIVE

of the highest standard and without fault • *His English was perfect.*

expert • *There is a great deal to learn from her expert approach.*

faultless • *faultless technique*

flawless • *her flawless complexion*

masterly • *a masterly performance*

polished • *polished promotional skills*

skilled • *a skilled repair job*

ANTONYM:

• *imperfect*

P

perfect ② ADJECTIVE

complete or absolute • They have a perfect right to say so.

absolute • absolute nonsense

complete • The resignation came as a complete surprise.

consummate • He acted the part with consummate skill.

sheer • an act of sheer desperation

unmitigated • Last year's crop was an unmitigated disaster.

utter • utter nonsense

perfect ③ VERB

to make something as good as it can be • The technique was perfected during the 1960s.

hone • a chance to hone their skills

improve • You must improve your French.

polish • He spent time polishing the script.

refine • Surgical techniques are constantly being refined.

perform ① VERB

to carry out a task or action • people who have performed acts of bravery

carry out • Police believe the attacks were carried out by a rival gang.

complete • She completed the test in record time.

do • He crashed trying to do a tricky manoeuvre.

execute • The landing was skilfully executed.

fulfil • Fulfil the tasks you have been allocated.

perform ② VERB

to act, dance or play music in

public • students performing Shakespeare's "Macbeth"

act • acting in Tarantino's films

do • I've always wanted to do a solo show on Broadway.

play • His ambition is to play the part of Dracula.

present • The company is presenting a new production of "Hamlet".

put on • The band are hoping to put on a UK show.

stage • The group staged their first play in the late 1990s.

perhaps ADVERB

maybe • Perhaps you're right.

conceivably • The mission could conceivably be accomplished in a week.

it could be • It could be he's upset at what you said.

maybe • Maybe she wants to be left alone.

possibly • Do you think that he could possibly be right?

period NOUN

a particular length of time • a period of a few months

interval • a long interval when no-one spoke

spell • a long spell of dry weather

stretch • an 18-month stretch in the army

term • a 5-year prison term

time • At 15 he left home for a short time.

while • I haven't seen him for a long while.

permanent ADJECTIVE

lasting for ever or present all

the time • *a permanent solution to the problem*
abiding • *one of his abiding interests*
constant • *Inflation is a constant threat.*
enduring • *an enduring friendship*
eternal • *the quest for eternal youth*
lasting • *We are well on our way to a lasting peace.*
perpetual • *a perpetual source of worry*

ANTONYM:
• temporary

permission NOUN
authorisation to do something • *He asked permission to leave the room.*
approval • *The plan will require official approval.*
assent (FORMAL) • *He requires the assent of parliament.*
authorisation • *his request for authorisation to use military force*
consent • *You can't go ahead without the owner's consent.*
go-ahead • *The government gave the go-ahead for five major road schemes.*
licence • *He has given me licence to do the job as I see fit.*

ANTONYM:
• ban

permit ① VERB
to allow something or make it possible • *The guards permitted me to bring my camera.*
allow • *Smoking will not be allowed.*

authorise • *They are expected to authorise the use of military force.*
enable • *The test should enable doctors to detect the disease early.*
give the green light to • *He has been given the green light to resume training.*
grant • *Permission was granted a few weeks ago.*
sanction • *The chairman will not sanction a big-money signing.*

ANTONYM:
• ban

permit ② NOUN
an official document allowing someone to do something • *a work permit*
authorisation • *We didn't have authorisation to go.*
licence • *a driving licence*
pass • *a rail pass*
passport • *My passport expires next year.*
permission • *Permission for the march has not been granted.*
warrant • *Police issued a warrant for his arrest.*

persecute VERB
to treat someone with continual cruelty and unfairness • *The government began by brutally persecuting the Church.*
hound • *He has been hounded by the press.*
ill-treat • *They were fined for ill-treating a horse.*
oppress • *Minorities here have been oppressed for generations.*

pick on • *She was repeatedly picked on by the manager.*
torment • *They were tormented by other pupils.*
torture • *He would not torture her further by trying to argue with her.*

person NOUN
a man, woman or child • *The amount of sleep we need varies from person to person.*
human • *the common ancestor of humans and the great apes*
human being • *This protein occurs naturally in human beings.*
individual • *the rights and responsibilities of the individual*
living soul • *The nearest living soul was 20 miles away.*
soul • *a tiny village of only 100 souls*

personal ADJECTIVE
belonging to a particular person or thing • *personal belongings*
individual • *Divide the vegetables among four individual dishes.*
own • *My wife decided I should have my own shop.*
particular • *his own particular style of preaching*
peculiar • *her own peculiar talents*
private • *my private life*
special • *Every person will have his or her own special problems.*

personality ① NOUN
a person's character and nature
• *She has such a kind, friendly personality.*
character • *a negative side to his character*
identity • *our own sense of cultural identity*
individuality • *People should be free to express their individuality.*
make-up • *There was some fundamental flaw in his make-up.*
nature • *She trusted people. That was her nature.*
psyche • *disturbing elements of the human psyche*

personality ② NOUN
a famous person in entertainment or sport
• *television personalities*
big name • *the big names in French cinema*
celebrity • *Hollywood celebrities*
famous name • *a famous name from Inter Milan's past*
household name • *The TV series that made him a household name.*
star • *film stars*

persuade VERB
to make someone do something by reason or charm • *He persuaded the company to sign him up.*
bring round (INFORMAL) • *We will do what we can to bring them round to our point of view.*
coax • *She coaxed Bobby into talking about himself.*
induce • *I would do anything to induce them to stay.*

P

sway • Don't ever be swayed by fashion.

talk into • He talked me into marrying him.

win over • By the end of the day he had won over the crowd.

persuasive ADJECTIVE

convincing • a persuasive argument against change

compelling • compelling reasons to attend

conclusive • conclusive proof

effective • an effective speaker

plausible • a plausible explanation

powerful • a powerful talk

winning • a winning speech

ANTONYM:
• unconvincing

pessimistic ADJECTIVE

believing that bad things will happen • a pessimistic view of life

despondent • despondent about losing their opening match of the season

gloomy • a gloomy outlook for the economy

glum • They are not entirely glum about the car industry's prospects.

hopeless • They were feeling hopeless about the future of the industry.

ANTONYM:
• optimistic

pest ① NOUN

an insect or animal that damages crops or livestock • 10% of the crop was lost to a pest called corn rootworm.

bane • The bane of farmers across the country is the badger.

blight • potato blight

scourge • This parasitic mite is the scourge of honey bees.

pest ② NOUN

an annoying person • I didn't want to be a cry baby or a pest.

bane • Weeds are the bane of many gardeners' lives.

bore • I don't enjoy his company. He's a bore and a fool.

nuisance • He could be a bit of a nuisance.

pain (INFORMAL) • She's been a real pain recently.

pain in the neck (INFORMAL) • I've always been a pain in the neck to publishers.

pester VERB

to bother someone continually • He gets fed up with people pestering him for money.

annoy • She kept on annoying me.

badger • She badgered her doctor time and again.

bother • I wish my little brother would stop bothering me.

bug (INFORMAL) • Stop bugging me.

drive someone up the wall (SLANG) • I sang in the bath and drove my sister up the wall.

get on someone's nerves (INFORMAL) • I was beginning to get on her nerves.

petty ① ADJECTIVE

small and unimportant • endless rules and petty regulations

insignificant • *In 1949, Bonn was a small, insignificant city.*
measly (INFORMAL) • *The average bathroom measures a measly 3.5 square metres.*
trifling • *The sums involved are trifling.*
trivial • *trivial details*
unimportant • *It was an unimportant job, and paid very little.*

petty ② ADJECTIVE
selfish and small-minded
• *I think that attitude is a bit petty.*
cheap • *politicians making cheap political points*
mean • *I'd feel mean saying no.*
small-minded • *their small-minded preoccupation with making money*

phone ① NOUN
a device that allows you to speak to someone in another place • *Will you please answer the phone.*
blower (BRITISH; INFORMAL)
• *Get on the blower and speak to the boss.*
mobile • *Can I borrow your mobile?*
mobile phone • *I lost my mobile phone at the weekend.*
smartphone • *The company announced that it will start making games for smartphones.*
telephone • *an old-fashioned black telephone*

phone ② VERB
to contact a person by phone • *Phone me when you get home.*

call • *You should call work to let them know you're ill.*
contact • *I've been trying to contact you all day.*
ring • *Joe rang the police station.*
Skype (TRADEMARK) • *They Skype their son in Australia every week.*
telephone • *Mary telephoned when you were out.*

phoney ADJECTIVE
(INFORMAL)
false and intended to deceive
• *a phoney accent*
bogus • *a bogus insurance claim*
counterfeit • *counterfeit currency*
fake • *fake certificates*
false • *a false name and address*
forged • *forged documents*
sham • *a sham marriage*
ANTONYM:
• *genuine*

pick ① VERB
to choose something • *He picked ten people to interview for six sales jobs.*
choose • *There are several options to choose from.*
decide upon • *He decided upon a career in publishing.*
hand-pick • *He was hand-picked for his job by the Admiral.*
opt for • *I think we should opt for a more cautious approach.*
select • *the party's policy of selecting candidates*
settle on • *We finally settled on the name "Clover" for our new puppy.*

P

pick ② VERB

to remove a flower or fruit with your fingers • He helps his mother pick fruit.

gather • We spent the afternoon gathering berries.

harvest • Many farmers are refusing to harvest the cane.

pluck • I plucked a lemon from the tree.

pick ③ NOUN

the best • the pick of the country's young athletes

elite • the elite of women's tennis

flower • the flower of the country's youth

pride • the hovercraft, once the pride of British maritime engineering

pick on VERB

to criticise someone unfairly or treat them unkindly • He complained of being picked on by his coach.

bait • He delighted in baiting his mother.

tease • She teased me mercilessly about going to Hollywood.

torment • They were tormented by other pupils.

picture ① NOUN

a drawing, painting or photograph • It's got a picture of me on the cover.

drawing • She did a drawing of me.

illustration • Tolkien's illustrations for The Hobbit

painting • his collection of Impressionist paintings

photograph • He wants to take some photographs of the house.

portrait • Velázquez's portrait of Pope Innocent X

selfie (INFORMAL) • James took a selfie with some young fans during a stoppage in play.

sketch • pencil sketches

RELATED WORD:
• ADJECTIVE pictorial

picture ② VERB

to imagine something clearly • He pictured her with long black hair.

conceive of • I can't conceive of doing work that doesn't interest me.

imagine • It's difficult to imagine anything coming between them.

see • A good idea, but can you see Taylor trying it?

visualise • He could not visualise her as old.

piece ① NOUN

a portion or part of something • a piece of cheese

bit • a bit of paper

chunk • He was accused of stealing a tin of pineapple chunks.

fragment • There were fragments of glass on the carpet.

part • The engine has got only three moving parts.

portion • Damage was confined to a small portion of the castle.

slice • a slice of bread

piece ② NOUN

something that has been

written, created or composed
• *his piece on climate change*

article • *a newspaper article*

composition • *Schubert's piano compositions*

creation • *The fashion designer's latest creations*

study • *Leonardo's studies of horsemen*

work • *In my opinion, this is Rembrandt's greatest work.*

piece together VERB
to assemble things or parts to make something complete • *Doctors painstakingly pieced together the broken bones.*

assemble • *He is assembling evidence concerning a murder.*

join • *Join all the sections together.*

mend • *I should have had it mended, but never got round to it.*

patch together • *A hasty deal was patched together.*

repair • *the cost of repairing earthquake damage*

restore • *The trust is playing a leading part in restoring old cinemas.*

pierce VERB
to make a hole in something with a sharp instrument • *Pierce the potato with a fork.*

bore • *tunnels bored into the foundations of the building*

drill • *I drilled five holes at equal distance.*

lance • *It's a painful experience having the boil lanced.*

penetrate • *The earth's atmosphere was penetrated by a meteor.*

puncture • *One of the tyres was punctured by a nail.*

pig NOUN
a farm animal kept for meat • *the number of pigs at the trough*

hog • *He's as fat as a hog.*

piggy (INFORMAL) • *These two piggies are going to market!*

porker • *a 30kg Vietnamese potbellied porker*

swine • *herds of oxen, sheep and swine*

RELATED WORDS:
• ADJECTIVE porcine
• MALE boar
• FEMALE sow
• YOUNG piglet
• COLLECTIVE NOUN litter
• HABITATION sty

pile ① NOUN
a quantity of things lying one on top of another • *a pile of books*

heap • *a compost heap*

hoard • *a hoard of jewels*

mound • *The bulldozers piled up huge mounds of dirt.*

mountain • *They have mountains of coffee to sell.*

stack • *a stack of magazines on the table*

pile ② NOUN
the raised fibres of a soft surface • *the carpet's thick pile*

down • *The whole plant is covered with fine down.*

P

fur • *This creature's fur is short and dense.*

nap • *The cotton is lightly brushed to heighten the nap.*

pile ③ VERB
to put things one on top of another • *A few newspapers were piled on the table.*

heap • *She heaped more carrots onto his plate.*

hoard • *They've begun to hoard gold and silver.*

stack • *They are stacked neatly in piles of three.*

pink NOUN OR ADJECTIVE

SHADES OF PINK
coral
flesh
fuchsia
oyster pink
rose
salmon
shell pink
shocking pink

pit NOUN
a large hole in something • *He lost his footing and began to slide into the pit.*

chasm • *Billy peered over the sheer drop into the chasm below.*

hole • *The builders had cut holes into the soft stone.*

pothole • *She told us to look out for potholes.*

pity ① VERB
to feel sorry for someone • *I don't know whether to hate or pity him.*

feel for • *She cried on the phone and I really felt for her.*

feel sorry for • *He felt sorry for the neighbours, who had to put up with all that noise.*

sympathise with • *I sympathise with you for your loss.*

pity ② NOUN
sympathy for other people's suffering • *She saw no pity in their faces.*

charity • *They showed a lack of charity and understanding to her.*

compassion • *his compassion for a helpless woman*

kindness • *He was treated with kindness by numerous officials.*

mercy • *Neither side showed any mercy.*

sympathy • *We expressed our sympathy for her loss.*

understanding • *We would like to thank them for their patience and understanding.*

pity ③ NOUN
a regrettable fact • *It's a pity they can't all have the same opportunities.*

crime (INFORMAL) • *It would be a crime to travel to Australia and not stop in Sydney.*

crying shame • *It would be a crying shame to split up a winning partnership.*

shame • *It's a shame it had to close.*

place ① NOUN
any point or area • *The pain is always in the same place.*

area • *a picnic area*

location • *The first thing she looked at was the office's location*

point • *The pain originated from a point in his right thigh.*
position • *the ship's position*
site • *a bat sanctuary with special nesting sites*
spot • *the island's top tourist spots*

place ② : take place VERB
to happen • *The meeting took place on Thursday.*
come about • *That came about when we went to Glastonbury last year.*
go on • *This has been going on for around a year.*
happen • *We cannot say for sure what will happen.*
occur • *The crash occurred when the crew shut down the wrong engine.*

place ③ VERB
to put something somewhere • *Chairs were placed in rows for the parents.*
deposit • *Imagine if you were suddenly deposited on a desert island.*
locate • *the best city in which to locate a business*
plant • *He planted his feet firmly to the spot.*
position • *plants which are carefully positioned in the alcove*
put • *She put the photograph on her desk.*
situate • *The hotel is situated next to the railway station.*

plain ① ADJECTIVE
very simple in style with no decoration • *It was a plain, grey stone house.*

austere • *The church was austere and simple.*
bare • *bare wooden floors*
spartan • *her spartan home in a tiny village*
stark • *a stark white, characterless fireplace*

ANTONYM:
• fancy

plain ② ADJECTIVE
obvious and easy to recognise or understand • *It was plain to him that I was lying about the day's events.*
clear • *The book is clear and readable.*
comprehensible • *a comprehensible manual*
distinct • *a distinct smell of burning coal*
evident • *His footprints were clearly evident in the heavy dust.*
obvious • *an obvious injustice*
unmistakable • *Ms Wynn's voice was unmistakable.*

plain ③ NOUN
TYPES OF PLAIN
flat
flatland
grassland
llano
lowland
mesa
plateau
prairie
savannah
steppe
tableland

P

plan ① NOUN
a way thought out to do
something • *a plan to beat last
year's fundraising target*
method • *He did it by his usual
method.*
proposal • *The proposals need
careful study.*
scheme • *The scheme was an
abject failure.*
strategy • *What should our
marketing strategy achieve?*
system • *the advantages of
the new system over the old
one*

plan ② NOUN
a detailed diagram of
something • *a detailed plan of
the prison*
blueprint • *a blueprint for a
new bathroom*
diagram • *a circuit diagram*
layout • *He tried to recall the
layout of the farmhouse.*
scale drawing • *scale drawings
of the building*

plan ③ VERB
to decide in detail what is to
be done • *when we plan road
construction*
arrange • *We arranged a social
event once a year.*
design • *He approached me to
design the restaurant.*
devise • *We devised a plan.*
draft • *The legislation was
drafted by the committee.*
formulate • *He formulated his
plan for escape.*

play ① VERB
to take part in games or use

toys • *Polly was playing with her
teddy bear.*
amuse yourself • *He amused
himself by rollerskating round the
building.*
entertain yourself • *I used to
entertain myself by building
model planes.*
frolic • *Tourists sunbathe and
frolic in the ocean.*
have fun • *having fun with your
friends*

play ② VERB
to take part in a sport or game
• *Alain was playing cards with
his friends.*
compete • *Eight entrants
competed for the prize.*
participate • *Sixteen teams
participated in the tournament.*
take on • *Scotland take on
South Africa at Murrayfield.*
take part • *The teams taking
part are cricket's bitterest enemies.*
vie with • *Arsenal are vying
with Chelsea for second spot in
the league.*

play ③ NOUN
a piece of drama performed
on stage, radio or television
• *Chekhov's best play*
comedy • *a romantic comedy*
drama • *He also wrote radio
dramas and film scripts.*
pantomime • *He regularly
performs in Christmas
pantomimes.*
show • *a one-woman show*
tragedy • *Shakespeare's tragedie*

plead VERB
to beg someone for somethin

• She pleaded with her daughter to come home.

appeal • The United Nations appealed for aid from the international community.

ask • I've asked you time and again not to do that.

beg • We are not going to beg for help any more.

beseech (LITERARY) • She beseeched him to show mercy.

implore • Opposition leaders implored the president to break the deadlock.

pleasant ① ADJECTIVE

enjoyable or attractive • I've got a pleasant little flat.

agreeable • workers in more agreeable and better-paid occupations

delightful • It was the most delightful garden I'd ever seen.

enjoyable • an enjoyable meal

lekker (SOUTH AFRICAN; SLANG) • a lekker little town

lovely • He had a lovely voice.

nice • It's nice to be here together again.

pleasurable • He found sailing more pleasurable than skiing.

ANTONYM:
• unpleasant

pleasant ② ADJECTIVE

friendly or charming • Ms Taylor had a pleasant face.

affable • He is an affable and approachable man.

amiable • She had been surprised at how amiable and polite he had seemed.

charming • He can be charming to his friends.

friendly • She has a friendly relationship with her customers.

likable or **likeable** • He's an immensely likable man.

nice • He's a nice fellow, very quiet and courteous.

ANTONYM:
• unpleasant

please VERB

to give pleasure to • I was tidying my bedroom to please mum.

amuse • The thought seemed to amuse him.

charm • He charmed all of us.

delight • music that has delighted audiences all over the world

entertain • Children's TV not only entertains but also teaches.

pleased ADJECTIVE

happy or satisfied • I'm pleased with the way things have been going.

contented • She had a contented smile on her face.

delighted • I know he will be delighted to see you.

glad • I'm glad he changed his mind in the end.

happy • She's a confident and happy child.

satisfied • satisfied customers

pleasure NOUN

a feeling of happiness and satisfaction • Everybody takes pleasure in eating.

amusement • Her impersonations provided great amusement.

P

enjoyment • *her enjoyment of the countryside*
happiness • *It was an occasion of pure happiness.*
joy • *tears of joy*
satisfaction • *job satisfaction*

plentiful ADJECTIVE
existing in large amounts
• *a plentiful supply*
abundant • *Birds are abundant in the tall vegetation.*
ample • *The design created ample space for a large kitchen.*
bountiful • *a bountiful harvest of fruits and vegetables*
copious • *She attended the lectures and took copious notes.*
infinite • *an infinite variety of landscapes*
ANTONYM:
• scarce

plenty NOUN
a lot of something • *There's plenty to go round.*
enough • *Have you had enough?*
great deal • *I've spent a great deal of time on this project.*
heaps (INFORMAL) • *You have heaps of time.*
lots (INFORMAL) • *He has made lots of amendments to the script.*
plethora • *a plethora of new products*

plot ① NOUN
a secret plan made by a group of people • *the plot to assassinate Martin Luther King*
conspiracy • *a conspiracy to steal nuclear missiles*
intrigue • *political intrigues*

plan • *a secret plan to persuade her parents to get a family dog*
scheme • *an elaborate scheme to dupe the police*

plot ② NOUN
the story of a novel or play
• *The film has a ludicrously complicated plot.*
narrative • *a fast-moving narrative*
scenario • *The movie's scenario is nonsensical.*
story • *I doubt the widespread appeal of this film's story.*
story line • *It sounds like a typical story line from a soap opera.*

plot ③ VERB
to plan something secretly with others • *Prosecutors allege the defendants plotted to overthrow the government.*
conspire • *The countries had secretly conspired to acquire nuclear weapons.*
hatch • *He hatched a plot to frame his enemy for the crime.*
plan • *I suspect they are secretly planning to raise taxes.*
scheme • *He claimed that they were scheming against him.*

plug ① NOUN
a small, round object for blocking a hole • *She put the plug in the sink and filled it with water.*
bung • *Remove the bung from the barrel.*
cork • *The message was found in a dark green bottle, sealed with a cork.*

stopper • *a bottle sealed with a cork stopper*

plug ② VERB
to block a hole with something • *working to plug a major oil leak*
block • *When the shrimp farm is built it will block the stream.*
fill • *Fill small holes with wood filler.*
seal • *She filled the containers and sealed them with a cork.*

plump ADJECTIVE
rather fat • *a plump little baby*
beefy (INFORMAL) • *beefy bodyguards*
burly • *burly shipyard workers*
chubby • *I was quite chubby as a child.*
fat • *I could eat what I liked without getting fat.*
stout • *He was a tall, stout man of sixty.*
tubby • *He's a bit on the tubby side.*

point ① NOUN
the purpose or meaning something has • *Cutting costs is not the point of the exercise.*
aim • *The aim of this book is to inform you.*
goal • *The goal is to raise a lot of money.*
intention • *It was never my intention to injure anyone.*
object • *It was his object in life to find the island.*
purpose • *He did not know the purpose of Vincent's visit.*

point ② NOUN
a quality or feature • *Tact was never her strong point.*
attribute • *Cruelty is a regrettable attribute of human behaviour.*
characteristic • *their physical characteristics*
feature • *It's one of my best features.*
quality • *mature people with leadership qualities*
side • *the dark side of his character*
trait • *Creativity is a human trait.*

point ③ NOUN
the thin sharp end of something • *the point of a needle*
nib • *the nib of my pen*
prong • *the prongs of a fork*
tip • *the tip of my scissors*

poison NOUN
a substance that can kill people or animals • *Mercury is a known poison.*
toxin • *the liver's ability to break down toxins*
venom • *the cobra's deadly venom*
RELATED WORD:
• ADJECTIVE toxic

poisonous ADJECTIVE
containing something that causes death or illness • *a large cloud of poisonous gas*
noxious • *Many household products give off noxious fumes.*
toxic • *The cost of cleaning up toxic waste.*

P

venomous • *The adder is Britain's only venomous snake.*

poke ① VERB
to jab or prod someone or something • *She poked a fork into the butternut squash.*
dig • *His companions were digging him in the ribs.*
elbow • *As I tried to get past him he elbowed me in the face.*
jab • *Somebody jabbed an umbrella into his leg.*
nudge • *She nudged me awake after I dozed off.*
prod • *He prodded Murray with his tennis racket.*
stab • *He stabbed at Frank with his forefinger.*

poke ② NOUN
a jab or prod • *She gave Richard a playful poke.*
dig • *She silenced him with a sharp dig in the small of the back.*
jab • *a quick jab of the brakes*
nudge • *She slipped her arm under his and gave him a nudge.*
prod • *She gave him a prod in the arm.*

polish ① VERB
to make smooth and shiny by rubbing • *He polished his shoes every morning.*
buff • *He was already buffing the car's hubs.*
shine • *Let him dust and shine the furniture.*
wax • *a Sunday morning spent washing and waxing the car*

polish ② VERB
to improve a skill or technique • *Polish up your writing skills.*
brush up • *She spent the summer brushing up on her driving.*
improve • *I want to improve my golf game.*
perfect • *We perfected a hand-signal system.*
refine • *Surgical techniques are constantly being refined.*

polish ③ NOUN
elegance or refinement • *The opera lacks the polish of his later work.*
class (INFORMAL) • *For sheer class, he is streets ahead of the other batsmen in the side.*
elegance • *The furniture combined practicality with elegance.*
finesse • *The simple cooking is carried out with great finesse.*
grace • *Ballet classes are important for learning poise and grace.*
refinement • *a woman who possessed both dignity and refinement*
style • *Paris, you have to admit, has style.*

polite ① ADJECTIVE
having good manners • *It's not polite to point at people.*
civil • *I have to force myself to be civil to him.*
courteous • *Her reply was courteous but firm.*
respectful • *Their children are always respectful to their elders.*
well-behaved • *well-behaved teenagers*

well-mannered • *a very pleasant and well-mannered student*

ANTONYM:
• rude

polite ② ADJECTIVE
cultivated or refined • *Certain words are not acceptable in polite society.*

cultured • *She is immensely cultured and well-read.*
genteel • *a genteel manner*
refined • *His speech and manner are very refined.*
sophisticated • *Recently her tastes have become more sophisticated.*
urbane • *She describes him as charming and urbane.*

politeness NOUN
the quality of being civil to someone • *She listened to him but only out of politeness.*

civility • *Handle customers with tact and courtesy.*
courtesy • *He did not even have the courtesy to reply to my message.*
decency • *He should have had the decency to inform me.*
etiquette • *the rules of diplomatic etiquette*

pollute VERB
to contaminate with something harmful • *Heavy industry pollutes our rivers with noxious chemicals.*

contaminate • *Have any fish been contaminated in the Arctic Ocean?*

infect • *a virus which is spread mainly by infected blood*
poison • *Drilling operations have poisoned the Nile delta.*
taint • *soils tainted with heavy metals*

pompous ADJECTIVE
behaving in a way that is too serious and self-important • *a pompous man with a high opinion of his own capabilities*

arrogant • *an air of arrogant indifference*
grandiose • *grandiose plans which never got off the ground*
ostentatious • *an ostentatious wedding reception*
pretentious • *Her response was full of pretentious nonsense.*
puffed up • *He is puffed up with his own importance.*

ponder VERB
to think about something deeply • *I'm continually pondering how to improve the team.*

brood • *I guess everyone broods over things once in a while.*
consider • *You have to consider the feelings of those around you.*
contemplate • *He lay in bed contemplating his future.*
mull over • *I'll leave you alone here so you can mull it over.*
reflect • *I reflected on the day's events.*
think • *I have often thought about this problem.*

poor ① ADJECTIVE
having little money • *He was one of thirteen children from a poor family.*

P

broke (INFORMAL) • *He was broke when I married him.*
destitute • *destitute people living on the streets*
hard up (INFORMAL) • *Her parents were very hard up.*
impoverished • *one of the most impoverished suburbs of Rio de Janeiro*
penniless • *a penniless refugee*
poverty-stricken • *a teacher of poverty-stricken kids*
ANTONYM:
• rich

poor ② ADJECTIVE
of a low quality or standard • *He was a poor actor.*
feeble • *a feeble attempt to save Bale's shot*
inferior • *The work was of inferior quality.*
mediocre • *His school record was mediocre.*
second-rate • *Passengers are fed up using a second-rate service.*
shoddy • *shoddy goods*
unsatisfactory • *questions to which he received unsatisfactory answers*

popular ① ADJECTIVE
liked or approved of by a lot of people • *These delicious pastries will be very popular.*
fashionable • *fashionable boutiques*
favourite • *Britain's favourite soap opera*
in demand • *Anne was much in demand as a lecturer.*
in favour • *He is now back in favour with the manager.*

sought-after • *one of the most sought-after new names in Hollywood*
well-liked • *She was very sociable and well-liked by the other students.*
ANTONYM:
• unpopular

popular ② ADJECTIVE
involving or intended for ordinary people • *the popular press*
common • *Much of the countryside has fallen out of common ownership and into private hands.*
conventional • *a respectable woman with conventional opinions*
general • *general awareness about bullying*
universal • *universal health care*

portion NOUN
a part or amount of something • *I have spent a considerable portion of my life here.*
bit • *I missed the first bit of the meeting.*
chunk • *Cut the melon into chunks.*
helping • *She gave them extra helpings of ice cream.*
part • *A large part of his earnings went on repaying the loan.*
piece • *Do you want another piece?*
segment • *the middle segment of his journey*

serving • *Each serving contains 240 calories.*

pose ① VERB
to ask a question • *When I finally posed the question "Why?", he merely shrugged.*
ask • *I wasn't the only one asking questions.*
put • *Some workers may be afraid to put questions publicly.*
submit • *Passengers are invited to submit questions.*

pose ② VERB
to pretend to be someone else • *The team posed as art collectors to trap the ringleaders.*
impersonate • *He was once jailed for impersonating a police officer.*
masquerade as • *He masqueraded as a doctor and fooled everyone.*
pass yourself off as • *He frequently passed himself off as a lawyer.*
pretend to be • *We spent the afternoon pretending to be foreign tourists.*

posh ① ADJECTIVE (INFORMAL)
smart, fashionable and expensive • *a posh hotel*
classy (INFORMAL) • *expensive cars with classy brand names*
elegant • *an elegant society ball*
exclusive • *a member of Britain's most exclusive club*
fashionable • *fashionable restaurants*
smart • *smart London dinner parties*
stylish • *stylish décor*

up-market • *an up-market agency aimed at professional people*

posh ② ADJECTIVE
upper-class • *He sounded very posh on the phone.*
aristocratic • *a wealthy, aristocratic family*
genteel • *a genteel manner*
upper-class • *upper-class speech*

ANTONYM:
• common

position ① NOUN
the place where someone or something is • *The ship's name and position were reported to the coastguard.*
location • *She knew the exact location of their headquarters.*
place • *The itch is always in the same place.*
point • *The pain originated from a point in his right thigh.*
whereabouts • *Finding his whereabouts proved surprisingly easy.*

position ② VERB
to put something somewhere • *Position trailing plants near the edges.*
arrange • *Arrange the books in neat piles.*
lay out • *Grace laid out the knives and forks at the table.*
locate • *the best city in which to locate a business*
place • *Chairs were placed in rows for the parents.*
put • *She put the photograph on her desk.*

P

positive ① ADJECTIVE

completely sure about something • *I was positive he'd known about that money.*

certain • *It wasn't a balloon – I'm certain about that.*

confident • *Ms Ryan is confident of success.*

convinced • *He was convinced that I was part of the problem.*

sure • *It is impossible to be sure about the value of the land.*

positive ② ADJECTIVE

providing definite proof of the truth or identity of something • *positive evidence*

clear • *a clear case of mistaken identity*

clear-cut • *The issue is not so clear-cut.*

conclusive • *Research on the matter is far from conclusive.*

concrete • *He had no concrete evidence.*

firm • *There is no firm evidence to prove this.*

positive ③ ADJECTIVE

tending to emphasise what is good • *I anticipate a positive response.*

constructive • *We welcome constructive criticism.*

helpful • *Camilla's helpful comments*

ANTONYM:
• negative

possess ① VERB

to have something as a quality • *He possesses both stamina and great technique.*

be blessed with • *She was blessed with a photographic memory.*

be born with • *Mozart was born with perfect pitch.*

enjoy • *I have always enjoyed good health.*

have • *They have talent in abundance.*

possess ② VERB

to own something • *He was said to possess a huge fortune.*

acquire • *I have acquired a new car.*

control • *He now controls the entire company.*

hold • *He does not hold a licence.*

occupy • *US forces now occupy part of the country.*

seize • *Troops have seized the airport and railway terminals.*

take over • *They plan to take over another airline.*

possession NOUN

ownership of something • *How did this picture come into your possession?*

control • *The restructuring involves his giving up control of the firm.*

custody • *She will have custody of their two children.*

ownership • *the growth of home ownership*

tenure • *his 28-year tenure of the house*

possessions PLURAL NOUN

the things owned by someone • *People had lost all their possessions.*

assets • *The group had assets worth over 10 million dollars.*
belongings • *I collected my belongings and left.*
effects • *His daughters were collecting his effects.*
estate • *She left her entire estate to a charity.*
property • *the rightful owner of the property*
things • *She told him to take all his things and not to return.*

possibility NOUN
something that might be true or might happen • *the possibility of a ban*
chance • *There's no chance of that happening.*
hope • *We had absolutely no hope of raising the money.*
likelihood • *the likelihood of infection*
odds • *What are the odds of that happening?*
prospect • *There is little prospect of peace.*
risk • *It reduces the risk of heart disease.*

possible ① ADJECTIVE
likely to happen or able to be done • *I am grateful to the staff for making this work possible.*
attainable • *I always thought promotion was attainable.*
feasible • *Whether such cooperation is feasible is a matter of doubt.*
practicable • *It was not reasonably practicable for Mr Tyler to attend.*

viable • *commercially viable products*
workable • *This isn't a workable solution in most cases.*
ANTONYM:
• impossible

possible ② ADJECTIVE
likely or capable of being true or correct • *It's possible there's an explanation for all this.*
conceivable • *It is just conceivable that a survivor might be found.*
imaginable • *a place of no imaginable strategic value*
likely • *Experts say a "yes" vote is still the likely outcome.*
potential • *the channel's potential audience*

postpone VERB
to put off to a later time • *The visit has been postponed until tomorrow.*
adjourn • *The proceedings have been adjourned until next week.*
defer • *Customers often defer payments for as long as possible.*
delay • *I wanted to delay my departure until June.*
put back • *The news conference has been put back a couple of hours.*
put off • *The Association has put off the event until October.*
shelve • *Sadly, the project has now been shelved.*

potential ① ADJECTIVE
possible but not yet actual
• *potential sources of finance*
likely • *A draw is the likely outcome.*

P

possible • *Her family is discussing a possible move to America.*

probable • *A bomb was the accident's most probable cause.*

potential ② NOUN
ability to achieve future success • *Denmark recognised the potential of wind energy early.*

ability • *You have the ability to become a good pianist.*

aptitude • *more aptitude for academic work than the others*

capability • *We experience differences in mental capability depending on the time of day.*

capacity • *people's creative capacities*

power • *the power of speech*

wherewithal • *She didn't have the financial wherewithal to do it.*

pour VERB
to flow quickly and in large quantities • *Blood was pouring from his broken nose.*

course • *The tears coursed down her cheeks.*

flow • *compressor stations that keep the gas flowing*

gush • *Piping-hot water gushed out.*

run • *Water was running down the walls.*

spout • *The water spouted 40 feet into the air.*

stream • *She came in, rain streaming from her clothes and hair.*

poverty NOUN
the state of being very poor • *Garvey died in loneliness and poverty.*

destitution • *refugees living in destitution*

hardship • *Many people are suffering economic hardship.*

insolvency • *Several companies are on the brink of insolvency.*

want • *We are fighting for freedom from want.*

power ① NOUN
control over people and activities • *a position of great power and influence*

ascendancy (FORMAL) • *The extremists in the party are gaining ascendancy.*

control • *He has been forced to give up control over the company.*

dominion (FORMAL) • *They truly believe they have dominion over us.*

sovereignty • *the resumption of Chinese sovereignty over Hong Kong in 1997*

supremacy • *The party has re-established its supremacy.*

power ② NOUN
authority to do something • *The police have the power of arrest.*

authority • *The judge had no authority to order a second trial.*

authorisation • *I don't have the authorisation to make such a decision.*

licence • *He has given me licence to do the job as I see fit.*

privilege • *the ancient powers and privileges of parliament*

right • *the right to vote*

power ③ NOUN
physical strength • *Power and bulk are vital to success in rugby.*

brawn • *He's got plenty of brains as well as brawn.*
might • *The might of the army could prove a decisive factor.*
strength • *He threw it forward with all his strength.*
vigour • *He blew his nose with great vigour.*

powerful ① ADJECTIVE
able to control people and events • *Russia and India, two large, powerful countries*
commanding • *We're in a more commanding position than we've been in for ages.*
dominant • *He was a dominant figure in the Italian film industry.*
influential • *She had been influential in shaping economic policy.*

powerful ② ADJECTIVE
physically strong • *It's such a big powerful dog.*
mighty • *a mighty river*
strapping • *He was a bricklayer – a big, strapping fellow.*
strong • *I'm not strong enough to carry him.*
sturdy • *The camera was mounted on a sturdy tripod.*
vigorous • *He was a vigorous, handsome young man.*
ANTONYM:
• weak

powerful ③ ADJECTIVE
having a strong effect • *a powerful argument*
compelling • *a compelling reason to leave*

convincing • *convincing evidence*
effective • *Antibiotics are effective against this organism.*
forceful • *forceful action to stop the suffering*
persuasive • *Mr. Knight made a persuasive case for removing the tax.*
telling • *Melanie spoke reasonably, carefully and with telling effect.*

powerless ADJECTIVE
unable to control or influence events • *I was powerless to save her.*
helpless • *Many people felt helpless against the violence.*
impotent • *She was shaking with impotent fury.*
incapable • *He is incapable as a manager.*

practical ① ADJECTIVE
involving experience rather than theory • *practical suggestions for more effective studying*
applied • *plans to put more money into applied research*
pragmatic • *a pragmatic approach to the problems of Latin America*

practical ② ADJECTIVE
likely to be effective • *The clothes are lightweight and practical for holidays.*
functional • *The design is functional but stylish.*
sensible • *sensible footwear*
ANTONYM:
• impractical

P

practical ③ ADJECTIVE

able to deal effectively with problems • *the practical common sense essential in management*

accomplished • *an accomplished cook*

experienced • *a team packed with experienced professionals*

proficient • *A great number of them are proficient in foreign languages.*

seasoned • *The author is a seasoned academic.*

skilled • *amateur but highly skilled observers of wildlife*

veteran • *a veteran broadcaster*

practice ① NOUN

something that people do regularly • *a public inquiry into bank practices*

custom • *I have tried to adapt to local customs.*

habit • *a survey on eating habits*

method • *her usual method of getting through the traffic*

routine • *We had to change our daily routine and lifestyle.*

way • *a return to the old ways of doing things*

practice ② NOUN

regular training or exercise • *I need more practice.*

drill • *The teacher ran them through the drill again.*

exercise • *Lack of exercise can lead to feelings of exhaustion.*

preparation • *Behind any successful event lie months of preparation.*

rehearsal • *rehearsals for a concert tour*

training • *her busy training schedule*

practise ① VERB

to do something repeatedly so as to gain skill • *Lauren practises the piano every day.*

polish • *They just need to polish their technique.*

rehearse • *She was in her room rehearsing her lines.*

train • *He was training for the new season.*

practise ② VERB

to take part in the activities of a religion, craft or custom • *Acupuncture has been practised in China for thousands of years.*

do • *I used to do karate.*

follow • *Do you follow any particular religion?*

observe • *American forces are observing Christmas quietly.*

praise ① VERB

to express strong approval of someone • *Many others praised Sanford for taking a strong stand.*

admire • *All those who knew him will admire him for his work.*

applaud • *He should be applauded for his courage.*

approve • *Not everyone approves of the festival.*

congratulate • *I must congratulate the organisers on a well-run event.*

pay tribute to • *He paid tribute to his captain.*

ANTONYM:
• criticise

praise ② NOUN
something said or written to show approval • She is full of praise for the range of services available.
accolade • the ultimate international accolade, the Nobel Peace Prize
approval • an obsessive drive to gain her mother's approval
commendation • They received a commendation from the Royal Society of Arts.
congratulation • I offered her my congratulations.
tribute • We marched past in tribute to our fallen comrades.
ANTONYM:
• criticism

precaution NOUN
an action intended to prevent something from happening • It's still worth taking precautions against accidents.
insurance • Farmers grew a mixture of crops as an insurance against crop failure.
preventative measure • a preventative measure against heart disease
protection • protection against damage to buildings
provision • People need to make decent provision for their retirement.
safeguard • legislation that offers safeguards against discrimination

precious ADJECTIVE
of great value and importance • precious jewels

expensive • an expensive new coat
invaluable • I was to gain invaluable experience over that year.
priceless • his priceless collection of Chinese art
prized • These shells were very highly prized by the indigenous population.
valuable • valuable books
ANTONYM:
• worthless

precise ADJECTIVE
exact and accurate • We may never know the precise details.
accurate • an accurate description of his attackers
actual • The actual number of victims is higher than statistics suggest.
correct • This information was correct at the time of going to press.
exact • The exact number of protest calls has not been revealed.
particular • a very particular account of events
specific • I asked him to be more specific.
very • Those were his very words.
ANTONYM:
• vague

predicament NOUN
a difficult situation • The decision will leave her in a peculiar predicament.
fix (INFORMAL) • The government has really got itself into a fix.

P

hot water (INFORMAL) • *His antics keep landing him in hot water with officials.*

jam (INFORMAL) • *We are in a real jam now.*

scrape (INFORMAL) • *He's had his fair share of scrapes with the law.*

tight spot (INFORMAL) • *This was one tight spot he couldn't get out of.*

predict VERB

to say that something will happen in the future • *The opinion polls are predicting a very close contest.*

forecast • *He forecasts that house prices will rise by 5% this year.*

foresee • *He did not foresee any problems.*

foretell • *prophets who have foretold the end of the world*

prophesy • *She prophesied a bad ending for the expedition.*

prediction NOUN

something that is forecast in advance • *He was unwilling to make a prediction for the coming year.*

forecast • *a forecast of heavy weather to come*

prophecy • *the interpreters of Biblical prophecy*

prefer VERB

to like one thing more than another thing • *Does he prefer a particular sort of music?*

be partial to • *I'm quite partial to mussels.*

favour • *Both sides favour a diplomatic solution.*

go for • *They went for a more up-market approach.*

incline towards • *The majority incline towards a forgiving attitude.*

like better • *I like the flat shoes better.*

prefix NOUN

PREFIXES

ante-
anti-
auto-
bi-
centi-
co-
contra-
de-
demi-
dis-
ex-
extra-
hyper-
in-
inter-
intra-
mega-
micro-
mid-
milli-
mini-
mono-
multi-
neo-
non-
over-
poly-
post-
pre-
pro-
pseudo-
re-

self-
semi-
step-
sub-
super-
tele-
trans-
tri-
ultra-
un-
under-
vice-

prejudice ① NOUN

an unreasonable or unfair
dislike or preference • prejudice
against workers over 45
bias • bias against women in the
workplace
partiality • She is criticised for
her one-sidedness and partiality.
preconception
• preconceptions about the sort
of people who did computing

prejudice ② NOUN

intolerance towards certain
people or groups • racial
prejudice
bigotry • religious bigotry
chauvinism • a campaign
against national chauvinism
discrimination
• discrimination against women
racism • the fight to rid sport of
racism
sexism • sexism in the
workplace

premonition NOUN

a feeling that something
unpleasant is going to happen
• He had a premonition that he
would never see her again.

foreboding • His triumph was
overshadowed by an uneasy
sense of foreboding.
funny feeling (INFORMAL)
• I have a funny feeling something
unpleasant is about to happen.
omen • Her appearance at this
moment is an omen of disaster.
sign • a sign of impending doom

preoccupied ADJECTIVE

totally involved with
something or deep in thought
• I am preoccupied with my
tennis career.
absorbed • They were
completely absorbed in each
other.
engrossed • Tom didn't notice
because he was too engrossed in
his work.
immersed • He's becoming
really immersed in his studies.
oblivious • When he was in his
car he was totally oblivious to
everybody else.
wrapped up • She's wrapped
up in her new career.

present ① ADJECTIVE

being at a place or event • He
had been present at the birth of
his son.
at hand • Having the right
equipment at hand will be very
useful.
here • He was here a minute
ago.
in attendance • Police and
several fire engines are in
attendance.
there • The group of old
buildings is still there today.

to hand • I haven't got the instructions to hand.

ANTONYM:
• absent

present ② NOUN
something given to someone
• a birthday present
bonsela (SOUTH AFRICAN)
• your kind bonsela to the hospital
donation • Employees make regular donations to charity.
gift • a Christmas gift
offering • a ritual in which each household brings an offering for the deities

present ③ VERB
to give something to someone
• The Mayor presented the prizes.
award • For his dedication he was awarded a medal of merit.
bestow • The Queen bestowed on him a knighthood.
donate • She frequently donates large sums to charity.
give • She gave me a pen for my birthday.
grant • France has agreed to grant him political asylum.
hand out • One of my jobs was to hand out the prizes.

press ① VERB
to apply force or weight to something • Press the blue button.
compress • Poor posture compresses the body's organs.
crush • Peel and crush the garlic.
mash • Mash the bananas with a fork.

push • She pushed the door open.
squeeze • He squeezed her arm reassuringly.

press ② VERB
to try hard to persuade someone to do something
• Trade Unions are pressing him to stand firm.
beg • I begged him to come back with me.
implore • "Tell me what to do!" she implored him.
petition • All the attempts to petition the government had failed.
plead • I pleaded to be allowed to go.
pressurise • He thought she was trying to pressurise him.
urge • He had urged her to come to Ireland.

pretend VERB
to claim or give the appearance of something untrue • She pretended to be asleep.
counterfeit • the coins he is alleged to have counterfeited
fake • He faked his own death last year.
falsify • He was charged with falsifying business records.
feign • The striker was accused of feigning injury.
pass yourself off as • She tried to pass herself off as an actor.

pretentious ADJECTIVE
making unjustified claims to importance • Many critics thought his work and ideas pretentious and empty.

affected • *She passed along with an affected air and a disdainful look.*

conceited • *I thought him conceited and arrogant.*

ostentatious • *an ostentatious wedding reception*

pompous • *He's pompous and has a high opinion of his own capabilities.*

snobbish • *a snobbish dislike for their intellectual inferiors*

pretty ① ADJECTIVE
attractive in a delicate way • *She's a very intelligent and pretty girl.*

attractive • *an attractive man*

beautiful • *a beautiful child*

cute • *a cute little baby*

lovely • *his lovely wife*

pretty ② ADVERB (INFORMAL)
quite or rather • *He spoke pretty good English.*

fairly • *Both ships are fairly new.*

kind of (INFORMAL) • *I was kind of embarrassed about it.*

quite • *It was quite hard.*

rather • *She's rather vain.*

prevent VERB
to stop something from happening • *the most practical way of preventing crime*

avert • *A fresh tragedy was narrowly averted yesterday.*

foil • *The plot was foiled by the police.*

hinder • *Research is hindered by lack of cash.*

impede • *Fallen rocks are impeding the progress of the rescue workers.*

stop • *a new diplomatic initiative to try to stop the war*

thwart • *Her ambition to become an artist was thwarted by failing eyesight.*

previous ADJECTIVE
happening or existing before something else • *the previous year*

earlier • *His earlier works include impressive still lifes.*

former • *a former president of Mexico*

one-time • *the country's one-time military rulers*

past • *a return to the turbulence of past centuries*

preceding • *This is examined in detail in the preceding chapter.*

prior • *I can't make it. I have a prior engagement.*

price ① NOUN
the amount of money paid for something • *a sharp increase in the price of petrol*

amount • *I was asked to pay the full amount.*

charge • *an annual management charge of 1.25%*

cost • *the cost of a loaf of bread*

fee • *the annual membership fee*

figure • *A figure of £2000 was mentioned.*

value • *The company's market value rose to 5.5 billion dollars.*

price ② VERB
to fix the price or value of something • *I just can't imagine why it has been priced at this level.*

cost • *We hope it won't cost too much.*

estimate • *His personal riches were estimated at $368 million.*

put a price on • *The company has refused to put a price on its bid.*

value • *I had my jewellery valued for insurance purposes.*

pride ① NOUN
a feeling of satisfaction about your achievements • *We take pride in offering you the highest standards.*

delight • *Haig took obvious delight in proving his critics wrong.*

pleasure • *Our first win gave me great pleasure.*

satisfaction • *His success was a great source of satisfaction to him.*

pride ② NOUN
an excessively high opinion of yourself • *His pride may still be his downfall.*

arrogance • *He has a swaggering arrogance.*

conceit • *She knew, without conceit, that she was considered a genius.*

egotism • *typical showbiz egotism*

smugness • *a trace of smugness in his voice*

snobbery • *intellectual snobbery*

vanity • *her vanity about her long hair*

ANTONYM:
• humility

priest NOUN

TYPES OF PRIEST
guru (HINDUISM AND SIKHISM)
high priest *or* high priestess
imam (ISLAM)
lama (BUDDHISM)
minister (CHRISTIANITY)
priest
rabbi (JUDAISM)
shaman *or* medicine man
vicar (CHRISTIANITY)

prim ADJECTIVE
behaving very correctly and easily shocked by anything rude • *We tend to assume the Victorians were very prim and proper.*

proper • *He was very pompous and proper.*

prudish • *I'm not prudish but I draw the line at that.*

puritanical • *She has a puritanical attitude towards work.*

strait-laced • *He is very strait-laced and narrow-minded.*

prime ① ADJECTIVE
main or most important • *a prime cause of brain damage*

chief • *The job went to one of his chief rivals.*

leading • *a leading industrial nation*

main • *the city's main tourist area*

principal • *our principal source of foreign exchange earnings*

prime ② ADJECTIVE
of the best quality • *prime beef*

best • *He'll have the best care.*

P

choice • *our choicest chocolates*
first-rate • *She's a first-rate officer.*
select • *With that historic win he now joins a select band of golfers.*
superior • *superior coffee beans*

primitive ADJECTIVE
very simple or basic • *a very small primitive cottage*
crude • *crude stone carvings*
rough • *a rough wooden table*
rude • *He constructed a rude cabin for himself.*
rudimentary • *The meals were made in a rudimentary kitchen.*
simple • *a simple shelter*

principal ADJECTIVE
main or most important • *Their principal concern is that of winning the election.*
chief • *his chief reason for withdrawing*
first • *The first duty of this government is to tackle poverty.*
foremost • *one of the world's foremost scholars of classical poetry*
main • *What are the main differences between them?*
major • *the major factor in her decision*
primary • *the primary cause of his problems*
prime • *Police will see me as the prime suspect!*

principle ① NOUN
a set of moral rules guiding personal conduct • *a woman of principle*

conscience • *the law on freedom of conscience and religious organisations*
integrity • *He has always been a man of integrity.*
morals • *public morals*
scruples • *a person with no moral scruples*
sense of duty • *He did it out of a sense of duty to his troops.*

principle ② NOUN
a general rule or scientific law • *the basic principles of marketing*
axiom • *the long-held axiom that education leads to higher income*
canon • *the canons of political economy*
doctrine • *religious doctrine*
fundamental • *the fundamentals of astronomy*
law • *the laws of motion*

printing NOUN
PRINTING WORDS
bold print
character
fount or font
italics
lower case
roman
typeface
type size
upper case

prison NOUN
a building where criminals are kept in captivity • *a high-security prison*
dungeon • *The castle's dungeons haven't been used for years.*

jail • *Three prisoners escaped from the jail.*
nick (BRITISH, AUSTRALIAN AND NEW ZEALAND; SLANG) • *I was banged up in the nick for six months.*
penal institution • *Thirty years in a penal institution is indeed a harsh penalty.*

prisoner NOUN
someone kept in prison or captivity • *top-security prisoners*
captive • *the difficulties of spending four months as a captive*
convict • *convicts serving life sentences*
hostage • *negotiations to release the hostages*

private ① ADJECTIVE
for few people rather than people in general • *a private bathroom*
exclusive • *Many of our cheeses are exclusive to our shops in Britain.*
individual • *Divide the vegetables among four individual dishes.*
personal • *It's for my own personal use.*
special • *her own special problems*

private ② ADJECTIVE
taking place among a small number of people • *They were married in a private ceremony.*
clandestine (FORMAL) • *He had a clandestine meeting with an enemy agent.*

confidential • *confidential information about her private life*
secret • *a secret hideaway*
ANTONYM:
• public

prize ① NOUN
a reward given to the winner of something • *She won first prize at the Leeds Piano Competition.*
accolade • *the ultimate international accolade, the Nobel Peace Prize*
award • *the Booker Prize, Britain's top award for fiction*
honour • *He was showered with honours – among them an Oscar.*
trophy • *They haven't won a trophy since 2006.*

prize ② ADJECTIVE
of the highest quality or standard • *a prize bull*
award-winning • *an award-winning restaurant*
first-rate • *a first-rate thriller writer*
outstanding • *an outstanding horse*
top • *Holland's top striker*

prize ③ VERB
to value highly • *These ornaments are prized by collectors.*
cherish • *We cherish our independence.*
esteem • *one of Europe's most esteemed awards*
treasure • *She treasures her memories of those joyous days.*
value • *I value the work he gives me.*

probability NOUN

the likelihood of something happening • *the probability of a serious earthquake*

chances • *The chances of success for the product are good.*

likelihood • *the likelihood of infection*

odds • *The odds are that you are going to fail.*

prospect • *the prospect for peace in the war-torn region*

probable ADJECTIVE

likely to be true or to happen • *a misunderstanding about the probable cost*

apparent • *There is no apparent reason for the crime.*

feasible • *Whether this is feasible is a matter of doubt.*

likely • *Further delays are likely.*

on the cards • *A promotion is definitely on the cards for you.*

plausible • *a plausible explanation*

ANTONYM:
• improbable

probably ADVERB

in all likelihood • *The wedding's probably going to be in late August.*

doubtless • *He will doubtless try to change my mind.*

in all probability • *Victory will, in all probability, earn France the title.*

likely • *The entire surplus will most likely be handed over.*

presumably • *The spear is presumably the murder weapon.*

problem ① NOUN

an unsatisfactory situation causing difficulties • *the economic problems of the inner city*

difficulty • *This company is facing great difficulties.*

predicament • *the once great club's current predicament*

quandary • *We're in a quandary over our holiday plans.*

trouble • *I had trouble parking this morning.*

problem ② NOUN

a puzzle that needs to be solved • *a mathematical problem*

conundrum • *an apparently insoluble conundrum*

puzzle • *The data has presented astronomers with a puzzle.*

riddle • *the riddle of the birth of the universe*

procedure NOUN

the correct or usual way of doing something • *He did not follow the correct procedure in applying for a visa.*

method • *new teaching methods*

policy • *It is our policy to prosecute shoplifters.*

practice • *a public inquiry into bank practices*

process • *the production process*

strategy • *a strategy for controlling malaria*

system • *an efficient filing system*

P

proceed ① VERB

to start doing or continue to do something • I had no idea how to proceed.

begin • He stood up and began to move about the room.

carry on • "Can I start with a couple of questions?"—"Carry on."

continue • I need some advice before I can continue with this task.

get under way • The court case got under way last autumn.

go on • Go on with your work.

start • I started to follow him up the stairs.

ANTONYM:
• cease

proceed ② VERB (FORMAL)

to move in a particular direction • She proceeded along the hallway.

advance • I advanced slowly, one step at a time.

continue • He continued rapidly up the path.

go on • They went on through the forest.

make your way • He made his way to the marketplace.

progress • She progressed slowly along the coast in an easterly direction.

travel • You can travel to Helsinki tomorrow.

process ① NOUN

a method of doing or producing something • The building process was spread over three years.

course of action • It is important that we take the right course of action.

means • The move is a means to fight crime.

method • new teaching methods

procedure • the correct procedure for applying for a visa

system • an efficient filing system

process ② VERB

to deal with or treat something • Your application is being processed.

deal with • the way that banks deal with complaints

dispose of • They disposed of the problem quickly.

handle • She didn't know how to handle the situation.

take care of • They left it to me to try and take care of everything.

produce ① VERB

to make something • Marmalade is produced from Seville oranges

construct • an inner frame constructed from timber

create • It was created from odds and ends.

invent • He invented the first electric clock.

make • One of my jobs was to make the tea.

manufacture • They manufacture plastics.

produce ② VERB

to bring out something so it can be seen or discussed • To hire a car you must produce a driving licence.

P

advance • *Many new theories have been advanced recently.*
bring forward • *We will bring forward new proposals for legislation.*
bring to light • *new evidence brought to light by the police*
put forward • *He has put forward new peace proposals.*

product NOUN
something that is made to be sold • *Many household products give off noxious fumes.*
commodity • *basic commodities such as bread and milk*
goods • *imported goods*
merchandise • *The club sells a wide range of merchandise.*
produce • *locally grown produce*

productive ① ADJECTIVE
producing a large number of things • *Training makes workers highly productive.*
fertile • *a product of his fertile imagination*
fruitful • *a landscape that was fruitful and lush*
prolific • *She is a prolific writer of novels and short stories.*
ANTONYM:
• unproductive

productive ② ADJECTIVE
bringing favourable results • *I'm hopeful the talks will be productive.*
constructive • *constructive criticism*
useful • *We made some progress during a useful exchange.*

valuable • *The experience was very valuable.*
worthwhile • *It had been a worthwhile discussion.*
ANTONYM:
• unproductive

profession NOUN
a job that requires advanced education or training • *Harper was a teacher by profession.*
business • *May I ask you what business you're in?*
career • *a career in journalism*
occupation • *her new occupation as an author*

proficient ADJECTIVE
able to do something well • *They tend to be proficient in foreign languages.*
able • *an able young rider*
accomplished • *an accomplished fundraiser*
adept • *an adept guitar player*
capable • *a very capable speaker*
competent • *a competent civil servant*
efficient • *a team of efficient workers*
skilful • *He is skilful at managing people.*
skilled • *a network of amateur but highly skilled observers of wildlife*
ANTONYM:
• incompetent

profit ① NOUN
money gained in business or trade • *The bank made pre-tax profits of $3.5 million.*

profit | 464

earnings • *her earnings as an accountant*
proceeds • *The proceeds from the concert will go to charity.*
revenue • *tax revenues*
surplus • *Japan's trade surplus*
takings • *the shop's weekly takings*

ANTONYM:
• loss

profit ② VERB

to gain or benefit from something • *They profited shamefully at the expense of my family.*
capitalise on • *The rebels are trying to capitalise on the public's discontent.*
exploit • *They are trying to exploit the troubles to their advantage.*
make the most of
• *Happiness is the ability to make the most of what you have.*
take advantage of • *She took advantage of his generosity.*

program NOUN

a set of instructions that a computer follows to perform a task • *a program to convert dollars to pounds*
app • *This app allows you to search by date or location.*
application • *a great application for editing photographs*
software • *a fairly simple software package*

programme ① NOUN

a planned series of events • *a programme of official engagements*

agenda • *This is sure to be an item on the agenda again next week.*
schedule • *We both have such hectic schedules.*
timetable • *We've finally managed to agree on a timetable for formal talks.*

programme ② NOUN

a broadcast on radio or television • *local news programmes*
broadcast • *a broadcast by the President*
show • *my favourite TV show*

progress ① NOUN

improvement or development • *progress in the treatment of diabetes*
advance • *dramatic advances in road safety*
breakthrough • *a breakthrough in their research*
headway • *The police are making little headway in the investigation.*
improvement • *considerable room for improvement in facilities for patients*

progress ② VERB

to become more advanced or skilful • *His reading is progressing well.*
advance • *Japan has advanced from a rural society to an industrial power.*
blossom • *In just a few years it has blossomed into an international event.*
develop • *workshops designed to develop skills*

improve • *Their French has improved enormously.*

prohibit VERB
to forbid something or make it illegal • *a law which prohibited trading on Sundays*

ban • *The country will ban smoking in all public places this year.*

forbid • *The country's constitution forbids the military use of nuclear energy.*

outlaw • *In 1975 gambling was outlawed.*

prevent • *Residents may be prevented from leaving the islands.*

ANTONYM:
• allow

prominent ① ADJECTIVE
important • *the children of very prominent or successful parents*

eminent • *an eminent scientist*

famous • *England's most famous modern artist*

important • *an important figure in the media*

notable • *the notable linguist, Henriette Walter*

noted • *a noted Hebrew scholar*

renowned • *Sir William Crookes, the renowned chemist*

well-known • *He liked to surround himself with well-known people.*

prominent ② ADJECTIVE
very noticeable, or sticking out a long way • *a prominent feature of the landscape*

conspicuous • *a conspicuous landmark*

eye-catching • *I outlined it in black to make it more eye-catching.*

jutting • *a jutting chin*

noticeable • *Squeezing spots only makes them more noticeable.*

obvious • *His cultural roots are most obvious in his poetry.*

pronounced • *The exhibition has a pronounced Scottish theme.*

striking • *a striking aspect of these statistics*

promise ① VERB
to say that you will definitely do or not do something • *I promise not to be back too late.*

assure • *She assured me that she would deal with the problem.*

give your word • *He had given us his word he would join the club.*

guarantee • *Most countries guarantee the right to free education.*

pledge • *They have pledged to support the opposition.*

vow • *I vowed that someday I would return to live in Europe.*

promise ② VERB
to show signs of • *This promised to be a very long night.*

hint at • *One finding hints at support for this theory.*

indicate • *His early work indicates talent.*

show signs of • *Developments in medical robotics are showing early signs of promise.*

P

promise ③ NOUN

an undertaking to do or not do something • *If you make a promise, you should keep it.*

assurance • *He gave written assurance that he would start work at once.*

guarantee • *They can give no guarantee that they will fulfil their obligations.*

pledge • *a pledge to step up cooperation between the two countries*

undertaking • *an undertaking that he would be a responsible parent*

vow • *I kept my marriage vows.*

promising ADJECTIVE

seeming likely to be good or successful • *a promising young footballer*

gifted • *She was proving to be a gifted pianist.*

rising • *a rising star in the world of photography*

talented • *the most talented students in the school*

up-and-coming • *an up-and-coming actor*

promote ① VERB

to encourage the progress or success of something • *All attempts to promote a ceasefire have failed.*

back • *She backed the new initiative enthusiastically.*

support • *He thanked everyone who had supported the strike.*

promote ② VERB

to encourage the sale of a product by advertising

• *She's in Europe promoting her new film.*

advertise • *She is contracted to advertise her beauty products.*

plug (INFORMAL) • *He was on the show to plug his latest film.*

publicise • *I was publicising the book in London.*

promote ③ VERB

to raise someone to a higher rank or position • *Fiona has been promoted twice in two years.*

elevate • *He was elevated to the post of Prime Minister.*

upgrade • *He was upgraded to supervisor.*

prompt ① VERB

to make someone decide to do something • *Falling rates of pay have prompted consumers to stop buying new cars.*

cause • *What caused you to change your mind?*

induce • *Many teachers were induced to take early retirement.*

inspire • *These herbs will inspire you to try out all sorts of dishes.*

motivate • *How do you motivate people to work hard?*

spur • *What spurs these firefighters to risk their lives?*

prompt ② VERB

to encourage someone to say something • *"What was that you were saying about a guided tour?" he prompted her.*

coax • *"Tell us what happened next," she coaxed me.*

remind • *"You stopped in the middle of your story," I reminded him.*

prompt ③ ADVERB
exactly at the time mentioned
• *The invitation specifies eight o'clock prompt.*
exactly • *He arrived at exactly five o'clock.*
on the dot • *At nine o'clock on the dot, they have breakfast.*
precisely • *The meeting began at precisely 4.00 pm.*
sharp • *She planned to get up at 8.00 sharp.*

prompt ④ ADJECTIVE
done without any delay • *a serious condition which needs prompt treatment*
immediate • *These incidents had an immediate effect.*
instant • *He took an instant dislike to this woman.*
instantaneous • *This would result in his instantaneous dismissal.*
quick • *hoping for a quick end to the dispute*
rapid • *their rapid response to the situation*
swift • *make a swift decision*

prone ① ADJECTIVE
having a tendency to be affected by or do something
• *She is prone to exaggeration.*
disposed • *I might have been disposed to like him in other circumstances.*
given • *I am not very given to emotional displays.*
inclined • *Nobody felt inclined to argue with Smith.*
liable • *equipment that is liable to break*

susceptible • *She's very susceptible to colds and flu.*

prone ② ADJECTIVE
lying flat and face downwards
• *We were lying prone on the grass.*
face down • *He was lying face down on his bed.*
prostrate • *The injured jockey lay prostrate on the ground.*

proof NOUN
evidence that confirms that something is true or exists
• *You have to have proof of residence in the state of Texas.*
confirmation • *further confirmation that house prices are no longer falling*
evidence • *To date there is no evidence to support this theory.*
testimony • *His testimony was an important element of the prosecution case.*
verification • *verification of her story*

proper ① ADJECTIVE
correct or most suitable • *the proper course of action*
appropriate • *a smart outfit appropriate to the job*
apt • *an apt title for the book*
correct • *the correct way to do things*
fitting • *His address was a fitting end to a bitter campaign.*
right • *He's the right man for the job.*
suitable • *She had no other dress suitable for the occasion.*
ANTONYM:
• *improper*

P

proper ② ADJECTIVE

accepted or conventional • *She wanted a proper wedding.*

accepted • *the accepted way of doing things*

conventional • *conventional surgical methods*

orthodox • *orthodox police methods*

property ① NOUN

the things that belong to someone • *her personal property*

assets • *The company has assets of 3.5 billion euros.*

belongings • *I collected my belongings and left.*

effects • *His daughters were collecting his effects.*

estate • *His estate was valued at $150,000.*

possessions • *People had lost their homes and all their possessions.*

property ② NOUN

a characteristic or quality • *Mint has powerful healing properties.*

attribute • *a normal attribute of human behaviour*

characteristic • *their physical characteristics*

feature • *a feature of the local culture*

hallmark • *His designs show a love of simplicity which is very much his hallmark.*

quality • *mature people with leadership qualities*

trait • *Creativity is a human trait.*

proportion NOUN

part of an amount or group • *a tiny proportion of the population*

percentage • *It has a high percentage of protein.*

quota • *Britain's fishing quota has been cut.*

segment • *a fast-growing segment of the market*

share • *I pay a share of the phone and gas bills.*

prospect NOUN

expectation or something anticipated • *There was no prospect of going home.*

expectation • *The hotel was being renovated in expectation of a tourist boom.*

hope • *There is little hope of improvement now.*

outlook • *Officials say the outlook for next year is gloomy.*

promise • *New Year brought the promise of better things to come.*

protect VERB

to prevent someone or something from being harmed • *Cash dispensers are protected by thick steel and glass.*

defend • *I had to defend myself against the attack.*

guard • *Soldiers guarded homes near the airport.*

safeguard • *action to safeguard the ozone layer*

shelter • *a wooden house, sheltered by a low pointed roof*

shield • *He shielded his head from the sun with a newspaper.*

protection NOUN
something that protects
• *Sheltered arcades offered protection from the sun.*
barrier • *a flood barrier*
buffer • *Keep savings as a buffer against unexpected cash needs.*
cover • *air cover for ground operations*
safeguard • *a safeguard against weeds*
shelter • *an air-raid shelter*

protest ① VERB
to disagree with someone or object to something • *She protested that she was a patriot, not a traitor.*
complain • *People always complain about the noise.*
disagree • *I disagree with that statement.*
disapprove • *Her mother disapproved of her friends.*
object • *We objected strongly but were outvoted.*
oppose • *Many parents oppose bilingual education in schools.*

protest ② NOUN
a strong objection • *The council has ignored their protests by backing the scheme.*
complaint • *the way that banks deal with complaints*
objection • *I questioned the logic of his objections.*
outcry • *The incident caused an international outcry.*

proud ADJECTIVE
feeling pleasure or satisfaction • *I was proud of our players today.*
gratified • *He was gratified by the audience's response.*
honoured • *I am honoured to work with her.*
pleased • *I was pleased to call him my friend.*

prove VERB
to provide evidence that something is definitely true
• *History will prove him to have been right all along.*
ascertain • *They had ascertained that he was not a spy.*
confirm • *X-rays confirmed that she had not broken any bones.*
demonstrate • *You have to demonstrate that you are reliable.*
establish • *The autopsy established the cause of death.*
verify • *I can verify that it takes about thirty seconds.*
ANTONYM:
• disprove

provide VERB
to make something available to someone • *I'll be glad to provide a copy of this.*
contribute • *NATO agreed to contribute troops and equipment.*
equip • *proposals to equip all officers with body armour*
furnish • *They'll be able to furnish you with the rest of the details.*
outfit • *They outfitted him with artificial legs.*
supply • *the blood vessels supplying oxygen to the brain*

P

provoke ① VERB

to try to make someone angry
• I didn't want to do anything to
provoke him.

anger • It's important not to
anger her.

annoy • You're just trying to
annoy me.

enrage (INFORMAL) • He enraged the
government by going back on the
agreement.

goad • My little brother was
always goading me.

insult • I didn't mean to insult you.

irritate • If you go on irritating
that dog, it'll bite you.

tease • I'm sorry, I shouldn't
tease you like that.

provoke ② VERB

to cause an unpleasant
reaction • His comments have
provoked a shocked reaction.

cause • These policies are likely
to cause problems.

evoke • The programme has
evoked a storm of protest.

produce • The decision produced
a furious reaction among fans.

prompt • The allegations
prompted an indignant response
from the accused.

rouse • This roused a feeling of
rebellion in him.

set off • The arrival of the supply
van set off a minor riot among
waiting villagers.

spark off • a political crisis
sparked off by religious violence

pry VERB

to try to find out about someone
else's private business • We do

not want people prying into our
business.

interfere • I wish everyone
would stop interfering and just
leave me alone.

intrude • The press were
intruding into my personal life.

poke your nose in
(INFORMAL) • Who asked you to
poke your nose in?

poke your nose into
(INFORMAL) • strangers who
poke their noses into our affairs

snoop (INFORMAL) • He was
snooping around Kim's hotel
room.

public ① NOUN

people in general • the public's
confidence in the government

masses • a quest to bring the
internet to the masses

nation • The President spoke to
the nation.

people • the will of the people

populace • a large proportion of
the populace

society • a menace to society

public ② ADJECTIVE

relating to people in general
• public support for the idea

civic • a sense of civic pride

general • The project should
raise general awareness about
bullying.

popular • Popular anger has
been expressed in
demonstrations.

universal • the universal
outrage at the deaths

public ③ ADJECTIVE

provided for everyone to use

or open to anyone • *public transport*

communal • *a communal dining room*

community • *a village community centre*

open to the public • *Part of the castle is now open to the public.*

universal • *universal health care*

ANTONYM:
• private

publicise VERB

to advertise something or make it widely known • *The author appeared on TV to publicise her book.*

advertise • *The product has been much advertised in specialist magazines.*

plug (INFORMAL) • *another celebrity plugging their latest book*

promote • *a tour to promote his second solo album*

publicity NOUN

information or advertisements about an item or event • *government publicity campaigns*

advertising • *perfume advertising in women's magazines*

plug (INFORMAL) • *The whole interview was an unashamed plug for her new book.*

promotion • *They've spent a lot of money on advertising and promotion.*

publish VERB

to make a piece of writing available for reading • *We publish a range of titles.*

bring out • *The newspapers all brought out special editions.*

post • *He posted a picture of himself holding a small piece of paper.*

print • *a letter printed in the Times yesterday*

put out • *a statement put out by the Iraqi news agency*

puff VERB

to breathe loudly and quickly with your mouth open • *I could see he was unfit, because he was puffing.*

breathe heavily • *She reached the top of the hill, breathing heavily.*

gasp • *He opened the window and gasped for air.*

pant • *Amy climbed rapidly until she was panting with the effort.*

wheeze • *His chest problems made him wheeze.*

pull ① VERB

to draw an object towards you • *a wooden plough pulled by oxen*

drag • *He dragged his chair towards the table.*

draw • *He drew his chair nearer the fire.*

haul • *A crane was used to haul the car out of the stream.*

tow • *They threatened to tow away my van.*

tug • *She kicked him, tugging his thick hair.*

yank • *She yanked open the drawer.*

ANTONYM:
• push

P

pull ② NOUN

the attraction or influence of something • *The pull of Mexico was too strong.*

attraction • *The attraction of Hollywood began to pall.*

lure • *The lure of rural life is as strong as ever.*

magnetism • *the sheer magnetism of his presence*

punctual ADJECTIVE

arriving or leaving at the correct time • *the world's most punctual airlines*

in good time • *It is now 5am and we are in good time.*

on time • *I'm generally early or on time for an appointment.*

prompt • *We expect you to be prompt for all your classes.*

punctuation NOUN

PUNCTUATION MARKS

apostrophe
asterisk
bracket
bullet point
colon
comma
dash
exclamation mark
full stop
hyphen
question mark
semicolon
slash
speech marks or quotation
 marks

punish VERB

to make someone suffer a penalty for some misbehaviour • *I got punished for insolence.*

discipline • *He was disciplined by his company but not dismissed.*

penalise • *Poor performance is not penalised in a formal way.*

rap someone's knuckles
• *The company got its knuckles rapped for this advertisement.*

sentence • *He has admitted the charge and will be sentenced later.*

throw the book at • *The football authorities seem certain to throw the book at him.*

punishment NOUN

a penalty for a crime or offence • *The punishment must always fit the crime.*

penalty • *One of those arrested could face the death penalty.*

retribution • *He didn't want any further involvement for fear of retribution.*

puny ADJECTIVE

very small and weak • *He's always been a puny lad.*

feeble • *He was ill and feeble.*

frail • *She lay in bed looking frail*

sickly • *He has been a sickly child*

skinny • *a skinny little boy*

weak • *His arms and legs were weak.*

pupil NOUN

a student taught at a school • *She is a model pupil.*

scholar (SOUTH AFRICAN) • *a bunch of rowdy scholars*

schoolboy • *a group of ten-year-old schoolboys*

schoolchild • *The bus was packed with schoolchildren.*

schoolgirl • *an appealing role model for schoolgirls*

student • *The students are sorted into three ability groups.*

pure ① ADJECTIVE
clean and free from harmful substances • *The water is pure enough to drink.*

clean • *Tiled kitchen floors are easy to keep clean.*

germ-free • *chlorine gas used to keep water germ-free*

pasteurised • *The milk is pasteurised to kill bacteria.*

spotless • *The living room was spotless.*

sterilised • *sterilised surgical equipment*

ANTONYM:
• impure

pure ② ADJECTIVE
complete and total • *a matter of pure luck*

absolute • *You're talking absolute nonsense.*

complete • *complete and utter rubbish*

outright • *an outright rejection of the deal*

sheer • *acts of sheer desperation*

unmitigated • *Last year's crop was an unmitigated disaster.*

utter • *This, of course, is utter nonsense.*

purple NOUN or ADJECTIVE

SHADES OF PURPLE
amethyst
aubergine
gentian
heather

heliotrope
indigo
lavender
lilac
magenta
mauve
mulberry
plum
puce
royal purple
violet

purpose ① NOUN
the reason for something • *What is the purpose of this meeting?*

aim • *the aim of the policy*

function • *Their main function is to raise capital for industry.*

intention • *The intention of the scheme is to encourage faster sales.*

object • *the object of the exercise*

point • *I don't see the point of it.*

reason • *What is the real reason for the delay?*

purpose ②: **on purpose** ADVERB
deliberately • *Did you do that on purpose?*

by design • *The pair met often – at first by chance but later by design.*

deliberately • *It looks as if the fire was started deliberately.*

intentionally • *I've never hurt anyone intentionally.*

knowingly • *He said that he'd never knowingly broken the law.*

purposely • *They are purposely withholding information.*

P

push ① VERB

to apply force to something in order to move it • *She pushed the door open.*

press • *He pressed his back against the door.*

ram • *He rammed the key into the lock.*

shove • *He shoved her aside.*

thrust • *They thrust him into the back of the jeep.*

ANTONYM:
• pull

push ② VERB

to persuade someone into doing something • *His mother pushed him into auditioning for a part.*

encourage • *She encouraged me to stick to the diet.*

persuade • *They persuaded him to moderate his views.*

press • *Trade unions are pressing him to stand firm.*

urge • *He had urged her to come to Ireland.*

pushy ADJECTIVE (INFORMAL)

unpleasantly forceful and determined • *a confident and pushy young woman*

aggressive • *a very aggressive business executive*

ambitious • *You have to be ambitious to make it in this business.*

assertive • *She encouraged her children to be more assertive.*

bossy (FORMAL) • *He remembers being rather bossy as a child.*

forceful • *Sarah is notorious for her forceful and quarrelsome nature.*

obtrusive • *"You are rude and obtrusive, Mr Smith," said Tommy.*

put ① VERB

to place something somewhere • *She put the photograph on the desk.*

deposit • *On his way out he deposited a glass in front of me.*

lay • *Lay a sheet of newspaper or the floor.*

place • *He placed it in the inside pocket of his jacket.*

position • *Plants were carefully positioned in the alcove.*

rest • *He rested his arms on the back of the chair.*

put ② VERB

to express something • *I think you put that very well.*

phrase • *I would have phrased quite differently.*

word • *You misinterpreted his letter, or else he worded it poorly*

put down VERB (INFORMAL)

to criticise someone and make them appear foolish • *I know that I do put people down occasionally.*

belittle • *She's always belittling her husband in public.*

criticise • *She rarely criticised any of her children.*

find fault with • *I wish you wouldn't find fault with me in front of the kids.*

humiliate • *Why would you try humiliate me in front of my friends*

put off VERB

to delay something • Ministers
have put off making a decision
until next month.

defer • Customers often defer
payment for as long as possible.

delay • She wants to delay the
wedding.

postpone • The visit has been
postponed indefinitely.

put back • The news conference
has been put back a couple of
hours.

put on ice • The decision has
been put on ice until October.

reschedule • Since I'll be away,
I'd like to reschedule the meeting.

put up with VERB

to tolerate something
disagreeable • They won't put
up with a return to the bad old
days.

abide • I can't abide arrogant
people.

bear • He can't bear to talk
about it.

stand • She cannot stand her boss.

stand for • We won't stand for it
any more.

stomach • He could not
stomach violence.

tolerate • She can no longer
tolerate the position she is in.

puzzle ① VERB

to perplex and confuse • There
was something about her that
puzzled me.

baffle • An apple tree producing
square fruit is baffling experts.

bewilder • His silence
bewildered her.

confuse • German politics
surprised and confused him.

mystify • The audience were
mystified by the plot.

stump • I was stumped by an
unexpected question.

puzzle ② NOUN

a game or question that
requires a lot of thought to
solve • a crossword puzzle

brain-teaser (INFORMAL)
• It took me ages to solve that
brain-teaser.

poser • Here is a little poser
for you.

problem • a mathematical
problem

riddle • See if you can answer
this riddle.

P

Qq

qualification ① NOUN
a skill or achievement • *His qualifications are impressive.*
ability • *a man of considerable abilities*
accomplishment • *Carl was proud of his son's accomplishments.*
achievement • *the highest academic achievement*
capability • *Her capabilities were not fully appreciated.*
quality • *Colley's leadership qualities*
skill • *a skill you can use*

qualification ② NOUN
something added to make a statement less strong • *The argument is not true without qualification.*
condition • *You can make any conditions you like.*
exception • *a major exception to this general argument*
modification • *to consider modifications to his proposal*
reservation • *men whose work I admire without reservation*

qualify VERB
to pass the tests necessary for an activity • *I qualified as a doctor 30 years ago.*

become licensed • *You can only become licensed by doing an accredited course.*
gain qualifications • *the opportunity to gain medical qualifications*
get certified • *They wanted to get certified as divers.*
graduate • *She graduated as a physiotherapist in 1960.*

quality ① NOUN
the measure of how good something is • *The quality of food is very poor.*
calibre • *a man of your calibre*
distinction • *a chef of great distinction*
grade • *high grade meat and poultry*
merit • *a work of real merit*
value • *He set a high value upon their friendship.*
worth • *a person's true worth*

quality ② NOUN
a characteristic of something • *These qualities are essential for success.*
aspect • *every aspect of our lives*
characteristic • *their physical characteristics*
feature • *the most striking feature of his work*
mark • *the mark of a great composer*
property • *the magnetic properties of iron*
trait • *the young Ms Rankine's personality traits*

quantity ① NOUN
an amount you can measure

or count • *a large quantity of fish*
amount • *a small amount of mayonnaise*
number • *There are a limited number of seats available.*
part • *the greater part of his wealth*
sum • *a large sum of money*

quantity ② NOUN
the amount of something that there is • *emphasis on quality rather than quantity*
extent • *the extent of the damage*
measure • *The government has had a fair measure of success.*
size • *He gauged the size of the audience.*
volume • *the sheer volume of traffic and accidents*

quarrel ① NOUN
an angry argument • *I had a terrible quarrel with my brother.*
argument • *an argument about money*
disagreement • *My instructor and I had a brief disagreement.*
dispute • *Brand eavesdropped on the petty dispute.*
feud • *a two-year feud between neighbours*
fight • *It was a silly fight about where we parked the car.*
row • *Maxine and I had a terrible row.*
squabble • *minor squabbles about phone bills*

quarrel ② VERB
to have an angry argument • *My brother quarrelled with my father.*
argue • *They were still arguing later.*
bicker • *They bickered endlessly over procedure.*
clash • *She had clashed with Doyle in the past.*
fall out (INFORMAL) • *Mum and I used to fall out a lot.*
fight • *The couple often fought with their son.*
row • *He had rowed with his girlfriend.*
squabble • *The children were squabbling over the remote control.*

queasy ADJECTIVE
feeling slightly sick • *He already felt queasy.*
ill • *I was feeling ill.*
nauseous • *The medication may make you feel nauseous.*
queer (OLD-FASHIONED) • *Twenty minutes later, he began to feel queer.*
sick • *The very thought of food made him feel sick.*
unwell • *He felt unwell this afternoon.*

query ① NOUN
a question • *If you have any queries, please contact us.*
inquiry • *I'll be happy to answer all your inquiries, if I can.*
question • *The President refused to answer further questions on the subject.*
ANTONYM:
• response

q

query ② VERB
to question something
because it seems wrong • No
one queried my decision.

challenge • The move was
challenged by two countries.

dispute • He disputed the
allegations.

object to • A lot of people
objected to the plan.

question • It never occurred to
me to question the doctor's
decisions.

question ① NOUN
a problem that needs to be
discussed • Can we get back to
the question of the car?

issue • What is your view on this
issue?

motion • The conference is now
debating the motion.

point • There is another point to
consider.

subject • He raised the subject
of money.

topic • the topic of where to go
on holiday

question ② VERB
to ask someone questions
• A man is being questioned by
police.

examine • Lawyers examined
the witnesses.

interrogate • I interrogated
everyone even slightly involved.

probe • tabloid journalists
probing us for details

quiz • She quizzed me quite
closely for a while.

ANTONYM:
• answer

question ③ VERB
to express doubts about
something • He never stopped
questioning his own beliefs.

challenge • Rose convincingly
challenged the story.

dispute • Nobody disputed that
Davey was clever.

distrust • I distrusted my ability
to keep quiet.

doubt • Nobody doubted his
sincerity.

query • No one queried my
decision.

suspect • Do we suspect the
motives of our friends?

quick ① ADJECTIVE
moving with great speed
• You'll have to be quick to catch
the flight.

brisk • a brisk walk

fast • a very fast driver

hasty • He spoke in a hasty,
nervous way.

rapid • a rapid rise through the
company

speedy • a speedy recovery

swift • She is as swift as an
arrow.

ANTONYM:
• slow

quick ② ADJECTIVE
lasting only a short time
• a quick chat

brief • a brief meeting

cursory • a cursory glance
inside the van

hasty • a hasty meal of bread
and soup

hurried • He ate a hurried
breakfast.

perfunctory • *With a perfunctory smile, she walked past Jessica.*

ANTONYM:
• long

quick ③ ADJECTIVE
happening without any delay
• *a quick response*
hasty • *This is no hasty decision.*
prompt • *Prompt action is needed.*
sudden • *this week's sudden cold snap*

quickly ADVERB
with great speed • *Stop me if I'm speaking too quickly.*
fast • *How fast were you driving?*
hastily • *sheltering in hastily erected tents*
hurriedly • *students hurriedly taking notes*
rapidly • *moving rapidly across the field*
speedily • *She speedily recovered herself.*
swiftly • *They had to act swiftly to save him.*

ANTONYM:
• slowly

quiet ① ADJECTIVE
making very little noise • *The children were quiet and contented.*
hushed • *Tales were exchanged in hushed tones.*
inaudible • *a tiny, almost inaudible squeak*
low • *I spoke in a low voice to Sullivan.*

silent • *He could speak no English and was silent.*
soft • *There was some soft music playing.*

ANTONYM:
• noisy

quiet ② ADJECTIVE
peaceful and calm • *a quiet evening at home*
calm • *The city seems relatively calm today.*
mild • *The night was mild.*
peaceful • *a peaceful old house*
restful • *a restful scene*
serene • *the beautiful, serene park*
tranquil • *a tranquil lake*

quiet ③ NOUN
silence or lack of noise • *The teacher called for quiet.*
calmness • *the calmness of this area*
peace • *I enjoy peace and quiet.*
serenity • *the peace and serenity of a tropical sunset*
silence • *There was a silence around the table.*
stillness • *the stillness of the summer night*
tranquillity • *the tranquillity of village life*

ANTONYM:
• noise

quit VERB
to leave a place or stop doing something • *Leigh quit his job as a salesman.*
discontinue • *Do not discontinue the treatment without seeing your doctor.*

q

give up • *She gave up smoking last year.*

leave • *He left school with no qualifications.*

resign • *Scott resigned from the firm.*

retire • *Littlejohn was forced to retire from the race.*

stop • *I stopped working last year to go travelling.*

quite ① ADVERB
fairly but not very • *He is quite old.*

fairly • *Both ships are fairly new.*

moderately • *a moderately attractive man*

rather • *I made some rather bad mistakes.*

reasonably • *I can dance reasonably well.*

somewhat • *He's somewhat deaf.*

quite ② ADVERB
completely and totally • *Jane lay quite still.*

absolutely • *I absolutely refuse to get married.*

completely • *something completely different*

entirely • *an entirely new approach*

fully • *He has still not fully recovered.*

perfectly • *They are perfectly safe to eat.*

totally • *The fire totally destroyed the house.*

quote VERB
to repeat the exact words someone has said • *She quoted a great line from Shakespeare.*

cite • *She cites a favourite poem by George Herbert.*

extract • *This material has been extracted from the handbook.*

recite • *They recited poetry to one another.*

repeat • *Could you repeat the whole interview word for word?*

Rr

race ① NOUN
a group of human beings with similar physical characteristics • *Discrimination on the grounds of race is illegal.*
ethnic group • *Ethnic group and nationality are often different.*
nation • *a mature and cultured nation*
people • *an address to the American people*

race ② VERB
to move very quickly • *When school was over, Kate raced home.*
dash • *He dashed upstairs.*
fly • *I must fly or I'll miss my train.*
hurry • *They hurried down the street.*
run • *The gunmen escaped by running into the woods.*
speed • *speeding along as fast as I could*
tear • *The door flew open and she tore into the room.*

racket ① NOUN
a lot of noise • *The racket went on past midnight.*
clamour • *She could hear a clamour in the road.*
commotion • *He heard a commotion outside.*
din • *make themselves heard over the din of the crowd*
hubbub • *His voice was drowned out by the hubbub of the fans.*
noise • *There was too much noise in the room.*
row • *"Whatever is that row?" she demanded.*
rumpus • *There was such a rumpus, she had to shout to make herself heard.*

racket ② NOUN
an illegal way of making money • *a protection racket*
enterprise • *a money-laundering enterprise*
fraud • *tax frauds*
scheme • *a quick money-making scheme*

rage ① NOUN
a feeling of very strong anger • *trembling with rage*
anger • *She felt deep anger at what he had said.*
frenzy • *Their behaviour drove her into a frenzy.*
fury • *Her face was distorted with fury and pain.*
wrath • *He incurred the wrath of the referee.*

rage ② VERB
to be angry or speak angrily about something • *He was raging at their lack of response.*
be furious • *He is furious at the way his wife has been treated.*
fume • *I was still fuming over her remark.*

r

rage ① NOUN

lose your temper • They had never seen me lose my temper before.

rave • She cried and raved for weeks.

storm • "It's a disaster!" he stormed.

rage ③ VERB

to continue with great force • The fire raged out of control.

be at its height • when the storm was at its height

rampage • a mob rampaging through the town

storm • armies storming across the continent

surge • The flood surged through the village.

raid ① VERB

to attack something by force • Soldiers raided the capital.

assault • Their stronghold was assaulted by pirates.

attack • We are being attacked!

break into • No-one saw them break into the warehouse.

invade • The invading army took all their food supplies.

plunder • plundering the homes of the inhabitants

raid ② NOUN

an attack on something • a bank raid

attack • a surprise attack on the house

break-in • The break-in occurred last night.

foray • Guerrillas made forays into the territory.

rain ① NOUN

water falling from the clouds • A spot of rain fell on her hand.

deluge • homes damaged in the deluge

downpour • A two-day downpour swelled water levels.

drizzle • The drizzle had stopped and the sun was shining.

rainfall • four years of below average rainfall

showers • bright spells followed by scattered showers

rain ② VERB

to fall from the sky in drops • It rained the whole weekend.

drizzle • It was starting to drizzle when I left.

pour • We drove all the way in pouring rain.

teem • It teemed the entire day.

raise ① VERB

to make something higher • a drive to raise standards of literacy

elevate • Emotional stress can elevate blood pressure.

heave • He heaved his leg into an easier position.

hoist • He climbed on the roof to hoist the flag.

lift • She lifted the last of her drink to her lips.

ANTONYM:
• lower

raise ② VERB

to look after children until they are grown up • the house where she was raised

bring up • She brought up four children single-handed.

nurture • *the best way to nurture a child to adulthood*
rear • *He reared his sister's family as well as his own.*

raise ③ VERB

to mention or suggest something • *He had raised no objections at the time.*
advance • *Some important ideas were advanced at the conference.*
bring up • *I hesitate to bring up this matter with you, but I have no choice.*
broach • *Eventually I broached the subject of her early life.*
introduce • *always willing to introduce a new topic*
moot • *The project was first mooted last year.*
suggest • *one possibility that might be suggested*

ramble ① NOUN

a long walk in the countryside • *They went for a ramble through the woods.*
excursion • *They organised an excursion into the hills.*
hike • *a long hike along the valley floor*
stroll • *The next day we took a stroll along the river bank.*
walk • *We often go for walks in the country.*

ramble ② VERB

to go for a long walk • *freedom to ramble across the moors*
amble • *ambling along a country lane*
stray • *You mustn't stray across the border.*

stroll • *whistling as he strolled along the road*
walk • *We finished the evening by walking along the beach.*
wander • *He loved to wander in the woods.*

ramble ③ VERB

to talk in a confused way • *He started rambling and repeating himself.*
babble • *She babbled on and on about the visitors.*
chatter • *I was so nervous that I chattered away like an idiot.*

rampage ① VERB

to rush about angrily or violently • *children rampaging round the garden*
go berserk • *The crowd went berserk at the sight of him.*
rage • *The castle was stormed by a raging mob.*
run amok • *a story about a giant ape running amok in New York*
run riot • *The emperor's army ran riot across the continent.*

rampage ②: on the rampage ADJECTIVE

rushing about in a wild and violent way • *a bull on the rampage*
amok • *An elephant ran amok and killed several people.*
berserk • *The fans went berserk and mobbed the stage.*
wild • *They just went wild after he left.*

random ① ADJECTIVE

not based on a definite plan

r

• random violence against innocent victims

aimless • after several hours of aimless searching

arbitrary • Arbitrary arrests and detention without trial were common.

haphazard • He had never seen such a haphazard approach to writing.

indiscriminate • the indiscriminate use of fertilisers

spot • picked up in a spot check

random ② : at random ADVERB

without any definite plan • chosen at random

aimlessly • wandering around aimlessly for hours

arbitrarily • The questions were chosen quite arbitrarily.

haphazardly • The books were stacked haphazardly on the shelves.

indiscriminately • This disease strikes indiscriminately.

randomly • a randomly selected sample

range ① NOUN

the maximum limits of something • Tactical nuclear weapons have shorter ranges.

bounds • the bounds of good taste

extent • the full extent of my knowledge

field • The subject covers a very wide field.

limits • outside the city limits

province • This doesn't fall within our province.

scope • He promised to widen the scope of their activities.

range ② NOUN

a number of different things of the same kind • a wide range of colours

assortment • There was a good assortment to choose from.

class • Cars in this class are expensive.

gamut • I experienced the whole gamut of emotions.

selection • a wide selection of delicious meals

series • a completely new model series

variety • The shop stocks a variety of local craft products.

range ③ VERB

to vary between two extremes • goods ranging between the everyday and the exotic

extend • The reclaimed land extends from here to the river.

go • Their sizes go from very small to enormous.

run • Accommodation runs from log cabins to high-standard hotels.

stretch • with interests that stretched from chemicals to sugar

vary • The cycle of sunspots varies between 8 to 15 years.

rank ① NOUN

someone's level in a group • He rose to the rank of captain.

class • relationships between social classes

echelon • the upper echelons of society

grade • *Staff turnover is high among the junior grades.*
level • *various levels of the judiciary system*
standing • *a woman of wealth and social standing*
station • *a humble station in life*
status • *promoted to the status of foreman*

rank ② NOUN

a row of people or things • *ranks of police in riot gear*
column • *a column of figures*
file • *They walked in single file to the top.*
line • *He waited in a line of slow-moving vehicles.*
row • *She lived in the middle of a row of pretty cottages.*

rank ③ ADJECTIVE

complete and absolute • *It was rank stupidity to go there alone.*
absolute • *not intended for absolute beginners*
complete • *her complete ignorance*
downright • *That was just downright rudeness.*
sheer • *his sheer stupidity*
unmitigated • *an unmitigated villain*
utter • *his utter disregard for other people*

rare ADJECTIVE

not common or frequent • *a rare species of bird*
exceptional • *in exceptional circumstances*
few • *Genuine friends are few.*
scarce • *Jobs are becoming increasingly scarce.*

sparse • *Information about the tests is sparse.*
sporadic • *occurring at only sporadic intervals*
uncommon • *The disease is uncommon in younger women.*
unusual • *an unusual variety but a very attractive one*
ANTONYM:
• common

rash ① ADJECTIVE

acting in a hasty and foolish way • *It would be rash to act on such flimsy evidence.*
foolhardy • *Some described his behaviour as foolhardy.*
hasty • *This is no hasty decision.*
impetuous • *As usual, he reacted in a heated and impetuous way.*
impulsive • *He is too impulsive to take this responsibility.*
reckless • *his reckless driving*

rash ② NOUN

an irritated area on your skin • *I noticed a rash on my leg.*
eruption • *an unpleasant skin eruption*
outbreak • *an outbreak of blisters around his mouth*

rash ③ NOUN

a large number of events happening together • *a rash of strikes*
epidemic • *A victim of the recent epidemic of shootings.*
flood • *a flood of complaints about the programme*
plague • *Last year there was a plague of burglaries.*

r

spate • *a spate of attacks on horses*

wave • *the current wave of violent attacks*

rate ① NOUN

the speed or frequency of something • *appearing at the rate of one a week*

frequency • *She phoned with increasing frequency.*

pace • *at an accelerated pace*

speed • *moving at the speed of light*

tempo • *They wanted to speed up the tempo of change.*

velocity • *changes in wind velocity*

rate ② NOUN

the cost or charge for something • *phone calls at cheap rates*

charge • *An annual charge will be made for this service.*

cost • *a low-cost mortgage*

fee • *The work will be invoiced at the usual fee.*

price • *falling share prices*

tariff • *How much you pay depends on your tariff.*

rate ③ VERB

to give an opinion of someone's qualities • *He was rated as one of the best.*

appraise • *She gave me an appraising glance.*

class • *classed as one of the top ten athletes*

consider • *I considered myself to be quite good at maths.*

count • *That would be counted as wrong.*

rank • *The hotel was ranked as one of the world's best.*

regard • *a highly regarded member of staff*

rather ADVERB

to a certain extent • *We got along rather well.*

fairly • *Both ships are fairly new.*

pretty (INFORMAL) • *I'm pretty tired now.*

quite • *The cottage looks quite ordinary from the road.*

relatively • *I think I'm relatively easy to get on with.*

slightly • *slightly startled by his sudden appearance*

somewhat • *He said, somewhat unconvincingly, that he would pay.*

rational ADJECTIVE

using reason rather than emotion • *to arrive at a rational conclusion*

enlightened • *enlightened companies who take a pragmatic view*

logical • *There must be a logical explanation for it.*

reasonable • *a perfectly reasonable decision*

sensible • *The sensible thing is to leave them alone.*

rave ① VERB

to talk in an uncontrolled way • *He started raving about being treated badly.*

babble • *She babbled on and on about her plans.*

rage • *He was raging at their lack of response.*

rant • *She started ranting about her boss's attitude.*

R

rave ② VERB (INFORMAL)
to be enthusiastic about
something • *She raved about
the facilities there.*

be wild about (INFORMAL)
• *He was just wild about the play.*
enthuse • *She enthused about
the local architecture.*
gush • *"It was brilliant!" he
gushed.*

reach ① VERB
to arrive somewhere • *He did
not stop until he reached the
door.*

arrive at • *They planted a flag
when they arrived at the top.*
get as far as • *If we get as far as
the coast we will be quite
satisfied.*
get to • *You must get to the end
before noon.*
make • *They didn't think they
would make the summit.*

reach ② VERB
to extend as far as something
• *Her cloak reached to the
ground.*

extend to • *The boundaries
extend to the edge of the lake.*
go as far as • *Try to make the
ball go as far as the trees.*

reach ③ VERB
to arrive at a certain stage or
level • *Unemployment has
reached record levels.*

arrive at • *to arrive at a false
conclusion*
attain • *He was close to
attaining his personal best.*
climb to • *Attendance climbed
to a record level this year.*

fall to • *Profits are expected to
fall to their lowest level.*
rise to • *She rose rapidly to the
top of her profession.*

reaction ① NOUN
a person's response to
something • *Reaction to the
visit was mixed.*

acknowledgment • *She made
no acknowledgment of my
question.*
answer • *In answer to
speculation in the press, she
declared her interest.*
feedback • *Continue to ask for
feedback on your work.*
response • *in response to a
request from the members*

reaction ② NOUN
a response to something
unpopular • *a reaction against
religious leaders*

backlash • *a backlash against
mass-produced goods*
counterbalance • *an
organisation set up as a
counterbalance to the official
group*

read ① VERB
to look at something written
• *I love to read in bed.*

glance at • *He just glanced
briefly at the article.*
look at • *She was looking at the
evening paper.*
pore over • *poring over a
dictionary*
scan • *There's only time to scan
through it quickly.*
study • *I'll study the text more
closely later.*

F

read ② VERB

to understand what someone means • *as if he could read her thoughts*

comprehend • *Her expression was difficult to comprehend.*

decipher • *She was still no closer to deciphering the code.*

interpret • *You have to interpret their gestures, too.*

ready ① ADJECTIVE

prepared for action or use • *The plums are ready to eat now.*

organised • *Everything is organised for the party tomorrow.*

prepared • *He was prepared for a tough fight.*

primed • *The other side is primed for battle.*

ripe • *Are those strawberries ripe yet?*

set • *We'll be set to go in five minutes.*

ready ② ADJECTIVE

willing to do something • *She was always ready to give interviews.*

agreeable • *We can go ahead if you are agreeable.*

eager • *Children are eager to learn.*

happy • *always happy to help*

keen • *He wasn't keen to get involved.*

willing • *questions which they were not willing to answer*

ready ③ ADJECTIVE

easily produced or obtained • *ready cash*

accessible • *The system should be accessible to everyone.*

available • *Food is available round the clock.*

convenient • *a convenient excuse*

handy • *Keep a pencil and paper handy.*

real ① ADJECTIVE

actually existing and not imagined • *You're dealing with real life now.*

actual • *She was the actual basis for the leading character.*

authentic • *containing authentic details of what happened*

concrete • *I don't have any concrete evidence.*

factual • *a factual account*

genuine • *His worries about the future were genuine ones.*

legitimate • *These are legitimate concerns.*

tangible • *I cannot see any tangible benefits in these changes.*

true • *the true story of his life*

ANTONYM:
• imaginary

real ② ADJECTIVE

genuine and not imitation • *Is that a real word?*

authentic • *an authentic French recipe*

bona fide • *We are happy to donate to bona fide charities.*

dinkum (AUSTRALIAN AND NEW ZEALAND; INFORMAL) • *a place which serves dinkum Aussie tucker*

genuine • *It's a genuine Rembrandt, all right.*

honest • *It was an honest attempt to set things right.*

rightful • *the rightful heir to the throne*

sincere • *His remorse was completely sincere, not just an act.*

true • *He is a true believer in human rights.*

unaffected • *her genuine and unaffected sympathy for the victims*

ANTONYM:
• fake

realise VERB
to become aware of something • *People don't realise how serious it is.*

appreciate • *He appreciates the difficulties we face.*

comprehend • *They do not comprehend the nature of the problem.*

grasp • *She still couldn't grasp what had really happened.*

recognise • *Of course I recognise that evil exists.*

understand • *I didn't understand what he meant until later.*

realistic ① ADJECTIVE
accepting the true situation • *It's only realistic to admit that things will go wrong.*

down-to-earth • *We welcomed her down-to-earth approach.*

level-headed • *a sensible, level-headed approach*

matter-of-fact • *He sounded matter-of-fact and unemotional.*

practical • *a highly practical attitude to life*

sensible • *I'm trying to persuade you to be more sensible.*

sober • *a more sober assessment of the situation*

realistic ② ADJECTIVE
true to real life • *His novels are more realistic than his short stories.*

authentic • *They have to look authentic.*

faithful • *faithful copies of old household items*

lifelike • *almost as lifelike as a photograph*

true • *It gave a true picture of how things were.*

reality NOUN
something that is true and not imagined • *Fiction and reality were increasingly blurred.*

authenticity • *The film's authenticity impressed the critics.*

fact • *No-one knew how much of what he said was fact.*

realism • *His stories had an edge of realism.*

truth • *I must tell you the truth about this situation.*

really ① ADVERB
very or certainly • *I've had a really good time.*

absolutely • *feeling absolutely exhausted*

certainly • *I am certainly getting tired of hearing about it.*

extremely • *My smartphone is extremely useful.*

r

remarkably • *They have been remarkably successful.*
terribly • *I'm terribly sorry to bother you.*
truly • *a truly splendid man*
very • *learning very quickly*

really ② ADVERB
in fact • *He didn't really love her.*
actually • *I pretended I was interested, but I was actually half asleep.*
in fact • *It sounds simple, but in fact it's very difficult.*
in reality • *He came across as streetwise, but in reality he was not.*
truly • *I truly never minded caring for Rusty.*

reason ① NOUN
the cause of something that happens • *for a multitude of reasons*
cause • *The true cause of the accident may never be known.*
grounds • *some grounds for optimism*
incentive • *There is no incentive to adopt these measures.*
motive • *Police have ruled out robbery as a motive.*
purpose • *the purpose of their visit*

reason ② NOUN
the ability to think • *a conflict between emotion and reason*
intellect • *good health and a lively intellect*
judgment • *His judgment was impaired.*
rationality • *We live in an era of rationality.*

reasoning • *a lack of sound reasoning and logic*
sense • *He should have had more sense.*

reason ③ VERB
to try to persuade someone of something • *It's better to reason with them than to use force.*
bring round (INFORMAL) • *We'll try to bring you round to our point of view.*
persuade • *I had to persuade him of the advantages.*
win over • *They still hoped to win him over to their way of thinking.*

reasonable ① ADJECTIVE
fair and sensible • *a reasonable sort of chap*
fair • *You can be sure she will be fair with you.*
moderate • *an easygoing man of very moderate views*
rational • *Please try to be rational about this.*
sane • *No sane person wishes to see a war.*
sensible • *She was a sensible girl and did not panic.*
sober • *We are now more sober and realistic.*
steady • *a politician who was steady almost to the point of being boring*
wise • *You're a wise old man: tell me what to do.*

reasonable ② ADJECTIVE
based on good reasoning • *It seems reasonable to expect rapid urban growth.*
justifiable • *I don't believe violence is ever justifiable.*

R

legitimate • *That's a perfectly legitimate fear.*
logical • *There was a logical explanation.*
sensible • *a sensible solution*
sound • *sound advice*
understandable • *His unhappiness was understandable.*

reasonable ③ ADJECTIVE
not too expensive • *His fees were quite reasonable.*
cheap • *She said she'd share a flat if I could find somewhere cheap enough.*
competitive • *homes offered for sale at competitive prices*
fair • *It's a fair price for a car like that.*
inexpensive • *an inexpensive divorce settlement*
low • *The low prices and friendly service made for a pleasant evening.*
modest • *a modest charge*

reassure VERB
to make someone feel less worried • *She reassured me that everything was fine.*
bolster • *measures intended to bolster morale*
cheer up • *I wrote it just to cheer myself up.*
comfort • *He tried to comfort her as far as he could.*
encourage • *Investors were encouraged by the news.*

rebel VERB
to fight against authority and accepted values • *I rebelled against everything when I was young.*

defy • *It was the first time she had defied her mother.*
mutiny • *Sailors mutinied against their officers.*
resist • *activists convicted of resisting apartheid*
revolt • *The islanders revolted against the prince.*

rebellion NOUN
an organised opposition to authority • *the ruthless suppression of the rebellion*
insurrection • *They were plotting to stage an armed insurrection.*
mutiny • *convicted of mutiny and high treason*
revolt • *The revolt ended in failure.*
revolution • *after the French Revolution*
uprising • *Isolated attacks turned into a full-scale uprising.*

receive ① VERB
to accept something from someone • *Did they receive my letter?*
accept • *They accepted the parcel gratefully.*
be given • *We were all given presents.*
get • *She got some lovely things.*
pick up • *He picked up an award for his performance.*
take • *Will you take this parcel for your neighbour?*

receive ② VERB
to experience something • *We received a very warm welcome.*
encounter • *He encountered some unexpected opposition.*

r

suffer • He suffered some bangs and bumps.
sustain • She had sustained a cut on her arm.
undergo • You may have to undergo a bit of teasing.

receive ③ VERB
to welcome visitors • You must be there to receive your guests.
entertain • She loved to entertain friends at home.
greet • They greeted the visitors at the door.
meet • I'll come down to meet you.
take in • The country took in many refugees.
welcome • Several people came by to welcome me.

recent ADJECTIVE
happening a short time ago • his most recent acquisition
current • a sound knowledge of current affairs
fresh • fresh footprints in the snow
new • the subject of a new film
present-day • Even by present-day standards these were large aircraft.
up-to-date • the most up-to-date computers

recession NOUN
a decline in economic conditions • companies which survived after the recession
decline • signs of economic decline
depression • the Great Depression of the 1930s
downturn • due to a sharp downturn in the industry

slump • Many jobs were lost during the slump.

reckon ① VERB (INFORMAL)
to think or believe something is the case • I reckon he's still fond of her.
assume • If mistakes occurred, they were assumed to be my fault.
believe • "You've never heard of him?"—"I don't believe so."
consider • Barbara considers that people who sell these birds are acting illegally.
judge • I would judge that my earnings are considerably below those of my sister.
suppose • I suppose I'd better do some homework.
think • I think the bus has already left.

reckon ② VERB
to calculate an amount • The figure is now reckoned to be 15%.
calculate • We calculate that the average size farm in the county is 65 acres.
count • The years before their arrival in prison are not counted as part of their sentence.
estimate • Analysts estimate its current popularity at around ten per cent.
figure out • I roughly figured out the total.
work out • It is proving hard to work out the value of their assets.

recognise ① VERB
to know who or what someone or something is • I recognised him at once.

R

identify • *She tried to identify the perfume.*
know • *You'd know him if you saw him again.*
place • *He couldn't place my voice immediately.*
spot • *I spotted the house quite easily.*

recognise ② VERB
to accept or acknowledge something • *He was recognised as an outstanding pilot.*
acknowledge • *Her great bravery was acknowledged.*
appreciate • *In time you'll appreciate his good points.*
honour • *achievements honoured with the Nobel Prize*
salute • *We salute your great courage.*

reconstruct ① VERB
to rebuild something that has been damaged • *The city centre has been completely reconstructed.*
rebuild • *The task of rebuilding would be very expensive.*
recreate • *They try to recreate the atmosphere of former times.*
regenerate • *the ability to regenerate damaged tissues*
renovate • *The hotel was being renovated.*
restore • *experts who specialise in restoring old furniture*

reconstruct ② VERB
to build up from small details • *The police reconstructed the scene of the crime.*
build up • *They built up an image of him from several different descriptions.*

deduce • *The date can be deduced from old documents.*
piece together • *It was easy to piece together the shattered fragments.*

record ① NOUN
a stored account of something • *medical records*
account • *The company keeps detailed accounts.*
archive • *Earlier issues are stored in the archives.*
file • *the right to inspect company files*
journal • *He kept a journal while he was travelling.*
minute • *Did you read the minutes of the last meeting?*
register • *a register of births, deaths and marriages*

record ② NOUN
what someone has done in the past • *You will be rejected if you have a criminal record.*
background • *His background was in engineering.*
career • *His career spoke for itself.*
curriculum vitae • *I must update my curriculum vitae.*
track record (INFORMAL) • *Her track record as a teacher was impeccable.*

record ③ VERB
to note and store information • *Her diary records her daily life in detail.*
blog • *If I'm being paid by a client, I don't blog about it.*
document • *All these facts have been well documented.*

r

enter • *All the names are entered in this book.*

log • *They log everyone who comes in or out.*

note • *I must note your birthday.*

register • *We registered his birth straight away.*

write down • *If I don't write it down, I'll forget it.*

recover ① VERB

to get better again • *He has still not fully recovered.*

convalesce • *those convalescing from illness or surgery*

get better • *He never really got better again.*

get well • *Get well soon!*

improve • *The condition of your hair will soon improve.*

recuperate • *recuperating from a serious injury*

revive • *Business soon revived once he came back.*

recover ② VERB

to get something back again • *They took legal action to recover the money.*

get back • *We got everything back after the burglary.*

recapture • *trying to recapture the atmosphere of our holiday*

recoup • *trying to recoup their losses*

regain • *It took him a while to regain his composure.*

retrieve • *I retrieved my bag from the back seat.*

recovery ① NOUN

the act of getting better again

• *He made a remarkable recovery after his illness.*

healing • *Adams claims that humour is an integral part of healing.*

improvement • *Germany is showing a perceptible improvement.*

recuperation • *great powers of recuperation*

revival • *little chance of a revival of interest*

recovery ② NOUN

the act of getting something back • *a reward for the recovery of the painting*

recapture • *An offensive was launched for the recapture of the airbase.*

reclamation • *the reclamation of dry land from the marshes*

restoration • *She owed the restoration of her sight to this remarkable technique.*

retrieval • *electronic storage and retrieval systems*

recruit ① VERB

to persuade people to join a group • *He helped to recruit volunteers.*

draft • *drafted into the armed forces*

enlist • *I had to enlist the help of six people to move it.*

enrol • *She enrolled me on her evening course.*

muster • *trying to muster support for the movement*

recruit ② NOUN

someone who has recently

joined a group • *the latest batch of recruits*
beginner • *The course is suitable for beginners.*
convert • *a recent convert to their religion*
novice • *I'm a novice at these things.*
trainee • *My first job was as a graduate trainee with a bank.*

red NOUN or ADJECTIVE

SHADES OF RED

burgundy
cardinal
carmine
cerise
cherry
claret
crimson
cyclamen
flame
fuchsia
magenta
maroon
poppy
raspberry
ruby
scarlet
strawberry
titian
vermilion

RELATED WORDS:
• ADJECTIVES rubicund, ruddy

reduce ① VERB

to make something smaller in size or amount • *Gradually reduce the dosage.*
curtail • *His powers will be severely curtailed.*
cut • *The first priority is to cut costs.*

cut down • *Try to cut down your coffee consumption.*
decrease • *The government plans to decrease interest rates.*
diminish • *to diminish the prestige of the monarchy*
lessen • *a diet that would lessen the risk of disease*
lower • *a commitment to lower taxes*
shorten • *taking steps to shorten queues*

ANTONYM:
• increase

reduce ② VERB

to bring to a weaker or inferior state • *The village was reduced to rubble.*
degrade • *I wouldn't degrade myself by accepting that offer.*
demote • *The French team have been demoted to second place.*
downgrade • *The hurricane has been downgraded to a tropical storm.*
drive • *a woman driven to selling off her jewellery to make ends meet*
force • *The men were so hungry they were forced to eat grass.*

refer ① VERB

to mention something • *In his speech, he referred to a recent trip to Canada.*
allude • *She alluded to his absence in vague terms.*
bring up • *Why are you bringing that up now?*
cite • *She cites a favourite poem by George Herbert.*
mention • *She did not mention her mother's illness.*

r

refer ② VERB
to look at to find something
out • I had to refer to the
manual.
consult • He had to consult a
dictionary.
look up • I looked up your file to
get your address.

refined ① ADJECTIVE
polite and well-mannered
• His speech and manner are very
refined.
civilised • the demands of
civilised behaviour
genteel • two ladies with
genteel manners and voices
gentlemanly • Sopwith
behaved in his usual gentlemanly
manner.
ladylike • They are models of
ladylike decorum.
polite • polite and correct
behaviour
ANTONYM:
• common

refined ② ADJECTIVE
processed to remove
impurities • refined sugar
distilled • distilled water
filtered • two pints of spring or
filtered water
processed • a diet high in
processed foods
pure • crisp pure air
purified • freshly purified
drinking water

reform ① NOUN
a major change or
improvement • radical
economic reforms

amendment • an amendment
to remove the ban on divorce
correction • a correction of
social injustice
improvement • She is pressing
for improvements to education.
rehabilitation • the
rehabilitation of young offenders

reform ② VERB
to make major changes or
improvements to something
• his plans to reform the economy
amend • They want to amend
the current system.
better • industrial action to
better their working conditions
correct • keen to correct
injustices
rectify • measures suggested to
rectify the financial situation
rehabilitate • a loan for
Bulgaria to rehabilitate its
railway system

refresh VERB
to make you feel more
energetic • A glass of fruit juice
will refresh you.
brace • a bracing walk
enliven • Music can enliven the
spirit.
rejuvenate • He was told that
the Italian climate would
rejuvenate him.
revive • The cold water revived
me a bit.
stimulate • a toner to stimulate
the skin

refuge NOUN
a place where you go for
safety • a mountain refuge
asylum • political asylum

harbour • *Patches of gorse were a great harbour for foxes.*
haven • *The island is a haven for international criminals.*
sanctuary • *a sanctuary from the outside world*
shelter • *an underground shelter*

refuse ① VERB
to say you will not do something • *He refused to speculate about the contents of the letter.*
abstain (FORMAL) • *people who abstain from eating meat*
decline • *He declined to comment on the story.*
withhold • *Financial aid for Britain has been withheld.*

refuse ② VERB
to say you will not allow or accept something • *He offered me a drink, which I refused.*
decline • *He declined their invitation.*
reject • *The court rejected their petition.*
spurn • *You spurned his last offer.*
turn down • *He has turned down the job.*
ANTONYM:
• accept

refuse ③ NOUN (FORMAL)
rubbish or waste • *a weekly collection of refuse*
garbage (INFORMAL) • *rotting piles of garbage*
junk (INFORMAL) • *What are you going to do with all that junk?*

litter • *If you see litter in the corridor, pick it up.*
rubbish • *They had piled most of their rubbish into yellow skips.*
trash • *I forgot to take out the trash.*
waste • *a law that regulates the disposal of waste*

regard ① VERB
to have particular views about someone or something • *I regard creativity as a gift.*
consider • *I consider activities such as jogging a waste of time.*
judge • *This may or may not be judged as reasonable.*
look on • *A lot of people looked on him as a healer.*
see • *I don't see it as my duty to take sides.*
think of • *We all thought of him as a father.*
view • *They view the United States as a land of opportunity.*

regard ② VERB (LITERARY)
to look at someone in a particular way • *She regarded him curiously for a moment.*
contemplate • *He contemplated her in silence.*
eye • *We eyed each other thoughtfully.*
gaze • *gazing at herself in the mirror*
look • *She looked at him earnestly.*
scrutinise • *She scrutinised his features to see if he was to be trusted.*
watch • *Chris watched him sipping his drink.*

r

region NOUN

a large area of land • *a remote mountainous region of Afghanistan*
area • *The area is renowned for its cuisine.*
district • *I drove around the business district.*
land • *a land permanently cloaked in mist*
locality • *All other factories in the locality went on strike.*
quarter • *We wandered through the Chinese quarter.*
sector • *the northeast sector of Bosnia*
territory • *the disputed territory on the border*
tract • *They cleared large tracts of forest.*
zone • *a different time zone*

regret ① VERB

to be sorry something has happened • *I gave in to him, and I have regretted it ever since.*
be sorry • *I'm sorry you feel that way about it.*
grieve • *grieving over the death of his wife*
lament • *We lament the loss of a fine novelist.*
mourn • *to mourn the loss of a loved one*
repent • *He repents his past sins.*

regret ② NOUN

the feeling of being sorry about something • *He expressed regret that he had caused any offence.*
grief • *his guilt and grief over the failed relationship*

pang of conscience • *He need not feel any pangs of conscience over his decision.*
penitence • *an abject display of penitence*
remorse • *He expressed remorse over his own foolishness.*
repentance • *an apparent lack of genuine repentance*
sorrow • *I feel real sorrow that my dad did this.*

regular ① ADJECTIVE

even or equally spaced • *soft music with a regular beat*
consistent • *a consistent heart rate*
constant • *a constant temperature*
even • *an even level of sound*
periodic • *Periodic checks are carried out.*
rhythmic • *the rhythmic beating of the drum*
steady • *a steady pace*
uniform • *The earth rotates on its axis at a uniform rate.*

ANTONYM:
• irregular

regular ② ADJECTIVE

usual or normal • *I was filling in for the regular bartender.*
customary • *her customary place at the table*
everyday • *part of everyday life*
habitual • *habitual practices*
normal • *a normal day*
ordinary • *It was just an ordinary weekend.*
routine • *a routine knee operation*
typical • *My typical day begins at 8.30.*

R

usual • *In a usual week I watch about 15 hours of television.*

reject VERB
to refuse to accept or agree to something • *We reject any suggestion that the law needs amending.*
decline • *They declined his proposal.*
deny • *He denied our offer of assistance.*
rebuff • *She rebuffed his advances.*
refuse • *He offered me a drink, which I refused.*
renounce (FORMAL) • *She renounced her parents' religion.*
say no to • *Just say no to drugs.*
spurn • *He spurned the advice of management consultants.*
turn down • *She turned down his offer of marriage.*
unfollow • *I found him boring so I unfollowed him.*
unfriend • *We fell out and she unfriended me.*
ANTONYM:
• accept

rejoice VERB
to be very happy about something • *Today we can rejoice in our success.*
be overjoyed • *I was overjoyed to see him.*
celebrate • *We should celebrate our victory.*
delight • *He delighted in her success.*
glory • *glorying in the achievement of his troops*

relation ① NOUN
a connection between two things • *This theory bears no relation to reality.*
bearing • *Diet has an important bearing on your general health.*
bond • *the bond between a mother and child*
connection • *Experts say there was no connection between the activity at the two volcanoes.*
correlation • *the correlation between unemployment and crime*
link • *a link between obesity and heart problems*
relationship • *the relationship between success and effort*

relation ② NOUN
a member of your family • *I was staying with relations in Atlanta.*
kin • *She has gone to live with her husband's kin.*
kinsman • *the prince who murdered his father and kinsmen*
kinswoman • *She was a kinswoman of the Duke of Portland.*
relative • *Get a relative to look after the children.*

relationship ① NOUN
the way people act towards each other • *He has a friendly relationship with his customers.*
affinity • *the natural affinity between the female members of the community*
association • *the association between the two countries*

r

relationship

bond • *The experience created a bond between us.*
connection • *He felt a personal connection with her.*
rapport • *He has a terrific rapport with kids.*

relationship ② NOUN

the connection between two things • *the relationship between humans and their environment*
connection • *the connection between age and ill-health*
correlation • *the correlation between unemployment and crime*
link • *the link between diet and health*
parallel • *the parallel between painting and music*

relax VERB

to be calm and become less worried • *I never have any time to relax.*
laze • *I'm just going to laze around and do nothing.*
rest • *Try to rest as much as you can.* **take it easy** • *the chance to just take it easy for a week or two*
unwind • *It helps them to unwind after a busy day at work.*

relaxed ① ADJECTIVE

calm and not worried or tense • *As soon as I made the decision, I felt more relaxed.*
at ease • *It is essential to feel at ease with your therapist.*
calm • *Diane felt calm and unafraid as she entered the courtroom.*

comfortable • *He liked me and I felt comfortable with him.*
cool • *He was marvellously cool, smiling as if nothing had happened.*
easy • *By then I was feeling a little easier about the situation.*
serene • *that serene smile of his*
unflustered • *He has a calm, unflustered temperament.*

ANTONYM:
• tense

relaxed ② ADJECTIVE

calm and peaceful • *The atmosphere at lunch was relaxed.*
calm • *The city appears relatively calm today.*
casual • *We have a very casual relationship.*
comfortable • *a comfortable silence*
informal • *an informal occasion*
peaceful • *Sundays are usually quiet and peaceful in our house.*

ANTONYM:
• tense

relay VERB

to give information to someone else • *She relayed the message, then frowned.*
communicate • *They successfully communicate their knowledge to others.*
convey (FORMAL) • *They have conveyed their views to the government.*
impart (FORMAL) • *the ability to impart knowledge*

release ① VERB

to set someone or something

free • *negotiations to release the hostages*

deliver • *I thank God for delivering me from that pain.*

discharge • *He may be discharged from hospital today.*

extricate • *They managed to extricate the survivors from the wreckage.*

free • *The government promised to free all political prisoners.*

let go • *They held him for three hours and then let him go.*

liberate • *liberated under the terms of the amnesty*

set free • *birds set free into the wild*

release ② VERB

to make something available • *The new album is released next week.*

issue • *He has issued a press statement.*

launch • *The company has just launched a new range of products.*

publish • *His latest book will be published in May.*

put out • *putting out a series of novels by Nobel prize winners*

release ③ NOUN

the setting free of someone or something • *his release from prison*

discharge • *a discharge from the army*

emancipation • *the emancipation of slaves in the 19th century*

freedom • *Hinckley campaigned for his freedom.*

liberation • *their liberation from a Nazi concentration camp*

liberty • *her television appearances pleading for his liberty*

relentless ADJECTIVE

never stopping or becoming less intense • *The pressure was relentless.*

incessant • *incessant rain*

nonstop • *nonstop background music*

persistent • *in the face of persistent criticism*

sustained • *a sustained attack*

unrelenting • *unrelenting protests*

unremitting • *the unremitting demands of duty*

relevant ADJECTIVE

connected with what is being discussed • *We have passed on all relevant information.*

applicable • *These fees are not applicable to mortgages in Scotland.*

apposite • *He could not think of anything apposite to say.*

appropriate • *The name seemed very appropriate.*

apt • *an apt comment*

pertinent • *She had asked some pertinent questions.*

ANTONYM:

• irrelevant

reliable ADJECTIVE

able to be trusted • *You have to demonstrate that you are reliable.*

dependable • *dependable information*

r

faithful • *a faithful friend*
safe • *It's all right, you're in safe hands.*
sound • *sound advice*
staunch • *a staunch supporter*
sure • *a sure sign of rain*
true • *a true account*
trustworthy • *a trustworthy and level-headed leader*

ANTONYM:
• unreliable

religion NOUN

RELIGIONS
animism
Baha'ism
Buddhism
Christianity
Confucianism
Hinduism
Islam
Jainism
Judaism
Rastafarianism
shamanism
Shinto
Sikhism
Taoism
Zen
Zoroastrianism or Zoroastrism

religious ① ADJECTIVE
connected with religion • *religious worship*
devotional • *an altar covered with devotional pictures*
divine • *a request for divine guidance*
doctrinal • *their doctrinal differences*
holy • *To Tibetans, this is a holy place.*
sacred • *Bach's sacred music*

scriptural • *scriptural and theological references*
spiritual • *We've got no spiritual values.*
theological • *theological studies*

religious ② ADJECTIVE
having a strong belief in a god or gods • *They are both very religious.*
devout • *She is a devout Catholic.*
God-fearing • *They brought up their children to be God-fearing Christians.*
godly • *a learned and godly preacher*
pious • *He was brought up by pious relatives.*
righteous • *struggling to be righteous and chaste*

reluctant ADJECTIVE
unwilling to do something • *He was reluctant to ask for help.*
averse • *I'm not averse to going along with the idea.*
disinclined • *He was disinclined to talk about himself.*
hesitant • *His advisers are hesitant to let the United States enter the conflict.*
loath • *The finance minister is loath to cut income tax.*
slow • *The world community ha been slow to respond to the crisi*
unwilling • *For months I had been unwilling to go through with it.*

ANTONYM:
• eager

remain ① VERB
to stay somewhere • *You'll have to remain in hospital for the time being.*
be left • *He was left in the car.*
linger • *I lingered for a few days until he arrived.*
stay behind • *I was told to stay behind after the class.*
wait • *Wait here until I come back.*

remain ② VERB
to stay the same • *The men remained silent.*
continue • *This state of affairs cannot continue.*
endure • *Somehow their friendship endures.*
go on • *The debate goes on.*
last • *Nothing lasts forever.*
stay • *They could stay afloat without swimming.*
survive • *companies which survived after the recession*

remainder NOUN
the part that is left of something • *He gulped down the remainder of his coffee.*
balance • *Pay the balance on delivery.*
last • *He finished off the last of the stew.*
others • *She took one and put the others back.*
remains • *tidying up the remains of their picnic*
remnants • *The remnants of the force were fleeing.*
rest • *I'm going to throw a party, then invest the rest of the money.*

remains PLURAL NOUN
the parts of something left over • *the remains of an ancient mosque*
debris • *screws, bolts and other debris from a scrapyard*
dregs • *Colum drained the dregs from his cup.*
leftovers • *Refrigerate any leftovers.*
relics • *a museum of war relics*
remnants • *Beneath the present church were remnants of Roman flooring.*
residue • *Discard the milky residue left behind.*
scraps • *the scraps from the dinner table*
vestiges • *an attempt to destroy the last vestiges of evidence*

remark ① VERB
to mention or comment on something • *She had remarked on the boy's improvement.*
comment • *So far, he has not commented on these reports.*
mention • *I mentioned that I didn't like jazz.*
observe • *"You're very pale," he observed.*
say • *"Well done," he said.*
state • *We stated that he had resigned.*

remark ② NOUN
something you say • *a vulgar remark*
comment • *his abrasive wit and caustic comments*
observation • *a few general observations*

r

statement • *That statement puzzled me.*
utterance • *admirers who hung on her every utterance*
word • *No-one had an unkind word to say about him.*

remember VERB
to bring to mind something from the past • *I do not remember the exact words.*
call to mind • *He invited the congregation to call to mind their sins.*
recall • *He tried to recall the layout of the farmhouse.*
recognise • *I don't recognise that name.*
retain • *information which can be retained in the memory*
ANTONYM:
• forget

remind VERB
to make someone remember something • *He reminds me of myself at that age.*
bring back to • *Talking about the accident brought it all back to me.*
jog someone's memory • *See if this picture helps jog your memory.*
make someone remember • *Your article made me remember my own traumas.*
put in mind • *His eagerness to please put her in mind of a puppy.*
refresh someone's memory • *I read through the list to refresh my memory.*

remote ① ADJECTIVE
far off in distance • *a remote farm in the hills*

distant • *in that distant land*
far-off • *start a new life in a far-off country*
inaccessible • *people living in inaccessible parts of the country*
isolated • *Many of the refugee villages are in isolated areas.*
lonely • *It felt like the loneliest place in the world.*
outlying • *Tourists can visit outlying areas by jeep.*

remote ② ADJECTIVE
far away in time • *It dates from the remote past.*
distant • *a glimpse into the more distant future*
far-off • *She has entirely forgotten those far-off days.*

remote ③ ADJECTIVE
not wanting to be friendly • *She looked beautiful, but at the same time so remote.*
aloof • *He seemed aloof, standing watching the others.*
cold • *What a cold, unfeeling character she was.*
detached • *He tries to remain emotionally detached from the prisoners.*
distant • *He is courteous but distant.*
reserved • *She's quite a reserved person.*
withdrawn • *Her sister had become withdrawn and moody.*

remote ④ ADJECTIVE
not very great • *The chances of his surviving are pretty remote.*
poor • *The odds of it happening again are very poor.*

R

slender • *There is a slender possibility that the plan might work.*

slight • *Is there even a slight hope that she might change her mind?*

slim • *There's still a slim chance that he may become Prime Minister.*

small • *There was still a small possibility that he might phone.*

remove VERB
to take something off or away • *I removed the splinter from her finger.*

delete • *He deleted files from the computer system.*

detach • *Detach and keep the bottom part of the form.*

eject • *He was ejected from the restaurant.*

eliminate • *Eliminate dairy products from your diet.*

erase • *She had erased the message.*

extract • *She is having a tooth extracted today.*

get rid of • *to get rid of raw sewage by pumping it out to sea*

take away • *She took away the tray.*

take off • *I won't take my coat off, I'm not staying.*

take out • *Take that dog out of here.*

withdraw • *She withdrew her hand from Roger's.*

renew VERB
to begin something again • *Syria renewed diplomatic relations with Egypt.*

begin again • *The audience began the slow handclap again.*

recommence • *He recommenced work on his novel.*

re-establish • *He had re-established his close friendship with Anthony.*

reopen • *It is feared that this issue could reopen the controversy.*

resume • *Rebels have refused to resume peace talks.*

renounce VERB (FORMAL)
to reject something or give it up • *She renounced terrorism.*

disown • *The comments were later disowned by an official spokesman.*

give up • *He did not want to give up his right to the title.*

reject • *children who reject their parents' political and religious beliefs*

relinquish • *He does not intend to relinquish power.*

renovate VERB
to repair an old building or machine • *They spent thousands renovating the house.*

do up • *his father's obsession with doing up old cars*

modernise • *plans to modernise the refinery*

recondition • *The company specialises in reconditioning photocopiers.*

refurbish • *This hotel has been completely refurbished.*

repair • *He has repaired the roof to make the house more windproof.*

r

restore • *The old town square has been beautifully restored.*

revamp • *plans to revamp the airport*

repair ① NOUN
something you do to mend something that is damaged • *The landlord carried out the repairs himself.*

darn • *a sock with a big darn in it*

mend • *Spray the area with paint to make the mend invisible.*

patch • *jackets with patches on the elbows*

restoration • *the restoration of a war-damaged building*

repair ② VERB
to mend something that is damaged • *The money will be used to repair faulty equipment.*

fix • *If something is broken, get it fixed.*

mend • *They mended it without charge.*

patch • *They patched the barn roof.*

patch up • *Patch up those holes.*

renovate • *They spent thousands renovating the house.*

restore • *experts who specialise in restoring ancient parchments*

repay VERB
to give back money which is owed • *It will take me years to repay the loan.*

pay back • *I'll pay you back that money tomorrow.*

refund • *Any extra that you have paid will be refunded to you.*

settle up • *If we owe you anything we can settle up when you come.*

repeat VERB
to say or write something again • *Since you didn't listen, I'll repeat that.*

echo • *"Are you frightened?"— "Frightened?" she echoed. "Of what?"*

reiterate • *The lawyer could only reiterate what he had said before.*

say again • *"I'm sorry," she said again.*

repel ① VERB
to horrify and disgust • *The thought of spiders repels me.*

disgust • *He disgusted everyone with his boorish behaviour.*

offend • *viewers who are easily offended*

revolt • *The smell revolted him.*

sicken • *What he saw there sickened him.*

ANTONYM:
• attract

repel ② VERB
to fight and drive back enemy forces • *troops along the border ready to repel an enemy attack*

drive off • *They drove the guerrillas off with infantry and air strikes.*

repulse • *Cavalry and artillery were sent to repulse the enemy forces.*

resist • *The tribe resisted the Spanish invaders.*

R

replace VERB
to take the place of something else • *the man who replaced him as England skipper*
succeed • *He was succeeded by his son.*
supersede • *Horses were superseded by cars.*
supplant • *Anger supplanted all other feelings.*
take over from • *the man taking over from Mr Berry as chairman*
take the place of • *Debit cards are taking the place of cash and cheques.*

replacement NOUN
a person or thing that takes the place of another • *He has nominated Adams as his replacement.*
proxy • *They must nominate a proxy to vote on their behalf.*
stand-in • *He was a stand-in for my regular doctor.*
substitute • *an artificial substitute for silk*
successor • *He recommended him as his successor.*
surrogate • *They had expected me to be a surrogate for my sister.*

reply ① VERB
to give someone an answer • *He did not even have the courtesy to reply to my message.*
answer • *He avoided answering the question.*
counter • *"It's not that simple," he countered in a firm voice.*
respond • *"Mind your manners!" I responded.*

retort • *"Nobody asked you," he retorted.*
return • *"I can manage," she returned coldly.*

reply ② NOUN
an answer given to someone • *There was a trace of irony in his reply.*
answer • *She could not give him a truthful answer.*
response • *His response was brusque.*
retort • *His sharp retort clearly made an impact.*

report ① VERB
to tell about or give an official account of something • *He reported the theft to the police.*
cover • *The US news media will cover the trial closely.*
describe • *His condition was described as "improving".*
inform of • *Inform the police of any suspicious activity.*
notify • *The skipper notified the coastguard of the tragedy.*
state • *The police stated that he had been arrested.*

report ② NOUN
an account of an event or situation • *reports of serious human rights violations*
account • *a dishonest account of events*
description • *a detailed description of the match*
statement • *a deliberately misleading statement*

represent ① VERB
to stand for something else

• This rune represents wealth and plenty.

mean • This tarot card means the death of your present situation.

stand for • The olive branch stands for peace.

symbolise • a scene which symbolises the movie's message

represent ② VERB
to describe something in a particular way • The popular press tends to represent him as a hero.

depict • Children's books usually depict farm animals as lovable.

describe • She was always described as an intellectual.

picture • In the American press she was pictured as a heroine.

portray • She was portrayed as a heartless, terrible woman.

show • He was shown as an intelligent and courageous man.

representative ① NOUN
a person who acts on behalf of another or others • Employees from each department elect a representative.

agent • You are buying direct, rather than through an agent.

delegate • a union delegate

deputy • I can't make it so I'll send my deputy.

proxy • They must nominate a proxy to vote on their behalf.

spokesman • the party's education spokesman

spokeswoman • a spokeswoman for her generation

representative ②
ADJECTIVE
typical of the group to which it belongs • fairly representative groups of adults

characteristic • a characteristic feature

illustrative • an illustrative example

typical • a typical Italian menu

reputation NOUN
the opinion that people have of a person or thing • The college has a good reputation.

character • a man of good character

name • I have disgraced the family's name.

renown • a singer of great renown

repute • a writer and scholar of some repute

standing • This has done nothing to improve his standing.

stature • his stature as the world's greatest cellist

request ① VERB
to ask for something politely or formally • She requested that the door be left open.

ask • The government is being asked to consider the plan.

beg • May I beg a favour of you?

seek • You should seek a medical opinion.

request ② NOUN
the action of asking for something politely or formally • France had agreed to his request for political asylum.

appeal • an appeal for witnesses to come forward

R

application • *Their application was vetoed.*

call • *calls to decrease income tax*

plea • *his plea for help in solving the killing*

require ① VERB
to need something • *A baby requires warmth and security.*

demand • *The task of reconstruction would demand patience and hard work.*

depend on • *I depend on this money to survive.*

be in need of • *The house was in need of modernisation.*

need • *He desperately needed money.*

want (INFORMAL) • *The windows wanted cleaning.*

require ② VERB
to say that someone must do something • *The rules require employers to provide safety training.*

compel • *legislation that would compel cyclists to wear a helmet*

demand • *This letter demands an immediate reply.*

direct • *a court order directing the group to leave the area*

instruct • *They have instructed their solicitor to sue for compensation.*

oblige • *This decree obliges unions to delay strikes.*

order • *The court ordered him to pay the sum in full.*

requirement NOUN
something that you must have or do • *The products met all legal requirements.*

demand • *the demands and challenges of his new job*

essential • *the basic essentials for bachelor life*

necessity • *food and other daily necessities*

need • *special nutritional needs*

specification • *These companies will have to meet new European specifications.*

research ① NOUN
the act of studying and finding out about something • *funds for research into dyslexia*

analysis • *They collected blood samples for laboratory analysis.*

examination • *a framework for the examination of these topics*

exploration • *an exploration of classical myths*

investigation • *Further investigation was hindered by the loss of all documentation.*

study • *The study demonstrated a link between obesity and heart problems.*

research ② VERB
to study and find out about something • *I'm researching for an article on New England.*

analyse • *We haven't had time to analyse those samples yet.*

examine • *The spacecraft will examine how solar wind affects earth's magnetic field.*

explore • *It would probably be wise to explore the matter further.*

google • *Google "Greek islands" and see what you can find.*

r

investigate • Gas officials are investigating the cause of the explosion.

study • She's been studying chimpanzees for thirty years.

resemblance NOUN
a similarity between two things • I can see a resemblance between you.

analogy • the analogy between learning and eating

correspondence • There's little correspondence between our lifestyles.

likeness • These myths have a startling likeness to one another.

parallel • There were parallels between the two cases.

similarity • similarities between mother and son

resemble VERB
to be similar to something else • Venison resembles beef in flavour.

bear a resemblance to • She bears a resemblance to Marilyn Monroe.

be like • The ground is like concrete.

be similar to • The game is similar to rounders.

look like • He looks like his father.

parallel • His fate paralleled that of his predecessor.

take after • You take after your grandmother.

resent VERB
to feel bitter and angry about something • I resent the slur on my integrity.

be angry about • I was angry at the way he spoke to me.

be offended by • She was offended by his comments.

dislike • I dislike his patronising attitude.

object to • I object to being treated like an idiot.

take offence at • She took offence at the implied criticism.

resentful ADJECTIVE
bitter about something that has happened • a sullen and resentful workforce

aggrieved • He is still aggrieved at the size of the fine.

angry • I was angry that I wasn't consulted.

bitter • a forsaken and bitter man

embittered • He had grown into an embittered, hardened adult.

huffy • He's so huffy if he doesn't get his own way.

indignant • They were indignant that they had not been consulted.

offended • He was offended at being left out.

resentment NOUN
a feeling of anger and bitterness • There is growing resentment against newcomers.

anger • Perhaps anger had clouded his vision.

animosity • The animosity between the two men grew.

bitterness • I feel bitterness towards the person who knocked me down.

R

grudge • *It was an accident and I bear no grudges.*

huff • *She went off in a huff.*

indignation • *He could hardly contain his indignation.*

rancour (FORMAL) • *There was no trace of envy or rancour in her face.*

reserve ① VERB

to keep for a particular person or purpose • *Hotel rooms have been reserved for us.*

hoard • *They've begun to hoard food and petrol.*

hold • *The information is held in a database.*

keep • *Grate the lemon zest and keep it for later.*

put by • *She had enough put by for her fare.*

save • *Save me a seat.*

set aside • *funds set aside for education*

stockpile • *People are stockpiling food for the coming winter.*

store • *potatoes stored for sale out of season*

reserve ② NOUN

a supply kept for future use • *a drain on the cash reserves*

cache • *a substantial cache of water*

fund • *a pension fund*

hoard • *a hoard of food and petrol*

stock • *stocks of paper and ink*

stockpile • *stockpiles of canned goods*

store • *a secret store of sweets*

supply • *food supplies*

resign ① VERB

to leave a job • *Scott resigned from the firm.*

abdicate • *The King abdicated to marry an American divorcee.*

hand in your notice • *I handed in my notice on Friday.*

leave • *I am leaving to become a teacher.*

quit • *He quit his job as an office manager.*

step down (INFORMAL) • *He headed the government until he stepped down in 1990.*

resign ②: **resign oneself** VERB

to accept an unpleasant situation • *She had resigned herself to losing her home.*

accept • *You've got to accept the fact that he's left you.*

bow • *He bowed to the inevitable and allowed her to go.*

reconcile yourself • *She had reconciled herself to never seeing him again.*

resist VERB

to refuse to accept something and try to prevent it • *They resisted our attempts to modernise.*

defy • *arrested for defying the ban on street trading*

fight • *He vigorously fought the proposal.*

oppose • *Many parents oppose bilingual education in schools.*

refuse • *The patient has the right to refuse treatment.*

struggle against • *nations struggling against Communist takeovers*

ANTONYM:
• accept

resolve ① VERB

to decide firmly to do something • *She resolved to report the matter.*

decide • *She decided to study chemistry.*

determine • *He determined to rescue his two countrymen.*

intend • *I intended to teach him a lesson he wouldn't forget.*

make up your mind • *Once he made up his mind to do it, there was no stopping him.*

resolve ② VERB

to find a solution to a problem • *We must find a way to resolve these problems.*

clear up • *The confusion was soon cleared up.*

find a solution to • *the ability to find an effective solution to the crisis*

overcome • *Find a way to overcome your difficulties.*

solve • *These reforms did not solve the problem of unemployment.*

sort out • *The two countries have sorted out their trade dispute.*

work out • *It seems like a nightmare, but I'm sure we can work it out.*

resolve ③ NOUN

absolute determination • *He doesn't weaken in his resolve.*

determination • *the expression of fierce determination on her face*

resolution • *"I'm going on a diet," she said with sudden resolution.*

tenacity • *Hard work and sheer tenacity are crucial to career success.*

respect ① VERB

to have a good opinion of someone • *I respect her talent as a pianist.*

admire • *I admire him for his honesty.*

have a good opinion of • *Nobody seems to have a good opinion of him.*

have a high opinion of • *She had a very high opinion of Neil.*

honour • *the Scout's promise to honour God and the Queen*

look up to • *He looks up to his dad.*

think highly of • *His boss thinks very highly of him.*

venerate (FORMAL) • *My father venerated General Eisenhower.*

ANTONYM:
• disrespect

respect ② NOUN

a good opinion of someone • *We have no respect for him at all.*

admiration • *I have always had the greatest admiration for him.*

esteem • *We have to win the trust and esteem of our clients.*

regard • *I hold her in high regard.*

reverence • *We did it out of reverence for the dead.*

ANTONYM:
• disrespect

respectable ① ADJECTIVE
considered to be acceptable and correct • *respectable families*
decent • *They married after a decent interval.*
good • *He comes from a good family.*
honourable • *His colleagues were honourable people.*
proper • *It was not proper for women to go on the stage.*
reputable • *a reputable firm*
upright • *an upright and trustworthy man*
worthy • *worthy citizens*

respectable ② ADJECTIVE
adequate or reasonable • *a respectable rate of economic growth*
appreciable • *making appreciable progress*
considerable • *a considerable amount*
decent • *a decent standard of living*
fair • *She had a fair command of English.*
reasonable • *He couldn't make a reasonable living from his writing.*

responsibility ① NOUN
the duty to deal with or take care of something • *The garden is your responsibility.*
duty • *My duty is to look after the animals.*

obligation • *You have an obligation to help him.*
onus • *The onus was on him to make sure he didn't fail.*

responsibility ② NOUN
the blame for something which has happened • *We must all accept responsibility for our mistakes.*
blame • *I'm not going to take the blame for this.*
fault • *This is all your fault.*
guilt • *He was not completely free of guilt.*
liability • *He admitted liability for the crash.*

responsible ① ADJECTIVE
being the person in charge of something • *The Cabinet is collectively responsible for policy.*
in charge • *I wish someone else was in charge of this inquiry.*
in control • *Who is in control of the operation?*

responsible ② ADJECTIVE
being to blame for something • *I hold you responsible for this mess.*
at fault • *I was not at fault as my vehicle was stationary.*
guilty • *I still maintain that I am not guilty.*
to blame • *Television is possibly to blame for this.*

responsible ③ ADJECTIVE
sensible and dependable • *He had to show that he would be a responsible parent.*
dependable • *a dependable, trustworthy teacher*

level-headed • *a sensible, level-headed approach*

reliable • *You have to demonstrate that you are reliable.*

sensible • *She's a sensible girl, if a bit headstrong.*

sound • *sound advice*

trustworthy • *He is a trustworthy leader.*

ANTONYM:
• irresponsible

rest ① NOUN
the remaining parts of something • *Take what you want and leave the rest.*

balance • *You pay half now and the balance on delivery.*

others • *She took one and put the others back.*

remainder • *He gulped down the remainder of his coffee.*

surplus • *Coat with seasoned flour, shaking off the surplus.*

rest ② NOUN
a period when you relax and do nothing • *I'll start again after a rest.*

break • *He needs to take a break from work.*

holiday • *I could really do with a holiday.*

leisure • *We get no leisure, no time off, no overtime pay.*

relaxation • *Make time for a bit of relaxation.*

respite • *a respite from the rush of everyday life*

rest ③ VERB
to relax and do nothing for a while • *He rested briefly before going on.*

have a break • *Paul felt he had to have a break.*

idle • *He sat idling in his room.*

laze • *lazing on the beach*

put your feet up • *Nobody's home, so I can put my feet up for a while.*

relax • *Guests can relax in the cosy bar.*

sit down • *I'll have to sit down for a minute.*

take it easy • *the chance to just take it easy for a couple of weeks*

restless ADJECTIVE
unable to sit still or relax • *She had been restless and irritable all day.*

edgy • *She was nervous and edgy, pacing up and down.*

fidgety • *bored, fidgety youngsters*

fretful • *The whole family was fretful and argumentative.*

jumpy • *If she can't get out she gets jumpy and irritable.*

on edge • *She's been on edge for weeks.*

unsettled • *The staff were unsettled and demoralised.*

restore ① VERB
to cause something to return to its previous state • *He was anxious to restore his reputation.*

re-establish • *an attempt to re-establish diplomatic relations*

reinstate • *the failure to reinstate the ceasefire*

reintroduce • *the plan to reintroduce wolves to the Highlands*

R

return • *their attempts to return the country to an agrarian economy*

restore ② VERB
to clean and repair something • *experts who specialise in restoring ancient parchments*

fix up • *It took us months to fix this house up.*

mend • *They finally got round to mending the roof.*

rebuild • *plans to rebuild the opera house*

reconstruct • *reconstructing paintings by old masters*

refurbish • *The city is refurbishing the cathedral's facade.*

renovate • *The hotel was being renovated in expectation of a tourist boom.*

repair • *The money will be used to repair faulty equipment.*

restrain VERB
to hold someone or something back • *He had to be restrained by his friends.*

contain • *He could hardly contain his rage.*

control • *She tried to control her excitement.*

curb • *You must curb your extravagant tastes.*

hamper • *I was hampered by a lack of information.*

hinder • *Research is hindered by lack of cash.*

hold back • *He could no longer hold back his laughter.*

inhibit • *factors which inhibit growth*

restrict VERB
to limit the movement or actions of someone or something • *laws to restrict foreign imports*

confine • *Keep your dog confined to the house.*

contain • *The curfew had contained the violence.*

hamper • *I was hampered by a lack of information.*

handicap • *handicapped by the terms of the contract*

impede • *Their work was being impeded by shortages of supplies.*

inhibit • *factors which inhibit growth*

limit • *He limited payments on the country's foreign debt.*

restrain • *the need to restrain wage rises*

restriction NOUN
a rule or situation that limits what you can do • *a speed restriction*

constraint • *financial constraints*

control • *a call for stricter gun control*

curb • *support for a curb on migration from neighbouring countries*

limitation • *A slipped disc causes severe limitation of movement.*

regulation • *regulations outlawing child labour*

restraint • *new restraints on trade unions*

stipulation • *The only dress stipulation was "no jeans".*

r

result ① NOUN

the situation that is caused by something • *the result of lengthy deliberation*

consequence • *This could have disastrous consequences for industry.*

effect • *the intended effect of the revised guidelines*

outcome • *The ultimate outcome will be different.*

product • *the product of five years' work*

upshot • *The upshot is that our employees are all unhappy.*

result ② VERB

to be caused by something • *The crash resulted from a defect in the aircraft.*

arise • *the publicity that arises from incidents of this kind*

derive • *Poor health often derives from poverty.*

develop • *a determination which has developed from his new-found confidence*

ensue • *If the system collapses, chaos will ensue.*

follow • *the consequences which followed his release from prison*

happen • *What will happen if the test proves positive?*

stem • *Her fear of flying stems from an incident in her youth.*

result in VERB

to cause something to happen • *50% of road accidents result in head injuries.*

bring about • *The Suez crisis brought about petrol rationing.*

cause • *The play caused a stir here.*

lead to • *brain damage which leads to paralysis*

retaliate VERB

to do something to someone in return for what they did • *The militia said it would retaliate against any attacks.*

get back (INFORMAL) • *a desire to get back at our enemies*

get even (INFORMAL) • *He wanted to get even with his former employers.*

get your own back (INFORMAL) • *the opportunity to get your own back*

hit back (INFORMAL) • *In this article he hits back at his critics.*

pay back • *I'll pay him back for what he's done.*

take revenge • *taking revenge for his father's murder*

retreat ① VERB

to move away from someone or something • *damage inflicted by the rebels as they retreated from the town*

back away • *He put up his hands in protest and began to back away.*

back off • *I stood up for myself and they backed off.*

draw back • *They drew back in fear.*

pull back • *Their forces have pulled back in all areas.*

withdraw • *Troops withdrew from the country last month.*

ANTONYM:
• advance

retreat ② NOUN

the action of moving away
from someone or something
• the long retreat from Moscow
departure • the departure of all
foreign forces from the country
evacuation • the evacuation of
British troops from Dunkirk
flight • my panicked flight from
London
withdrawal • French
withdrawal from Algeria
ANTONYM:
• advance

retreat ③ NOUN

a quiet place you can go to
• He spent the day hidden away
in his country retreat.
haven • The hotel is a haven of
tranquillity.
refuge • a refuge from the harsh
realities of the world
sanctuary • a sanctuary
located on an island

return ① VERB

to go back to a place • The
plane failed to return at the
scheduled time.
come back • He said he'd come
back later.
go back • I love going back
home.
reappear • He reappeared two
nights later.
turn back • We've come too far
now to turn back.

return ② VERB

to give something back • They
guarantee to return your original
investment.

give back • He is refusing to
give the dog back.
pay back • You have to pay back
the loan, plus an arrangement
fee.
refund • The company will
refund the full cost.
repay • I can afford to repay the
loan.

reveal ① VERB

to tell people about
something • They were not
ready to reveal any of the details.
announce • She was planning
to announce her engagement.
disclose • He will not disclose
the name of his patient.
divulge • I do not want to
divulge where the village is.
get off your chest
(INFORMAL) • I feel it's done me
good to get it off my chest.
let on • She never let on that
anything was wrong.

reveal ② VERB

to uncover something that is
hidden • The carpet was
removed to reveal the original
pine floor.
bring to light • The truth is
unlikely to be brought to light.
lay bare • His real motives were
laid bare.
uncover • Auditors said they
had uncovered evidence of
fraud.
unearth • Quarry workers have
unearthed the skeleton of a
mammoth.
unveil • The statue will be
unveiled next week.

r

revenge ① NOUN
vengeance for wrongs or
injury received • *acts of
revenge*
reprisal • *Witnesses are
unwilling to testify through fear
of reprisals.*
retaliation • *The attack was in
retaliation for his murder.*
retribution • *They did not want
their names used for fear of
retribution.*
vengeance • *He swore
vengeance on everyone involved
in the murder.*

revenge ② VERB
to take vengeance on
someone • *to revenge himself on
the press*
avenge • *He was trying to
avenge the death of his friend.*
get even (INFORMAL) • *I'm
going to get even with you for
this.*
get your own back
(INFORMAL) • *I simply want to
get my own back on him.*
hit back (INFORMAL) • *He hit
back at those who criticised him.*
pay back • *Some day I'll pay you
back for this.*
retaliate • *I was sorely tempted
to retaliate.*

reverse ① VERB
to change into something
different or contrary • *They
won't reverse the decision to
increase prices.*
change • *They should change
the law to make this practice
illegal.*

invalidate • *A contract signed
now might be invalidated at a
future date.*
overrule • *In 1998 the Court of
Appeal overruled the decision.*
overturn • *When the
parliament overturned his
decision, he backed down.*
retract • *He was asked to
retract his comments but
refused.*

reverse ② NOUN
the opposite of what has just
been said or done • *The reverse
seldom applies.*
contrary • *There are no
indications she will quit, quite
the contrary.*
converse • *In fact, the converse
is true.*
opposite • *When I told him to
do something he always did the
opposite.*

review ① NOUN
a critical assessment of a book
or performance • *We've never
had a good review in the music
press.*
commentary • *He'll be writing
a weekly commentary on
American culture.*
criticism • *literary criticism*
notice • *Richards's solo work
received good notices.*

review ② NOUN
a general survey or report
• *a review of safety procedures*
analysis • *an analysis of
American trade policy*
examination • *an examination
of the top 250 companies*

report • *the committee's annual report*
study • *a recent study of treatments for back pain*
survey • *a survey of 250 businessmen*

revise VERB
to alter or correct something • *The second edition was completely revised.*
amend • *They voted unanimously to amend the constitution.*
correct • *time spent correcting his students' work*
edit • *We have the right to edit this book once it's finished.*
refresh • *The page refreshes every three minutes.*
revamp • *It is time to revamp the system.*
update • *He was back in the office, updating the work schedule.*

revive VERB
to make or become lively or active again • *an attempt to revive the Russian economy*
rally • *Markets began to rally worldwide.*
resuscitate • *a bid to resuscitate the weekly magazine*

reward NOUN
something given in return for a service • *As a reward for good behaviour, treat your child to a new toy.*
bonus • *We don't get a Christmas bonus any more.*
bounty • *They paid bounties to people to give up their weapons.*

payment • *Players now expect payment for interviews.*
prize • *He won first prize.*

rhythm NOUN
a regular movement or beat • *His body twists and sways to the rhythm.*
beat • *the thumping beat of rock music*
pulse • *the repetitive pulse of the drum beat*
tempo • *Elgar supplied his works with precise indications of tempo.*
time • *A reel is in four-four time.*

rich ① ADJECTIVE
having a lot of money and possessions • *You're going to be a very rich man.*
affluent • *an affluent neighbourhood*
loaded (SLANG) • *Of course he can afford it. He's loaded.*
opulent • *his opulent lifestyle*
prosperous • *The youngest son of a relatively prosperous family*
wealthy • *a wealthy international businessman*
well off • *My grandparents were quite well off.*
ANTONYM:
• poor

rich ② ADJECTIVE
abundant in something • *Bananas are rich in vitamin A.*
abundant • *the earth's most abundant natural resources*
fertile • *a fertile imagination*
plentiful • *a plentiful supply of vegetables*

rid: get rid of VERB

to remove or destroy
something • *a senior manager
who wanted to get rid of him*
dispose of • *He disposed of the
murder weapon.*
dump • *We dumped our bags at
the hotel.*
eject • *Officials used guard dogs
to eject the protestors.*
jettison • *The crew jettisoned
excess fuel.*
remove • *Most of her fears had
been removed.*
weed out • *We must weed these
people out as soon as possible.*

ridiculous ADJECTIVE

very foolish • *It is ridiculous to
suggest we are having a romance.*
absurd • *absurd claims to have
met big stars*
laughable • *He claims the
allegations are "laughable".*
ludicrous • *It's a completely
ludicrous idea.*
preposterous • *their
preposterous claim that they had
unearthed a plot*

right ① ADJECTIVE

in accordance with the facts
• *That clock never tells the right
time.*
accurate • *an accurate record of
events*
correct • *The correct answers
can be found at the bottom of the
page.*
exact • *I can't remember the
exact words of the song.*
factual • *His version of events is
not strictly factual.*

genuine • *a genuine eyewitness
account*
precise • *Officials did not give
precise figures.*
strict • *The book is not a
biography in the strict sense of
the word.*
true • *The true cost often differs
from that.*
valid • *Your point is a valid one.*
ANTONYM:
• wrong

right ② ADJECTIVE

most suitable • *The time is right
for our escape.*
acceptable • *This was beyond
the bounds of acceptable
behaviour.*
appropriate • *an appropriate
outfit for the occasion*
desirable • *This goal is neither
achievable nor desirable.*
done • *It just isn't done to
behave like that in public.*
fit • *a subject which is not fit for
discussion*
fitting • *a fitting end to an
exciting match*
okay or **OK** (INFORMAL) • *Is it
okay if I bring a friend with me?*
proper • *It was not thought
proper for a woman to appear on
the stage.*
seemly (OLD-FASHIONED)
• *the rules of civility and seemly
conduct*
suitable • *the most suitable
man for the job*

right ③ NOUN

what is just and fair • *At least
he knew right from wrong.*

equity • *Income should be distributed with some sense of equity.*
fairness • *a decision based not on fairness but on expediency*
honour • *His whole life was dominated by his sense of honour.*
integrity • *They always strove to maintain a high level of integrity.*
justice • *He has no sense of justice or fair play.*
legality • *They are expected to observe the principles of legality.*
morality • *standards of morality and justice in society*
virtue • *Virtue is not confined to the Christian world.*

right-wing ADJECTIVE
believing in capitalist policies • *some right-wing politicians*
conservative • *the conservative manifesto*
Tory (BRITISH) • *a senior Tory peer*

rigid ① ADJECTIVE
unchangeable and often considered severe • *Hospital routines for nurses are very rigid.*
fixed • *fixed laws*
inflexible • *Workers said the system was too inflexible.*
set • *They have very set ideas about how to achieve this.*
strict • *a strict diet*
stringent • *stringent rules*

rigid ② ADJECTIVE
not easy to bend • *rigid plastic containers*
firm • *a firm platform*
hard • *Something cold and hard pressed into his back.*

solid • *The concrete will stay as solid.*
stiff • *Her fingers were stiff with cold.*
ANTONYM:
• flexible

ring ① VERB
to make a loud clear sound • *He heard the school bell ring.*
chime • *The clock chimed three o'clock.*
clang • *A little later the church bell clanged.*
peal • *Church bells pealed at the stroke of midnight.*
resonate • *a strap hung with bells and resonating gongs*
toll • *The pilgrims tolled the bell.*

ring ② NOUN
an object or group of things in the shape of a circle • *a ring of blue smoke*
band • *a black arm-band*
circle • *Cut out four circles of pastry.*
hoop • *a steel hoop*
loop • *a loop of garden hose*
round • *small fresh rounds of goats' cheese*

ring ③ NOUN
a group of people involved in an illegal activity • *a smuggling ring*
band • *a small band of plotters*
cell • *a cell of neo-Nazis*
clique • *A small clique of people is trying to take over the party.*
syndicate • *a major crime syndicate*

r

riot ① NOUN

a disturbance made by an
unruly mob • *a prison riot*

anarchy • *a decade of civil war
and anarchy*

disorder • *mass public
disorder*

disturbance • *Three people
were injured in a violent
disturbance outside a pub.*

mob violence • *last week's
mob violence in Bucharest*

strife • *communal strife in Los
Angeles*

riot ② VERB

to take part in a riot • *They
rioted in protest against the
Government.*

go on the rampage • *Rock
fans went on the rampage after a
concert.*

rampage • *A curfew was
imposed as gangs rampaged
through the streets.*

run riot • *hooligans running riot
in the streets*

take to the streets • *Workers
and students took to the streets
in protest.*

rise ① VERB

to move upwards • *Wilson
watched the smoke rise from the
fire.*

ascend • *He held her hand as
they ascended the steps.*

climb • *We climbed up the steps
on to the bridge.*

go up • *He went up the ladder
quickly.*

move up • *They moved up to
second place after their win.*

rise ② VERB

to increase • *House prices are
expected to rise this year.*

go up • *Prices must have gone
up since then.*

grow • *The Chinese economy
continues to grow.*

increase • *the decision to
increase prices*

intensify • *The conflict is bound
to intensify.*

mount • *For several hours the
tension mounted.*

ANTONYM:
• fall

rise ③ NOUN

an increase in something • *a rise
in prices*

improvement • *a major
improvement in standards*

increase • *a substantial
increase in workload*

upsurge • *an upsurge of interest
in books*

ANTONYM:
• fall

risk ① NOUN

a chance that something
unpleasant might happen
• *That's a risk I'm happy to take.*

danger • *the dangers of
smoking*

gamble • *Booking a holiday can
be a gamble.*

peril • *the perils of starring in a
TV commercial*

pitfall • *the pitfalls of working
abroad*

risk ② VERB

to do something knowing

that something unpleasant
might happen • *If he doesn't
play, he risks losing his place in
the team.*
chance • *No assassin would
chance a shot from amongst that
crowd.*
dare • *Few people dared go
anywhere on foot.*
gamble • *gambling his life
savings on the stock market*
jeopardise • *The talks may still
be jeopardised by disputes.*
put in jeopardy • *A series of
setbacks have put the whole
project in jeopardy.*

rival ① NOUN
the person someone is
competing with • *He is well
ahead of his nearest rival.*
adversary • *political
adversaries*
antagonist • *Greece's key
rival and chief antagonist,
Turkey*
challenger • *his only challenger
for the presidency*
opponent • *He's a tough
opponent but I'm too good for
him.*

rival ② VERB
to be the equal or near equal
of • *As a holiday destination,
South Africa rivals Kenya for
weather.*
be a match for • *On our day we
are a match for anyone.*
equal • *The victory equalled
Portugal's best in history.*
match • *I think we matched
them in every department.*

river NOUN
TYPES OF RIVER
beck
brook
burn (SCOTTISH)
creek
estuary
rivulet
stream
tributary
watercourse
waterway

road NOUN
a route used by travellers and
vehicles • *There was very little
traffic on the roads.*
motorway • *Britain's first
motorway, the M1*
route • *the most direct route to
the town centre*
street • *He walked briskly down
the street.*
track • *a rough mountain track*

rob VERB
to take something from a
person illegally • *He was beaten
senseless and robbed of all his
money.*
burgle • *He admitted that he
was trying to burgle the surgery.*
con (INFORMAL) • *The
businessman had conned him of
$10,000.*
defraud • *charges of conspiracy
to defraud the government*
loot • *thugs who have looted
shops*
steal from • *trying to steal from
a woman in the street*
swindle • *two executives who
swindled their employer*

romantic ADJECTIVE

connected with love • *a romantic relationship*

amorous • *The object of his amorous intentions is Wendy.*

loving • *a loving husband*

tender • *They embraced and kissed. It was a tender moment.*

room ① NOUN

a separate section in a building • *You can stay in my spare room.*

chamber • *the council chamber*

office • *I'm in the office at the end of the corridor.*

room ② NOUN

unoccupied space • *There wasn't enough room for his gear.*

capacity • *a seating capacity of 17,000*

elbow room • *There wasn't too much elbow room in the cockpit.*

space • *the high cost of office space*

rot ① VERB

to become rotten • *The grain started rotting in the silos.*

decay • *The bodies buried in the fine ash slowly decayed.*

decompose • *The debris slowly decomposes into compost.*

fester • *The wound is festering and gangrene has set in.*

spoil • *Fats spoil by becoming rancid.*

RELATED WORD:
• ADJECTIVE putrid

rot ② NOUN

the condition that affects things when they rot • *The timber frame was not protected against rot.*

decay • *tooth decay*

deterioration • *gum deterioration*

mould • *He scraped the mould off the cheese.*

rotten ① ADJECTIVE

decayed and no longer of use • *The front bay window is rotten.*

bad • *That milk in the fridge is bad.*

decayed • *teeth so decayed they need to be pulled*

decomposed • *The body was too badly decomposed to be identified at once.*

mouldy • *mouldy bread*

sour • *sour milk*

rotten ② ADJECTIVE

(INFORMAL)

of very poor quality • *It's a rotten idea.*

inferior • *overpriced and inferior products*

lousy (SLANG) • *The menu is limited and the food is lousy.*

poor • *The match was very poor.*

unsatisfactory • *if you have obtained unsatisfactory goods or services*

rough ① ADJECTIVE

uneven and not smooth • *My bicycle bumped along the rough ground.*

bumpy • *bumpy cobbled streets*

craggy • *craggy mountains*

rocky • *a bleak and rocky shore*

rugged • *a remote and rugged plateau*

R

uneven • *The ball bobbled awkwardly on the uneven surface.*

ANTONYM:
• smooth

rough ② ADJECTIVE
difficult or unpleasant
• *Teachers have been given a rough time.*

difficult • *It's been a difficult month for us.*

hard • *I've had a hard life.*

tough • *She had a pretty tough childhood.*

unpleasant • *The last few weeks here have been very unpleasant.*

rough ③ ADJECTIVE
only approximately correct
• *At a rough guess it is five times more profitable.*

approximate • *The times are approximate only.*

estimated • *There are an estimated 90,000 gangsters in the country.*

sketchy • *a sketchy account of the incident*

vague • *She could only give a vague description of the intruder.*

round ① ADJECTIVE
shaped like a ball or a circle
• *She has a round attractive face.*

circular • *a circular hole twelve feet wide*

cylindrical • *a cylindrical container*

rounded • *a low rounded hill*

spherical • *gold spherical earrings*

round ② NOUN
one of a series of events • *After round three, two Americans shared the lead.*

lap • *the last lap of the race*

period • *the second period of extra time*

session • *The World Champion was ahead after the first two sessions.*

stage • *the second stage of the Tour de France*

route NOUN
a way from one place to another • *the direct route to the town centre*

channel • *a safe channel avoiding the reefs*

course • *The ship was on a course that followed the coastline.*

itinerary • *The next place on our itinerary was Silistra.*

path • *We followed the path along the clifftops.*

road • *The coastal road is longer, but more scenic.*

way • *I'm afraid I can't remember the way.*

routine ① ADJECTIVE
ordinary, and done regularly
• *a series of routine medical tests*

everyday • *an everyday occurrence*

normal • *The hospital claimed they were following their normal procedure.*

ordinary • *It was just an ordinary weekend for us.*

regular • *one of the regular checks we carry out*

routine
standard • *It was standard practice for untrained clerks to do this work.*
typical • *This was a fairly typical morning scene in our house.*
usual • *The usual methods were not effective.*

routine ② NOUN
the usual way or order someone does things • *The players had to change their daily routine.*
order • *Babies respond well to order in their daily lives.*
pattern • *All three attacks followed the same pattern.*
practice • *a public inquiry into bank practices*
procedure • *The White House said there would be no change in procedure.*
programme • *It is best to follow some sort of structured programme.*
schedule • *He has been forced to adjust his schedule.*
system • *an efficient filing system*

row ① NOUN
several things arranged in a line • *He was greeted by a row of glum faces.*
bank • *a bank of video screens*
column • *a column of figures*
line • *a sparse line of spectators*
queue • *a queue of shoppers*
rank • *a rank of taxis*

row ② NOUN
a serious disagreement • *This could provoke a major diplomatic row with France.*
altercation • *He had an altercation with the umpire.*
argument • *an argument about money*
quarrel • *I had a terrible quarrel with my brother.*
squabble • *There have been minor squabbles about phone bills.*

rowdy ADJECTIVE
rough and noisy • *He complained to the police about rowdy neighbours.*
boisterous • *Most of the children were noisy and boisterous.*
noisy • *My neighbours are a noisy bunch.*
unruly • *a mother accompanied by her ghastly unruly child*
wild • *They loved fast cars and wild parties.*

royal ADJECTIVE
concerning a king or a queen or their family • *the royal yacht*
imperial • *the Imperial palace in Tokyo*
regal • *Never has she looked more regal.*
sovereign • *the Queen's sovereign authority*

rubbish ① NOUN
unwanted things or waste material • *tons of rubbish waiting to be dumped*
garbage • *I found all kinds of garbage left behind by the tide.*
litter • *fines for dropping litter*
refuse (FORMAL) • *The Council made a weekly collection of refuse.*

R

trash • *The yards are overgrown and covered with trash.*

waste • *the safe disposal of toxic waste*

rubbish ② NOUN

foolish words or speech • *Don't talk rubbish!*

drivel • *mindless drivel*

garbage (INFORMAL) • *I personally think this is complete garbage.*

gibberish • *When he did speak to her, he spoke gibberish.*

nonsense • *all that poetic nonsense about love*

rude ① ADJECTIVE

not polite • *He is rude to her friends.*

disrespectful • *They shouldn't treat their mother in this disrespectful way.*

impertinent • *I don't like being asked impertinent questions.*

impudent • *his rude and impudent behaviour*

insolent • *a defiant, almost insolent look*

ANTONYM:
• polite

rude ② ADJECTIVE

unexpected and unpleasant • *a rude awakening*

abrupt • *The recession brought an abrupt end to his happiness.*

unpleasant • *an unpleasant surprise*

violent • *violent mood swings*

ruin ① VERB

to destroy or spoil something • *The crops have been ruined.*

break • *He's broken all his toys.*

damage • *This could damage our chances of winning.*

destroy • *a recipe for destroying the economy*

devastate • *A fire had devastated large parts of the castle.*

impair • *The flavour is impaired by overcooking.*

mar • *The celebrations were marred by violence.*

mess up • *He's messed up his whole career.*

spoil • *Don't let a stupid mistake spoil your life.*

undo • *He intends to undo everything I have fought for.*

wreck • *He wrecked the garden.*

ruin ② NOUN

the state of being destroyed or spoiled • *The vineyards were falling into ruin.*

decay • *The house fell into a state of decay.*

destruction • *the destruction caused by the rioters*

devastation • *A bomb brought chaos and devastation to the city centre yesterday.*

disrepair • *Many of the buildings had fallen into disrepair.*

downfall • *His lack of experience led to his downfall.*

fall • *the fall of the Roman Empire*

ruin ③ NOUN

the remaining parts of a severely damaged thing • *the burnt-out ruins of houses*

r

remains • *the remains of an ancient mosque*

shell • *the shells of burned buildings*

wreck • *We thought of buying the house as a wreck and doing it up.*

rule ① NOUN

a statement of what is allowed • *This was against the rules.*

decree • *a decree lifting sanctions against China*

guideline • *Are there strict guidelines for animal experimentation?*

law • *inflexible moral laws*

order • *He was sacked for disobeying orders.*

regulation • *new safety regulations*

rule ②: as a rule ADVERB

usually or generally • *As a rule, I eat my meals in front of the TV.*

generally • *It is generally true that the darker the fruit the higher its iron content.*

mainly • *Mainly I work alone.*

normally • *Normally, the transport system carries 50,000 passengers a day.*

on the whole • *Their goods are, on the whole, of a very high standard.*

usually • *She is usually a calm and diplomatic woman.*

rule ③ VERB

to govern people • *For four centuries, he says, foreigners have ruled Angola.*

administer • *calls for the UN to administer the country until the election*

be in power • *They were in power for eighteen years.*

govern • *The citizens are thankful they are not governed by a dictator.*

lead • *He led the country between 1949 and 1984.*

reign • *Henry II reigned from 1154 to 1189.*

ruler NOUN

a person who rules or commands • *He was a weak-willed and indecisive ruler.*

commander • *He is commander of the US Fifth Fleet.*

governor • *He was governor of the province in the late 1970s.*

head of state • *the heads of state of all the countries in the European Union*

leader • *the leader of the German Social Democratic Party*

monarch • *the coronation of the new monarch*

sovereign • *the first British sovereign to set foot on Spanish soil*

rumour NOUN

a story which may or may not be true • *persistent rumours of quarrels within the movement*

gossip • *We spent the first hour exchanging gossip.*

hearsay • *Much of what was reported to them was hearsay.*

whisper • *I've heard a whisper that the Bishop intends to leave.*

word • *What's the latest word from Washington?*

run ① VERB

to move on foot at a rapid pace

• I excused myself and ran back to the telephone.

bolt • The pig rose, squealing, and bolted.

gallop • The horses galloped away.

jog • He could scarcely jog around the block that first day.

sprint • She sprinted to the car.

run ② VERB
to manage • He ran a small hotel.

administer • the authorities who administer the island

be in charge of • He is in charge of public safety.

control • He now controls a large retail development empire.

direct • Christopher will direct day-to-day operations.

look after • I look after his finances for him.

manage • Within two years he was managing the store.

rush ① VERB
to move fast or do something quickly • Someone rushed out of the building.

dash • She dashed in from the garden.

fly • I must fly or I'll miss my train.

gush • Piping-hot water gushed out.

hasten • One of them hastened towards me.

hurry • She had to hurry home to look after her son.

race • He raced across town to her house.

run • I excused myself and ran to the door.

scurry • Reporters scurried to get to the phones.

shoot • The car shot out of a junction and smashed into them.

rush ② VERB
to force into immediate action without sufficient preparation • Ministers won't be rushed into a response.

hurry • I don't want to hurry you.

hustle • You won't hustle me into making a commitment.

press • attempting to press me into making a statement

pressurise • Do not be pressurised into making your decision immediately.

push • Don't be pushed into signing anything.

rush ③ NOUN
a state of hurrying • the rush not to be late for school

bustle • the bustle of modern life

dash • a 160-mile dash to the hospital

hurry • Eric left the house in a hurry.

race • a race to get the work finished before the deadline

scramble • the scramble to get a seat on the early morning flight

stampede • There was a stampede for the exit.

r

Ss

sack ① VERB (INFORMAL)
to dismiss from a job • *sacked for punching his boss*
discharge • *discharged from the army*
dismiss • *the power to dismiss employees*
fire (INFORMAL) • *He was fired for poor timekeeping.*

sack ②: the sack NOUN (INFORMAL)
dismissal from a job • *He got the sack after three months.*
discharge • *He plans to appeal his discharge.*
dismissal • *the case for his dismissal*
termination of employment (FORMAL)
• *wrongful termination of employment*

sacrifice ① VERB
to give something up • *She sacrificed her family life for her career.*
forego • *If we forego our summer holiday we can afford a car.*
forfeit • *The company is forfeiting safety for the sake of profit.*
give up • *I gave up my job to be with you.*

surrender • *We have surrendered our political authority for economic gain.*

sacrifice ② NOUN
the action of giving something up • *He was willing to make any sacrifice for peace.*
renunciation • *religious principles of renunciation and dedication*
self-denial • *an unprecedented act of self-denial*

sad ① ADJECTIVE
feeling unhappy about something • *The loss of our friendship makes me sad.*
blue • *I don't know why I'm feeling so blue today.*
dejected • *Everyone has days when they feel dejected.*
depressed • *She's depressed about this whole situation.*
dismal • *What are you all looking so dismal about?*
down • *The elderly man sounded really down.*
downcast • *a downcast expression*
gloomy • *Don't look so gloomy, Mr Todd. I'll do my best for you.*
glum • *a row of glum faces*
grief-stricken • *comforting the grief-stricken relatives*
low • *He used to listen when I was feeling low.*
melancholy (LITERARY)
• *melancholy thoughts*
mournful • *the mournful expression on his face*
unhappy • *I hate to see you so unhappy.*

wistful • *I found myself feeling wistful at the memory of him.*

ANTONYM:
• happy

sad ② ADJECTIVE
making you feel unhappy
• *a sad song*
depressing • *a depressing film*
dismal • *a dark, dismal day*
gloomy • *a gloomy tale of a poor orphan*
harrowing • *a harrowing documentary about the First World War*
heart-rending • *heart-rending pictures of the victims*
melancholy • *the melancholy music used throughout the film*
mournful • *a mournful ballad*
moving • *a deeply moving account of her life*
pathetic • *the pathetic sight of oil-covered sea birds*
poignant • *a poignant love story*
tragic • *his tragic death*
upsetting • *I'm afraid I have some upsetting news for you.*

adness NOUN
the feeling of being unhappy
• *I said goodbye with a mixture of sadness and joy.*
dejection • *a feeling of dejection and despair*
depression • *plunged into the deepest depression*
despondency • *Deep despondency set in again.*
melancholy (LITERARY)
• *Dean had shaken off his melancholy.*

unhappiness • *His unhappiness shows in his face.*

ANTONYM:
• happiness

safe ① ADJECTIVE
not causing harm or danger
• *This is a safe place for tourists to visit.*
harmless • *harmless substances*
innocuous • *Both mushrooms look innocuous but are in fact deadly.*

ANTONYM:
• dangerous

safe ② ADJECTIVE
not in any danger • *I felt warm and safe with him.*
all right • *I'll be all right on my own.*
in safe hands • *It's all right, you're in safe hands.*
okay or **OK** (INFORMAL)
• *Could you check that the baby's okay?*
out of danger • *We were not out of danger yet.*
out of harm's way • *I'm keeping him well out of harm's way.*
protected • *Keep the plants dry and protected from frost.*
safe and sound • *I'm hoping he will come home safe and sound.*
secure • *I would like to feel financially secure.*

safeguard ① VERB
to protect something
• *international action to safeguard the ozone layer*

defend • *his courage in defending religious and civil rights*

guard • *He closely guarded her identity.*

look after • *People tend to look after their own property.*

preserve • *We need to preserve the forest.*

protect • *What can we do to protect ourselves against heart disease?*

save • *This machine could help save babies from cot death.*

shield • *They moved to shield their children from adverse publicity.*

safeguard ② NOUN

something that protects people or things • *adequate safeguards for civil liberties*

barrier • *a barrier against the outside world*

cover • *Airlines are required to provide cover against such incidents.*

defence • *The immune system is our main defence against disease.*

protection • *Innocence is no protection from the evils in our society.*

safety NOUN

the state of being safe from harm or danger • *I was very anxious about her safety.*

immunity • *natural immunity to the disease*

protection • *protection from harmful rays*

security • *a false sense of security*

ANTONYM:
• danger

salty ADJECTIVE

tasting of or containing salt • *a good rasher of salty bacon*

brak (SOUTH AFRICAN) • *the brak shallow water near the dam wall*

briny • *the flow of the briny water*

salted • *100 grams of slightly salted butter*

same ADJECTIVE

exactly like one another • *The two words sound the same but have different spellings.*

alike • *No two families are alike.*

equal • *Mix equal quantities of soy sauce and rice vinegar.*

equivalent • *A kilogram is equivalent to 2.2 pounds.*

identical • *Nearly all the houses were identical.*

indistinguishable • *Her voice is indistinguishable from her sister's.*

ANTONYM:
• different

sanction ① VERB

to officially approve of or allow something • *He is ready to sanction the use of force.*

allow • *I cannot be seen to allow any criminal activity.*

approve • *The parliament has approved a programme of economic reforms.*

authorise • *We are willing to authorise a police raid.*

back • *persuading the government to back the plan*

endorse • *policies endorsed by the voting public*

permit • *The board will not permit the sale to go through.*

support • *The party is under pressure to support the ban.*

ANTONYM:
• veto

sanction ② NOUN

official approval of something • *The king could not enact the law without the sanction of parliament.*

approval • *The chairman has given his approval.*

authorisation • *You will need the authorisation of a parent or guardian.*

backing • *He said the president had the backing of his government.*

blessing • *With the blessing of the White House, the group is meeting to identify more budget cuts.*

permission • *Finally she gave permission for him to marry.*

support • *The prime minister gave his support to the reforms.*

sanctions PLURAL NOUN

penalties for countries which break the law • *The United States is considering imposing sanctions against the regime.*

ban • *After four years, he lifted the ban.*

boycott • *the lifting of the economic boycott against the country*

embargo • *They called on the government to lift its embargo on trade with the country.*

penalties • *legally binding penalties against treaty violators*

sane ① ADJECTIVE

having a normal healthy mind • *This was not the act of a sane person.*

lucid • *She was lucid right up until her death.*

normal • *the question of what constitutes normal behaviour*

rational • *He seemed perfectly rational to me.*

sane ② ADJECTIVE

showing good sense • *a sane and practical policy*

judicious (FORMAL) • *the judicious use of military force*

level-headed • *a sensible, level-headed approach*

rational • *a rational analysis*

reasonable • *a reasonable course of action*

sensible • *the sensible thing to do*

sound • *sound advice*

sarcastic ADJECTIVE

saying the opposite of what you mean to make fun of someone • *A sarcastic remark was on the tip of her tongue.*

caustic • *his abrasive wit and caustic comments*

ironic • *an ironic remark*

sardonic • *a sardonic sense of humour*

satirical • *a satirical TV show*

satisfactory ADJECTIVE

acceptable or adequate • *a satisfactory explanation*

acceptable • *The air pollution exceeds acceptable levels.*

s

adequate • *One in four people are without adequate homes.*
all right • *The meal was all right, but nothing special.*
good enough • *He's not good enough for you.*
passable • *She speaks passable French.*
sufficient • *One teaspoon of sugar should be sufficient.*
ANTONYM:
• unsatisfactory

satisfied ADJECTIVE
happy because you have got what you want • *We are not satisfied with these results.*
content • *I'm perfectly content where I am.*
contented • *She led a quiet, contented life.*
happy • *I'm not happy with the situation.*
pleased • *He seemed pleased with the arrangement.*
ANTONYM:
• disappointed

satisfy ① VERB
to give someone as much of something as they want • *a solution which I hope will satisfy everyone*
gratify • *He was gratified by the audience's response.*
indulge • *I don't believe in indulging children.*
please • *Our prime objective is to please our customers.*

satisfy ② VERB
to convince someone of something • *He had to satisfy*

the doctors that he was fit to play.
convince • *trying to convince the public that its product is safe*
persuade • *I had to persuade him of the advantages.*
put someone's mind at rest • *He has done his best to put my mind at rest.*
reassure • *I tried to reassure them, but they knew I was lying.*

satisfy ③ VERB
to fulfil a requirement • *Candidates must satisfy the conditions for admission.*
fulfil • *All the minimum requirements were fulfilled.*
meet • *The current arrangements are inadequate to meet their needs.*

savage ① ADJECTIVE
cruel and violent • *a savage attack*
barbaric • *a particularly barbaric act of violence*
barbarous • *the barbarous customs of earlier times*
brutal • *a very brutal murder*
cruel • *the cruel practice of bullfighting*
ferocious • *the most ferocious violence ever seen on the streets of London*
inhuman • *the inhuman slaughter of these beautiful creatures*
vicious • *a vicious blow to the head*
violent • *violent crimes*

savage ② NOUN
a violent and uncivilised perso

• They really are a bunch of savages.
barbarian • They considered Charles's followers to be uncouth barbarians.
beast • You beast! Let me go!
brute • He was a brute and he deserved his fate.
lout • an ill-tempered lout
monster • These men were total monsters.

savage ③ VERB
to attack and bite someone • He was savaged to death by the animal.
attack • A lion attacked him when he was a child.
bite • Every year thousands of children are bitten by dogs.
maul • The dog went berserk and mauled all the girls.

save ① VERB
to rescue someone or something • He saved my life.
come to someone's rescue • His uncle came to his rescue.
deliver • I was relieved to be delivered from the pain.
redeem • to redeem souls from purgatory
rescue • rescued from the flames
salvage • salvaging equipment from the wreckage

save ② VERB
to keep someone or something safe • a new machine which could save babies from cot death
keep safe • to keep my home safe from germs

preserve • preserving old buildings
protect • What can we do to protect ourselves from heart disease?
safeguard • measures to safeguard the ozone layer

save ③ VERB
to keep something for later use • They are saving for a house.
hoard • They've begun to hoard food and petrol.
keep • Grate the lemon zest and keep it for later.
put by • He's putting his money in a deposit account.
reserve • Drain the fruit and reserve the juice.
set aside • £130 million would be set aside for repairs to schools.
ANTONYM:
• waste

say ① VERB
to speak words • She said they were very impressed.
▶ see Word Study **say**, page 723

say ② NOUN
a chance to express your opinion • voters who want a say in the matter
voice • Parents are given a voice in decision-making.
vote • Every employee had a vote in the company's future.

saying NOUN
a well-known sentence or phrase • the saying "charity begins at home"
adage • the old adage, "the show must go on"

S

axiom • *the long-held axiom that education leads to higher income*

maxim • *I believe in the maxim "If it ain't broke, don't fix it".*

proverb • *an old Chinese proverb*

scarce ADJECTIVE

rare or uncommon • *Jobs are becoming increasingly scarce.*

few • *Our options are few.*

rare • *Puffins are now rare in this country.*

uncommon • *an extreme but by no means uncommon case*

unusual • *To be appreciated as a parent is quite unusual.*

ANTONYM:

common

scare ① VERB

to frighten someone • *You're scaring me.*

alarm • *We could not see what had alarmed me.*

frighten • *He knew that Soli was trying to frighten him.*

give someone a fright • *The snake moved and gave everyone a fright.*

intimidate • *Jones had set out to intimidate and dominate Paul.*

startle • *Sorry, I didn't mean to startle you.*

terrify • *Flying terrifies him.*

terrorise • *pensioners terrorised by anonymous phone calls*

unnerve • *We were unnerved by the total silence.*

scare ② NOUN

a short period of feeling very frightened • *We got a bit of a scare.*

fright • *the last time I had a real fright*

shock • *It gave me quite a shock to see his face on the screen.*

start • *The sudden noise gave me quite a start.*

scare ③ NOUN

a situation where people worry about something • *Despite the health scare there are no plans to withdraw the drug.*

alert • *a security alert*

hysteria • *Everyone was getting carried away by the hysteria.*

panic • *the panic over GM foods*

scary ADJECTIVE (INFORMAL)

frightening • *Prison is going to be a scary thing for him.*

alarming • *an alarming report on the rise of street crime*

chilling • *a chilling account of the accident*

creepy (INFORMAL) • *places that are really creepy at night*

eerie • *the eerie dark path*

frightening • *a very frightening experience*

hair-raising • *a hair-raising encounter with a wild boar*

spooky • *The whole place has a slightly spooky atmosphere.*

terrifying • *I find it terrifying to be surrounded by a crowd of people.*

unnerving • *It is very unnerving to find out that someone you know is carrying the virus.*

scatter VERB

to throw or drop things all over an area • *She scattered the petals over the grave.*

shower • *They showered confetti over the newlyweds.*
sow • *Sow the seeds in a warm place.*
sprinkle • *Sprinkle a tablespoon of sugar over the fruit.*
throw about • *They started throwing food about.*
ANTONYM:
• gather

scene ① NOUN
a picture or view of something • *a village scene*
landscape • *Arizona's desert landscape*
panorama • *a panorama of fertile valleys*
view • *a view of the lake*

scene ② NOUN
the place where something happens • *the scene of the crime*
location • *filmed in an exotic location*
place • *Can you show me the place where the attack happened?*
setting • *Rome is the perfect setting for romance.*
site • *the site of the battle*
spot • *the ideal spot for a picnic*

scene ③ NOUN
an area of activity • *the music scene*
arena • *the political arena*
business • *the potential to revolutionise the publishing business*
environment • *the Japanese business environment*
world • *the fashion world*

scenery NOUN
the things you see in the countryside • *Drive slowly down the lane enjoying the scenery.*
landscape • *Arizona's desert landscape*
panorama • *admiring the distant mountain panorama*
surroundings • *a holiday home in beautiful surroundings*
terrain • *The terrain changed from arable land to desert.*
view • *The view from our window was spectacular.*

scold VERB
to tell someone off • *She scolded her daughter for being cheeky.*
chide • *Cross chided himself for worrying.*
lecture • *My mother always used to lecture me about not eating properly.*
rebuke • *I turned to him and sharply rebuked him.*
reprimand • *reprimanded for talking in the corridor*
tell off (INFORMAL) • *The teacher really told her off.*
tick off (INFORMAL) • *ticked off for being late*

scorn ① NOUN
great contempt felt for something • *The proposal was greeted with scorn.*
contempt • *I treated this remark with the contempt it deserved.*
derision • *shouts of derision*
disdain • *Janet looked at him with disdain.*

s

mockery • *his mockery of all things English*

scorn ② VERB
to treat with great contempt • *Eleanor scorns the work of others.*
despise • *She secretly despises him.*
disdain • *He disdained politicians.*
look down on • *I wasn't successful so they looked down on me.*
slight • *He felt slighted by this treatment.*

scornful ADJECTIVE
showing contempt for something • *He is deeply scornful of his rivals.*
contemptuous • *She gave a contemptuous little laugh.*
disdainful • *He is disdainful of politicians.*
scathing • *He made some scathing comments about the design.*
sneering • *a sneering tone*
supercilious • *His manner is supercilious and arrogant.*
withering • *Her mother gave her a withering look.*

scrape ① VERB
to rub a rough or sharp object against something • *We had to scrape the frost from the windscreen.*
graze • *He had grazed his knees a little.*
scour • *Scour the pans.*
scratch • *The branches scratched my face and hands.*

scuff • *scuffed shoes*
skin • *I found that I had skinned my knuckles.*

scrape ② VERB
to make a harsh noise by rubbing • *his shoes scraping across the ground*
grate • *His chair grated as he got to his feet.*
grind • *Blocks of ice ground against each other.*
rasp • *The blade rasped over his skin.*
scratch • *He scratched his knife over the worktop.*

scream ① VERB
to shout or cry in a high-pitched voice • *If he says that again, I shall scream.*
cry • *a crying baby*
howl • *He howled like a wounded animal.*
screech • *"Get me some water!" screeched.*
shout • *I shouted at mother to get the police.*
shriek • *She shrieked and leapt from the bed.*
squeal • *Jennifer squealed with delight.*
yell • *I pushed him away, yelling abuse.*

scream ② NOUN
a loud, high-pitched cry • *Hild let out a scream.*
cry • *a cry of horror*
howl • *a howl of rage*
screech • *The figure gave a screech.*
shriek • *a shriek of joy*
squeal • *the squeal of piglets*

yell • *Something brushed Bob's face and he let out a yell.*

scrounge VERB (INFORMAL)
to get something by asking rather than working for it • *He's always scrounging lifts.*

beg • *They managed to beg a lift from a passing fisherman.*

bludge (AUSTRALIAN AND NEW ZEALAND; INFORMAL) • *They've come here to bludge food and money.*

cadge (INFORMAL) • *Can I cadge a ride into town?*

sponge (INFORMAL) • *I got tired of him sponging off me and threw him out.*

scruffy ADJECTIVE
dirty and untidy • *four scruffy youths*

ragged • *a ragged band of men*

seedy • *his seedy clothes*

shabby • *a shabby, tall man with dark eyes*

tatty • *a tatty old cardigan*

unkempt • *His hair was unkempt and filthy.*

ANTONYM:
• smart

scrutinise VERB
to examine something very carefully • *She scrutinised his features.*

examine • *He examined her passport.*

inspect • *Cut the fruit in half and inspect the pips.*

pore over • *We spent hours poring over the files.*

scan • *She kept scanning the crowd for Paul.*

search • *Her eyes searched his face.*

study • *Debbie studied the document for a moment.*

scungy ADJECTIVE
(AUSTRALIAN AND NEW ZEALAND; SLANG)
dirty • *living in some scungy flat on the outskirts of town*

dirty • *He was wearing a dirty old mac.*

filthy • *This flat is so filthy I can't possibly stay here.*

foul • *foul polluted water*

seedy • *a seedy flat*

sleazy • *sleazy bars*

sordid • *sordid little rooms*

squalid • *a squalid bedsit*

search ① VERB
to look for something • *The security forces are searching for the missing men.*

comb • *Police combed the woods for the murder weapon.*

forage • *foraging for food*

fossick (AUSTRALIAN AND NEW ZEALAND) • *to help Gaston fossick for food around the hut*

google • *I went straight home from the party and googled him.*

hunt • *hunting for a job*

look • *He's looking for a way out of this situation.*

scour • *They had scoured the intervening miles of moorland.*

seek • *the man he had been seeking for weeks*

sift • *sifting through the wreckage for clues*

search ② NOUN
the action of looking for

something • *Police will resume the search today.*

hunt • *the hunt for my lost boy*

quest • *his quest to find true love*

secret ADJECTIVE

known about by only a few people • *a secret location*

closet (INFORMAL) • *a closet Fascist*

confidential • *a confidential report*

covert • *She gave him a covert glance.*

furtive • *furtive meetings*

hidden • *a hidden camera*

undercover • *undercover FBI agents*

underground • *the underground communist movement*

RELATED WORD:
• ADJECTIVE cryptic

secretive ADJECTIVE

hiding your feelings and intentions • *Jake was very secretive about his family affairs.*

cagey (INFORMAL) • *He is cagey about what he was paid for the business.*

reserved • *He was unemotional and reserved.*

reticent • *She is very reticent about her achievements.*

section NOUN

one of the parts into which something is divided • *this section of the motorway*

division • *the company's sales division*

instalment • *Payment can be made in instalments.*

part • *the upper part of the body*

piece • *The equipment was taken down the shaft in pieces.*

portion • *I had learnt a portion of the Koran.*

segment • *the third segment of the journey*

secure ① VERB (FORMAL)

to manage to get something • *His achievements helped him to secure the job.*

acquire • *General Motors recently acquired a 50% stake in the company.*

gain • *Hard work may not be enough to gain a place at university.*

get • *I got a job at the sawmill.*

obtain • *He tried to obtain a false passport.*

procure (FORMAL) • *trying to procure the release of the hostages*

secure ② VERB

to make something safe • *We need to secure the building against attack.*

fortify • *British soldiers are working to fortify the airbase.*

make impregnable • *Their intention was to make the old fort impregnable.*

make safe • *Crime Prevention Officers will suggest ways to make your home safe.*

strengthen • *In the 14th century they strengthened this wall against raiders.*

secure ③ VERB

to fasten or attach something firmly • *The frames are secured by rails to the wall.*

attach • *The gadget can be attached to any vertical surface.*
bind • *Bind the ends of the cord together with thread.*
fasten • *Her long hair was fastened by an elastic band.*
fix • *He fixed a bayonet to the end of his rifle.*
lock • *Are you sure you locked the front door?*
moor • *She moored her barge on the river bank.*
tie up • *They dismounted and tied up their horses.*
ANTONYM:
• release

secure ④ ADJECTIVE
tightly locked or well protected • *Make sure your home is as secure as possible.*
fortified • *The door is fortified against flooding.*
impregnable • *The old castle was completely impregnable against raids.*
protected • *the right of women to be protected from harassment*
safe • *We want to go to a football match knowing we are safe from hooliganism.*
shielded • *The company is shielded from takeover attempts.*

secure ⑤ ADJECTIVE
firmly fixed in place • *Shelves are only as secure as their fixings.*
fastened • *Make sure the safety belt is fastened.*
firm • *If you have to climb up, use a firm platform.*
fixed • *Check the holder is fixed in its place on the wall.*

locked • *Leave doors and windows locked.*
solid • *I yanked on the bracket to see if it was solid.*
stable • *The structure must be stable.*
tight • *He kept a tight hold of her arm.*

secure ⑥ ADJECTIVE
feeling safe and happy • *She felt secure when she was with him.*
confident • *In time he became more confident.*
protected • *It's good to have a place in which you feel protected and loved.*
reassured • *I feel much more reassured when I've been for a health check.*
relaxed • *There are very few people he feels relaxed with.*
safe • *With my family I felt warm and safe.*
ANTONYM:
• insecure

see ① VERB
to look at or notice something • *Did you see what happened?*
behold • *She looked into his eyes and beheld madness.*
discern • *We could just discern the outline of the island.*
glimpse • *She glimpsed the man's face briefly.*
look • *She turned to look at him.*
notice • *She noticed a bird sitting on the roof.*
observe • *He observed a reddish spot on the planet's surface.*

s

perceive • *Infants start to perceive objects at a very early age.*

sight • *A fleet of French ships was sighted.*

spot • *I think he spotted me but didn't want to be seen.*

see ② VERB
to realise or understand something • *I see what you mean.*

appreciate • *He appreciates the difficulties.*

comprehend • *They do not comprehend the nature of the problem.*

follow • *Do you follow what I'm saying?*

get • *You don't seem to get the point.*

grasp • *They have not grasped the seriousness of the crisis.*

realise • *They realised too late that they were wrong.*

understand • *I'm not sure I understand.*

see ③ VERB
to find something out • *I'll see what's happening outside.*

ascertain • *Ascertain what services your bank provides.*

determine • *The investigation will determine what really happened.*

discover • *Try to discover what you are good at.*

find out • *Watch the next episode to find out what happens.*

seek ① VERB
to try to find something

• *The police were still seeking information.*

be after • *At last I found what I was after.*

hunt • *Police are hunting for clues.*

look for • *I'm looking for a lost child.*

search for • *searching for answers*

seek ② VERB
to try to do something • *De Gaulle sought to reunite the country.*

aim • *We aim to raise funds for charity.*

aspire to • *He aspired to work in music journalism.*

attempt • *He was forever attempting to arrange deals.*

endeavour • *They are endeavouring to protect trade union rights.*

strive • *The school strives to treat pupils as individuals.*

try • *We are trying to bring about a better world.*

seem VERB
to appear to be • *He seemed such a quiet man.*

appear • *She appeared euphoric.*

give the impression • *He gave the impression of being the perfect husband.*

look • *The cottage looks quite ordinary from the road.*

look like • *You look like a nice guy.*

seize ① VERB
to grab something firmly • *He seized the phone.*

grab • *I grabbed him by the neck.*
grasp • *He grasped both my hands.*
snatch • *Mick snatched the cards from Archie's hand.*

seize ② VERB
to take control of something
• *Rebels have seized the airport.*
annex • *the plan to invade and annex Kuwait*
appropriate • *The land was appropriated by Communists.*
confiscate • *His goods were confiscated and he was ordered to pay a fine.*
hijack • *Almost 250 trucks were hijacked.*
impound • *The ship was impounded under the terms of the trade embargo.*

select ① VERB
to choose something • *They selected only the brightest pupils.*
choose • *Houston was chosen as the site for the conference.*
decide on • *I'm still trying to decide on an outfit for the wedding.*
opt for • *You may wish to opt for one method straight away.*
pick • *He had picked ten people to interview for the jobs.*
settle on • *I finally settled on the estate car because it was so roomy.*
single out • *His boss has singled him out for a special mission.*
take • *"I'll take the grilled tuna," she told the waiter.*

select ② ADJECTIVE
of good quality • *a select band of top-ranking sportsmen*
choice • *We use only the choicest ingredients.*
exclusive • *Britain's most exclusive club*
first-class • *a first-class hotel*
first-rate • *The first-rate cast includes many famous names.*
hand-picked • *a hand-picked series of timeless classics*
prime • *one of the City's prime sites, with a view of several historic buildings*
special • *a special group of government officials*
superior • *a superior range of products*

selfish ADJECTIVE
caring only about yourself
• *his greedy and selfish behaviour*
egoistic or **egoistical**
• *egoistic motives*
egotistic or **egotistical** • *an intensely egotistic streak*
greedy • *greedy bosses awarding themselves big pay rises*
self-centred • *He was self-centred, but he wasn't cruel.*

sell ① VERB
to let someone have something in return for money • *I just sold my car.*
deal in • *They deal in antiques.*
hawk • *vendors hawking trinkets*
peddle • *arrested for peddling drugs*

s

trade in • *They trade in spices and all kinds of grain.*

ANTONYM:
• buy

sell ② VERB
to have available for people to buy • *a little shop that sells teapots*

deal in • *a business dealing in honey*

stock • *The shop stocks a variety of local craft products.*

trade in • *a company that trades in sporting memorabilia*

ANTONYM:
• buy

send ① VERB
to arrange for something to be delivered • *He sent a basket of fruit and a card.*

dispatch • *He dispatched a telegram of congratulations.*

forward • *A letter was forwarded from the clinic.*

remit • *Many immigrants regularly remit money to their families.*

send ② VERB
to transmit a signal or message • *The pilot was trying to send a distress signal.*

broadcast • *to broadcast a message to a whole group of people at once*

stream • *All four matches will be streamed live.*

transmit • *the most efficient way to transmit data*

senior ADJECTIVE
the highest and most

important in an organisation • *senior jobs*

best • *These officers have traditionally taken the best jobs.*

better • *Well-qualified women are now attaining better positions.*

high-ranking • *a high-ranking officer in the medical corps*

superior • *negotiations between crew members and their superior officers*

ANTONYM:
• junior

sense ① NOUN
a feeling you have about something • *an overwhelming sense of guilt*

consciousness • *a consciousness of tension*

feeling • *It gave me a feeling of satisfaction.*

impression • *The music creates an impression of menace.*

sense ② NOUN
the ability to think and behave sensibly • *He had the good sense to call me at once.*

brains (INFORMAL) • *At least I had the brains to keep quiet.*

common sense • *completely lacking in common sense*

intelligence • *He didn't have the intelligence to understand what was happening.*

judgment • *I respect his judgment.*

reason • *a conflict between emotion and reason*

wisdom • *the wisdom that comes with age*

sense ③ VERB
to become aware of
something • *She sensed he
wasn't telling her the whole
story.*
  be aware of • *He was aware of
her anger.*
  feel • *Suddenly, I felt a presence
behind me.*
  get the impression • *I get the
impression he's lying.*
  have a hunch • *Lowe had a
hunch he was on to something.*
  realise • *We realised something
was wrong.*

sensible ADJECTIVE
showing good sense and
judgment • *a sensible,
level-headed approach*
  down-to-earth • *the most
down-to-earth person I've ever
met*
  judicious (FORMAL) • *the
judicious use of military force*
  practical • *practical
suggestions*
  prudent • *It is prudent to start
any exercise programme
gradually.*
  rational • *a rational decision*
  sound • *sound advice*
  wise • *a wise move*
ANTONYM:
• *foolish*

sensitive ADJECTIVE
easily upset about something
• *He was sensitive about his
height.*
  easily offended • *I keep a
sense of humour, and I am not
easily offended.*

easily upset • *He remained
deeply neurotic and easily upset.*
  thin-skinned • *I'm too
thin-skinned – I want everyone to
like me.*
  touchy • *She is very touchy
about being photographed.*

sentimental ADJECTIVE
expressing exaggerated
sadness or tenderness
• *sentimental love stories*
  maudlin • *Jimmy turned
maudlin after three drinks.*
  mushy (INFORMAL) • *I go
completely mushy when I see a
baby.*
  nostalgic • *nostalgic for the
good old days*
  sloppy (INFORMAL) • *I hate
sloppy romantic films.*
  slushy (INFORMAL) • *slushy
ballads*

separate ① ADJECTIVE
not connected to something
else • *The question muddles up
two separate issues.*
  detached • *a detached house*
  disconnected • *sequences of
disconnected events*
  discrete • *two discrete sets of
nerves*
  divorced • *speculative theories
divorced from reality*
  isolated • *He lives as if isolated
from the rest of the world.*
  unconnected • *The two
murders are unconnected.*
ANTONYM:
• *connected*

separate ② VERB
to end a connection between

s

people or things • Police moved in to separate the two groups.

detach • Three of the carriages on the train became detached.

disconnect • Make sure supply plugs are disconnected from the mains.

divide • This was a ruse to divide them.

ANTONYM:
• connect

separate ③ VERB
to end a relationship or marriage • Her parents separated when she was very young.

break up • She hadn't used his name since they broke up.

divorce • We divorced ten years ago.

part • He is parting from his wife.

split up • I split up with my boyfriend last year.

sequence ① NOUN
a number of events coming one after another • an unbroken sequence of victories

chain • the chain of events leading to the assassination

course • a course of injections

cycle • the cycle of birth, growth, decay and death

progression • The story of American freedom is anything but a linear progression.

series • a series of explosions

string • a string of burglaries

succession • He took a succession of jobs that stood him in good stead.

sequence ② NOUN
a particular order in which things are arranged • the colour sequence: yellow, orange, purple, blue

arrangement • a simple arrangement of coloured tiles

order • Music shops should arrange their recordings in alphabetical order.

pattern • a systematic pattern of behaviour

progression • the natural progression of the seasons

structure • The bricks had been arranged in a regular structure.

series NOUN
a number of things coming one after the other • a series of loud explosions

chain • a bizarre chain of events

run • The England skipper is haunted by a run of low scores.

sequence • a sequence of novels

string • a string of burglaries

succession • He had a succession of jobs.

serious ① ADJECTIVE
very bad and worrying • They survived their serious injuries.

acute • an acute attack of appendicitis

alarming • the alarming increase in the number of casualties

bad • a bad bout of flu

critical • He remains in a critical condition in hospital.

dangerous • His wound proved more dangerous than it seemed at first.

extreme • *the most extreme case doctors have ever seen*

grave (FORMAL) • *We are all in grave danger.*

grievous • *grievous wounds*

grim • *Our situation is grim indeed.*

intense • *Intense fighting has broken out in the capital.*

precarious • *He is in a very precarious position.*

severe • *a severe shortage of drinking water*

worrying • *It is a worrying situation.*

serious ② ADJECTIVE
important and deserving careful thought • *I regard this as a serious matter.*

crucial • *Negotiations were at a crucial stage.*

deep • *This novel raises deep questions about the nature of faith.*

difficult • *The government faces even more difficult problems.*

far-reaching • *His actions will have far-reaching consequences.*

grave (FORMAL) • *a grave situation*

important • *We've got more important things to worry about now.*

momentous • *the momentous decision to go to war*

pressing • *a pressing problem*

profound • *a man who thinks about the more profound issues of life*

significant • *the most significant question of all*

urgent • *He is not equipped to deal with an urgent situation like this.*

weighty • *a weighty problem*

ANTONYM:
• trivial

serious ③ ADJECTIVE
sincere about something • *I was not quite sure whether he was serious.*

earnest • *It is my earnest hope that we can work things out.*

genuine • *a genuine offer*

heartfelt • *a full and heartfelt apology*

honest • *He looked at me in honest surprise.*

in earnest • *I can never tell if he is in earnest or not.*

resolute • *He was resolute about his ideals.*

resolved • *They are quite resolved about their decision.*

sincere • *He's sincere in his views.*

serious ④ ADJECTIVE
quiet and not laughing much • *He's quite a serious person.*

earnest • *She looked up at me with an earnest expression.*

grave • *He was looking unusually grave.*

humourless • *a dour, humourless man*

pensive • *We're both in a pensive mood today.*

sober • *sad, sober faces*

solemn • *His solemn little face broke into a smile.*

staid • *a staid country doctor*

stern • *a stern headmaster feared by all the pupils*

S

set ① NOUN

a group of things that belong
together • *a set of tools*

batch • *the latest batch of
recruits*

kit • *I forgot my gym kit.*

outfit • *She was wearing a
brand new outfit.*

series • *a series of books
covering the history of aviation*

set ② VERB

to put or place something
somewhere • *He set his case
down on the floor.*

deposit • *Imagine if you were
suddenly deposited on a desert
island.*

lay • *Lay a sheet of newspaper on
the floor.*

locate • *The restaurant is
located near the cathedral.*

place • *She placed a mug of
coffee in front of him.*

position • *Plants were
carefully positioned in the
alcove.*

put • *He put the photograph on
the desk.*

rest • *He rested one of his
crutches against the rail.*

stick • *Just stick your bag down
anywhere.*

set ③ ADJECTIVE

fixed and not varying • *a set
charge*

arranged • *We arrived at the
arranged time.*

established • *the established
order*

firm • *a firm booking*

fixed • *a fixed rate of interest*

predetermined • *His destiny
was predetermined from the
moment of his birth.*

scheduled • *The plane failed to
return at the scheduled time.*

set on ADJECTIVE

determined to do something
• *She was set on going to the
States.*

bent on • *He's bent on revenge.*

determined • *His enemies are
determined to ruin him.*

intent on • *an actor who was
intent on making a comeback*

settle ① VERB

to put an end to an argument
or problem • *The dispute has
been settled.*

clear up • *Eventually the
confusion was cleared up.*

decide • *None of the cases had
been decided.*

dispose of • *the way in which
you disposed of that problem*

put an end to • *I just want to
put an end to this situation.*

reconcile • *urging the two
parties to reconcile their
differences*

resolve • *They hoped the crisis
could be resolved peacefully.*

straighten out • *doing their best
to straighten out this confusion*

settle ② VERB

to decide or arrange
something • *Let's settle where
we're going tonight.*

agree • *We haven't agreed a
date yet.*

arrange • *Have you arranged
our next appointment?*

decide on • *They decided on an evening to meet.*
determine • *The final wording had not yet been determined.*
fix • *He's going to fix a time when I can see him.*

settle ③ VERB
to make your home in a place • *refugees settling in Britain*
make your home • *those who had made their homes in China*
move to • *His family moved to New Zealand when he was 12.*
people • *The plateau was peopled by nomadic tribes.*
populate • *The island was populated by Native Americans.*

set up VERB
to make arrangements for something • *setting up a system of communication*
arrange • *We have arranged a series of interviews.*
establish • *We have established links with industry and commerce.*
install • *I'm having cable installed next week.*
institute • *to institute better levels of quality control*
organise • *a two-day meeting organised by the UN*

sever VERB
to cut something off • *The tail of the plane was severed from the fuselage.*
chop off • *Peel the parsnips and chop off the root.*
hack off • *They hacked off the branches.*

lop off • *Somebody had lopped the heads off our tulips.*

several ADJECTIVE
indicating a small number • *several boxes filled with albums*
assorted • *overnight stops in assorted hotels*
some • *some cheers from the gallery*
sundry • *He has won sundry music awards.*
various • *a dozen trees of various sorts*

severe ① ADJECTIVE
extremely bad or unpleasant • *severe cash flow problems*
acute • *an acute economic crisis*
critical • *if the situation becomes critical*
deep • *We will be in deep trouble if this goes on.*
dire • *This would have dire consequences for domestic peace.*
extreme • *people living in extreme poverty*
grave (FORMAL) • *He said the situation was very grave.*
intense • *A number of people collapsed in the intense heat.*
serious • *The government faces very serious difficulties.*
terrible • *terrible injuries*
ANTONYM:
• *mild*

severe ② ADJECTIVE
stern and harsh • *This was a dreadful crime and a severe sentence is necessary.*
disapproving • *Janet gave him a disapproving look.*

S

grim • Her expression was grim and unpleasant.

hard • His father was a hard man.

harsh • the cold, harsh cruelty of her husband

stern • He said stern measures would be taken.

strict • My parents were very strict.

shabby ① ADJECTIVE

ragged and worn in appearance • a shabby overcoat

dilapidated • a dilapidated old building

ragged • dressed in a ragged coat

scruffy • a scruffy basement flat in London

seedy • his seedy clothes

tatty • a tatty old cardigan

threadbare • a square of threadbare carpet

worn • a worn corduroy jacket

shabby ② ADJECTIVE

behaving meanly and unfairly • shabby treatment

contemptible • contemptible behaviour

despicable • a despicable thing to do

dirty • That was a dirty trick.

mean • It was mean of you to hurt her like that.

rotten (INFORMAL) • That's a rotten thing to say!

shake ① VERB

to move something from side to side or up and down • You have to shake the bottle before use.

agitate • Gently agitate the water.

brandish • He appeared brandishing a knife.

flourish • He flourished his glass to make the point.

wave • The crowd were waving flags and cheering.

shake ② VERB

to move from side to side or up and down • The whole building shook with the force of the blast.

jolt • The train jolted again.

quake • The whole mountain quaked.

quiver • Her bottom lip began to quiver.

shiver • shivering with fear

shudder • Elaine shuddered with cold.

tremble • The leaves trembled in the breeze.

vibrate • The engine began to vibrate alarmingly.

shake ③ VERB

to shock and upset someone • The news shook me quite a bit.

distress • Her death had profoundly distressed me.

disturb • dreams so vivid that they disturb me for days

rattle (INFORMAL) • He was obviously rattled by events.

shock • Pictures of emaciated prisoners shocked the world.

unnerve • unnerved by the sight

upset • I was too upset to speak

shaky ADJECTIVE

weak and unsteady • threatening an already shaky economy

rickety • *Mona climbed the rickety wooden stairway.*

tottering • *the baby's first tottering steps*

trembling • *She held out one frail, trembling hand.*

unstable • *an unstable lamp on top of an old tea-chest*

unsteady • *His voice was unsteady.*

wobbly • *I'm sorry, this table's a bit wobbly.*

shame ① NOUN
a feeling of guilt or embarrassment • *She felt a deep sense of shame.*

embarrassment • *He turned red with embarrassment.*

humiliation • *the humiliation of having to ask for money*

ignominy • *the ignominy of being excluded*

shame ② NOUN
something that makes people lose respect for you • *I don't want to bring shame on the family.*

discredit • *It was to his discredit that he did nothing.*

disgrace • *He had to resign in disgrace.*

dishonour • *his sense of dishonour at his brother's conduct*

scandal • *They kept quiet about the deal for fear of scandal.*

shame ③ VERB
to make someone feel ashamed • *Her son's behaviour had shamed her.*

disgrace • *I have disgraced my country.*

embarrass • *It embarrassed him that he had no idea of what was going on.*

humiliate • *Why would you try to humiliate me in front of my friends?*

shameless ADJECTIVE
behaving badly without showing any shame • *shameless dishonesty*

barefaced • *a barefaced lie*

brazen • *a brazen theft*

flagrant • *a flagrant violation of the law*

unabashed • *an unabashed egotist*

unashamed • *blatant, unashamed hypocrisy*

shape ① NOUN
the outline of something • *a round shape*

contours • *the contours of the mountains*

figure • *a trim figure*

form • *the form of the human body*

lines • *The belt spoilt the lines of her long dress.*

outline • *the dim outline of a small boat*

shape ② VERB
to make something in a particular form • *Shape the dough into a loaf.*

fashion • *buttons fashioned from bone*

form • *The polymer is formed into a thin sheet.*

make • *gold made into wedding rings*

model • *She began modelling animals from clay.*

s

mould • *Mould the cheese into small ovals.*

share ① VERB
to divide something between two or more people • *We shared a takeaway pizza.*
divide • *The prize money was divided between the two winners.*
split • *We split the bill between us.*

share ② NOUN
a portion of something • *a share of the profits*
allotment • *a daily allotment of 85 grams of bread*
portion • *his portion of the inheritance*
quota • *a quota of four tickets per person*
ration • *their daily ration of water*

sharp ① ADJECTIVE
having a fine cutting edge or point • *a sharp knife*
jagged • *jagged rocks*
keen • *a keen edge*
pointed • *pointed teeth*
razor-sharp • *the razor-sharp blade*

ANTONYM:
• blunt

sharp ② ADJECTIVE
quick to notice or understand things • *a sharp intellect*
alert • *Alert security guards foiled the robbery.*
astute • *He made a series of astute business decisions.*
bright • *an exceptionally bright child*

observant • *an observant eye*
perceptive • *a perceptive gaze*
quick • *His quick mind soon grasped the situation.*
quick-witted • *He is very alert and quick-witted.*

sharp ③ ADJECTIVE
sudden and significant • *a sharp rise in prices*
abrupt • *Their friendship came to an abrupt end.*
marked • *a marked increase in crimes against property*
sudden • *a sudden change in course*

sheer ① ADJECTIVE
complete and total • *acts of sheer desperation*
absolute • *I think it's absolute nonsense.*
complete • *He shook his head in complete bewilderment.*
pure • *To have an uninterrupted night's sleep was pure bliss.*
total • *This is total madness!*
unqualified • *It has been an unqualified disaster.*
utter • *a look of utter confusion*

sheer ② ADJECTIVE
vertical • *There was a sheer drop just outside my window.*
perpendicular • *the perpendicular wall of sandstone*
steep • *a narrow valley with steep sides*
vertical • *The climber inched up a vertical wall of rock.*

sheer ③ ADJECTIVE
very light and delicate • *sheer black tights*

delicate • *delicate fabric*
fine • *a fine, pale grey material*
lightweight • *lightweight materials with Lycra*
thin • *the thin silk of her blouse*

ANTONYM:
• thick

shelter ① NOUN

a place providing protection
• *a bus shelter*
hostel • *She spent two years living in a hostel.*
refuge • *a mountain refuge*
sanctuary • *His church became a sanctuary for people fleeing the civil war.*

shelter ② NOUN

protection from bad weather or danger • *the hut where they were given food and shelter*
asylum • *refugees who sought political asylum*
cover • *They ran for cover from the storm.*
harbour • *Patches of gorse were a great harbour for foxes.*
haven • *The island is a haven for international criminals.*
protection • *Riot shields acted as protection against the attack.*
refuge • *They took refuge in an old barn.*
safety • *the safety of one's own home*
sanctuary • *Some of them sought sanctuary in the church.*

shelter ③ VERB

to stay somewhere in order to be safe • *a man sheltering in a doorway*
hide • *They hid behind a wall.*

huddle • *She huddled inside the porch.*
take cover • *We took cover under a tree when it started to rain.*

shelter ④ VERB

to hide or protect someone
• *A neighbour sheltered the boy for seven days.*
harbour • *He was accused of harbouring terrorist suspects.*
hide • *They hid me until the coast was clear.*
protect • *A purple headscarf protected her against the wind.*
shield • *He shielded his head from the sun with a sack.*

shine VERB

to give out a bright light • *The sun is shining.*
beam • *The spotlight beamed down on the stage.*
gleam • *The moonlight gleamed on the water.*
glow • *The lantern glowed softly in the darkness.*
radiate • *the amount of light radiated by an ordinary light bulb*
shimmer • *The lake shimmered in the sunlight.*
sparkle • *Diamonds sparkled on her wrists.*

shining ADJECTIVE

giving out or reflecting light
• *shining stainless steel tables*
bright • *a bright star*
brilliant • *brilliant sunshine*
gleaming • *gleaming headlights*
luminous • *the luminous dial on the clock*

s

radiant • He saw a figure surrounded by a radiant light.
shimmering • a shimmering gold fabric
sparkling • elegant cutlery and sparkling crystal

shock ① NOUN

a sudden upsetting experience • The extent of the damage came as a shock.
blow • It was a terrible blow when he was made redundant.
bombshell • His departure was a bombshell for the team.
distress • She wanted to save her mother all the distress she could.
trauma • the trauma of losing a parent

shock ② VERB

to make you feel upset • I was shocked by his appearance.
numb • numbed by suffering and terror
paralyse • He stood paralysed with horror.
shake • The news of her death has shaken us all.
stagger • The judge said he was staggered by the defendant's callousness.
stun • Audiences were stunned by the film's violent ending.
traumatise • My wife was traumatised by the experience.

shock ③ VERB

to offend because of being rude or immoral • She is very easily shocked.
appal • I was appalled by her rudeness.

disgust • He disgusted everyone with his boorish behaviour.
offend • Many people are offended by strong swearwords.
outrage • They were outraged by his racist comments.

shop NOUN

a place where things are sold • I had to race round the shops.
boutique • He owns a jewellery boutique.
market • He sold fruit on a stall at the market.
store • Within two years he was managing the store.
supermarket • Most of us do our food shopping in the supermarket.

shore NOUN

TYPES OF SHORE
bank
beach
coast
foreshore
front
lakeside
sands
seaboard
seashore
shingle
strand
waterside

short ① ADJECTIVE

not lasting very long • a short break
brief • a brief meeting
fleeting • a fleeting glimpse
momentary • a momentary lapse of reason
short-lived • a short-lived craz

ANTONYM:
• long

short ② ADJECTIVE
small in height • *a short, elderly man*
▶ see Word Study **short**, page 727

ANTONYM:
• tall

short ③ ADJECTIVE
not using many words • *a short speech*
brief • *a brief description*
concise • *a concise summary*
succinct • *a succinct account*
terse • *a terse comment*

shortage NOUN
a lack of something • *a shortage of funds*
dearth • *the dearth of good fiction by English authors*
deficiency • *tests for vitamin deficiency*
lack • *I was hampered by a lack of information.*
scarcity • *a scarcity of water*
shortfall • *a shortfall in income*
want • *a want of manners and charm*

ANTONYM:
• abundance

shorten VERB
to make something shorter • *Smoking can shorten your life.*
abbreviate • *He abbreviated his name to Alec.*
cut • *The film was cut to two hours.*
trim • *I need to get my hair trimmed.*

ANTONYM:
• lengthen

shout ① NOUN
a loud call or cry • *I heard a distant shout.*
bellow • *a bellow of rage*
cry • *She gave a cry of horror.*
roar • *a roar of approval*
scream • *screams of terror*
yell • *He let out a yell of delight.*

shout ② VERB
to call or cry loudly • *He shouted something to his brother.*
bawl • *Laura and Peter were bawling at each other.*
bellow • *He bellowed orders down the phone.*
call • *He could hear them calling his name.*
cry • *"You're under arrest!" he cried.*
roar • *"I'll kill you for that!" he roared.*
scream • *screaming at them to get out of my house*
yell • *She pushed him away, yelling abuse.*

show ① VERB
to prove something • *Tests show that he has an allergy to peanuts.*
demonstrate • *The study demonstrated a link between obesity and heart problems.*
prove • *History will prove him to be right.*

show ② VERB
to do something in order to teach someone else • *I'll show you how to set the timer.*

s

demonstrate • *She demonstrated how to make ice cream.*

instruct • *He instructed us on how to give first aid.*

teach • *She taught me how to ride.*

show ③ VERB
to display a quality or characteristic • *Her sketches showed artistic promise.*

demonstrate • *He has demonstrated his ability.*

display • *He displayed remarkable courage.*

indicate • *Her choice of words indicated her real feelings.*

manifest (FORMAL) • *Fear can manifest itself in many ways.*

reveal • *His reaction revealed a lack of self-confidence.*

show ④ NOUN
a public exhibition • *a fashion show*

display • *a gymnastics display*

exhibition • *an art exhibition*

presentation • *Julie's successful presentation to the board*

show ⑤ NOUN
a display of a feeling or quality • *a show of affection*

air • *an air of indifference*

display • *a display of remorse*

pose • *a pose of injured innocence*

pretence • *They have given up all pretence of neutrality.*

semblance • *trying to maintain a semblance of order*

shrewd ADJECTIVE
showing intelligence and good judgment • *a shrewd businessman*

astute • *an astute judge of character*

canny • *He was far too canny to give himself away.*

crafty • *He is a clever man and a crafty politician.*

perceptive • *a perceptive analysis of the situation*

sharp • *He is very sharp, and a quick thinker.*

smart • *a very smart move*

shrill ADJECTIVE
high-pitched and piercing • *the shrill whistle of the engine*

penetrating • *a penetrating voice*

piercing • *a piercing squawk*

sharp • *the sharp cry of a vixen*

shrink VERB
to become smaller • *All my jumpers have shrunk in the wash.*

contract • *The ribcage expands and contracts as you breathe.*

diminish • *The threat of war has diminished.*

dwindle • *The factory's workforce has dwindled from 4000 to 200.*

get smaller • *Electronic systems are getting smaller.*

narrow • *The gap between the two parties has narrowed.*

ANTONYM:
• grow

shut ① VERB
to close something • *Someone had forgotten to shut the door.*

close • *If you are cold, close the window.*

fasten • *He fastened the diamond clasp of the necklace.*

slam • *He slammed the gate shut behind him.*

ANTONYM:
• open

shut ② ADJECTIVE

closed or fastened • *A smell of burning came from behind the shut door.*

closed • *All the exits were closed.*

fastened • *The pockets are fastened with buttons.*

sealed • *a sealed envelope*

ANTONYM:
• open

shy ADJECTIVE

nervous in the company of other people • *a shy, quiet-spoken girl*

bashful • *Offstage, he is bashful and awkward.*

reserved • *He was unemotional and reserved.*

retiring • *He was the quiet, retiring type.*

self-conscious • *I felt a bit self-conscious in my swimming costume.*

timid • *a timid little boy*

ANTONYM:
• bold

sick ① ADJECTIVE

unwell or ill • *a ward full of very sick people*

ailing • *She tenderly nursed her ailing mother.*

laid up (INFORMAL) • *I was laid up in bed for weeks.*

poorly (BRITISH; INFORMAL) • *I called Julie and she's still poorly.*

under the weather

(INFORMAL) • *Are you still a bit under the weather?*

unwell • *She had been unwell for some time.*

ANTONYM:
• well

sick ② ADJECTIVE

feeling as if you are going to vomit • *The very thought of food made him sick.*

ill • *The smell of petrol always makes me feel ill.*

nauseous • *These drugs may make you feel nauseous.*

queasy • *The motion of the ship was already making him queasy.*

sick ③: sick of ADJECTIVE

(INFORMAL)

tired of something • *I'm sick of your complaints.*

bored • *I'm getting bored with the whole business.*

fed up • *He is fed up with this country.*

tired • *I am tired of this music.*

weary • *She was weary of being alone.*

side ① NOUN

the edge of something • *Her head hung over the side of the bed.*

edge • *She fell over the edge of the balcony.*

verge • *He parked on the verge of the road.*

RELATED WORD:
• ADJECTIVE lateral

s

side ② NOUN

one of two groups involved in a dispute or contest • *Both sides began to prepare for battle.*

camp • *Most of his supporters had now defected to the opposite camp.*

faction • *leaders of the warring factions*

party • *the candidates for the three main parties*

team • *Both teams played well.*

side with VERB

to support someone in an argument • *Louise always sided with her sister.*

agree with • *She's bound to agree with her husband.*

stand up for • *I was the one who always stood up for my mother.*

support • *a fellow prisoner who supported her*

take the part of • *Why do you always take his part?*

sight ① NOUN

the ability to see • *My sight is so bad now that I can't read any more.*

eyesight • *He suffered from weak eyesight.*

visibility • *Visibility was very poor.*

vision • *It can cause blindness or serious loss of vision.*

RELATED WORDS:
• ADJECTIVES optical, visual

sight ② NOUN

something you see • *It was a ghastly sight.*

display • *These flowers make a colourful display in spring.*

scene • *a bizarre scene*

spectacle • *an impressive spectacle*

sight ③ VERB

to see something or someone • *He had been sighted in Cairo.*

see • *I saw a deer in the woods today.*

spot • *I drove round till I spotted her.*

sign ① NOUN

a mark or symbol • *The negative number is preceded by a minus sign.*

character • *the characters used in the hallmarking system*

emblem • *a small yellow hammer-and-sickle emblem*

logo • *the company's logo*

mark • *Put a tick mark against the statements you agree with.*

symbol • *the chemical symbol for mercury*

sign ② NOUN

a notice put up to give a warning or information • *a sign saying that the highway was closed*

board • *He studied the destination board on the front of the bus.*

notice • *a notice saying "no entry"*

placard • *The protesters sang songs and waved placards.*

sign ③ NOUN

evidence of something • *the first signs of recovery*

clue • *the only real clue that something was wrong*

evidence • *There has been no evidence of criminal activity.*

hint • *He showed only the slightest hint of emotion.*

indication • *All the indications suggest that he is the murderer.*

symptom • *typical symptoms of stress*

token • *a token of goodwill*

trace • *No traces of violence were found on the body.*

signal ① NOUN

something which is intended to give a message • *a distress signal*

beacon • *an emergency beacon*

cue • *He gave me my cue to speak.*

gesture • *She made a menacing gesture with her fist.*

sign • *They gave him the thumbs-up sign.*

signal ② VERB

to make a sign as a message to someone • *He was frantically signalling to her to shut up.*

beckon • *I beckoned her over.*

gesticulate • *He was gesticulating at a hole in the ground.*

gesture • *I gestured towards the house, and he went in.*

motion • *He motioned to her to go behind the screen.*

nod • *They nodded goodnight to the security man.*

sign • *She signed to me to come near.*

wave • *He waved the servants out of the tent.*

significant ADJECTIVE

large or important • *This drug seems to have a significant effect on the disease.*

considerable • *Doing it properly makes considerable demands on our time.*

important • *The strike represents an important challenge to the government.*

impressive • *an impressive achievement*

marked • *a marked increase in crimes against property*

notable • *With a few notable exceptions, doctors are a pretty sensible lot.*

pronounced • *The exhibition has a pronounced Scottish theme.*

striking • *The most striking feature of these statistics is the rate of growth.*

ANTONYM:
• insignificant

silence ① NOUN

an absence of sound • *There was a momentary silence.*

calm • *He liked the calm of the evening.*

hush • *A hush fell over the crowd.*

lull • *a lull in the conversation*

peace • *I love the peace of the countryside.*

quiet • *The quiet of the flat was very soothing.*

stillness • *An explosion shattered the stillness of the night air.*

ANTONYM:
• noise

S

silence ② NOUN

an inability or refusal to talk
• *breaking his silence for the first time about the incident*
dumbness • *I was temporarily traumatised into dumbness.*
muteness • *He retreated into stubborn muteness.*
reticence • *Fran didn't seem to notice my reticence.*
speechlessness • *He was shy to the point of speechlessness.*

silence ③ VERB

to make someone or something quiet • *The shock silenced her completely.*
deaden • *We hung up curtains to try and deaden the noise.*
gag • *I gagged him with a towel.*
muffle • *You can muffle the sound with absorbent material.*
quiet • *A look from her mother quieted her at once.*
quieten • *She tried to quieten her breathing.*
stifle • *He put his hand to his mouth to stifle a giggle.*
still • *He raised a hand to still Alex's protest.*
suppress • *She barely suppressed a gasp.*

silent ① ADJECTIVE

not saying anything • *The class fell silent as the teacher entered.*
dumb • *We were all struck dumb for a moment.*
mute • *a mute look of appeal*
speechless • *speechless with rage*
taciturn • *a taciturn man with a solemn expression*

wordless • *They exchanged a wordless look of understanding.*

silent ② ADJECTIVE

making no noise • *The room was silent except for the ticking of the clock.*
hushed • *the vast, hushed space of the cathedral*
quiet • *a quiet engine*
soundless • *My bare feet were soundless on the carpet.*
still • *The room was suddenly still.*

ANTONYM:
• noisy

silly ADJECTIVE

foolish or ridiculous • *I know it's silly to get so upset.*
absurd • *He found fashion absurd.*
daft (BRITISH; INFORMAL)
• *That's a daft question.*
foolish • *It is foolish to risk injury.*
idiotic • *What an idiotic thing to say!*
inane • *He stood there with an inane grin on his face.*
ridiculous • *a ridiculous suggestion*
stupid • *a stupid mistake*

similar ADJECTIVE

like something else • *an accident similar to Hakkinen's*
alike • *You two are very alike.*
analogous • *a ritual analogous to those of primitive tribal cultures*
comparable • *paying the same wages for work of comparable value*

like • They're as like as two peas in a pod.
uniform • droplets of uniform size

ANTONYM:
• different

similarity NOUN
the quality of being like something else • the similarity of our backgrounds
analogy • There is an analogy between learning and eating.
likeness • These myths have a startling likeness to one another.
resemblance • I could see the resemblance to his grandfather.
sameness • He grew bored by the sameness of the speeches.

ANTONYM:
• difference

simple ① ADJECTIVE
easy to understand or do • a simple task
easy • This ice cream maker is cheap and easy to use.
elementary • elementary computer skills
straightforward • It was a straightforward question.
uncomplicated • an uncomplicated story
understandable • He writes in a clear, understandable style.

ANTONYM:
• complicated

simple ② ADJECTIVE
plain in style • a simple but stylish outfit
basic • an extremely basic hotel room

classic • classic designs which will fit in anywhere
clean • the clean lines of Shaker furniture
plain • Her dress was plain but hung well on her.
severe • hair scraped back in a severe style

ANTONYM:
• elaborate

simplify VERB
to make something easier to do or understand • measures intended to simplify the procedure
make simpler • restructuring the tax system to make it simpler
streamline • an effort to cut costs and streamline operations

sin ① NOUN
wicked and immoral behaviour • preaching against sin
crime • a life of crime
evil • You can't stop all the evil in the world.
offence • an offence which can carry the death penalty
wickedness • a sign of human wickedness
wrong • I intend to right that wrong.

sin ② VERB
to do something wicked and immoral • I admit that I have sinned.
do wrong • They have done wrong and they know it.

sincere ADJECTIVE
saying things that you really mean • my sincere apologies

s

genuine • *a display of genuine emotion*
heartfelt • *heartfelt sympathy*
real • *the real affection between them*
wholehearted • *a wholehearted and genuine response*

ANTONYM:
• insincere

single ① ADJECTIVE
only one and no more • *A single shot was fired.*
lone • *A lone police officer guarded the doors.*
one • *I just had one drink.*
only • *My only regret is that I never knew him.*
sole • *the sole survivor of the accident*
solitary • *There is not one solitary scrap of evidence.*

single ② ADJECTIVE
not married • *I'm surprised you're still single.*
unattached • *I only know two or three unattached people.*
unmarried • *an unmarried friend*

single ③ ADJECTIVE
for one person only • *a single room*
individual • *an individual portion*
separate • *separate beds*

singular ADJECTIVE (FORMAL)
unusual and remarkable • *a smile of singular sweetness*
exceptional • *children with exceptional ability*

extraordinary • *The task requires extraordinary patience and endurance.*
rare • *a leader of rare strength and instinct*
remarkable • *a remarkable achievement*
uncommon • *She read Cecilia's letter with uncommon interest.*
unique • *a woman of unique talent and determination*
unusual • *He had an unusual aptitude for mathematics.*

sinister ADJECTIVE
seeming harmful or evil • *There was something cold and sinister about him.*
evil • *an evil smile*
forbidding • *a huge, forbidding building*
menacing • *His dark eyebrows gave him a menacing look.*
ominous • *A dark and ominous figure stood in the doorway.*
threatening • *his threatening appearance*

situation NOUN
what is happening • *a serious situation*
case • *a clear case of mistaken identity*
circumstances • *I wish we could have met in happier circumstances*
plight • *the plight of Third World countries*
scenario • *a nightmare scenario*
state of affairs • *This state of affairs cannot continue.*

size ① NOUN
how big or small something is • *the size of the audience*

dimensions • *He considered the dimensions of the problem.*
extent • *the extent of the damage*
proportions • *In the tropics, plants grow to huge proportions.*

size ② NOUN
the fact of something being very large • *the sheer size of Australia*
bulk • *Despite his bulk, he moved gracefully.*
immensity • *The immensity of the universe is impossible to grasp.*

skilful ADJECTIVE
able to do something very well • *the country's most skilful politician*
able • *a very able businessman*
accomplished • *an accomplished pianist*
adept • *an adept diplomat*
competent • *a competent and careful driver*
expert • *He is expert at handling complex negotiations.*
masterly • *a masterly performance*
proficient • *proficient with computers*
skilled • *a skilled carpenter*
ANTONYM:
• incompetent

skill NOUN
the ability to do something well • *This task requires great skill.*
ability • *a man of considerable abilities*
competence • *his high professional competence*

dexterity • *Reid's dexterity on the guitar*
expertise • *the expertise to deal with these problems*
facility • *a facility for languages*
knack • *the knack of getting on with people*
proficiency • *basic proficiency in English*

skilled ADJECTIVE
having the knowledge to do something well • *skilled workers, such as plumbers*
able • *an able craftsman*
accomplished • *an accomplished pianist*
competent • *a competent and careful driver*
experienced • *lawyers who are experienced in these matters*
expert • *It takes an expert eye to see the symptoms.*
masterly • *the artist's masterly use of colour*
professional • *professional people like doctors and engineers*
proficient • *He is proficient in several foreign languages.*
skilful • *the artist's skilful use of light and shade*
trained • *Our workforce is highly trained.*
ANTONYM:
• incompetent

skinny ADJECTIVE
extremely thin • *a skinny little boy*
bony • *a long bony finger*
emaciated • *television pictures of emaciated prisoners*
lean • *a tall, lean figure*

s

scrawny • *the vulture's scrawny neck*

thin • *He is small and very thin with white skin.*

underfed • *Kate still looks pale and underfed.*

undernourished
• *undernourished children*

ANTONYM:
• *plump*

slander ① NOUN
something untrue and malicious said about someone • *He is now suing the company for slander.*

libel • *defendants seeking damages for libel*

scandal • *She loves spreading scandal.*

slur • *a vicious slur on his character*

smear • *He called the allegation "an evil smear".*

slander ② VERB
to say untrue and malicious things about someone • *He has been charged with slandering the Prime Minister.*

libel • *The newspaper which libelled him had to pay compensation.*

malign • *He claims he is being unfairly maligned.*

smear • *an attempt to smear their manager*

sleep ① NOUN
the natural state of rest in which you are unconscious • *They were exhausted from lack of sleep.*

doze • *I had a doze after lunch.*

hibernation • *Many animals go into hibernation during the winter.*

kip (BRITISH; SLANG) • *Mason went home for a couple of hours' kip.*

nap • *I might take a nap for a while.*

slumber • *He had fallen into exhausted slumber.*

snooze (INFORMAL) • *a little snooze after dinner*

sleep ② VERB
to rest in a natural state of unconsciousness • *The baby slept during the car journey.*

doze • *He dozed in an armchair.*

hibernate • *Dormice hibernate from October to May.*

kip (BRITISH; SLANG) • *He kipped on my sofa last night.*

slumber • *The girls were slumbering peacefully.*

snooze (INFORMAL) • *Mark snoozed in front of the television*

take a nap • *Try to take a nap every afternoon.*

sleepy ① ADJECTIVE
tired and ready to go to sleep • *Do you feel sleepy during the day?*

drowsy • *This medicine may make you feel drowsy.*

lethargic • *He felt too lethargic to get dressed.*

sluggish • *I was still feeling sluggish after my nap.*

sleepy ② ADJECTIVE
not having much activity or excitement • *a sleepy little village*

dull • *a dull town*

quiet • *a quiet rural backwater*

slender ① ADJECTIVE

attractively thin • *a tall, slender woman*

lean • *Like most athletes, she was lean and muscular.*

slight • *She is small and slight.*

slim • *a young man with a slim build.*

slender ② ADJECTIVE

small in amount or degree • *He won, but only by a slender majority.*

faint • *They now have only a faint chance of survival.*

remote • *a remote possibility*

slight • *There is a slight improvement in his condition.*

slim • *a slim hope*

small • *a small chance of success*

slight ADJECTIVE

small in amount or degree • *a slight dent*

insignificant • *an insignificant amount*

minor • *a minor inconvenience*

negligible • *The strike will have a negligible impact.*

small • *It only makes a small difference.*

trivial • *trivial details*

ANTONYM:

• large

slip ① VERB

to go somewhere quickly and quietly • *Amy slipped downstairs and out of the house.*

creep • *I crept up to my room.*

sneak • *Sometimes he would sneak out to see me.*

steal • *They can steal away at night to join us.*

slip ② NOUN

a small mistake • *There must be no slips.*

blunder • *an embarrassing blunder*

error • *a tactical error*

mistake • *Many people are anxious about making mistakes in grammar.*

slogan NOUN

a short easily-remembered phrase • *a poster with the slogan, "Your country needs you"*

jingle • *a catchy advertising jingle*

motto • *"Who Dares Wins" is the motto of the Special Air Service.*

slope ① NOUN

a flat surface with one end higher than the other • *The street is on a slope.*

gradient • *a steep gradient*

incline • *The car was unable to negotiate the incline.*

ramp • *There is a ramp allowing access for wheelchairs.*

slope ② VERB

to be at an angle • *The bank sloped sharply down to the river.*

fall • *The road fell steeply.*

rise • *The climb is arduous, rising steeply through thick bush.*

slant • *His handwriting slanted to the left.*

slouch VERB

to stand or sit with your

shoulders and head drooping forwards • *She had started to slouch in front of her computer.*

droop • *If you are unhappy, your shoulders may droop.*

lounge • *They lounged in the shade.*

slump • *Don't slump over your desk to write.*

stoop • *He stooped a little and walked with some difficulty.*

slow ADJECTIVE
moving or happening with little speed • *slow, regular breathing*

gradual • *Losing weight is a gradual process.*

leisurely • *He walked at a leisurely pace.*

lingering • *a lingering goodbye*

ponderous • *His steps were heavy and ponderous.*

sluggish • *a sluggish stream*

unhurried • *She rose with unhurried grace.*

ANTONYM:
• fast

slow (down) VERB
to go or cause to go more slowly • *The car slowed and then stopped.*

check • *attempts to check the spread of the virus*

decelerate • *He decelerated when he saw the warning sign.*

slowly ADVERB
not quickly or hurriedly • *He turned and began to walk away slowly.*

by degrees • *By degrees, the tension passed out of him.*

gradually • *Their friendship gradually deepened.*

unhurriedly • *The islanders drift along unhurriedly from day to day.*

ANTONYM:
• quickly

sly ADJECTIVE
cunning and deceptive • *She is devious, sly and manipulative.*

crafty • *a crafty villain*

cunning • *Some of these kids can be very cunning.*

devious • *an extremely dangerous, evil and devious man*

scheming • *You're a scheming little rat, aren't you?*

underhand • *underhand tactics*

wily • *a wily politician*

small ① ADJECTIVE
not large in size, number or amount • *a small child*
▶ see Word Study **small**, page 728

ANTONYM:
• large

small ② ADJECTIVE
not important or significant • *small changes*

inconsequential • *a seeming inconsequential event*

insignificant • *an insignificant village in the hills*

little • *Fancy making such a fuss over such a little thing!*

minor • *a minor detail*

negligible • *The impact of the strike will be negligible.*

petty • *Rows would start over the most petty things.*

slight • *It will only make a slight difference.*
trifling • *These are trifling objections.*
trivial • *Let's not get bogged down in trivial details.*
unimportant • *a comparatively unimportant event*

smart ① ADJECTIVE
clean and neat in appearance • *a smart navy blue outfit*
chic • *chic Parisian women*
elegant • *Patricia looked beautiful and elegant, as always.*
neat • *a neat grey flannel suit*
spruce • *Chris was looking spruce in his uniform.*
stylish • *stylish white shoes*
ANTONYM:
• scruffy

smart ② ADJECTIVE
clever and intelligent • *a smart idea*
astute • *a series of astute business decisions*
bright • *She is not very bright.*
canny • *He was far too canny to give himself away.*
clever • *Nobody disputed that Davey was clever.*
ingenious • *an ingenious plan*
intelligent • *Dolphins are an intelligent species.*
shrewd • *a shrewd businessman*
ANTONYM:
• dumb

smell ① NOUN
the quality of something which you sense through your nose • *a smell of damp wood*

aroma • *the aroma of fresh bread*
fragrance • *the fragrance of his cologne*
odour • *a disagreeable odour*
perfume • *enjoying the perfume of the lemon trees*
pong (BRITISH AND AUSTRALIAN; INFORMAL) • *What's that horrible pong?*
reek • *the reek of rotting wood*
scent • *flowers chosen for their scent*
stench • *a foul stench*
stink • *the stink of smoke and burnt plastic*

smell ② VERB
to become aware of the smell of something • *I could smell liquor on his breath.*
scent • *The dog had scented something in the bushes.*
sniff • *He opened his window and sniffed the air.*

smelly ADJECTIVE
having a strong unpleasant smell • *smelly socks*
foul • *His breath was foul.*
reeking • *reeking drains*
stinking • *piles of stinking rubbish*
ANTONYM:
• fragrant

smile ① VERB
to move the corners of your mouth upwards because you are pleased • *When he saw me, he smiled and waved.*
beam • *She beamed at him in delight.*
grin • *He grinned broadly.*

smirk • *The two men looked at me, nudged each other and smirked.*

smile ② NOUN

the expression you have when you smile • *She gave me a big smile.*

beam • *a strange beam of satisfaction on his face*

grin • *She looked at me with a sheepish grin.*

smirk • *a smirk of triumph*

smooth ADJECTIVE

not rough or bumpy • *a smooth wooden surface*

glassy • *glassy green pebbles*

glossy • *glossy dark fur*

polished • *He slipped on the polished floor.*

silky • *The sauce should be silky in texture.*

sleek • *her sleek, waist-length hair*

ANTONYM:
• rough

smug ADJECTIVE

pleased with yourself • *They looked at each other in smug satisfaction.*

complacent • *an aggravating, complacent little smile*

conceited • *They had grown too conceited and pleased with themselves.*

self-satisfied • *a self-satisfied little snob*

superior • *He stood there looking superior.*

snag NOUN

a small problem or disadvantage • *The snag was that he had no transport.*

catch (INFORMAL) • *It sounds too good to be true – what's the catch?*

difficulty • *The only difficulty may be the price.*

disadvantage • *The disadvantage is that this plant needs frequent watering.*

drawback • *The flat's only drawback was its size.*

problem • *The only problem about living here is the tourists.*

sneak ① VERB

to go somewhere quietly • *Sometimes he would sneak out to see me.*

lurk • *I saw someone lurking outside.*

sidle • *He sidled into the bar, trying to look inconspicuous.*

slip • *Amy slipped downstairs and out of the house.*

steal • *They can steal out and join us later.*

sneak ② VERB

to put or take something somewhere secretly • *I sneaked the books out of the library.*

slip • *He slipped me a note.*

smuggle • *We smuggled a camera into the concert.*

spirit • *treasures spirited away to foreign museums*

sneaky ADJECTIVE

doing things secretly or being done secretly • *He only won by using sneaky tactics.*

crafty • *the crafty methods used by salesmen to get people to sign*

deceitful • *They claimed the government had been deceitful.*

devious • *He was devious, saying one thing to me and another to her.*
dishonest • *It would be dishonest to mislead people in that way.*
mean • *That was a mean trick.*
slippery • *She's a slippery customer, and should be watched.*
sly • *He's a sly devil.*
untrustworthy • *His opponents say he's untrustworthy.*

snooper NOUN
a person who interferes in other people's business • *a tabloid snooper*
meddler • *a meddler in the affairs of state*
stickybeak (AUSTRALIAN AND NEW ZEALAND; INFORMAL) • *She's just an annoying stickybeak.*

soak VERB
to make something very wet • *The water had soaked his jacket.*
bathe • *Bathe the infected area in a salt solution.*
permeate • *The water had permeated the stone.*
steep • *green beans steeped in olive oil*
wet • *Wet the hair and work the shampoo through it.*

sociable ADJECTIVE
enjoying the company of other people • *She's usually outgoing and sociable.*
friendly • *The people here are very friendly.*

gregarious • *I'm not a gregarious person.*
outgoing • *He was shy and she was very outgoing.*

society ① NOUN
the people in a particular country or region • *a major problem in society*
civilisation • *an ancient civilisation*
culture • *people from different cultures*

society ② NOUN
an organisation for people with the same interest or aim • *the school debating society*
association • *the Football Association*
circle • *a local painting circle*
club • *He was at the youth club.*
fellowship • *the Visual Arts Fellowship*
group • *an environmental group*
guild • *the Screen Writers' Guild*
institute • *the Women's Institute*
league • *the World Muslim League*
organisation • *student organisations*
union • *the International Astronomical Union*

soft ① ADJECTIVE
not hard, stiff or firm • *a soft bed*
flexible • *a flexible material*
pliable • *a pliable dough*
squashy • *a squashy tomato*
supple • *supple leather*
yielding • *yielding cushions*
ANTONYM:
• hard

s

soft ② ADJECTIVE

quiet and not harsh • *a soft tapping at my door*

gentle • *a gentle voice*

low • *She spoke to us in a low whisper.*

mellow • *mellow background music*

muted • *Their loud conversation became muted.*

quiet • *He always spoke in a quiet tone to which everyone listened.*

subdued • *His voice was more subdued than usual.*

software NOUN

computer programs used on a particular system • *software for mobile phones*

app • *an app telling you where your seat is*

application • *Download the application here.*

code • *Developers have to produce code that works in any browser.*

program • *a program to convert dollars into pounds*

soil ① NOUN

the surface of the earth • *The soil is reasonably moist after the rain.*

clay • *a thin layer of clay*

dirt • *The bulldozers piled up huge mounds of dirt.*

earth • *a huge pile of earth*

ground • *a hole in the ground*

soil ② VERB

to make something dirty • *He looked at her as though her words might soil him.*

dirty • *He was afraid the dog's hairs might dirty the seats.*

foul • *The cage was fouled with droppings.*

pollute • *chemicals which pollute rivers*

smear • *The pillow was smeared with make-up.*

spatter • *Her dress was spattered with mud.*

stain • *Some foods can stain the teeth.*

ANTONYM:
• clean

solemn ADJECTIVE

not cheerful or humorous • *a taciturn man with a solemn expression*

earnest • *Ella was a pious, earnest woman.*

grave (FORMAL) • *He was looking unusually grave.*

serious • *She looked at me with big, serious eyes.*

sober • *sad, sober faces*

staid • *He is boring, old-fashioned, and staid.*

solid ① ADJECTIVE

hard and firm • *a block of solid wax*

firm • *a firm mattress*

hard • *The snow was hard and slippery.*

solid ② ADJECTIVE

not likely to fall down • *a solid structure*

stable • *stable foundations*

strong • *a strong fence*

sturdy • *The camera was mounted on a sturdy tripod.*

substantial • *The posts are made of concrete and are fairly substantial.*

solitude NOUN
the state of being alone • *He went to the cottage for a few days of solitude.*
isolation • *the isolation he endured while in captivity*
loneliness • *I have a fear of loneliness.*
privacy • *the privacy of my own room*
seclusion • *She lived in seclusion with her husband.*

solve VERB
to find the answer to a problem or question • *attempts to solve the mystery*
clear up • *During dinner the confusion was cleared up.*
crack • *He finally managed to crack the code.*
decipher • *trying to decipher the symbols on the stone tablets*
get to the bottom of • *The police wanted to get to the bottom of the case.*
resolve • *Scientists hope this will finally resolve the mystery.*
work out • *I've worked out where I'm going wrong.*

sometimes ADVERB
now and then • *During the summer, I sometimes have hay fever.*
at times • *The debate was highly emotional at times.*
every now and then • *He checks up on me every now and then.*

every so often • *Every so often he does something silly.*
from time to time • *I go back to see my mum from time to time.*
now and again • *I enjoy a day out now and again.*
now and then • *These people like a laugh now and then.*
occasionally • *I know that I do put people down occasionally.*
once in a while • *It does you good to get out once in a while.*

soon ADVERB
in a very short time • *You'll be hearing from us very soon.*
any minute now • *Any minute now she's going to start crying.*
before long • *Interest rates will come down before long.*
in a minute • *I'll be with you in a minute.*
in the near future • *The controversy is unlikely to be resolved in the near future.*
presently • *I'll deal with you presently.*
shortly • *The trial will begin shortly.*
ANTONYM:
• later

sophisticated ① ADJECTIVE
having refined tastes • *a charming, sophisticated companion*
cosmopolitan • *The family are rich and extremely cosmopolitan.*
cultivated • *an elegant and cultivated woman*
cultured • *He is immensely cultured and well-read.*

s

refined • *a woman of refined tastes*
urbane • *a polished, urbane manner*

sophisticated ② ADJECTIVE

advanced and complicated • *a sophisticated piece of equipment*
advanced • *the most advanced optical telescope in the world*
complex • *complex machines*
complicated • *a complicated voting system*
elaborate • *an elaborate design*
intricate • *intricate controls*
refined • *a more refined engine*

ANTONYM:
• simple

sore ADJECTIVE

causing pain and discomfort • *a sore throat*
inflamed • *Her eyes were red and inflamed.*
painful • *a painful knock on the knee*
raw • *Her hands were rubbed raw by the rope.*
sensitive • *the pain of sensitive teeth*
smarting • *My eyes were smarting from the smoke.*
tender • *My stomach feels very tender.*

sorrow ① NOUN

deep sadness or regret • *a time of great sorrow*
grief • *Their grief soon gave way to anger.*
heartache • *suffering the heartache of a divorce*
melancholy (LITERARY) • *She has an air of melancholy.*

misery • *All his money brought him nothing but misery.*
mourning • *a day of mourning*
pain • *My heart is full of pain.*
regret • *She accepted his resignation with regret.*
sadness • *It is with a mixture of sadness and joy that I say farewell.*
unhappiness • *I had a lot of unhappiness in my adolescence.*
woe (FORMAL) • *a tale of woe*

ANTONYM:
• joy

sorrow ② NOUN

things that cause deep sadness and regret • *the joys and sorrows of family life*
hardship • *One of the worst hardships is having so little time with my family.*
heartache • *all the heartaches of parenthood*
misfortune • *She seems to enjoy the misfortunes of others.*
trouble • *She told me all her troubles.*
woe (FORMAL) • *He did not tell his friends about his woes.*
worry • *a life with no worries*

ANTONYM:
• joy

sorry ① ADJECTIVE

feeling sadness or regret • *I'm terribly sorry to bother you.*
apologetic • *"I'm afraid I can't help," she said with an apologetic smile.*
penitent • *He sat silent and penitent in a corner.*
regretful • *Now I'm totally regretful I did it.*

remorseful • *He was genuinely remorseful.*

repentant • *repentant sinners*

sorry ② ADJECTIVE
feeling sympathy for someone
• *I was sorry to hear about your accident.*

moved • *I'm moved by what you say.*

sympathetic • *She gave me a sympathetic glance.*

sorry ③ ADJECTIVE
in a bad condition • *He was in a pretty sorry state when we found him.*

deplorable • *living in deplorable conditions*

miserable • *a miserable existence*

pathetic • *the pathetic sight of oil-covered sea birds*

pitiful • *a pitiful creature*

poor • *the poor condition of the pitch*

sad • *a sad state of affairs*

wretched • *the wretched victims of war*

sort ① NOUN
one of the different kinds of something • *a dozen trees of various sorts*

brand • *his favourite brand of toothpaste*

category • *The topics were divided into six categories.*

class • *a better class of restaurant*

group • *Weathermen classify clouds into several different groups.*

kind • *different kinds of roses*

make • *a certain make of car*

species • *400 species of fungi have been recorded.*

style • *Several styles of hat were available.*

type • *What type of dog should we get?*

variety • *many varieties of birds*

sort ② VERB
to arrange things into different kinds • *He sorted the material into three folders.*

arrange • *Arrange the books in neat piles.*

categorise • *ways to categorise information*

classify • *Rocks can be classified according to their mode of origin.*

divide • *The subjects were divided into four groups.*

grade • *musical pieces graded according to difficulty*

group • *The fact sheet is grouped into seven sections.*

separate • *His work can be separated into three main categories.*

sound ① NOUN
something that can be heard
• *the sound of laughter*

din • *make themselves heard over the din of the crowd*

hubbub • *the hubbub of excited conversation*

noise • *The noise was deafening.*

racket • *the racket of drills and electric saws*

tone • *the clear tone of the bell*

ANTONYM:
• silence

RELATED WORDS:
• ADJECTIVES acoustic, sonic

s

sound ② VERB
to produce or cause to
produce a noise • *A young man
sounded the bell.*
blow • *A guard was blowing his
whistle.*
chime • *He heard the doorbell
chime.*
clang • *The church bell clanged.*
peal • *Church bells pealed at the
stroke of midnight.*
ring • *She heard the school bell
ringing.*
set off • *Any escape sets off the
alarm.*
toll • *The pilgrims tolled the
bell.*

sound ③ ADJECTIVE
healthy, or in good condition
• *His body was still sound.*
all right • *Does the roof seem all
right?*
fine • *She told me her heart was
perfectly fine.*
fit • *Exercise is the first step to a
fit body.*
healthy • *His once healthy mind
was deteriorating.*
in good condition • *The
timbers were all in good
condition.*
intact • *The boat did not appear
damaged and its equipment
seemed intact.*
robust • *He is in robust health
for a man of his age.*

sound ④ ADJECTIVE
reliable and sensible • *a sound
financial proposition*
down-to-earth • *Their ideas
seem very down-to-earth.*

good • *Give me one good reason
why I should tell you.*
reasonable • *a perfectly
reasonable decision*
reliable • *It's difficult to give a
reliable estimate.*
sensible • *sensible advice*
solid • *good solid information*
valid • *Both sides made some
valid points.*

sour ① ADJECTIVE
having a sharp taste • *The
stewed apple was sour even with
sugar added.*
acid • *The liquid had an acid
taste.*
bitter • *a bitter drink*
pungent • *a pungent sauce*
sharp • *a clean, sharp flavour*
tart • *the tart qualities of citrus
fruit*
ANTONYM:
• sweet

sour ② ADJECTIVE
unpleasant in taste because
no longer fresh • *This cream's
gone sour.*
curdled • *curdled milk*
off • *This meat's gone off.*
rancid • *rancid butter*

sour ③ ADJECTIVE
bad-tempered and unfriendly
• *a sour expression*
disagreeable • *a shallow,
disagreeable man*
embittered • *an embittered
former employee*
jaundiced • *a jaundiced
attitude*
tart • *a tart reply*

source NOUN

the place where something comes from • *the source of his confidence*

beginning • *the beginning of all the trouble*

cause • *the cause of the problem*

derivation • *The derivation of the name is obscure.*

origin • *the origin of life*

originator • *the originator of the theory*

souvenir NOUN

something you keep as a reminder • *a souvenir of our holiday*

keepsake • *a cherished keepsake*

memento • *a memento of the occasion*

relic • *the threadbare teddy bear, a relic of childhood*

reminder • *a permanent reminder of this historic event*

space ① NOUN

an area which is empty or available • *a car with plenty of interior space*

accommodation • *We have accommodation for six people.*

capacity • *the capacity of the airliner*

room • *no room to manoeuvre*

RELATED WORD:
• ADJECTIVE spatial

space ② NOUN

the gap between two things • *the space between the two tables*

blank • *I've left a blank here for your signature.*

distance • *the distance between the island and the mainland*

gap • *The wind was tearing through gaps in the window frames.*

interval • *the intervals between the trees*

space ③ NOUN

a period of time • *two incidents in the space of a week*

interval • *a long interval of silence*

period • *for a limited period only*

span • *The batteries have a life span of six hours.*

time • *At 15 he left home for a short time.*

while • *Sit down for a while.*

spacious ADJECTIVE

having or providing a lot of space • *a spacious lounge*

ample • *the city's ample car parks*

broad • *a broad expanse of green lawn*

expansive • *an expansive play area*

extensive • *The palace stands in extensive grounds.*

huge • *a huge apartment overlooking the park*

large • *a large detached house*

vast • *a vast chamber*

spare ① ADJECTIVE

in addition to what is needed • *Luckily I had a spare pair of glasses.*

extra • *Allow yourself some extra time in case of emergencies.*

free • *I'll do it as soon as I get some free time.*

s

superfluous • *I got rid of all my superfluous belongings.*
surplus • *They sell their surplus produce.*

spare ② VERB
to make something available • *Can you spare some money for a cup of tea?*
afford • *It's all I can afford to give you.*
give • *It's good of you to give me some of your time.*
let someone have • *I can let you have some milk and sugar.*

spare ③ VERB
to save someone from an unpleasant experience • *I wanted to spare her that suffering.*
let off (INFORMAL) • *I'll let you off this time.*
pardon • *Relatives had begged authorities to pardon him.*
relieve of • *a machine which relieves you of the drudgery of housework*
save from • *I was trying to save you from unnecessary worry.*

sparkle VERB
to shine with small bright points of light • *Diamonds sparkled on her wrists.*
gleam • *sunlight gleaming on the water*
glisten • *The wall glistened with frost.*
glitter • *A million stars glittered in the black sky.*
shimmer • *In the distance the lake shimmered.*

twinkle • *The old man's eyes twinkled.*

speak VERB
to use your voice to say words • *She turned to look at the person who was speaking.*
▶ see Word Study **say**, page 723

special ① ADJECTIVE
more important or better than others of its kind • *You are very special to me.*
exceptional • *children with exceptional ability*
important • *This is an important occasion.*
significant • *of significant importance*
unique • *a unique talent*
ANTONYM:
• ordinary

special ② ADJECTIVE
relating to one person or group in particular • *the special needs of the chronically sick*
characteristic • *a characteristic feature*
distinctive • *the distinctive smell of chlorine*
individual • *Each family needs individual attention.*
particular • *This is a question of particular importance for us.*
peculiar • *This is not a problem peculiar to London.*
specific • *the specific needs of elderly people*
ANTONYM:
• general

specify VERB
to state or describe

something precisely • *Specify which size and colour you want.*
be specific about • *She was never very specific about her date of birth.*
indicate • *Please indicate your preference below.*
name • *The victims of the fire have been named.*
spell out • *He spelled out the reasons why he was leaving.*
state • *Please state your name.*
stipulate • *His duties were stipulated in the contract.*

spectator NOUN
a person who watches something • *Spectators lined the route.*
bystander • *an innocent bystander*
eyewitness • *Eyewitnesses say the suspect then fled the scene.*
observer • *a disinterested observer*
onlooker • *A small crowd of onlookers was there to greet her.*
witness • *There were scores of witnesses.*

speech NOUN
a formal talk given to an audience • *He delivered his speech in French.*
address • *an address to the American people*
discourse • *a lengthy discourse on strategy*
lecture • *a series of lectures on art*
talk • *a talk on Celtic mythology*

speed ① NOUN
the rate at which something moves or happens • *a top speed of 200 mph*
haste • *the old saying "more haste, less speed"*
hurry • *the hurry and excitement of the city*
momentum • *This campaign is gaining momentum.*
pace • *He walked at a leisurely pace.*
rapidity • *My moods alternate with alarming rapidity.*
swiftness • *Time is passing with incredible swiftness.*
velocity • *the velocity of light*

speed ② VERB
to move quickly • *The pair sped off when the police arrived.*
career • *His car careered into a river.*
flash • *The bus flashed past me.*
gallop • *galloping along the corridor*
race • *He raced across town.*
rush • *He rushed off, closely followed by Kemp.*
tear • *Miranda tore off down the road.*

spin VERB
to turn quickly around a central point • *as the earth spins on its axis*
pirouette • *She pirouetted in front of the mirror.*
revolve • *The satellite revolves around the planet.*
rotate • *rotating propellers*
turn • *a turning wheel*

S

whirl • *The fallen leaves whirled around.*

spirit ① NOUN
the part of you that is not physical • *His spirit had left his body.*
life force • *the life force of all animate things*
soul • *praying for the soul of her dead husband*

spirit ② NOUN
a ghost or supernatural being • *a protection against evil spirits*
apparition • *an apparition of her dead son*
ghost • *the premise that ghosts exist*
phantom • *People claimed to have seen the phantom.*
spectre • *a spectre from the other world*
sprite • *a water sprite*

spirit ③ NOUN
liveliness and energy • *They played with spirit.*
animation • *They both spoke with animation.*
energy • *At 80 her energy is amazing.*
enthusiasm • *They seem to be lacking in enthusiasm.*
fire • *His performance was full of fire.*
force • *She expressed her feelings with some force.*
vigour • *We resumed the attack with renewed vigour.*
zest • *He threw himself into the project with typical zest.*

spite ① : in spite of
PREPOSITION
even though something is the case • *In spite of all the gossip, Virginia stayed behind.*
despite • *They manage to enjoy life despite adversity.*
even though • *They did it even though I warned them not to.*
notwithstanding
• *Notwithstanding his age, Sikorski had an important job.*
regardless of • *He led from the front, regardless of the danger.*
though • *I enjoy painting, though I am not very good at it.*

spite ② NOUN
a desire to hurt someone • *He just did it out of spite.*
ill will • *He didn't bear anyone any ill will.*
malevolence • *a streak of malevolence*
malice • *There was no malice in her voice.*
spitefulness • *petty spitefulness*
venom • *His wit had a touch of venom about it.*

spiteful ADJECTIVE
saying or doing nasty things to hurt people • *a stream of spiteful telephone calls*
catty (INFORMAL) • *She's always making catty remarks.*
cruel • *They gave him a cruel nickname.*
malevolent • *a malevolent stare*
malicious • *spreading malicious gossip*

S

nasty • *What nasty little snobs you all are.*
snide • *He made a snide comment about my family.*
venomous • *a venomous attack*
vindictive • *How can you be so vindictive?*

splendid ① ADJECTIVE
very good indeed • *I've had a splendid time.*
cracking (BRITISH, AUSTRALIAN AND NEW ZEALAND; INFORMAL) • *It's a cracking script.*
excellent • *The recording quality is excellent.*
fantastic (INFORMAL) • *a fantastic combination of colours*
fine • *a fine little fellow*
glorious • *a glorious career*
great (INFORMAL) • *a great bunch of guys*
marvellous • *a marvellous thing to do*
wonderful • *a wonderful movie*

splendid ② ADJECTIVE
beautiful and impressive • *a splendid old mansion*
gorgeous • *a gorgeous Renaissance building*
grand • *a grand hotel*
imposing • *imposing wrought-iron gates*
impressive • *an impressive spectacle*
magnificent • *magnificent views across the valley*
superb • *The hotel has a superb isolated location.*

split ① VERB
to divide into two or more parts • *The ship split in two.*

diverge • *Their paths began to diverge.*
fork • *Ahead of us, the road forked.*
part • *For a moment the clouds parted.*
separate • *Fluff the rice with a fork to separate the grains.*

split ② VERB
to have a crack or tear • *His trousers split.*
burst • *A water pipe has burst.*
come apart • *My jacket's coming apart at the seams.*
crack • *A gas main cracked.*
rip • *I felt the paper rip as we pulled in opposite directions.*

split ③ NOUN
a crack or tear in something • *There's a split in my mattress.*
crack • *The larvae burrow into cracks in the floor.*
fissure • *Water trickled out of fissures in the limestone.*
rip • *the rip in her new jacket*
tear • *the ragged edges of a tear*

split ④ NOUN
a division between two things • *the split between rugby league and rugby union*
breach • *a serious breach in relations between the two countries*
breakup • *the breakup of the Soviet Union in 1991*
divergence • *a divergence between France and its allies*
division • *the conventional division between "art" and "life"*
rift • *There is a rift between us and the rest of the family.*

s

spoil | 580

schism • *the schism which divided the Christian world*

spoil ① VERB
to damage or destroy something • *Don't let it spoil your holiday.*

damage • *This could damage our chances of winning.*

destroy • *His criticism has destroyed my confidence.*

harm • *This product harms the environment.*

impair • *The flavour is impaired by overcooking.*

mar • *The celebrations were marred by violence.*

mess up • *He's messed up his life.*

ruin • *My wife was ruining her health through worry.*

wreck • *the injuries which nearly wrecked his career*

spoil ② VERB
to give someone everything they want • *Grandparents often spoil their grandchildren.*

cosset • *We did not cosset our children.*

indulge • *a heavily indulged youngest daughter*

pamper • *pampered pets*

spoilsport NOUN
a person who spoils other people's fun • *They made me feel like a spoilsport for saying no.*

misery (BRITISH; INFORMAL) • *the miseries in the government*

wowser (AUSTRALIAN; SLANG) • *a small group of wowsers*

spooky ADJECTIVE
eerie and frightening • *The whole place had a slightly spooky atmosphere.*

creepy (INFORMAL) • *a place that is really creepy at night*

eerie • *The wind made eerie noises in the trees.*

frightening • *Whenever I fall asleep, I see these frightening faces.*

ghostly • *The moon shed a ghostly light on the fields.*

haunted • *a haunted house*

scary (INFORMAL) • *a scary ruined castle*

supernatural • *The blade glowed with a supernatural light.*

uncanny • *The strange, uncanny feeling was creeping all over me.*

spot ① NOUN
a small, round mark on something • *a navy blue dress with white spots*

blemish • *A small blemish spoiled the surface.*

blot • *an ink blot*

blotch • *His face was covered in red blotches.*

mark • *a little red mark on my neck*

smudge • *There was a dark smudge on his forehead.*

speck • *a speck of dirt*

spot ② NOUN
a location or place • *an out-of-the-way spot*

location • *The hotel is in a superb isolated location.*

place • *Jerusalem is Christianity most venerated place.*

point • *the point where the rive had burst its banks*

position • She moved the body to a position where it would not be seen.

scene • He left a note at the scene of the crime.

site • plans to construct a temple on the site

spot ③ VERB

to see or notice something • Her drama teacher spotted her ability.

catch sight of • I caught sight of an ad in the paper.

detect • The test should enable doctors to detect the disease early.

discern • I did not discern any change.

observe • Can you observe any difference?

see • I can see a resemblance between you.

sight • A fleet of French ships was sighted.

spread ① VERB

to open out or extend over an area • He spread his coat over the bed.

extend • The new territory would extend over one-fifth of Canada's land mass.

fan out • She spun, and her dress's full skirt fanned out in a circle.

open • She opened her arms and gave me a big hug.

sprawl • The recreation area sprawls over 900 acres.

unfold • When the bird lifts off, its wings unfold to a six-foot span.

unfurl • We began to unfurl the sails.

unroll • I unrolled my sleeping bag.

spread ② VERB

to put a thin layer on a surface • Spread the bread with the cream cheese.

apply • Apply the preparation evenly over the wood's surface.

coat • Coat the fish with the paste.

cover • I covered the table with a cloth.

overlay • The floor was overlaid with rugs.

plaster • She plastered herself in sun lotion.

smear • Smear a little oil over the inside of the bowl.

smother • He likes to smother his bread with butter.

spread ③ VERB

to reach or affect more people gradually • The sense of fear is spreading in the neighbourhood.

circulate • Rumours were circulating that the project was to be abandoned.

grow • Opposition grew and the government agreed to negotiate.

expand • The industry is looking for opportunities to expand into other countries.

increase • The population continues to increase.

proliferate • the free internet services that are proliferating across the world

travel • News of his work travelled all the way to Asia.

s

spread ④ NOUN

the extent or growth of something • *the gradual spread of information*

diffusion • *the development and diffusion of ideas*

expansion • *the rapid expansion of private health insurance*

extent • *the growing extent of the problem*

growth • *the growth of nationalism*

increase • *an increase of violence along the border*

progression • *This drug slows the progression of HIV.*

proliferation • *the proliferation of nuclear weapons*

upsurge • *the upsurge in interest in these books*

squabble ① VERB

to quarrel about something trivial • *Mum and Dad squabble all the time.*

argue • *They went on arguing all the way down the road.*

bicker • *The two women bickered constantly.*

fall out (INFORMAL) • *Mum and I used to fall out a lot.*

feud • *feuding neighbours*

fight • *Mostly, they fight about paying bills.*

quarrel • *At one point we quarrelled over something silly.*

row • *They rowed all the time.*

wrangle • *The two sides spend their time wrangling over procedural problems.*

squabble ② NOUN

a quarrel • *There have been minor squabbles about phone bills.*

altercation • *an altercation with the referee*

argument • *a heated argument*

barney (BRITISH, AUSTRALIAN AND NEW ZEALAND; INFORMAL) • *We had such a barney that we nearly split up.*

disagreement • *My instructor and I had a brief disagreement.*

dispute • *a dispute between the two countries over farm subsidies*

fight • *He had a big fight with his dad that night.*

quarrel • *I had a terrible quarrel with my brother.*

row • *A man had been stabbed to death in a family row.*

tiff • *She was walking home after a tiff with her boyfriend.*

staff NOUN

the people who work for an organisation • *She made little effort to socialise with other staff.*

employees • *We want to make sure our employees are happy.*

personnel • *An announcement was made to all personnel.*

team • *The team worked well under his direction.*

workers • *weekend and night-shift workers*

workforce • *a sullen and resentful workforce*

stage ① NOUN

a part of a process • *the closing stages of the race*

lap • *The first lap was clocked at under a minute.*

period • *We went through a period of unprecedented change.*

phase • *a passing phase*

point • *a critical point in the campaign*

step • *the next step in the process*

stage ② VERB

to organise something • *Workers have staged a number of one-day strikes.*

arrange • *We're arranging a surprise party for her.*

engineer • *He was the one who engineered the merger.*

mount • *a security operation mounted by the army*

orchestrate • *a carefully orchestrated campaign*

organise • *a two-day meeting organised by the UN*

stain ① NOUN

a mark on something • *grass stains*

blot • *an ink blot*

mark • *I can't get this mark to come off.*

spot • *brown spots on the skin caused by the sun*

stain ② VERB

to make a mark on something • *Some foods can stain the teeth.*

dirty • *Sheets can be reused until they are damaged or dirtied.*

mark • *the places where Steve's boots had marked the wood*

soil • *a soiled white apron*

spot • *her coat was spotted with blood*

stale ADJECTIVE

no longer fresh • *a lump of stale bread*

flat • *flat lemonade*

old • *mouldy old cheese*

sour • *sour milk*

stagnant • *stagnant water*

ANTONYM:
• fresh

standard ① NOUN

a particular level of quality or achievement • *There will be new standards of hospital cleanliness.*

calibre • *the high calibre of these researchers*

criterion • *The most important criterion for entry is excellence in your chosen field.*

guideline • *The accord lays down guidelines for the conduct of government agents.*

level • *The exercises are marked according to their level of difficulty.*

norm • *the commonly accepted norms of democracy*

quality • *Everyone can improve their quality of life.*

requirement • *These products meet all legal requirements.*

standard ② ADJECTIVE

usual, normal and correct • *It was standard practice for them to consult the parents.*

accepted • *It is accepted wisdom that the state of your body impacts on your state of mind.*

correct • *the correct way to produce a crop of tomato plants*

customary • *It is customary to offer a drink or a snack to guests.*

normal • *Some shops were closed, but that's quite normal for a Thursday.*

orthodox • *orthodox police methods*

regular • *This product looks and tastes like regular lemonade.*

usual • *It is usual to tip waiters.*

standards PLURAL NOUN
moral principles of behaviour • *My father has always had high moral standards.*

ethics • *the difference between our personal and social ethics*

ideals • *The party has drifted too far from its socialist ideals.*

morals • *Western ideas and morals*

principles • *He refused to do anything that went against his principles.*

rules • *They were expected to adhere to the rules of the convent.*

scruples • *a man with no moral scruples*

values • *the values of liberty and equality*

star NOUN
a famous person • *a film star*

celebrity • *A host of celebrities attended the premiere.*

idol • *the city's greatest soccer idol*

luminary (LITERARY) • *The event attracted such pop luminaries as Madonna.*

stare VERB
to look at something for a long time • *He stared at the floor, lost in meditation.*

gaze • *gazing at herself in the mirror*

look • *He looked at her with open hostility.*

start ① VERB
to begin to take place • *School starts again next week.*

arise • *A conflict is likely to arise.*

begin • *A typical day begins at 8.30.*

come into being • *The festival came into being in 1986.*

come into existence • *a club that came into existence only 30 years ago*

commence (FORMAL) • *The programme will commence at 6.30.*

get under way • *The game got under way.*

originate • *The disease originated in Africa.*

ANTONYM:
• finish

start ② VERB
to begin to do something • *Susie started to cry.*

begin • *He began to groan with pain.*

commence (FORMAL) • *They commenced a systematic search.*

embark on • *He's embarking on a new career as a writer.*

proceed • *He proceeded to prove me wrong.*

set about • *How do you set about getting a mortgage?*

ANTONYM:
• stop

S

start ③ VERB

to cause something to begin
• *a good time to start a business*

begin • *The US is prepared to begin talks immediately.*

create • *Criticism will only create feelings of failure.*

establish • *The school was established in 1899.*

found • *Baden-Powell founded the Boy Scouts in 1908.*

get going • *I've worked hard to get this business going.*

inaugurate (FORMAL) • *the company which inaugurated the first scheduled international flight*

initiate • *They wanted to initiate a discussion.*

instigate • *The violence was instigated by a few people.*

institute • *We have instituted a number of measures.*

introduce • *The government has introduced other money-saving schemes.*

launch • *The police have launched an investigation into the incident.*

open • *We opened the service with a hymn.*

pioneer • *the man who invented and pioneered DNA testing*

set in motion • *Several changes have already been set in motion.*

set up • *A committee was set up to arbitrate in the dispute.*

trigger • *Nuts can trigger an allergic reaction in some people.*

ANTONYM:
• stop

start ④ NOUN

the beginning of something
• *His career had an auspicious start.*

beginning • *the beginning of all the trouble*

birth • *the birth of modern art*

commencement (FORMAL)
• *Applicants should be at least 16 before the commencement of the course.*

dawn • *the dawn of a new age*

foundation • *the foundation of the National Organisation for Women*

inauguration (FORMAL) • *the inauguration of new exam standards*

inception (FORMAL) • *Since its inception the company has produced 53 different aircraft designs.*

initiation • *There was a year between initiation and completion.*

onset • *the onset of puberty*

opening • *the opening of the trial*

outset • *There were lots of problems from the outset.*

ANTONYM:
• finish

state ① NOUN

the condition or circumstances of something
• *the pathetic state of the rail network*

circumstances • *He's in desperate circumstances.*

condition • *He remains in a critical condition in hospital.*

plight • *the plight of Third World countries*

position • *We are in a privileged position.*

predicament • *the once great club's current predicament*

shape • *Her finances were in terrible shape.*

situation • *a precarious situation*

state ② NOUN

a country • *the state of Denmark*

country • *a country where alcohol is prohibited*

kingdom • *The kingdom's power declined.*

land • *in that distant land*

nation • *a leading nation in world politics*

republic • *In 1918, Austria became a republic.*

state ③ VERB

to say something, especially in a formal way • *Please state your occupation.*

affirm • *a speech in which he affirmed his policies*

articulate • *an attempt to articulate his feelings*

assert • *He asserted his innocence.*

declare • *He declared that he would fight on.*

express • *He expressed regret that he had caused any offence.*

say • *The police said he had no connection with the security forces.*

specify • *Please specify your preferences below.*

statement NOUN

a short written or spoken piece giving information • *He was angry when he made that statement.*

account • *He gave a detailed account of what happened that night.*

announcement • *He made his announcement after talks with the President.*

bulletin • *A bulletin was released announcing the decision.*

declaration • *a public declaration of support*

explanation • *They have given no public explanation for his dismissal.*

proclamation • *The proclamation of independence was broadcast over the radio.*

report • *A press report said that at least six people had died.*

testimony • *His testimony was an important part of the prosecution case.*

status NOUN

a person's social position • *the status of children in society*

position • *a privileged position*

prestige • *to diminish the prestige of the monarchy*

rank • *He was stripped of his rank*

standing • *This has done nothing to improve his standing.*

stay VERB

to remain somewhere • *She stayed in bed till noon.*

hang around (INFORMAL) • *I can't hang around here all day*

linger • *I lingered on for a few days until he arrived.*

loiter • *We loitered around looking in shop windows.*
remain • *You'll have to remain in hospital for the time being.*
tarry • *The shop's aim is to persuade you to tarry and spend.*
wait • *I'll wait here till you come back.*

steadfast ADJECTIVE
refusing to change or give up • *He remained steadfast in his belief.*
constant • *He has been her constant companion for the last four months.*
faithful • *this party's most faithful voters*
firm • *He held a firm belief in the afterlife.*
immovable • *On one issue, however, she was immovable.*
resolute • *a decisive and resolute international leader*
staunch • *a staunch supporter of these proposals*
steady • *He was firm and steady, unlike many men she knew.*
unshakeable • *his unshakeable belief in the project*

steady ① ADJECTIVE
continuing without interruptions • *a steady rise in profits*
consistent • *consistent support*
constant • *under constant pressure*
continuous • *Japanese-style programmes of continuous improvement*
even • *an even level of sound*
nonstop • *nonstop background music*
regular • *a regular beat*
uninterrupted • *28 years of uninterrupted growth*

steady ② ADJECTIVE
not shaky or wobbling • *O'Brien held out a steady hand.*
firm • *Make sure the tree is securely mounted on a firm base.*
secure • *Check joints are secure and the wood is sound.*
stable • *stable foundations*

steady ③ VERB
to prevent something from shaking or wobbling • *Two men were steadying a ladder.*
brace • *the old timbers which braced the roof*
secure • *The frames are secured by horizontal rails.*
stabilise • *gyros which stabilise the platform*
support • *Thick wooden posts support the ceiling.*

steal ① VERB
to take something without permission • *He was accused of stealing a tin of pineapple chunks.*
appropriate • *Several other companies have appropriated the idea.*
nick (BRITISH, AUSTRALIAN AND NEW ZEALAND; SLANG) • *I nicked that money from the till.*
pilfer • *Staff were pilfering behind the bar.*
pinch (INFORMAL) • *Someone's pinched my wallet.*

S

swipe (SLANG) • *Did you just swipe that book?*

take • *The burglars took anything they could carry.*

steal ② VERB
to move somewhere quietly and secretly • *They can steal out and join us later.*

creep • *We crept away under cover of darkness.*

slip • *I wanted to duck down and slip past but they saw me.*

sneak • *Sometimes he would sneak out to see me.*

tiptoe • *She slipped out of bed and tiptoed to the window.*

steep ① ADJECTIVE
rising sharply and abruptly • *a steep hill*

sheer • *a sheer drop*

vertical • *The slope was almost vertical.*

ANTONYM:
• gradual

steep ② ADJECTIVE
more expensive than is reasonable • *steep prices*

excessive • *excessive charges*

extortionate • *an extortionate rate of interest*

high • *high loan rates*

unreasonable • *unreasonable interest charges*

steep ③ VERB
to soak something in a liquid • *green beans steeped in olive oil*

immerse • *Immerse the gammon in cold water to remove the salt.*

marinate • *Marinate the chicken for at least four hours.*

soak • *Soak the beans overnight.*

sterile ① ADJECTIVE
free from germs • *Protect the cut with a sterile dressing.*

antiseptic • *an antiseptic hospital room*

germ-free • *Keep your working surfaces germ-free.*

sterilised • *a sterilised laboratory*

sterile ② ADJECTIVE
unable to produce • *These chemicals can cause fish to become sterile.*

barren • *a barren mare*

unproductive • *70 million acres of unproductive land*

ANTONYM:
• fertile

stick ① NOUN
a long, thin piece of wood • *crowds armed with sticks and stones*

bat • *a baseball bat*

cane • *He wore a grey suit and leaned heavily on his cane.*

mace • *a statue of a king holding a golden mace*

pole • *He reached up with a hooked pole to roll down the shutter.*

rod • *a witch-doctor's rod*

truncheon • *a police officer's truncheon*

twig • *the sound of a twig breaking underfoot*

wand • *You can't wave a magic wand and make everything okay.*

stick ② VERB

to thrust something somewhere • *They stuck a needle in my back.*

dig • *She dug her spoon into the moussaka.*

insert • *He inserted the key into the lock.*

jab • *A needle was jabbed into my arm.*

poke • *He poked his finger into the hole.*

push • *She pushed her thumb into his eye.*

put • *Just put it through my letter-box when you're finished with it.*

ram • *He rammed the jacket under the seat.*

shove • *We shoved a copy of the newsletter beneath their door.*

stuff • *I stuffed my hands in my pockets.*

thrust • *A small aerial thrust up from the grass verge.*

stick ③ VERB

to attach • *Stick down any loose bits of flooring.*

attach • *We attach labels to things before we file them away.*

bond • *Strips of wood are bonded together.*

fix • *Fix the photo to the card using double-sided tape.*

fuse • *The scientists fused immune cells with cancer cells.*

glue • *Glue the fabric around the window.*

paste • *The children were busy pasting stars on to a chart.*

stick ④ VERB

to become attached • *The soil stuck to my boots.*

adhere (FORMAL) • *Small particles adhere to the seed.*

bond • *Diamond does not bond well with other materials.*

cling • *His sodden trousers were clinging to his shins.*

fuse • *The flakes fuse together and produce ice crystals.*

stick ⑤ VERB

to jam or become jammed • *The dagger stuck tightly in the silver scabbard.*

catch • *His jacket buttons caught in the net.*

jam • *Every few moments the machinery became jammed.*

lodge • *The car has a bullet lodged in the passenger door.*

snag • *The fishermen said their nets kept snagging on submerged objects.*

sticky ADJECTIVE

covered with a substance that sticks to other things • *She thrust her hand into the sticky mess.*

adhesive • *adhesive tape*

tacky • *covered with a tacky resin*

stiff ① ADJECTIVE

firm and not easily bent • *stiff metal wires*

firm • *a firm mattress*

hard • *the hard wooden floor*

rigid • *a rigid plastic container*

solid • *a block of solid wax*

taut • *He lifted the wire until it was taut.*

ANTONYM:

• limp

s

stiff ② ADJECTIVE
not friendly or relaxed • *the rather stiff and formal surroundings of the Palace*
cold • *Sharon was very cold with me.*
forced • *a forced smile*
formal • *His voice was grave and formal.*
stilted • *Our conversation was stilted and polite.*
unnatural • *a strained and unnatural atmosphere*
wooden • *a wooden performance*

stiff ③ ADJECTIVE
difficult or severe • *a stiff exam*
arduous • *an arduous undertaking*
difficult • *a difficult job*
exacting • *exacting standards*
formidable • *a formidable task*
hard • *a hard day's work*
rigorous • *rigorous military training*
tough • *a tough challenge*

still ADJECTIVE
not moving • *The air was still.*
calm • *the calm waters of the harbour*
inert • *He covered the inert body with a blanket.*
motionless • *He stood there, motionless.*
stationary • *The train was stationary for 90 minutes.*
tranquil • *a tranquil lake*

stock ① NOUN
shares bought in an investment company • *the buying of stocks*

bonds • *the recent sharp decline in bond prices*
investments • *Earn a rate of return of 8% on your investments.*
shares • *He was keen to buy shares in the company.*

stock ② NOUN
the total amount of goods for sale in a shop • *The shop withdrew a quantity of stock from sale.*
goods • *Are all your goods on display?*
merchandise (FORMAL) • *25% off selected merchandise*

stock ③ NOUN
a supply of something • *Troops have seized a large stock of weapons.*
reserve • *65% of the world's oil reserves*
reservoir • *the body's short-term reservoir of energy*
stockpile • *a stockpile of food for the winter*
store • *my secret store of chocolate biscuits*
supply • *What happens when food supplies run low?*

stock ④ NOUN
an animal or person's ancestors • *We are both from working-class stock.*
ancestry • *a family who can trace their ancestry back to the sixteenth century*
descent • *All the contributors were of African descent.*
extraction • *Her father was of Italian extraction.*

lineage • *a respectable family of ancient lineage*
origin • *people of Asian origin*
parentage • *She's a Londoner of mixed parentage.*

stock ⑤ VERB
to keep a stock of goods to sell • *The shop stocks a wide range of paint.*
deal in • *They deal in kitchen equipment.*
sell • *It sells everything from hair ribbons to oriental rugs.*
supply • *We supply office furniture and accessories.*
trade in • *He had been trading in antique furniture for 25 years.*

stock ⑥ ADJECTIVE
commonly used • *National security is the stock excuse for government secrecy.*
hackneyed • *It may be an old hackneyed phrase, but it's true.*
overused • *an overused catch phrase*
routine • *We've tried all the routine methods of persuasion.*
standard • *the standard ending for a formal letter*
stereotyped • *stereotyped ideas about women*
typical • *the typical questions journalists ask celebrities*
usual • *He came out with all the usual excuses.*

stockpile ① VERB
to store large quantities of something • *People are stockpiling food for the winter.*

accumulate • *Some people get rich by accumulating wealth very gradually.*
amass • *It is best not to enquire how he amassed his fortune.*
collect • *Two young girls were collecting firewood.*
gather • *We gathered enough wood to last the night.*
hoard • *They've begun to hoard food and petrol.*
save • *Scraps of material were saved for quilts.*
stash (INFORMAL) • *He had stashed money in an offshore account.*
store up • *Investors were storing up cash in anticipation of disaster.*

stockpile ② NOUN
a large store of something • *stockpiles of fuel*
arsenal • *a formidable arsenal of facts*
cache • *a substantial cache of documents*
hoard • *a hoard of silver and jewels worth $40m*
reserve • *The country's reserves of food are running low.*
stash (INFORMAL) • *a secret stash of treasure*
stock • *our existing stocks of food*
store • *his secret store of sweets*

stocky ADJECTIVE
short but solid-looking • *a stocky, middle-aged man*
chunky • *the chunky South African tennis player*
solid • *a solid build*

sturdy • *a short, sturdy woman in her early sixties*

stomach NOUN
the front part of the body around the waist • *Breathe out and flatten your stomach.*

belly • *He patted his belly in satisfaction.*

paunch • *Nicholson surveyed his spreading paunch.*

puku (NEW ZEALAND) • *a pain in my puku*

tummy (INFORMAL) • *I'd like a flatter tummy, but then who wouldn't?*

stop ① VERB
to cease doing something • *I stopped working last year to go travelling.*

cease • *A small number of firms have ceased trading.*

cut out (INFORMAL) • *Will you cut out that racket?*

desist • *I will be boycotting the country's products until it desists from whaling.*

discontinue • *Do not discontinue the treatment without talking to your doctor.*

end • *public pressure to end the embargo*

quit • *He's trying to quit smoking.*

ANTONYM:
• start

stop ② VERB
to come to an end • *He prayed for the blizzard to stop.*

cease • *At one o'clock the rain ceased.*

come to an end • *An hour later, the meeting came to an end.*

conclude • *The evening concluded with dinner and speeches.*

end • *The talks ended in disagreement.*

finish • *The teaching day finishes at around 4 pm.*

halt • *Discussions have halted again.*

ANTONYM:
• start

stop ③ VERB
to prevent something • *measures to stop the trade in ivory*

arrest • *trying to arrest the bleeding*

check • *a policy to check fast population growth*

prevent • *the most practical way of preventing crime*

store ① NOUN
a supply kept for future use • *I have a store of food and water here.*

cache • *their cache of treasures*

fund • *an extraordinary fund of energy*

hoard • *a hoard of supplies*

reserve • *the world's oil reserves*

reservoir • *the body's short-term reservoir of energy*

stock • *stocks of paper and ink*

stockpile • *a stockpile of fuel*

supply • *food supplies*

store ② NOUN
a place where things are kept • *a grain store*

depot • *a government food depot*

storeroom • a storeroom filled with furniture
warehouse • a carpet warehouse

store ③ VERB
to keep something for future use • The information can be stored in a computer.
hoard • They've begun to hoard food and petrol.
keep • Grate the lemon zest and keep it for later.
save • His allotment of gas had to be saved for emergencies.
stash (INFORMAL) • He had stashed money away in a secret offshore account.
stockpile • People are stockpiling food for the coming winter.

story NOUN
a tale told or written to entertain people • a poignant love story
account • a true account
anecdote • her store of theatrical anecdotes
legend • an old Scottish legend
narrative • a fast-moving narrative
tale • a fairy tale
yarn • a children's yarn about giants

straight ① ADJECTIVE
upright or level • Keep your arms straight.
erect • The upper back and neck are held in an erect position.
even • to ensure an even hem
horizontal • a horizontal line
level • a completely level base

perpendicular • Position your body perpendicular with the slope.
upright • He sat in an upright position in his chair.
vertical • Keep the spine vertical.
ANTONYM:
• crooked

straight ② ADJECTIVE
honest, frank and direct • They wouldn't give me a straight answer.
blunt • She is blunt about her personal life.
candid • I haven't been completely candid with you.
forthright • a forthright reply
frank • a frank discussion
honest • Please be honest with me.
outright • This was outright rejection.
plain • plain talking
point-blank • a point-blank refusal

straightforward ① ADJECTIVE
easy and involving no problems • The question seemed straightforward enough.
basic • The film's story is pretty basic.
easy • The shower is easy to install.
elementary • elementary computer skills
lo-fi • books on how to start your own lo-fi radio station
routine • a fairly routine procedure

s

straightforward

simple • *simple advice on filling in your tax form*

uncomplicated • *good British cooking with its uncomplicated, natural flavours*

ANTONYM:
• complicated

straightforward ②
ADJECTIVE

honest, open and frank • *I liked his straightforward, intelligent manner.*

candid • *I haven't been completely candid with you.*

direct • *He avoided giving a direct answer.*

forthright • *He was known for his forthright manner.*

frank • *They had a frank discussion about the issue.*

honest • *I was totally honest about what I was doing.*

open • *He had always been open with her.*

plain • *I believe in plain talking.*

straight • *He never gives a straight answer to a straight question.*

ANTONYM:
• devious

strain ① NOUN

worry and nervous tension • *the stresses and strains of a busy career*

anxiety • *Her voice was full of anxiety.*

pressure • *the pressure of work*

stress • *the stress of exams*

tension • *Laughing relieves tension and stress.*

strain ② VERB

to make something do more than it is able to do • *You'll strain your eyes reading in this light.*

overwork • *Too much food will overwork your digestive system.*

tax • *He is beginning to tax my patience.*

strange ① ADJECTIVE

unusual or unexpected • *A strange thing happened.*

abnormal • *an abnormal fear of spiders*

bizarre • *a bizarre scene*

curious • *a curious mixture of ancient and modern*

extraordinary • *an extraordinary occurrence*

funny • *a funny feeling*

odd • *There was something odd about her.*

peculiar • *It tasted very peculiar.*

queer (OLD-FASHIONED) • *I think there's something a bit queer going on.*

uncommon • *A 15-year lifespan is not uncommon for a dog.*

weird • *He's a really weird guy.*

strange ② ADJECTIVE

new or unfamiliar • *alone in a strange country*

alien • *transplanted into an alien culture*

exotic • *filmed in an exotic location*

foreign • *This was a foreign country, so unlike his own.*

new • *I'm always open to new experiences.*

S

novel • *a novel idea*
unfamiliar • *visiting an unfamiliar city*

strength ① NOUN
physical energy and power • *an astonishing display of physical strength*
brawn • *He's got plenty of brains as well as brawn.*
might • *the full might of the army*
muscle • *demonstrating both muscle and skill*
stamina • *The race requires a lot of stamina.*
ANTONYM:
• weakness

strength ② NOUN
the degree of intensity • *an indication of the strength of feeling among parents*
force • *the force of his argument*
intensity • *the intensity of their emotions*
potency • *the extraordinary potency of his personality*
power • *the overwhelming power of love*
vehemence • *I was surprised by the vehemence of his criticism.*
vigour • *We resumed the attack with renewed vigour.*
ANTONYM:
• weakness

strengthen ① VERB
to give something more power • *This move will strengthen his political standing.*
consolidate • *to consolidate an already dominant position*

encourage • *encouraged by the shouts of their supporters*
harden • *evidence which hardens suspicions about their involvement*
stiffen • *This only stiffened his resolve to quit.*
toughen • *new laws to toughen police powers*
ANTONYM:
• weaken

strengthen ② VERB
to support the structure of something • *The builders had to strengthen the joists with timber.*
bolster • *steel beams used to bolster the roof*
brace • *tottering pillars braced by scaffolding*
fortify • *citadels fortified by high stone walls*
reinforce • *They had to reinforce the walls with exterior beams.*
support • *the thick wooden posts that supported the ceiling*
ANTONYM:
• weaken

stress ① NOUN
worry and nervous tension • *the stresses and strains of a busy career*
anxiety • *Her voice was full of anxiety.*
hassle (INFORMAL) • *I don't think it's worth the money or the hassle.*
pressure • *I felt the pressure of being the first woman in the job.*
strain • *She was tired and under great strain.*

tension • *Laughing relieves tension.*

worry • *It was a time of worry for us.*

stress ② VERB

to emphasise something • *The leaders have stressed their commitment to the talks.*

accentuate • *make-up which accentuates your best features*

emphasise • *He flourished his glass to emphasise the point.*

repeat • *We are not, I repeat not, in the negotiating process.*

underline • *The report underlined his concern about falling standards.*

stretch ① VERB

to extend over an area or time • *an artificial reef stretching the length of the coast*

continue • *The road continued into the distance.*

cover • *The oil slick covered a total area of seven miles.*

extend • *The caves extend for some 18 kilometres.*

go on • *The dispute looks set to go on into the new year.*

hang • *The branches hang right down to the ground.*

last • *His difficulties are likely to last well beyond childhood.*

reach • *a caravan park which reached from one end of the bay to the other*

spread • *The estuary spreads as far as the eye can see.*

stretch ② VERB

to reach out with part of your body • *She arched her back and stretched herself.*

extend • *Stand straight with your arms extended at your sides.*

reach • *He reached up for an overhanging branch.*

straighten • *Point your toes and straighten both legs slowly.*

ANTONYM:
• bend

stretch ③ NOUN

an area of land or water • *It's a very dangerous stretch of road.*

area • *extensive mountainous areas of Europe and South America*

expanse • *a huge expanse of grassland*

extent • *a vast extent of fertile country*

sweep • *The ground fell away in a broad sweep down the river.*

tract • *They cleared large tracts of forest for farming.*

stretch ④ NOUN

a period of time • *He would study for eight hour stretches.*

period • *a long period of time*

run • *The show will transfer to the West End, after a month's run in Birmingham.*

space • *They've come a long way in a short space of time.*

spell • *a long spell of dry weather*

stint • *He is coming home after a five-year stint abroad.*

term • *the full term of her pregnancy*

time • *doing very little exercise for several weeks at a time*

strict ① ADJECTIVE

very firm in demanding

obedience • *My parents were very strict.*
authoritarian • *He has an authoritarian approach to parenthood.*
firm • *the guiding hand of a firm father figure*
rigid • *a rigid hospital routine*
rigorous • *rigorous military training*
stern • *Her mother was stern and hard to please.*
stringent • *stringent rules*

strict ② ADJECTIVE
precise and accurate • *The book is not a biography in the strict sense of the word.*
accurate • *an accurate record of events*
exact • *I do not remember the exact words.*
meticulous • *meticulous attention to detail*
particular • *very particular dietary requirements*
precise • *precise instructions*
true • *a true account*

strive VERB
to make a great effort to achieve something • *He strives hard to keep himself fit.*
attempt • *He attempted to smile, but found it difficult.*
do your best • *I'll do my best to find out.*
do your utmost • *She was certain he would do his utmost to help her.*
endeavour (FORMAL) • *They are endeavouring to protect trade union rights.*

make an effort • *He made no effort to hide his disappointment.*
seek • *We have never sought to impose our views.*
try • *He tried to block her advancement in the Party.*

strong ① ADJECTIVE
having powerful muscles • *a strong, robust man*
athletic • *He was tall and athletic.*
brawny • *a brawny young rugby player*
burly • *a big, burly man*
muscular • *Like most female athletes, she was lean and muscular.*
powerful • *a powerful bodybuilder*
strapping • *She was a tall, strapping woman.*
well-built • *a fit, well-built runner*
ANTONYM:
• weak

strong ② ADJECTIVE
able to withstand rough treatment • *a strong casing, which won't crack or chip*
durable • *made of durable plastic*
hard-wearing • *hard-wearing cotton overalls*
heavy-duty • *a heavy-duty canvas bag*
reinforced • *reinforced concrete supports*
sturdy • *a camera mounted on a sturdy tripod*
substantial • *a substantial boat with a powerful rigging*

S

tough • *a tough vehicle designed for all terrains*
well-built • *You need a well-built fence all round the garden.*
ANTONYM:
• fragile

strong ③ ADJECTIVE
great in degree or intensity • *Despite strong opposition, she was victorious.*
acute • *an acute feeling of embarrassment*
ardent • *an ardent admirer*
deep • *a deep resentment*
fervent • *a fervent hope for peace*
fierce • *He inspires fierce loyalty in his friends.*
intense • *an intense dislike of jazz*
keen • *a keen interest in tennis*
passionate • *a passionate believer in justice*
profound • *a profound distrust of bankers*
vehement • *the government's most vehement critic*
violent • *His plans met with violent hostility.*
zealous • *her zealous religious beliefs*
ANTONYM:
• faint

structure ① NOUN
the way something is made or organised • *the structure of this molecule*
arrangement • *an intricate arrangement of treadles, rods and cranks*

construction • *The chairs were light in construction but very strong.*
design • *The shoes were of good design and good quality.*
make-up • *the chemical make-up of the oceans and atmosphere*
organisation • *the organisation of the economy*

structure ② NOUN
something that has been built • *The museum is an impressive structure.*
building • *an ugly modern building*
construction • *an impressive steel and glass construction*
edifice • *historic edifices in the area*

struggle ① VERB
to try hard to do something • *They had to struggle to make ends meet.*
strain • *straining to lift heavy weights*
strive • *He strives hard to keep himself fit.*
toil • *toiling to make up for lost time*
work • *I had to work hard for everything I've got.*

struggle ② NOUN
something that is hard to achieve • *Life became a struggle for survival.*
effort • *It was an effort to finish in time.*
labour • *weary from their labours*
toil • *another day of toil and strife*

work • *It's been hard work, but rewarding.*

stubborn ADJECTIVE
determined not to change or give in • *a stubborn character who is used to getting his own way*

dogged • *his dogged insistence on his rights*

inflexible • *His opponents viewed him as dogmatic and inflexible.*

obstinate • *a wicked and obstinate child*

tenacious • *a tenacious and persistent interviewer*

wilful • *a headstrong and wilful young woman*

stuck-up ADJECTIVE
(INFORMAL)
proud and conceited • *She was famous, but she wasn't a bit stuck-up.*

arrogant • *He was so arrogant, he never even said hello to me.*

conceited • *He's a very conceited young man.*

disdainful • *She cast a disdainful glance at me.*

haughty • *She looks haughty, but when you get to know her, she's very friendly.*

proud • *He's too proud to use public transport.*

snobbish • *I'd expected her to be snobbish, but she was warm and welcoming.*

study ① VERB
to spend time learning about something • *He is studying History and Economics.*

learn • *I'm learning French.*
read up • *She spent a year reading up on farming techniques.*
swot (BRITISH, AUSTRALIAN AND NEW ZEALAND; INFORMAL) • *swotting for their finals*

study ② VERB
to look at something carefully • *He studied the map in silence.*
contemplate • *He contemplated his hands, frowning.*
examine • *He examined her passport and stamped it.*
pore over • *We spent hours poring over travel brochures.*

study ③ NOUN
the activity of learning about a subject • *the serious study of medieval architecture*
lessons • *He was lagging behind in his lessons.*
research • *funds for research into AIDS*
school work • *She buried herself in school work.*
swotting (BRITISH, AUSTRALIAN AND NEW ZEALAND; INFORMAL) • *She put her success down to last-minute swotting.*

stuff ① NOUN
a substance or group of things • *"That's my stuff," he said, pointing to a bag.*
apparatus • *all the apparatus you'll need for the job*
belongings • *I collected my belongings and left.*
equipment • *outdoor playing equipment*

s

stuff | 600

gear • *fishing gear*
kit • *I forgot my gym kit.*
material • *organic material*
substance • *The substance that's causing problems comes from barley.*
tackle • *Martin kept his fishing tackle in his room.*
things • *Sara told him to take all his things and not to return.*

stuff ② VERB
to push something somewhere quickly and roughly • *He stuffed the newspapers into a litter bin.*
cram • *I crammed her hat into a waste-basket.*
force • *I forced the key into the ignition.*
jam • *Pete jammed his hands into his pockets.*
push • *Someone had pushed a tissue into the keyhole.*
ram • *He rammed his clothes into a drawer.*
shove • *We shoved a newsletter beneath their door.*
squeeze • *I squeezed everything into my rucksack.*
thrust • *She thrust a stack of photos into my hands.*

stuff ③ VERB
to fill something with a substance or objects • *He stood there, stuffing his mouth with popcorn.*
cram • *I crammed my bag full of clothes and set off.*
fill • *I filled the box with polystyrene chips.*

load • *They loaded all their equipment into backpacks.*
pack • *a lorry packed with explosives*

stuffy ① ADJECTIVE
formal and old-fashioned • *his lack of stuffy formality*
dull • *They are nice people but rather dull.*
formal • *an austere and formal family*
old-fashioned • *She was condemned as an old-fashioned prude.*
staid • *He is boring, old-fashioned and staid.*
strait-laced • *She is very strait-laced and narrow-minded.*

stuffy ② ADJECTIVE
not containing enough fresh air • *It was hot and stuffy in the classroom.*
close • *The atmosphere was close.*
heavy • *The air was heavy, moist and sultry.*
muggy • *It was muggy and overcast.*
oppressive • *The little room was windowless and oppressive*
stale • *A layer of smoke hung in the stale air.*
stifling • *the stifling heat of the room*

stupid ADJECTIVE
lacking intelligence or good judgment • *How could I have been so stupid?*
absurd • *absurd ideas*
daft (BRITISH; INFORMAL) • *That's a daft question.*

s

dim • *He is rather dim.*
foolish • *It is foolish to risk injury.*
idiotic • *What an idiotic thing to say!*
inane • *She's always asking inane questions.*
obtuse (FORMAL) • *It should be obvious even to the most obtuse person.*
thick • *I must have seemed incredibly thick.*

ANTONYM:
• clever

stupidity NOUN
lack of intelligence or good judgment • *I was astonished by his stupidity.*
absurdity • *the absurdity of the suggestion*
folly • *the danger and folly of taking drugs*
foolishness • *He expressed remorse over his own foolishness.*
inanity • *The inanity of the conversation.*
silliness • *He sounded quite exasperated by my silliness.*

sturdy ADJECTIVE
strong and unlikely to be damaged • *The camera was mounted on a sturdy tripod.*
durable • *Fine china is surprisingly durable.*
hardy • *a hardy breed of cattle*
robust • *very robust, simply-designed machinery*
solid • *The car feels very solid.*
substantial • *Jack had put on weight – he seemed more substantial.*
stout • *a stout oak door*

strong • *a strong casing which won't crack or chip*
well-built • *Mitchell is well-built and of medium height.*

ANTONYM:
• fragile

style ① NOUN
the way in which something is done • *a dictatorial management style*
approach • *his blunt approach*
manner • *a satire in the manner of Dickens*
method • *a new method of education*
mode • *a cheap and convenient mode of transport*
technique • *his driving technique*
way • *He had a strange way of talking.*

style ② NOUN
smartness and elegance • *She has not lost her grace and style.*
chic • *French designer chic*
elegance • *Princess Grace's understated elegance*
flair • *dressed with typical Italian flair*
sophistication • *to add a touch of sophistication to any wardrobe*
taste • *impeccable taste*

subdue VERB
to bring people under control by force • *The government have not been able to subdue the rebels.*
crush • *ruthless measures to crush the revolt*
defeat • *an important role in defeating the rebellion*

s

overcome • working to overcome the enemy forces

overpower • The police eventually overpowered him.

quell • tough new measures to quell the disturbances

vanquish (LITERARY) • his vanquished foe

subject ① NOUN

the thing or person being discussed • They exchanged views on a wide range of subjects.

issue • an issue that had worried him for some time

matter • I don't want to discuss the matter.

object • the object of much heated discussion

point • There is another point to consider.

question • the difficult question of unemployment

theme • The book's central theme is power.

topic • The weather is a constant topic of conversation.

subject ② VERB

to make someone experience something • He was subjected to constant interruptions.

expose • people exposed to high levels of radiation

put through • She was put through the ordeal of a trial.

submit ① VERB

to accept or agree to something unwillingly • I submitted to their requests.

agree • Management has agreed to the union's conditions.

bow • Some shops are bowing to consumer pressure and stocking the product.

capitulate • He capitulated to their ultimatum.

comply • The commander said his army would comply with the ceasefire.

give in • Officials say they won't give in to the workers' demands.

surrender • We'll never surrender to these terrorists.

yield (FORMAL) • She yielded to her mother's nagging and took the child to a specialist.

ANTONYM:
• resist

submit ② VERB

to formally present a document or proposal • They submitted their reports to the Chancellor.

hand in • I'm supposed to hand in my dissertation on Friday.

present • The group intends to present this petition to the parliament.

propose • He has proposed a bill to abolish the House of Commons.

put forward • He has put forward new peace proposals.

send in • Applicants are asked to send in a CV and covering letter.

table • They've tabled a motion criticising the Government for its actions.

tender • She tendered her resignation.

ANTONYM:
• withdraw

substance NOUN
a solid, powder, liquid or gas
• *Poisonous substances should be labelled as such.*
element • *a chart of the chemical elements*
fabric • *Condensation will rot the fabric of the building.*
material • *an armchair of some resilient plastic material*
stuff • *The stuff from which the universe is made*

substitute ① VERB
to use one thing in place of another • *You can substitute honey for the sugar.*
exchange • *exchanging one set of problems for another*
interchange • *Meat can be interchanged with pulses as a source of protein.*
replace • *We dug up the concrete and replaced it with grass.*
swap • *Some hostages were swapped for convicted prisoners.*
switch • *They switched the tags on the cables.*

substitute ② NOUN
something used in place of another thing • *an artificial substitute for silk*
deputy • *I can't make it so I'll send my deputy.*
proxy • *They must nominate a proxy to vote on their behalf.*
replacement • *He has nominated Adams as his replacement.*
representative • *Employees from each department elect a representative.*

surrogate • *They had expected me to be a surrogate for my sister.*

subtract VERB
to take one number away from another • *If you subtract 3 from 5 you get 2.*
deduct • *Marks will be deducted for spelling mistakes.*
take away • *Take away the number you first thought of.*
take from • *Take the 5% discount from the total amount due.*

ANTONYM:
• add

succeed ① VERB
to achieve the result you intend • *To succeed, you must learn to overcome obstacles.*
be successful • *We must help our clubs to be successful in Europe.*
do well • *Their team did well.*
flourish • *The business flourished.*
make it (INFORMAL) • *It is hard for actors to make it in Hollywood.*
prosper • *His teams have always prospered in cup competitions.*
thrive • *The company has thrived by selling cheap, simple products.*
triumph • *a symbol of good triumphing over evil*
work • *The plan worked.*

ANTONYM:
• fail

s

succeed ② VERB

to be the next person to have someone's job • *David is almost certain to succeed him as chairman.*

replace • *the man who replaced him as England skipper*

take over from • *Last year she took over from Bauman as chief executive.*

success ① NOUN

the achievement of a goal, fame or wealth • *Do you believe that work is the key to success?*

celebrity • *I never expected this kind of celebrity when I was writing my novel.*

eminence • *a pilot who achieved eminence in the aeronautical world*

fame • *her rise to fame as a dramatist*

prosperity • *the country's economic prosperity*

triumph • *last year's Republican triumph in the elections*

victory • *Union leaders are heading for victory in their battle over workplace rights.*

wealth • *His hard work brought him wealth and respect.*

ANTONYM:
• failure

success ② NOUN

a person or thing achieving popularity or greatness • *Everyone knows her says she will be a huge success.*

celebrity • *At the age of 12, Dan is already a celebrity.*

hit • *The song became a massive hit.*

sensation • *the film that turned her into an overnight sensation*

star • *I always knew she would be a star.*

triumph • *a triumph of modern surgery*

winner • *Selling was my game and I intended to be a winner.*

ANTONYM:
• failure

successful ADJECTIVE

having achieved what you intended to do • *Mr Singh was a highly successful salesman.*

flourishing • *a flourishing business*

lucrative • *a lucrative career*

profitable • *a profitable exchange of ideas*

rewarding • *a rewarding investment*

thriving • *a thriving housebuilding industry*

top • *a top model*

sudden ADJECTIVE

happening quickly and unexpectedly • *a sudden cry*

abrupt • *Her idyllic world came to an abrupt end when her parents died.*

hasty • *his hasty departure*

quick • *I had to make a quick decision.*

swift • *a swift blow to the stomach*

unexpected • *His death was totally unexpected.*

ANTONYM:
• gradual

suffer VERB
to be affected by pain or something unpleasant • *I knew he was suffering some discomfort.*
bear • *He bore his trials with dignity and grace.*
endure • *The writer endured a harsh life.*
experience • *Widows seem to experience more distress than do widowers.*
go through • *I wouldn't like to go through that again.*
sustain • *He had sustained massive facial injuries.*
undergo • *He had to undergo a thorough examination.*

sufficient ADJECTIVE
being enough for a purpose • *He had sufficient time to prepare his speech.*
adequate • *an adequate income*
ample • *an ample supply of petrol*
enough • *enough cash to live on*
ANTONYM:
• insufficient

-uffix NOUN
SUFFIXES
-able
-ence
-er
-est
-ful
-hood
-ise or -ize
-ism
-less
-like
-logy or -ology
-ly
-ness
-phobia
-ship
-ward or -wards

suggest ① VERB
to mention something as a possibility or recommendation • *Clive suggested going out for tea.*
advise • *I advise you to keep quiet.*
advocate • *Mr Jones advocates longer school days.*
propose • *And where do you propose building such a huge thing?*
recommend • *I have no qualms about recommending this approach.*

suggest ② VERB
to hint that something is the case • *Reports suggested the factory would close.*
hint • *The President hinted that he might make some changes.*
imply • *The tone of the report implied that his death was inevitable.*
indicate • *She has indicated that she may resign.*
insinuate • *an article which insinuated that he was lying*
intimate • *He did intimate that he is seeking legal action.*

suggestion ① NOUN
an idea mentioned as a possibility • *practical suggestions*

s

plan • The government is being asked to consider the plan.
proposal • the proposal to do away with nuclear weapons
proposition • a business proposition
recommendation • a range of recommendations for change

suggestion ② NOUN
a slight indication of something • a suggestion of dishonesty
hint • He showed only the slightest hint of emotion.
indication • He gave no indication of remorse.
insinuation • The insinuation is that I have something to hide.
intimation • He did not give any intimation that he was going to resign.
trace • No traces of violence were found on the body.

suit VERB
to be acceptable • They will only move if it suits them.
be acceptable to • The name chosen had to be acceptable to everyone.
do • A holiday at home will do me just fine.
please • I'll leave when it pleases me and not before.
satisfy • Nothing you can do will satisfy him.

suitable ADJECTIVE
right or acceptable for a particular purpose
• Conditions were not suitable for life to flourish.

acceptable • a mutually acceptable new contract
appropriate • an appropriate outfit for the occasion
apt • an apt name
fit • the suggestion that she is not a fit candidate
fitting • a fitting end to the drama
proper • It was not thought proper for a woman to be on stage.
right • He always said just the right thing.
satisfactory • a satisfactory arrangement
ANTONYM:
• unsuitable

sulky ADJECTIVE
showing annoyance by being silent and moody • I was quite sulky, so I didn't take part in games.
huffy • What are you being so huffy about?
moody • Her sister had become withdrawn and moody.
petulant • He's just being childish and petulant.
resentful • a resentful workforce
sullen • He lapsed into a sullen silence.

summary NOUN
a short account of something main points • a summary of th report
outline • an outline of the proposal
review • a film review
rundown • Here's a rundown the options.

summing-up • *The judge concluded his summing-up.*
synopsis • *a brief synopsis of the book*

sum up VERB

to describe briefly • *He summed up his weekend in one word: "Disastrous".*
recapitulate • *Let's just recapitulate the essential points.*
summarise • *The article can be summarised in three sentences.*

superb ADJECTIVE

very good indeed • *With superb skill, he managed to make a perfect landing.*
breathtaking • *The house has breathtaking views.*
excellent • *You've done an excellent job.*
exquisite • *His photography is exquisite.*
magnificent • *a magnificent country house*
marvellous • *She is a marvellous cook.*
outstanding • *an outstanding performance*
splendid • *a splendid Victorian mansion*
superior • *a superior blend of the finest coffee beans*
unrivalled • *He has an unrivalled knowledge of British politics.*
wonderful • *The sun setting over the mountains was a wonderful sight.*

superior ① ADJECTIVE

better than other similar things • *superior coffee beans*

better • *I'd like to move to a better area.*
choice • *the choicest cuts of meat*
de luxe • *a de luxe model*
exceptional • *children with exceptional ability*
first-rate • *a first-rate thriller*
surpassing • *her surpassing achievements*
unrivalled • *colour printing of unrivalled quality*

ANTONYM:
• inferior

superior ② ADJECTIVE

showing pride and self-importance • *He stood there looking superior.*
condescending • *I'm fed up with your condescending attitude.*
disdainful • *She passed along with a disdainful look.*
haughty • *He spoke in a haughty tone.*
lofty • *lofty disdain*
patronising • *his patronising attitude to the homeless*
snobbish • *a snobbish dislike for their intellectual inferiors*
stuck-up (INFORMAL) • *She was a famous actor, but she wasn't a bit stuck-up.*
supercilious • *His manner is supercilious and arrogant.*

superior ③ NOUN

a person in a higher position than you • *his immediate superior*
boss • *Her boss was very supportive.*

s

manager • *His plans found favour with his manager.*

senior • *He was described by his seniors as a model officer.*

supervisor • *Each student has a supervisor.*

ANTONYM:
• inferior

supervise VERB
to oversee a person or activity • *He supervised more than 400 volunteers.*

be in charge of • *He is in charge of the whole project.*

direct • *Christopher will direct day-to-day operations.*

have charge of • *He has charge of a three-acre estate.*

keep an eye on • *I told you to keep an eye on the children.*

manage • *I manage a small team of workers.*

oversee • *an architect to oversee the work*

run • *Each teacher will run a different workshop.*

supplement ① VERB
to add to something to improve it • *I suggest supplementing your diet with vitamin A.*

add to • *A good bathroom adds to the value of any house.*

augment • *a way to augment the family income*

complement • *an in-work benefit that complements earnings*

reinforce • *measures which will reinforce their current strengths*

top up • *compulsory contributions to top up pension schemes*

supplement ② NOUN
something added to something else • *a supplement to their basic pension*

addition • *an addition to the existing system*

appendix • *The report includes a six-page appendix.*

complement • *The photographs are a perfect complement to the text.*

extra • *an optional extra*

supplies PLURAL NOUN
food or equipment for a particular purpose • *I had only two pints of water in my emergency supplies.*

equipment • *vital medical equipment*

provisions • *provisions for two weeks*

rations • *Aid officials said food rations had been distributed.*

stores • *an important part of a ship's stores*

supply ① VERB
to provide someone with something • *an agreement not to supply chemical weapons*

equip • *plans for equipping the island with water*

furnish • *They'll be able to furnish you with the details.*

give • *We'll give you all the information you need.*

provide • *They'll provide all the equipment.*

S

supply ② NOUN

an amount of something
available for use • *a plentiful
supply of vegetables*
cache • *their cache of treasures*
fund • *an extraordinary fund of
energy*
hoard • *a hoard of food and
petrol*
reserve • *The Gulf has 65% of
the world's oil reserves.*
stock • *stocks of paper and ink*
stockpile • *a stockpile of fuel*
store • *I have a store of food and
water here.*

support ① VERB

to agree with someone's ideas
or aims • *We supported his
political campaign.*
back • *a new witness to back his
claim*
champion • *He passionately
championed the cause.*
defend • *He defended all of
Clarence's decisions, right or
wrong.*
promote • *He continued to
promote the idea of Scottish
autonomy.*
second • *The Prime Minister
seconded the call for discipline.*
side with • *accused of siding
with terrorists*
uphold • *We uphold the
capitalist free economy.*

ANTONYM:
• oppose

support ② VERB

to help someone in difficulties
• *Try to support each other when
one of you is feeling down.*

encourage • *When things aren't
going well, he encourages me.*
help • *He'd do anything to help
a friend.*

support ③ VERB

to hold something up from
underneath • *Thick wooden
posts support the ceiling.*
bolster • *steel beams used to
bolster the roof*
brace • *The roll-over bar braces
the car's structure.*
hold up • *Her legs wouldn't hold
her up.*
prop up • *Use sticks to prop the
plants up.*
reinforce • *They had to
reinforce the walls with exterior
beams.*

support ④ NOUN

an object that holds
something up • *the metal
supports which hold up the
canvas*
brace • *He will have to wear a
neck brace for several months.*
foundation • *the foundation on
which the bridge was built*
pillar • *the pillars supporting
the roof*
post • *The device is fixed to a
post.*
prop • *a structural part such as
a beam or prop*

supporter NOUN

a person who agrees with or
helps someone • *He is a strong
supporter of the plan.*
adherent (FORMAL)
• *Communism was gaining
adherents in Latin America.*

advocate • *a strong advocate of free market policies*

ally • *a close political ally*

champion • *a champion of women's causes*

fan • *fans of this football club*

follower • *followers of the Dalai Lama*

sponsor • *the first sponsor of Buddhism in Japan*

suppose VERB
to think that something is probably the case • *Where do you suppose he has gone?*

assume • *I assume you have permission to be here?*

believe • *We believe them to be hidden somewhere in the area.*

expect • *I don't expect you've had much experience in the job yet.*

guess • *I guess you're right.*

imagine • *We tend to imagine that the Victorians were prim and proper.*

presume • *I presume you're here on business.*

think • *Do you think she was embarrassed?*

supposed ① ADJECTIVE
planned, expected or required to do something • *You're not supposed to leave a child on its own.*

expected • *You were expected to arrive much earlier than this.*

meant • *Parties are meant to be fun.*

obliged • *He is legally obliged to declare his interests.*

required • *Will I be required to come to every meeting?*

supposed ② ADJECTIVE
generally believed or thought to be the case • *What is his son supposed to have said?*

alleged • *The accused is alleged to have killed a man.*

assumed • *As usual, the mistakes were assumed to be my fault.*

believed • *He is believed to have died in 1117.*

meant • *They are meant to be one of the top teams in the world.*

presumed • *This area is presumed to be safe.*

reputed • *The monster is reputed to live in the deep waters of a Scottish loch.*

rumoured • *They are rumoured to be on the verge of splitting up.*

suppress ① VERB
to prevent people from doing something • *international attempts to suppress organised crime*

crush • *a plan to crush the uprising*

quash • *It may help to quash these rumours.*

quell • *The army moved in to quell the uprising.*

stamp out • *steps to stamp out bullying in schools*

stop • *measures to stop the trade in ivory*

suppress ② VERB
to stop yourself from expressing a feeling or reaction • *She barely suppressed a gasp.*

S

conceal • Robert could not conceal his relief.

contain • He could hardly contain his rage.

curb • He curbed his temper.

repress • people who repress their emotions

restrain • unable to restrain her anger

smother • I smothered a chuckle.

stifle • Miller stifled a yawn and looked at his watch.

supreme ADJECTIVE
of the highest degree or rank • They conspired to seize supreme power.

chief • his chief rival

foremost • the world's foremost scientists

greatest • the city's greatest soccer idol

highest • the highest academic achievement

leading • the world's leading basketball players

paramount • a factor of paramount importance

pre-eminent • a pre-eminent political figure

principal • the principal reason

top • the president's top military advisers

ultimate • the ultimate international accolade, the Nobel Prize

sure ① ADJECTIVE
having no doubts • She was no longer sure how she felt about him.

certain • certain of getting a place on the team

clear • He is not clear on how he will go about it.

convinced • He is convinced it's your fault.

definite • a definite answer

positive • I'm positive it will happen.

satisfied • We must be satisfied that the treatment is safe.

ANTONYM:
• unsure

sure ② ADJECTIVE
reliable or definite • a sure sign that something is wrong

definite • a definite advantage

dependable • dependable information

foolproof • a foolproof system

infallible • an infallible eye for detail

reliable • a reliable source

trustworthy • trustworthy reports

undeniable • a sad but undeniable fact

surprise ① NOUN
something unexpected • The resignation came as a complete surprise.

bombshell • His departure was a bombshell for the team.

revelation • Degas's work had been a revelation to her.

shock • I got a shock when I saw her.

start • You gave me quite a start.

surprise ② NOUN
the feeling caused by something unexpected • an exclamation of surprise

s

amazement • He stared in baffled amazement.
astonishment • "What?" Meg asked in astonishment.
incredulity • The announcement has been met with incredulity.
wonder • Cross shook his head in wonder.

surprise ③ VERB

to give someone a feeling of surprise • I was surprised by the vehemence of his criticism.
amaze • Most of the cast were amazed by the play's success.
astonish • I was astonished to discover his true age.
astound • He was astounded at the result.
jolt • Henderson was jolted by the news.
stagger • I was staggered by his reaction.
stun • Audiences were stunned by the film's tragic end.
take aback • Derek was taken aback when a man answered the phone.

surrender ① VERB

to agree that the other side has won • We'll never surrender to the terrorists.
capitulate • They had no choice but to capitulate.
give in • She gave in to him on everything.
submit • I refuse to submit to their demands.
succumb (FORMAL) • The Minister said his country would never succumb to pressure.

yield (FORMAL) • The government had to yield to local opinion.

surrender ② VERB

to give something up to someone else • We have surrendered our political authority for economic gain.
cede • After the war, Spain ceded the island to America.
give up • She is loath to give up her hard-earned liberty.
relinquish • He does not intend to relinquish power.
renounce • He renounced his claim to the throne.
yield (FORMAL) • He was obliged to yield territory to France.

surrender ③ NOUN

a situation in which one side gives in to the other • unconditional surrender
capitulation • the German capitulation at the end of the First World War
submission • The army intends to starve the city into submission.

surround VERB

to be all around a person or thing • He was surrounded by bodyguards.
encircle • A forty-foot-high concrete wall encircles the jail.
enclose • The land was enclosed by a fence.
encompass • the largest lake in Canada wholly encompassed by a town
envelop • The rich smell of the forest enveloped us.

hem in • *a valley hemmed in by mountains*

surroundings PLURAL NOUN

the area and environment around a person or place • *He felt a longing for familiar surroundings.*

background • *a fitting background for her beauty*

environment • *a safe environment for marine mammals*

location • *filmed in an exotic location*

neighbourhood • *living in an affluent neighbourhood*

setting • *Rome is the perfect setting for romance.*

survive VERB

to live or exist in spite of difficulties • *companies which survived after the recession*

endure • *Somehow their friendship endures.*

last • *Nothing lasts forever.*

live • *having lived through the 1930s depression*

outlive • *They have outlived the horror of the war.*

pull through • *He should pull through okay.*

suspect ① VERB

to think something is likely • *I suspect they are secretly planning to raise taxes.*

believe • *Police believe the attacks were carried out by a rival gang.*

feel • *I somehow feel he was involved.*

guess • *As you probably guessed, I don't like him much.*

suppose • *The problem is more complex than he supposes.*

suspect ② VERB

to have doubts about something • *He suspected her motives.*

distrust • *I don't have any particular reason to distrust them.*

doubt • *Do you doubt my word?*

mistrust • *He mistrusts all journalists.*

suspect ③ ADJECTIVE

not to be trusted • *a rather suspect holy man*

dodgy (BRITISH, AUSTRALIAN AND NEW ZEALAND; INFORMAL) • *a dodgy car dealer*

doubtful • *These details are of doubtful origin.*

dubious • *dubious practices*

fishy (INFORMAL) • *There's something very fishy about it.*

questionable • *the questionable motives of politicians*

suspicion ① NOUN

a feeling of mistrust • *I was always regarded with suspicion because of my background.*

distrust • *an instinctive distrust of authority*

doubt • *I have my doubts about his ability to govern.*

misgiving • *His first words filled us with misgiving.*

mistrust • *a deep mistrust of banks*

scepticism • *The report has been greeted with scepticism.*

s

suspicion ② NOUN

a feeling that something is true • *I have a strong suspicion they are lying.*
hunch • *Lowe had a hunch he was on to something.*
idea • *I had an idea that he joined the army later.*
impression • *I get the impression he's hiding something.*

suspicious ① ADJECTIVE

feeling distrustful of someone or something • *He was rightly suspicious of their motives.*
apprehensive • *She was apprehensive of strangers.*
distrustful • *Voters are deeply distrustful of all politicians.*
doubtful • *At first I was doubtful about their authenticity.*
sceptical • *Other archaeologists are sceptical about his findings.*
wary • *Many people are wary of lawyers.*

suspicious ② ADJECTIVE

causing feelings of distrust • *suspicious circumstances*
dodgy (BRITISH, AUSTRALIAN AND NEW ZEALAND; INFORMAL) • *He was a bit of a dodgy character.*
doubtful • *selling something of doubtful quality*
dubious • *This claim seems to us rather dubious.*
fishy (INFORMAL) • *There's something fishy going on here.*
funny • *There's something funny about him.*

questionable • *the questionable motives of politicians*
shady (INFORMAL) • *shady deals*
suspect • *The whole affair has been highly suspect.*

swap VERB

to replace one thing for another • *Some hostages were swapped for convicted prisoners.*
barter • *bartering wheat for cotton and timber*
exchange • *exchanging one set of problems for another*
interchange • *Meat can be interchanged with pulses as a source of protein.*
switch • *They switched the tags on the cables.*
trade • *They traded land for goods and money.*

sweet ① ADJECTIVE

containing a lot of sugar • *a mug of sweet tea*
cloying • *a cloying apricot chutney*
sugary • *a sugary meringue pie*
sweetened • *sweetened shortcrust pastry*

ANTONYM:
• sour

sweet ② ADJECTIVE

having a pleasant smell • *the sweet smell of roses*
aromatic • *a plant with aromatic leaves*
fragrant • *fragrant clover*
perfumed • *perfumed soaps*
sweet-smelling • *cottage gardens filled with sweet-smelling flowers and herb*

S

sweet ③ ADJECTIVE
pleasant-sounding and
tuneful • *the sweet sounds of
children's singing*
harmonious • *harmonious
sounds*
mellow • *mellow background
music*
melodious • *The melodious
tones of the organ echoed around
the great cathedral.*
musical • *He had a soft, musical
voice.*
tuneful • *The band were noted
for their tuneful backing vocals.*

sweet ④ NOUN
a sweet-tasting thing such as
a toffee • *His sack was full of
packets of sweets.*
candy (AMERICAN) • *We were
sick after eating some syrupy
candies she had made.*
confectionery • *The company
specialises in selling confectionery
from all over the world.*
lolly (AUSTRALIAN AND NEW
ZEALAND) • *Avoid feeding him
too many lollies.*
sweetie • *She presented him
with a jar of his favourite
sweeties as a thank-you.*

swerve VERB
to change direction suddenly
to avoid hitting something
• *He swerved to avoid a truck.*
swing • *The car swung off the
road.*
turn • *He turned sharply to
the left.*
veer • *The vehicle veered out
of control.*

swift ADJECTIVE
happening or moving very
quickly • *make a swift decision*
brisk • *walking at a brisk pace*
express • *a special express
service*
fast • *The question is how fast
the process will be.*
hurried • *a hurried breakfast*
prompt • *Prompt action is
needed.*
quick • *The country has been
developing at a very quick pace.*
rapid • *Will the Tunnel provide
more rapid transport than
ferries?*
speedy • *We wish Bill a speedy
recovery.*
ANTONYM:
• slow

symbol NOUN
a design or idea used to
represent something • *the
chemical symbol for mercury*
emblem • *His badge bore a
small yellow hammer-and-sickle
emblem.*
emoticon • *He signed off with a
happy-face emoticon.*
figure • *the figure of a
five-pointed star*
logo • *the company's logo*
mark • *a mark of identification*
representation • *This rune is a
representation of a spearhead.*
sign • *a multiplication sign*
token • *He gave her a ring as a
token of his love.*

sympathy NOUN
kindness and understanding
towards someone in trouble

S

• My heartfelt sympathy goes out to all the relatives.

compassion • I was impressed by the compassion he showed for a helpless animal.

empathy • They displayed an admirable understanding of the crime and empathy with the victim.

pity • He showed no pity for his victims.

understanding • I'd like to thank you for your patience and understanding.

system NOUN
an organised way of doing or arranging something • the advantages of the new system over the old one

arrangement • an intricate arrangement of treadles, rods and cranks

method • the methods employed in the study

procedure • This is now the standard procedure.

routine • his daily routine

structure • the structure of local government

technique • a new technique for processing sound

Tt

tact NOUN
the ability not to offend people • He has handled the affair with great tact.

delicacy • Both countries are behaving with rare delicacy.

diplomacy • It took all Minnelli's diplomacy to get him to return.

discretion • I appreciate your discretion.

sensitivity • The police treated the victims with great sensitivity.

tactful ADJECTIVE
showing tact • Sorry, that wasn't a very tactful question.

diplomatic • She is very direct. I tend to be more diplomatic.

discreet • They were gossipy and not always discreet.

sensitive • his sensitive handling of the situation

ANTONYM:
• tactless

take ① VERB
to require something • He takes three hours to get ready.

demand • The task of rebuilding would demand much patience.

require • The race requires a lot of stamina.

take ② VERB

to carry something • *I'll take these papers home and read them.*

bear (FORMAL) • *They bore the hardwood box into the kitchen.*

bring • *He poured a cup for Dena and brought it to her.*

carry • *She carried the shopping from the car.*

convey (FORMAL) • *The minibus conveyed us to the city centre.*

ferry • *A plane arrives to ferry guests to the island.*

fetch • *Sylvia fetched a towel from the bathroom.*

transport • *They use tankers to transport the oil to Los Angeles.*

take ③ VERB

to lead someone somewhere • *She took me to a Mexican restaurant.*

bring • *Come to my party and bring a friend with you.*

conduct (FORMAL) • *He asked if he might conduct us to the ball.*

escort • *I escorted him to the door.*

guide • *a young Egyptologist who guided us through the tombs*

lead • *She led the paramedics to the site of the crash.*

usher • *I ushered him into the office.*

take care of ① VERB

to look after someone or something • *There was no-one to take care of the children.*

care for • *They hired a nurse to care for her.*

look after • *I love looking after the children.*

mind • *Jim will mind the shop while I'm away.*

nurse • *All the years he was sick, my mother had nursed him.*

protect • *He vowed to protect her all the days of her life.*

tend • *He tends the flower beds that he has planted.*

watch • *Are parents expected to watch their children 24 hours a day?*

ANTONYM:
• neglect

take care of ② VERB

to deal with a problem, task or situation • *"Do you need clean sheets?"—"No, Mrs May took care of that."*

attend to • *We have business to attend to first.*

cope with • *A new system has been designed to cope with the increased demand.*

deal with • *the way that banks deal with complaints*

handle • *She handled the president's travel arrangements during the campaign.*

manage • *He tries to manage all the household expenses on very little.*

see to • *While I saw to the luggage, Frank took the children home.*

take in ① VERB

to deceive someone • *He was a real charmer who totally took me in.*

con (INFORMAL) • The British public has been conned by the government.
deceive • He has deceived us all.
dupe • Some offenders dupe the psychologists who assess them.
fool • Art dealers fool a lot of people.
mislead • It appears we were misled by a professional con artist.
trick • He'll be upset when he finds out how you tricked him.

take in ② VERB
to understand something • She seemed to take in all he said.
absorb • It will take time for us to absorb the news.
appreciate • She never really appreciated the bitterness of the conflict.
assimilate • My mind could only assimilate one of these ideas at a time.
comprehend • He failed to comprehend the significance of this remark.
digest • They need time to digest the information they have learned.
get • You just don't get what I'm saying, do you?
grasp • The Government has not yet grasped the seriousness of the crisis.
understand • They are too young to understand what is going on.

talent NOUN
a natural ability • Both her children have a talent for music.

ability • Her drama teacher spotted her ability.
aptitude • Alan has no aptitude for music.
capacity • people's creative capacities
flair • a dentist with a flair for invention
genius • his genius for chess
gift • a gift for teaching
knack • He's got the knack of getting people to listen.

talk ① VERB
to say things • They were talking about American food.
▶ see Word Study **say**, page 723

talk ② NOUN
a conversation • We had a long talk about her father.
chat • I had a chat with him.
chatter • idle chatter
conversation • We had a long conversation.

talk ③ NOUN
an informal speech • a talk about dyslexia
address • an address to the American people
discourse • a lengthy discourse on strategy
lecture • a series of lectures
sermon • a church sermon
speech • He delivered his speec in French.

talkative ADJECTIVE
talking a lot • His eyes grew bright and he suddenly became very talkative.
chatty • She's quite a chatty person.

communicative • She has become a lot more communicative.
long-winded • I hope I'm not being too long-winded.

tall ADJECTIVE
higher than average • tall buildings
high • a high wall
lanky • He was six foot four, all lanky and leggy.
lofty • lofty ceilings
soaring • the soaring spires of churches like St Peter's
towering • towering cliffs of black granite
ANTONYM:
• short

tangle ① NOUN
a mass of long things knotted together • a tangle of wires
jumble • a jumble of twisted tubes
knot • Her hair was full of knots.
mass • a flailing mass of arms and legs
mat • the thick mat of sandy hair on his chest
muddle • The back of the tapestry was a muddle of threads.
web • a thick web of fibres

tangle ② VERB
to twist together or catch someone or something • Dolphins can get tangled in fishing nets and drown.
catch • a fly caught in a spider's web
jumble • The wires were all jumbled together and tied in a knot.

knot • The kite strings had got knotted together.
twist • Her hands began to twist the handles of the bag.

task NOUN
a job that you have to do • Walker had the task of breaking the bad news.
assignment • written assignments and practical tests
chore • household chores
duty • I carried out my duties conscientiously.
job • He was given the job of tending the fire.
mission • Salisbury sent him on a diplomatic mission to North America.
undertaking • Organising the show has been a massive undertaking.

taste ① NOUN
the flavour of something • I like the taste of strawberries.
flavour • a crumbly texture with a strong flavour
tang • the tang of lemon

taste ② NOUN
a small amount of food or drink • He added some hot sauce and took a taste.
bite • Chew each mouthful fully before the next bite.
mouthful • She gulped down a mouthful of coffee.
sip • a sip of water

taste ③ NOUN
a liking for something • a taste for adventure
appetite • his appetite for success

t

fondness • *I've always had a fondness for jewels.*

liking • *She had a liking for good clothes.*

penchant (FORMAL) • *He had a penchant for playing jokes on people.*

tasteless ① ADJECTIVE
having little flavour • *The fish was mushy and tasteless.*

bland • *It tasted bland, like warmed cardboard.*

insipid • *a rather insipid meal*

ANTONYM:
• tasty

tasteless ② ADJECTIVE
vulgar and unattractive • *a house crammed with tasteless ornaments*

flashy • *a flashy sports car*

garish • *garish bright red boots*

gaudy • *her gaudy floral hat*

tacky (INFORMAL) • *tacky holiday souvenirs*

tawdry • *a tawdry seaside town*

vulgar • *a very vulgar house*

ANTONYM:
• tasteful

tasty ADJECTIVE
having a pleasant flavour • *The food was very tasty.*

appetising • *a choice of appetising dishes*

delicious • *a wide selection of delicious desserts*

lekker (SOUTH AFRICAN; SLANG) • *a lekker meal*

luscious • *luscious fruit*

palatable • *a very palatable starter*

tax ① NOUN
money paid to the government • *the tax on new cars*

duty • *customs duties*

excise • *These products are excused VAT and excise.*

levy (FORMAL) • *an annual motorway levy on all drivers*

tariff • *America wants to eliminate tariffs on items such as electronics.*

tax ② VERB
to make heavy demands on someone • *They must be told not to tax your patience.*

drain • *conflicts that drain your energy*

exhaust • *She has exhausted my sympathy.*

sap • *The illness sapped his strength.*

strain • *The volume of flights is straining the air traffic control system.*

stretch • *The drought there is stretching American resources to their limits.*

teach VERB
to instruct someone how to do something • *She taught Julie to read.*

coach • *She coached the basketball team.*

drill • *He drills the choir to a high standard.*

educate • *He was educated at Haslingden Grammar School.*

instruct • *He instructed family members in nursing techniques.*
school • *She had been schooled to take over the family business.*
train • *They train teachers in counselling skills.*
tutor • *She was tutored at home by her parents.*

teacher NOUN
someone who teaches something • *a geography teacher*
coach • *her drama coach*
don • *a Cambridge don*
guru • *a religious guru*
instructor • *a driving instructor*
lecturer • *a lecturer in law*
master • *a retired maths master*
mistress • *like a school mistress presiding over an exam*
professor • *a professor of economics*
tutor • *He surprised his tutors by failing the exam.*

team ① NOUN
a group of people • *the football team*
band • *a band of rebels*
crew • *the ship's crew*
gang • *a gang of workmen*
group • *The students work in groups.*
side • *Italy were definitely the better side.*
squad • *the England under-21 squad*
troupe • *troupes of travelling actors*

team ② or **team up** VERB
to work together • *A friend suggested that we team up for a working holiday.*

collaborate • *The two men met and agreed to collaborate.*
cooperate • *They would cooperate in raising their child.*
join forces • *The groups joined forces to fight against the ban.*
link up • *the first time the two presenters have linked up*
pair up • *On the show, professionals and celebrities pair up to dance.*
unite • *The two parties have been trying to unite.*
work together • *We have always wanted to work together.*

tear ① NOUN
a hole in something • *I peered through a tear in the curtains.*
hole • *the hole in my shoe*
ladder • *There was a ladder in her tights.*
rip • *the rip in her new jacket*
rupture • *a rupture in the valve*
scratch • *I pointed to a number of scratches in the tile floor.*
split • *the split in his trousers*

tear ② VERB
to make a hole in something • *She nearly tore my overcoat.*
ladder • *after she laddered her tights*
rip • *I tried not to rip the paper.*
rupture • *a ruptured appendix*
scratch • *Knives will scratch the worktop.*
shred • *They may be shredding documents.*
split • *I'd split my trousers.*

tear ③ VERB
to go somewhere in a hurry

t

• He tore through busy streets in a high-speed chase.

charge • He charged through the door.

dart • Ingrid darted across the deserted street.

dash • He dashed upstairs.

fly • She flew to their bedsides when they were ill.

race • He raced across town.

shoot • Another car shot out of a junction.

speed • A low shot sped past Lukic.

zoom • We zoomed through the gallery.

tease VERB
to make fun of someone • He used to tease me about wanting to act.

make fun of • The kids at school made fun of me and my Cockney accent.

mock • Don't mock me!

needle (INFORMAL) • He used to enjoy needling people.

taunt • Other youths taunted him about his clothes.

tell ① VERB
to let someone know something • They told us the dreadful news.

inform • My daughter informed me that she was getting married.

notify • We have notified the police.

tell ② VERB
to give someone an order • A passer-by told the driver to move his car.

command • He commanded his troops to attack.

direct (FORMAL) • They have been directed to give special attention to the problem.

instruct • The family has instructed solicitors to sue the company.

order • He ordered his men to cease firing.

tell ③ VERB
to judge something correctly • I could tell he was scared.

discern • It was hard to discern why this was happening.

see • I could see she was lonely.

temporary ADJECTIVE
lasting a short time • a temporary loss of memory

ephemeral (FORMAL) • a reminder that earthly pleasures are ephemeral

fleeting • a fleeting glimpse

interim • an interim measure

momentary • a momentary lapse

passing • a passing phase

provisional • a provisional coalition government

transient (FORMAL)
• Modelling is a transient career.

transitory • the transitory nature of political success

ANTONYM:
• permanent

tempt VERB
to persuade someone to do something • Children not attending schools may be tempted into crime.

entice • *She resisted attempts to entice her into politics.*
lure • *Her old boss tried to lure her back with promises of a senior position.*
seduce • *We are seduced into buying all these items.*

tend ① VERB
to happen usually or often • *I tend to forget things.*
be apt • *She was apt to raise her voice.*
be inclined • *He was inclined to self-pity.*
be liable • *equipment that is liable to break*
be prone • *Older people are more prone to insomnia.*
have a tendency • *Shetland jumpers have a tendency to be annoyingly itchy.*

tend ② VERB
to look after someone or something • *the way we tend our cattle*
care for • *They hired a nurse to care for her.*
look after • *I love looking after the children.*
nurse • *In hospital they nursed me back to health.*
take care of • *There was no one else to take care of the animals.*

tendency NOUN
behaviour that happens very often • *a tendency to be critical*
inclination • *his artistic inclinations*
leaning • *their socialist leanings*
propensity • *his propensity for violence*

tender ① ADJECTIVE
showing gentle and caring feelings • *tender, loving care*
affectionate • *She gave him an affectionate smile.*
caring • *He is a lovely boy, and very caring.*
compassionate • *a deeply compassionate film*
gentle • *Michael's voice was gentle and consoling.*
kind • *She is warmhearted and kind to everyone and everything.*
loving • *He was a most loving husband and father.*
sensitive • *He was always so sensitive.*
warm • *She was a very warm person.*
ANTONYM:
• tough

tender ② ADJECTIVE
painful and sore • *My tummy felt very tender.*
aching • *The weary holidaymakers soothed their aching feet in the sea.*
bruised • *bruised legs*
inflamed • *Her eyes were inflamed.*
painful • *Her glands were swollen and painful.*
raw • *the drag of the rope against the raw flesh of my shoulders*
sensitive • *Ouch! I'm sorry, my lip is still a bit sensitive.*
sore • *My chest is still sore from the surgery.*

tender ③ VERB
to offer something such as an

t

apology or resignation • She tendered her resignation.

hand in • All the opposition members have handed in their resignation.

offer • May I offer my sincere condolences?

tender ④ NOUN

a proposal to provide something at a price • Builders will be asked to submit a tender for the work.

bid • a successful bid to host the Olympic Games

estimate • The firm is preparing an estimate for the work.

package • We opted for the package submitted by the existing service provider.

submission • A written submission has to be prepared.

tense ① ADJECTIVE

nervous and unable to relax • Never had she seen him so tense.

anxious • She had become very anxious and alarmed.

edgy • She was nervous and edgy, pacing about the room.

jittery (INFORMAL) • Investors have become jittery about the country's economy.

jumpy • I told myself not to be so jumpy.

nervous • It has made me very nervous about going out.

uptight (INFORMAL) • Penny never got uptight about exams.

ANTONYM:
• calm

tense ② ADJECTIVE

causing anxiety • the tense atmosphere at the talks

anxious • They had to wait ten anxious days.

nerve-racking • It was more nerve-racking than taking a World Cup penalty.

stressful • a stressful job

tense ③ ADJECTIVE

having tight muscles • She lay, eyes shut, body tense.

rigid • Andrew went rigid whenever he saw a dog.

strained • His shoulders were strained with effort.

taut • when muscles are taut or cold

tight • It is better to stretch the tight muscles first.

ANTONYM:
• relaxed

term ① NOUN

a fixed period of time • a 12-month term of service

period • for a limited period only

session • The parliamentary session ends on October 4th.

spell • a six-month spell of practical experience

stretch • He did an 18-month stretch in prison.

time • He served the time of his contract and then left the company.

term ② NOUN

a name or word for a particular thing • the medical term for heart attack

designation • *Level Four Alert is a designation reserved for very serious incidents.*
expression • *She used some remarkably coarse expressions.*
name • *The correct name for this condition is bovine spongiform encephalopathy.*
word • *The word ginseng comes from the Chinese "Shen-seng".*

terms PLURAL NOUN
conditions that have been agreed • *the terms of the merger agreement*
conditions • *They may be breaching the conditions of their contract.*
provisions • *the provisions of the Amsterdam treaty*
proviso • *He left me the house with the proviso that it had to stay in the family.*
stipulations • *He left, violating the stipulations of his parole.*

terrible ① ADJECTIVE
serious and unpleasant • *a terrible illness*
appalling • *an appalling headache*
awful • *an awful crime*
desperate • *a desperate situation*
dreadful • *a dreadful mistake*
frightful (OLD-FASHIONED) • *He got himself into a frightful muddle.*
horrendous • *horrendous injuries*
horrible • *a horrible mess*
horrid (OLD-FASHIONED) • *What a horrid smell!*
rotten (INFORMAL) • *What rotten luck!*

terrible ② ADJECTIVE
of very poor quality • *my cousin's terrible haircut*
abysmal • *The standard of play was abysmal.*
appalling • *Her singing is appalling.*
awful • *Jeans look awful on me.*
dire • *Most of the poems were dire.*
dreadful • *My financial situation is dreadful.*
horrible • *a horrible meal*
rotten (INFORMAL) • *I think it's a rotten idea.*
ANTONYM:
• excellent

territory NOUN
the land that a person or country controls • *gangs fighting to defend their territories*
area • *They claim that the entire area belongs to Syria.*
country • *He is an ambassador to a foreign country.*
district • *Stick to your own district and stay out of ours.*
domain • *He surveyed his domain from the roof of the castle.*
dominion • *men who ruled their dominions with ruthless efficiency*
land • *New mines were discovered on what had been Apache land.*
province • *debates about the political future of their province*

t

state • *This state remains suspended from the Commonwealth.*

test ① VERB
to find out what something is like • *travelling to Holland to test a British-built boat*
assess • *The test was to assess aptitude rather than academic achievement.*
check • *It's worth checking each item for obvious flaws.*
try • *Howard wanted to try a new restaurant.*
try out • *London Transport hopes to try out the system in September.*

test ② NOUN
an attempt to test something • *the banning of nuclear tests*
assessment • *He was remanded for assessment by doctors.*
check • *regular checks on his blood pressure*
trial • *clinical trials*

texture NOUN
the way that something feels • *Her skin is pale, the texture of fine wax.*
consistency • *Mix the dough to the right consistency.*
feel • *Linen raincoats have a crisp, papery feel.*

theft NOUN
the crime of stealing • *the theft of classified documents*
robbery • *The man was serving a sentence for robbery.*
stealing • *She was jailed for six months for stealing.*

thieving • *an ex-con who says he's given up thieving*

theory NOUN
an idea that explains something • *Darwin's theory of evolution*
conjecture (FORMAL) • *That was a conjecture, not a fact.*
hypothesis (FORMAL) • *Different hypotheses have been put forward.*
supposition • *As with many such suppositions, no one had ever tested it.*
surmise (FORMAL) • *His surmise proved correct.*

therefore ADVERB
as a result • *Muscles need lots of fuel and therefore burn lots of calories.*
as a result • *I slept in, and, as a result, I was late for work.*
consequently • *He's more experienced, and consequently earns a higher salary.*
for that reason • *I'd never met my in-laws before. For that reason, I was a little nervous.*
hence (FORMAL) • *These products are all natural, and hence, better for you.*
so • *I was worried about her, so I phoned to check how she was.*
thus • *His men were getting tired, and thus, careless.*

thesaurus NOUN
PARTS OF A DICTIONARY OR THESAURUS
antonym
definition

entry
example
headword
homonym
homophone
inflection
label
part of speech
pronunciation
root word
synonym
word derivation

thick ① ADJECTIVE
measuring a large distance
from side to side • *a thick stone
wall*
fat • *a fat book*
wide • *a desk that was almost as
wide as the room*
ANTONYM:
• thin

thick ② ADJECTIVE
containing little water • *thick
soup*
clotted • *clotted cream*
concentrated • *a glass of
concentrated orange juice*
condensed • *tins of condensed
milk*
ANTONYM:
• watery

thick ③ ADJECTIVE
grouped closely together
• *thick dark hair*
bristling • *a bristling
moustache*
dense • *a large dense forest*
lush • *the lush green meadows*
luxuriant • *the luxuriant foliage
of Young Island*

ANTONYM:
• sparse

thicken VERB
to become thicker • *The clouds
thickened.*
clot • *The patient's blood refused
to clot.*
condense • *Water vapour
condenses to form clouds.*
congeal • *The gravy started to
congeal.*
set • *as the jelly starts to set*
ANTONYM:
• thin

thief NOUN
someone who steals
something • *a car thief*
burglar • *Burglars broke into
their home.*
crook (INFORMAL) • *a petty
crook*
mugger (INFORMAL) • *after
being threatened by a mugger*
pickpocket • *a gang of
pickpockets*
robber • *armed robbers*
shoplifter • *a persistent
shoplifter*

thin ① ADJECTIVE
measuring a small distance
from side to side • *The material
was too thin.*
fine • *the fine hairs on her arms*
narrow • *a narrow strip of land*
slim • *a slim volume of verse*
ANTONYM:
• thick

thin ② ADJECTIVE
not carrying a lot of fat • *a tall,
thin man with grey hair*

t

emaciated • *emaciated prisoners*
lean • *lean athletes*
skinny • *a skinny body*
slender • *a slender waist*
slim • *a slim figure*
ANTONYM:
• fat

thin ③ ADJECTIVE
containing a lot of water • *thin soup*
dilute or **diluted** • *a dilute solution of bleach*
runny • *a runny soft cheese*
watery • *a mug of watery hot chocolate*
weak • *a cup of weak tea*
ANTONYM:
• thick

thing NOUN
a physical object • *What's that thing doing here?*
article • *household articles*
object • *everyday objects such as wooden spoons*

things PLURAL NOUN
someone's clothes or belongings • *Sara told him to take all his things with him.*
belongings • *I collected my belongings and left.*
effects • *His daughters were collecting his effects.*
gear (INFORMAL) • *They helped us put our gear back into the van.*
possessions • *People had lost all their possessions.*
stuff • *Where have you put all your stuff?*

think ① VERB
to consider something • *Let's think what we can do next.*
consider • *The government is being asked to consider the plan.*
contemplate • *He cried as he contemplated his future.*
deliberate • *She deliberated over the decision for a good few years.*
meditate • *He meditated on the problem.*
mull over • *I'll leave you alone so you can mull it over.*
muse (LITERARY) • *Many of the papers muse on the fate of the President.*
ponder • *I'm continually pondering how to improve the team.*
reflect • *I reflected on the child's future.*

think ② VERB
to believe something • *I think she has a secret boyfriend.*
believe • *Experts believe that the drought will be extensive.*
consider • *He considers that this is the worst recession this century.*
deem (FORMAL) • *Many people have ideas that their society deems to be dangerous.*
hold • *The theory holds that minor events are the trigger for larger events.*
imagine • *I imagine he was just showing off.*
judge • *He judged that this was the moment to say what had to be said.*

reckon (INFORMAL) • *Toni reckoned that it must be about three o'clock.*

thorough ADJECTIVE
careful and complete • *a thorough examination*
complete • *a complete overhaul of the engine*
comprehensive • *a comprehensive guide to the region*
exhaustive • *exhaustive enquiries*
full • *Mr Primakov gave a full account of his meeting with the President.*
intensive • *four weeks of intensive study*
meticulous • *A happy wedding day requires meticulous planning.*
painstaking • *a painstaking search*
scrupulous • *Observe scrupulous hygiene when preparing and cooking food.*

thought ① NOUN
an idea or opinion • *his thoughts on love*
idea • *his ideas about democracy*
notion • *We each have a notion of what kind of person we'd like to be.*
opinion • *most of those who expressed an opinion*
view • *Make your views known to your MP.*

thought ② NOUN
the activity of thinking • *After much thought I decided to end my marriage.*

consideration • *There should be careful consideration of the BBC's future role.*
contemplation • *He was lost in contemplation of the landscape.*
deliberation • *the result of lengthy deliberation*
meditation • *He stared at the floor, lost in meditation.*
reflection • *after days of reflection*
thinking • *This is definitely a time for decisive action and quick thinking.*

thoughtful ① ADJECTIVE
quiet and serious • *He was looking very thoughtful.*
contemplative • *a quiet, contemplative sort of chap*
pensive • *He looked unusually pensive before the start.*
reflective • *I walked on in a reflective mood.*

thoughtful ② ADJECTIVE
showing consideration for others • *a thoughtful and caring man*
attentive • *an attentive husband*
caring • *a caring son*
considerate • *the most considerate man I've ever known*
kind • *She is warmhearted and kind to everyone.*
ANTONYM:
• thoughtless

thoughtless ADJECTIVE
showing a lack of consideration • *It was thoughtless of her to mention it.*

t

insensitive • *My husband is very insensitive about my problem.*

tactless • *a tactless remark*

ANTONYM:
• thoughtful

threat ① NOUN
a statement that someone will harm you • *death threats*

menace • *demanding money with menaces*

threatening remark • *He was overheard making threatening remarks to the couple.*

threat ② NOUN
something that seems likely to harm you • *the threat of tropical storms*

hazard • *a health hazard*

menace • *a menace to the public*

risk • *a fire risk*

threaten ① VERB
to promise to do something bad • *She threatened to report him to the headteacher.*

make threats to • *He denied that he had made threats to cut their funding.*

menace • *They are being menaced by armed rebels.*

threaten ② VERB
to be likely to cause harm • *The newcomers threaten the livelihood of the workers.*

endanger • *Toxic waste could endanger lives.*

jeopardise • *He has jeopardised the future of his government.*

put at risk • *If they have the virus, they are putting patients at risk.*

put in jeopardy • *A series of setbacks have put the whole project in jeopardy.*

thrifty ADJECTIVE
careful not to waste money or resources • *Britain became a nation of thrifty consumers and bargain hunters.*

careful • *He's very careful with his money.*

economical • *a very economical way to travel*

frugal • *a frugal lifestyle*

prudent • *the need for a much more prudent use of energy*

thrill ① NOUN
a feeling of excitement • *the thrill of waking up on Christmas morning*

high (INFORMAL) • *the high of a win over New Zealand*

kick (INFORMAL) • *I got a kick out of seeing my name in print.*

thrill ② VERB
to cause a feeling of excitement • *It thrilled me to see her looking so happy.*

excite • *I only take on work that excites me.*

give a kick (INFORMAL) • *It gave me a kick to actually meet her.*

thrive VERB
to be successful • *His company continues to thrive.*

do well • *Connie did well at school.*

flourish • *Art still flourishes in the ghetto.*

prosper • *His teams have always prospered in cup competitions.*

throw VERB
to make something move through the air • *throwing a tennis ball against a wall*

cast • *He cast the stone away.*

chuck (INFORMAL) • *He chucked the paper in the bin.*

fling • *Peter flung his shoes into the corner.*

hurl • *She hurled her racket down on the court.*

lob • *She lobbed a snowball at them.*

pitch • *Simon pitched the empty bottle into the lake.*

sling • *He took off his anorak and slung it into the back seat.*

toss • *She tossed her suitcase onto one of the beds.*

thug NOUN
a very violent person • *a gang of armed thugs*

bandit • *terrorist acts carried out by bandits*

hooligan • *severe measures against soccer hooligans*

tough • *The neighbourhood toughs beat them both up.*

tsotsi (SOUTH AFRICAN)
• *Many are too terrified of local tsotsis to protest.*

tidy ① ADJECTIVE
arranged in an orderly way
• *a tidy desk*

neat • *She put her clothes in a neat pile.*

orderly • *a beautiful, clean and orderly city*

ANTONYM:
• untidy

tidy ② VERB
to make something neat • *He tidied his garage.*

spruce up • *Many buildings have been spruced up.*

straighten • *straightening cushions and organising magazines*

ANTONYM:
• mess up

tie ① VERB
to fasten something • *They tied the ends of the bag securely.*

bind • *Bind the ends of the cord together with thread.*

fasten • *instructions on how to fasten the strap to the box*

knot • *He knotted the laces securely together.*

lash • *The shelter is built by lashing poles together.*

rope • *I roped myself to the chimney.*

secure • *He secured the canvas straps as tight as they would go.*

tether • *tethering his horse to a tree*

truss • *She trussed him quickly with a stolen bandage.*

ANTONYM:
• untie

tie ② VERB
to have the same score
• *Rafferty tied with Nobilo.*

be level • *At the end of 90 minutes the teams were level.*

t

draw • *Holland and Ireland drew 1–1.*

tie ③ NOUN

a connection with something • *I had very close ties with the family.*

affiliation • *They asked her what her political affiliations were.*

affinity • *He has a close affinity with the landscape.*

bond • *The experience created a special bond between us.*

connection • *The police say he had no connection with the security forces.*

relationship • *family relationships*

tight ① ADJECTIVE

fitting closely • *The shoes are too tight.*

constricted • *His throat began to feel swollen and constricted.*

cramped • *families living in cramped conditions*

snug • *a snug black T-shirt*

ANTONYM:
• loose

tight ② ADJECTIVE

firmly fastened • *a tight knot*

firm • *He managed to get a firm grip of it.*

secure • *Check joints are secure and the wood is sound.*

tight ③ ADJECTIVE

not slack or relaxed • *Pull the elastic tight.*

rigid • *I went rigid with shock.*

taut • *The clothes line is pulled taut and secured.*

tense • *A bath can relax tense muscles.*

ANTONYM:
• slack

tilt ① VERB

to raise one end of something • *Leonard tilted his chair back on two legs.*

incline • *Jack inclined his head.*

lean • *Lean the plants against a wall.*

slant • *The floor slanted down to the window.*

slope • *The bank sloped down sharply to the river.*

tip • *She had to tip her head back to see him.*

tilt ② NOUN

a raised position • *the tilt of the earth's axis*

angle • *The boat is now leaning at a 30 degree angle.*

gradient • *a gradient of 1 in 3*

incline • *at the edge of a steep incline*

slant • *The house is on a slant.*

slope • *The street must have been on a slope.*

time ① NOUN

a particular period • *I enjoyed my time in Durham.*

interval • *a long interval of silence*

period • *a period of calm*

spell • *a brief spell teaching*

stretch • *an 18-month stretch in the army*

while • *They walked on in silence for a while.*

RELATED WORD:
• ADJECTIVE temporal

time ② VERB
to plan when something will happen • *We had timed our visit for March 7.*
schedule • *The rocket was scheduled to blast off at 04:38.*
set • *A court hearing has been set for December 16.*

timid ADJECTIVE
lacking courage or confidence • *a timid child*
bashful • *Offstage, he is bashful and awkward.*
cowardly • *I was too cowardly to complain.*
diffident • *Helen was diffident and reserved.*
nervous • *a very nervous woman*
shy • *a shy, quiet-spoken girl*
ANTONYM:
• bold

tiny ADJECTIVE
very small • *The living room is tiny.*
diminutive • *a diminutive figure standing at the entrance*
microscopic • *a microscopic amount of the substance*
miniature • *He looked like a miniature version of his brother.*
minute • *Only a minute amount is needed.*
negligible • *The pay that the soldiers received was negligible.*
wee (SCOTTISH) • *a wee boy*
ANTONYM:
• huge

tire VERB
to use a lot of energy • *If driving tires you, take the train.*

drain • *My emotional turmoil had drained me.*
exhaust • *Walking in deep snow had totally exhausted him.*
fatigue • *He is easily fatigued.*

tired ADJECTIVE
having little energy • *She was too tired to take a shower.*
drained • *as United stalked off, stunned and drained*
drowsy • *He felt pleasantly drowsy.*
exhausted • *She was too exhausted and distressed to talk.*
fatigued • *Winter weather can leave you feeling fatigued.*
sleepy • *I was beginning to feel sleepy.*
tuckered out (AMERICAN, AUSTRALIAN AND NEW ZEALAND; INFORMAL) • *You must be tuckered out after that bus trip.*
weary • *a weary traveller*
worn out • *He's just worn out after the drive.*

together ① ADVERB
with other people • *We went on long bicycle rides together.*
collectively • *The Cabinet is collectively responsible for policy.*
en masse • *The people marched en masse.*
in unison • *Michael and the landlady nodded in unison.*
jointly • *an agency jointly run by New York and New Jersey*
shoulder to shoulder • *They could fight shoulder to shoulder against a common enemy.*

t

side by side • *areas where different nationalities live side by side*

together ② ADVERB

at the same time • *Three horses crossed the finish line together.*

as one • *The 40,000 crowd rose as one.*

at once • *You can't do two things at once.*

concurrently (FORMAL) • *There were three races running concurrently.*

simultaneously • *The two guns fired almost simultaneously.*

with one accord • *With one accord they turned and walked back.*

tolerable ① ADJECTIVE

able to be tolerated • *The pain was tolerable.*

acceptable • *a mutually acceptable new contract*

bearable • *A cool breeze made the heat bearable.*

ANTONYM:
• unbearable

tolerable ② ADJECTIVE

fairly satisfactory • *a tolerable salary*

acceptable • *We've made an acceptable start.*

adequate • *The level of service was adequate.*

okay or **OK** (INFORMAL) • *For a fashionable restaurant like this the prices are okay.*

passable • *Ms Campbell speaks passable French.*

reasonable • *able to make a reasonable living from his writing*

so-so (INFORMAL) • *Their lunch was only so-so.*

tolerant ADJECTIVE

accepting of different views and behaviour • *a more tolerant attitude towards other religions*

broad-minded • *a very fair and broad-minded man*

liberal • *She is known to have liberal views on divorce.*

open-minded • *I am very open-minded about that question.*

understanding • *Fortunately for John, he had understanding parents.*

ANTONYM:
• narrow-minded

tolerate ① VERB

to accept something you disagree with • *We will not tolerate such behaviour.*

accept • *Urban dwellers often accept noise as part of city life.*

put up with • *You're late again and I won't put up with it.*

tolerate ② VERB

to accept something unpleasant • *She can no longer tolerate the position that she's*

bear • *He can't bear to talk about it.*

endure • *unable to endure the pain*

stand • *He can't stand being cold.*

tomb NOUN

a burial chamber • *Carter discovered Tutankhamun's tomb*

grave • *They used to visit her grave twice a year.*

mausoleum • *the elaborate mausoleums of the Paris cemetery*

sarcophagus • *an Egyptian sarcophagus*

sepulchre (LITERARY) • *the ornate lid of the sepulchre*

vault • *the family vault*

too ① ADVERB
also or as well • *You were there too.*

as well • *She published historical novels as well.*

besides • *You get to sample lots of baking and take home cookies besides.*

in addition • *There are, in addition, other objections to the plan.*

into the bargain • *The machine can play CDs into the bargain.*

likewise • *She sat down and he did likewise.*

moreover • *He didn't know, and moreover, he didn't care.*

too ② ADVERB
more than a desirable or acceptable amount • *You've had too many late nights.*

excessively • *He had an excessively protective mother.*

over- • *I didn't want to seem over-eager.*

overly • *Most people consider him to be overly ambitious.*

unduly • *She's unduly concerned with what people think of her.*

unreasonably • *These prices seem unreasonably high to me.*

tool NOUN
a hand-held instrument for doing a job • *The best tool for the purpose is a pair of shears.*

implement • *knives and other useful implements*

instrument • *instruments for cleaning and polishing teeth*

utensil • *cooking utensils*

top ① NOUN
the highest part of something • *I waited at the top of the stairs.*

apex • *at the very apex of the pyramid*

brow • *the brow of the hill*

crest • *the crest of the wave*

crown • *the crown of the head*

culmination • *the culmination of his career*

head • *A different name was placed at the head of the chart.*

height • *at the height of his success*

high point • *the high point of his movie career*

peak • *at the peak of the morning rush hour*

pinnacle • *the pinnacle of sporting achievement*

ridge • *He died after falling from a ridge on Mount Snowdon.*

summit • *the summit of the mountain*

zenith (LITERARY) • *His career is now at its zenith.*

ANTONYM:
• bottom

top ② NOUN
the lid of a container • *a bottle top*

t

cap • *She unscrewed the cap of her water bottle.*
lid • *the lid of the jar*
stopper • *a scent bottle with a stopper in blue frosted glass*

top ③ ADJECTIVE
being the best of its kind
• *She was the top student in physics.*
best • *the best pupil of his year*
chief • *one of the world's chief nuclear scientists*
elite • *the elite troops of the presidential bodyguard*
foremost • *the foremost urban painter of his age*
head • *He was head boy when he was at school.*
highest • *He achieved one of the highest positions in the land.*
lead • *She has landed the lead role in a major film.*
leading • *a leading member of the community*
pre-eminent • *a pre-eminent political figure*
premier • *the country's premier theatre company*
prime • *The store will be built in a prime location.*
principal • *the principal singer with the Royal Opera House*

top ④ VERB
to be greater than something
• *The temperature topped 90 degrees.*
cap • *He capped his display with two fine goals.*
exceed • *Its research budget exceeds $700 million a year.*

go beyond • *This goes beyond anything I've ever attempted before.*
outstrip • *Demand is outstripping supply.*
surpass • *He has surpassed the record of nine wins in one season.*

top ⑤ VERB
to be better than someone or something • *You'll never manage to top that story.*
beat • *Nothing beats a nice, long bath at the end of a day.*
better • *As an account of adolescence, this novel cannot be bettered.*
eclipse • *Nothing is going to eclipse winning the Olympic title*
improve on • *We need to improve on our performance against France.*
outdo • *Both sides are trying to outdo each other.*
surpass • *He was determined to surpass the achievements of his brothers.*

total ① NOUN
several things added together
• *The companies have a total of 1776 employees.*
aggregate • *three successive defeats by an aggregate of 12 goals*
sum • *the sum of all the angles*
whole • *taken as a percentage of the whole*

total ② ADJECTIVE
complete in all its parts • *a total failure*
absolute • *absolute beginners*
complete • *a complete mess*

out-and-out • *an out-and-out lie*

outright • *an outright rejection of the deal*

unconditional • *unconditional surrender*

undivided • *You have my undivided attention.*

unmitigated • *an unmitigated failure*

unqualified • *an unqualified success*

utter • *utter nonsense*

total ③ VERB
to reach the sum of • *Their debts totalled over 300,000 dollars.*

add up to • *Profits can add up to millions of dollars.*

amount to • *Spending on sports-related items amounted to £9.75 billion.*

come to • *That comes to over a thousand pounds.*

touch ① VERB
to put your hand on something • *Don't touch that dial.*

feel • *The doctor felt his head.*

finger • *He fingered the few coins in his pocket.*

handle • *Wear rubber gloves when handling cat litter.*

touch ② VERB
to come into contact with • *Annie lowered her legs until her feet touched the floor.*

brush • *Something brushed against her leg.*

graze • *A bullet had grazed his arm.*

meet • *when the wheels meet the ground*

RELATED WORD:
• ADJECTIVE **tactile**

touch ③ VERB
to emotionally affect someone • *I was touched by his kindness.*

affect • *Jazza was badly affected by his divorce.*

move • *These stories surprised and moved me.*

stir • *She stirred something very deep in me.*

touching ADJECTIVE
causing sadness or sympathy • *a touching tale*

affecting (LITERARY) • *an affecting memorial to Countess Rachel*

moving • *It was a moving moment for Marianne.*

poignant • *a poignant love story*

touchy ADJECTIVE
easily upset • *She is very touchy about her past.*

easily offended • *viewers who are easily offended*

sensitive • *Some people are very sensitive about their appearance.*

toey (AUSTRALIAN AND NEW ZEALAND; SLANG) • *Don't be so toey.*

tough ① ADJECTIVE
able to put up with hardship • *She is tough and ambitious.*

hardened • *hardened criminals*

hardy • *a hardy race of pioneers*

resilient • *a good soldier, calm and resilient*

t

robust • *Perhaps men are more robust than women?*
rugged • *Rugged individualism forged America's frontier society.*
strong • *Eventually I felt strong enough to look at him.*

tough ② ADJECTIVE
difficult to break or damage • *beans with a rather tough outer skin*
durable • *Fine bone china is both strong and durable.*
hard-wearing • *hard-wearing cotton shirts*
leathery • *leathery skin*
resilient • *an armchair of some resilient plastic material*
robust • *very robust machinery*
rugged • *You need a rugged, four-wheel drive vehicle.*
solid • *The car feels very solid.*
strong • *a strong casing, which won't crack or chip*
sturdy • *The camera was mounted on a sturdy tripod.*
ANTONYM:
• fragile

tough ③ ADJECTIVE
full of hardship • *She had a pretty tough childhood.*
arduous • *an arduous journey*
difficult • *We're living in difficult times.*
exacting • *an exacting task*
hard • *a hard life*
ANTONYM:
• easy

trace ① VERB
to look for and find something

• *Police are trying to trace the owner.*
locate • *We've simply been unable to locate him.*
track down • *She had spent years trying to track down her parents.*

trace ② NOUN
a sign of something • *No trace of his father had been found.*
evidence • *He'd seen no evidence of fraud.*
hint • *I saw no hint of irony on her face.*
indication • *He gave no indication of remorse.*
record • *There's no record of any marriage or children.*
sign • *Sally waited for any sign of illness.*
suggestion • *a faint suggestion of a tan*
whiff • *Not a whiff of scandal has ever tainted his private life.*

trace ③ NOUN
a small amount of something • *to write without a trace of sensationalism*
dash • *a story with a dash of mystery*
drop • *a drop of sherry*
remnant • *Beneath the present church were remnants of Roman flooring.*
suspicion • *large blooms of white with a suspicion of pale pink*
tinge • *Could there have been a slight tinge of envy in Eva's voice?*
touch • *a touch of flu*

T

vestige • *the last vestige of a UN force that once numbered 30,000*

trade ① NOUN
the buying and selling of goods • *foreign trade*
business • *a career in business*
commerce • *They have made their fortunes from industry and commerce.*

RELATED WORD:
• ADJECTIVE mercantile

trade ② NOUN
the kind of work someone does • *He learnt his trade as a diver in the North Sea.*
business • *the music business*
line • *Are you in the publishing line too?*
line of work • *In my line of work I often get home too late for dinner.*
occupation • *her new occupation as an author*
profession • *Harper was a teacher by profession.*

trade ③ VERB
to buy and sell goods • *They had years of experience of trading with the West.*
deal • *They deal in antiques.*
do business • *the different people who did business with me*
traffic • *those who traffic in illegal drugs*

trader NOUN
someone who trades in goods • *a timber trader*
broker • *a financial broker*

dealer • *dealers in commodities*
merchant • *a grain merchant*

tradition NOUN
a long-standing custom • *the rich traditions of Afro-Cuban music*
convention • *It's just a social convention that men don't wear skirts.*
custom • *an ancient Japanese custom*

traditional ADJECTIVE
existing for a long time • *her traditional Indian dress*
conventional • *conventional research methods*
established • *the established church*

ANTONYM:
• unconventional

tragic ADJECTIVE
very sad • *a tragic accident*
distressing • *distressing news*
heartbreaking • *They suffered a heartbreaking defeat on penalties.*
heart-rending • *heart-rending pictures of refugees*

train VERB
to teach someone how to do something • *We train them in bricklaying and other building techniques.*
coach • *He coached the basketball team.*
drill • *He drills the choir to a high standard.*
educate • *I was educated at the local grammar school.*

t

instruct • *All their members are instructed in first aid.*

school • *He has been schooled to take over the family business.*

teach • *This is something they teach us to do in our first year.*

tutor • *She decided to tutor her children at home.*

transfer VERB

to move something from one place to another • *It's easy to transfer money between accounts.*

carry • *I carried the box to the table.*

download • *You can download free games from this website.*

move • *I think we should move the TV to the other side of the room.*

upload • *The boy uploaded a video of the puppies to the internet.*

transform VERB

to change something completely • *This technology has transformed our society.*

alter • *New curtains can completely alter the look of a room.*

change • *alchemists attempting to change base metals into gold*

convert • *They have converted the church into a restaurant.*

reform • *He was totally reformed by this experience.*

revolutionise • *a device which will revolutionise the way you cook*

transparent ADJECTIVE

able to be seen through • *a sheet of transparent plastic*

clear • *a clear glass panel*

crystalline (LITERARY) • *crystalline lakes*

sheer • *a sheer black shirt*

translucent • *translucent corrugated plastic*

ANTONYM:
• opaque

transport ① NOUN

the moving of goods and people • *The prices quoted include transport costs.*

removal • *the furniture removal business*

shipment • *transported to the docks for shipment overseas*

transportation • *the transportation of refugees*

transport ② VERB

to move people or goods somewhere • *They use tankers to transport the oil to Los Angeles.*

carry • *The ship could carry seventy passengers.*

convey (FORMAL) • *a branch line to convey fish direct to Billingsgate*

ship • *the food being shipped to Iraq*

transfer • *She was transferred to another hospital.*

trap ① NOUN

a device for catching animals • *a rabbit trap*

net • *a fishing net*

snare • *a snare for catching bir*

trap ② VERB
to catch animals • *The locals were encouraged to trap and kill the birds.*
catch • *an animal caught in a trap*
corner • *like a cornered rat*
snare • *He'd snared a rabbit earlier in the day.*

trap ③ VERB
to trick someone • *Were you trying to trap her into making some admission?*
dupe • *a plot to dupe stamp collectors into buying fake rarities*
trick • *His family tricked him into signing the document.*

trash ① NOUN
waste material • *He picks up your trash on Mondays.*
garbage • *rotting piles of garbage*
refuse • *a weekly collection of refuse*
rubbish • *They had piled most of their rubbish into yellow skips.*
waste • *a law that regulates the disposal of waste*

trash ② NOUN
something of poor quality • *Don't read that awful trash.*
garbage (INFORMAL) • *He spends his time watching garbage on TV.*
rubbish • *He described her book as absolute rubbish.*

travel VERB
to make a journey somewhere

• *You had better travel to Helsinki tomorrow.*
go • *We went to Rome.*
journey (FORMAL) • *He intended to journey up the Amazon.*
make your way • *He made his way home at last.*
take a trip • *We intend to take a trip there sometime.*

treacherous ① ADJECTIVE
likely to betray someone • *He denounced the party's treacherous leaders.*
disloyal • *disloyal Cabinet colleagues*
faithless • *betrayed by their faithless queen*
unfaithful • *his unfaithful servant*
untrustworthy • *Jordan has tried to brand his opponents as untrustworthy.*

ANTONYM:
• **loyal**

treacherous ② ADJECTIVE
dangerous or unreliable
• *treacherous mountain roads*
dangerous • *a dangerous stretch of road*
hazardous • *hazardous seas*
perilous (LITERARY) • *The roads grew even steeper and more perilous.*

treasure VERB
to consider something very precious • *He treasures his friendship with her.*
cherish • *The previous owners had cherished the house.*
hold dear • *forced to renounce everything he held most dear*

prize • one of the gallery's most prized possessions
value • if you value your health

treat ① VERB

to behave towards someone • Artie treated most other people with indifference.
act towards • the way you act towards other people
behave towards • He always behaved towards me with great kindness.
deal with • She has to deal with homeless young people.

treat ② VERB

to give someone medical care • the doctor who treated her
care for • They hired a nurse to care for her.
nurse • All the years he was sick my mother had nursed him.

trendy ADJECTIVE (INFORMAL)

fashionable • a trendy night club
fashionable • a very fashionable place to go on holiday
in (SLANG) • what's in and what's not
in fashion • Calf-length skirts are in fashion this season.
in vogue • African art is in vogue at the moment.
latest • the latest thing in camera technology
stylish • This city has got a lot more stylish in recent years.

tribute NOUN

something that shows admiration • Police paid tribute to her courage.
accolade (FORMAL) • To play for your country is the ultimate accolade.
compliment • We consider it a compliment to be called "conservative".
honour • Only two writers are granted the honour of a solo display.
praise • That is high praise indeed.
testimony • a testimony to her dedication

trick ① NOUN

something that deceives someone • We are playing a trick on a man who keeps bothering me.
con (INFORMAL) • Slimming snacks that offer miraculous weight loss are a con.
deception • the victim of a cruel deception
hoax • a bomb hoax
ploy • a cynical marketing ploy
ruse • This was a ruse to divide them.

trick ② VERB

to deceive someone • They tricked me into giving them all my money.
con (INFORMAL) • We have been conned for 20 years.
deceive • He deceived me into thinking the money was his.
dupe • I was duped into letting them in.
fool • They tried to fool you into coming after us.

take in (INFORMAL) • *I wasn't taken in for a minute.*

tricky ADJECTIVE
difficult to do or to deal with • *This could be a very tricky problem.*

complex • *the whole complex issue of crime and punishment*

complicated • *a complicated operation*

delicate • *This brings us to the delicate question of his future.*

difficult • *It was a difficult decision to make.*

hard • *That's a hard question to answer.*

problematic • *It's a very problematic piece to play.*

puzzling • *a puzzling case to solve*

sensitive • *The death penalty is a very sensitive issue.*

trip ① NOUN
a journey to a place • *a business trip*

excursion • *a coach excursion to Trondheim*

jaunt • *a jaunt in the car*

journey • *the journey to Bordeaux*

outing • *a school outing*

voyage • *Columbus's voyage to the West Indies*

trip ② VERB
to fall over • *I tripped on the stairs.*

fall over • *Plenty of top skiers fell over.*

lose your footing • *He lost his footing and slid into the water.*

stumble • *He stumbled and almost fell.*

triumph ① NOUN
a great success • *The championships proved to be a personal triumph for the coach.*

success • *The jewellery was a great success.*

victory • *a victory for common sense*

ANTONYM:
• failure

triumph ② VERB
to be successful • *a symbol of good triumphing over evil*

come out on top (INFORMAL) • *The only way to come out on top is to adopt a different approach.*

prevail • *I do hope he will prevail over the rebels.*

succeed • *if they can succeed in America*

win • *The top four teams all won.*

ANTONYM:
• fail

trivial ADJECTIVE
not important • *She doesn't concern herself with such trivial details.*

insignificant • *The dangers are insignificant compared with those of smoking.*

minor • *a minor inconvenience*

negligible • *The strike will have a negligible impact.*

paltry • *They had no interest in paltry domestic concerns.*

petty • *I wouldn't indulge in such petty schoolboy pranks.*

t

slight • It's only a slight problem.

trifling • The sums involved were trifling.

unimportant • Too much time is spent discussing unimportant matters.

ANTONYM:
• important

trouble ① NOUN
a difficulty or problem
• financial troubles

bother • Vince is having a spot of bother with the law.

difficulty • economic difficulties

hassle (INFORMAL) • We had loads of hassles trying to find somewhere to rehearse.

problem • The main problem is unemployment.

trouble ② VERB
to make someone feel worried
• He was troubled by the lifestyle of his son.

agitate • The thought agitates her.

bother • Is something bothering you?

disturb • dreams so vivid that they disturb me for days

worry • I didn't want to worry you.

trouble ③ VERB
to cause someone inconvenience • Can I trouble you for some milk?

bother • I don't know why he bothers me with this kind of rubbish.

disturb • a room where you won't be disturbed

impose upon • I was afraid you'd feel we were imposing on you.

inconvenience • He promised to be quick so as not to inconvenience them further.

put out • Please don't put yourself out on my account.

true ① ADJECTIVE
not invented • The film is based on a true story.

accurate • an accurate assessment of the situation

correct • a correct diagnosis

factual • any comparison that is not strictly factual

ANTONYM:
• inaccurate

true ② ADJECTIVE
real or genuine • She was a true friend.

authentic • authentic Italian food

bona fide • We are happy to donate to bona fide charities.

genuine • There was a risk of genuine refugees being returned to Vietnam.

real • No, it wasn't a dream. It was real.

ANTONYM:
• false

trust VERB
to believe that someone will do something • The president can't be trusted.

count on • I can always count on you to cheer me up.

depend on • *You can depend on me.*

have confidence in • *We have the utmost confidence in your abilities.*

have faith in • *I have no faith in him any more.*

place your trust in • *I would never place my trust in one so young.*

rely upon • *I know I can rely on you to sort it out.*

trusty ADJECTIVE
considered to be reliable • *a trusty member of the crew*

dependable • *a dependable and steady worker*

faithful • *his faithful black Labrador*

firm • *Betty became a firm friend of the family.*

reliable • *the problem of finding reliable staff*

solid • *one of my most solid supporters*

staunch • *He proved himself a staunch ally.*

true • *a true friend*

trustworthy • *trying to find a trustworthy adviser*

truth NOUN
the facts about something • *Marcel is keen to get to the truth of what happened.*

fact • *How much was fact and how much fancy no one knew.*

reality • *Fiction and reality were increasingly blurred.*

RELATED WORDS:
• ADJECTIVES veritable, veracious

try ① VERB
to make an effort to do something • *I tried hard to persuade him to stay.*

attempt • *They are accused of attempting to smuggle weapons into the country.*

endeavour (FORMAL) • *I will endeavour to arrange it.*

make an attempt • *He made three attempts to break the record.*

make an effort • *He made no effort to hide his disappointment.*

seek • *We have never sought to impose our views.*

strive • *The school strives to treat pupils as individuals.*

try ② VERB
to test the quality of something • *Howard wanted to try a new restaurant.*

check out • *We went to the club to check it out.*

sample • *We sampled a selection of different bottled waters.*

test • *The drug was tested on rats.*

try out • *London Transport hopes to try out the system in September.*

try ③ NOUN
an attempt to do something • *After a few tries he pressed the right button.*

attempt • *a deliberate attempt to destabilise the defence*

effort • *his efforts to improve*

endeavour (FORMAL) • *His first endeavours in the field were wedding films.*

t

go (INFORMAL) • She won on her
first go.
shot (INFORMAL) • I have had a
shot at professional cricket.

tubby ADJECTIVE
rather fat • He's a bit on the
tubby side.
chubby • She was very chubby
as a child.
fat • He was short and fat.
overweight • He has to work
hard to avoid being overweight.
plump • a plump, pretty baby
with curly hair
podgy • Eddie is a little podgy
round the middle.
portly • a portly gentleman
stout • His wife was a small,
stout woman.

tug ① VERB
to give something a quick,
hard pull • A little boy tugged at
her skirt excitedly.
drag • He grabbed my ankle and
dragged me back.
draw • She took his hand and
drew him along.
haul • I gripped his wrist and
hauled him up.
heave • They heaved the last
bag into the van.
jerk • He jerked his hand out of
mine angrily.
pluck • The beggar plucked at
her sleeve as she passed.
pull • She pulled down the hem of
her skirt over her knees.
wrench • The horse wrenched
its head free.
yank • He grabbed my arm and
yanked me out of the car.

tug ② NOUN
a quick, hard pull • He felt a tug
at his arm.
heave • With a mighty heave,
she pulled herself away from him.
jerk • He gave a sudden jerk of
the reins.
pull • Give the cord three sharp
pulls.
wrench • He lowered the flag
with a quick wrench.
yank • He gave the phone a
savage yank.

tune NOUN
a series of musical notes • She
was humming a merry little tune.
melody • a beautiful melody
strains • She could hear the tiny
strains of a chamber orchestra.

turn ① VERB
to change the direction or
position of something • She
had turned the bedside chair to
face the door.
rotate • Take each foot in both
your hands and rotate it.
spin • He spun the wheel sharply
and made a U-turn.
swivel • She swivelled her chair
round.
twirl • Bonnie twirled her empty
glass in her fingers.
twist • She twisted her head
sideways.

turn ② VERB
to become or make
something different • A hobby
can be turned into a career.
change • She has now
changed into a happy,
self-confident woman.

convert • *a table that converts into an ironing board*
mutate • *Overnight, the gossip begins to mutate into headlines.*
transform • *the speed at which your body transforms food into energy*

turn ③ NOUN
someone's right or duty to do something • *Tonight it's my turn to cook.*
chance • *All eligible people would get a chance to vote.*
go • *Whose go is it?*
opportunity • *Now is your opportunity to say you've always wanted.*

twist ① VERB
to turn something round • *Her hands began to twist the handles of the bag.*
bend • *Bend the bar into a horseshoe.*
curl • *She sat with her legs curled under her.*
twine • *He had twined his chubby arms around Vincent's neck.*
weave • *He weaves his way through a crowd.*
wring • *She wrung her hands together and shook her head.*

twist ② VERB
to bend into a new shape • *The car was left a mess of twisted metal.*
distort • *A painter may exaggerate or distort shapes and forms.*
mangle • *the mangled wreckage*
screw up • *Amy screwed up her face.*

twist ③ VERB
to injure a part of your body • *I've twisted my ankle.*
sprain • *He fell and sprained his wrist.*
wrench • *He had wrenched his back badly from the force of the fall.*

two-faced ADJECTIVE
not honest in dealing with other people • *a two-faced, manipulative woman*
deceitful • *a deceitful, conniving liar*
dishonest • *He's been dishonest in his dealings with us both.*
disloyal • *I can't stand people who are disloyal.*
false • *He had been betrayed by his false friends.*
hypocritical • *a hypocritical and ambitious careerist*
insincere • *They are still widely seen as insincere and untrustworthy.*
treacherous • *He has been consistently treacherous to both sides.*

type NOUN
a group of things that have features in common • *There are various types of dog suitable as pets.*
brand • *his favourite brand of toothpaste*
breed • *a rare breed of cattle*
class • *a better class of restaurant*
group • *Weather forecasters classify clouds into several different groups.*

t

kind • *I don't like that kind of film.*
make • *He'll only drive a certain make of car.*
sort • *a dozen trees of various sorts*
species • *a rare species of moth*
style • *Several styles of hat were available.*
variety • *Many varieties of birds live here.*

typical ADJECTIVE
having the usual characteristics of something • *a typical American child*
average • *The average adult man burns 1500 to 2000 calories per day.*
characteristic • *a characteristic feature of the landscape*
normal • *a normal day*
regular • *He describes himself as just a regular guy.*
representative • *fairly representative groups of adults*
standard • *It was standard practice in cases like this.*
stock • *He had a stock answer for all problems.*
usual • *a neighbourhood beset by all the usual inner-city problems*

ANTONYM:
• uncharacteristic

Uu

ugly ADJECTIVE
having a very unattractive appearance • *She makes me feel dowdy and ugly.*
plain • *a shy, plain girl with a pale complexion*
unattractive • *painted in an unattractive shade of green*
unsightly • *The view was spoiled by some unsightly houses.*

ANTONYM:
• beautiful

ultimate ① ADJECTIVE
being the final one of a series • *It is not possible to predict the ultimate outcome.*
eventual • *Reunification is the eventual aim.*
final • *the fifth and final day*
last • *This is his last chance to do something useful.*

ultimate ② ADJECTIVE
the most important or powerful • *the ultimate goal of any player*
greatest • *Our greatest aim was to take the gold medal.*
paramount • *His paramount ambition was to be an actor.*
supreme • *the supreme test of his abilities*

utmost • *This has to be our utmost priority.*

ultimate ③ NOUN
the finest example of something • *This hotel is the ultimate in luxury.*
epitome • *She was the epitome of the successful businesswoman.*
extreme • *This was shyness taken to the extreme.*
height • *the height of bad manners*
peak • *roses at the peak of perfection*

unaware ADJECTIVE
not knowing about something • *Many people are unaware of how much they eat.*
ignorant • *They are completely ignorant of the relevant facts.*
oblivious • *John appeared oblivious to his surroundings.*
unconscious • *totally unconscious of my presence*
unsuspecting • *The cars were then sold to unsuspecting buyers.*

ANTONYM:
• aware

unbearable ADJECTIVE
too unpleasant to be tolerated • *Life was unbearable for the remaining citizens.*
intolerable • *The heat and humidity were intolerable.*
oppressive • *An oppressive sadness weighed upon him.*
unacceptable • *She condemned the group's unacceptable behaviour.*

ANTONYM:
• tolerable

unbelievable ① ADJECTIVE
extremely great or surprising • *He showed unbelievable courage.*
colossal • *There has been a colossal waste of public money.*
incredible • *You're always an incredible help on these occasions.*
stupendous • *It cost a stupendous amount of money.*

unbelievable ② ADJECTIVE
so unlikely it cannot be believed • *He came up with some unbelievable story.*
implausible • *a film with an implausible ending*
improbable • *highly improbable claims*
inconceivable • *It was inconceivable that he'd hurt anyone.*
incredible • *It seems incredible that anyone would want to do that.*
preposterous • *The whole idea was preposterous.*
unconvincing • *In response he was given the usual unconvincing excuses.*

ANTONYM:
• believable

uncertain ① ADJECTIVE
not knowing what to do • *For a moment he looked uncertain as to how to respond.*
doubtful • *He was a bit doubtful about starting without her.*
dubious • *We were a bit dubious about it at first.*

u

uncertain

    unclear • *I'm unclear about where to go.*

    undecided • *Even then she was still undecided about her future plans.*

    ANTONYM:
    • certain

uncertain ② ADJECTIVE

not definite • *facing an uncertain future*

    ambiguous • *The wording of the contract was ambiguous.*

    doubtful • *The outcome of the match is still doubtful.*

    indefinite • *suspended for an indefinite period*

    indeterminate • *a woman of indeterminate age*

    ANTONYM:
    • certain

unclear ADJECTIVE

confusing and not obvious • *It is unclear how much popular support they have.*

    ambiguous • *in order to clarify the earlier ambiguous statement*

    confused • *The situation remains confused, as no clear victor has emerged.*

    vague • *The description was pretty vague.*

    ANTONYM:
    • clear

uncomfortable ①

ADJECTIVE

feeling or causing discomfort • *an uncomfortable bed*

    awkward • *Its shape made it awkward to carry.*

    cramped • *living in very cramped conditions*

    disagreeable • *designed to make flying a less disagreeable experience*

    ill-fitting • *Walking was difficult because of her ill-fitting shoes.*

    painful • *a painful back injury*

    ANTONYM:
    • comfortable

uncomfortable ②

ADJECTIVE

not relaxed or confident • *Talking about money made her uncomfortable.*

    awkward • *Offstage, he is bashful and awkward.*

    embarrassed • *an embarrassed silence*

    ill at ease • *I always feel ill at ease in their company.*

    self-conscious • *She was always self-conscious about her height.*

    uneasy • *He looked uneasy and refused to answer any more questions.*

    ANTONYM:
    • comfortable

uncommon ① ADJECTIVE

not happening or seen often • *This type of injury is uncommon among athletes.*

    exceptional • *These are exceptional circumstances.*

    extraordinary • *an act of extraordinary generosity*

    few • *Genuine friends are few.*

    infrequent • *one of the infrequent visitors to the island*

U

out of the ordinary • *My story is nothing out of the ordinary.*
rare • *a rare occurrence*
scarce • *places where jobs are scarce*
sparse • *Traffic is sparse on this stretch of road.*
unusual • *an unusual sight these days*

ANTONYM:
• common

uncommon ② ADJECTIVE

unusually great • *She had read Cecilia's last letter with uncommon interest.*
acute • *He has an acute dislike of children.*
exceptional • *a woman of exceptional beauty*
extraordinary • *a young player of extraordinary energy*
extreme • *regions suffering from extreme poverty*
great • *They share a great love of Bach's music.*
intense • *intense heat*
remarkable • *a musician of remarkable talent*

unconscious ① ADJECTIVE

in a state similar to sleep • *By the time the ambulance arrived, he was unconscious.*
asleep • *They were fast asleep in their beds.*
senseless • *He was beaten senseless and robbed of all his money.*
stunned • *stunned by a blow to the head*

ANTONYM:
• conscious

unconscious ② ADJECTIVE

not aware of what is happening • *quite unconscious of their presence*
oblivious • *He seemed oblivious of his surroundings.*
unaware • *He was unaware of the chaos he was causing.*
unknowing • *unknowing accomplices in his crimes*
unsuspecting • *She was an unsuspecting victim of his deceit.*

ANTONYM:
• aware

uncover ① VERB

to find something out • *Auditors said they had uncovered evidence of fraud.*
bring to light • *The truth is unlikely to be brought to light.*
expose • *His lies were exposed in court.*
reveal • *He will reveal the truth behind the scandal.*
show up • *His true character has been shown up for what it is.*
unearth • *a campaign to unearth supposed conspiracies*

uncover ② VERB

to remove the lid or cover from something • *When the seedlings sprout, uncover the tray.*
expose • *The wreck was exposed by the action of the tide.*
lay bare • *Layers of paint and flaking plaster were laid bare.*
open • *I opened a new jar of coffee.*
reveal • *His shirt was open, revealing a tattooed chest.*

u

unearth • *Quarry workers have unearthed the skeleton of a mammoth.*

unveil • *The statue will be unveiled next week.*

unwrap • *unwrapping Christmas presents*

under PREPOSITION
at a lower level than something • *a labyrinth of tunnels under the ground*

below • *The sun had already sunk below the horizon.*

beneath • *the frozen grass crunching beneath his feet*

underneath • *people trapped underneath the wreckage*

ANTONYM:
• above

undergo VERB
to have something happen to you • *He had to undergo major surgery.*

be subjected to • *She was subjected to constant interruptions.*

endure • *The company endured heavy losses.*

experience • *They seem to experience more distress than the others.*

go through • *I wouldn't like to go through that again.*

suffer • *The peace process had suffered a serious setback.*

undermine VERB
to make something less secure or strong • *You're trying to undermine my confidence again.*

impair • *Their actions will impair France's national interests.*

sap • *I was afraid the illness had sapped my strength.*

subvert • *an attempt to subvert their culture from within*

weaken • *Her authority had been fatally weakened.*

ANTONYM:
• strengthen

understand ① VERB
to know what someone means • *Do you understand what I'm saying?*

catch on (INFORMAL) • *I didn't catch on immediately to what he meant.*

comprehend • *Whenever she failed to comprehend, she just laughed.*

follow • *I don't follow you at all.*

get • *Did you get that joke?*

grasp • *He instantly grasped that they were talking about him.*

see • *"I see," she said at last.*

take in • *too much to take in at once*

understand ② VERB
to know why or how something is happening • *too young to understand what's going on*

appreciate • *You must appreciate how important this is.*

comprehend • *I just cannot comprehend your viewpoint.*

fathom • *His attitude was hard to fathom.*

grasp • *We immediately grasped the seriousness of the crisis.*

realise • *People just don't realise how serious it could be.*

understand ③ VERB
to hear of something • *I understand she hasn't been well.*
believe • *She's coming back tomorrow, I believe.*
gather • *We gather the report is critical of the judge.*
hear • *I hear you've been having some problems.*
learn • *On learning who he was, I wanted to meet him.*

understanding ① NOUN
a knowledge of something • *a basic understanding of computers*
appreciation • *some appreciation of the problems of consumers*
comprehension • *completely beyond our comprehension*
grasp • *a good grasp of foreign languages*
knowledge • *I have no knowledge of his business affairs.*
perception • *Her questions showed a shrewd perception.*

understanding ② NOUN
an informal agreement • *There was an understanding between us.*
accord (FORMAL) • *trying to reach an accord*
agreement • *A new defence agreement was signed last month.*
pact • *an electoral pact between the parties*

understanding ③
ADJECTIVE
having a sympathetic nature • *Fortunately he had understanding parents.*

compassionate • *a deeply compassionate man*
considerate • *They should be more considerate towards the prisoners.*
sensitive • *He was always sensitive and caring.*
sympathetic • *a sympathetic listener*

undertaking NOUN
a task which you have agreed to do • *Organising the show has been a massive undertaking.*
affair • *It's going to be a tricky affair to arrange.*
business • *Livestock farming is an arduous and difficult business.*
endeavour • *an endeavour that was bound to end in failure*
enterprise • *a risky enterprise such as horse breeding*
job • *What made you decide to take this job on?*
operation • *the man in charge of the entire operation*
project • *I can't take responsibility for such a huge project.*
task • *a task I do not feel equipped to take on*
venture • *a venture that few were willing to invest in*

uneasy ADJECTIVE
worried that something may be wrong • *I was very uneasy about these developments.*
agitated • *She seemed agitated about something.*
anxious • *He admitted he was still anxious about the situation.*
nervous • *Consumers say they*

u

are nervous about their jobs.
perturbed • *I am not too perturbed at this setback.*
worried • *If you're worried about it, just ask for more details.*
ANTONYM:
• comfortable

unemployed ADJECTIVE
not having a job • *an unemployed mechanic*
idle • *He has been idle for almost a month.*
jobless • *One in four people are now jobless.*
redundant • *aid for the 30,000 redundant miners*
ANTONYM:
• employed

uneven ① ADJECTIVE
having an unlevel or rough surface • *I tripped and fell on an uneven pavement.*
bumpy • *bumpy cobbled streets*
not level • *It was hard to walk because the road was not level.*
not smooth • *The icing isn't smooth enough.*
rough • *She picked her way across the rough ground.*
ANTONYM:
• level

uneven ② ADJECTIVE
not the same or consistent • *six lines of uneven length*
fluctuating • *a fluctuating temperature*
inconsistent • *Their performance was inconsistent over the whole season.*
irregular • *at irregular intervals*

patchy • *Her career has been patchy.*
variable • *The potassium content of food is very variable.*
ANTONYM:
• even

unexpected ADJECTIVE
not considered likely to happen • *His death was completely unexpected.*
astonishing • *What an astonishing piece of good luck!*
chance • *a chance meeting*
surprising • *a most surprising turn of events*
unforeseen • *The show was cancelled due to unforeseen circumstances.*

unfailing ADJECTIVE
continuous and not weakening as time passes • *his unfailing cheerfulness*
constant • *They were under constant pressure.*
endless • *his endless demands for attention*
unremitting • *her unremitting efforts*

unfair ADJECTIVE
without right or justice • *It was unfair that he should suffer so much.*
unjust • *an unjust decision*
wrong • *It would be wrong to allow the case to go any further.*
wrongful • *his claim for wrongful dismissal*
ANTONYM:
• fair

unfamiliar ADJECTIVE
not having been seen or heard of before • *She grew many plants which were unfamiliar to me.*
alien • *transplanted into an alien culture*
exotic • *filmed in an exotic location*
foreign • *This was a foreign country, so unlike his own.*
new • *This was a new experience for me.*
novel • *having to cope with many novel situations*
strange • *All these faces were strange to me.*
unknown • *I'd discovered a writer quite unknown to me.*

unfriendly ADJECTIVE
not showing any warmth or kindness • *He can expect an unfriendly welcome.*
aloof • *His manner was aloof.*
antagonistic • *They were always antagonistic to newcomers.*
cold • *She was a cold, unfeeling woman.*
disagreeable • *He may be clever but he's most disagreeable.*
hostile • *The prisoner eyed him in hostile silence.*
unkind • *They're always unkind to newcomers.*

ANTONYM:
• friendly

ungrateful ADJECTIVE
not appreciating the things you have • *the most miserable and ungrateful people on earth*

unappreciative • *He was unappreciative of our efforts.*
unthankful • *mercenary players and unthankful supporters*

ANTONYM:
• grateful

unhappy ADJECTIVE
feeling sad or depressed • *He was a shy, sometimes unhappy man.*
depressed • *She's depressed about this whole situation.*
despondent • *After the interview John was despondent.*
down • *They felt really down after they spoke to him.*
miserable • *My job made me really miserable sometimes.*
sad • *I felt sad to leave our little house.*

ANTONYM:
• happy

unhealthy ① ADJECTIVE
likely to cause illness • *an unhealthy lifestyle*
bad for you • *the argument that eating meat is bad for you*
harmful • *Try to avoid harmful habits like smoking.*
insanitary • *the insanitary conditions of slums*
noxious • *factories belching out noxious fumes*
unwholesome • *an epidemic originating from the unwholesome food they ate*

ANTONYM:
• healthy

u

unhealthy ② ADJECTIVE
not well • *an unhealthy-looking man with a bad complexion*
ailing • *The President is said to be ailing.*
crook (AUSTRALIAN AND NEW ZEALAND; INFORMAL) • *I'm sorry to hear you've been crook, mate.*
ill • *He didn't look at all ill when I last saw him.*
not well • *When I'm not well, she looks after me.*
poorly (BRITISH; INFORMAL) • *She's still poorly after that bout of pneumonia.*
sick • *He's very sick and he needs treatment.*
unwell • *an infection which could make you very unwell*
ANTONYM:
• healthy

unimportant ADJECTIVE
having little significance or importance • *The difference in their ages seemed unimportant at the time.*
insignificant • *In 1949, Bonn was a small, insignificant city.*
minor • *a minor inconvenience*
paltry • *They had little interest in paltry domestic concerns.*
slight • *We have a slight problem.*
trivial • *She waved aside the trivial details.*
ANTONYM:
• important

uninterested ADJECTIVE
not interested in something • *I'm completely uninterested in anything you have to say.*

apathetic • *apathetic about politics*
bored • *She looked bored with the whole performance.*
impassive • *He remained impassive while she ranted on.*
indifferent • *He is totally indifferent to our problems.*
nonchalant • *"Suit yourself," I said, trying to sound nonchalant.*
passive • *That passive attitude of his drives me mad.*
unconcerned • *She is unconcerned about anything except herself.*
ANTONYM:
• interested

union ① NOUN
an organisation of people or groups with mutual interests • *a trades union*
association • *a member of several different associations*
coalition • *governed by a coalition of three parties*
confederation • *a confederation of mini-states*
federation • *a federation of six separate agencies*
league • *the League of Nations*

union ② NOUN
the joining together of two or more things • *The majority voted for union with Russia.*
amalgamation • *an amalgamation of two organisations*
blend • *a blend of traditional charm and modern amenities*
combination • *the combination of science and art*

fusion • *fusions of jazz and pop*
mixture • *a mixture of nuts,
raisins and capers*

unite VERB
to join together and act as a
group • *We must unite to fight
our common enemy.*
collaborate • *They all
collaborated on the project.*
combine • *The companies have
combined to form a
multinational.*
join • *People of all kinds joined to
make a dignified protest.*
join forces • *The two parties are
joining forces.*
link up • *the first time the two
armies have linked up*
merge • *The media group hopes
to merge with its rival company.*
pull together • *The staff and
management are pulling together
to save the company.*
work together • *industry and
government working together*
ANTONYM:
• divide

universal ADJECTIVE
relating to everyone or to the
whole universe • *These
programmes have a universal
appeal.*
common • *The common view is
that it is a good thing.*
general • *This project should
raise general awareness about
the problem.*
unlimited • *destruction on an
unlimited scale*
widespread • *Food shortages
are widespread.*

worldwide • *the fear of a
worldwide epidemic*

unkind ADJECTIVE
lacking in kindness and
consideration • *It's very unkind
to describe her in those terms.*
cruel • *Children can be so cruel.*
malicious • *spreading
malicious gossip*
mean • *I'd feel mean saying no.*
nasty • *What nasty little snobs
you are!*
spiteful • *How can you say such
spiteful things about us?*
thoughtless • *a small minority
of thoughtless and inconsiderate
people*
ANTONYM:
• kind

unknown ADJECTIVE
not familiar or famous • *He was
an unknown writer at that time.*
humble • *He started out as a
humble fisherman.*
obscure • *an obscure Greek
composer*
unfamiliar • *There were several
unfamiliar names on the list.*
unsung • *among the unsung
heroes of our time*
ANTONYM:
• famous

unlike PREPOSITION
different from • *She was unlike
him in every way.*
different from • *I've always felt
different from most people.*
dissimilar to • *a cultural
background not dissimilar
to our own*

u

distinct from • *Their cuisines
are quite distinct from each other.*
divergent from (FORMAL)
• *That viewpoint is not much
divergent from that of his
predecessor.*
far from • *His politics are not all
that far from mine.*
ANTONYM:
• like

unlikely ADJECTIVE
probably not true or likely to
happen • *a military coup seems
unlikely*
implausible • *a film with an
implausible ending*
incredible • *an incredible pack
of lies*
unbelievable • *I know it
sounds unbelievable, but I wasn't
there that day.*
unconvincing • *He came up
with a very unconvincing excuse.*
ANTONYM:
• likely

unlucky ADJECTIVE
having bad luck • *He was
unlucky not to score during the
first half.*
cursed • *the most cursed family
in history*
hapless • *a hapless victim of
chance*
luckless • *the luckless parents
of a difficult child*
unfortunate • *Some unfortunate
person nearby could be injured.*
wretched • *wretched people
who had to sell or starve*
ANTONYM:
• lucky

unnecessary ADJECTIVE
completely needless • *He
frowns upon unnecessary expense.*
needless • *causing needless
panic*
pointless • *pointless meetings*
uncalled-for • *uncalled-for
rudeness*
ANTONYM:
• necessary

unpleasant ① ADJECTIVE
causing feelings of discomfort
or dislike • *It has a very
unpleasant smell.*
bad • *I have some bad news.*
disagreeable • *a disagreeable
experience*
distasteful • *I find her gossip
distasteful.*
nasty • *This divorce could turn
nasty.*
repulsive • *repulsive fat white
slugs*
unpalatable • *Only then did I
learn the unpalatable truth.*
ANTONYM:
• pleasant

unpleasant ② ADJECTIVE
rude or unfriendly • *a
thoroughly unpleasant person*
disagreeable • *He may be
clever, but he's a very
disagreeable man.*
horrid (OLD-FASHIONED) • *I
must have been a horrid little girl.*
objectionable • *His tone was
highly objectionable.*
obnoxious • *Clarissa's
obnoxious brother James*
rude • *He was frequently
rude to waiters.*

U

unfriendly • spoken in a rather unfriendly voice

ANTONYM:
• pleasant

unpopular ADJECTIVE
disliked by most people • an unpopular idea
detested • The rebels toppled the detested dictator.
disliked • one of the most disliked choices on offer
shunned • the shunned former minister
undesirable • all sorts of undesirable effects on health

ANTONYM:
• popular

unpredictable ADJECTIVE
unable to be foreseen
• Britain's notoriously unpredictable weather
chance • A chance meeting can change your life.
doubtful • The outcome remains doubtful.
hit and miss (INFORMAL)
• Farming can be a very hit and miss affair.
unforeseeable • unforeseeable weather conditions

ANTONYM:
• predictable

unsatisfactory ADJECTIVE
not good enough • His work was judged unsatisfactory.
disappointing • The results were disappointing.
inadequate • The problem goes far beyond inadequate staffing.

mediocre • a mediocre string of performances
poor • Her school record was poor at first.
unacceptable • The quality of his work was unacceptable.

ANTONYM:
• satisfactory

unsteady ADJECTIVE
not held or fixed securely and likely to fall over • a slightly unsteady item of furniture
precarious • The beds are precarious-looking hammocks strung from the walls.
rickety • She stood on a rickety old table.
shaky • He climbed up the shaky ladder to the scaffold.
tottering • a tottering pile of bricks
unsafe • That bridge looks decidedly unsafe to me.
unstable • funds used to demolish dangerously unstable buildings
wobbly • cat-scratched upholstery and wobbly chairs

ANTONYM:
• steady

unsuitable ADJECTIVE
not appropriate for a purpose
• Her shoes were unsuitable for walking any distance.
improper • an improper diet
inappropriate • inappropriate use of the internet
unacceptable • using completely unacceptable language
unfit • unfit for human habitation

u

untidy ADJECTIVE

ANTONYM:
• suitable

untidy ADJECTIVE
not neatly arranged • The place
quickly became untidy.
bedraggled • My hair was a
bedraggled mess.
chaotic • The chaotic mess of
papers on his desk
cluttered • There was no space
on the cluttered worktop.
jumbled • We moved our
supplies into a jumbled heap.
messy • She was a good, if
messy, cook.
unkempt • the unkempt grass
in front of the house

ANTONYM:
• tidy

untrue ADJECTIVE
not true • The allegations were
completely untrue.
erroneous (FORMAL) • an
erroneous description
false • He gave a false name and
address.
fictitious • the source of the
fictitious rumours
inaccurate • the passing on of
inaccurate or misleading
information
incorrect • an incorrect account
of the sequence of events
misleading • It would be
misleading to say we were
friends.
mistaken • I had a mistaken
idea of what had happened.

ANTONYM:
• true

unusual ADJECTIVE
not occurring very often
• many rare and unusual plants
curious • a curious mixture of
ancient and modern
exceptional • exceptional
circumstances
extraordinary • What an
extraordinary thing to happen!
rare • one of the rarest species in
the world
uncommon • It's a very
uncommon surname.
unconventional • produced by
an unconventional technique

ANTONYM:
• common

unwell ADJECTIVE
ill or sick • He felt unwell and had
to go home early.
ailing • The President is said to
be ailing.
crook (AUSTRALIAN AND
NEW ZEALAND; INFORMAL)
• I'm sorry to hear you've been
crook, mate.
ill • Payne was seriously ill with
pneumonia.
poorly (BRITISH; INFORMAL)
• Julie is still poorly after her bout
of flu.
queasy • I always feel queasy on
boats.
sick • He's very sick and he needs
treatment.

ANTONYM:
• well

unwilling ADJECTIVE
not wanting to do something
• an unwilling participant in
school politics

averse • I'm not averse to going along with the suggestion.
grudging • a grudging acceptance of the situation
loath • She is loath to give up her hard-earned liberty.
reluctant • They were reluctant to get involved at first.

ANTONYM:
• willing

unwise ADJECTIVE
foolish or not sensible • It would be unwise to expect too much of her.
daft (BRITISH; INFORMAL)
• You'd be daft to get on the wrong side of him.
foolish • It was foolish to risk injury like that.
idiotic • What an idiotic thing to do!
irresponsible • irresponsible plans for tax cuts
rash • Don't panic or do anything rash.
senseless • It would be senseless to try and stop him now.
silly • You're not going to go and do something silly, are you?
stupid • I've had enough of your stupid suggestions.

ANTONYM:
• wise

upkeep NOUN
the process and cost of maintaining something • The money will be used for the upkeep of the grounds.
keep • He does not contribute towards his keep.

maintenance • the regular maintenance of government buildings
overheads • We must cut our overheads or we shall have to close.
preservation • the preservation of historical sites
running • The running of the house took up all her time.

upset ① ADJECTIVE
feeling unhappy about something • She was very upset when she heard the news.
agitated • in an excited and agitated state
distressed • The animals were distressed by the noise.
frantic • frantic with worry
hurt • I was very hurt when they refused.
troubled • He sounded deeply troubled.
unhappy • The divorce made him very unhappy.

upset ② VERB
to make someone worried or unhappy • The whole incident upset me terribly.
agitate • The thought agitates her.
bother • Don't let his manner bother you.
distress • The whole thing really distressed him.
disturb • These dreams disturb me for days afterwards.
grieve • deeply grieved by their suffering
ruffle • She doesn't get ruffled by anything.

u

upset ③ VERB

to turn something over accidentally • *Don't upset that pile of papers.*

capsize • *He capsized the boat through his carelessness.*

knock over • *The kitten knocked over the vase.*

overturn • *She overturned her glass of water as she stood up.*

spill • *The waiter spilled the drinks all over the table.*

urge ① NOUN

a strong wish to do something • *stifling the urge to scream*

compulsion • *a compulsion to write*

desire • *I had a strong desire to help and care for people.*

drive • *a demonic drive to succeed*

impulse • *Peter resisted an impulse to smile.*

longing • *his longing to return home*

wish • *She had a genuine wish to make amends.*

urge ② VERB

to try hard to persuade someone • *He urged the government to change the law.*

beg • *I begged him to leave me alone.*

beseech (LITERARY) • *Her eyes beseeched him to show mercy.*

implore • *He left early, although they implored him to stay.*

plead • *kneeling on the floor pleading for mercy*

press • *The unions are pressing him to stand firm.*

urgent ADJECTIVE

needing to be dealt with quickly • *an urgent need for food and water*

compelling • *There are compelling reasons to act swiftly.*

immediate • *The immediate problem is transportation.*

imperative • *It is imperative we end up with a win.*

pressing • *one of our most pressing problems*

use ① VERB

to perform a task with something • *Use a sharp knife to trim the edges.*

apply • *The company applies this technology to solve practical problems.*

employ • *the methods employed in the study*

operate • *Can you operate the coffee machine?*

utilise • *The body utilises many different minerals.*

use ② NOUN

the act of using something • *the use of force*

application • *Her theory was put into practical application.*

employment • *the employment of completely new methods*

operation • *the operation of the computer mouse*

usage • *Parts of the motor wore out because of constant usage.*

use ③ NOUN

the purpose for which something is used • *of no practical use whatsoever*

end • *The police force was manipulated for political ends.*
object • *the object of the exercise*
point • *I don't see the point of a thing like that.*
purpose • *It is wrong to use it for military purposes.*

useful ADJECTIVE

something which helps or makes things easier • *a great deal of useful information*
beneficial • *It may be beneficial to study the relevant guidelines.*
effective • *Antibiotics are effective against this organism.*
helpful • *a number of helpful booklets*
practical • *practical suggestions for healthy eating*
valuable • *Here are a few valuable tips to help you to succeed.*
worthwhile • *a worthwhile source of income*

ANTONYM:
• useless

useless ADJECTIVE

not suitable or useful • *We realised that our money was useless here.*
futile • *It would be futile to make any further attempts.*
impractical • *A tripod is impractical when following animals on the move.*
unproductive • *increasingly unproductive land*
unsuitable • *This tool is completely unsuitable for use with metal.*

worthless • *The old skills are worthless now.*

ANTONYM:
• useful

usual ADJECTIVE

done or happening most often • *sitting at his usual table*
accustomed • *She acted with her accustomed shrewdness.*
common • *the commonest cause of death*
customary • *It's customary to offer guests a drink.*
habitual • *He soon recovered his habitual geniality.*
normal • *That's quite normal for a Friday.*
regular • *samples from one of their regular suppliers*
standard • *It was standard practice to put them outside.*

utter ADJECTIVE

complete or total • *scenes of utter chaos*
absolute • *This is absolute madness!*
complete • *a complete mess*
consummate • *a consummate professional*
out-and-out • *an out-and-out lie*
outright • *an outright rejection of the deal*
perfect • *a perfect stranger*
pure • *She did it out of pure malice.*
sheer • *an act of sheer stupidity*
thorough • *She is a thorough snob.*
total • *a total failure*

u

Vv

vague ADJECTIVE
not clearly expressed or clearly
visible • *vague promises about
raising standards*
hazy • *Many details remain hazy.*
indefinite • *at some indefinite
time in the future*
indistinct • *The lettering was
worn and indistinct.*
loose • *a loose translation*
uncertain • *Students are facing
an uncertain future.*
unclear • *The proposals were
sketchy and unclear.*
ANTONYM:
• definite

vain ① ADJECTIVE
very proud of your looks or
qualities • *I think he is shallow
and vain.*
conceited • *They had grown too
conceited and pleased with
themselves.*
egotistical • *an egotistical
show-off*
ostentatious • *He was
generous with his money without
being ostentatious.*
proud • *She was said to be proud
and arrogant.*
stuck-up (INFORMAL) • *She
was a famous actor, but she
wasn't a bit stuck-up.*

vain ② ADJECTIVE
not successful in achieving
what was intended • *He made
a vain effort to cheer her up.*
abortive • *the abortive coup
attempt*
fruitless • *It was a fruitless
search.*
futile • *their futile attempts to
avoid publicity*
unproductive • *an
unproductive strategy*
useless • *a useless punishment
which fails to stop crime*
ANTONYM:
• successful

vain ③ : **in vain** ADJECTIVE
unsuccessful in achieving
what was intended • *Her
complaints were in vain.*
fruitless • *Four years of
negotiation were fruitless.*
to no avail • *His protests were
to no avail.*
unsuccessful • *Previous
attempts have been unsuccessfu*
wasted • *Their efforts were
wasted.*

valley NOUN
TYPES OF VALLEY
canyon
chasm
coomb
cwm (WELSH)
dale
defile
dell
depression
dingle
glen
gorge

gulch
gully
hollow
ravine
strath (SCOTTISH)
vale

valuable ① ADJECTIVE
having great importance or usefulness • The experience was very valuable.
beneficial • Using computers has a beneficial effect on learning.
helpful • a number of helpful booklets
important • Her sons are the most important thing in her life.
prized • one of the gallery's most prized possessions
useful • a mine of useful information
worthwhile • a worthwhile source of income

ANTONYM:
• useless

valuable ② ADJECTIVE
worth a lot of money • valuable old books
costly • a small and costly bottle of scent
expensive • exclusive, expensive possessions
precious • rings set with precious jewels

ANTONYM:
• worthless

valuables PLURAL NOUN
the things you own that cost a lot of money • Leave your valuables in the hotel safe.

heirlooms • family heirlooms
treasures • The house was full of art treasures.

value ① NOUN
the importance or usefulness of something • Studies are needed to see if these therapies have any value.
advantage • the great advantage of this method
benefit • They see no benefit in waiting any longer.
effectiveness • the effectiveness of the new system
importance • They have always placed great importance on live performances.
merit • the artistic merit of their work
use • This is of no use to anyone.
usefulness • the usefulness of the internet in disseminating new ideas
virtue • the great virtue of modern technology
worth • This system has already proved its worth.

value ② NOUN
the amount of money that something is worth • The value of his house has risen by more than 100%.
cost • the cost of a loaf of bread
market price • buying shares at the current market price
price • a sharp increase in the price of petrol
selling price • the average selling price of a new home
worth • He sold the car for less than half its worth.

v

value ③ VERB

to appreciate something and think it is important • *Do you value your friends enough?*

appreciate • *I would appreciate your advice.*

cherish • *Cherish every moment you have with your children.*

have a high opinion of • *Your boss seems to have a high opinion of you.*

prize • *These items are prized by collectors.*

rate highly • *He is an excellent keeper and I rate him highly.*

respect • *I respect his talent as a pianist.*

treasure • *memories I will treasure for the rest of my life*

value ④ VERB

to decide how much money something is worth • *I have had my jewellery valued for insurance purposes.*

appraise • *He was called in to appraise and sell the cottage.*

assess • *Experts are now assessing the cost of the restoration.*

cost • *an operation costed at around $649m*

estimate • *a personal fortune estimated at more than $400m*

evaluate • *The company needs to evaluate the cost of leasing the building.*

price • *The property was priced at less than £1m.*

vanish ① VERB

to disappear • *The moon vanished behind a cloud.*

become invisible • *The plane became invisible in the clouds.*

be lost to view • *They watched the ship until it was lost to view.*

disappear • *The aircraft disappeared off the radar.*

fade • *We watched the harbour fade into the mist.*

recede • *Gradually Luke receded into the distance.*

ANTONYM:

• appear

vanish ② VERB

to cease to exist • *Dinosaurs vanished from the earth millions of years ago.*

become extinct • *Without help, these animals will become extinct.*

cease • *At one o'clock the rain ceased.*

cease to exist • *Without trees the world as we know it would cease to exist.*

die out • *Britain's bear population died out about 2,000 years ago.*

dissolve • *The crowds dissolve and we were alone.*

evaporate • *All my pleasure evaporated when I saw him.*

fade away • *Her black mood faded away.*

go away • *All she wanted was for the pain to go away.*

melt away • *All my cares melted away.*

pass • *Breathe deeply and the panic attack will pass.*

vanquish VERB (LITERARY)

to defeat someone complete

• a happy ending in which the hero vanquishes the monsters

beat • the team that beat us in the finals

conquer • a great warrior who conquers the enemies of his people

crush • their bid to crush the rebels

defeat • His guerrillas defeated the colonial army in 1954.

overcome • They overcame the opposition to win the cup.

rout • the battle at which the Norman army routed the English

trounce • Australia trounced France by 60 points to 4.

variation NOUN

a change from the normal or usual pattern • a variation of the same route

alteration • some alterations in your diet

change • a change of attitude

departure • Her new novel is a departure from her previous work.

deviation • Deviation from the norm is not tolerated.

difference • a noticeable difference in his behaviour

diversion • a welcome diversion from the daily grind

ariety ① NOUN

a number of different kinds of things • a wide variety of readers

array • an attractive array of bright colours

assortment • an assortment of ets

collection • a huge collection of books

medley • a medley of vegetables

mixture • a mixture of sweets

range • a range of sun-care products

variety ② NOUN

a particular type of something • a new variety of celery

category • There are three broad categories of soil.

class • several classes of butterflies

kind • different kinds of roses

sort • several articles of this sort

strain • a new strain of the virus

type • What type of dog was it?

various ADJECTIVE

of several different types • trees of various sorts

assorted • swimsuits in assorted colours

different • different brands of drinks

disparate • the disparate cultures of India

diverse • Society is more diverse than ever before.

miscellaneous • a hoard of miscellaneous junk

sundry • sundry journalists and lawyers

vary ① VERB

to change to something different • weather patterns vary greatly

alter • During the course of a day the light alters constantly.

alternate • My moods alternate with alarming rapidity.

change • My feelings haven't changed.

fluctuate • Weight may fluctuate markedly.

vary ② VERB

to introduce changes in
something • *Vary your routes as
much as possible.*

alternate • *Alternate the chunks
of fish with chunks of vegetable.*

diversify • *They decided to
diversify their products.*

modify • *The government
refuses to modify its position.*

vast ADJECTIVE

extremely large • *farmers who
own vast stretches of land*

colossal • *a colossal statue*

enormous • *The main bedroom
is enormous.*

giant • *a giant meteorite
heading for the earth*

gigantic • *a gigantic shopping
mall*

great • *a great hall as long as a
church*

huge • *a huge crowd*

immense • *an immense castle*

massive • *a massive theme park*

ANTONYM:

• tiny

verdict NOUN

a decision or opinion on
something • *The doctor's
verdict was that he was fine.*

conclusion • *I've come to the
conclusion that she's lying.*

decision • *The editor's decision
is final.*

finding • *The court announced
its findings.*

judgment • *My judgment is that
things are going to get worse.*

opinion • *You should seek a
medical opinion.*

very ADVERB

to a great degree • *very bad
dreams*

deeply • *I was deeply sorry to
hear about your loss.*

extremely • *My smartphone is
extremely useful.*

greatly • *I was greatly relieved
when he finally arrived.*

highly • *Mr Singh was a highly
successful salesman.*

really • *I know her really well.*

terribly • *I'm terribly sorry to
bother you.*

veto ① VERB

to forbid something • *Treasury
officials vetoed the plans.*

ban • *The authorities have
banned the advertisement.*

forbid • *Carver was forbidden to
attend any of the society's
meetings.*

prohibit • *The government
intends to prohibit all trade with
the country.*

veto ② NOUN

the act of forbidding or power
to forbid something • *Dr. Bake
has the power of veto.*

ban • *the arms ban on the
Bosnian government*

prohibition • *a prohibition on
nuclear testing*

victory NOUN

a success in a battle or
competition • *his 15th
consecutive victory in a doubles
final*

laurels • *A former British
champion took the laurels in
this event.*

success • *league and cup successes*
superiority • *United Nations air forces won air superiority.*
triumph • *last year's Republican triumph in the elections*
win • *eight wins in nine games*
ANTONYM:
• *defeat*

view ① NOUN
a personal opinion • *his political views*
attitude • *other people's attitudes towards you*
belief • *people's beliefs about crime*
conviction • *a firm conviction that things have improved*
feeling • *It is my feeling that Klein is right.*
opinion • *a favourable opinion of our neighbours*
point of view • *an unusual point of view on the subject*

view ② NOUN
the things you can see from a particular place • *There was a beautiful view from the window.*
aspect • *the Yorkshire hills which give the cottage a lovely aspect*
landscape • *Arizona's desert landscape*
panorama • *a panorama of fertile valleys*
perspective • *the aerial perspective of St Paul's Cathedral*
scene • *Wright surveyed the scene from his chosen seat.*
spectacle • *a sweeping spectacle of rugged peaks*

view ③ VERB
to think of something in a particular way • *They viewed me with contempt.*
consider • *We consider them to be our friends.*
deem (FORMAL) • *His ideas were deemed unacceptable.*
judge • *His work was judged unsatisfactory.*
regard • *They regard the tax as unfair.*

viewpoint NOUN
an attitude towards something • *We all have our own personal viewpoints.*
attitude • *other people's attitudes towards you*
belief • *people's beliefs about crime*
conviction • *a very personal, political conviction*
feeling • *What are your feelings on this matter?*
opinion • *a favourable opinion of our neighbours*
point of view • *an unusual point of view on the subject*

violence ① NOUN
behaviour which is intended to hurt people • *Twenty people were killed in the violence.*
bloodshed • *The government must avoid further bloodshed.*
brutality • *the brutality of the war in Vietnam*
cruelty • *Human beings are capable of such cruelty to each other.*
force • *If you use any force, I shall inform the police.*

V

savagery • *acts of vicious savagery*

terrorism • *political terrorism in the 19th century*

violence ② NOUN

force and energy • *Amy spoke with sudden violence.*

fervour • *views he had put forward with fervour*

force • *She expressed her feelings with some force.*

harshness • *the harshness of her words*

intensity • *His voice hoarsened with intensity.*

severity • *the severity of her scoldings*

vehemence • *Tweed was taken aback by her vehemence.*

violent ① ADJECTIVE

intending to hurt or kill people • *violent criminals*

bloodthirsty • *a bloodthirsty monster*

brutal • *a brutal crime*

cruel • *He is cruel towards animals.*

murderous • *a murderous bank robber*

savage • *savage warriors*

vicious • *He was a cruel and vicious man.*

ANTONYM:
• gentle

violent ② ADJECTIVE

happening unexpectedly and with great force • *violent storms*

powerful • *He was caught in a powerful blow.*

raging • *a raging flood*

rough • *A wooden ship sank in rough seas.*

strong • *strong winds and rain*

turbulent • *the turbulent events of the century*

wild • *the wild gales sweeping up from the channel*

violent ③ ADJECTIVE

said, felt or done with great force • *the violent reaction to his plans*

acute • *pain which grew more and more acute*

furious • *a furious row*

intense • *a look of intense dislike*

powerful • *a powerful backlash against the government*

severe • *a severe emotional shock*

strong • *strong words*

virtue ① NOUN

the quality of doing what is morally right • *He is a paragon of virtue.*

goodness • *He has faith in human goodness.*

integrity • *He was praised for his fairness and integrity.*

morality • *standards of morality and justice in society*

virtue ② NOUN

an advantage something has • *the virtue of neatness*

advantage • *the advantages of the new system*

asset • *The one asset the job provided was contacts.*

attribute • *a player with every attribute you could want*

merit • *the merits of various football teams*

plus (INFORMAL) • *The nutrients in milk have pluses and minuses.*
strength • *the strengths and weaknesses of our position*

virtue ③: by virtue of
PREPOSITION
because of • *The article stuck in my mind by virtue of one detail.*
as a result of • *People will feel better as a result of their efforts.*
because of • *She was promoted because of her experience.*
by dint of • *He succeeds by dint of hard work.*
on account of • *The city is popular with tourists on account of its many museums.*
thanks to • *Thanks to recent research, new treatments are available.*

visible ① ADJECTIVE
able to be seen • *The warning lights were clearly visible.*
clear • *the clearest pictures ever of Pluto*
conspicuous • *He felt more conspicuous than he'd have liked.*
distinguishable • *colours just distinguishable in the dark*
in sight • *There wasn't another vehicle in sight.*
observable • *the observable part of the Universe*
perceptible • *Daniel gave a barely perceptible nod.*

ANTONYM:
• invisible

visible ② ADJECTIVE
noticeable or evident • *There was little visible excitement.*

apparent • *There is no apparent reason for the crime.*
evident • *He ate with evident enjoyment.*
manifest (FORMAL) • *his manifest enthusiasm*
noticeable • *subtle but noticeable changes*
obvious • *There are obvious dangers.*
plain • *It is plain a mistake has been made.*

vision ① NOUN
a mental picture in which you imagine things • *my vision of the future*
conception • *my conception of a garden*
daydream • *He learned to escape into daydreams.*
dream • *his dream of becoming a pilot*
fantasy • *fantasies of romance and true love*
ideal • *your ideal of a holiday*
image • *an image in your mind of what you are looking for*

vision ② NOUN
the ability to imagine future developments • *a total lack of vision and imagination*
foresight • *They had the foresight to invest in technology.*
imagination • *He had the imagination to foresee dangers.*
insight • *the development of insight and understanding*
intuition • *Her intuition told her something was wrong.*

vision ③ NOUN
an experience in which you see things others cannot

V

• She was convinced her visions were real.

apparition • One of the women was the apparition he had seen.

hallucination • The drug can cause hallucinations.

illusion • Perhaps the footprint was an illusion.

mirage • The girl was a mirage, created by his troubled mind.

phantom • People claimed to have seen the phantom.

spectre • a spectre from the other world

visit ① VERB

to go to see and spend time with someone • He wanted to visit his brother in Sydney.

call on • Don't hesitate to call on me.

go to see • I'll go to see him in the hospital.

look up • She looked up friends she had not seen for a while.

visit ② NOUN

a trip to see a person or place • Helen had recently paid him a visit.

call • He decided to pay a call on Tommy.

stay • An experienced guide is provided during your stay.

stop • The last stop in Mr Cook's tour was Paris.

vital ① ADJECTIVE

necessary or very important • a blockade which cut off vital fuel supplies

central • He is central to the whole project.

critical • This decision will be critical to our future.

crucial • the man who played a crucial role in the negotiations

essential • It is essential that you see a doctor soon.

important • the most important piece of evidence in the case

indispensable • an indispensable piece of equipment

necessary • the skills necessary for survival

pivotal • He played a pivotal role in the match.

vital ② ADJECTIVE

energetic and full of life • Illness has diminished a once vital person.

active • an active youngster

dynamic • a dynamic and exciting place

energetic • She became a shadow of her happy, energetic self.

lively • a lively personality

spirited • the spirited hero of this film

sprightly • You're sprightly this morning.

vivacious • She is vivacious and charming.

ANTONYM:
• dull

vomit VERB

to have food and drink come back up through the mouth • Any product made from milk made him vomit.

be sick • She was sick in the handbasin.

bring up • *Certain foods are difficult to bring up.*
regurgitate • *swallowing and regurgitating large quantities of water*

vote ① NOUN
a decision made by allowing people to state their preference • *Do you think we should have a vote on that?*
ballot • *The result of the ballot will be known soon.*
plebiscite (FORMAL) • *A plebiscite made Hitler the Chancellor.*
polls • *In 1945, Churchill was defeated at the polls.*
referendum • *Estonia planned to hold a referendum on independence.*

vote ② VERB
to indicate a choice or opinion • *It seems that many people would vote for the opposition.*
cast a vote • *90% of those who cast a vote*
go to the polls • *Voters are due to go to the polls on Sunday.*
opt • *The mass of Spaniards opted for democracy.*
return • *Members will be asked to return a vote for or against the motion.*

vote ③ VERB
to suggest that something should happen • *I vote that we all go to Holland.*
propose • *I propose that we all try to get some sleep.*
recommend • *I recommend that he be sent home early.*

suggest • *I suggest we go round the table and introduce ourselves.*

vulgar ① ADJECTIVE
socially unacceptable or offensive • *vulgar language*
coarse • *coarse humour*
rude • *a rude gesture*
uncouth • *that oafish, uncouth person*
ANTONYM:
• refined

vulgar ② ADJECTIVE
showing a lack of taste or quality • *I think it's a very vulgar house.*
common • *She could be a little common at times.*
flashy • *flashy clothes*
gaudy • *a gaudy purple-and-orange hat*
tacky (INFORMAL) • *wearing tacky red sunglasses*
tasteless • *a house with tasteless decor*
tawdry • *a tawdry seaside town*
ANTONYM:
• sophisticated

vulnerable ADJECTIVE
weak and without protection • *vulnerable elderly people*
exposed • *The west coast is very exposed to Atlantic winds.*
sensitive • *Most people are highly sensitive to criticism.*
susceptible • *an area that is susceptible to attack*
weak • *He spoke up for the weak and defenceless.*

v

Ww

wait ① VERB
to spend time before
something happens • *Wait
until we get there.*
linger • *I lingered on for a few
days until he arrived.*
pause • *The crowd paused for a
minute, wondering what to do
next.*
remain • *You'll have to remain in
hospital for the time being.*
stand by • *Ships are standing by
to evacuate the people.*
stay • *Stay here while I go for
help.*

wait ② NOUN
a period of time before
something happens • *They
faced a three-hour wait before
they could leave.*
delay • *The accident caused
some delay.*
interval • *a long interval when
no-one spoke*
pause • *There was a pause
before he replied.*

wake VERB
to make or become conscious
again after sleep • *It was still
dark when he woke.*
awake • *We were awoken by
the doorbell.*

come to • *When she came to she
found it was raining.*
rouse • *We roused him at seven
so he would be on time.*
stir • *She shook him and he
started to stir.*
waken • *wakened by the
thunder*

walk ① VERB
to go on foot • *I walked slowly
along the road.*
▶ see Word Study **walk**, page 729

walk ② NOUN
a journey made by walking
• *We'll have a quick walk while
it's fine.*
hike • *a long hike in the country*
march • *a day's march north of
their objective*
ramble • *They went for a ramble
through the woods.*
stroll • *After dinner we took a
stroll around the city.*
trek • *He's on a trek across the
Antarctic.*

walk ③ NOUN
the way someone moves
when walking • *Despite his
gangling walk he was a good
dancer.*
carriage • *her regal carriage*
gait • *an awkward gait*
pace • *moving at a brisk pace
down the road*
stride • *He lengthened his stride
to catch up with her.*

wander VERB
to move about in a casual way
• *They wandered aimlessly
around the village.*

cruise • *A police car cruised by.*
drift • *The balloon drifted slowly over the countryside.*
ramble • *freedom to ramble across the moors*
range • *They range widely in search of food.*
roam • *Barefoot children roamed the streets.*
stroll • *We strolled down the street, looking at the shops.*

want ① VERB
to feel a desire for something
• *I want a red car for a change.*
covet • *He coveted his boss's job.*
crave • *Sometimes she still craved chocolate.*
desire • *He could make them do whatever he desired.*
wish • *I don't wish to know that.*

want ② VERB
to need something • *My hair wants cutting.*
be deficient in • *Their diet was deficient in vitamins.*
demand • *The task of reconstruction demanded much sacrifice.*
lack • *training to give him the skills he lacked*
need • *My car needs servicing.*
require • *He knows exactly what is required of him.*

want ③ NOUN
a lack of something • *becoming weak from want of rest*
absence • *a complete absence of evidence*

deficiency • *They did blood tests for signs of vitamin deficiency.*
lack • *He got the job in spite of his lack of experience.*
scarcity • *an increasing scarcity of water*
shortage • *A shortage of funds is holding them back.*
ANTONYM:
• abundance

war ① NOUN
a period of armed conflict between countries • *The war dragged on for five years.*
combat • *men who died in combat*
conflict • *The conflict is bound to intensify.*
fighting • *He was killed in the fighting which followed the treaty.*
hostilities • *in case hostilities break out*
strife • *The country was torn with strife.*
warfare • *chemical warfare*
ANTONYM:
• peace
RELATED WORDS:
• ADJECTIVES belligerent, martial

war ② VERB
to engage in armed conflict
• *The two countries had been warring with each other for years.*
battle • *Thousands of people battled with the police.*
clash • *The two armies clashed at first light.*

w

fight • *The tribe fought with its rivals.*

warm ① ADJECTIVE
having some heat but not hot
• *a warm spring day*
balmy • *balmy summer evenings*
heated • *a heated swimming pool*
lukewarm • *Heat the milk until lukewarm.*
pleasant • *After a chilly morning, the afternoon was very pleasant.*
tepid • *a bath full of tepid water*

ANTONYM:
• cold

warm ② ADJECTIVE
friendly and affectionate • *a warm and likable personality*
affectionate • *with an affectionate glance at her children*
amiable • *He was very amiable company.*
cordial • *We were given a most cordial welcome.*
friendly • *All her colleagues were very friendly.*
genial • *a warm-hearted friend and genial host*
loving • *He is a loving husband and father.*

ANTONYM:
• unfriendly

warm ③ VERB
to heat something gently
• *The sun came out and warmed his back.*

heat • *Heat the bread in the oven.*
heat up • *The fire soon heated up the room.*
melt • *He melted the butter in a small pan.*
thaw • *Always thaw pastry thoroughly.*
warm up • *You must begin gently to warm up the muscles.*

ANTONYM:
• cool

warn VERB
to give advance notice of something unpleasant • *I warned him about those loose tiles.*
alert • *The siren alerted them to the danger.*
caution • *Their reaction cautioned him against any further attempts.*
forewarn • *We were forewarned of what to expect.*
notify • *The weather forecast notified them of the coming storm.*

warning NOUN
something that tells people of possible danger • *advance warning of the attack*
alarm • *They heard the fire alarm and ran to safety.*
alert • *a security alert*
caution • *a note of caution*
notice • *three months' notice*
premonition • *He had a premonition of bad news.*

wary ADJECTIVE
showing lack of trust in something • *She was wary of marriage.*

cautious • *His experience has made him cautious.*
distrustful • *Voters are deeply distrustful of all politicians.*
guarded • *The boy gave him a guarded look.*
suspicious • *He was rightly suspicious of their motives.*
vigilant • *He warned the public to be vigilant.*

wash ① VERB
to clean something with water • *He got a job washing dishes.*
bathe • *She bathed her blistered feet.*
cleanse • *the correct way to cleanse the skin*
launder • *freshly laundered shirts*
rinse • *Rinse several times in clear water.*
scrub • *I was scrubbing the bathroom floor.*
shampoo • *You must shampoo your hair first.*

wash ② VERB
to carry something by the force of water • *washed ashore by the waves*
carry off • *The debris was carried off on the tide.*
erode • *Exposed soil is quickly eroded by wind and rain.*
sweep away • *The floods swept away the houses by the river.*

waste ① VERB
to use too much of something unnecessarily • *I wouldn't waste my money on something like that.*

fritter away • *He just fritters his time away.*
squander • *He had squandered his chances of winning.*
throw away • *You're throwing away a good opportunity.*
ANTONYM:
• save

waste ② NOUN
using something excessively or unnecessarily • *What a complete waste of money!*
extravagance • *widespread tales of his extravagance*
misuse • *This project is a misuse of public funds.*
squandering • *a squandering of his valuable time*

waste ③ ADJECTIVE
not needed or wanted • *waste paper*
leftover • *leftover pieces of fabric*
superfluous • *She got rid of many superfluous belongings.*
unused • *spoiled or unused ballot papers*

wasteful ADJECTIVE
using something in a careless or extravagant way • *wasteful duplication of effort*
extravagant • *an extravagant lifestyle*
uneconomical • *the uneconomical duplication of jobs*
ANTONYM:
• thrifty

watch ① NOUN
a period of time when a guard

w

is kept on something • *Keep a close watch on the prisoners.*
observation • *In hospital she'll be under observation night and day.*
supervision • *A toddler requires close supervision.*
surveillance • *kept under constant surveillance*

watch ② VERB
to look at something for some time • *I don't watch television very often.*
gaze at • *gazing at herself in the mirror*
look at • *They looked closely at the insects.*
observe • *Researchers observed the behaviour of small children.*
pay attention • *Pay attention or you won't know what to do.*
see • *We went to see the semi-finals.*
view • *The police have viewed the video recording of the incident.*

watch ③ VERB
to look after something • *You must watch the baby carefully.*
guard • *They were guarded the whole time they were there.*
look after • *I looked after her cat while she was away.*
mind • *Can you mind the store for a couple of hours?*
take care of • *Can you take care of the kids for a while?*

watch out VERB
to be careful or alert for something • *You have to watch out for snakes in the swamp.*

be alert • *The bank is alert to the danger.*
be watchful • *Be watchful for any warning signs.*
keep your eyes open • *They kept their eyes open for any troublemakers.*
look out • *What are the symptoms to look out for?*

waterfall NOUN
TYPES OF WATERFALL
cascade
cataract
chute
fall
linn (SCOTTISH)
rapids
torrent
white water

wave ① VERB
to move or flap to and fro • *The doctor waved a piece of paper at him.*
brandish • *He appeared brandishing a knife.*
flap • *He flapped his hand at me to be quiet.*
flourish • *He flourished his glass to emphasise the point.*
flutter • *a fluttering white lace handkerchief*
shake • *Shake the rugs well to air them.*

wave ② NOUN
a ridge of water on the surface of the sea • *the sound of the waves breaking on the shore*
breaker • *The foaming breakers crashed on to the beach.*

W

ripple • *gentle ripples on the surface of the lake*

swell • *We bobbed gently on the swell of the incoming tide.*

wave ③ NOUN
an increase in a type of activity • *the crime wave*

flood • *a flood of complaints about the programme*

movement • *a growing movement towards democracy*

rush • *He felt a sudden rush of panic at the thought.*

surge • *the recent surge in inflation*

trend • *This is a growing trend.*

upsurge • *There was an upsurge of business confidence after the war.*

way ① NOUN
a manner of doing something • *an excellent way of cooking meat*

approach • *different approaches to gathering information*

manner • *in a friendly manner*

means • *The move is a means to fight crime.*

method • *using the latest teaching methods*

procedure • *He failed to follow the correct procedure when applying for a visa.*

technique • *The tests were performed using a new technique.*

way ② NOUN
the customs or behaviour of a person or group • *Their ways are certainly different.*

conduct • *People judged him by his social skills and conduct.*

custom • *an ancient Japanese custom*

manner • *His manner was rather abrupt.*

practice • *a public enquiry into bank practices*

style • *Behaving like that isn't his style.*

way ③ NOUN
a route taken to a particular place • *I can't remember the way.*

channel • *a safe channel avoiding the reefs*

course • *The ship was on a course that followed the coastline.*

lane • *the busiest shipping lanes in the world*

path • *The lava annihilates everything in its path.*

road • *the road into the village*

route • *the most direct route to the town centre*

weak ① ADJECTIVE
lacking in strength • *She had a weak heart.*

delicate • *She was physically delicate and often unwell.*

faint • *Feeling faint is one of the symptoms of angina.*

feeble • *feeble and unable to walk far*

frail • *in frail health*

puny • *He was puny as a child but grew up to be a top athlete.*

sickly • *a sickly baby with no resistance to illness*

w

wasted • *muscles which were wasted through lack of use*

ANTONYM:
• strong

weak ② ADJECTIVE
likely to break or fail • *a weak economy*

deficient • *The plane had a deficient landing system.*

faulty • *The money will be used to repair faulty equipment.*

inadequate • *inadequate safety measures*

weak ③ ADJECTIVE
easily influenced by other people • *He was a weak man who wouldn't stick his neck out.*

powerless • *a powerless ruler governed by his advisers*

spineless • *bureaucrats and spineless politicians*

ANTONYM:
• resolute

weaken VERB
to make or become less strong • *His authority was weakened by their actions.*

diminish • *to diminish the prestige of the monarchy*

fail • *His strength began to fail after a few hours.*

flag • *Her enthusiasm was in no way flagging.*

lessen • *The drugs lessen the risk of an epidemic.*

reduce • *Reduced consumer demand caused the company to collapse.*

sap • *I was afraid the illness had sapped my strength.*

undermine • *They were accused of trying to undermine the government.*

wane • *His interest in sport began to wane.*

ANTONYM:
• strengthen

weakness ① NOUN
a lack of physical or moral strength • *His extreme weakness caused him to collapse.*

defect • *a serious character defect*

flaw • *His main flaw is his bad temper.*

fragility • *They are at risk because of the fragility of their bones.*

frailty • *the triumph of will over human frailty*

imperfection • *He concedes that there are imperfections in the system.*

vulnerability • *the extreme vulnerability of the young chicks*

ANTONYM:
• strength

weakness ② NOUN
a great liking for something • *a weakness for chocolate*

fondness • *a fondness for modern art*

liking • *a liking for tripe and onions*

passion • *His other great passion was his motorbike.*

penchant (FORMAL) • *a stylist woman with a penchant for dark glasses*

ANTONYM:
• dislike

wealth ① NOUN
a large amount of money
• *Economic reform brought them wealth.*

affluence • *the trappings of affluence*

fortune • *He made a fortune in the property boom.*

means • *a person of means*

money • *All that money brought nothing but sadness and misery.*

prosperity • *Japan's economic prosperity*

riches • *His Olympic medal brought him fame and riches.*

substance • *run by local men of substance*

wealth ② NOUN
a lot of something • *a wealth of information*

abundance • *This area has an abundance of safe beaches.*

bounty • *autumn's bounty of fruits and berries*

plenty • *He grew up in a time of plenty.*

store • *She dipped into her store of theatrical anecdotes.*

ANTONYM:
• shortage

wealthy ADJECTIVE
having plenty of money • *She came from a very wealthy background.*

affluent • *living in an affluent neighbourhood*

comfortable • *from a stable, comfortable family*

opulent • *Most of the cash went on supporting his opulent lifestyle.*

prosperous • *The place looks more prosperous than ever.*

rich • *I'm going to be very rich one day.*

well-to-do • *a rather well-to-do family in the shipping business*

ANTONYM:
• poor

wear ① VERB
to be dressed in something
• *He was wearing a brown uniform.*

be clothed in • *She was clothed in a flowered dress.*

be dressed in • *The women were dressed in their finest attire.*

don • *The police responded by donning riot gear.*

have on • *I had my new shoes on that night.*

put on • *He had to put on his glasses to read the paper.*

sport (INFORMAL) • *sporting a red tie*

wear ② VERB
to become worse in condition with use or age • *The old stone steps were worn in the middle.*

corrode • *The underground pipes were badly corroded.*

erode • *Exposed rock is quickly eroded by wind and rain.*

fray • *fraying edges on the stair carpet*

rub • *The inscription had been rubbed smooth by generations of hands.*

wash away • *The topsoil had been washed away by the incessant rain.*

w

wear ③ NOUN

the type of use which causes something to be damaged • The tyres showed signs of wear.

corrosion • Zinc is used to protect other metals from corrosion.

deterioration • The building is already showing signs of deterioration.

erosion • erosion of the river valleys

use • The carpet must be able to cope with heavy use.

wear out VERB

to make someone tired • The past few days have really worn me out.

exhaust • The long working day exhausted him.

tire • If driving tires you, take the train.

weary • wearied by the constant demands on his time

weary ADJECTIVE

very tired • She sank to the ground, too weary to walk another step.

drained • He's always completely drained after a performance.

exhausted • She was too exhausted and upset to talk.

fatigued • Winter weather can leave you feeling fatigued.

tired • He was too tired even to take a shower.

tuckered out (AMERICAN, AUSTRALIAN AND NEW ZEALAND; INFORMAL) • You must be tuckered out after that bus trip.

worn out • He's just worn out after the long drive.

weather NOUN

TYPES OF WEATHER

cloud
drought
fog
freeze
frost
hail
haze
heatwave
ice
lightning
rain
sleet
snow
sunshine
thaw
thunder

WORDS USED TO DESCRIBE THE WEATHER

arctic
balmy
baltic
blustery
breezy
clammy
clear
close
cloudy
cold
drizzly
dry
dull
fine
foggy
freezing
hot
humid
icy

mild
misty
muggy
overcast
rainy
showery
snowy
stormy
sultry
sunny
thundery
wet
windy

WORDS FOR RAIN AND SNOW

drizzle
rain
shower
sleet
slush
snow

WORDS FOR STORM

blizzard
hailstorm
snowstorm
squall
storm
superstorm
tempest
thunderstorm

WORDS FOR WIND

breeze
cyclone
gale
gust
hurricane
squall
tornado
twister
typhoon
whirlwind
wind

WORDS FOR FOG

fog
haar
haze
mist
pea-souper
smog

weird ADJECTIVE

strange or odd • *I had such a weird dream last night.*
bizarre • *his bizarre behaviour*
curious • *What a curious thing to say!*
extraordinary • *an extraordinary occurrence*
funny • *There's something funny about him.*
odd • *an odd coincidence*
peculiar • *It tasted very peculiar.*
queer (OLD-FASHIONED) • *I think there's something queer going on here.*
singular (FORMAL) • *I can't think where you got such a singular notion.*
strange • *Didn't you notice anything strange about her?*

ANTONYM:
• ordinary

well ① ADVERB

in a satisfactory way • *The interview went well.*
satisfactorily • *The system should work satisfactorily.*
smoothly • *So far, the operation is going smoothly.*
splendidly • *They have behaved splendidly.*
successfully • *The changeover is working successfully.*

w

well ② ADVERB

with skill and ability • *He draws well.*

ably • *He was ably assisted by the other members of staff.*

adequately • *He speaks French very adequately.*

admirably • *dealing admirably with a difficult situation*

competently • *They handled the situation very competently.*

effectively • *In the first half he operated effectively in defence.*

efficiently • *He works efficiently and accurately.*

expertly • *Shopkeepers expertly rolled spices up in bay leaves.*

professionally • *These tickets have been forged very professionally.*

skilfully • *He skilfully exploited his company's strengths.*

ANTONYM:
• badly

well ③ ADVERB

fully and with thoroughness • *They should be well washed and well dried.*

amply • *I was amply rewarded for my trouble.*

closely • *He studied the documents closely.*

completely • *Make sure you defrost it completely.*

fully • *The new system is now fully under way.*

highly • *one of the most highly regarded authors*

meticulously • *He had planned his trip meticulously.*

rigorously • *Their duties have not been performed as rigorously as they might have been.*

thoroughly • *Add the oil and mix thoroughly.*

well ④ ADVERB

in a kind way • *He treats his employees well.*

compassionately • *He always acted compassionately towards her.*

considerately • *I expect people to deal with me considerately and fairly.*

favourably • *Large companies are treated more favourably than small shopkeepers.*

humanely • *They treat their livestock humanely.*

kindly • *Children are capable of behaving kindly.*

with consideration • *He was treated with consideration and kindness.*

well ⑤ ADJECTIVE

having good health • *I'm not very well today.*

blooming • *She felt confident, blooming and attractive.*

fit • *He keeps himself really fit.*

healthy • *Most people want to be healthy and happy.*

in good condition • *He's in good condition for his age.*

in good health • *He seemed to be in good health and spirits.*

robust • *He's never been a very robust child.*

sound • *a sound body*

strong • *Eat well and you'll soon be strong again.*

ANTONYM:
• sick

wet ① ADJECTIVE
covered in liquid • *Don't get your feet wet.*
damp • *Her hair was still damp.*
drenched • *getting drenched by icy water*
moist • *The soil is reasonably moist after the September rain.*
saturated • *The filter has been saturated with oil.*
soaked • *soaked to the skin*
sodden • *I slipped on the sodden grass.*
waterlogged • *The game was called off because the pitch was waterlogged.*

ANTONYM:
• dry

wet ② ADJECTIVE
in rainy weather conditions
• *It was a miserable wet day.*
humid • *hot and humid weather conditions*
misty • *The air was cold and misty.*
rainy • *The rainy season starts in December.*
showery • *The day had been showery with sunny intervals.*

ANTONYM:
• dry

wet ③ VERB
to put liquid on to something
• *Wet the edges and stick them together.*
dampen • *You must dampen the laundry before you iron it.*

irrigate • *irrigated by a system of interconnected canals*
moisten • *Take a sip of water to moisten your throat.*
soak • *The water had soaked his jacket and shirt.*
spray • *It can spray the whole field in half an hour.*
water • *We have to water the plants when the weather is dry.*

ANTONYM:
• dry

whim NOUN
a sudden fancy for something
• *We decided to go more or less on a whim.*
craze • *the latest fitness craze*
fad (INFORMAL) • *just a passing fad*
fancy • *I had a fancy for some strawberries.*
impulse • *He resisted the impulse to buy a new one.*
urge • *He had an urge to open a shop of his own.*

white NOUN OR ADJECTIVE
SHADES OF WHITE
cream
ecru
ivory
magnolia
off-white
oyster white
pearl
snow-white

whole ① ADJECTIVE
indicating all of something
• *We spent the whole summer abroad.*

complete • *The list filled a complete page.*

entire • *There are only ten in the entire country.*

full • *a full week's notice*

total • *The evening was a total fiasco.*

uncut • *the uncut version of the film*

undivided • *He has my undivided loyalty.*

whole ② NOUN

the full amount of something • *the whole of Asia*

aggregate • *the aggregate of the individual scores*

all • *All is not lost.*

everything • *Everything that happened is my fault.*

lot • *He lost the lot within five minutes.*

sum total • *The small room contained the sum total of their possessions.*

total • *The eventual total was far higher.*

wicked ① ADJECTIVE

very bad or evil • *That was a wicked thing to do.*

atrocious • *He had committed atrocious crimes against the refugees.*

bad • *Please forgive our bad behaviour.*

depraved • *the work of depraved criminals*

evil • *the country's most evil terrorists*

sinful • *"This is a sinful world," he said.*

vicious • *He was a cruel and vicious man.*

wicked ② ADJECTIVE

mischievous in an amusing or attractive way • *She always felt wicked when eating chocolate.*

impish • *an impish sense of humour*

mischievous • *like a mischievous child*

naughty • *He could be so naughty when he was younger.*

wide ① ADJECTIVE

measuring a large distance from side to side • *It should be wide enough to give plenty of working space.*

ample • *a large woman with an ample figure*

baggy • *He was wearing ridiculously baggy trousers.*

broad • *His shoulders were broad and his waist narrow.*

expansive • *The park has swings and an expansive play area.*

extensive • *The grounds were more extensive than the town itself.*

full • *She was wearing a dress with a full skirt.*

immense • *an immense body of water*

large • *This fish lives mainly in large rivers and lakes.*

roomy • *I like roomy jackets with big pockets.*

spacious • *The house has a spacious kitchen.*

sweeping • *the long sweeping curve of the bay*

vast • *The farmers there own vast stretches of land.*

voluminous • *a voluminous trench coat*

ANTONYM:
• narrow

wide ② ADJECTIVE

extensive in scope • *a wide range of colours*

ample • *There is ample scope here for the imagination.*

broad • *A broad range of issues was discussed.*

catholic • *He has very catholic tastes in music.*

comprehensive • *a comprehensive guide to the region*

encyclopedic • *He has an encyclopedic knowledge of the subject.*

exhaustive • *The author's treatment of the topic is exhaustive.*

extensive • *The question has received extensive press coverage.*

far-ranging • *the plan to introduce far-ranging reforms*

immense • *an immense range of holiday activities*

inclusive • *an inclusive survey*

large • *a large selection of goods at reasonable prices*

vast • *a vast range of products*

wide-ranging • *The aims of the redesign are wide-ranging but simple.*

ANTONYM:
• narrow

wide ③ ADVERB

as far as possible • *Open wide!*

completely • *He opened the map out completely so we could see.*

fully • *Extend the aerial fully.*

right out • *Spread it right out to the edges.*

widespread ADJECTIVE

existing over a large area • *Food shortages are widespread.*

broad • *The agreement won broad support among the people.*

common • *the common view that treatment is ineffective*

extensive • *The storm caused extensive damage.*

pervasive • *the pervasive influence of the army in national life*

prevalent • *a style of art that became prevalent in the 1980s*

rife • *Bribery and corruption were rife in the industry.*

wild ① ADJECTIVE

not cultivated or domesticated • *a meadow of wild flowers*

fierce • *Fierce hyenas scavenged for food after the kill.*

free • *stunning pictures of wild and free animals*

natural • *In the natural state this animal is not ferocious.*

uncultivated • *developed from an uncultivated type of grass*

undomesticated • *These cats lived wild and were completely undomesticated.*

untamed • *the untamed horses of the Camargue*

warrigal (AUSTRALIAN; LITERARY) • *a warrigal mare*

W

wild ② ADJECTIVE
in stormy conditions • They
were not deterred by the wild
weather.
howling • a howling gale
raging • The trip involved
crossing a raging torrent.
rough • The two ships collided in
rough seas.
stormy • a dark and stormy
night
violent • That night they were
hit by a violent storm.

wild ③ ADJECTIVE
without control or restraint
• wild with excitement
boisterous • Most of the
children were noisy and
boisterous.
rowdy • The television
coverage revealed their rowdy
behaviour.
turbulent • five turbulent years
of rows and reconciliations
uncontrolled • His
uncontrolled behaviour disturbed
the entire group.
wayward • wayward children
with a history of emotional
problems

will ① VERB
to leave something to
someone when you die • He
had willed his fortune to his
daughter.
bequeath • She bequeathed her
collection to the local museum.
leave • Everything was left to
the housekeeper.
pass on • He passed on much of
his estate to his eldest son.

will ② NOUN
the strong determination to
achieve something • the will to
win
determination
• Determination has always been
a part of his make-up.
purpose • They are
enthusiastic and have a sense
of purpose.
resolution • He began to form a
resolution to clear his name.
resolve • This will strengthen
the public's resolve.
willpower • succeeding by sheer
willpower

will ③ NOUN
what someone wants • the
will of the people
choice • It's your choice.
inclination • She showed no
inclination to go.
mind • You can go if you have a
mind to do so.
volition • a product of our
volition
wish • done against my wishes
RELATED WORD:
• ADJECTIVE voluntary

willing ADJECTIVE
ready and eager to do
something • a willing helper
agreeable • We can go ahead if
you are agreeable.
eager • Children are eager to
learn.
game (INFORMAL) • He still ha
new ideas and was game to try
them.
happy • That's a risk I'm happy
to take.

prepared • *I'm not prepared to take orders from her.*
ready • *ready to die for their beliefs*
ANTONYM:
• unwilling

win ① VERB
to defeat your opponents
• *The top four teams all won.*
be victorious • *Despite the strong opposition she was victorious.*
come first • *They unexpectedly came first this year.*
prevail • *the votes he must win in order to prevail*
succeed • *the skills and qualities needed to succeed*
triumph • *a symbol of good triumphing over evil*
ANTONYM:
• lose

win ② VERB
to succeed in obtaining something • *moves to win popular support*
achieve • *We have achieved our objective.*
attain • *He's half-way to attaining his pilot's licence.*
gain • *After three weeks the hostages finally gained their freedom.*
get • *My entry got a commendation this year.*
secure (FORMAL) • *Her achievements helped secure her the job.*

win ③ NOUN
a victory in a contest • *a run of seven games without a win*

success • *his success in the Monaco Grand Prix*
triumph • *their World Cup triumph*
victory • *the 3–1 victory over Switzerland*
ANTONYM:
• defeat

winner NOUN
a person who wins something
• *The winners will be notified by post.*
champion • *a former Olympic champion*
conqueror • *This time they easily overcame their former conquerors.*
victor • *He emerged as the victor by the second day.*
ANTONYM:
• loser

wisdom NOUN
judgment used to make sensible decisions • *the wisdom that comes from experience*
discernment • *Her keen discernment made her an excellent collector.*
insight • *a man of considerable insight and diplomatic skills*
judgment • *He respected our judgment on this matter.*
knowledge • *the quest for scientific knowledge*
reason • *a conflict between emotion and reason*
ANTONYM:
• foolishness

RELATED WORD:
• ADJECTIVE sagacious

w

wise ADJECTIVE
able to make use of
experience and judgment
• *a wise old man*

informed • *an informed guess
at his wealth*

judicious (FORMAL) • *the
judicious use of military force*

perceptive • *the words of a
perceptive political
commentator*

rational • *You must look at both
sides before you can reach a
rational decision.*

sensible • *The sensible thing is
to leave them alone.*

shrewd • *a shrewd deduction
about what was going on*

ANTONYM:
• foolish

wish ① NOUN
a desire for something • *She
was sincere in her wish to make
amends.*

desire • *her desire for a room of
her own*

hankering • *She had always
had a hankering to be an actor.*

hunger • *a hunger for success*

longing • *He felt a longing for
familiar surroundings.*

urge • *He had an urge to open a
shop of his own.*

want • *Supermarkets respond
to the wants of their
customers.*

wish ② VERB
to want something • *We
wished to return.*

desire • *He was bored and
desired to go home.*

hunger • *She hungered for
adventure.*

long • *I'm longing for the
holidays.*

thirst • *thirsting for knowledge*

want • *people who know exactly
what they want in life*

yearn • *The younger ones
yearned to be part of a normal
family.*

withdraw ① VERB
to take something out • *He
withdrew some money from the
bank.*

draw out • *I'll have to draw out
some of my savings.*

extract • *She extracted another
dress from the wardrobe.*

remove • *I removed the splinter
from her finger.*

take out • *There was a fee for
taking out money from the
account.*

withdraw ② VERB
to back out of an activity
• *They withdrew from the
conference.*

back out • *He backed out of the
agreement.*

leave • *Davis left the game to go
to hospital.*

pull out • *The general pulled out
of the talks after two days.*

retire • *The jury retired three
hours ago.*

retreat • *retreating from the
harsh realities of life*

wither ① VERB
to become weaker and fade
away • *Will the company flouris
or wither?*

decline • *The church's influence has declined.*

fade • *Prospects for peace have already started to fade.*

wither ② VERB
to shrivel up and die • *Crops withered under the sun.*

droop • *plants drooping in the heat*

shrivel • *They watched their crops shrivel and die in the drought.*

wilt • *The roses wilted the day after she bought them.*

witness ① NOUN
someone who has seen something happen • *The police appealed for witnesses to come forward.*

bystander • *Seven other innocent bystanders were injured.*

eyewitness • *Eyewitnesses say the soldiers opened fire on the crowd.*

observer • *A casual observer would not have noticed them.*

onlooker • *a small crowd of onlookers*

spectator • *carried out in full view of spectators*

witness ② VERB
to see something happening • *Anyone who witnessed the attack should call the police.*

be present at • *Many men are now present at the birth of their children.*

observe • *Observe how it looks from all sides.*

see • *I saw him do it.*

watch • *She had watched them leaving the hotel before the accident.*

witty ADJECTIVE
amusing in a clever way • *He's so witty I could listen to him for hours.*

amusing • *He provided an irreverent and amusing commentary to the film.*

brilliant • *a brilliant after-dinner speaker*

clever • *He raised some smiles with several clever lines.*

funny • *a film packed with incredibly funny dialogue*

humorous • *a satirical and humorous parody*

sparkling • *He's famous for his sparkling conversation.*

woman NOUN
an adult female human being • *women over 75 years old*

female • *The average young female is fairly affluent.*

girl • *a night out with the girls*

lady • *Your table is ready, ladies, so please come through.*

lass • *a lass from the country*

sheila (AUSTRALIAN AND NEW ZEALAND; INFORMAL) • *his role as a sheila in his own play*

vrou (SOUTH AFRICAN) • *Have you met his vrou yet?*

ANTONYM:
• man

wonder ① VERB
to think about something with curiosity • *I wondered what that noise was.*

W

ask yourself • *You have to ask yourself what this really means.*

ponder • *pondering how to improve the team*

puzzle • *Researchers continue to puzzle over the origins of the disease.*

speculate • *He refused to speculate about the contents of the letter.*

wonder ② VERB

to be surprised and amazed • *He wondered at her anger.*

be amazed • *Most of the cast were amazed by the play's success.*

be astonished • *I was astonished to discover his true age.*

boggle • *The mind boggles at what might be in store for us.*

marvel • *We marvelled at her endless energy.*

wonder ③ NOUN

something that amazes people • *one of the wonders of nature*

marvel • *a marvel of high technology*

miracle • *It's a miracle no one was killed.*

phenomenon • *a well-known geographical phenomenon*

spectacle • *a spectacle not to be missed*

wonderful ① ADJECTIVE

extremely good • *It's wonderful to see you.*

excellent • *The recording quality is excellent.*

great (INFORMAL) • *a great bunch of guys*

marvellous • *What a marvellous time we had!*

superb • *The hotel has a superb isolated location.*

tremendous • *I thought it was a tremendous book.*

wonderful ② ADJECTIVE

very impressive • *The sunset was a truly wonderful sight.*

amazing • *containing some amazing special effects*

astounding • *The results are quite astounding.*

incredible • *The intensity of colour was incredible.*

magnificent • *magnificent views across the valley*

remarkable • *It was a remarkable achievement to complete the course.*

word ① NOUN

PARTS OF A WORD

capital letter
consonant
grapheme
letter
phoneme
prefix
suffix
syllable
vowel

RELATED WORDS:
• ADJECTIVES lexical, verbal

word ② NOUN

a remark • *I'd like to say a word of thanks to everyone who helped m*

comment • *He left without an further comment.*

remark • Apart from that one remark, he stayed quiet all evening.

statement • Verity issued a brief statement to the press.

utterance • a crowd of admirers who hung on his every utterance

word ③ NOUN

a brief conversation • James, could I have a quick word with you?

chat • We need to have a chat about the arrangements some time.

conversation • He recalled his brief conversation with the Queen.

discussion • We had a very short discussion about what to do.

talk • I bumped into him yesterday and we had a quick talk.

word ④ NOUN

a message • Since then we've had no word from them.

announcement • There has been no formal announcement from either government.

bulletin • A spokesperson said no bulletin would be issued.

communication • The ambassador brought a communication from the President.

information • They will issue written information in due course.

intelligence • He wanted to pass this intelligence on to her.

message • Did he leave any message for me?

news • Is there any news from the embassy?

word ⑤ NOUN

a promise or guarantee • He gave me his word that he would be there.

assurance • Do I have your assurance that you'll take responsibility?

oath • She gave her solemn oath not to tell anyone.

pledge • He gave his personal pledge that he would help.

promise • I'll support you – you have my promise on that.

word of honour • I want your word of honour that you'll respect my anonymity.

work ① VERB

to do the tasks required of you • I had to work twelve hours a day.

labour • peasants labouring in the fields

slave • slaving over a hot stove

slog away • They are still slogging away at algebra.

toil • Workers toiled long hours in the mills.

ANTONYM:

• laze

work ② NOUN

someone's job • She's trying to find work.

craft • He learned his craft from an expert.

employment • unable to find employment

job • I got at a job at the sawmill.

w

livelihood • *fishermen who depend on the seas for their livelihood*

occupation • *Please state your occupation.*

profession • *a dentist by profession*

work ③ NOUN

the tasks that have to be done • *Sometimes he had to take work home.*

assignment • *written assignments and practical tests*

business • *We have business to attend to first.*

chore • *We share the household chores.*

duty • *My duty is to look after the animals.*

job • *It turned out to be a bigger job than expected.*

task • *catching up with administrative tasks*

yakka (AUSTRALIAN AND NEW ZEALAND; INFORMAL) • *a decade of hard yakka on the land*

worker NOUN

a person who works • *seeking a reliable research worker*

craftsman • *furniture made by a local craftsman*

employee • *Many of its employees are women.*

labourer • *a farm labourer*

workman • *Workmen are building a steel fence.*

work out ① VERB

to find the solution to something • *It took us some time to work out what was happening.*

calculate • *First, calculate your monthly living expenses.*

figure out • *You don't need to be a detective to figure that one out.*

resolve • *They hoped the crisis could be quickly resolved.*

solve • *We'll solve the case ourselves and surprise everyone.*

work out ② VERB

to happen in a certain way • *Things didn't work out that way after all.*

develop • *Wait and see how the situation develops.*

go • *Did it all go well?*

happen • *Things don't happen the way you want them to.*

turn out • *Sometimes life doesn't turn out as we expect.*

worn-out ① ADJECTIVE

no longer usable because of extreme wear • *a worn-out pair of shoes*

broken-down • *Broken-down cars lined the road.*

tattered • *tattered clothes*

threadbare • *a square of threadbare carpet*

worn • *Worn tyres cost lives.*

worn-out ② ADJECTIVE

extremely tired • *You must be worn-out after the journey.*

exhausted • *too exhausted to do any more*

fatigued • *Winter weather can leave you feeling fatigued.*

prostrate • *He lay prostrate with exhaustion.*

tired • *I need to rest because I'm tired.*

weary • *a weary traveller*

worried ADJECTIVE
being anxious about
something • *His parents were
worried about his lack of
progress.*
anxious • *I was very anxious
about her safety.*
bothered • *I'm not bothered
about it at all.*
concerned • *a phone call from a
concerned neighbour*
nervous • *Consumers say they
are nervous about their jobs.*
troubled • *He was troubled by
the lifestyle of his son.*
uneasy • *an uneasy feeling
that everything was going
wrong*
ANTONYM:
• unconcerned

worry ① VERB
to feel anxious about
something • *Don't worry, it's
bound to arrive soon.*
be anxious • *They admitted
they were still anxious about the
situation.*
brood • *constantly brooding
about his family*
feel uneasy • *I felt very uneasy
at the lack of response.*
fret • *You mustn't fret about
someone else's problems.*

worry ② VERB
to disturb someone with a
problem • *I didn't want to worry
the boys with this.*
bother • *I hate to bother you
again so soon.*
hassle (INFORMAL) • *Then my
boss started hassling me.*

pester • *I wish they'd stop
pestering me for an answer.*
plague • *I'm not going to plague
you with more questions.*
trouble • *Don't trouble me while
I'm working.*

worry ③ NOUN
a feeling of anxiety • *a major
source of worry*
anxiety • *anxieties about
money*
apprehension • *real anger
and apprehension about the
future*
concern • *growing concern for
the environment*
fear • *His fears might be
groundless.*
misgiving • *She had some
misgivings about what she was
about to do.*
unease • *a deep sense of unease
about the coming interview*

worsen VERB
to become more difficult
• *My relationship with my
mother worsened.*
decline • *Hourly output
declined in the third quarter.*
degenerate • *The whole tone of
the campaign began to
degenerate.*
deteriorate • *The weather
conditions are deteriorating.*
go downhill (INFORMAL)
• *Things have gone steadily
downhill since he left.*
ANTONYM:
• improve

worship ① VERB
to praise and revere something

w

• People go to church to pray and worship their god.

glorify • The monks devoted their days to glorifying God.

honour • the Scout's promise to honour God

praise • She asked the church to praise God.

pray to • They prayed to their gods to bring them rain.

venerate (FORMAL) • the most venerated religious figure in the country

ANTONYM:
• dishonour

worship ② VERB

to love and admire someone
• She had worshipped him from afar for years.

adore • an adoring husband

idolise • She idolised her father as she was growing up.

love • He genuinely loved and cherished her.

ANTONYM:
• despise

worship ③ NOUN

a feeling of love and admiration for something • the worship of the ancient Roman gods

admiration • Her eyes widened in admiration.

adoration • He had been used to adoration all his life.

adulation • The book was received with adulation by the critics.

devotion • flattered by his devotion

homage • The emperor received the homage of every prince.

praise • singing hymns in praise of their god

PLACES OF WORSHIP
altar
basilica (CHRISTIANITY)
cathedral (CHRISTIANITY)
chapel (CHRISTIANITY)
church (CHRISTIANITY)
gurdwara (SIKHISM)
meeting house (QUAKERISM)
mosque (ISLAM)
pagoda (HINDUISM AND BUDDHISM)
shrine
synagogue (JUDAISM)
tabernacle (JUDAISM AND CHRISTIANITY)
temple

worthless ADJECTIVE

having no real value or worth
• a worthless piece of junk

meaningless • their sense of a meaningless existence

paltry • a paltry amount

poor • a poor reward for his effort

trifling • We were paid a trifling sum.

trivial • She would go to the doctor for any trivial complaint.

useless • I felt useless and a failure.

valueless • commercially valueless trees

ANTONYM:
• valuable

write VERB

to record something in writing • Write your name and address on a postcard and send it to us.

inscribe • *Their names were inscribed on the front of the pillar.*
record • *Her letters record the domestic and social details of her life.*
take down • *notes taken down in shorthand*

writing NOUN

TYPES OF WRITING
autobiography
ballad
biography
blog *or* weblog
column
dissertation
editorial
epitaph
essay
fable
feature
fiction
legend
letter
lyric
memoir
myth
narrative
non-fiction
novel
obituary
parable
play
poem
report
review
rhyme
riddle
script
story
thesis
verse

STYLES USED IN WRITING
alliteration
cliché
idiom
metaphor
narrative
parody
pun
satire
simile

FEATURES OF WRITING
character
dialogue
imagery
motif
plot
setting
subplot
theme

wrong ① ADJECTIVE
not correct or truthful • *That was the wrong answer.*
false • *We don't know if the information is true or false.*
faulty • *His diagnosis was faulty from the outset.*
incorrect • *a decision based on figures which were incorrect*
mistaken • *a mistaken view of the situation*
unsound • *The thinking is good-hearted, but muddled and unsound.*
untrue • *The remarks were completely untrue.*

ANTONYM:
• right

wrong ② ADJECTIVE
morally unacceptable • *It's wrong to hurt people.*

w

bad • I may have some faults but I'm not a bad person.

crooked • crooked business deals

evil • the country's most evil criminals

illegal • It is illegal to intercept radio messages.

immoral • Many would consider such practices immoral.

unfair • It was unfair that he should suffer so much.

unjust • unjust treatment

ANTONYM:
• right

wrong ③ NOUN

an unjust action • the wrongs of our society

abuse • controversy over human rights abuses

crime • crimes against humanity

grievance • He had a deep sense of grievance.

injustice • A great injustice had been done to him in the past.

sin • He admitted the many sins of his youth.

Yy

yellow NOUN or ADJECTIVE

SHADES OF YELLOW

amber
canary yellow
champagne
citrus yellow
daffodil
gold
lemon
mustard
primrose
saffron
sand
straw
topaz

yes INTERJECTION

an expression used to agree with something or say it is true • "Are you a friend of his?"—"Yes."

aye (SCOTTISH; INFORMAL) • "Can I borrow this?"—"Aye, but want it back."

okay • "Will we leave now?"—"Okay, if you like."

sure • "Can I come too?"— "Sure."

ya (SOUTH AFRICAN) • "Are you a runaway?"—"Ya," the child replied.

yeah (INFORMAL) • Yeah, I thi we've met once.

yup (INFORMAL) • *"Coming for a swim?"—"Yup, why not?"*

ANTONYM:
• no

yokel NOUN
a person who lives in the country • *a bunch of those yokels*
bushie or **bushy** (AUSTRALIAN AND NEW ZEALAND; INFORMAL) • *"I'm a bit of a bushie at heart,"* she said.
countryman • *They are true old-fashioned countrymen.*
peasant • *In rural Mexico a peasant is rarely without his machete.*

young ① ADJECTIVE
not yet mature • *young people*
adolescent • *He spent his adolescent years playing guitar.*
immature • *an immature female whale*
infant • *his infant daughter*
junior • *a junior member of the family*
juvenile • *a juvenile delinquent*
little • *What were you like when you were little?*
youthful • *the youthful stars of the film*

ANTONYM:
• old

young ② PLURAL NOUN
the babies an animal has • *The hen may not be able to feed its young.*
babies • *animals making nests for their babies*
brood • *a hungry brood of fledglings*

family • *a family of weasels*
litter • *a litter of pups*
little ones • *a family of elephants with their little ones*
offspring • *female rats' offspring*

Zz

zero NOUN
nothing or the number 0 • *I will
now count from zero to ten.*
nil • *They beat Argentina one-nil.*
nothing • *Some weeks I earn
nothing.*
nought • *How many noughts
are there in a million?*

zoom VERB
to move very quickly • *They
zoomed to safety.*
dart • *Ingrid darted across the
street.*
fly • *She flew downstairs.*
shoot • *Another car shot out of a
junction.*
speed • *A shot sped past the
keeper.*

Word Studies

BAD

BAD is such a commonly used word that it has come to lose much of its effectiveness. Depending on the sense and context of what you are saying, there are many other much more expressive words that can be used instead.

1. If you are describing something that has a harmful effect, you could try:
    - extremely **damaging**
    - **destructive** effect
    - **detrimental** impact
    - **harmful** consequences
    - **unhealthy** lifestyle
    - **unpleasant** side effects

2. If you are describing something upsetting, you could try:
    - **distressing** images
    - **disturbing** news
    - **grim** days
    - **painful** memories
    - a **traumatic** period
    - an **unsettling** atmosphere
    - an **upsetting** experience

3. If you are describing physical pain, you could try:
    - an **acute** attack
    - an **agonising** injury
    - **excruciating** pain
    - **intense** cramps
    - a **painful** knee
    - **serious** back problems
    - **severe** stomach pains
    - a **terrible** migraine

4. If you are describing something of poor quality,
   you could try:
   • a **defective** engine
   • a **deficient** diet
   • **faulty** goods
   • an **imperfect** copy
   • an **inadequate** response
   • an **inferior** product
   • a **pathetic** excuse
   • **poor** housing
   • a **sorry** effort
   • an **unsatisfactory** reply

5. If you are describing someone or something that lacks
   skill, you could try:
   • an **incompetent** worker
   • an **inept** performance
   • a **poor** judge
   • a **useless** committee

6. If you are describing something or someone evil,
   you could try:
   • **corrupt** practices
   • **criminal** actions
   • **depraved** criminals
   • an **evil** tyrant
   • an **immoral** act
   • **sinful** behaviour
   • a **villainous** character
   • a **wicked** stepmother

BIG

Try not to use **BIG** to describe the size or importance of a person or thing. Use one of the many alternatives available.

1. If you are describing the size of something, you could try:
    - *a **colossal** statue*
    - *an **enormous** building*
    - *a **gigantic** creature*
    - *a **great** forest*
    - *a **huge** cake*
    - *an **immense** wall*
    - *a **large** map*
    - *a **massive** display*
    - *a **significant** difference*
    - *a **vast** cathedral*

2. If you are describing the importance of something or someone, you could try:
    - *an **eminent** politician*
    - *an **important** influence*
    - *an **influential** figure*
    - *a **leading** thinker*
    - *a **major** role*
    - *a **powerful** president*
    - *the **principal** guest*
    - *a **prominent** scientist*
    - *a **significant** investor*

3. If you are describing an important issue or problem, you could try:
    - *a **critical** moment*
    - *a **grave** crisis*
    - *a **momentous** decision*
    - *a **serious** disadvantage*
    - *an **urgent** need*
    - *a **weighty** problem*

BREAK

There are lots of words you can use instead of **BREAK** to give additional information about the way in which something breaks or is broken.

1. If something hard **cracks**, or you **crack** it, it becomes slightly damaged, with lines appearing on its surface:
   • *The ice **cracked** but did not give way.*

2. If something **fractures**, or you **fracture** it, it gets a slight crack in it:
   • *You've **fractured** a rib.*

3. If something **snaps**, or you **snap** it, it breaks suddenly, with a sharp cracking noise:
   • *She gripped the pipe in both hands, trying to **snap** it in half.*

4. If something **splits**, or you **split** it, it breaks into two or more parts:
   • *In the severe gale, the ship **split** in two.*

5. If something **splinters**, or you **splinter** it, it breaks into thin, sharp pieces:
   • *The ruler **splintered** into pieces.*

6. If something **fragments**, or is **fragmented**, it breaks or separates into small parts:
   • *The rock began to **fragment** and crumble.*

7. If something **shatters**, it breaks into many small pieces:
   • *Safety glass won't **shatter** if it's hit.*

8. If you **smash** something, or it **smashes**, it breaks into many small pieces, often because it has been hit or dropped:
   • *Two glasses fell off the table and **smashed** into pieces.*

CRY

If you want to give a little more detail about how a person cries, there are words you can use instead of **CRY**.

1. If you **weep**, you cry. This is quite a literary word:
   • The woman began to **weep** uncontrollably.

2. If you **whimper**, you make a low, unhappy sound as if you are about to cry:
   • He huddled in a corner, **whimpering** with fear.

3. If you **sob**, you cry in a noisy way, with short breaths:
   • Her sister broke down and began to **sob** into her handkerchief.

4. If you **blubber**, you cry noisily and in an unattractive way:
   • To our surprise, he began to **blubber** like a child.

5. If you **howl** or **wail**, you cry with a long, loud noise:
   • The baby was **howling** in the next room.
   • The woman was **wailing** for her lost child.

6. If you **bawl**, you cry very loudly:
   • One of the toddlers was **bawling**.

CUT

There are many useful alternatives for **CUT**, depending on what is being cut, what device is doing the cutting, and how deep the cutting is.

1. If you **nick** something, you make a small cut on its surface:
   • *He nicked his chin while he was shaving.*

2. If you **score** something, you cut a line or lines on its surface:
   • *Lightly score the surface of the fruit with a cook's knife.*

3. If you **slit** something, you make a long narrow cut in it:
   • *He began to slit open each envelope.*

4. If you **clip** something, you cut small pieces from it in order to shape it:
   • *I saw an old man out clipping his hedge.*

5. If you **trim** something, you cut off small amounts of it to make it look neater:
   • *I have my hair trimmed every eight weeks.*

6. If you **slice** something, you cut it into thin pieces:
   • *I sliced the bread and cheese for the sandwiches.*

7. If you **chop** something, you cut it into pieces with strong downward movements of a knife or axe:
   • *You will need to chop the onions very finely.*

EAT

Instead of using **EAT**, use one of the many other words that describe how a person eats.

1. If you **consume** something, you eat it. This is a formal word:
   • *Andrew would consume nearly a pound of cheese a day.*

2. When an animal **feeds**, or **feeds on** something, it eats:
   • *After a few days the caterpillars stopped feeding.*
   • *Slugs feed on decaying plant material.*

3. If you **swallow** something, you make it go from your mouth into your stomach:
   • *Snakes swallow their prey whole.*

4. If you **chew** something, you break it up with your teeth so that it is easier to swallow:
   • *I pulled out a filling while I was chewing a toffee.*

5. If you **nibble** food, you eat it by biting very small pieces of it, perhaps because you are not very hungry:
   • *She nibbled at a piece of dry toast.*

6. If you **munch** food, you eat it by chewing it slowly, thoroughly, and rather noisily:
   • *Luke munched his sandwiches appreciatively.*

7. If you **gobble**, **guzzle**, **wolf (down)** or **scoff** food, you eat it quickly and greedily. **Wolf (down)** and **scoff** are informal words:
   • *Pete gobbled all the stew before anyone else arrived.*
   • *I couldn't believe how quickly they guzzled chocolate.*
   • *I was back in the changing room wolfing sandwiches.*
   • *You greedy so-and-so! You've scoffed the lot!*

8. If you **devour** something, you eat it quickly and eagerly:
   • *She devoured half an apple pie.*

GOOD

Like **bad**, **GOOD** is used in so many ways to describe so many things that it has lost much of its effectiveness. Explore the wide range of alternative words available.

1. If you are describing the quality of something, you could try:
   • an **acceptable** standard
   • an **excellent** meal
   • a **fine** match
   • a **first-class** game
   • a **first-rate** dinner
   • a **great** concert
   • a **splendid** hotel
   • a **superb** performance

2. If you are describing an experience, you could try:
   • an **agreeable** evening
   • a **delightful** party
   • an **enjoyable** trip
   • a **lovely** holiday in Paris
   • a **pleasant** stay

3. If you are describing someone's behaviour, you could try:
   • **disciplined** behaviour
   • a **docile** child
   • three **obedient** sons
   • an **orderly** queue
   • **well-behaved** pupils

4. If you are describing someone who is skilled at something, you could try:
   • an **able** student
   • an **accomplished** pianist
   • He is **adept** at manipulating the press.
   • a **capable** employee
   • a **clever** negotiator

709

GOOD

- *a **competent** worker*
- *an **efficient** manager*
- *an **expert** painter*
- *a **first-rate** teacher*
- *a **proficient** driver*
- *a **skilled** carpenter*
- *a **talented** musician*

5. If you are describing an effect, you could try:
   - ***advantageous** changes*
   - ***beneficial** effects*
   - ***favourable** conditions*
   - ***positive** results*

6. If you are describing advice or an idea, you could try:
   - ***constructive** input*
   - *a **helpful** suggestion*
   - *a **judicious** approach*
   - ***practical** help*
   - *a **prudent** strategy*
   - *a **sensible** way*
   - ***sound** advice*
   - *a **useful** tip*
   - *a **wise** plan*

7. If you are describing a person or an action, you could try:
   - *a **benevolent** parent*
   - *a **charitable** donation*
   - *a **considerate** son*
   - *a **generous** nature*
   - *a **humane** person*
   - *a **kind** woman*
   - *a **kind-hearted** friend*
   - *an **obliging** neighbour*
   - *a **thoughtful** child*

HAPPY

There are many other words you can use in your writing in order to avoid using **HAPPY**.

1. If you would like to describe someone or something as displaying a cheerful nature or mood, you could try:
    - a **cheerful** disposition
    - a **cheery** face
    - You're very **chirpy** today.
    - a **jolly** character
    - a **merry** laugh
    - her unfailingly **sunny** nature

2. If you would like to describe something that causes joy, you could try:
    - the **agreeable** task
    - their **blissful** marriage
    - a truly **festive** occasion
    - a **gratifying** relationship
    - a **joyful** event
    - the **joyous** news
    - a **pleasurable** memory

3. If you would like to describe a feeling of joy at something, you could try:
    - They are **delighted** with their new home.
    - I was **ecstatic** to see George again.
    - She was **elated** that she had won.
    - He is understandably **euphoric** at the result.
    - We are all **glad** to be back.
    - She takes a **joyful** pride in her work.
    - They were **jubilant** over their victory.
    - The sisters are **overjoyed** to be reunited.
    - The players are **over the moon** with this result.
    - We're very **pleased** at the news.
    - I'm just **thrilled** about the job.

HIT

There is a wide range of words you can use instead of **HIT**, allowing you to find the one that describes exactly what is happening.

1. If you **strike** something, you hit it deliberately and with force. This is a formal word:
    • She stepped forward and **struck** the gong.

2. If you **tap** something, you hit it with a quick light blow or series of blows:
    • **Tap** the egg gently with a teaspoon to crack the shell.

3. If you **rap** something, or **rap on** it, you hit it with a series of quick blows:
    • He **rapped** the glass with the knuckles of his right hand.

4. If you **slap** or **smack** something or someone, you hit them with the palm of your hand:
    • She **slapped** me on the back and said, 'It's nice to see you again.'

5. If you **swat** something such as an insect, you hit it with a quick, swinging movement using your hand or a flat object:
    • Every time a fly came near, I **swatted** it with a newspaper.

6. If you **knock** something such as a door or window, you hit it, usually several times, to attract someone's attention:
    • She went to his apartment and **knocked** the door loudly.

7. If you **beat** something, you hit it hard, usually several times or continuously for a period of time:
    • a circle of men **beating** drums

8. If you **hammer** something, you hit it hard several times to make a noise:
    • We had to **hammer** the door and shout to attract their attention

9. If you **pound** something, you hit it with great force, usually loudly and repeatedly:
   • *He pounded the table with both fists.*

10. If you **batter** something, you hit it very hard, using your fists or a heavy object:
    • *He battered the empty oil drum with a club.*

11. If you **bang** a part of your body, you accidentally knock it against something and hurt it:
    • *She'd fainted and banged her head.*

12. If you **belt** someone, you hit them very hard. This is an informal word:
    • *She drew back her fist and belted the other boxer.*

13. If you **bash** something, you hit it hard. This is an informal word:
    • *The car bashed into a lamppost.*

14. If you **whack** something, you hit it hard. This is an informal word:
    • *He whacked the ball straight into the net.*

15. If you **wallop** something or someone, you hit them very hard, often causing a dull sound. This is an informal word:
    • *Jerry walloped Tom over the head with a frying pan.*

16. If you **thump** something or someone, you hit them hard, usually with your fist:
    • *He thumped my shoulder affectionately, nearly knocking me over.*

17. If you **punch** something or someone, you hit them hard with your fist:
    • *The referee awarded a penalty when the defender punched the ball.*

INTERESTING

There are many other words you can use in your writing to avoid repeating the word **INTERESTING** too often.

1. If you are describing something that arouses your interest, you could try:
   - some **appealing** ideas
   - the computer game's **arresting** storyline
   - an **attractive** basis for a TV show
   - **captivating** music
   - the **intriguing** character of the author
   - an **inviting** topic for a speech
   - the **tantalising** prospect of a new album from the band

2. If you are describing something that holds your interest for a long time, you could try:
   - an **absorbing** conversation
   - a **compelling** series
   - an **enchanting** ballet
   - her **engaging** new novel
   - **engrossing** entertainment
   - an **enthralling** book
   - a **gripping** story
   - an **involving** drama
   - a **spellbinding** performance

3. If you are describing something that inspires your thinking or enthusiasm, you could try:
   - a **challenging** documentary
   - an imaginative and **entertaining** film
   - an **exciting** plan
   - a **fascinating** insight into the past
   - a truly **inspiring** read
   - one of the writer's most **moving** poems
   - a **stimulating** visit to India
   - a **thought-provoking** newspaper article

Rather than using **LAUGH**, try one of the alternatives to express exactly how a person is laughing.

1. If you **chuckle**, you laugh quietly:
    • I **chuckled** to myself at the look on his face.

2. If you **chortle**, you laugh in a pleased or amused way:
    • He sat there **chortling** at my predicament.

3. If you **snigger**, you laugh in a quiet, sly way, perhaps at something rude or unkind:
    • The boys **sniggered** when the teacher dropped his glasses on the floor.

4. If you **giggle**, you laugh in a high-pitched way because you are nervous or embarrassed:
    • They followed me around, **giggling** every time I spoke.

5. If you **titter**, you give a short, nervous laugh, often because you are embarrassed:
    • The audience began to **titter** when the speaker couldn't find his notes.

6. If you **cackle**, you laugh in a loud, harsh and unpleasant way, often at something bad which happens to someone else:
    • Her staff all **cackled** when they heard that she had been fired.

7. If you **guffaw**, **howl** or **roar**, you laugh very loudly because you think something is very funny:
    • They **guffawed** at the comedian's jokes.
    • The crowd **howled** at his antics.
    • We **roared** when she told us the story.

LOOK

All the words below mean **LOOK**, but each one expresses a slightly different way of looking. Find the one that captures just what you mean.

1. If you **glance**, **peek** or **peep** at something, you look at it quickly, and often secretly:
    • *He glanced at his watch as she spoke.*
    • *She peeked at him through the curtains.*
    • *He peeped at me to see if I was watching him.*

2. If you **scan** something written, you look at it quickly:
    • *She scanned the advertisement pages of the newspapers.*

3. If you **eye** or **regard** someone or something, you look at them carefully:
    • *The waiters eyed him with suspicion.*
    • *He regarded me curiously.*

4. If you **gaze** or **stare** at someone or something, you look at them steadily for a long time, for example because you find them interesting or because you are thinking about something else. **Staring** is often thought to be rude, but **gazing** is not:
    • *She sat gazing into the fire for a long time.*
    • *They stared silently into each other's eyes.*

5. If you **observe** or **watch** someone or something, you look at them for a period of time to see what they are doing or what is happening:
    • *A man was observing him from across the square.*
    • *I hate people watching me while I eat.*

6. If you **survey** or **view** someone or something, you look at the whole of them carefully:
    • *He stood up and surveyed the crowd.*
    • *The guests went to view the presents, which were set out on a table.*

7. If you **examine**, **scrutinise** or **study** something, you look at it very carefully, often to find out information from it:
   • He **examined** all the evidence.
   • He **scrutinised** her passport and stamped it.
   • We **studied** the menu for several minutes.

8. If you **glare**, **glower** or **scowl** at someone, you stare at them angrily:
   • He **glared** resentfully at me.
   • She stood **glowering** at me with her arms crossed.
   • She **scowled** at the two men as they came into the room.

9. If you **peer** or **squint** at something, you try to see it more clearly by narrowing or screwing up your eyes as you look at it:
   • He was **peering** at me through the keyhole.
   • She **squinted** at the screen, trying to read what was on it.

10. If you **gape** at someone or something, you look at them in surprise, usually with your mouth open:
    • She was **gaping** at the wreckage, lost for words.

11. If you **goggle** at someone or something, you look at them with your eyes wide open, usually because you are surprised by them:
    • He **goggled** at me in disbelief.

MOVE

There are many ways to **MOVE**, and as many words to describe the way it is done. Use one of the alternatives below.

1. When a person **crawls**, they move forwards on their hands and knees:
    • As he tried to **crawl** away, he was spotted by his captors.

2. If a person or animal **creeps** somewhere, they move quietly and slowly:
    • I tried to **creep** upstairs without being heard.

3. To **inch** somewhere means to move there very carefully and slowly:
    • He began to **inch** along the ledge.

4. If you **edge** somewhere, you move very slowly in that direction:
    • He **edged** closer to the telephone.

5. If a person or animal **slithers** somewhere, they move by sliding along the ground in an uneven way:
    • Robert lost his footing and **slithered** down the bank.

6. If you **wriggle** somewhere, for example through a small gap, you move there by twisting and turning your body:
    • I **wriggled** through a gap in the fence.

7. When people or small animals **scamper** or **scuttle** somewhere, they move there quickly with small, light steps:
    • The children got off the bus and **scampered** into the playground.
    • The crabs **scuttled** along the muddy bank.

8. When people or small animals **scurry** somewhere, they move there quickly and hurriedly, often because they are frightened:
    • The attack began, sending residents **scurrying** for cover.

9. If you **hurry**, **race** or **rush** somewhere, you go there as quickly as you can:
    • Claire **hurried** along the road.
    • He **raced** across town to the hospital.
    • A schoolgirl **rushed** into a burning building to save a baby.

10. If you **hasten** somewhere, you hurry there. This is a literary word:
    • He **hastened** along the corridor to Grace's room.

11. If you **dash**, **dart** or **shoot** somewhere, you run or go there quickly and suddenly:
    • She jumped up and **dashed** out of the room.
    • The girl turned and **darted** away through the trees.
    • They had almost reached the boat when a figure **shot** past them.

12. If you say that someone or something **flies** in a particular direction, you are emphasising that they move there with a lot of speed and force:
    • I **flew** downstairs to answer the door.

13. If you **tear** somewhere, you move there very quickly, often in an uncontrolled or dangerous way:
    • Without looking to left or right, he **tore** off down the road.

14. If you **jog**, you run slowly:
    • She **jogged** off in the direction he had indicated.

15. If you **sprint**, you run as fast as you can over a short distance:
    • The sergeant **sprinted** to the car.

16. If you **gallop**, you run somewhere very quickly:
    • They were **galloping** round the garden playing football.

17. If a person or animal **bolts**, they suddenly start to run very fast, often because something has frightened them:
    • I made some excuse and **bolted** towards the exit.

NICE

Instead of using **NICE**, think carefully about what you are trying to describe. Is it a person, object, quality or event? Then consider the many alternatives you can use.

1. If you are describing someone's appearance, you could try:
   - an **attractive** face
   - a **beautiful** baby boy
   - a very **cute** toddler
   - her **dishy** brother
   - a **good-looking** guy
   - her **gorgeous** boyfriend
   - a **handsome** man
   - a **lovely** woman
   - two **pretty** girls

2. If you are describing an object, place or view, you could try:
   - a **beautiful** old church
   - a **charming** little fishing village
   - a **delightful** room
   - a **lovely** walled garden
   - a **pretty** cottage

3. If you are describing an item of clothing, you could try:
   - a **chic** black suit
   - an **elegant** evening dress
   - a **fetching** outfit
   - a **smart** wool jacket
   - She wears such **stylish** clothes.

4. If you are describing an event or occasion, you could try:
   - a very **agreeable** dinner party
   - a **delightful** wedding
   - an **enjoyable** evening
   - a **fantastic** party
   - a **lovely** holiday
   - a **pleasurable** experience

5. If you are describing someone's personality, you could try:
   - *an **amiable** woman*
   - *a **considerate** neighbour*
   - *always **friendly** to strangers*
   - *unfailingly **good-natured***
   - ***kind** to everyone*
   - *a **kindly** man*
   - *an immensely **likeable** chap*
   - *a **thoughtful** girl*

6. If you are describing food or drink, you could try:
   - *an **appetising** smell*
   - *some **delectable** raspberries*
   - *a **delicious** meal*
   - *a bowl of **luscious** peaches*
   - *a **mouthwatering** dessert*
   - *a **tasty** soup*

7. If you are describing the weather, you could try:
   - *a **beautiful** morning*
   - *a **fine** afternoon*
   - *a **glorious** summer day*

8. If you are describing a room or house, you could try:
   - *a **comfortable** bungalow*
   - *a **cosy** sitting room*
   - *a **homely** atmosphere*
   - *a **welcoming** home*

OLD

Whether you are writing about an **OLD** person or an **OLD** thing, there are other words you can use to make your writing more interesting.

1. If you are describing someone who has lived for a long time, you could try:
   - *an **aged** parent*
   - *an **elderly** man*
   - ***senior** citizens*
   - *a **venerable** professor*

2. If you are describing something in the past, you could try:
   - *relics of **ancient** cultures*
   - *rituals of a **bygone** civilisation*
   - *an **earlier** marriage*
   - *the **early** days of advertising*
   - *his **ex**-wife*
   - *a **former** colleague*
   - *in **olden** times*
   - ***one-time** president*
   - ***past** grievances*
   - ***previous** tenants*
   - ***prior** arrangements*
   - *those **remote** days of the Wild West*

If you avoid **SAY**, you can be more creative by using one of the words which describe the way in which a person says something.

1. If someone **utters** sounds or words, they say them. This is a literary word:
    • *They left without **uttering** a single word.*

2. If you **remark** that something is the case, you say that it is the case:
    • *'I don't see you complaining,' he **remarked**.*

    If you **state** something, you say it in a formal or definite way:
    • *Could you please **state** your name for the record?*

    If you **mention** something, you say something about it, usually briefly:
    • *He never **mentioned** that he was married.*

    If you **note** something, you mention it in order to bring people's attention to it:
    • *'It's already getting dark,' he **noted**.*

    If you **observe** that something is the case, you make a comment about it, especially when it is something you have noticed or thought about a lot:
    • *'He's a very loyal friend,' Daniel **observed**.*

    If you **point out** a fact or mistake, you tell someone about it or draw their attention to it:
    • *'You've not done so badly out of the deal,' she **pointed out**.*

    If you **announce** something, you tell people about it publicly or officially:
    • *'We're engaged!' she **announced**.*

    If someone **asserts** a fact or belief, they state it firmly:
    • *'The facts are clear,' the Prime Minister **asserted**.*

SAY

10. If you **declare** that something is true, you say that it is true in a firm, deliberate way:
    • *'I'm absolutely thrilled with the result,'* he **declared**.

11. If you **interrupt**, you say something while someone else is speaking:
    • *'I don't think you quite understand,'* James **interrupted**.

12. When people **natter**, they talk casually for a long time about unimportant things:
    • *Susan and Jim were still **nattering** when I left.*

13. If you **inquire** about something, you ask for information about it. This is a formal word:
    • *'Is something wrong?'* he **inquired**.

14. To **query** or **question** means to ask a question:
    • *'Can I help you?'* the assistant **queried**.
    • *'What if something goes wrong?'* he **questioned** anxiously.

15. When you **respond** to something that has been said, you react to it by saying something yourself:
    • *'Are you well enough to carry on?'* he asked. *'Of course,'* she **responded** scornfully.

16. To **retort** means to reply angrily to someone. This is a formal word:
    • *'I don't agree,'* James said. *'Who cares what you think?'* she **retorted**.

17. If someone **babbles**, they talk in a confused or excited way:
    • *'I'm so excited I don't know what I'm doing,'* I **babbled**.

18. If you **chatter**, you talk quickly and excitedly about thing which are not important:
    • *Everyone was **chattering** away in different languages.*

19. If you **gabble**, you say things so quickly that it is difficult for people to understand you:
   • *Marcello sat on his knee and **gabbled** excitedly.*

20. If you **prattle**, you talk a great deal about something unimportant:
   • *She was **prattling** on about this show she had watched the night before.*

21. If someone **rambles**, they talk but do not make much sense because they keep going off the subject:
   • *The old man **rambled** about his feud with his neighbours.*

22. If someone **breathes** something, they say it very quietly. This is a literary word:
   • *'Oh, thank God you're here,' he **breathed**.*

23. When you **whisper**, you say something very quietly, using your breath rather than your throat:
   • *'Keep your voice down,' I **whispered**.*

24. If you **hiss** something, you say it forcefully in a whisper:
   • *'Stay here and don't make a sound,' he **hissed**.*

25. If you **mumble**, you speak very quietly and not at all clearly, so that your words are hard to make out:
   • *'I didn't know I was meant to do it,' she **mumbled**.*

26. If you **murmur** something, you speak very quietly, so that not many people can hear you:
   • *'How convenient,' I **murmured**.*

27. If you **mutter**, you speak very quietly, often because you are complaining about something:
   • *'Oh great,' he **muttered**, 'That's all I need.'*

28. If you **croak** something, you say it in a low, rough voice:
   • *'Water!' he **croaked**.*

SAY

Word Studies

29. If you **grunt** something, you say it in a low voice, often because you are annoyed or not interested:
    • *'Rubbish,'* I **grunted**, *'You just didn't try hard enough.'*

30. If you **rasp** something, you say it in a harsh, unpleasant voice:
    • *'Get out of my sight,'* he **rasped**.

31. If you **wheeze** something, you say it with a whistling sound, for example because you cannot get your breath:
    • *'I'm really out of condition,'* I **wheezed**.

32. If you **gasp** something, you say it in a short, breathless way, especially because you are shocked or in pain:
    • *'What do you mean?'* she **gasped**.

33. If you **pant** something, you say it while breathing loudly and quickly with your mouth open because you have been doing something energetic:
    • *'Let me get my breath back,'* he **panted**.

34. If you **groan** or **moan** something, you say it in a low voice usually because you are unhappy or in pain:
    • *'My leg – I think it's broken,'* Eric **groaned**.
    • *'I can't stand it any longer,'* she **moaned**.

35. When someone **growls** something, they say it in a low, rough and angry voice:
    • *'I ought to kill you for this,'* Sharpe **growled**.

36. If you **snarl** something, you say it in a fierce, angry way:
    • *'Get out of here,'* he **snarled**.

37. If you **snap** at someone, you speak to them in a sharp, unfriendly way:
    • *'Of course you can't have it,'* he **snapped**.

The are a number of words you can use instead of **SHORT**, although you should be aware that some are more likely to hurt a person's feelings than others.

1. A **little** or **small** person is not large in physical size:
   • *He was too **little** to reach the books on the top shelf.*
   • *She is **small** for her age.*

2. A **diminutive** person is very small:
   • *a **diminutive** figure standing at the entrance*

3. A **tiny** person is extremely small:
   • *Though she was **tiny**, she had a loud voice.*

4. If you describe a woman as **petite**, you are politely saying that she is small and not fat. This is a complimentary word:
   • *a **petite** young woman*

5. If you describe someone as **dumpy**, you mean they are short and plump. This is an uncomplimentary word:
   • *a **dumpy** character in a baggy tracksuit*

6. If you describe someone as **squat**, you mean that they are short and thick, usually in an unattractive way:
   • *Eddie was a **squat** fellow in his mid-forties.*

SMALL

Before using **SMALL** in your writing, think about what you are describing, and then try one of the alternatives offered here.

1. If you are describing an object or the physical size of something, you could try:
   • a **little** table
   • a **miniature** camera
   • a pair of **minuscule** shorts
   • a **minute** amount
   • a **tiny** room

2. If you are describing an area, you could try:
   • a **little** distance from the station
   • a **narrow** space
   • a **restricted** habitat

3. If you are describing the size of a person, you could try:
   • a **diminutive** figure
   • a **dumpy** man
   • too **little** to reach the shelf
   • a **petite** woman
   • a **short** fellow
   • a **tiny** girl

4. If you are describing a person's age, you could try:
   • my **baby** brother
   • an **infant** prodigy
   • Her boys are only **little**.
   • a **young** child

Instead of using **WALK**, use another word that describes exactly how the person walks.

1. If you **step** in a particular direction, you move your foot in that direction:
 • *I stepped carefully over the piles of rubbish.*

2. If you **tread** in a particular way, you walk in that way. This is quite a literary word:
 • *She trod carefully across the grass.*

If you **amble** or **stroll**, you walk in a slow, relaxed way:
 • *We ambled along the beach hand in hand.*
 • *They strolled down the High Street, looking in shop windows.*

If you **saunter**, you walk in a slow, casual way:
 • *He was sauntering along as if he had all the time in the world.*

If you **wander**, you walk around in a casual way, often without intending to go anywhere in particular:
 • *Khachi was wandering aimlessly about in the garden.*

If you **tiptoe**, you walk very quietly without putting your heels on the ground, so as not to be heard:
 • *She slipped out of bed and tiptoed to the window.*

If you **toddle**, you walk unsteadily, with short quick steps. This word is most often used of babies or small children:
 • *My daughter toddles around after me wherever I go.*

If you **pace**, you walk up and down a small area, usually because you are anxious or impatient:
 • *As he waited, he paced nervously around the room.*

If you **stride**, you walk with quick, long steps:
 • *He turned abruptly and strode off down the corridor.*

10. If you **march**, you walk quickly and in a determined way, perhaps because you are angry:
    • *She marched into the office and demanded to see the manager.*

11. If you **stamp**, you put your feet down very hard when you walk, usually because you are angry:
    • *'I'm leaving!' she shouted as she stamped out of the room.*

12. If you **flounce**, you walk quickly and with exaggerated movements, in a way that shows you are annoyed or upset about something:
    • *He flounced out of the room in a huff.*

13. If you **stalk**, you walk in a stiff, proud or angry way:
    • *She stalked out of the meeting, slamming the door.*

14. If you **lurch**, you walk with sudden, jerky movements:
    • *He lurched around the room in pain and astonishment.*

15. If you **stagger** or **totter**, you walk very unsteadily:
    • *She staggered and had to hold onto chair for support.*
    • *I had to totter around on crutches for six weeks.*

16. If you **reel**, you walk about in an unsteady way as if you are going to fall:
    • *He lost his balance and reeled back.*

17. If you **stumble**, you trip while you are walking and almost fall:
    • *I stumbled over a stack of books in the doorway.*

18. If you **plod**, **tramp** or **trudge**, you walk slowly, with heavy steps, often because you are tired:
    • *He plodded about after me, looking bored.*
    • *They spent all day tramping through the snow.*
    • *We had to trudge all the way back up the hill.*